FORMAL TECHNIQUES IN
ARTIFICIAL INTELLIGENCE
A Sourcebook

STUDIES IN COMPUTER SCIENCE AND ARTIFICIAL INTELLIGENCE

6

Editors:

R.B. Banerji
Saint Joseph's University
Philadelphia

H. Kobayashi
Princeton University
Princeton

U. Montanari
Università di Pisa
Pisa

M. Nivat
Université Paris VII
Paris

NORTH-HOLLAND – AMSTERDAM • NEW YORK • OXFORD • TOKYO

FORMAL TECHNIQUES IN ARTIFICIAL INTELLIGENCE
A Sourcebook

edited by

Ranan B. BANERJI

*Department of Mathematics
 and Computer Science
Saint Joseph's University
Philadelphia, PA, U.S.A.*

1990

NORTH-HOLLAND – AMSTERDAM • NEW YORK • OXFORD • TOKYO

006.3
F 723

ELSEVIER SCIENCE PUBLISHERS B.V.
Sara Burgerhartstraat 25
P.O. Box 211, 1000 AE Amsterdam, The Netherlands

Distributors for the United States and Canada:

ELSEVIER SCIENCE PUBLISHING COMPANY, INC.
655 Avenue of the Americas
New York, N.Y. 10010, U.S.A.

Library of Congress Cataloging-in-Publication Data

Formal techniques in artificial intellligence : a sourcebook / edited
  by Ranan B. Banerji.
      p.   cm. -- (Studies in computer science and artificial
  intelligence ; 6)
    Includes bibliographical references.
    ISBN 0-444-88130-1
    1. Artificial intelligence.   I. Banerji, Ranan B., 1928-
  II. Series.
  Q335.F674 1990
  006.3--dc20   89-23117
                                                             CIP

ISBN: 0 444 88130 1

PRINTED IN THE NETHERLANDS

Editor's Preface

The idea for this collection of introductory surveys was conceived during the IJCAI meeting at Milano in August 1987. Drs. Arjen Sevenster of North-Holland and I were discussing how most books on Artificial Intelligence did not discuss the subject from a firm theoretical basis in the model of modern computer science. We conceded that there were some such books. There were, for instance, good books on mechanical deduction and on areas of non-standard logics as applied to Artificial Intelligence. My own book was mentioned, but we soon agreed that it also was limited, mostly to problems, games and learning and even there was beginning to get a little behind the times, in view of the recent advances in the area of learning. Moreover, there were now areas of endeavor outside the ones mentioned which have reached sufficient maturity as can be discussed in book form, and with mathematical precision.

We fell to talking then on what an ideal up-to-date book on Artificial Intelligence would look like: it soon became obvious that if such a book restricted itself to tight and precise discussions, a large amount of present and past work would be extremely hard to discuss. And quite satisfactory books already existed which did quite competent jobs on informal discussions of AI programs - to the extent that informal discussions are feasible for such formal objects as computer programs.

So we felt that if scientific precision was to be the major thrust of a book, then extensive coverage of all approaches would not be feasible and if one drops the requirement of precision of discussion, then acceptably good and up-to-date books are already available. So we decided to limit our discussion to the feasibility of a book on those areas of Artificial Intelligence which have been attacked from the traditional mathematical and computer-scientific viewpoints. We began to enumerate such areas and concluded that sufficient amount of precise results in these were available that one could write a book on such topics. But equal justice to all the topics would be very difficult. All the fields were sufficiently new and specialized: it would be a herculean task for one person to do a competent job on all of them. The idea of a book written by many different specialists seemed feasible. I was requested by Drs. Sevenster to coordinate the writing of such a volume. I felt that to bring about such a book would be an extremely useful thing to do and that I would be proud to be associated with such an effort.

We decided that the book would be a book of surveys as opposed to a book about individual research: there were enough conference proceedings and journals that describe individual research results. But we also agreed that these surveys should not be what one might call annotated bibliographies: ones that introduce the topics of the field only superficially and interrelate them, leaving the reader to go to the cited publications for information in depth. We wanted to maintain some semblance to a textbook: there would be enough introduction to the basic techniques of the fields to facilitate further reading. We decided to call the articles "Introductory Surveys" What we wanted were articles which would serve as very terse texts in the field, from which the reader could comfortably move into the literature.

The topics we chose are almost exactly reflected in the table of contents. We have been lucky in having been able to get competent scholars to agree to spend the time and effort involved in writing the different chapters of this book. There have been times when I despaired of covering one field or another, occassionally considering reformatting available material into the format needed if the book had to be published at an early date. But I received enough help from active people in the field - even when they could not help in the actual writing or reviewing, they helped me in locating proper authors. My hope is that their efforts and mine will prove of value.

As a person who still maintains keen interest in the field and is still active at some level, it behooves me to make some comments on how I view the field at present and how the sub-areas chosen here contribute to it. Needless to say, if the book fails to address some areas, or addresses them only partially, the fault lies with my selection process: authors did cooperate marvelously, except in cases where the idiosyncracies of academia prevented them from helping even when they wanted to. (One surprizing fact that emerged is that many leading universities did not consider good exposition to be as important as new results when it came to quality judgement for a faculty member. This lop-sided view of "scholarly quality" probably is a result of the strong influence of the demand for project-oriented science that is made by many funding agencies and their reviewers. Although Universities pride themselves - deservedly - as centers of scholarship, it can probably be understood why they cannot avoid this pressure from the real world in their reward structure. Dissemination of truth for society has to take a back seat to the advancement of truth for the elite).

My own interest and abilities lie in the areas of problem solving, games and learning. Let me initially comment on these. It will be noticed that the book does not contain any discussion on what in the area of problem-solving is called "Theory of Heuristic Search" The reason is two-fold. First, there is an excellent book on Heuristics by Prof. Judea Pearl of UCLA. Secondly, although there have been later work and indeed much good work, my personal belief is that the work in this area will not prove to be of permanent value. The success of using heuristic evaluation functions depend much more on the quality of the heuristic used than on the precise way in which the search algorithm uses the heuristic (assuming, of course, that the search algorithm is at least a complete one: some of the algorithms mentioned in AI textbooks are not). Different search algorithms do have somewhat different efficiencies, and there are questions of balancing space and time efficiencies. But these differences do not alleviate the inefficiencies caused by an inaccuracy in the heuristic function. Pearl has shown, for instance, that to lead to a polynomial search time, the accuracy of the heuristic function can not be allowed to increase any faster than logarithmically as the distance from the goal increases. The main challenge, then, is in the discovery of a heuristic function than in the improvement of the search algorithm.

On the other hand, there has been work on problem solving independent of what today is called the heuristic function (i.e. an estimate of the distance from the goal). The general problem solver predates the A^* algorithm and has been improved and anlyzed by many authors since then. Much of the work has been carried out with precision, and there has been a recent trend at correlating the concepts there to standard algebraic concepts. One of the articles in this book is an exposition of this new algebraic point of view and an exposition of the existing work from that vantage point (to the extent that this could be done with precision). Where precision could not be achieved, the surveyed work has been described in its original formalism. It is my belief that the algebraic approach holds promise. I am aware of some unpublished work where this point of view has been pursued to formalize explanation-based learning.

On the subject of explanation-based learning, I feel keenly aware that this book has not been able to address this new and promising area. It is my belief that the sub-area of explanation based learning called Explanation- based Generalization (EBG) is presently being pursued with sufficient precision and clarity. This applies especially to the recent works of the students of Prof. Tom Mitchell of Carnegie Mellon University. It is unfortunate that I became conscious of some of these developments only after the book was already on its way to completion. It is my belief that eventually there will be a bridge established between EBG and refinement.

The last sentence needs some clarification. In the area of learning (from examples - some prefer to call this "similarity-based" learning), a basic concept is that of the partial order of implication between representations (related to what is called the Version Space following Mitchell). A number of learning techniques which "learn in the limit" move through this partial order by a process that Dr. Philip Laird of NASA (one of the contributors to this volume) calls "refinement" The representations need not be in any standard logical calculus. Nor do they need to represent sets. If one considers the EBG process from this point of view, then one needs to set up a partial order between proofs, i.e. to define in a useful fashion as to when one proof is a "generalization" of another. I do not believe we have yet studied what the word "generalization" means when applied to proofs. But when one looks at the present formal work on EBG, one begins to form ideas on what kind of properties such generalizations should have. Refinement theory may well play a role here.

Much of this book seems to be on Logic and its extensions and variations. The chapter on Heuristics is algebraic in nature and the chapter on learning has strong combinatorial and statistical overtones to its logic- related techniques. But logic, which a few years ago was held to be irrelevant to the 20th century in some A.I. circles, seems to be influencing the field very strongly. However, this logic is by no means always classical first order predicate logic. The chapter on qualitative physics, for instance, would indicate a syntax very similar to algebra in nature (though the traditional syntax-semantics dichotomy has not quite been formalized in this area). The logic on which program verification and synthesis is based (as exemplified in the paper on metamathematical metods), while classical in its essential form, has incorporated many structures which are used in a way different from the way it is done classically. The way refinement is done in the work on Induction and Learning can be used in any partially ordered structure as long as the semantic interpretation makes sense. The work on non-monotonic logics (which seem almost imperative in intelligent data bases) also is indegenous to the field of Artificial Intelligence. We have been fortunate in having been able to incorporate surveys on these areas in this volume.

The reason for the development of specialized logics is not far to seek. Classical logic was developed to have mathematical functions and relations as interpetations. In computer science there is need for distinguishing algorithms from the functions they represent: definitions of functions (which are also modeled in recursive function theory) is an important part of computer science. The many new syntactic approaches are in recognition of this fact. The other fact is that while proofs and calculations were matters of metamathetical discussions in the field of classical metamathematics, now there is a need for carrying them out in actuality. And the experience in this area has been that this process in its full strength is extremely inefficient when done by a machine without human intervention. Moreover, here as in all areas of Artificial Intelligence, the efficiency of the proof process as well as the intuitive clarity with which the process can be humanly controlled is heavily dependent on the way the one designs the axioms describing a problem. This has led to a greater emphasis on designing logical systems specifically geared to the purposes to which they are to be applied.

There is one area where such a special purpose logic has been developed to a degree as to make it an almost independent new system. I am referring here to logics where equalities are the only predicates. The axioms of equality have always been a challenge to designers of theorem provers. The workers in equational theories (theories of varieties, if you will) have faced that challenge by isolating that problem and attacking it with special tools designed specifically for it. This volume contains two articles on this area. I have hopes that techniques developed here will some day enrich more general theorem provers. Theorem provers based entirely on term-rewriting techniques have indeed been contemplated.

When I was beginning to think of the book, I had almost decided against including any survey on theorem proving in classical logic. This is one of the oldest formal areas of A.I, and is rich in techniques and results. For a while I did not believe that justice could be done to the area without writing another book on it, and good books did exist. I was lucky in being able to find an author who could write a comprehensive up-to-date discussion of the field within the confines of a few pages.

Many among the older activists in A.I. came into the field during the initial excitement around the device called "perceptron" They remember the promises made and the results obtained. They would also remeber how both good and bad theory grew around the concept and how experimental work promised much more than theory predicted could be done. To many of them, the present excitement around neural networks can not but have a familiar ring. However, there are significant differences between the sixties and the eighties. We have discovered techniques for analyzing algorithms for correctness. A comprehensive theory of computational complexity has developed so instead of merely claiming that a process converges correctly, one can investigate the time it takes for the process to converge. A solid theory of parallel computation has been initiated. There is thus hope that neural network-like devices can be understood and analyzed much more precisely than could be done thirty years ago. One of the articles in this volume brings the reader abreast of our present state of knowledge regarding the ability and speed of neural networks as parallel computational devices. The author of the article informs me, to my great gratification, that he is planning a book based on this article.

This volume has not been as good at addressing another important question regarding neural nets, however: it would be useful to know more about the algorithms one uses to adjust weights on the axons to the neurons to bring about the phenomenon of learning. Although some very promising experimental results have been published on the capabilities of various learning algorithms, I am personally not aware of any precise discussion of their convergence and efficiency. If there are, the fault for not having included such results in this book is mine. It is definitely my fault also that two recent techniques for the anlysis of neural nets have not been covered in this book because at the time of the design of the volume, I was personally not aware of them. I am referring to some of the analysis that has been going on, considering a neural net as a control device, studying the trajectory and steady states of such devices in response to different inputs. Also, some effort has been going on to study neural networks as randomly connected devices, using the techniques of statistical thermodynamics. These are certainly promising new avenues of study which have veered away from the conventional wisdom of the field and will bear watching. I apologize that we have not been able to get the reader started on this path of study. It is my understanding that Dr. Kamp of the Philips Research Laboratories in Brussels is planning a new book in these areas, so at least one source book will also be available soon.

I bear an unrepayable debt of gratitude to all the authors of this volume for their help and cooperation. Drs. Arjen Sevenster has encouraged and helped the venture at every stage. Ms. Janet Mitchell, Ms. Titia Kraaij of Elsevier and their indefatigable staff have been of great support in making the manuscript presentable in appearence and technically complete: if there have been lapses in this, the fault is the editor's not the technical editors'.

In spite of all the help, the book has its faults. Some I have mentioned, others I am not aware of. I apologize in advance to the readers for these.

There will, of course be many to whom the book will appear entirely irrelevant to the cutting edge of AI. To them also I extend my apologies.

Contents

Editor's Preface   v

Term Rewriting and Equational Reasoning
J. Avenhaus and K. Madlener   1

Implementing Metamathematics as an Approach to Automatic
  Theorem Proving
R.L. Constable and D.J. Howe   45

Qualitative Physics
S.D. Grantham and L.H. Ungar   77

Automatic Generation of Heuristics
J.P.E. Hodgson   123

A Survey of Computational Learning Theory
P.D. Laird   173

A Primer on the Complexity Theory of Neutral Networks
I. Parberry   217

Mechanical Theorem Proving
D.A. Plaisted   269

Semantic Issues in Deductive Databases and Logic Programs
H. Przymusinska and T. Przymusinski   321

An Introduction to Unification Theory
J.H. Siekmann   369

Index   425

Formal Techniques in Artificial Intelligence
A Sourcebook. R.B. Banerji (editor)
© Elsevier Science Publishers B.V. (North-Holland), 1990

Term Rewriting and Equational Reasoning

J. Avenhaus, K. Madlener

Fachbereich Informatik
Universität Kaiserslautern
6750 Kaiserslautern
Germany

This paper presents a survey on term rewriting. Term rewriting is a technique that can be applied to reasoning in structures defined by equations, and therefore, this survey is intended for those who are interested in deduction based on mathematical logic. Like most surveys ours does not contain any new results; instead it gives an overview on the fundamental techniques used in term rewriting, and it presents some of the important applications of term rewriting.

The basic idea of rewriting is the following: Let S be a set of syntactic objects, e.g., first order terms on a given signature, formulae of the predicate calculus, polynomial expressions, or programs in a given programming language, and let $\sim$ be an equivalence relation on S, which in a way gives the semantics of the objects in S. Then the validity problem is the problem to decide whether two syntactic objects s and t from S have the same meaning, i.e., whether they are equivalent modulo $\sim$. To solve this problem we may proceed as follows. An ordering > is defined on S such that > is well-founded. If $s(1) > s(2)$, we say that $s(2)$ is simpler than $s(1)$. Now given s and t we replace s and t by simpler objects $s(1)$ and $t(1)$, respectively, such that s and $s(1)$ and t and $t(1)$, respectively, are equivalent. This process is called simplification or rewriting. Repeating this process we obtain two sequences $s > s(1) > s(2) > ... > s(i)$ and $t > t(1) > t(2) > ... > t(j)$. Under certain conditions this sequences will end with identical objects, i.e., $s(i) = t(j)$, if and only if s and t are equivalent.

Evans [62] was one of the first to apply this technique to algebraic structures. He noticed that some algebraic structures are defined by systems E of equations having the following property: the set of equations E can be oriented into a system of rewrite rules R such that the process of rewriting by R yields unique normal forms. This gives a way to effectively perform computations in these structures.

Already Newman [172] had noticed that confluence and termination are the key properties for a rewriting system R to guarantee that R yields unique normal forms. Thus, a fundamental problem that we will address is the problem of how to verify whether a rewriting system R is confluent and terminating.

If a rewriting system R obtained from a set of equations E is not confluent and terminating, there might still exist another rewriting system R_1 that is confluent and terminating, and that defines the same equivalence relation as the set of equations E. In their seminal paper [142] Knuth and Bendix developed a method - called completion - which in many cases allows to transform a system of equations E into an equivalent rewriting system R which is confluent and terminating. If on input E the process of completion succeeds then the validity problem for E, i.e. E-equality, is decidable. Thus, completion can be seen as a preprocessing which, in case it succeeds, yields an algorithm for the validity problem for E.

By now the technique of rewriting has found many applications.
Originally, it was applied only to sets of equations over an unstructured universe. This allows to deal with first order logic with equality and without predicate symbols. Later on the technique of rewriting has been extended to conditional rewriting, which can be used to deal with sets of conditional equations, and order sorted rewriting, which allows to structure the universe into different sorts and to build sort hierarchies. It is well-known that sorts and sort hierarchies can be used to formulate certain problems in a natural way by coding taxonomial information (or knowledge) into the syntax of the description. This may reduce the complexity of solving these problems considerably.

There are many applications of the technique of rewriting. In this survey we will deal with the following: proving inductive theorems, solving equations, logic programming, first order theorem proving, and computing in algebraic structures.

Obviously, we cannot present all these topics in full detail here; rather we will outline the basic ideas and give pointers to the literature. In fact, we will not even be able to explicitly mention all the relevant work in this field, but we hope that our list of references will guide the interested reader to find the relevant papers on the topic of his interest.

This paper is organized as follows. After an introduction in Chapter 1 the basic completion procedure is presented in Chapter 2. Chapter 3 then presents some important extensions, and in Chapter 4 some of the applications of the technique of rewriting are described.

1. Introduction

Rewrite systems are used to reason about and to compute within structures defined by equations. These structures and equations may come from very different areas of application like universal algebra, specification of data types or theorem proving.

Let us start with two examples, one from universal algebra and one from algebraic specification:

(1) E_1: $\quad$ x∗1 $\quad = \quad$ x

$\qquad\qquad$ x∗x^{-1} $\quad = \quad$ 1

$\qquad\qquad$ (x∗y)∗z $= \quad$ x∗(y∗z)

$\quad$ This system E_1 describes the variety of groups.

(2) E_2: $\quad$ app(nil,z) = z

$\qquad\qquad$ app(cons(x,y),z) = cons(x,app(y,z))

$\quad$ This system E_2 describes the concatenation of two lists.

Among the most important problems in this context are

- computation of normal forms, i.e. representatives for E-equal terms
- deciding validity of an equation s = t in all (or some) models of E
- solving an equation s = t in all (or some) models of E.

For instance 1∗x = x can be proved in E_1 by "replacing equals by equals" and hence holds in all models of E_1. However, associativity of concatenation of lists, i.e. the equation app(app(x,y),z) = app(x,app(y,z)), does not hold in all models of E_2, but it holds in the models programmers are interested in, i.e. in the initial model of E_2.

Rewriting systems are based on two fundamental methods: simplification and completion. Simplification or rewriting is used for the computation of normal forms and completion is used to get systems in which these normal forms are unique. Many problems in structures defined by equations can be solved using rewrite systems. We will start with ordinary equational systems and develop the basic concepts. Various applications require extensions of the basic concepts and methods. This leads to equational rewriting, unfailing completion, conditional rewriting and order sorted rewriting. In some applications only a restricted form of confluence is needed, e.g. when proving equations in the initial model; here only ground confluence is required.

1.1.   Equational Systems

In order to introduce the basic concepts we want to explain in this paper we use the area of algebraic data type specification as motivation (Guttag [86]). In this approach the data are abstractly given as terms over some signature. Different terms may denote the same data object, and which terms denote the same object is defined by equations. Furthermore equations are used to define operations on the data objects. A simple example of this is the specification of lists given in the introduction. This example shows also that one needs different sorts of objects, say natural numbers and lists of natural numbers. This leads to the following definitions.

A **signature** $\Sigma = (S,F)$ consists of a set S of sort symbols and a set F of function symbols or operators. Each operator f has a fixed arity $s_1,...,s_n \to s$, $s_i,s \in S$ indicating the sorts of its arguments and the output sort. Operators of arity $\to s$ are called constants. Let T(F) denote the set of "correct terms" that can be constructed using F, i.e. every constant a: $\to s$ is a term of sort s and, if f: $s_1 ... s_n \to s$ and t_i are terms of sort s_i, then $f(t_1,...,t_n)$ is a term of sort s. These terms are called **ground terms**.

To describe a relation between these ground terms we use equations and variables. For each $s \in S$ let V_s be a set of variables (of sort s), let V be the union of these V_s and let T(F,V) be the set of terms built from F and V. We write $s \equiv t$ if s and t are syntactically equal.

An **equation** $s = t$ is a pair of terms where s and t have the same sort. If E is a set of equations, then (Σ,E) is called an **abstract data type specification**.

As an example we give a specification of the integers with the successor function s, the predecessor function p, the addition + and the unary minus op. We need just one sort and the following equations

E: $x+0 = x$ $p(s(x)) = x$

$x+s(y) = s(x+y)$ $s(p(x)) = x$

$x+p(y) = p(x+y)$ $op(0) = 0$

$op(s(x)) = p(op(x))$

$op(p(x)) = s(op(x))$

The set of equations E defines a syntactical equalitity relation $=_E$ on T(F,V). To explain this we fix the following terminology. We write $s \to t$ to indicate that the equation $s = t$ in E is to be applied from left to right: Given a term t' and a position p in t' such that the subterm t'/p of t' at position p can be matched by s, i.e. $t'/p \equiv \sigma(s)$ for some substitution σ. Let $t'' \equiv t'[p \leftarrow \sigma(t)]$ be the term obtained from t' by replacing the subterm $\sigma(s)$ with $\sigma(t)$. Then we write $t' \rightarrow_E t''$. We write $t' \leftrightarrow_E t''$ to indicate that one equation in E is applied in either direction. Now let $=_E$ be the reflexive and transitive closure of $\leftrightarrow_E$, i.e. $=_E$ is as usual defined by the concept of "replacing equals by equals".

The relation $=_E$ is syntactically defined. One has also a semantical definition of E-equality as it is well known from logic: We write $E \models t' = t''$ if the equation $t' = t''$ holds in every model of E. The fundamental result of Birkhoff assures that both notions coincide.

Theorem (Birkhoff [23]) $t' =_E t''$ iff $E \models t' = t''$

For any set E of equations, we use the operational definition $=_E$ for E-equality. A proof of $t' =_E t''$ is a sequence $t' \equiv t_0 \leftrightarrow_E t_1 \leftrightarrow_E ... \leftrightarrow_E t_n \equiv t''$.   As an example, in the specification of integers we can easily prove $p(op(p(x)) =_E s(op(s(x)))$: $p(op(p(x))) \leftrightarrow_E op(s(p(x))) \leftrightarrow_E op(x) \leftrightarrow_E op(p(s(x))) \leftrightarrow_E s(op(s(x)))$.
It is a little bit harder to find a proof for $x =_E (x^{-1})^{-1}$ in the group example.

A fundamental problem now is the **validity problem** for E:
INPUT: $s,t \in T(F,V)$
QUESTION: $s =_E t$?

It is well known that this problem is undecidable in general. It is semi-decidable if E is a finite or at least a semi-decidable set of equations. But of course, there are important equational systems E which have a decidable validity problem. The fundamental approach of Knuth and Bendix [142] to deal with the validity problem in an equational system E was to transform E into a system R of ordered equations such that $s =_E t$ iff there is a "rewrite" proof in R of the form

$$s \rightarrow_R s_1 \rightarrow_R ... \rightarrow_R s_n \equiv t_m \,_R\leftarrow ... \,_R\leftarrow t_1 \,_R\leftarrow t$$

This means, the equations in R are always applied from left to right and the proof has the special form indicated above. An oriented equational system is called a term rewriting system.

1.2   Term Rewriting Systems

Given a signature (S,F), a rule $l \rightarrow r$ is an oriented equation such that every variable occurring in term r also occurs in term l. A **term rewriting system** R is a set of rules. It defines the

rewrite relation $\to_R$ as in Section 1.1, i.e. $s \to_R t$ if there is a rule $l \to r$ in R, a position p in s
and a substitution σ with $s/p \equiv \sigma(l)$ and $t \equiv s[p \leftarrow \sigma(r)]$.

We denote by $\xrightarrow{+}_R$ the transitive, by $\xrightarrow{*}_R$ the reflexive and transitive and by $\xleftrightarrow{*}_R$ the
symmetric, reflexive and transitive closure of $\to_R$. A term t is **reducible** in R if $t \to_R s$ for
some term s. If $t \xrightarrow{*} s$ and s is irreducible, then s is a **normal form** of t. Two terms s and t
are **joinable** if they are reducible to a common term, i.e. $s \xrightarrow{*}_R u$ and $t \xrightarrow{*} u$ for some u.
We write $s \downarrow t$ in this case.

If R is regarded as an equational system, then the validity problem can be solved by rewriting
if every term t has a unique normal form $t \downarrow$ and $t \downarrow$ can be computed from t. This leads to the
following definition.

Definition: A term rewriting system R is **terminating** (or **Notherian**) if it allows no
infinite sequences $t_0 \to_R t_1 \to_R t_2 \to_R \dots$. It is called **confluent** if $t \xrightarrow{*}_R t_1$ and $t \xrightarrow{*}_R t_2$
implies that t_1 and t_2 are joinable. R is called **convergent** if it is both, terminating and
confluent.

One can easily prove that the confluence property is equivalent to the Church-Rosser
property i.e.: $s \xleftrightarrow{*} t$ implies $s \downarrow t$. This gives

Fact: If R is convergent, then every term t has a unique normal form $t \downarrow$.

           So, $s \xleftrightarrow{*}_R t$ iff $s \downarrow \equiv t \downarrow$.

If R is a recursive set of rewrite rules and R is convergent, then $t \downarrow$ can be computed for every
term t. This solves the validity problem for E if $=_E = \xleftrightarrow{*}_R$. The Knuth-Bendix completion
procedure attempts to compute such a system R for E. Of course, this cannot succeed for
every input E. One reason is that E may have an unsolvable validity problem. Another reason
is that E may contain equations that cannot be described by a terminating rewriting system, a
simple example is the AC-theory $x+y = y+x$ and $(x+y)+z = x+(y+z)$. We will see later how
to deal with the latter case.

It turns out that the Knuth-Bendix approach is successful in many important applications. As
an example look at the specification of integers. If we orient all the equations from left to
right, then the resulting system R is already convergent. For instance, for $t_1 \equiv p(op(p(x)))$
and $t_2 \equiv s(op(s(x)))$ we have $t_1 \xrightarrow{*}_R op(x)$ and $t_2 \xrightarrow{*}_R op(x)$. This proves $t_1 =_E t_2$. In
contrast, orienting all equations in the group example from left to right does not result in a
confluent term rewriting system. But the Knuth-Bendix procedure produces a finite
convergent system R by adding new rules.

2.   Completion

Completion addresses the following problem: Given an equational system E, compute an equivalent rewriting system R which is convergent. By equivalence of E and R we mean $=_E = \xleftrightarrow{*}_R$. Let us outline the basic ideas for completion.

As we have seen, convergence splits into two parts: termination and confluence. Termination can be guaranteed by means of a reduction ordering > on terms: If $l > r$ for all rules $l \to r$ in R then R is terminating. We will deal with termination in Section 2.2.

Now assume R is terminating. Then confluence is equivalent to a weaker condition called local confluence. If R is finite, then local confluence can be tested, and if R is not locally confluent then a non-joinable pair (s,t) with $s \xleftrightarrow{*}_R t$ can be computed. The completion algorithm systematically generates all these pairs, adds new rules to R and so tries to compute a confluent system R' which is equivalent to R.

So completion works by computing a sequence $(E_i;R_i)$ of equational and rewriting systems such that

i)   E is equivalent to $E_i \cup R_i$.

ii) R_i is terminating.

iii)   In the limit: $E^\infty = \emptyset$ and R^∞ is convergent.

2.1   Confluence

In general it is undecidable whether a rewriting system R is confluent (Huet [99]). But, already (Newman [172]) noticed that confluence is equivalent to the weaker property of local confluence if R is terminating. And, local confluence can be tested for a finite and terminating R.

Let us write $\to$ for $\to_R$. In fact, the following result is true for any binary relation $\to$ on any set M.

A relation $\to$ is **confluent** if $t_1 \xleftarrow{*} t \xrightarrow{*} t_2$ implies $t_1 \downarrow t_2$. It is **locally confluent** if $t_1 \leftarrow t \to t_2$ implies $t_1 \downarrow t_2$. Notice that local confluence only deals with "local divergence" $t_1 \leftarrow t \to t_2$ while confluence deals with general divergence $t_1 \xleftarrow{*} t \xrightarrow{*} t_2$. This can be visualized by the following diagram

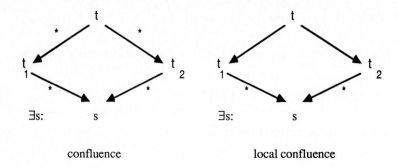

confluence   local confluence

Now we have

Diamond Lemma (Newman [172])
A terminating relation $\rightarrow$ is confluent iff it is locally confluent.

The following example shows that termination is really needed for this lemma:

$$a \leftarrow b \underset{\leftarrow}{\overset{\rightarrow}{}} c \rightarrow d$$

Here $\rightarrow$ is locally confluent but not confluent since $a \overset{*}{\leftarrow} b \overset{*}{\rightarrow} d$, but not $a{\downarrow}d$.

For a finite system R there are in general infinitely many local divergences $t_1 \leftarrow t \rightarrow t_2$. The Critical-Pair-Lemma of Knuth and Bendix allows to reduce the test for local confluence for R to the joinability of a finite number of "critical pairs".

A critical pair comes from a minimal term to which two rules are applicable: Let $l \rightarrow r$ and $s \rightarrow t$ be two rules in R. By renaming of variables we may assume that they do not share common variables. We say that l overlaps s if for some subterm s/p of s, $s/p \notin V$, the terms s/p and l are unifiable, say by most general unifier σ. Then $\sigma(s)$ is the overlap and it can be rewritten by $l \rightarrow r$ and $s \rightarrow t$ giving $\sigma(t) \leftarrow \sigma(s) \rightarrow \sigma(s[p \leftarrow r])$. Then $<\sigma(t), \sigma(s[p \leftarrow r])>$ is a **critical pair**. Let CP(R) be the set of all critical pairs for R.

Notice that a rule may overlap with itself and that any pair of rules defines only finitely many critical pairs. So CP(R) is finite for finite R.

Critical Pair Lemma (Knuth and Bendix [142])
For any rewriting system R, if $t_1 \underset{R}{\leftarrow} t \rightarrow_R t_2$, then either t_1 and t_2 are joinable in R or $t_1 \leftrightarrow_{CP(R)} t_2$.

So, if all critical pairs of R are joinable, then $t_1 \underset{R}{\leftarrow} t \rightarrow_R t_2$ implies $t_1 \downarrow t_2$ and R is locally confluent. This gives

Theorem (Knuth and Bendix [142])
A terminating rewriting system R is confluent iff all pairs in CP(R) are joinable.

Clearly, if R is finite and terminating, then it can be tested whether all critical pairs are joinable.

Let us look at an example. The group axioms can be oriented to R = $\{x*1 \rightarrow x, x*x^{-1} \rightarrow 1,$ $(x*y)*z \rightarrow x*(y*z)\}$. The second and the third rule produce $x*(x^{-1}*z) \leftarrow (x*x^{-1})*z \rightarrow 1*z$. Since $x*(x^{-1}*z)$ and $1*z$ are not joinable, R is not locally confluent. On the other hand, the system R obtained by ordering all equations of the specification of the integers from left to right is locally confluent. It is terminating and hence convergent.

Let us conclude this section with some decidability results. Confluence of rewriting systems is undecidable even in the restricted case where all operations have arity $s \rightarrow s$, i.e. are monadic. This is in essence string rewriting, see (Book [24]). Confluence on ground terms is undecidable even if R is terminating (Kapur et.al. [131]). On the other hand, if R consists only of finitely many ground rules (i.e. containing no variable), then confluence becomes decidable, see (Oyamaguchi [182]) and (Dauchet et.al. [43]).

2.2   Termination

In the previous section we assumed R to be terminating. In general it is undecidable whether a given rewriting system R is terminating even if all its operators are monadic, but for ground systems R termination is decidable (Huet and Lankford [102]). However, there are useful tools to prove termination for non-ground systems. The most important ones are reduction orderings on T(F,V). By an ordering we mean a transitive and irreflexive binary relation.

An ordering > on T(F,V) is a **reduction ordering** if

(1)   > is well founded, i.e. there is no infinite chain $t_1 > t_2 > ...$
(2)   > is compatible with substitutions, i.e. $s > t$ implies $\sigma(s) > \sigma(t)$
(3)   > is compatible with the term structure, i.e. $s > t$ implies $t_0[p \leftarrow s] > t_0[p \leftarrow t]$.

Now one has

Theorem:
A rewriting system R is terminating iff there is a reduction ordering $>$ such that $l > r$ for every rule $l \to r$ in R.

There are several schemes to construct reduction orderings. For an excellent treatment of termination see (Dershowitz [50]). Here we give only an idea of how to construct them. We distinguish two classes of orderings, one defines the order on the terms directly (syntactic orderings) and the other one uses a well-known ordered structure to define the ordering (semantic orderings). The first class contains for example the recursive path ordering RPO (Dershowitz [47]) and the recursive decomposition ordering RDO (Jouannaud et. al. [114]). These orderings are easy to handle since they are based on a partial order $\cdot>$ on the operators (precedence). If an equation appears which is unorientable one can refine the precedence to orient it. This results in a refinement of the term ordering. The well-foundedness of these orderings is based on a deep result of Kruskal [146].They form a powerful class of orderings which are frequently used for orienting equations.

The polynomial orderings form a class of semantic orderings, see (Lankford [152]) and (Ben Cherifa and Lescanne [20]). Here a polynomial $p_f(x_1,...,x_n)$ with positive coefficients is associated to every n-ary operator f. This defines a mapping φ from T(F,V) to the set of polynomials. A polynomial $p(x)$ is greater than $q(x)$ if $p(x) > q(x)$ for all $x \in A$ and a suitable subset $A \subseteq N$. Now an ordering $>$ is defined on T(F,V) by $s > t$ iff $\varphi(s) > \varphi(t)$. As an example, look at the monoid axioms $1*x = x$, $x*1 = x$, $(x*y)*z = x*(y*z)$. If we define $p_1 = 1$ and $p_*(x,y) = 2x+y$ then the induced ordering orients the equations to $x*1 \to x$, $1*x \to x$, $(x*y)*z \to x*(y*z)$. Polynomial orderings can also be used to prove termination of rewriting systems modulo equational theories (see Section 3.2).

2.3 Completion Procedures

In this section we want to discuss the transformation of an equational system E into an equivalent convergent rewrite system R. This transformation is called a completion procedure and is essentially based on the fact, that a terminating rewrite system is confluent if all its critical pairs are joinable. Termination is guaranteed by orienting all rules according to a fixed reduction ordering $>$, i.e. $l > r$ for all rules $l \to r$. So a completion procedure takes E and $>$ as input.

The simplest form of a completion procedure would be the following:

1. Orient all equations in E according to $>$ and let the result be R_0. If an equation cannot be oriented, abort without result. (Notice that $>$ is a partial order, so pairs may be incomparable.)

2. Compute R_{i+1} from R_i as follows:

   For every R_i-critical pair $\langle t_1, t_2 \rangle$ compute a R_i-normal form $\langle t_1\downarrow, t_2\downarrow \rangle$. If $t_1\downarrow \neq t_2\downarrow$ orient this pair according to $>$ and collect these rules in R'. If orientation is not possible, abort. Set $R_{i+1} := R_i \cup R'$. Stop with result R_i if $R_i = R_{i+1}$.

This procedure is very inefficient, but it shows the typical characteristics of a completion procedure, namely

a) It may stop successfully, abort or run forever.

b) If it stops at step i, then R_i is a convergent rewrite system equivalent to E.

c) If it runs forever, then the limit system $R^\infty = \bigcup_{i\geq 0} R_i$ is a convergent infinite rewrite system equivalent to E.

There has been considerable effort to devise efficient completion procedures and to avoid abortion. The key ideas to improve efficiency are to keep the actual system R_i as small as possible and to minimize the number of critical pairs to be considered. For this the unresolved critical pairs are collected in a set E_i of equations, and R_i is simplified as much as possible in the following sense:

A system R is **interreduced** if for all $l \to r$ in R

i) r is irreducible in R and

ii) l is irreducible in $R-\{l \to r\}$.

The interreduced form of a convergent system R is unique up to variable renaming (Avenhaus [2], Metevier [167]). A rewrite system is called **canonical** if it is convergent and interreduced.

It turns out that it is hard to directly prove the correctness of variations of completion procedures that include interreduction and restricted critical pairs criteria (Huet [100]). To overcome this difficulty (Bachmair, Dershowitz, Hsiang [10]) have developed an abstract framework for completion based on the concept of **proof transformation**. Completion steps correspond to the application of inference rules on pairs (E,R), where E is an equational system and R is a rewrite system. Transformations $(E,R) \vdash (E',R')$ are done so that proofs $s \xleftrightarrow{*}_{E\cup R} t$ become simpler. The simpliest proofs are the rewrite proofs, i.e. proofs of the form $s \xrightarrow{*}_R \circ {}_R\xleftarrow{*} t$. So the transformation $(E_0,R_0) \vdash (E_1,R_1) \vdash ... \vdash (E_n,R_n)$ will lead to $E_n = \emptyset$ with R_n convergent, if this is possible.

The relation ⊢ is defined by the following inference rules (we use $s \doteq t$ for $s = t$ or $t = s$).

Deduce	$(E,R) \vdash (E \cup \{s = t\},R)$	if $<s,t> \in CP(R)$
Simplify	$(E \cup \{s \doteq t\};R) \vdash (E \cup \{s = u\},R)$	if $t \to_R u$
Delete	$(E \cup \{s = s\},R) \vdash (E,R)$	
Orient	$(E \cup \{s \doteq t\},R) \vdash (E,R \cup \{s \to t\})$	if $s > t$
Reduce 1	$(E,R \cup \{s \to t\}) \vdash (E,R \cup \{s \to u\})$	if $t \to_R u$
Reduce 2	$(E,R \cup \{s \to t\}) \vdash (E \cup \{u = t\},R)$	if $s \to_R u$,
		by $l \to r$ in R with $s \triangleright l$.

The first four rules are enough for completion, and the Reduce-rules are used for interreduction and hence for gaining efficiency. Deduce is used to introduce critical pairs as equations, and Simplify, Delete, and Orient are used to transform the critical pairs into rules, if necessary. Reduce 1 simplifies the right-hand side of a rule and Reduce 2 simplifies the left-hand side of a rule. This is only allowed if the left hand side l of the rule $l \to r$ used to reduce s is smaller than s in a certain ordering. To be precise, $s \triangleright l$ means that $\sigma(l)$ is a subterm of s for some σ but not vice versa.

A **completion sequence** is a sequence (E_i,R_i), $i \in I$, $I \subseteq N$ with $(E_i,R_i) \vdash (E_{i+1},R_{i+1})$. (We always assume $I = N$ and extend a finite sequence by repeating the last (E_i,R_i) for finite I). Such a sequence defines the sets of **persistent equations** and **persistent rules** namely $E^\infty = \bigcup_{i \geq 0} \bigcap_{j \geq i} E_j$, $R^\infty = \bigcup_{i \geq 0} \bigcap_{j \geq i} R_j$, respectively.

Let $(E_o,R_o) := (E,\emptyset)$. We want R^∞ to be a convergent rewrite system for E. To achieve this goal, we have to guarantee that all equations are resolved and that all critical pairs are considered.

Definition: A completion sequence (E_i,R_i), $i \geq 0$ is **fair** if

a) $E^\infty = \emptyset$ and   b) $CP(R^\infty) \subseteq \bigcup_{i \geq 0} E_i$.

A **completion procedure** is any program which, with an equational system E and a reduction ordering > as input, either computes a fair completion sequence starting with $(E_o,R_o) = (E,\emptyset)$ or fails. The main result in (Bachmair et. al. [10]) is that a completion procedure with input (E,>) either fails or computes a convergent rewrite system R^∞ for E. Moreover, if no Reduce rule is applicable to $(\emptyset,R^\infty)$, then R^∞ is even canonical.

Let us outline the main ideas for the proof of this result. Let (E_i,R_i), $i \geq 0$ be a fair completion sequence starting with $(E,\emptyset)$. It is easy to prove by induction that

(i) $=_E = \xleftrightarrow{*}_{E_i \cup R_i}$ for all $i \in I$ and

(ii) $l > r$ for all $l \to r$ in R_i.

Hence $=_E \supseteq \xleftarrow{*}\rightarrow_{R^\infty}$ and R^∞ is terminating.

To prove $=_E \subseteq \xleftarrow{*}\rightarrow_{R^\infty}$ and the confluence of R^∞ an ordering on "justified proofs" is introduced as follows: A **justified proof** of s $\xleftarrow{*}\rightarrow_{E \cup R}$ t is a sequence $t_o, t_1, ..., t_n$ such that $s \equiv t_o$, $t \equiv t_n$ and $t_i \rightarrow_R t_{i+1}$ or $t_{i+1} \rightarrow_R t_i$ or $t_i \leftrightarrow_E t_{i+1}$, and as justification the positions p_i and the used rules/ equations (l_i, r_i) in $E \cup R$ used in step i are given.

From the given reduction ordering > a Noetherian ordering $>_c$ on justified proofs is defined such that rewrite proofs s $\xrightarrow{*} \circ \xleftarrow{*}$ t are minimal among all proofs of s $\xleftarrow{*}\rightarrow$ t.

Lemma (Bachmair et. al. [10]). Let (E_i, R_i) i $\geq$ 0 be a fair completion sequence and $\mathcal{P}$ a proof of s $\xleftarrow{*}\rightarrow_{Ei \cup Ri}$ t, such that $\mathcal{P}$ is not a rewrite proof. Then there is a j $\geq$ i and a proof $\mathcal{P'}$ of s $\xleftarrow{*}\rightarrow_{Ej \cup Rj}$ t with $\mathcal{P} >_c \mathcal{P'}$.

This gives

Theorem (Bachmair et. al. [10]). Let $\mathcal{A}$ be a completion procedure that does not fail on input (E,>). If s $=_E$ t, then $\mathcal{A}$ produces a pair (E_i, R_i) such that s and t are R_i-joinable. In particular $\mathcal{A}$ computes a convergent rewrite system R^∞ for E.
Thus completion provides a semi-decision procedure for E-validity if it does not fail and a decision procedure for E-validity if it halts successfully.

2.4 Two examples

a) Let E be given by E = { -(x*y) = (-x)*y, -(x*y) = x*(-y), (x*y)*z = x*(y*z)}.
These equations may be oriented using a variant of an RPO ordering into the following rules
(1)	-(x*y)	$\rightarrow$ (-x)*y
(2)	-(x*y)	$\rightarrow$ x*(-y)
(3)	(x*y)*z	$\rightarrow$ x*(y*z)

Computing critical pairs between these rules yields

(4)   (-x)*y $\rightarrow$ x*(-y)   from critical pair between (1) and (2)

Rule (1) gets simplified with (4) giving

(1')   -(x*y) $\rightarrow$ x*(-y)   which is in fact rule (2)

The critical pairs between (3) and (3), (2) and (3) and (3) and (4) are all joinable using (2), (3), and (4). As an example consider the superposition between (3) and (4) which yields the critical pair (x*(-y))*z and (-x)*(y*z). Both terms reduce to x*(y*(-z)).

Thus the system R' containing rules (2), (3), and (4) is convergent.

b) In contrast to the successful completion in a) consider the rules

1) $(x+y)+z$ → $x+(y+z)$
2) $f(x) + f(y)$ → $f(x+y)$

Overlapping rules 1) and 2) gives the overlap $(f(x) + f(y)) + z$ and the critical pair
$<f(x) + (f(y) + z), f(x+y) + z>$. Using the lexicographical RPO with precedence + ·> f
this critical pair after reduction is transformed into the rule

3.1) $f(x+y)+z → f(x) + (f(y) + z)$

Overlapping rules 2) and 3.1) gives the overlap $f(f(x) + f(y)) +z$ and the rule $f^2(x+y) + z →$
$f^2(x) + (f^2(y) + z)$. Continuing this process we get the infinite sequence of rules

3.n) $f^n(x+y) + z → f^n(x) + (f^n(y) + z)$ $n ≥ 1$

In this sequence the rule 3.n+1) is generated by overlapping rule 2) into 3.n). One can easily
show that in the infinite system $R^∞$ consisting of the rules 1), 2) and 3.n) all critical pairs are
joinable. Hence $R^∞$ is convergent.

This example shows that completion can run forever without failure and so produce an
infinite convergent rewriting system $R^∞$. This example also shows the great influence of the
reduction order to the completion process: If we use as ordering the RPO with precedence
f ·> +, then completion stops immediately with the second rule oriented in the other
direction.

3.   Extensions

There are many reasons to extend the basic rewriting approach discussed in Chapter 2. Two
of them are failure and divergence of the completion procedure, but also an extension of the
expressive power of the language of equations is desirable. Let us outline the most important
directions of extensions.

1. Extensions to avoid failure of the completion procedure:

As described earlier a completion procedure may fail because no equation can be ordered by the used ordering. In some cases a refinement of the ordering may help, but in some cases it is in principle impossible to order equations without violating the termination property. The most prominent examples are those where some binary operators are commutative or associative and commutative. If E contains a set A of unorientable equations, then A may be split from E and rewriting modulo the congruence generated by A can be done. To do so, one needs unification and matching modulo A. But only for few theories A unification and matching algorithms modulo A are known. A slightly more general approach is to use globally finite rewriting systems. We discuss these topics in Section 3.1. An even more general approach is to use unorientable equations for generating critical pairs only, but not for rewriting. We discuss this "unfailing completion" in Section 3.2.

2. Increasing expressibility of the equational systems:

Especially in software specification one needs two extensions, namely conditional equations and order sorted equational specification. This allows in many cases more succinct descriptions of the algebraic structure. We discuss conditional rewriting in Section 3.4 and order sorted rewriting in Section 3.5.

3. Restricting confluence:

In connection with verification of software only confluence on ground terms is required. So, specialized criteria for ground confluence are of interest in this setting. This will be discussed in Section 4.1. In some cases confluence on just one congruence class is required. For example, if there is an operator "-" such that $s =_E t$ is equivalent to $s\text{-}t =_E 0$ - as in the case of groups or rings - then only confluence on the congruence class $[0]$ is enough to solve E-validity. Some applications of restricted confluence will be quoted in Section 4.

3.1   Rewriting Modulo a Congruence

In this section we consider the following situation: Given an equational system $E \cup A$, where A is a relatively simple subsystem of $E \cup A$ which admits no convergent rewrite system but generates only finite congruence classes. Then one can do "rewriting modulo A" and look for a rewriting system R which is "convergent modulo A". In this way $E \cup A$-validity can be reduced to A-validity. As pointed out earlier, the most important application is that A is an AC-theory. This problem was studied in (Huet [99]) for left linear rewrite systems (i.e. every variable in a left-hand side l of a rule in R appears only once in l) and for the general case in (Peterson and Stickel [193]) and (Jouannaud and Kirchner [110]). There a completion procedure is developed and a detailed analysis is given on which critical pairs are needed for testing confluence. (Bachmair and Dershowitz [8]) extend the inference rule approach based on proof simplification to rewriting modulo A.

Let $\sim_A$ be the congruence generated by A. One way to define **rewriting modulo** A is to do rewriting on the A-congruence classes. This is reflected by the rewrite relation $\rightarrow_{R/A} = \sim_A \circ \rightarrow_R \circ \sim_A$, i.e. $s \rightarrow_{R/A} t$ if $s \sim_A s' \rightarrow_R t' \sim t$ for some terms s' and t'. This rewrite relation is costly to implement, for in order to rewrite a term s one has to search through the whole A-congruence class of s for a term s' to which a rule $l \rightarrow r$ in R can be applied. To avoid this, one may restrict the application of A-equations to that subterm s/p to which the rule $l \rightarrow r$ is applied. This leads to the rewrite relation $s \rightarrow_{R,A} t$ iff $s/p \sim_A \sigma(l)$ and $t \equiv s[p \leftarrow \sigma(r)]$ for some position p in s, some rule $l \rightarrow r$ in R and some substitution σ. The problem to find for two terms s_o and l a substitution σ with $s_o \sim_A \sigma(l)$ is called matching modulo A. If A is an AC-theory then this problem is relatively simple.

In (Jouannaud and Kirchner [110]) an abstract theory of R-convergence modulo A is developed. Here we line out the basic tools to prove that $\rightarrow_{R,A}$ is convergent modulo A.

R is **convergent modulo A** if

i) $s \xleftarrow{*}\rightarrow_{R \cup A} t$ implies $s -\xrightarrow{*}_{R,A} s'$, $t -\xrightarrow{*}_{R,A} t'$ and $s' \sim_A t'$ for some terms s', t' (Church-Rosser property).

ii) there is no infinite chain $t_1 \rightarrow_{R/A} t_2 \rightarrow_{R/A} t_3 \rightarrow_{R/A} \cdots$ (termination property).

A test for the Church-Rosser property splits into two parts, **local confluence** modulo A and **local coherence** modulo A. This is defined in the next diagram.

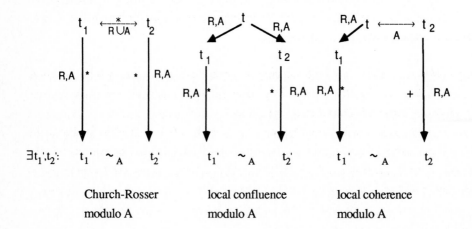

Church-Rosser   local confluence   local coherence
modulo A   modulo A   modulo A

Using these definitions one can prove the following result

Theorem (Jouannaud and Kirchner [110]):
If $\rightarrow_{R/A}$ is terminating, then R has the Church-Rosser property modulo A iff R is locally confluent and locally coherent modulo A.

To test local confluence and local coherence modulo A one has to compute the critical pairs. This needs unification modulo A , see (Siekmann [213]) for this problem. If R is finite and unification modulo A is finitary, then the set CP(R,A) of critical pairs also is finite. For details see (Jouannaud and Kirchner [110]).

A way to deal with unorientable equations without the need of matching and unification modulo a congruence is to use globally finite rewriting systems. A system R is **globally finite** if for all terms t the set $\{t' \mid t \xrightarrow{*}_R t'\}$ is finite. If R can be split into $R = R_c \cup R_r$ where R_c contains the cyclic and R_r the reducing rules, i.e. R_r is terminating, then the notions of local confluence and local coherence may be used to get criteria for confluence modulo R_c. The advantage of this approach is that no matching and no unification modulo a congruence is needed. The disadvantage is that completion often leads to infinite systems, so rewriting modulo A tends to be more succinct. For inductive proofs however where only ground confluence is required this approach is very useful, see (Göbel [78, 80]).

3.2   Unfailing Completion

Completion may fail due to the fact that equations appear which are unorientable by the fixed reduction ordering >. One way to deal with this difficulty was described before, namely to start with a weak reduction ordering and to make it stronger whenever an unorientable equation appears. This technique is supported by precedence based orderings, but is not able to avoid failure in general.

It is known that for a fixed ordering > a (not necessarily finite) convergent rewrite system R compatible with > exists if every E-congruence class has a unique >-minimal element (Avenhaus [2], Metevier [167]). Let this be the case.
It may happen that some completion sequence starting with (E,Ø) fails while another stops with success (Dershowitz et. al. [56], Avenhaus [1]). So backtracking can be helpful. Nevertheless the next example shows that even with backtracking one can fail in finding a convergent system:

R_1: $f(x,y) \to h(x,c)$ $g(h(x,c)) \to h(x,c)$ $h(c,c) \to c$

                $f(x,y) \to h(c,y)$ $g(h(c,x)) \to c$ $g(c) \to c$

We use the recursive path ordering RPO with precedence $f \rightsquigarrow h$. Starting with $(E_1,R_1) = (\varnothing,R_1)$ no completion step is possible because $h(x,c)$ and $h(c,y)$ are incomparable. (In fact, these two terms are comparable with no reduction ordering at all.). On the other hand, for

R: $f(x,y) \to c$ $h(x,c) \to c$

            $g(c) \to c$ $h(c,x) \to c$

we have $\overset{*}{\leftrightarrow}_R = \overset{*}{\leftrightarrow}_{R1}$ and R is convergent and compatible with >.

To overcome such problems an extension of completion, called **unfailing completion**, has been developed (Hsiang, Rusinowitch [98], Bachmair et. al. [11]) based on earlier methods from (Lankford [149]). Clearly, such a method cannot always find a convergent system R equivalent to E, since such a system may not exist. But it will find a rewrite system R equivalent to E and compatible with > which is ground confluent, i.e. R is confluent on the set of ground terms. The basic idea is to use both sides of unorientable equations in the completion process for critical pair generation but not to use these equations for simplification.

This results in a new inference rule for the completion process:

Deduce U   (E;R) $\vdash$ (E $\cup$ {s = t},R) if $s \leftrightarrow_E u \leftrightarrow_E t$

If > can be extended to a total simplification ordering on ground terms, then any fair completion sequence results in a ground confluent R^∞. This method can be extended to define a refutationally complete procedure for E-validity (Bachmair et al. [10],[11]).

3.3   Conditional Rewriting

Conditional equations are frequently used in the specification of abstract data types, not only because they allow the common definition by cases, but also because they allow more succinct descriptions. We write C $\Rightarrow$ s = t for a conditional equation and s = t if the condition C is empty.

The following example specifies the integers with predecessor, successor and the less-than relation <.

Example:

(1)		$0 < 0$	$=$ false
(2)		$0 < s(0)$	$=$ true
(3)		$s(x) < y$	$=$ $x < p(y)$
(4)		$p(x) < y$	$=$ $x < s(y)$
(5)	$x<y = \text{true} \Rightarrow$	$x<s(y)$	$=$ true
(6)	$y<x = \text{false} \Rightarrow$	$y<p(x)$	$=$ false
(7)		$s(p(x))$	$=$ x
(8)		$p(s(x))$	$=$ x

We restrict ourselves to the case where the condition C is a finite conjunction of equations $C \equiv u_1 = v_1 \wedge ... \wedge u_n = v_n$. A conditional equation $C \Rightarrow s = t$ is implicitely regarded as universally quantified. So we are dealing with Horn clause logic and the initial model of a finite set of conditional equations exists.

A conditional equation $C \Rightarrow l = r$ is transformed into a conditional rule $C \Rightarrow l \rightarrow r$ by orienting the equation $l = r$ acccording to some fixed order. A **conditional rewrite system** R is a set of conditional rules $C \Rightarrow l \rightarrow r$ such that any variable occurring in r, u_i or v_i is also contained in l.

There are several possibilities to define the rewrite relation $\rightarrow_R$ defined by R, according to how the condition C is to be evaluated, see (Kaplan [118]), (Dershowitz, et al. [57],[58]). Evaluating the condition $u_i = v_i$ by $u_i \xleftarrow{*}_R v_i$ leads to the fact that the one step rewrite relation $\rightarrow_R$ may be undecidable. So one evaluates $u_i = v_i$ by $u_i \downarrow v_i$ and defines $s \rightarrow_R t$ iff there is a rule $u_1 = v_1 \wedge ... \wedge u_n = v_n \Rightarrow l \rightarrow r$, a position p in s and substitution σ with $s/p \equiv \sigma(l)$, $\sigma(u_i) \downarrow \sigma(v_i)$ and $t \equiv s[p \leftarrow \sigma(r)]$.

Note that rewriting $s \rightarrow_R t$ calls recursively the rewrite relation $\rightarrow_R$ for verifying the conditions $u_i \downarrow v_i$. This recursive definition may lead to infinite computations for just one rewrite step. To avoid this, one assumes that u_i, v_i, $r < l$ for some reduction ordering. It is then easy to see that in this case the relation $\rightarrow_R$ is decidable and that R is terminating.

The next question is how to test confluence. This is again based on critical pairs. Assume $C \Rightarrow l_1 \rightarrow r_1$ and $D \Rightarrow l_2 \rightarrow r_2$ are two conditional rules, that l_1/p and l_2 are unifiable by most general unifier σ and that $<s,t>$ is the corresponding critical pair. $\sigma(C) \wedge \sigma(D): \{s,t\}$ is then a **contextual critical pair** .

As an example let R be the conditional rewrite system for the specification of integers from the beginning of this section where all the equations $C \Rightarrow 1 = r$ are oriented from left to right into $C \Rightarrow 1 \rightarrow r$. Then the rules (4) and (6) produce the contextual critical pair

$$p(x) < z = \text{false} \quad : \quad \{x < s(p(z)), \text{ false}\}$$

A contextual critical pair $u_1 = v_1 \wedge ... \wedge u_n = v_n : \{s,t\}$ is **joinable** if for every substitution σ satisfying the conditions $\sigma(u_i) \downarrow \sigma(v_i)$ we have $\sigma(s) \downarrow \sigma(t)$. Clearly, the condition that every contextual critical pair of R is joinable is a necessary condition for R to be locally confluent. But this condition is not sufficient for confluence. There exists a terminating conditional rewriting system R such that all contextual critical pairs are joinable but R is not locally confluent (Dershowitz et. al. [58]).

But if one restricts attention to **reductive systems** R, i.e. for some reduction ordering > we have $1 > r, 1 > u_i, 1 > v_i$ for every rule $u_1 = v_1 \wedge ... \wedge u_n = v_n \Rightarrow 1 \rightarrow r$, the above criterion is necessary and sufficient, see (Kaplan [119]), (Jouannaud and Waldmann [116]) and (Dershowitz et. al. [58]).

Theorem:

A reductive conditional rewriting system is confluent iff all its contextual critical pairs are joinable.

For a more detailed discussion on confluence of conditional rewriting systems see (Dershowitz et. al. [58]).

For the completion procedure one has to test whether a contextual critical pair C: {s,t} is joinable and if not, to add new conditional equations. This causes problems since one has to test for every substitution σ whether it satisfies $\sigma(s) \downarrow \sigma(t)$ whenever it satisfies C. A rough way to deal with this problem is to add $C \Rightarrow s = t$ whenever one cannot prove either $s \downarrow t$ or that no σ satisfies C. Another problem is that a conditional equation $C \Rightarrow s = t$ cannot be ordered into a reductive conditional rule $C \Rightarrow s \rightarrow t$ if the condition C is not smaller than s. See (Ganzinger [72]) and (Kounalis and Rusinowitch [144]) for techniques to transform a system of conditional equations into a confluent conditional rewrite system.

3.4   Order Sorted Rewriting

In the previous sections we have considered equational systems that allow data of different sorts, but the sorts were unrelated, i.e. it was impossible to express the fact that some sort is a subsort of another sort. Such an equational system is called many sorted. In this section we allow sorts to be ordered.

The possibility to have sort hierarchies is very useful in the specification of data types. It is possible to deal with partial functions by specifying their domain as a subsort. For example the pop-operation is only defined on stacks which are non-empty. So one can declare the sort NONEMPTY-STACK as a subsort of sort STACK and declare pop: NONEMPTY-STACK → STACK. This also helps to avoid conditional equations. In theorem proving the introduction of appropriate subsorts may allow to encode a lot of information in the signature and thus to reduce the search space.

An **order sorted specification** consists of an order sorted signature (S,F,<) and a set E of equations. Here < is a partial order on the set S of sorts. A sort declaration has the form $s_1 < s_2$ and indicates that all data (terms) of sort s_1 are also of sort s_2. An operator declaration has the form f: $s_1 \dots s_n$ → s as before, but there may be several declarations for the same operator f (overloading). This defines in a natural way the set T(F,V) of terms over the S-indexed set of variables V. If a term t has sort s_1 and $s_1 < s_2$ then t has also sort s_2. As an example one can specify the integers with the not-greater-then relation ≤ by

sorts:	NEG < INAT,	ZERO < INAT,	INAT < INT
	ZERO < NAT,	POS < NAT,	NAT < INT

variables: x,y: INT , i: NAT n: NEG

ops:	0: → ZERO	
	s: NAT → POS	s: INT → INT
	p: INAT → NEG	p: INT → INT
	+: INT,INT → INT	+: NAT,NAT → NAT
	+: POS,NAT → POS	+: NAT,POS → POS
	true,false: → BOOL	≤: INT,INT → BOOL
eqns:	p(s(x)) = x	p(x) ≤ y = x ≤ s(y)
	s(p(x)) = x	s(x) ≤ y = x ≤ p(y)
	x+0 = x	0 ≤ i = true
	x+s(y) = s(x+y)	0 ≤ n = false
	x+p(y) = p(x+y)	

Given a set E of equations over a signature Σ = (S,F,<) one can define in a natural way the Σ-algebras and the models of E (Goguen et. al. [82]). We write E ⊨ s = t if the equation s = t holds in all models of E. We write s ↔$_E$ t if s can be transformed into t by one application of an equation in E. (Notice that a well-formed term s may be transformed into a non-well-formed term by an application of an equation. But ↔$_E$ is a relation on the set

T(F,V) of well-formed terms). If R is a set of rules (oriented equations) then $\to_R$ is defined analogously.

In the many sorted case we have $E \models s = t$ iff $s \xleftarrow{*}\to_E t$ by Birkhoffs Theorem. Unfortunately, this does not hold in general for the order sorted case as the following example of (Smolka et. al. [217]) shows

sorts:	$A < B$		
ops:	$a, a': \to A$	$b: \to B$	$f: A \to A$
eqns:	$a = b$	$a' = b$	

We have $E \models f(a) = f(a')$ but not $f(a) \xleftarrow{*}\to_E f(a')$, due to the fact that a proof of $f(a) \xleftarrow{*}\to_E f(a')$ would need $f(b)$ which is not a well-formed term.

We now assume that the set E of equations is transformed into a set R of rules by orienting the equations. R is called **compatible** if the application of a rule transforms every well-formed term into a well-formed term, i.e., if $s/p \equiv \sigma(l)$ then $s[p \leftarrow \sigma(r)]$ is well-formed for every rule $l \to r$ and every substitution σ. Then we have the soundness and completeness of rewriting (Smolka et. al. [217]).

Theorem:
If R is compatible and confluent , then
$$R \models s = t \quad \text{iff} \quad s \downarrow t \quad \text{iff} \quad s \xleftarrow{*}\to_R t$$
for all $s, t \in T(F,V)$.

To test whether R is locally confluent one defines the critical pairs of two rules $l_1 \to r_1$ and $l_2 \to r_2$ exactly as in the many sorted case. But notice that here order sorted unification is needed. This may result in the fact that unification is no more unitary and one has to consider a complete set of unifiers for l_1/p and l_2 that subsume all unifiers of l_1/p and l_2.

If R is not compatible one cannot hope that R is locally confluent if all critical pairs are confluent. So one restricts to **sort decreasing** rewriting systems R, i.e. one requires that for every rule $l \to r$ in R and every substitution σ, if $\sigma(l)$ has sort s then $\sigma(r)$ has sort s. In this case R is compatible and one has the following result, see (Smolka et. al., [217]).

Theorem:
Let R be sort decreasing. Then R is locally confluent iff all critical pairs are joinable.

It is decidable whether a rewriting system R is sort decreasing. If R is terminating then the test for confluence depends on the ability to compute critical pairs and this depends on the ability to compute a complete set of order sorted unifiers for two terms s and t.

In order to not get too difficult unification problems one restricts attention to **regular** signatures (S,F,<), i.e., i) < is actually a partial ordering on S and ii) every term has a unique least sort according to this partial ordering. For a finite regular signature the unification problem is decidable and for every unifiable pair s,t there is a finite set of complete unifiers which can be computed. So confluence of R is decidable in this case if R is terminating.

For a fundamental treatment of order sorted equational computation we refer to (Smolka et. al. [217]). For order sorted Knuth-Bendix completion see (Gnaedig et. al. [76]). An early reference to order sorted rewriting is (Cunningham and Dick [40]).

4.   Applications

In this section we describe some of the various applications of rewrite methods to equational reasoning. The most important application is deciding (semi deciding) validity of equations in all or some models of an equational theory. If the equational system E can be transformed into an equivalent convergent rewrite system, then validity of equations in all models of E can be decided. The unfailing version of completion can be used as a semi decision procedure without failure provided some weak conditions on the ordering used are satisfied. We will describe the application of the completion method for proving equations in the initial model of an equational theory, i.e. by doing proofs by consistency.

Because validity and satisfiability are related, we will also describe some techniques for solving equations in models of an equational theory based on rewriting notions.

Some applications of rewrite methods to first order theorem proving will be presented. First order formulae can be seen as polynomials in an appropriate boolean ring and the question whether a formula is a theorem can be reduced to the question whether 1 is in the ideal generated by certain polynomials associated to the formula. This approach relates first order theorem proving with the ideal membership problem for certain boolean rings which can be solved by computing Gröbner bases.

In fact it turned out that rewriting modulo AC, which contains the case of commutative rings, is one of the most fruitful applications of rewriting techniques to equational reasoning. New applications of Gröbner bases in computational geometry and geometrical theorem proving are described in (Buchberger [34]). Rewriting in algebraic structures like rings, groups and monoids have been extensively studied. For a survey see (Le Chenadec [161]). It turns out that for some algebraic structures like rings and monoids the general approach using signatures, terms and equational axioms involves considerably many unnecessary computational steps. For many such structures canonical representatives for the elements are given and it is sometimes easier to define rewriting using these representatives. This is the case for finitely presented commutative rings, and for monoids. In the former case polynomials with coefficients in **Z**, and in the latter case strings over a finite alphabet can be used as the primitive representations of elements. We will discuss polynomial rewriting and string rewriting as a method for solving problems in rings and monoids.

We will not discuss here applications of rewriting to equational and logic programming, one of the originating sources of rewriting. In particular, for the applications of completion to program synthesis see e.g. (Dershowitz [50],[52]).

4.1   Proving Theorems in the Initial Model

In many applications not the validity of equations in every model of an equational system is required but only validity of equations in the standard model, i.e. the initial model of E. We define s = t to be an **inductive theorem** of E if for all ground-substitutions σ we have $\sigma(s) =_E \sigma(t)$. Recall that σ is a ground-substitution if $\sigma(x)$ is a ground term for all x such that $\sigma(x) \neq x$. We will write $s =_{\mathcal{I}(E)} t$ if s = t is an inductive theorem of E.

Example: Natural Numbers with addition and multiplication.

E: add(x,0) = x   add(x,s(y)) = s(add(x,y))
         mul(x,0) = 0   mul(x,s(y)) = add(x,mul(x,y))

Here the equations
       add(x,y) = add(y,x)   and   mul(x,y) = mul(y,x)
are not theorems of E, i.e. these equations do not hold in every model of E. But these equations are inductive theorems of E, they hold in the intended model of natural numbers.

Proving inductive theorems normally requires structural - or more general - Noetherian induction. (Musser [169]) first suggested to use a completion procedure to prove such theorems, see also (Goguen [81]). This approach has been called "inductionless induction" in (Lankford [154]) and "proof by consistency" in (Kapur and Musser [124]).

The basic idea for proofs of this kind is the following: The equation s = t is an inductive theorem of E iff for all ground terms u,v we have u $=_E$ v iff u $=_{E_0}$ v, where $E_0 = E \cup \{s=t\}$. This means that the equation s = t does not introduce inconsistencies on the set of ground terms.

Now suppose R is a canonical rewrite system for E and completion leads to a canonical rewrite system R^∞ for E_0. The test whether for ground terms u $=_{E_0}$ v implies u $=_E$ v leads to the following notion introduced in (Jouannaud and Kounalis [111]): A term t is **inductively R-reducible** if for each ground substitution σ the term σ(t) is R-reducible. Using this notion the following theorem holds: see e.g. (Jouannaud and Kounalis, [111]).

Theorem: Let R be a canonical rewriting system for E and R^∞ the result of a fair completion sequence without failure starting with $E_0 = E \cup \{s = t\}$. Then s $=_{\mathcal{I}(E)}$ t iff the left-hand side of every rule in R^∞ is inductively R-reducible.

So the completion procedure and its generalizations can be used to prove inductive theorems. By the theorem these proofs are reduced to some tests for inductive R-reducibility.

For finite R inductive reducibility is decidable (Plaisted [194]), (Kapur et al. [134]). If R is left-linear inductive reduciblity can be decided more efficiently (Jouannaud and Kounalis [111]). In some important applications the operators can be split into constructors and defined function symbols. In this case there exist even more efficient algorithms for testing inductive reducibility, see e.g. (Nipkow and Weikum [173]).

Proving inductive theorems is of great importance for many applications, e.g. for proving properties of specifications and equational programs. A lot of research has been done to improve the method and to extend its applicability.

The main obstacle for applying this method is the search space, which for proofs by consistency may be very large. Especially, the completion procedure with input R $\cup$ {s = t} may run forever or abort. (Fribourg [68]) noticed that for completion one may restrict the computation of critical pairs to those at "inductively complete" positions. This tries to mimic classical structural induction proofs. (Göbel [79]) uses a different approach to restrict the critical pairs and (Küchlin [148]) refines the techniques of Fribourg. Both approaches lead to a system R^∞ which is confluent on ground terms only. (Göbel [80]) developes methods to compute for a globally finite system R an equivalent R_o that is ground confluent. When applied to inductive proofs one can use inductive lemmata for simplification. See (Bachmair [5]) for generalizations and the problem of avoiding abortion.

The method also applies if some operators are associative and commutative. One has to use rewriting and completion modulo an AC-theory. See (Goguen [81]), (Lankford [154]), (Jounnaud and Kounalis [111]) and for experiments (Huet and Hullott [101]). For conditional rewriting systems, the method has also been adapted. (Ganzinger [71],[72]) studies ways to find ground confluent conditional rewrite systems and to use inductive lemmata for simplification. (Padawitz [183]) studies Horn clause logic with equality and develops a method to prove inductive theorems. He gives a general framework incorporating conditional rewriting, distinction by cases and Noetherian induction. See (Padawitz [184],[186]) for a survey and further results.

4.2   Solving Equations and Logic Programming

In this section we describe rewrite techniques for solving equations in an equational theory T, a problem which is also known as unification of terms modulo T. These techniques naturally generalize to the use of rewrite systems as a combination of logic and functional programming.

We assume T to be given by a canonical rewriting system R. A solution to an equation $s = t$ is any substitution σ such that $\sigma(s) =_R \sigma(t)$, σ is called an **R-unifier**. Two questions are interesting, namely to decide whether there is a solution at all and if possible to represent and compute all possible solutions.
A set U of R-unifiers is a **complete set of R-unifiers** if for every R-unifier σ there is an element $\tau \in U$ and a substitution σ' with $\sigma = \sigma' \cdot \tau$.

Example:
a)   Let T be given by
   R: $h(h(x)) \rightarrow h(x)$, $h(a) \rightarrow a$
   The equation $f(x) = f(h(x))$ has solutions $\sigma_1 = \{x \leftarrow a\}$, $\sigma_2 = \{x \leftarrow h(z)\}$
   Even more, $U = \{\sigma_1, \sigma_2\}$ is a complete set of R-unifiers.
b)   Let T be given by
   R: $g(f(x)) \rightarrow g(x)$.
   The equation $g(x) = g(o)$ has no finite complete set of R-unifiers, but $U = \{\sigma_i \mid i \geq 0\}$
   with $\sigma_i = \{x \leftarrow f^i(o)\}$ is an infinite complete set of R-unifiers.

Solving equations by using the "narrowing" technique was used by (Fay [64]), (Lankford and Ballantine [157]) and (Hullot [105]), and was optimized by (Rety [204]). The basic idea involved is the following: Assume σ is an R-unifier of s and t, i.e. $\sigma(s) =_R \sigma(t)$. Since R is canonical, there must be a term u such that $\sigma(s) \xrightarrow{*}_R u \xleftarrow{*}_R \sigma(t)$. This means either $\sigma(s) \equiv \sigma(t)$ or the term $\sigma(s = = t)$ is R-reducible. (We consider here = = as a new symbol not appearing in R). We may assume that s,t are R-irreducible, for otherwise we replace s,t by their normal forms. If s,t are unifiable under the empty theory, i.e. $\sigma'(s) \equiv \sigma'(t)$ for some σ', then the most general unifier σ_0 is unique (up to renaming of variables) and can easily be computed by standard algorithms. If this is the case we have a solution. If s,t are not unifiable, then s,t have to be instantiated by a substitution Θ_1 such that $\Theta_1 (s = = t)$ is R-reducible. The problem s = = t is replaced by $s_1 = = t_1$, where $s_1 \equiv \Theta_1(s)$, $t_1 \equiv \Theta_1(t)$. This process builts up a search tree and it can be shown, see e.g. (Hullot [105]), that this search tree leads to all solutions of s = t. Let us discuss some details.

We write $u \rightsquigarrow_\Theta v$ if for some $l \rightarrow r$ in R some subterm u/p unifies with l by mgu Θ and v is $v \equiv \Theta(u)[p \leftarrow \Theta(r)]$. Notice that $\rightsquigarrow$ generalizes $\rightarrow$, since $u \rightsquigarrow v$ is actually a reduction step $u \rightarrow v$ if Θ is a match, i.e., $u/p \equiv \Theta(l)$, and not a real unifier of u/p and l. In general Θ is called the **narrowing** substitution.

A **narrowing sequence** has the form $s_0 = = t_0 \rightsquigarrow_{\Theta 1} s_1 = = t_1 \rightsquigarrow_{\Theta 2} \cdots \rightsquigarrow_{\Theta n} s_n = = t_n$ such that s_n, t_n are unifiable under the empty theory by mgu τ. Let $\Theta = \Theta_n \circ \ldots \circ \Theta_1$. It is easy to see that $\sigma = \tau \circ \Theta$ is an R-solution for $s_0 = t_0$, i.e. $\sigma(s_0) =_R \sigma(t_0)$ which proves that the narrowing procedure is correct. The procedure is also complete: If σ is a R-solution for $s_0 = t_0$, then there is a narrowing sequence as above such that σ is an instantiation of a solution $\tau \circ \Theta$, i.e. $\sigma = \sigma' \circ \tau \circ \Theta$ for some σ'.

For details of the outlined procedure and for refinements and improvements the interested reader may consult (Hullot [105]) and (Rety [204]). Hullot restricts narrowing steps to so-called "basic" positions but rules in R are not allowed to simplify the actual equation to be solved. Rety combines basic narrowing with simplification and proves its completeness.

A narrowing sequence may be infinite even if R is terminating. As an example let
R: $g(f(z)) \rightarrow g(z)$,   then
       $g(x) = = 0 \rightsquigarrow g(x) = = 0 \rightsquigarrow g(x) = = 0 \ldots$
where in each step the substitution $x \leftarrow f(x)$ and the rule from R is used for simplification. In (Rety et al.[205]) such situations are considered and methods are developed to deal with infinite rational search trees.

4.3   First-Order Theorem Proving

(Hsiang [94]) was the first to develop a theorem prover for first-order logic based on rewriting systems. Boolean functions have unique normal form representations as Shegalkin polynomials using the operators · for "and" and + for "exclusive or". Hsiang gave the following canonical rewrite system BA for these polynomials:

$$
\begin{aligned}
\text{BA::}\quad \neg X &\to X + 1 \\
X \vee Y &\to (X{\cdot}Y) + X{+}Y \\
X \supset Y &\to (X{\cdot}Y) + X{+}1 \\
X \cdot 1 &\to X \qquad\qquad\qquad X + 0 \to X \\
X \cdot X &\to X \qquad\qquad\qquad X + X \to 0 \\
X \cdot 0 &\to 0 \qquad\qquad\quad (X{+}Y){\cdot}Z \to (X{\cdot}Z) + (Y{\cdot}Z)
\end{aligned}
$$

Here the operators + and · are associative and commutative, 1 represents *true* and 0 represents *false* . The rules allow the translation of boolean formulae into boolean polynomials.

This system allows theorem proving in propositional calculus by rewriting: s and t are logically equivalent iff $s \xrightarrow{*}_{BA} u \; {}_{BA}\xleftarrow{*} t$ for some term u. In particular s is a tautology iff $s \xrightarrow{*}_{BA} 1$. Notice that an irreducible term u is a flat polynomial of the form $u \equiv 0$ or $u \equiv m_1 + ... + m_k$ where the m_i are monomials of the form $m_i \equiv 1$ or $m_i \equiv x_{i1} x_{i2} ... x_{ik}$. Here the x_{ij} are variables of the propositional calculus.

Applying BA to a quantifier-free formula from first-order logic also results in a flat polynomial of this type. Here the indeterminates x are the atomic formulae $P(t_1,...,t_n)$ where P is a predicate symbol and the t_i are terms. Terms may contain individual variables $y_1,...,y_n$.

Theorem proving in first-order logic using this approach proceeds as follows:
A formula A is a theorem iff ¬A is unsatisfiable. By standard methods ¬A can be transformed into a quantifier-free formula B such that ¬A is unsatisfiable iff $\forall y_1 ... y_n$: B is unsatisfiable. So it remains to give a procedure to test whether $\forall y_1 ... y_n$: B is unsatisfiable for quantifier free formulae B. There are different approaches to solve this problem using rewriting. Perhaps the conceptually simpliest one is based on the following

Theorem. $\forall y_1 ... y_n$: B is unsatisfiable iff $1 =_E 0$ where $E = BA \cup \{B = 1\}$.

So in order to prove that $\forall y_1 \ldots y_n$: B is unsatisfiable one starts a fair AC-completion procedure with E = BA $\cup$ {B = 1} and an ordering > such that t > 1 > 0 for every term t different from 0 and 1. It will produce $1 \to 0$ iff $\forall y_1 \ldots y_n$: B is unsatisfiable, see (Bachmair and Dershowitz [7]).

The problem with this general result is that the fairness criterion stated earlier in this paper will result in a rather inefficient algorithm. (Hsiang [94]) uses a very restricted form of completion. His procedure is very close to the classical resolution method and the proof that his procedure is complete (in the sense $1 \to 0$ will be generated if $\forall y_1 \ldots y_n$: B is unsatisfiable) is based on semantic trees as in classical theorem proving.

(Kapur and Narendran [128]) transform the formula A to be proved into a set of equations $p_i = 0$, i = 1,...,n where the p_i are flat polynomials as indicated above. They pointed out the close relationship to Buchberger's algorithm for computing Gröbner bases in polynomial rings over a field K. For K = F_2 = {0,1} they prove that A is a theorem iff 1 is in the ideal generated by the polynomials $p_1,...,p_n$ and $X^2 + X$.

(Müller [168]) also transforms the formula A to be proved into a system of polynomial equations E = {$p_i = 0 \mid i = 1,...,n$} such that A is a theorem iff E is solvable. A solution for E is any truth assignment Θ to the ground atoms such that $\Theta(\sigma(p_i)) = 1$, i = 1,...,n for every ground substitution σ. A specialized completion procedure is proposed to construct a complete theorem prover that allows to simplify the data basis by rewriting. It is extended to handle also equality.

4.4 Rewriting in Algebraic Structures

The study of algebraic structures defined by equations has been one of the most important application field for rewriting methods. In order to compute effectively in finitely presented structures one has to have structures with solvable word problems. This is one of the main reasons for the intensive study of the word problem for these structures and there are a lot of undecidability results e.g. for finitely presented monoids and groups. Nevertheless there are large classes of finitely presented structures for which the word problem is algorithmically solvable. For commutative monoids and some classes of groups the rewriting approach has been used successfully .

Using the Knuth-Bendix completion procedure canonical systems for different varieties have been found, see e.g. (Le Chenadec [161]). In particular for monoids and groups we have the well-known systems

M: $(x*y)*z \rightarrow x*(y*z)$ G: $x*1 \rightarrow x$ $1*x \rightarrow x$

   $x*1 \rightarrow x$ $x*x^{-1} \rightarrow x$ $x^{-1}*x \rightarrow 1$

   $1*x \rightarrow x$ $x*(x^{-1}*y) \rightarrow y$ $x^{-1}*(x*y) \rightarrow y$

                                                $1^{-1} \rightarrow 1$

                                                $(x*y)*z \rightarrow x*(y*z)$

                                                $(x*y)^{-1} \rightarrow y^{-1}*x^{-1}$

                                                $(x^{-1})^{-1} \rightarrow x$

These systems can be used to prove equations which hold in all monoids and groups, respectively. Usually a particular monoid or group can be described by a finite set of generators Σ and a finite set of defining relations R. Defining relations are equations of the form u = v where u and v are ground terms, i.e. they are built only from 1, the constants in Σ, and the monoid or group operations, respectively. For solving the word problem for such a structure a ground convergent system is sufficient. One way to complete such a system would be to run a completion procedure with the ground equations together with M or G. This approach has the disadvantage of being unnecessarily inefficient since it does not use explicitly the information that the structure under consideration is a monoid or a group.

A monoid M_R given by a presentation $(\Sigma;R)$ is isomorphic to the quotient $\Sigma^*/=_R$ of the free monoid Σ^* generated by Σ and $=_R$ the congruence generated by R. The elements of Σ^* are strings (words) over the alphabet Σ, so elements of M are equivalence classes [w] for $w \in \Sigma^*$. If we can effectively associate to every equivalence class [w] a unique representative w↓, then the word problem for M is solvable. One possibility of choosing a representative is to take a minimal element in the equivalence class with respect to some well-founded ordering < on Σ^*. **String rewriting** is now a method for effectively computing this minimal representative. The main idea here is again to orient the equations in R and to apply the resulting rules to the strings in Σ^*. To be more precise a **string-rewriting system** R on Σ is a subset of $\Sigma^* \times \Sigma^*$ the elements of which are called rewrite rules. R induces a **reduction relation** $\xrightarrow{*}_R$ on Σ^* which is the reflexive transitive closure of the single-step reduction relation $\rightarrow_R$: for all $u,v \in \Sigma^*$, $(l,r) \in R$: $ulv \rightarrow_R urv$. It also induces a congruence relation $\xleftrightarrow{*}_R$ on Σ^*, the **Thue congruence** generated by R which is indeed $=_R$. A word $u \in \Sigma^*$ is called **irreducible** if there is no word $v \in \Sigma^*$ such that $u \rightarrow_R v$. The set of all irreducible words is denoted by IRR(R). The notions of termination and confluence for term rewriting systems can be carried over straightforward to string rewriting systems. As pointed out in Section 2 termination and confluence are in general undecidable properties, even for string rewriting systems. Also, the confluence of terminating string rewriting systems can be localized and characterized through a critical pair lemma as in 2.1.

Since string rewriting systems can be seen as special term rewriting systems where $F = \Sigma$ contains only monadic operators, all techniques which work for general term rewriting systems can be used for string rewriting systems. In particular a specialized completion procedure using the critical pairs for string rewriting can be designed and used to get a convergent string rewriting system for a monoid M. For a convergent string rewriting system R the set IRR(R) is a set of representatives for the monoid M_R. Further if R is finite, then for each word $u \in \Sigma^*$, the irreducible word $u\downarrow$ in $[u]$ can effectively be computed from u. Thus, the word problem for M_R is effectively decidable.

Among the most extensively studied string rewriting systems are those where the rules are oriented by decreasing length of the words, i.e. length reducing - or at most length preserving - rules. Convergent systems with this ordering have been called Church-Rosser systems by R. Book and have been used to study language properties of the equivalence classes. Further restrictions on R like **special**, where $R \subseteq \Sigma^+ \times \{1\}$, or **monadic**, where the right-hand sides of rules are letters or the empty word have been considered. A very good survey on results for such systems is given in (Book [26]).

String rewriting systems are easier to handle than general term rewriting systems, but they have been very useful to show some limitations of the general rewriting techniques. One result of this type is the following observation due to (Kapur and Narendran [129]):
There exists a finite presentation $(\Sigma;R)$ such that the word problem for the monoid M_R is easily decidable, but the congruence $\overset{*}{\leftarrow}\to_R$ cannot be generated by a finite canonical string-rewriting system on Σ. In fact the monoid M_R with $\Sigma = \{a,b\}$ and $R = \{(aba,bab)\}$ has this property. (Jantzen [108]) gave another example with $\Sigma = \{a,b\}$ and $J = \{(abba,1)\}$. Here the monoid M_J is a group and there is no finite canonical string-rewriting system on Σ which generates the same congruence. For both examples it is easy to find canonical string rewriting systems over a larger alphabet which present the same monoid.

A long standing question was whether every finitely presented monoid with a decidable word problem does have some presentation by a finite canonical string-rewriting system. This has been answered negatively by (Squier [218]). For a positive result in this direction using 2-level string rewriting systems, see (Bauer [16]).

String rewriting for solving the word problem in finitely presented groups has a long tradition. (Dehn [44]) gave a solution of the word problem for small cancellation groups based on rewriting. In fact he proved that for these groups a string rewriting system can be defined which is confluent on the equivalence class of 1. Hence the problem w = 1 is decidable for this class of groups. This is enough for deciding the word problem in groups, since u = v iff uv^{-1} = 1. Specialized completion procedures for groups have been considered, see e.g. (Le Chenadec [161]) where a detailed discussion of Dehn´s algorithm and a list of canonical group presentations is given.

The classification of groups having canonical presentations is under current study. One important question is to find algebraic characterizations for those classes of groups that can be presented by certain types of finite canonical string-rewriting systems. A result in this direction is given in (Avenhaus et. al.[3]) where groups having monadic canonical group presentations are shown to be free products of free and finite groups. For a survey of results in this area see (Madlener and Otto [165]).

In the field of commutative algebra a different kind of rewriting namely polynomial rewriting has been considered.

For commutative rings with unity the following canonical system with AC-operators + and * was given by (Peterson and Stickel [193]).

R: $x+0 \rightarrow x$

      $(-x)+x \rightarrow 0$ $x+(-y)+y \rightarrow x$

      $1*x \rightarrow x$ $x*(y+z) \rightarrow (x*y) + (x*z)$

      $-0 \rightarrow 0$ $-(x+y) \rightarrow (-x) + (-y)$

      $-(-x) \rightarrow x$ $x*(-y) \rightarrow -(x*y)$

      $x*0 \rightarrow 0$

This canonical system motivates also the usual notation for ring elements as "polynomials" of the form $\alpha = \Sigma_i \, \varepsilon_i \, \alpha_1^{n1} \, ... \, \alpha_k^{nk}$, where ε_i indicates the presence or absence of the inverse operator - , each α_i is either a variable or a generator of the ring and $n_i \in \mathbf{N}$. A more concrete representation for the ground terms for a finitely presented commutative ring with generators $a_1,...,a_n$ can be defined by taking the elements of the polynomial ring $\mathbf{Z}[a_1,...,a_n]$ as representatives. For $\alpha = \Sigma \, \varepsilon_i \, m_i$ just take $\Sigma \, \alpha_j \, m_{ij}$, where $\alpha_j \in \mathbf{Z}$ is the result of collecting equal terms m_{ij} in α using the usual operations in $\mathbf{Z}$. The terms m_{ij} can be seen as words in the generators a_i and they can be ordered in decreasing order with respect to the degree and lexicographic orderings of words. Thus the degree of a polynomial is the maximum degree of its monomials and we may speak of the head monomial $\alpha_1 m_{i1}$ of polynomial p.

A finitely presented commutative ring is then a quotient of the polynomial ring in the generators $a_1,...,a_n$ modulo the ideal generated by the defining relations which are now of the form $p_i = 0$ for some polynomials p_i. The polynomials p_i define a reduction relation on the polynomial ring by subtracting from the element being reduced an appropriate multiple of one of the p_i. This is done in a way which guarantees the termination property of the reduction relation. A set of polynomials is a (weak) **Gröbner basis** if the reduction relation is confluent (confluent on the ideal generated by the set). Having a set of polynomials B which is a Gröbner basis for the ideal allows to solve the ideal membership problem for the ideal since $p \in (B)$ iff $p \xrightarrow{*}_B 0$, and hence the word problem for the finitely presented commutative ring is solvable.

The effective construction of Gröbner bases for finitely generated ideals in different polynomial rings has been intensively studied. It was initiated by Buchberger´s celebrated result for computing a finite Gröbner basis in polynomial rings over fields. His algorithm is based on a completion approach in which divergencies are localized by overlaps between head monomials of polynomials in the actual basis and resolved into new polynomials from the ideal when necessary. This completion procedure has the advantage that it always terminates giving a Gröbner basis for the input ideal. For a very good survey of polynomial rewriting and its relation to term rewriting, see (Buchberger [33]) and for using the Gröbner basis approach to solve other problems in commutative algebra, see (Buchberger [32]).

The application of Gröbner basis methods to theorem proving has been pointed out by (Kapur and Narendran [128]) where Boolean rings are used. In the last years applications to geometry theorem proving based on a method introduced by Wu, see (Chou [38]) have been considered. Here geometrical statements are translated into polynomial equations and a geometrical theorem is translated into some hypotheses which are polynomial equations and a conclusion which is also a polynomial equation. The theorem holds if the conclusion vanishes at all points on which the hypotheses vanish.

There are two difficulties with this approach. First, it is not complete since algebraically closed fields have to be considered and secondly, most geometrical theorems are only true for the general case. It may happen that they are false for degenerate situations, e.g. when circles have radius zero or lines become parallel. The Gröbner bases method can handle degenerate situations automatically giving some subsidiary conditions under which the theorem becomes true.

For a description of applications of Gröbner bases in non linear computational geometry, see (Buchberger [34]).

References:

In the references the following common abbreviations for Conferences and Journals will be used:

CAAP   Colloquium on Trees in Algebra and Programming

CADE   International Conference on Automated Deduction

ICALP   Colloquium on Automata, Languages and Programming

LICS   IEEE Symposium on Logic in Computer Science

RTA   Rewriting Techniques and Applications

J. ACM   Journal of the Association for Computing Machinery

J. CSS   Journal of Computer and System Sciences

IPL   Information and Processing Letters

LNCS   Lecture Notes in Computer Science (Springer Berlin)

[1]   Avenhaus, J., On the Termination of the Knuth-Bendix Completion Algorithm, Report 120/84, Universität Kaiserslautern, FB Informatik.
[2]   Avenhaus, J., On the Descriptive Power of Term Rewriting Systems, J. Symbolic Comp. 2 (1986), pp. 109-122.
[3]   Avenhaus, J., Madlener, K., Otto, F., Groups Presented by Finite Two-Monadic Church-Rosser Thue Systems, Trans. Amer. Math. Soc. 297 (1986), pp. 427-443.
[4]   Bachmair, L., Proof Methods for Equational Theories, Ph.D. Thesis, Dept. of Computer Science, U.of Illinois, Urbana, 1987.
[5]   Bachmair, L., Proof by Consistency in Equational Theories, 3rd LICS   (1988), pp. 228-233.
[6]   Bachmair, L., Dershowitz, N., Commutation, Transformation and Termination, 8th CADE (1986), LNCS 230, pp. 5-20.
[7]   Bachmair, L., Dershowitz, N., Completion for Rewriting Modulo a Congruence, 2nd RTA (1987), LNCS 256, pp. 192-203.
[8]   Bachmair, L., Dershowitz, N., Inference Rules for Rewrite-Based First-Order Theorem Proving, 2nd LICS (1987), pp. 331-337.
[9]   Bachmair, L., Dershowitz, N., Critical Pair Criteria for Completion, J. Symbolic Comp. 6 (1988), pp. 1-18.
[10] Bachmair, L., Dershowitz, N., Hsiang, J., Orderings for Equational Proofs, 1st LICS (1986), pp. 346-357.
[11] Bachmair, L., Dershowitz, N., Plaisted, D.A., Completion without Failure, Coll. on the Resolution of Equations in Algebraic Structures, Austin (1987), Academic Press, NY 1989.
[12] Bachmair, L., Plaisted, D.A.,Termination Orderings for Associative-Commutative Rewriting Systems, J. Symbolic Comp. 1 (1985), pp. 329-349.
[13] Baeten, J.C., Bergstra, J.A., Klop, J.W., Term Rewriting Systems with Priorities, 2nd RTA (1987), LNCS 256, pp. 83-94.
[14] Ballantyne, M., Butler, G., Lankford, D., Applications of Term Rewriting Systems to Finitely Presented Abelian Groups, Memo MTP-16, Mathematics Department, Louisiana Tech. University, Ruston, LA, Sept. 1981.
[15] Ballantyne, A.M., Lankford, D.S., New Decision Algorithms for Finitely Presented Commutative Semigroups, Math. and Comp. with Appl. 7 (1981), pp. 159-165.

[16] Bauer, G., N-Level Rewriting Systems, Theoret. Comp. Sci. 40 (1985), pp. 85-99.

[17] Bauer, G., Otto, F., Finite Complete Rewriting Systems and the Complexity of the Word Problem, Acta Informatica 21 (1984), pp. 521-540.

[18] Bellegarde, F.,Lescanne P., Transformation Orderings, 12th CAAP, TAPSOFT (1987), LNCS 249, pp.69-80.

[19] Benanav, D., Kapur, D., Narendran, P., Complexity of Matching Problems, 1st RTA (1985), LNCS 202, pp. 417-429.

[20] Ben Cherifa, A., Lescanne, P., Termination of Rewriting Systems by Polynomial Interpretations and its Implementation, Science of Computer Programming 9 (1987), pp. 137-160.

[21] Benninghofen B., Kemmerich S., Richter M.M., Systems of Reductions, LNCS 277, Springer, Berlin (1987).

[22] Bergstra, J.A., Klop, J.W., Conditional Rewrite Rules: Confluence and Termination, J. Comp. Syst. Sci. 32 (1986), 323-362.

[23] Birkhoff, G., On the Structure of Abstract Algebras, Proc. of the Cambridge Phil. Soc. 31 (1935), pp. 433-454.

[24] Book, R.V., Confluent and Other Types of Thue Systems, JACM 29 (1982), pp. 171-182.

[25] Book, R.V., The Power of the Church-Rosser Property for String Rewriting Systems, 6th CADE (1982), LNCS 138, pp. 360-368 .

[26] Book, R.V., Thue Systems as Rewriting Systems, 1st RTA (1985), LNCS 202, also in J. Symbolic Comp. 3 (1987), pp. 39-68.

[27] Boudol, G., Computational Semantics of Terms Rewriting Systems, Algebraic Methods in Semantics (M. Nivat, J. Reynolds (eds)), Cambridge Univ. Press, Cambridge (1985), pp. 169-236.

[28] Bousdira,W., Remy, J.L., Hierarchical Contextual Rewriting with Several Levels, 1st Int. Workshop on Conditional Term Rewriting Systems, Orsay, France, (1987), LNCS 308, pp. 15-30.

[29] Boyer, R.R., Moore, J.S., A Computational Logic, Academic Press (1979).

[30] Brand, D., Darringer, J.A., Joyner Jr, W.H., Completeness of Conditional Reductions, Report RC 7404, IBM Thomas J. Watson Research Center (1978) also Proc.Symp. Automatic Deduction (1979).

[31] Buchberger, B., A Critical-Pair/Completion Algorithm for Finitely Generated Ideals in Rings, Proc. Logic and Machines (1983), LNCS 171, pp. 137-161.

[32] Buchberger, B., Gröbner Bases: An Algorithmic Method in Polynomial Ideal Theory, in Multidimensional Systems Theory (N.K. Bose (ed.)) D. Reichel, Dordrecht (1985), pp. 184-229.

[33] Buchberger, B., History and Basic Features of the Critical-Pair/Completion Procedure, J. Symbolic Comp. 3 (1987), pp. 3-38.

[34] Buchberger, B., Applications of Gröbner Bases in Non-Linear Computational Geometry, Trends in Computer Algebra (1987), LNCS 296 , pp. 52-80.

[35] Buchberger, B., Loos, R., Algebraic Simplification, in Computer Algebra - Symbolic and Algebraic Computation (B. Buchberger, G. Collins, R. Loos (eds.)), Springer, Wien-NY (1982), pp. 11-43.

[36] Burstall, R.M., Proving Properties of Programs by Structural Induction, Computer Journal 12 (1969), pp. 41-48.

[37] Chou, S.C., An Introduction to Wu's Method for Mechanical Theorem Proving in Geometry, J. Automat. Reas. 4 (1988), pp. 237-267.

[38] Chou, S.C., Mechanical Geometry Theorem Proving, D. Reichel, Dordrecht (1988).

[39] Comon, H., Sufficient Completeness, Term Rewriting Systems and "Anti-Unification", 8th CADE (1986), LNCS 230, pp. 128-140.

[40] Cunningham, R.J., Dick, A.J.J., Rewrite Systems on a Lattice of Types, Acta Informatica 22 (1985), pp. 149-169.

[41] Darlington, J.L., Automatic Theorem Proving with Equality Substitutions and Mathematical Induction, Machine Intelligence 3 (1968), pp. 113-127.

[42] Dauchet, M., Termination of Rewriting is Undecidable in the One Rule Case,
      Proc. 14 MFCS (1988), LNCS 324, pp. 262-268.
[43] Dauchet, M., Tison, S., Heuillard, T., Lescanne, P., Decidability of the
      Confluence of Ground Term Rewriting Systems, 2nd LICS (1987), pp.
      353-359.
[44] Dehn, M., Über unendliche diskontinuierliche Gruppen, Math. Analen 71 (1911),
      pp. 116-144.
[45] Dershowitz, N., A Note on Simplification Orderings, IPL 9 (1979), pp. 212-215.
[46] Dershowitz, N., Termination of Linear Rewriting Systems, 8th ICALP (1981),
      LNCS 115, pp. 448-458.
[47] Dershowitz, N., Orderings for Term-Rewriting Systems, Theoret. Comp. Sci. 17
      (1982), pp. 279-301.
[48] Dershowitz, N., Equations as Programming Language, 4th Jerusalem Conf. on
      Inf. Technolgy, IEEE Comp. Soc (1984), pp. 114-124.
[49] Dershowitz, N., Synthesis by Completion, IJCAI (1985), pp. 208-214.
[50] Dershowitz, N., Termination, 1st RTA (1985), LNCS 202, pp. 180-224 and J.
      Symbolic Comp. 3 (1987), pp. 69-116.
[51] Dershowitz, N., Completion and its Applications, Coll. on the Resolution of
      Equations in Algebraic Structures (1987), Academic Press, NY (1989).
[52] Dershowitz, N., Hsiang, J., Refutational Theorem Proving with Oriented
      Equations, Coll. on the Resolution of Equations in Algebraic Structures (1987),
      Academic Press, NY (1989).
[53] Dershowitz, N., Jouannaud, J.P., Rewriting Systems, Handbook of Computer
      Science, North Holland (1989), to be published.
[54] Dershowitz, N., Manna, Z., Proving Termination with Multiset Orderings,
      Comm. of the ACM 22 (1979), pp. 465-476.
[55] Dershowitz, N., Marcus, L., Tarlecki, A., Existence, Uniqueness, and
      Construction of Rewrite Systems, SIAM J. Comput.17 (1988), pp. 629-639.
[56] Dershowitz, N., Okada, M., Proof-Theoretic Techniques for Term Rewriting
      Theory, 3rd LICS (1988), pp. 104-111.
[57] Dershowitz, N., Okada, M., Sivakumar, G., Canonical Conditional Rewrite
      Systems, 9th CADE (1988), LNCS 310, pp. 538-549.
[58] Dershowitz, N., Okada, M., Sivakumar, G., Confluence of Conditional Rewrite
      Systems, 1st Int. Workshop on Conditional Term Rewriting Systems (1987),
      LNCS 308 (1988), pp. 31-44.
[59] Dershowitz, N., Plaisted, D.A., Logic Programming cum Applicative
      Programming, IEEE '85 Symp. on Logic Programming (1985), pp. 54-66.
[60] Dick, A.J.J. , Eril-Equational Reasoning: An Interactive Laboratory, EUROCAL
      '85 (1985), LNCS 204, pp. 400-401.
[61] Drosten, K., Towards Executable Specifications Using Conditional Axioms,
      STACS '84 (1984), LNCS 166, pp. 85-96.
[62] Evans, T., The Word Problem for Abstract Algebras, 5th London Math. Soc. 26
      (1951), pp. 64-71.
[63] Fages, F., Huet, G., Unification and matching in equational theories, CAAP
      (1983), LNCS 159, pp. 205-220.
[64] Fay, M., First Order Unification in an Equational Theory, 4th CADE (1979), pp.
      161-167.
[65] Forgaard, R., Detlefs, D., An Incremental Algorithm for Proving Termination of
      Term Rewriting Systems, 1st RTA (1985), LNCS 202, pp. 255-270.
[66] Fribourg, L., Oriented Equational Clauses as a Programming Language, J. Logic
      Programming '84 (1984), pp. 165-177.
[67] Fribourg, L., Slog: A Logic Programming Language Interpreter Based on Causal
      Superposition and Rewriting, IEEE Symp. on Logic Programming (1985), pp.
      172-184.
[68] Fribourg, L., A Strong Restriction of the Inductive Completion Procedure, 13 th
      ICALP (1986), LNCS 226, pp. 105-115.

[69]   Futatsugi, K., Goguen, J.A., Jouannaud,J.P., Meseguer, J., Principles of OBJ2.
       CRIN Report 84-R-066, Nancy, France (1984).
[70]   Gallier, J., Narendran, P., Plaisted, D., Raatz, S., Synder, W., Finding
       Canonical Rewriting Systems Equivalent to a Finite Set of a Ground Equations in
       Polynomial Time, 9th CADE (1988), LNCS 310, pp. 182-196.
[71]   Ganzinger, H., Ground Term Confluence in Parametric Conditional Equational
       Specifications, 4th STACS (1987), LNCS 247, pp. 286-298.
[72]   Ganzinger, H., A Completion Procedure for Conditional Equations, 1st Int.
       Workshop on Conditional Term Rewriting Systems 1987, LNCS 308 (1988), pp.
       62-83.
[73]   Ganzinger, H., Giegerich, R., A Note on Termination in Combinations of
       Heterogeneous Term Rewriting Systems, Bull. EATCS 31 (1987), pp. 22-28.
[74]   Geser, A., Hussmann, H., Mueck, A., A Compiler for a Class of Conditional
       Term Rewriting Systems, 1st Int. Workshop on Conditional Term Rewriting
       Systems 1987, LNCS 308 (1988), pp. 84-90.
[75]   Gilman, R.H., Presentations of Groups and Monoids, J. Algebra 57 (1979), pp.
       544-554.
[76]   Gnaedig, I., Kirchner, C., Kirchner, H., Equational Completion in Order-Sorted
       Algebras, CAAP (1988), LNCS 299, pp. 165-184.
[77]   Gnaedig, I., Lescanne, P., Proving Termination of Associative Commutative
       Rewriting Systems by Rewriting, 8th CADE (1986), LNCS 230, pp. 52-61.
[78]   Göbel, R., Completion of Globally Finite Term Rewriting Systems for Inductive
       Proofs, SEKI-Projekt SEKI-Report SR-86-06, also Proc., 9th GWAI (1985),
       Springer, IFB 118, pp. 101-110.
[79]   Göbel, R., A Specialized Knuth-Bendix Algorithm for Inductive Proofs, Proc.
       Combinatorial Algorithms in Algebraic Structures, Otzenhausen (1985), Uni.
       Kaiserslautern (Germany).
[80]   Göbel, R., A Completion Procedure for Generating Ground Confluent Term
       Rewriting Systems, Dissertation, U. Kaiserslautern (Germany) 1987, partially in
       Ground Confluence, 2nd RTA (1987), LNCS 256, pp. 156-167.
[81]   Goguen, J.A., How to Prove Algebraic Inductive Hypotheses without Induction,
       5th CADE (1980), LNCS 87, pp. 356-373.
[82]   Goguen, J.A., Jouannaud, J.P., Meseguer, J., Operational Semantics for
       Order-Sorted Algebra, 12th ICALP (1985), LNCS 194, pp. 221-231.
[83]   Goguen, J., Kirchner, C., Kirchner, H., Megrelis, A., Meseguer, J., Winkler,
       T., An Introduction to OBJ 3, Centre de Recherche en Informatique de Nancy,
       88-R-001 (1988).
[84]   Goguen, J.A., Meseguer, J., Completeness of Many-Sorted Equational Logic,
       Houston Journal of Math. 11 (1985), pp.307-334.
[85]   Gramlich, B., Denzinger, J.,   Efficient AC-Matching Using Constraint
       Propagation, SEKI-Report SR-88-15, FB Informatik, Uni. K'lautern
       (Germany), 1988.
[86]   Guttag, J.V., Abstract Data Types and the Development of Data Structures,
       Communications of the ACM 20 (1976), pp. 396-404.
[87]   Guttag, J.V., Kapur, D., Musser, D.R., On Proving Uniform Termination and
       Restricted Termination of Rewriting Systems, SIAM J. Comput. 12 (1983), pp.
       189-214.
[88]   Henkin, L., The Logic of Equality, Math.Monthly (1977), pp.597-612.
[89]   Hermann, M., Vademecum of Divergent Term Rewriting Systems, CRIN
       88-R-082, Vandoeuvre, France (1988).
[90]   Hermann, M., Privara, I., On Nontermination of Knuth-Bendix Algorithm, 13th
       ICALP (1986), LNCS 226, pp. 146-156.
[91]   Hermann, M., Kirchner, C., Kirchner, H., Implementations of Term Rewriting
       Systems, CRIN 89, Vandoeuvre, France (1989) to appear.
[92]   Hoffmann, C.M., O'Donnell, M.J., Programming with Equations, Transactions
       on Programming Languages and Systems (1982), pp. 83-112.

[93]   Hsiang, J., Two Results in Term Rewriting Theorem Proving, 1st RTA (1985), LNCS 202, pp. 301-324.
[94]   Hsiang, J., Refutational Theorem Proving Using Term-Rewriting Systems. Ph.D.Thesis, U. of Illinois Urbana 1982, see also Artificial Intelligence 25 (1985), pp. 255-300.
[95]   Hsiang, J., Rewrite Method for Theorem Proving in First Order Theory with Equality, J. Symbolic Comp. (1987), pp. 133-151.
[96]   Hsiang, J., Dershowitz, N., Rewrite Methods for Clausal and Non-Clausal Theorem Proving, 10th ICALP (1983), LNCS 154, pp. 331-346.
[97]   Hsiang, J., Rusinowitch, M., A New Method for Establishing Refutational Completeness in Theorem Proving, 8th CADE (1986), LNCS 230, pp. 141-52.
[98]   Hsiang, J., Rusinowitch, M., On Word Problems in Equational Theories, 14th ICALP (1987), LNCS 267, pp. 54-71.
[99]   Huet, G., Confluent Reductions: Abstract Properties and Applications to Term Rewriting Systems, J. ACM 27 (1980), pp. 797-821.
[100] Huet, G., A Complete Proof of the Correctness of the Knuth-Bendix Completion Algorithm, JCSS 23 (1981), pp. 11-21.
[101] Huet, G., Hullot, J.M., Proofs by Induction in Equational Theories with Constructors, 21th FOCS (1980), pp. 96-107, also in JCSS 25 (1982), pp. 239-266.
[102] Huet, G., Lankford, D., On the Uniform Halting Problem for Term Rewriting Systems, INRIA Report No. 283, Le Chesnay, France (1978).
[103] Huet, G., Levy, J.J., Call by Need Computations in Non-Ambiguous Linear Term Rewriting Systems, INRIA Report No. 359, Le Chesnay, France (1979).
[104] Huet, G., Oppen, D.C., Equations and Rewrite Rules: A Survey in R. Book ed. Formal Language: Theory Perspective and Open Problems, Academic Press, NY (1980), pp. 349-405.
[105] Hullot, J.M., Canonical Forms and Unification, 5th CADE (1980), LNCS 87, pp. 318-334.
[106] Hullot, J.M., Associative-Commutative Pattern Matching, IJCAI (1979), pp. 406-412.
[107] Hullot, J.M., A Catalogue of Canonical Term Rewriting Systems, Technical Report CSC-113, SRI International (1980).
[108] Jantzen, M., Confluent String Rewriting, EATCS Monographs 14, Springer 1988.
[109] Jouannaud, J.P., Confluent and Coherent Equational Term Rewriting System, Application to Proofs in Abstract Data Types, 8th CAAP (1983), LNCS 59, pp. 269-283.
[110] Jouannaud, J.P., Kirchner, H., Completion of a Set of Rules Modulo a Set of Equations, SIAM J. Comput. 15 (1986), pp. 1155-1194.
[111] Jouannaud, J.P., Kounalis, E., Automatic Proofs by Induction in Equational Theories without Constructors, 1st LICS (1986), pp. 358-366.
[112] Jouannaud, J.P., Lescanne, P., On Multiset Orderings, IPL 15 (1982), pp. 57-63.
[113] Jouannaud, J.P., Lescanne, P., Rewriting Systems, Technology and Science of Informatics 6 (1987), pp. 181-199.
[114] Jouannaud, J.P., Lescanne, P., Reinig, F., Recursive Decomposition Ordering, Formal Description of Programming Concepts-2, ed. by D. Bjorner (1983), pp. 331-346.
[115] Jouannaud, J.P., Munoz, M., Termination of a Set of Rules Modulo a Set of Equations, 7 th CADE (1984), LNCS 170, pp. 175-193.
[116] Jouannaud, J.P., Waldmann, B., Reductive Conditional Term Rewriting Systems, Proc.of the third IFIP Conf.on Formal Description of Prog.Concepts, Ebberup, Denmark (1986).
[117] Kandri-Rody, A., Kapur, D., Computing a Gröbner Basis of a Polynomial Ideal Over a Euclidean Domain, J. Symbolic Comp. 6 (1988), pp. 37-57.

[118] Kaplan, S., Conditional Rewrite Rules, Theo. Comp. Sci. 33 (1984), pp. 175-193.

[119] Kaplan, S., Simplifying Conditional Term Rewriting Systems: Unification, Termination and Confluence, J. Symbolic Comp. 4 (1987), pp. 295-334.   [120] Kaplan, S., A Compiler for Conditional Term Rewriting Systems, 2nd RTA (1987), LNCS 256, pp. 25-41.

[121] Kaplan, S., Choquer, M., On the Decidability of Quasi-Reducibility, Bull. EATCS 28 (1986), pp. 32-34.

[122] Kaplan, S, Remy, J.L., Completion Algorithms for Conditional Rewriting Systems, Coll. on the Resolution of Equations in Algebraic Structures, Austin 1987, Academic Press, NY (1989).

[123] Kapur, D., Krishnamurthy, B., A Natural Proof System Based on Rewriting Techniques, 7th CADE (1984), LNCS 170, pp. 53-64.

[124] Kapur, D., Musser, D.R., Proof by Consistency, Artificial Intelligence 31 (1987), pp. 125-157.

[125] Kapur, D., Musser, D.R., Inductive Reasoning with Incomplete Specifications, 1st LICS (1986), pp. 367-377.

[126] Kapur, D., Musser, D.R., Narendran, P., Only Prime Superpositions Need be Considered in the Knuth-Bendix Completion Procedure, J.Symbolic Comp. 6 (1988), pp. 19-36.

[127] Kapur, D., Narendran, P., The Knuth Bendix Completion Procedure and Thue Systems, Proc. 3th Conf. Foundations of Computer Science and Software Engineering, Bangalore, India (1983).

[128] Kapur, D., Narendran, P., An Equational Approach to Theorem Proving in First-Order Predicate Calculus, 9th IJCAI (1985), pp. 1146-1153.

[129] Kapur, D., Narendran, P., A Finite Thue System with Decidable Word Problem and without Equivalent Finite Canonical System, Theoret. Comput. Sci. 35 (1985), pp. 337-344.

[130] Kapur, D., Narendran, P., NP-Completeness of the Set Unification and Matching Problems, 8th CADE (1986), LNCS 230, pp. 489-495.

[131] Kapur, D., Narendran, P., Otto, F., On Ground-Confluence of Term Rewriting Systems, Technical Report, 87-6 SUNY, Albany (1987).

[132] Kapur, D., Narendran, P., Sivakumar, G., A Path Ordering for Proving Termination of Term Rewriting Systems, 10th CAAP (1985), pp. 173-187.

[133] Kapur, D., Narendran, P., Zhang, H., On Sufficient-Completeness and Related Properties of Term Rewriting Systems, Acta Informatica 24 (1987), pp. 395-415.

[134] Kapur, D., Narendran, P., Zhang, H., Proof by Induction Using Test Sets, 8th CADE (1986), LNCS 230, pp. 99-117.

[135] Kapur, D., Srivas, M., A Rewrite Rule Based Approach for Synthesizing Abstract Data Types, TAPSOFT '85, Berlin, (1985).

[136] Kirchner, C., Methods and Tools for Equational Unification, Coll. on the Resolution of Equations in Algebraic Structures, Austin 1987, Academic Press, NY (1989).

[137] Kirchner, H., A General Inductive Completion Algorithm and Applications to Abstract Data Types, 7th CADE (1984), LNCS 170, pp. 282-302.

[138] Kirchner, H., Schematization of Infinite Sets of Rewrite Rules, Application to the Divergence of Completion Processes, 2nd RTA (1987), LNCS 256, 180-191.

[139] Kirchner, C., Kirchner, H., Implementation of a General Completion Procedure Parameterized by Built-In Theories and Strategies EUROCAL (1985), LNCS 204, pp. 402-404.

[140] Kirchner, C., Kirchner, H., Meseguer, J., Operational Semantics of OBJ-3, 15th ICALP (1988), LNCS 317, pp. 287-301.

[141] Klop, J.W., Term Rewriting Systems: A Tutorial, Bull. EATCS 32 (1987), pp. 143-183.

[142] Knuth, D.E., Bendix, P.B., Simple Word Problems in Universal Algebras. Computational Problems in Abstract Algebra, ed.: J. Leech, Pergamon Press (1970), pp. 263-297.

[143] Kouanlis,E.,Completeness in Data Type Specifications, EUROCAL (1985), LNCS 204, pp. 348-362.

[144] Kounalis, E., Rusinowitch, M., On Word Problems in Horn Theories, 9th CADE (1988), LNCS 310, pp. 527-537.

[145] Krishnamoorthy, M.S., Narendran, P., On Recursive Path Ordering, Theoret. Comp. Sci. 40 (1985), pp. 323-328.

[146] Kruskal, J.B., The Theory of Well-Quasi-Ordering: A Frequently Discovered Concept, J. Combinatorial Theory, Ser. A 13 (1972), pp. 297-305.

[147]. Küchlin, W., A Theorem-Proving Approach to the Knuth-Bendix Completion Algorithm, EUROCAM (1982), LNCS 144, pp. 101-108.

[148] Küchlin, W., Inductive Completion by Ground Proof Transformation. Coll. on the Resolution of Equations in Algebraic Structures, Austin 1987, Academic Press, NY (1989).

[149] Lankford, D.S., Canonical Algebraic Simplification in Computational Logic, Report ATP-25, Univ. of Texas, Math. Dept., Automatic Theorem Proving Project, Austin (1975).

[150] Lankford, D.S., Canonical Inference. Report ATP-32, Univ. of Texas, Math.Dept., Automatic Theorem Proving Project, Austin (1975).

[151] Lankford, D.S., Some Approaches to Equality for Computational Logic: A Survey and Assessment Report ATP-36, Univ. of Texas, Math. Dept., Automatic Theorem Proving Project, August (1977).

[152] Lankford, D.S., On Proving Term Rewriting Systems are Noetherian, Memo MTP-3, Mathematics Department, Louisiana Tech. University, Ruston, LA (1979).

[153] Lankford, D.S., Some New Approaches to the Theory and Applications of Conditional Term Rewriting Systems, Memo MTP-6, Mathematics Department, Louisiana Tech. University, Ruston, LA (1979).

[154] Lankford, D.S., A Simple Explanation of Inductionless Induction, Memo MTP-14, Mathematics Department, Louisiana Techn. University, Ruston, LA (1981).

[155] Lankford, D.S., Ballantyne, A.M., Decision Procedures for Simple Equational Theories with Permutative Axioms: Complete Sets of Permutative Reductions, Report ATP-37, Univ. of Texas, Dept. of Math. and Comp. Sci., Austin (1977).

[156] Lankford, D.S., Ballantyne, A.M., Decision Procedures for Simple Equational Theories with a Commutative Axiom: Complete Sets of Commutative Reductions, Report ATP-39, Univ. of Texas, Dept. of Math. and Comp. Sci., Austin (1977).

[157] Lankford, D.S., Ballantyne, A.M., The Refutation Completeness of Blocked Permutative Narrowing and Resolution, 4th CADE (1979), pp. 53-59.

[158] Lescanne, P., Computer Experiments with the REVE Term Rewriting System Generator, Proc.10 ACM POPL Symp. Austin (1983), pp. 99-108.

[159] Lescanne, P., Uniform Termination of Term Rewriting Systems, Recursive Decomposition Ordering with Status, 9th CAAP (1984), pp. 184-194.

[160] Lescanne, P., Divergence of the Knuth-Bendix Completion Procedure and Termination Orderings, Bull. EATCS 30 (1986), pp. 80-83.

[161] Le Chenadec, Ph., Canonical Forms in Finitely Presented Algebras, 7th CADE (1984), LNCS 170, see also Research Notes in TCS, Pitman and Wiley, London (1985).

[162] Llopis de Trias, R., An Overview of Completion Algorithms, EUROCAL (1985), LNCS 204, pp. 424-428.

[163] Loos, R., Term Reduction Systems and Algebraic Algorithms, Proc. 5th GI Workshop on AI (1981), pp. 214-234.

[164] Madlener, K., Otto, F., Groups Presented by Certain Classes of Finite Length-Reducing String-Rewriting Systems, 2nd RTA (1987), LNCS 256, pp. 133-144.

[165] Madlener, K., Otto, F., About the Descriptive Power of Certain Classes of Finite String-Rewriting Systems, Theoret. Comp. Sci., to appear 1989.

[166] Martin, U., Extension Functions for Multiset Orderings, IPL 26 (1987), pp. 181-186.

[167] Metivier, Y., About the Rewriting Systems Produced by the Knuth-Bendix Completion Algorithm, IPL 16 (1983), pp. 31-34.

[168] Mueller, J., Theorem Proving with Rewrite Techniques - Methods, Strategies, Comparisons, Dissertation FB Informatik, U. Kaiserslautern, Germany (1988).

[169] Musser, D.R., On Proving Inductive Properties of Abstract Data Types, Proc. 7 ACM Symp. on Principles of Programming Languages (1980), pp. 154-162.

[170] Navarro, M., Orejas, F., On the Equivalence of Hierarchical and Non-Hierarchical Rewriting on Conditional Term Rewriting Systems, EUROSAM (1984), LNCS 174, pp. 74-85.

[171] Narendran, P., Otto, F., Preperfectness is Undecidable for Thue Systems Containing only Length-Reducing Rules and a Single Commutation Rule, IPL 29 (1988), pp. 125-130.

[172] Newman, M.H.A., On Theories with a Combinatorial Definition of "Equivalence", Ann. of Math. 43 (1942), pp. 223-243.

[173] Nipkow, T., Weikum, G., A Decidability Result about Sufficient Completeness of Axiomatically Specified Abstract Data Types, Proc. 6th GI Conference (1983), LNCS 145, pp. 257-268.

[174] Nutt, W., Rety, P., Smolka, G., Basic Narrowing Revisited, SEKI-Report SR-87-07, FB Informatik, Uni. K'lautern (1987), to appear in JSC.

[175] O'Dunlaing, C., Infinite Regular Thue Systems, Theoret. Comp. Sci. (1983), pp. 171-192.

[176] O'Donnell, M.J., Term-Rewriting Implementation of Equational Logic Programming, 2nd RTA (1987), LNCS 256, pp. 1-12.

[177] O'Donnell, M.J., Computing in Systems Described by Equations (1977), LNCS 58, Springer, Berlin (1977).

[178] Okada, M., A Logic Analysis on Theory of Conditional Rewriting, 1st Int. Workshop on Conditional Term Rewriting Systems (1987), LNCS 308, pp. 179-198.

[179] Orejas, F., Theorem Proving in Conditional Equational Theories, 1st Int.Workshop on Conditional Term Rewriting Systems (1987).

[180] Otto, F., Deciding Algebraic Properties of Monoids Presented by Finite Church-Rosser Thue Systems, 1st RTA (1985), LNCS 202, pp. 95-106.

[181] Otto, F., On Deciding the Confluence of a Finite String-Rewriting System on a Given Congruence Class, J. CSS 35 (1987), pp. 285-310.

[182] Oyamaguchi, M., The Church-Rosser Property for Ground Term-Rewriting Systems is Decidable, Theoret. Comp. Sci. 49 (1987), pp. 43-79.

[183] Padawitz, P., Computing in Horn Clause Theories, EATCS Monographs 16, Springer (1988).

[184] Padawitz, P., Can Inductive Proofs Be Automated ?, Bull. EATCS 35 (1988), pp. 163-170.

[185] Padawitz, P., Can Inductive Proofs Be Automated ?, Part II, Bull. EATCS 37 (1989), pp. 168-174.

[186] Padawitz, P., Inductive Proofs by Resolution and Paramodulation, CAAP (1989) to appear.

[187] Pan, L., Applications of Rewriting Techniques, A Dissertation Ph. Math., Uni. of Cal., Santa Barbara (1985).

[188] Paul, E., Proof by Induction in Equational Theories with Relations Between Constructors, 9th CAAP (1984), pp. 211-226.

[189] Paul, E., A New Interpretation of the Resolution Principle, 7th CADE (1984), pp. 333-355.

[190] Pedersen, J., Confluence Methods and the Word Problem in Universal Algebra, Ph. D. Thesis, Emory Univ., Dept. Math. and Comp. Sci., Atlanta (1984).

[191] Pelin, A., Computing with Conditional Rewrite Rules, 1st Int. Workshop on Conditional Term Rewriting Systems (1987), LNCS 308, pp. 197-211.

[192] Peterson, G.E., A Technique for Establishing Completeness Results in Theorem Proving with Equality, SIAM J. on Computing 12 (1983), pp. 82-100.

[193] Peterson, G.E., Stickel, M.E., Complete Sets of Reductions for Some Equational Theories, J. ACM. 28 (1981), pp. 233-264.

[194] Plaisted, D.A., Semantic Confluence Tests and Completion Methods, Information and Control 65 (1985), pp. 182-215.

[195] Plaisted, D.A., A Simple Non-Termination Test for the Knuth-Bendix Method, 8th CADE (1986), LNCS 230, pp. 79-88.

[196] Plaisted, D.A., A Logic for Conditional Term Rewriting Systems, 1st Int. Workshop on Condition Term Rewriting Systems (1987), LNCS 308, pp. 212-227.

[197] Plotkin, G.D., Building-In Equational Theories, Machine Intelligence 7 (1972), pp. 73-90.

[198] Qian, Z., Structured Contextual Rewriting, 2nd RTA (1987), LNCS 256, pp. 168-179.

[199] Raoult, J.C., Finiteness Results on Rewriting Systems, RAIRO Theor. Inf. 15 (1981), pp. 373-391.

[200] Raoult, J.C., On Graph Rewriting, Theoret. Comp. Sci. 32 (1984), pp. 1-24.

[201] Raoult, J.C., Proving Open Properties by Induction, IPL 29 (1988), pp. 19-23.

[202] Remy, J.L., Etude des Systemes de Reecriture Conditionnels et Applications aux Types Abstraits Algebriques, These d'Etat de L'Institut National Polytechnique de Lorraine, Nancy 1982.

[203] Remy, J.L., Comon, H., How to Characterize the Language of Ground Normal Forms, INRIA, Report 676 (1987).

[204] Rety, P., Improving Basic Narrowing Techniques, 2nd RTA (1987), LNCS 256, pp. 228-241.

[205] Rety, P., Kirchner, C., Kirchner, H., Lescanne, P., Narrower: A New Algorithm for Unification and its Application to Logic Programming, 1st RTA (1985), LNCS 202, pp. 141-157.

[206] Robinson, J.A., A Machine-Oriented Logic Based on the Resolution Principle, J. ACM 12 (1965), pp. 23-41.

[207] Robinson, G., Wos, L., Paramodulation and Theorem-Proving in First Order Theories with Equality, Machine Intelligence 4 (1969), pp. 135-150.

[208] Rosen, B.K., Tree-Manipulating Systems and Church-Rosser Theorems, J. ACM 20 (1973), pp. 160-187.

[209] Rusinowitch, M., Path of Subterms Ordering and Recursive Decomposition Ordering Revisited, J. Symbolic Comp. 3 (1987), pp. 117-131.

[210] Rusinowitch, M., On Termination of the Direct Sum of Term Rewriting Systems, IPL 26 (1987), pp. 65-70.

[211] Sethi, R., Testing for the Church-Rosser Property, J. ACM 21 (1974), pp. 671-679.

[212] Shankar, N., A Mechanical Proof of the Church-Rosser Theorem, J. ACM 35 (1988), pp. 475-522.

[213] Siekmann, J., Unification Theory, this Volume.

[214] Siekmann, J., Szabo, P., A Noetherian and Confluent Rewrite System for Idempotent Semigroups, Semigroup Forum 25 (1982), pp. 83-110.

[215] Slagle, J.R., Automated Theorem-Proving for Theories with Simplifiers, Commutativity, and Associativity, J. ACM 21 (1974), pp. 622-642

[216] Smolka, G., Order-Sorted Horn Logic: Semantics and Deduction, SEKI-Report SR-86-17, FB Informatik, Uni. Kaiserslautern, Germany (1986).

[217] Smolka, G., Nutt, W., Goguen, J.A., Meseguer, J., Order-Sorted Equational Computation, SEKI-Report SR-87-14, FB Informatik, Uni. Kaiserslautern, (1987), also in Coll. on the Resolution of Equations in Algebraic Structures, Academic Press, NY (1989).

[218] Squier, C., Otto, F., The Word Problem for Finitely Presented Monoids and Finite Canonical Rewriting Systems, 2nd RTA (1987), LNCS 256, pp. 74-82.

[219] Staples, J., Church-Rosser Theorems for Replacement Systems, Algebra and Logic, J. Crossley (ed.) (1975), LNCS 450, pp. 291-309.

[220] Steinbach, J., Comparison of Simplification Orderings, SEKI-Report SR-88-02, FB Informatik, Uni. Kaiserslautern, Germany (1988), also to appear in 3nd RTA 1989.

[221] Stickel, M.E., A Unification Algorithm for Associative-Commutative Functions, J. ACM 28 (1981), pp. 423-434.

[222] Thatte, S., A Refinement of Strong Sequentiality for Term Rewriting with Constructors, Information and Computation 72 (1987), pp. 46-65.

[223] Toyama, Y., How to Prove Equivalence of Term Rewriting Systems without Induction, 8th CADE (1986), LNCS 230, pp. 118-127.

[224] Toyama, Y., Counterexamples to Termination for the Direct Sum of Term Rewriting Systems, IPL 25 (1987), pp. 141-143.

[225] Toyama, Y., On the Church-Rosser Property for the Direct Sum of Term Rewriting Systems, J. ACM 34 (1987), pp. 128-143.

[226] Toyama, Y., Confluent Term Rewriting Systems with Membership Conditions, 1st Int. Workshop on Conditional Term Rewriting Systems (1987), LNCS 308, pp. 228-234.

[227] Toyama, Y., Klop, J.W., Barendregt, H.P., Termination for the Direct Sum of Left-Linear Term Rewriting Systems, Expanded Version of the IEICE Technical Report COMP-88, July 1988, also 3rd RTA (1989) to appear.

[228] Walther, Ch., Argument-Bounded Algorithms as a Basis for Automated Termination Proofs, 9th CADE (1988), LNCS 310, pp. 602-621.

[229] Winkler, F., Reducing the Complexity of the Knuth-Bendix Completion Algorithm: A "Unification" of Different Approaches, EUROCAL (1985), LNCS 204, pp. 378-389.

[230] Winkler, F., Buchberger, B., A Criterion for Eliminating Unnecessary Reductions in the Knuth-Bendix Algorithm, Proc. Coll. Algebra, Combinatorics and Logic in Computer Science, Györ, Hungary (1983).

[231] Zhang, H., Kapur, D., First-Order Theorem Proving Using Conditional Rewrite Rules, 9th CADE (1988), LNCS 310, pp.1-20.

[232] Zhang, H., Kapur, D., Krishnamoorthy, M.S., A Mechanizable Induction Principle for Equational Specifications, 9th CADE (1988), LNCS 310, pp.162-181.

[233] Zhang, H., Remy, J.L., Contextual Rewriting, 1st RTA (1985), LNCS 202, pp. 46-62.

Formal Techniques in Artificial Intelligence
A Sourcebook. R.B. Banerji (editor)
© Elsevier Science Publishers B.V. (North-Holland), 1990

Implementing Metamathematics as an Approach to Automatic Theorem Proving*

Robert L. Constable   *Douglas J. Howe*[†]

Abstract

A simple but important algorithm used to support automated reasoning is called *matching*: given two terms it produces a substitution, if one exists, that maps the first term to the second. In this paper the matching algorithm is used to illustrate the approach to automating reasoning suggested in the title. In Section 3 the algorithm is derived and verified in the Nuprl proof development system following exactly an informal presentation of it in Section 2.

The example serves to introduce a particular automated reasoning system, Nuprl, as well as the idea of deriving programs from constructive proofs. The treatment of this example also suggests how these systems can be soundly extended by the addition of constructive metatheorems about themselves to their libraries of results.

1   Introduction

People use computers to do all sorts of things, from the mundane to the miraculous. Among the enduring uncommon uses are game playing, notably chess, and *theorem proving*. Clearly chess is interesting, but why has theorem proving remained active? We can make an argument that theorem proving is a significant activity, and if computers can help when it really counts, society will be better off. Some people are interested in it for exactly those reasons. They apply automated theorem proving in such areas as *program verification* and *hardware verification*. There are now companies whose employees make a living from this activity. But these people are mostly newcomers to the subject (see [21] for a recent survey). We might call them *logic engineers*.

There are other motives for studying theorem proving by computer. Indeed, efforts to employ computers in the enterprise have from the beginning brought into proximity researchers of diverse interests. There are those interested in studying intelligence, especially reasoning. They argue that reasoning and problem solving are critical to intelligence and that proving theorems is intelligent behavior. People with those interests will usually associate themselves with the study of artificial intelligence. Prominent pioneers in their ranks are the likes of Allen Newell, Herbert Simon, and John McCarthy. On the other hand, the subject has attracted applied logicians who study proof systems and algorithms for finding proofs. These people want to test their algorithms; their goal is to prove a lot of theorems fast, regardless of how. They are not necessarily concerned with emulating

*This research was supported in part by NSF grant CCR-8616552 and ONR grant N00014-88-K-0409

[†]Authors' address: Department of Computer Science, Cornell University, Ithaca NY 14853

human thought processes unless those processes are effective in proving theorems. This early dichotomy among people "in the area" is well-known and amply referenced [9]. The contrast in the early days of the subject was between A.I. programs such as Logic Theorist [26] and fast decision procedures like Wang's [32]. Besides Hao Wang, there are people like J.A. Robinson and Martin Davis in the latter group.

Nowadays another group has become involved. They see the possibility of building a variety of tools which are especially suited to helping people use computers to prove theorems. The important point for them is that theorem proving is a complex information processing task and the computer offers new ways to perform it. The goal is to allow anyone, logician or A.I. researcher, to easily test ideas for proving theorems. This is a newer concern. The authors started in this area along with Joseph Bates and others at Cornell who will be referenced in the course of this article. One of the pioneers here was Robin Milner and his LCF group [14,27].

In short, let us say that since 1950 it has been a goal of A.I. to find architectures for intelligence. Systems like Logic Theorist, GPS and now Soar [29] are built to achieve this goal. Since the late 1950's there has been the goal to "prove lots of theorems". Systems like the Argonne prover [33], the Boyer & Moore prover [4] and others are oriented this way. Since the 1970's there has been the goal to apply the technology, as in Gypsy [13], and to build systems that allow easy expression of a wide variety of strategies (including in the limit those from A.I.), as in LCF and Nuprl [8].

A great deal of practical work has been put into meeting these basic goals. Now there is another goal, made possible by the substantial body of experimental results; it is to *understand* the experimental results, to develop a *theory of theorem proving*. In fact, one of the deepest results in computing theory arose precisely in pursuit of this aim. S.A. Cook proved that the tautology problem is essentially the same as the problem of membership in languages accepted by nondeterministic polynomial time Turing machines. This led Cook to propose the now famous $P = NP$ problem which lies at the heart of theoretical computer science.

Because so much is known about logic and its algorithmic content, there are many compelling questions about the automation of theorem proving—questions about why an algorithm works on one class of problems but not on another, questions about those characteristics of a sentence or its partial proof which tell an experienced prover what to do next, questions about the cost of proving a result relative to a library of results, questions about the limits to feasible automation. There is the hope that the answers to these questions may provide answers to deeper questions about the requirements for an intelligent system.

In this article we will describe the enterprise of automated theorem proving in a context that suggests an outline of a *theory of theorem proving* and suggests an organization of the various existing methods that facilitates the computer scientist's goal of providing a general environment for the empirical study of the subject. The basic idea is that automated theorem proving can be seen as the implementation of a constructive *metamathematics*. In metamathematics one proves theorems about doing mathematics. Some of these theorems have interesting computational content, such as a result claiming that a theory is decidable or a result saying that any proof of a theorem of one form can be converted to one of another form (say from prenex form into nonprenex form). We will show how some theorem proving algorithms can be understood as implementations of theorems about proofs and formulas. Especially noteworthy are results of the second author on term rewriting [17].

One of the critical reasons for adopting this point of view is that much of the knowledge we discover about theorem proving is potentially useful to the automated system itself. In order to be used by machines, the knowledge must be formalized. Conversely, the more we can say about the algorithms we use, the more effectively we can use them. This suggests that we want to develop them in the context of a formal theory. Related reasons for doing this are discussed by Davis and Schwartz [10], Boyer and Moore [5] and Shankar [30].

One of the major advantages of formalizing knowledge about theorem proving is that we can use it to extend the stock of derived rules of inference. This in some cases allows us to avoid running theorem-proving algorithms. This point will be mentioned again in Section 3.3. To the extent that results from other parts of mathematics are useful in theorem proving, as in the use of graph algorithms in congruence closure, we want to be able to prove that they are correct and preserve the correctness of the logic when they are used in derived inference rules.

The rest of the paper is organized as follows. First we develop some informal metatheory, focusing on two particular metatheorems. One of these yields an algorithm for first-order matching. The computational content of the other is a tableau decision procedure for propositional formulas. We then present a formalization of the development of the match algorithm that was carried out in the Nuprl proof development system. This formalization is based directly on the informal account.

2 Informal Constructive Metamathematics

2.1 Preliminaries

To begin we establish some basic definitions and notations. The type of integers is denoted *int* and its elements are $0, +1, -1, \ldots$. When dealing with syntactic matters it is convenient to have a type *atom* of atomic symbols or (or "atoms"). Its elements are denoted "*id*" where *id* is a character string. We assume that an equality relation is provided on this type; we write it as $a = b$ *in atom*. We also assume that equality is *decidable*. This is expressed by saying that for all atoms a and b, either $a = b$ *in atom* or not. In general we treat the word *or* (and its symbolic form $\vee$) *constructively*; that is, when we say $P \vee Q$ for P and Q statements, we mean that either P or Q is true and we know which one. The classical meaning of *or*, as in the phrase "P *or* Q *classically*", can be taken as an abbreviation of *not (not P and not Q)*. We sometimes write *not* as $\neg$, so that $\neg P$ is *not P*. We will often abbreviate *and* by & and "for all x of type A" by $\forall x : A$. So "for all x of type A, $P(x)$ or $Q(x)$ classically" is written as

$$\forall x : A. \ \neg(\neg P(x) \vee \neg Q(x)).$$

We will always specify the classical *or* explicitly when we need it; otherwise *or* has its constructive meaning which, as we have just seen, is convenient for expressing the notion that a relation is *decidable*.[1]

Given two types A and B, their *cartesian product* is denoted $A\#B$ and consists of pairs $\langle a, b \rangle$ where a is in A and b is in B. Thus $int\#atom$ contains elements like $\langle 0, "0" \rangle$.

---

[1]In the case of the integers, we can either take equality as a primitive decidable relation, $x = y$ *in int*, or we could define it inductively. We take it as primitive. In order to take these equality relations as primitive, there must be an algorithm for deciding them. In the case of integers and atoms this is obvious.

The type $A \to B$ denotes the *computable functions* from A to B. These are denoted as $\lambda x.exp$ for *exp* an expression denoting an object of type B. If f is a function in $A \to B$ and a belongs to A, then $f(a)$ is the *application* of f to a and is a value in B. If we want to talk about noncomputable functions, then we treat them as single-valued relations over $A\#B$. That is, a relation F contained in $A\#B$ is a *classical function* if and only if for all $\langle a, b\rangle$ and $\langle a', b'\rangle$ in F, if $a = a'$ in A, then $b = b'$ in B.

The *domain* of a classical function F is defined as the set of all a in A for which we can find an element b in B such that $\langle a, b\rangle$ is in F. Symbolically we write the phrase "we can find an element b in B such that $R(x)$" as $\exists x{:}\,B.\ R(x)$. We denote the set of all elements x of A such that $R(x)$ holds as $\{\, x{:}\,A \mid R(x)\,\}$. So the domain of a classical function F is

$$\{\, x{:}\,A \mid \exists\, y{:}\,B.\ \langle x, y\rangle\ in\ F\,\}.$$

Another familiar (but little-used in this paper) classical concept is the *classical domain* of F. This consists of those elements of A for which it is not impossible to find a corresponding element of B, that is, for which a range element *classically exists*. To say that there exists classically an element y of type B such that $R(y)$ is to say $\neg(\forall\, y{:}\,B.\ \neg R(y))$. We denote this as $E\, y{:}\,B.\ R(y)$. So the classical domain of F is

$$\{\, x{:}\,A \mid E\, y{:}\,B.\ \langle x, y\rangle\ in\ F\,\}.$$

Another important way to build types from others is to unite them. Given types A and B we write their *disjoint union* as $A|B$. It is essential that we can tell for any element of $A|B$ whether it is from A or B. One way to do this is to write the elements of the union so that we can tell. We take the elements to be $inl(a)$ and $inr(b)$ for a in A and b in B. The operator inl stands for *inject left* while $inr(b)$ stands for *inject right*. So even when we form the type $A|A$, we can tell for any element of this union whether it is a "left a" or a "right a". In set theory the disjoint union is usually defined from the ordinary union by providing a scheme for tagging elements (see [3]).

For any type A, another important type built from it are lists of elements from A. The type is denoted A *list*. All nonempty lists are built from the empty list which is denoted *nil* (regardless of the type A). If a is an element of A, then $a.nil$ is a nonempty list. The dot operation is sometimes called *cons* for *construction*. In general given a list t and an element h of A, $h.t$ is a list with h as its *head* and t as its *tail*. It is convenient to write the list $a_1.a_2.\cdots.a_n.nil$ as $(a_1, \ldots, a_n)$. We sometimes do this in the informal mathematics. Below we will see how the type A *list* is a special case of the more general notion of an inductively defined type.

One important kind of construction arises from the inductive nature of lists. We can build an object incrementally from the elements of a list following the same pattern used to build the list. That is, a list starts from the empty list *nil*. Suppose that corresponding to it we can specify some object, such as the integer 0. Given a list t, we extend it by adjoining an element to form $h.t$. In the same way, given a value associated with t, say its length v, we can build a value associated with $h.t$ incrementally, say by adding one to v, thereby associating $v + 1$ to $h.t$. This process of associating a value with a list is sometimes called *primitive recursion on lists* or *list recursion* or *list induction*. One way of writing it is illustrated by the following definition of the length of a list.

$$len(nil)\ =\ 0$$
$$len(h.t)\ =\ 1 + len(t)$$

The critical components in this definition are an expression b for the value in the base case, names for the components of the arbitrary list, say h for its head and t for its tail, a name v for the value associated with t, and finally an expression e telling how to build a new value given h, t and v. In the example, e is $1 + v$; generally it is an expression in h, t and v. Instead of writing such recursion equations we use a linear format to present the information:

$$list\_ind(l; b; h, t, v.e)$$

(*list_ind* for "list induction"). In this format, l is the list expression; b is an expression defining an object, say of type T, in the base case, and e is an expression which defines an object, of type T, in the induction case. The expression e can refer to the variables h, t and v. These variable occurrences of h, t and v before e are *binding occurrences*, and they *bind* in e. The definition of length in this format is

$$list\_ind(l; 0; \ h, t, v. \ v + 1).$$

This *list_ind* form specifies a computation when we give the explicit rules for evaluating it. To write these rules we need an informal notation for substitution. Given an expression t with a free variable x, and a term s, then $t[s/x]$ denotes the expression t with s substituted for each occurrence of x in t. More generally, if $x_1, \ldots, x_n$ are variables and $s_1, \ldots, s_n$ are terms, then $t[s_1/x_1, \ s_2/x_2, \ldots, s_n/x_n]$ represents the simultaneous substitution of each s_i for x_i. A formal definition of substitution is given later. With this notation the rules are:

$$list\_ind(nil; b; h, t, v.e) \ = \ b$$
$$list\_ind(a.l; b; \ h, t, v.e) \ = \ l[a/h, \ l/t, \ list\_ind(l; b; h, t, v.e)/v].$$

For example,

$$list\_ind(a.nil; \ 0; \ h, t, v. \ v + 1) \ = \ list\_ind(nil; \ 0; \ h, t, v. \ v + 1) + 1$$
$$= \ 0 + 1$$
$$= \ 1$$

One of the fundamental concepts in logic is that of an *inductively defined* type. For instance, the types of lists, terms, formulas and proofs are each defined inductively. One of the simplest inductively defined types is that of lists over a type A. Above we said that *nil* is a list; this is the *base case* of the definition. And we said that if a is in A and if l is an A list, then $a.l$ is an A list. In general, a type is specified inductively if we show how to build an element of the type given other elements of it. Also in general there is a *base case* which does not involve using other elements of the type to build new ones; for lists it is the clause saying that *nil* is a list.

The typical informal presentation of an inductively defined set I has this pattern:

[base case:]   if b is in B then b is in I
[inductive cases:]   if $t_1, \ldots, t_n$ are in I and a is in A then $f(t_1, \ldots, t_n, a)$ is in I
$$\vdots$$
  if $s_1, \ldots, s_p$ are in I and c is in C then $g(s_1, \ldots, s_p, c)$ is in I.

There is also an extremal clause saying that nothing is in I unless it is required to be there by the base and inductive clauses.

It is well-known that so called *positive inductive* definitions can be interpreted as least fixed points of monotone operators on a set (for example, see [1,24,23]). We will present only positive inductive definitions without parameters. A wider class could be defined [23], but there is no need for it here.

The syntactic style of our definitions is derived from the fixed point idea. We write the type as $rec(T.\ F(T))$ where $F(T)$ is some expression in which T occurs positively[2]. This suggests the equation $T = F(T)$. One subclass of expressions in which T occurs only positively are those built from T and other previously defined types using only the operators of cartesian product and disjoint union. For example, A *list* can be defined as $rec(T.\ \{\ nil\ \}\ |\ A\#T)$. The type of binary trees with leaves in a type A is $rec(T.\ A\ |\ T\#T)$.

One of the most important properties of inductively defined types I is that we can prove statements of the form $\forall x\colon I.\ G(x)$ by induction on I. Informally the rule for the type $I = rec(T.\ F(T))$ is this. To prove $\forall x\colon I.\ G(x)$, we assume as an induction hypothesis that we are given an arbitrary subset S of I and that $G(x)$ is true for all $x \in S$, and then show that $G(z)$ holds for all $z \in F(S)$. The arbitrary subset is presented as $\{\ v\colon I\ |\ P(v)\ \}$ where P is an arbitrary predicate on I.

2.2   Syntax

We now present some basic definitions which allow us to talk about terms, logical formulas, free variables, substitution of terms for variables and pattern matching of one formula against another. The basic concept is that of a term; formulas are a special case. We do not treat binding operators, such as quantifiers.

The type of terms is inductively defined. We have in mind terms such as x, $sin(x)$, $equal(x,y)$, $plus(x,y)$, $implies(x,y)$, $implies(equal(x,plus(y,1)),\ equal(plus(y,1),x)))$. We say that the words *sin, equal, plus, implies* are *function symbols*. A simple definition of terms would be to say that a variable is a term, and if $t_1,\dots,t_n$ are terms and f is a function symbol, then $f(t_1,\dots,t_n)$ is a term. But the important point for manipulating terms is not the particular way of displaying them but rather the component parts and a means of accessing them. So for a composite term such as $f(t_1,\dots,t_n)$, the components are f and the list $(t_1,\dots,t_n)$. The important feature of a variable is that it is the base case of the definition. So the official definition of a term is that it is a variable or it is a pair $\langle f,l \rangle$ where f is a function symbol and l is a list of terms. This is the mathematical definition, but we can agree to display a composite term as $f(l)$.

If we let *Var* be the set of variables and *Fun* the set of function symbols, then the type *Term* is defined as[3]

$$rec(Term.\ Var\ |\ (Fun\#\ Term\ list)).$$

---

[2]In the special case treated here, all occurrences are positive. But in Nuprl [8,23] a much wider class of terms is allowed.

[3]Usually different kinds of characters are used for variables and function symbols, say $x, y, z, x_1, y_1, z_1, \dots$ for variables and $f_1, f_2, \dots$ for functions. We adopt the convention that any *atomic symbol* can serve as either a function or a variable. These atomic symbols come from the set *atom*. One can tell which is intended because variables occur without arguments while functions always have them. Another departure from custom is that we allow the same symbol to appear as a function or a variable and as a function taking different numbers of arguments. Thus $f(f(f),f)$ is a legitimate term, a way of writing $\langle f, (\langle f, (f) \rangle), f \rangle$. This term can be interpreted in numerous ways; one possibility is that f is treated as three different objects, one a variable, one a function of one argument and one a function of two arguments. So the above term is like $f_2(f_1(f),f)$. But these are matters of meaning which we do not discuss now. We are concerned only with the *syntax* of terms.

The induction principle for terms is given by the principle for this recursive type. We use it to prove the following theorem.

Theorem 1 *For all propositional functions P on terms, if $\forall x$: Var. $P(x)$, and if for all Term lists l and function symbols f, whenever $P(t)$ holds for all terms on l then $P(f(l))$, then $\forall t$: Term. $P(t)$.*

2.2.1 Term structure

We frequently carry out proofs or constructions based on the structure of a term. To facilitate them we introduce a case discriminator written as

$$case\ t:\ y \to a;\ f.l \to b.$$

This means that if the term t is a variable then the value is a, where in the expression a, y stands for the variable; if the term is composite then the value is b where f and l are names in b of the function symbol and subterm list respectively. This case analysis is used together with induction on term structure to define concepts on terms. For example, here is a definition of the notion that a variable x occurs in a term t.

Definition A variable x *occurs in* a term t, abbreviated $x \epsilon t$, if in the case that t is a variable y then $y = x$, and in the case that t is $f(l)$, then x occurs in some term u of l.

The form of inductive arguments on term structure is clarified by seeing the computational meaning of induction. The induction rule defined above is not only a way to prove properties of terms, but it is also a method of computing based on the structure of a term, just as mathematical induction is a way of computing based on the structure of natural numbers. The computational form associated with induction on terms is denoted $rec\_ind(t; h, x.\ b)$. To compute by "recursion induction" on a term t, we compute the expression b with the term t substituted for x and the entire rec_ind form substituted for h. Both h and x are bound variables whose scope is b. Let us consider this form for the notion of x occurs in t. The expression b is a case discriminator on x, precisely,

$$rec\_ind(t;\ occurs,\ z\ .\ case\ z:\ y \to x{=}y;$$
$$f,l \to for\ some\ u\ on\ l.\ occurs(u))$$

The general rule for evaluating the recursion induction form $rec\_ind(t; h, z.\ b)$ is that it reduces to

$$b[t/z, (\lambda w.\ rec\_ind(w; h, z.\ b))/h].$$

So in the case of a term such as $f(x, v)$ the computation of the recursive definition x *occurs in $f(x,v)$* is the following:

$$rec\_ind(f(x,v);\ occurs,z.\ case\ z:\ y \to x{=}y$$
$$f,l \to for\ some\ u\ in\ l.\ occurs(u))$$

reduces to (letting *occurs* denote $\lambda w.\ rec\_ind(w; \ldots)$)

$$case\ f(x,v):\ y \to x{=}y$$
$$f,l \to for\ some\ u\ in\ l.\ occurs(u)$$

which reduces to

> *for some u in (x,v). occurs(u).*

Taking u to be x results in

> *case x: y* → *x=y*
> *f,l* → *....*

In this case the term is a variable and the form reduces to

$$x = x$$

which is true. So x does occur in $f(x, v)$.

2.2.2   Substitutions

We want to study the substitution of terms for variables in terms, as in substituting 2 for x in $3 * x = z$ to obtain $3 * 2 = z$. A substitution will be defined as a list of pairs of a variable with a term, such as

$$(\langle x, 2 \rangle, \langle y, z \rangle, \langle z, x + y \rangle).$$

Thus a substitution is an element of the type *Var# Term list*. Call this type *Sub*.

Given a substitution s and a variable x we write $s(x)$ to designate the term paired with x (the first if there is more than one). This notion can be defined precisely by a list induction form, namely

$$s(x) = list\_ind(s; x; h, tl, v. \; if \; h.1 = x \; then \; h.2 \; else \; v).$$

(Recall that $h.1$ and $h.2$ select the first and second members of a pair respectively.)

The application of a substitution s to a term t is written $s(t)$; it is defined by induction on the structure of t. If t is a variable y, then $s(t)$ is $s(y)$. If t is f, l, then $s(t)$ is obtained by applying s to each element of the list l. If we let $map(s, l)$ denote the function that applies s to each term on the list l, then $s(t)$ is

$$rec\_ind(t; \; h, z. \; case \; z: \; y \to s(y) \; ; \; f, l \to f(map(s, l))).$$

Abbreviate $map(s, l)$ by $s(l)$.

The *domain* of a substitution is those variables that appear as the first element of a pair. We write $x \; \epsilon \; dom(s)$ to indicate that x is in the domain of substitution s. We say that s_1 is a *sub-substitution* of s_2, written $s_1 \subset s_2$, if for every variable x such that $x \; \epsilon \; dom(s_1)$, $x \; \epsilon \; dom(s_2)$ and $s_1(x) = s_2(x)$. We say that a substitution is *minimal*, $min(s)$, if no variable occurs twice on the left side of a pair.

2.2.3   Matching

We are now ready to discuss the problem of (first–order) matching. This is a basic issue in automated reasoning; for instance see [6,11,2,33]. We say that term t_1 matches t_2 if there is a substitution s such that $s(t_1) = t_2$. For example, $f(x, \; g(y, z))$ matches $f(g(y, z), g(y, z))$ using the substitution $(\langle x, g(y, z) \rangle)$. But $f(x, y)$ does not match $g(x, y)$ because the outer operators are different. We want to prove that for all terms t_1 and t_2 either t_1 matches t_2, and we can find a minimal substitution s such that $s(t_1) = s(t_2)$, or no substitution will produce a match. More precisely, define $match?(t_1)$ if for every $t_2 \in Term$

$$\exists\, s\colon Sub.\ s(t_1) = s(t_2)\ \&\ min(s)\ \&\ \forall x\colon Var.\ x{\in}dom(s) \Leftrightarrow x{\in}t_1)$$
$$\lor\ \forall\, s\colon Sub.\ \neg(s(t_1) = s(t_2)).$$

The main theorem can now be stated.

Theorem 2 *(match_thm):* $\forall\, t\colon Term.\ match?(t).$

The main idea of the proof is to check the outer structure of t_1 and t_2. If t_1 is a variable, then the pair $\langle t_1, t_2 \rangle$ is the substitution. Otherwise t_1 is compound, say $\langle f_1, l_1 \rangle$. If t_2 is a variable then there is no match, so assume it has the form $\langle f_2, l_2 \rangle$. If $f_1 \neq f_2$, then there is no substitution, otherwise the result depends on the result of trying to match l_1 and l_2. Suppose l_1 is *nil*. If l_2 is also *nil* then the empty substitution matches t_1 and t_2, otherwise there is no match. Suppose l_1 is $a_1.u_1$; if l_2 is *nil* then there is no match so suppose l_2 is $a_2.u_2$. First match a_1 and a_2. If they do not match, then neither do t_1 and t_2. Suppose they do, and let s be the substitution so that $s(a_1) = a_2$. Now try recursively to match u_1 and u_2. If these do not match, then neither do t_1 and t_2. If s' matches them, then we see whether s and s' are compatible substitutions, *i.e.* whether they agree on common variables. If they do, then the final substitution is a union of s and s'. If they are incompatible, then we must argue that no match exists.

2.3   Semantics

One account of the meaning of sentences in formal logic is that they denote a *truth value*. The meaning of operations that combine sentences, such as *and, or, implies* and *not* can in this account be explained as operations on truth values. For example, P and Q is a true sentence if P is true and Q is true; whereas it is false when one of P or Q is false. We develop next a brief account of the semantics of the propositional connectives $\&$, $\lor$, $\Rightarrow$ and $\neg$. Syntactic matters are covered completely by treating these operators as function symbols. The terms built from these operators are called *propositional formulas*. For example, the *contrapositive law* of logic usually written

$$(p \Rightarrow q) \Rightarrow (\neg q \Rightarrow \neg p)$$

is written as the term

$$imp(imp(p, q),\ imp(not(q), not(p))).$$

To assert this as a law is to say that its truth value is *true* regardless of the values of the variables p, q which stand for arbitrary propositions. We will express this precisely by defining a function that takes as arguments a propositional formula and an assignment of truth values to the variables of the formula, and returns the truth value of the formula given the assignment. An assignment is simply a substitution in which each term is a constant, either *true* or *false*. That is,

$$Assignment\ =\ \{\, s\colon Sub \mid for\ all\ p\ in\ s.\ p.2 = true \lor p.2 = false \,\}.$$

The value of a formula f under a truth assignment $a \in Assignment$, written $value(a, f)$, is

$$case\ f\ ;\ x \to a(x)\ ;\ op, l \to case\ op:\quad and \to value(a, l.1)\ \&\ value(a, l.2)$$
$$or \to value(a, l.1) \lor value(a, l.2)$$
$$imp \to \neg value(a, l.1) \lor value(a, l.2)$$
$$not \to \neg value(a, l.1),$$

where $l.1$ and $l.2$ here are the first and second elements of the list l, and the operators &, $\lor$, $\Rightarrow$ and $\neg$ are functions computing the appropriate truth values. A formula f is *valid* or a *tautology* if for every assignment a, $value(a, f) = true$. An assignment a *falsifies* f if $value(a, f) = false$.

2.3.1   Decision procedure for validity

We want to show that we can decide for any propositional formula whether or not it is valid. Moreover, we want the computational content of the argument to be a special algorithm called a *tableau decision* procedure [31,16]. One elegant way to express the procedure is in terms of a pair of formula lists called a *sequent*.

$$Sequent\ =\ (Term\ list)\#(Term\ list)$$

If H and G are lists of terms, then we sometimes write the sequent containing them as $H \gg G$, calling H the *hypothesis list* and G the *goal list*. We extend the notions of truth and validity to sequents by taking $H \gg G$ to be true if the conjunction of the elements of H implies the disjunction of those of G. This can be made formal with the following definitions.

$$conj(H)\ =\ list\_ind(H;\ true;\ h, t, v.\ and(h, v))$$
$$disj(H)\ =\ list\_ind(H;\ false;\ h, t, v. or(h, v))$$
$$svalue(a, \langle H, G \rangle)\ =\ value(a,\ imp(conj(H), disj(G)))$$
$$\langle H, G \rangle\ is\ valid\ \Leftrightarrow\ \forall a{:}\ Assignment.\ svalue(a, \langle H, G \rangle) = true$$

With these definitions, the exact result we want is:

$$\forall s{:} Sequent.\ valid(s) \lor \exists a{:} Assignment.\ (svalue(a, s) = false)$$

The method of proof will be to decompose s into smaller sequents which have the property. We show that if the smaller sequents are valid, so is the original, and if the smaller sequents are falsifiable, then so is the original. Here follows a typical step of the argument.

For example, given a sequent $H \gg (A \Rightarrow B)$ we form the smaller sequent $A, H \gg B$. If this is valid, then so is the original. If assignment a falsifies this smaller sequent, then it gives value true to A and all elements of H and *false* to B. But such an assignment will falsify $H \gg (A \Rightarrow B)$ because it assigns *true* to H and *false* to $(A \Rightarrow B)$.

One of the key features of the argument is the definition of a *smaller* sequent. Notice that in going from $H \gg (A \Rightarrow B)$ to $A, H \gg B$ one occurrence of an operator has been eliminated. Thus the "over-all number of operators" is decreasing. We write $s' < s$ if s' has fewer operators than s.

Theorem 3 *(Validity is Decidable):*

$$\forall s{:} Sequent.\ valid(s) \lor \exists a{:} Assignment.\ (svalue(a, s) = false)$$

Proof. The proof is by induction on the number of operators in s. Let s be an arbitrary sequent, say $s = \langle H, G \rangle$. The induction hypothesis is:

$$\forall s': Sequent. \ s' < s \Rightarrow P(s').$$

Suppose that all formulas of s are atomic (so there are no s' where $s' < s$). Either H and G are disjoint or there is some formula f in both H and G. In the case that H and G are disjoint, there is an assignment which assigns *false* to all variables of G and *true* to all variable of H. Under this assignment $svalue(a, s) = false$ by definition of *svalue*. If f occurs in both H and G, then $\langle H, G \rangle$ is valid because each assignment that assigns value *true* to f in H will make $disj(G)$ true as well.

Now suppose that there is at least one formula f of H or G which is compound. The argument proceeds by cases on the *location* and *structure* of f. Let us assume first that the goal G has a compound formula, and that f is the first compound formula (from the left).

G1. If f is $f_1 \vee f_2$ then form G' from G by replacing f by f_1, f_2. Let $s' = \langle H, G' \rangle$ and notice that $s' < s$, so that by the induction hypothesis the theorem holds for s'. If s' is valid, then clearly s is as well, and if a falsifies s' then it falsifies s as well.

G2. If f is $f_1 \& f_2$ then form G_1 by replacing f by f_1 and form G_2 by replacing f by f_2. Let $s_1 = \langle H, G_1 \rangle$ and $s_2 = \langle H, G_2 \rangle$. Notice that $s_1 < s$ and $s_2 < s$, so the theorem is true s_1 and s_2.

If both s_1 and s_2 are valid, then clearly s is as well. If one of them, without loss of generality say s_1, is falsifiable using a, then a falsifies s as well.

G3. If f is $(f_1 \Rightarrow f_2)$ then replace f in G by f_2 to obtain G' and add f_1 to H to form H'. Let $s' = \langle H', G' \rangle$. Suppose s' is valid, and suppose that the assignment a makes H true. If $a(f_1) = false$ then G is true, so suppose $a(f_1) = true$. H' must then be true. Since s' is valid G' must be true under a hence so must G.

If s' is falsifiable by a, then the same a falsifies s because f_1 is true and f_2 is false, so $(f_1 \Rightarrow f_2)$ is false along with all the other formulas of G.

G4. If f is $\neg f_1$ then replace f in G by *false* to form G' and add f_1 to H to form H'. Let $s' = \langle H', G' \rangle$. We can now argue as in the previous case.

Now suppose there is no compound formula in G, but there is one in H, say f. Consider the possible forms of f.

H1. If f is $f_1 \vee f_2$ then replace f by f_1 in H to form H_1 and by f_2 to form H_2. Let $s_1 = \langle H_1, G \rangle$ and $s_2 = \langle H_2, G \rangle$. Notice that $s_1 < s$ and $s_2 < s$, so the theorem is true for s_1 and s_2. If both s_1 and s_2 are valid, then so is s. If either s_1 or s_2 is falsified by a, then the same a falsifies s.

H2. If f is $f_1 \& f_2$ then replace it in H by f_1, f_2 to form H' and let $s' = \langle H', G \rangle$. If s' is valid, then clearly s is as well. If s' is falsifiable by assignment a, then a falsifies s since the truth values of H and H' are the same.

H3. If f is $(f_1 \Rightarrow f_2)$ then replace f by f_2 to create H' and add f_1 to G to create G'. Let $s_1 = \langle H', G \rangle$ and $s_2 = <H'', G'>$ where H'' is H without f. If both s_1 and s_2 are valid, then we argue that s is valid. Consider any assignment which makes H true. Then f is made true which means either f_2 is true or both f_1 and f_2 are false. If f_2 is true then so is H' so from the validity of s_1 we know that G is true. If both f_1 and f_2 are false, then since s_2 is valid and H'' is true, some element of G must be true.

If one of s_1 or s_2 is falsifiable by a, then s will be. Suppose s_1 is falsifiable. Then f_2 and hence f will have value *true* under a, but G will be false, so s is false. On the other hand, if s_2 is falsifiable by a, then f_1 has the value *false*. But then in s, f will get value true and all formulas of G will remain false.

H4. If f is $\neg f_1$ then remove f from H to obtain H' and add f_1 to G to obtain G'. Let $s' = \langle H', G' \rangle$. If s' is valid, then s is as well, that is, when $\neg f_1$ gets the value *true* in H, then f_1 gets the value *false*, so in G' some other formula must get the value *true*, and this is the formula true in G. If s' is falsifiable by a, then H' is true but G' is not. Thus f_1 gets the value *false*, so H is true and all formulas of G remain false.

Qed.

Notice that the proof of this theorem is constructive. It implicitly gives an algorithm to decide validity, and the algorithm is the tableau procedure. In the next section we show how to formalize the theorem on matching in the constructive type theory of Nuprl. The formal library follows very closely the informal development.

3   Formal Metamathematics

A system that supports our approach to automatic theorem proving should have several properties. First, it should be based on a rich formal logic that allows direct expression of metamathematical ideas. Since we are interested in the computational content of metamathematics, the logic should be constructive, so that, for example, in asserting that a theory is decidable we are also implicitly asserting that there is a procedure for deciding when a given sentence is true. We want to apply the computational content of our metamathematics in the construction of proofs, so the system should be able to extract the algorithms that are implicit in our theorems.

Since programs are to be extracted from metatheorems, and since we must be certain that these programs are correct so that logical soundness is preserved, the metatheorems must be formally proven. Since programs are determined by proofs, we will often want to construct formal proofs that follow a specific outline. For example, in proving that any propositional formula is either valid or not, we gave an argument that implicitly constructs a tableau decision procedure. Ideally we would like to be able to construct the formal proof by supplying the proof we want at as high a level as possible, with the system taking care of the detailed reasoning necessary to complete the proof.

The Nuprl proof development system[8] goes a good part of the way toward satisfying the above properties. Nuprl's logic was designed as a foundation for constructive mathematics, and there is little doubt that it is sufficiently expressive for the applications we have in mind. By design it has an extraction property; complete proofs yield programs in a direct and natural manner. The extent to which Nuprl allows direct expression of and high-level natural reasoning about metamathematics is difficult to quantify. We will not do so, but will instead give an extended example of formal metamathematics in Nuprl. In particular, most of the rest of this section is devoted to describing a formal proof we have carried out in Nuprl of the theorem about matching that was discussed earlier.

The formal proof, which was developed specifically for this paper, took about a day to construct using Nuprl. A complete listing of the proof can be obtained from the authors. The actual Nuprl-readable version is available with the distribution of the Nuprl system.

Before we can proceed with the example, we need to give a brief description of Nuprl. After the example, we discuss how programs such as matching can be incorporated in Nuprl's own inference mechanisms.

3.1   Nuprl

Nuprl [8] is a system that has been developed at Cornell by a team of researchers, and is intended to provide an environment for the solution of formal problems, especially those where computational aspects are important. One of the main problem-solving paradigms that the system supports is that of *proofs-as-programs*, where a program specification takes the form of a mathematical proposition implicitly asserting the existence of the desired programs. Such a proposition can be formally proved, with computer assistance, in a manner resembling conventional mathematical arguments. The system can extract from the proof the implicit computational content, which is a program that is guaranteed to meet its specification.

The logical basis of Nuprl is a constructive type theory that is a descendent of a type theory of Martin-Löf [22]. We will not give details of the type theory except as necessary in the discussion of the match example, and in particular we will not discuss how notions of logic are expressed in the type theory (but we used informally the basic concepts of this type theory in section 2.2). Higher-order logic is defined directly in terms of types and can be used abstractly. When we refer to "formulas" or "propositions" below we mean these defined notions, and often the statements we make about formulas will be true of types in general. The following account is somewhat loose; a complete account of the type theory and system is contained in the Nuprl book [8].

The inference rules of Nuprl deal with *sequents*, which are objects of the form

$$H_1 , \ H_2 , \ \dots , \ H_n \ >> \ P$$

where P is a formula and where each H_i is either a formula or a variable declaration of the form $x : T$ for x a variable and T a type. The H_i are referred to as *hypotheses*, and P is called the *conclusion* of the sequent. Sequents, in the context of a proof, are also called *goals*. A sequent is true if the conclusion is true whenever the hypotheses are. We take truth here to be constructive, so that a true sequent comes with a procedure giving its computational content. An important point about the rules of Nuprl is that they preserve constructive truth, so that from a complete proof of a sequent $>>P$ the computational content of P can be computed.

A proof in Nuprl is a tree-structured object where each node has associated with it a sequent and a rule. We call rules in Nuprl *refinement* rules because we think of them as being applied backwards: given a goal, we *refine* it by using an inference rule whose conclusion matches the goal, obtaining *subgoals* which are the premises of the rule. The children of a node in a proof tree are the subgoals which result from the application of the refinement rule of the node. A key feature of Nuprl's proof structure is that a refinement rule need not be just a primitive inference rule, but can also be a *tactic* written in the programming language ML [14]. As with a primitive refinement rules, the application of a tactic to a goal produces subgoals. Because of ML's strong typing property, it is guaranteed that the subgoals imply the goal. When a tactic is used to refine a goal, the rule at the new node of the proof tree will show the text of the tactic. This gives a means for constructing higher level proofs that can serve as explanations of formal arguments.

Suppose we have proven a theorem

```
∀i,j,m,n: Int. i≤j & m≤n => m+i≤n+j
```

and named it mono. An example of a refinement step using a tactic which applies this theorem is the following.[4]

```
x:Int, 0≤x  >>   x+2 ≤ 2*x+2    BY (Lemma 'mono' ...)
    x:Int, 0≤x  >>   x ≤ 2*x
```

The tactic Lemma computes the necessary terms and applies the rules necessary to instantiate the theorem. The three dots after the tactic indicate that a general purpose tactic called the *autotactic* was applied after Lemma. In this example, the autotactic proved the most trivial subgoals produced by Lemma (that x, 2*x and 2 are integers and that 2≤2). The result of the refinement is the single subgoal shown.

Interactions with Nuprl are centred on the *library*. A library contains an ordered collection of definitions, theorems, and other objects. New objects are constructed using special-purpose window-oriented editors. The text editor, together with the definition facility, permit very readable notations for objects of Nuprl's type theory. The proof editor is used to construct proofs in a top-down manner, and to view previously constructed proofs. Proofs are retained by the system, and can be later referred to either by the user, or by tactics.

3.2   A Formal Account of Matching

In Section 2.2 we gave an informal type-theoretic account of first-order matching. We have implemented a formalization of this account in Nuprl. The complete Nuprl library containing this formalization can be divided into two parts. The first part, consisting of about 150 objects, is of a general nature. It contains definitions and simple theorems pertaining to the representation of logic within Nuprl. It also contains a minimal development of the theory of lists. The second part is particular to the formalization of matching; it contains about 40 definitions and theorems, most of which concern substitution and the syntax of terms.

The description that follows consists of three parts. First is a brief discussion of the tactics that were used in building the proofs in this library. Next is a presentation of the definitions and the simple theorems leading up to the main results of the library. Last is a detailed description of the proofs of the three main theorems of the library. In particular, we will examine one of the proofs in its entirety in order to give an idea of the character of reasoning about formal metatheory in Nuprl. These three parts constitute a complete description of the library, in that all definitions and theorems not in the general portion of the library will be at least stated.

---

[4]We will use typewriter typeface when presenting objects constructed (or hypothetically constructed) with the Nuprl system.

The definitions, theorems and proof steps that we show below appear much as they would on the screen of a Nuprl session, although a few liberties have been for the sake of readability. In particular, a few variables were renamed, and a quirk of the system whereby display forms associated with definitions were occasionally lost was manually corrected for. Also, the syntax of Nuprl definitions was slightly altered for compactness. The notations for defined terms, including the special symbols for quantification, *etc.*, are exactly as they appear in the system.

3.2.1 Preliminaries

A tactic in Nuprl is an ML program that, when applied to a sequent, either *fails* or returns a list of subgoal sequents. Over the last several years a rather large collection of tactics has been built up at Cornell. Some of these are described in [17]. Only a few of these need to be described here. Little detail will be given, but it should be enough so that their use in the proof steps we give later will be understandable.

The bulk of the work in proving the theorems in our library, in terms of number inference steps taken, is done by two general tactics. The first of these, the *autotactic*, was mentioned above. The autotactic is usually able to completely prove subgoals involving typechecking (showing that a term is in a certain type or that a formula is well-formed—these properties are recursively undecidable in Nuprl because of the generality of the type theory) and simple kinds of simple integer arithmetic and propositional reasoning. Associated with definitions in the library are theorems which give a type for the defined term; these types are used by the autotactic in proving the numerous typechecking subgoals that arise. The autotactic is usually effective in hiding the details of the type theory from the user; for example, there are no typechecking subgoals in the proofs of the main theorems described below. The autotactic is usually invoked via a Nuprl definition: when $(T \ \ldots)$ appears in a proof, it means that the autotactic was applied after the tactic T.

The other general tactic is called Simp and is used to simplify terms. This tactic can be updated from the library (through a special kind of library object that can contain an ML form) with new simplification clauses in two basic ways. First, one can specify that a theorem be used for simplification. The theorem should be a universally quantified formula of the form

$$A_1 \Rightarrow A_2 \Rightarrow \ldots \Rightarrow A_n \Rightarrow R(a, b)$$

where R is an equivalence relation (such as if-and-only-if or Nuprl's built-in equality). The simplifier will then always try to rewrite terms matching a to an instance of b. Second, one can directly specify a simplification that is computationally justified (where one term can be obtained from another by a sequence of forward or backward computation steps). For example, one can specify that the length |h.1| of a list with head h always be simplified to |1|+1. The "general" portion of the match library contains numerous updates to the simplifier, mostly for propositions and some for list theory. Like the autotactic, the simplifier is invoked by a definition: the notation $(T \ \ldots +s)$ indicates that the simplifier and autotactic were both applied after T. One of the variants of this has sc in place of +s; this means the simplifier was applied to the just the conclusions of the subgoals produced by T.

Several other tactics use information from the library. Induction is used to perform induction on a variable appearing in a goal. If there is an induction principle in the library for the type of the variable, that is used, otherwise the type should be a primitive one (not a definition instance) for which there is an induction rule. Unroll is similar to induction except that no induction hypothesis is generated. Finally, Decide takes a formula P and performs a case analysis on whether or not P is true. Decidability ($P \lor \neg P$) is non-trivial in Nuprl, and Decide attempts to use theorems of the appropriate form to justify the case analysis.

There are quite a few tactics for purely logical reasoning; most of these are simple. For example, ILeft reduces proving a disjunction to proving the left disjunct, and ITerm reduces proving an existentially quantified term $\exists x : T.\ P(x)$) to proving $P(t)$ for some supplied term t. ("I" is for introduction). For analysing hypotheses there are various "elimination" tactics: E applies to most kinds of formula and performs one step of analysis; SomeE applies to "some" (or "exists") formulas; and EOn (which requires a term argument) applies to universally quantified formulas. HypCases uses a universally quantified disjunction in the hypothesis list to perform a case analysis; it takes a list of terms as arguments to instantiate the quantified variables with. The most powerful tactic for logical reasoning is Backchain which uses (universally quantified) implications in the hypothesis list in a search for a complete proof. For example, if the conclusion of a sequent is Q and $P \Rightarrow Q$ is a hypothesis, then it reduces proving Q to proving P and then attempts to recursively prove Q; if this fails it tries another hypothesis of a similar form.

There are several simple tactics for lemma application. One of these is Lemma, an example application of which was given above. FLemma does a forward-reasoning analogue of what Lemma does. For example, if the theorem referred to is $P \Rightarrow Q$ and P is a (specified) hypothesis, then Q is added as a new hypothesis. Finally, CaseLemma uses a named lemma to determine a case analysis.

Finally, there are a few miscellaneous tactics that should be mentioned. First, the tactic Thin and its variants are used to remove unwanted hypotheses from a goal. AndThin takes a tactic that applies to hypotheses, applies it to a hypothesis and then discards the hypothesis. The so-called *tactical* THEN is used to combine tactics; if T_1 and T_2 are tactics then the tactic T_1 THEN T_2 first applies T_1 then applies T_2 to the resulting subgoals. The last tactic we discuss is Expand. This tactic takes a list of names of definitions and expands all instances of those definitions in the goal.

3.2.2 Definitions and Simple Theorems

Since the definitions given in Section 2.2 are given in type-theoretic terms, their formalizations are almost identical. In particular, the explanations given there still apply, so we will do little more here than to simply present the formal versions. In Nuprl a definition generally consists of two objects. One object is used to establish the defined term (and usually to give it a type), and the other is used to attach a notation or display form to the definition. For brevity we will present definitions by collapsing these two objects into one, just giving the notation and the term it denotes.

The simple theorems given below were easy to prove, and we will only present a proof of one of them. These theorems required on average about five steps each to prove. What a "step" is is not well-defined since we can always collapse an entire proof into a single step by composing all the tactics used in the proof. We will rely on our description of some representative proofs to convey what a typical step is in this setting.

The definitions for syntax are straightforward. We first define the types of representatives of functions and variables in terms of Nuprl's type of atoms (character strings).

```
Var == Atom
Fun == Atom
```

The type of term representatives is a recursive type of syntax trees:

```
Term == rec(T. Var | Fun # T list).
```

The equality relations for terms and lists of terms are frequently used, so definitions are made for them.

```
t1=t2 == t1=t2 in Term
l1=l2 == l1=l2 in Term list
```

Note that ambiguities in notations are acceptable in Nuprl (since definition instances do not have to be parsed). The "injections" or "term constructors" are defined by

```
x == inl(x)
f(l) == inr(<f,l>)
```

We prove an induction principle and a useful special case of it:

```
>> ∀P:Term->U1. (∀x:Var. P(x))
           => (∀l:Term list. ∀f:Fun. (∀t:l. P(t)) => P(f(l)))
           => ∀t:Term. P(t)
>> ∀P:Term->U1. ∀x:Var. P(x)
           => ∀l:Term list. ∀f:Fun. P(f(l))
           => ∀t:Term. P(t)
```

Here the proposition ∀t:l. P(t) asserts that P(t) is true for every member t of the list l. The first of these theorems can be read as "The property P of terms is true for all terms if (1) it is true for all variables and (2) if f is a member of Fun and l is a list of terms satisfying P then P is true of $f(l)$". For our purposes, the type U1 can be thought of as the type of all propositions.

The form for case analysis of terms is the following.

```
case t: x→a; f,l→b == decide(t; x.a; ap. let f,l=ap in b)
```

This uses the type theory's operators for analyzing a member of a disjoint union and for decomposing a pair. As in Section 2.2, we can now define when a variable *occurs* in a term.

```
x∈t == rec_ind(t; P,z. case z: y → y=x; f,l→ ∃u:l. P(u))
```

We also define a version of this predicate for lists

```
x∈l == ∃t:l. x∈t
```

so that a variable occurs in a list if it occurs in some member of the list. For this definition, as with other defined recursive functions and predicates, we add appropriate clauses to the simplifier. For example, we want any term of the form x∈f(l) to simplify to x∈l.

The type of substitutions and the application of a substitution to a variable and a term are defined as before. We also define application to a list of terms.

```
Sub == Var#Term list
s(x) == list_ind(s; x; h,ll,v. if h.1=x then h.2 else v)
s(t) == rec_ind(t; h,z. case z: x→s(x); f,l→f(map(h,l)))
s(l) == map(λt.s(t), l)
```

As in Section 2.2, the notations .1 and .2 denote projections from a pair, and map(h,l) applies the function h to every element of the list l.

We will need several predicates on substitutions. In particular, we define when a variable is in the domain of a substitution, when one substitution is contained in another, when a substitution is minimal (that is, no two pairs in it have the same variable component) and when two substitutions are inconsistent (that is, disagree on some variable in both their domains).

```
x∈dom(s) == ∃p:s. p.1=x
s1⊏s2 == ∀x:Var. x∈dom(s1) => x∈dom(s2) & s1(x)=s2(x)
min(s) == list_ind(s; True; h,l,v. ¬(h.1∈dom(l)) & P)
ncst(s1,s2) == ∃x:Var. x∈dom(s1) & x∈dom(s2) & ¬(s1(x)=s2(x))
```

Finally, it will be handy to have the following definition for the main theorem.

```
match?(t1) == ∀t2:Term. ∃s:Sub. s(t1)=t2 & min(s)
                                  & ∀x:Var. x∈dom(s) <=> x∈t1
              V ∀s:Sub. ¬(s(t1)=t2)
```

Thus match?(t1) asserts that for every t2 either there is a minimal matching substitution or there is no matching substitution. The minimality and the condition that a variable be in the domain of the substitution exactly if it occurs in t are required for our inductive proof to go through. We also have a version of the above definition for lists.

```
match?(l1) ==  ∀l2:Term list. ∃s:Sub. s(l1)=l2 & min(s)
                                    & ∀x:Var. x∈dom(s) <=> x∈l1
               V ∀s:Sub. ¬(s(l1)=l2)
```

This list version is defined simply for convenience, as will be made clear when we present the proof of the main theorem.

The following seven simple lemmas are incorporated into the simplifier and never have to be explicitly referred to. The fifth of these may look trivial; this is because we have used the same display form for term equality as for equality in Var.

```
>> ∀x,y:Var. ∀s:Sub. ∀t:Term. x=y => (<x,t>.s)(y) = t
>> ∀x,y:Var. ∀s:Sub. ∀t:Term. ¬(x=y) => (<x,t>.s)(y) = s(y)
>> ∀x,y:Var. ∀s:Sub. ∀t:Term. x=y => x∈dom((<y,t>).s) <=> True
>> ∀x,y:Var. ∀s:Sub. ∀t:Term. ¬(x=y) => x∈dom((<y,t>).s) <=> x∈dom(s)
>> ∀x,y:Var. x=y <=> x=y
>> ∀f1,f2:Fun. ∀l1,l2:Term list. f1(l1)=f2(l2) <=> f1=f2 & l1=l2
>> ∀x:Var. ∀f:Fun. ∀l:Term list. x=f(l) <=> False
```

The following is the first theorem we prove that has an interesting computational interpretation. Constructively it means that we can decide whether or not two terms are equal. From the proof of this theorem Nuprl can extract a decision procedure.

```
    * top
    >> ∀x:Var. ∀s:Sub. ¬(x∈dom(s)) ∨ ∃t:Term. x∈dom(s) & s(x)=t

    BY (On 's' Induction ...+s)

    1* 1. x: Var
       2. s: Sub
       3. p: Var#Term
       4. ¬(x∈dom(s)) ∨ ∃t:Term. x∈dom(s) & s(x)=t
       >> ¬(p.1=x ∨ x∈dom(s))
            ∨ ∃t:Term. (p.1=x ∨ x∈dom(s)) & (p.s)(x)=t
```

Figure 1: Proof by induction on s.

```
    >> ∀t1,t2:Term. t1=t2 ∨ ¬(t1=t2)
```

The next two theorems establish that the value of a substitution on a term (list) is characterized by its values on the variables occurring in the term (list).

```
    >> ∀s1,s2:Sub. ∀t:Term.
          s1(t)=s2(t) <=> (∀x:Var. x∈t => s1(x)=s2(x))
    >> ∀l:Term list. ∀s1,s2:Sub.
          s1(l)=s2(l) <=> (∀x:Var. x∈l => s1(x)=s2(x))
```

The computational content of the next simple theorem is a procedure which "looks up" a binding for a variable x in a substitution s, producing an indication of whether or not the variable is in the domain of s and in the former case giving the term bound to x.

```
    >> ∀x:Var. ∀s:Sub. ¬(x∈dom(s)) ∨ ∃t:Term. x∈dom(s) & s(x)=t
```

For future reference, the name of this theorem is sub_lookup. The proof is short and is given in its entirety as Figures 1 to 4. The figures show the proof steps as they would appear to a Nuprl user except that to save space we have removed from some steps some of the hypotheses that appear in earlier steps.

The first step in the proof is in Figure 1 and is by induction on the list s. This figure shows the goal sequent, then the rule applied, in this case a tactic, and then the subgoal sequent with its hypothesis list numbered and displayed vertically. The asterisk at the top left is Nuprl's indication that the proof is complete, and top is the tree address of the proof node within the proof tree for the theorem. Note that in this step the simplifier and autotactic together automatically proved the base case and left the remaining subgoal in a simplified form. The step applied to this subgoal is shown in Figure 2. Here we decompose ("eliminate") the pair p (and thin, or discard, its hypothesis) and then perform some reduction steps to simplify the subgoal. The next step is shown in Figure 3. In this goal we know that the property we are proving is inductively true of s, and we have to prove it for <x1,t1>.s. We want to do a case analysis on whether x1=x, so we use the tactic Decide. The negative case was proved automatically, and we are left with a simple subgoal in the other case. The last step (Figure 4) is trivial.

The structure of the program extracted from this proof is determined by the steps we have shown. The first step (using induction) introduces list recursion. In the next step, the

```
* top 1
3. p: Var#Term
4. ¬(x∈dom(s)) ∨ ∃t:Term. x∈dom(s) & s(x)=t
>> ¬(p.1=x ∨ x∈dom(s))
   ∨ ∃t:Term. p.1=x ∨ x∈dom(s) & p.s(x)=t

BY (AndThin E 3 THEN Reduce ...)

1* 4. x1: Var
   5. t1: Term
   >> ¬(x1=x ∨ x∈dom(s))
      ∨ ∃t:Term.  (x1=x ∨ x∈dom(s)) & (<x1,t1>.s)(x)=t
```

Figure 2: Let x1 and t1 be the components of p.

```
* top 1 1
3. ¬(x∈dom(s)) ∨ ∃t:Term. x∈dom(s) & s(x)=t
4. x1: Var
5. t1: Term
>> ¬(x1=x ∨ x∈dom(s))
   ∨ ∃t:Term.  (x1=x ∨ x∈dom(s)) & (<x1,t1>.s)(x)=t

BY (Decide 'x1=x' ...+s)

1* 5. x1=x
   6. ¬(x∈dom(s)) ∨ ∃t:Term. x∈dom(s) & s(x)=t
   >> ∃t:Term. t1=t
```

Figure 3: Case analysis on whether or not x1=x.

```
* top 1 1 1
5. x1=x
6. ¬(x∈dom(s)) ∨ ∃t:Term. x∈dom(s) & s(x)=t
>> ∃t:Term. t1=t

BY (ITerm 't1' ...)
```

Figure 4: Take t to be t1.

induction hypothesis corresponds to a recursive call of the function we are constructing. To lookup the value of x in p.s we first decompose the pair p into its components x1 and t1. The use of Decide in the next step corresponds to the introduction of an "if-then-else" expression whose condition is x1=x. In the case where x1 is not equal to x, a recursive call is made (that is, the induction hypothesis is used, automatically). In the other case we return the value t1.

The last theorems in our library before the three main theorems (which are discussed below) are added to the simplifier and forgotten.

```
>> ∀s1,s2:Sub. ∀x:Var. ∀t:Term.
      s1⊂s2 => (<x,t>.s1 ⊂ <x,t>.s2 <=> True)
>> ∀s1,s2:Sub. ∀x:Var. ∀t:Term.
      s1⊂s2 => ¬(x∈dom(s1)) => (s1 ⊂ <x,t>.s2 <=> True)
>> ∀s1,s2:Sub. ∀x:Var. ∀t:Term.
    s1⊂s2 => x∈dom(s2) => s2(x)=t => (<x,t>.s1 ⊂ s2 <=> True)
```

3.2.3 Matching

The match procedure is mostly the product of the last three theorems in the library.

```
>> ∀s1,s2:Sub. min(s1) & min(s2)
    => ncst(s1,s2)
        ∨ ∃s:Sub. min(s) & s1⊂s & s2⊂s
                  & ∀x:Var. x∈dom(s) => x∈dom(s1) ∨ x∈dom(s2)
>> ∀l:Term list. (∀t:l. match?(t)) => match?(l)
>> ∀t:Term. match?(t)
```

The names of these theorems in the library are sub_union, lmatch_thm and match_thm respectively. The proof of the first theorem has 23 steps, the proof of the second has 25, and the last has 13. Space limitations prevent us from presenting all of these proofs, so we will instead give the complete proof of the last theorem and just give some of the highlights of the other two. The level of inference in the three proofs is roughly the same.

The proof of match_thm is given in Figures 5 to 17. This proof is rather self explanatory, so not much additional explanation will be given. The first step (Figure 5) is by induction on t. The proof of the base case (where t is a variable) is easy and is contained in Figures 6 and 7. The first step in the proof of the induction step (Figure 8) is to apply the second of the three "main" theorems listed above, and then (Figure 9) we expand the definition of match?. In the next step (Figure 10) we "unroll" t2, doing a case analysis on whether t2 is a variable or an application. The variable case is easy (Figure 11). In the other case (Figure 12) we do a case analysis on whether the function parts of the two terms are the same.

The case where they are not the same is proved in one step (Figure 13). When they are the same we need to know if one argument list matches the other (Figure 14). When it does, we get the required matching substitution (Figure 15). Otherwise, we obtain a contradiction (Figures 16 and 17).

We finish our presentation of the formalization of the matching algorithm by briefly discussing the other two major theorems of the library. For one we will just describe the

```
            * top
            >> ∀t:Term. match?(t)

            BY (On 't' Induction ...)

            1* 1. x: Var
               >> match?(x)

            2* 1. l: Term list
               2. f: Fun
               3. ∀t:l. match?(t)
               >> match?(f(l))
```

Figure 5: Proof by induction on t.

```
* top 1
1. x: Var
>> match?(x)

BY (Expand ''matchp'' ...+s)

1* 1. x: Var
   2. t2: Term
   >> ∃s:Sub. s(x)=t2 & min(s) & ∀x1:Var. x1∈dom(s) <=> x=x1
      ∨ ∀s:Sub. ¬(s(x)=t2)
```

Figure 6: Use the definition of match?.

```
* top 1 1
1. x: Var
2. t2: Term
>> ∃s:Sub. s(x)=t2 & min(s) & ∀x1:Var. x1∈dom(s) <=> x=x1
   ∨ ∀s:Sub. ¬(s(x)=t2)

BY (ILeft THENM ITerm '[<x,t2>]' ...+s)
```

Figure 7: The left disjunct is true: take s to be [<x,t2>].

```
                * top 2
                1. 1: Term list
                2. f: Fun
                3. ∀t:1. match?(t)
                >> match?(f(1))

                BY (FLemma 'lmatch_thm' [3] ...) THEN Thin 3

                1* 3. match?(1)
                   >> match?(f(1))
```

Figure 8: By lmatch_thm and 3 we have match?(1).

```
        * top 2 1
        1. 1: Term list
        2. f: Fun
        3. match?(1)
        >> match?(f(1))

        BY (Expand ''matchp'' ...+s)

        1* 3. t2: Term
           4. match?(1)
           >> ∃s:Sub. f(s(1))=t2 & min(s) & ∀x:Var. x∈dom(s) <=> x∈l
              ∨ ∀s:Sub. ¬(f(s(1))=t2)
```

Figure 9: Use the definition of matchp.

```
        * top 2 1 1
        3. t2: Term
        4. match?(1)
        >> ∃s:Sub. f(s(1))=t2 & min(s) & ∀x:Var. x∈dom(s) <=> x∈l
           ∨ ∀s:Sub. ¬(f(s(1))=t2)

        BY (On 't2' Unroll ...)

        1* 4. x: Var
           >> ∃s:Sub. f(s(1))=x & min(s) & ∀x:Var. x∈dom(s) <=> x∈l
              ∨ ∀s:Sub. ¬(f(s(1))=x)

        2* 4. 12: Term list
           5. f2: Fun
           >> ∃s:Sub. f(s(1))=f2(12) & min(s) & ∀x:Var. x∈dom(s) <=> x∈l
              ∨ ∀s:Sub. ¬(f(s(1))=f2(12))
```

Figure 10: Case analysis on the term kind of t2.

```
* top 2 1 1 1
4. x: Var
>> ∃s:Sub. f(s(1))=x & min(s) & ∀x:Var. x∈dom(s) <=> x∈l
   ∨ ∀s:Sub. ¬(f(s(1))=x)

BY (IRight ...+s)
```

Figure 11: In this case there are no matching substitutions.

```
* top 2 1 1 2
4. 12: Term list
5. f2: Fun
>> ∃s:Sub. f(s(1))=f2(12) & min(s) & ∀x:Var. x∈dom(s) <=> x∈l
   ∨ ∀s:Sub. ¬(f(s(1))=f2(12))

BY (Decide 'f=f2' ...)

1* 6. f=f2
   >> ∃s:Sub. f(s(1))=f2(12) & min(s) & ∀x:Var. x∈dom(s) <=> x∈l
      ∨ ∀s:Sub. ¬(f(s(1))=f2(12))

2* 6. ¬(f=f2)
   >> ∃s:Sub. f(s(1))=f2(12) & min(s) & ∀x:Var. x∈dom(s) <=> x∈l
      ∨ ∀s:Sub. ¬(f(s(1))=f2(12))
```

Figure 12: Either f=f2 or not.

```
* top 2 1 1 2 2
3. match?(1)
4. 12: Term list
5. f2: Fun
6. ¬(f=f2)
>> ∃s:Sub. f(s(1))=f2(12) & min(s) & ∀x:Var. x∈dom(s) <=> x∈l
   ∨ ∀s:Sub. ¬(f(s(1))=f2(12))

BY (IRight ...+s)
```

Figure 13: Clearly no match in this case.

```
* top 2 1 1 2 1
3. match?(1)
6. f=f2
>> ∃s:Sub. f(s(1))=f2(12) & min(s) & ∀x:Var. x∈dom(s) <=> x∈1
   ∨ ∀s:Sub. ¬(f(s(1))=f2(12))


BY (Expand ''lmatchp'' THEN HypCases ['12'] 3 ...)


1* 6. ∃s:Sub. s(1)=12 & min(s) & ∀x:Var. x∈dom(s) <=> x∈1
   >> ∃s:Sub. f(s(1))=f2(12) & min(s) & ∀x:Var. x∈dom(s) <=> x∈1
      ∨ ∀s:Sub. ¬(f(s(1))=f2(12))


2* 6. ∀s:Sub. ¬(s(1)=12)
   >> ∃s:Sub. f(s(1))=f2(12) & min(s) & ∀x:Var. x∈dom(s) <=> x∈1
      ∨ ∀s:Sub. ¬(f(s(1))=f2(12))
```

Figure 14: By 3 either 1 matches 12 or not.

```
* top 2 1 1 2 1 1
5. f=f2
6. ∃s:Sub. s(1)=12 & min(s) & ∀x:Var. x∈dom(s) <=> x∈1
>> ∃s:Sub. f(s(1))=f2(12) & min(s) & ∀x:Var. x∈dom(s) <=> x∈1
   ∨ ∀s:Sub. ¬(f(s(1))=f2(12))


BY ((OnLast (SomeE ''s'') THEN ILeft THENM ITerm 's' ...) ...sc)
```

Figure 15: Let s match 1 with 12. Then s matches f(1) and f2(12).

```
* top 2 1 1 2 1 2
5. f=f2
6. ∀s:Sub. ¬(s(1)=12)
>> ∃s:Sub. f(s(1))=f2(12) & min(s) & ∀x:Var. x∈dom(s) <=> x∈1
   ∨ ∀s:Sub. ¬(f(s(1))=f2(12))


BY (IRight ...+s)


1* 5. s: Sub
   6. s(1)=12
   7. ∀s1:Sub. ¬(s1(1)=12)
   >> False
```

Figure 16: 1 does not match 12, so there is no matching substitution.

```
* top 2 1 1 2 1 2 1
5. s: Sub
6. s(1)=12
7. ∀s1:Sub. ¬(s1(1)=12)
8. f=f2
>> False

BY (EOn 's' 7 ...) THEN (Contradiction ...)
```
Figure 17: A match for f(1) and f2(12) would match 1 and 12.

```
* top 2 1 1
1. l: Term list
2. t: Term
3. match?(t)
4. match?(l)
5. 12: Term list
>> ∃s:Sub. s(t).s(1)=12 & min(s) & (∀x:Var. x∈dom(s) <=> x∈t ∨ x∈l)
   ∨ ∀s:Sub. ¬(s(t).s(1)=12)

BY (On '12' Unroll ...sc)

1* 6. t2: Term
   >> ∃s:Sub. s(t)=t2 & s(1)=12 & min(s)
            & (∀x:Var. x∈dom(s) <=> x∈t ∨ x∈l)
      ∨ ∀s:Sub. ¬(s(t)=t2 & s(1)=12)
```
Figure 18: In the induction step. s.

computational content of its proof, and for the other we will show the steps of the proof that are computationally the most important.

The theorem sub_union says that any two minimal substitutions s1 and s2 are either inconsistent or can be combined into a minimal subsitution (the "union"). We limit our discussion of the proof of this theorem to describing the algorithm embodied in it. The union of the empty list and s2 is s2. The union of <x,t>.s1 and s2 is computed as follows. By sub_lookup (whose proof was given above), x is either in the domain of s2, in which case s2(x)=t2 for some t2, or it is not. In the first case, if t is not equal to t2 then the substitutions are inconsistent, otherwise the result is just the recursively computed union of s1 and s2. In the second case, the result is <x,t>.s where s is the union of s1 and s2.

Figures 18 to 21 show some of the steps of lmatch_thm. To save space we have occasionally elided the conclusion of a subgoal when it is the same as the conclusion of the goal. The proof is by induction on the term list 1. Figure 18 shows the first major step in the induction step. In this step, we are assuming that we know how to match t and l when possible and must show that t.l can be matched against an arbitrary 12 when possible. The step is to do a case analysis on whether 12 is empty or not. In Figure 19, we have an arbitrary t2 and 12 and must show that t.l can be matched against t2.12 when possible.

```
* top 2 1 1 1
3. match?(t)
4. match?(l)
5. 12: Term list
6. t2: Term
>> ∃s:Sub. s(t)=t2 & s(l)=12 & min(s)
           & (∀x:Var. x∈dom(s) <=> x∈t V x∈l)
    V ∀s:Sub. ¬(s(t)=t2 & s(l)=12)

BY (Expand ''matchp lmatchp'' THEN HypCases ['t2'] 3 ...)

1* 6. ∃s:Sub. s(t)=t2 & min(s) & ∀x:Var. x∈dom(s) <=> x∈t
   >> ...

2* 6. ∀s:Sub. ¬(s(t)=t2)
   >> ...
```

Figure 19: Does t match t2?.

We do this by cases on whether t matches t2. If it doesn't, then no subsitution matches
t.1 to t2.12. Otherwise, we proceed by cases on whether 1 matches 12 (Figure 20).   If
it does, then we proceed by cases on whether the substitutions s1 and s2 matching t to
t2 and 1 to 2 respectively can be combined (Figure 21).   If they can, then we have the
desired substitution. If not (the first subgoal in Figure 21), then s1 and s2 are inconsistent
and we can prove that there is no matching substitution by using hypotheses 8 and 12 and
the two lemmas that characterize the application of a substitution to a term or term list
by its values on variables that occur in the term or term list.

3.3   Applying Formal Metamathematics

How can these results be applied to Nuprl itself? One method is to define the type of
terms to match exactly the terms of Nuprl. Then the theorems such as the match theorem
apply to Nuprl itself. In this form they are *enlightening* but not *useful*. To make them
useful it must be possible to apply them in proving theorems.

One way to do this is outlined in the second author's thesis [17]. The idea there
is to directly connect terms with the objects they denote. He defines a type of term
representatives similar to the type *Term* defined in this paper and a function that maps a
term representative to the object it represents. This function is called *val* because it can
be thought of as mapping a term representative to its *value*.

To see how the function *val* allows us to make the connection we want, consider the
example of constructing term rewriting procedures in Nuprl (that is procedures mapping
terms to terms that preserve equality). If we construct a function f in Nuprl of type
$Term \to Term$ and prove that it respects *values*, so that $val(t) = val(f(t))$ for all members
t of *Term*, then we can prove theorems in Nuprl using f as term-rewriting function. In
the course of a proof, if we want to use f on some term a appearing in the goal, we first
determine a representative t in *Term* for a. We then evaluate $f(t)$, getting a new member
t' of *Term*. Because of the property known of f, we know that $val(t')$ is equal a and so we

```
* top 2 1 1 1 1
3. ∀12:Term list. ∃s:Sub. s(1)=12 & min(s) & (∀x:Var. x∈dom(s) <=> x∈l)
              ∨ ∀s:Sub. ¬(s(1)=12)
6. ∃s:Sub. s(t)=t2 & min(s) & (∀x:Var. x∈dom(s) <=> x∈t)
>> ∃s:Sub. s(t)=t2 & s(1)=12 & min(s) & (∀x:Var. x∈dom(s) <=> x∈t ∨ x∈l)
   ∨ ∀s:Sub. ¬(s(t)=t2 & s(1)=12)

BY (HypCases ['12'] 3 ...)


1* 6. ∃s:Sub. s(1)=12 & min(s) & ∀x:Var. x∈dom(s) <=> x∈l
   >> ...

2* 6. ∀s:Sub. ¬(s(1)=12)
   >> ...
```

Figure 20: Does 1 match 12?.

can substitute it for a. These steps have in effect rewritten a.

This approach is called *partial reflection*. In [17] is an extensive implementation of this approach. The partial reflection mechanism is developed completely within Nuprl, and several substantial applications are made. Note that matching is central to term rewriting, since the basic operation is applying a rewrite rule. A rewrite rule, in terms of our type *Term*, is a pair $\langle t, t' \rangle$ of terms containing variables, where all the variables of t' occur in t. A term u can be rewritten to a term u' via the rule $\langle t, t' \rangle$ if there is a substitution s for the variables of t such that u' is obtained by replacing an occurrence of $s(t)$ in u by $s(t')$. Thus to determine whether the rewrite rule applies to a term u, t must be matched against subterms of u. The development in [17] contains a substantial term rewriting system; this includes a formal treatment of matching similar to the one we developed for this paper, although the term structure there is somewhat different.

Another method of proceeding is to formalize the metatheory of Nuprl, making the types of terms and proof two of the basic types. The work here in proving metatheorems is about the same as in the partial reflection setting, and proofs in the formal metatheory, call it *Nuprl*$_1$, are just as enlightening. But now the connection to the base theory, call it *Nuprl*$_0$, is built-in. The algorithms extracted from a metatheorem about matching can be directly applied because they are about *Nuprl*$_0$ terms. Some of the details of this approach are presented in [20,19].

Acknowledgements

We would like to thank David Basin and Wilfred Chen for their helpful suggestions, and Elizabeth Maxwell for her help in preparing this document.

```
* top 2 1 1 1 1 1
5. ∃s:Sub. s(t)=t2 & min(s) & (∀x:Var. x∈dom(s) <=> x∈t)
6. ∃s:Sub. s(1)=12 & min(s) & (∀x:Var. x∈dom(s) <=> x∈1)
>> ∃s:Sub. s(t)=t2 & s(1)=12 & min(s) & (∀x:Var. x∈dom(s) <=> x∈t ∨ x∈1)
   ∨ ∀s:Sub. ¬(s(t)=t2 & s(1)=12)

BY (SomeE ''s2'' 6 THEN SomeE ''s1'' 5 THEN
    CaseLemma 'sub_union' ['s1';'s2']...)

1* 5. s2: Sub
   6. s2(1)=12
   7. min(s2)
   8. ∀x:Var. x∈dom(s2) <=> x∈1
   9. s1: Sub
   10. s1(t)=t2
   11. min(s1)
   12. ∀x:Var. x∈dom(s1) <=> x∈t
   13. ncst(s1,s2)
   >> ...

2* 5. s2: Sub
   6. s2(1)=12
   7. min(s2)
   8. ∀x:Var. x∈dom(s2) <=> x∈1
   9. s1: Sub
   10. s1(t)=t2
   11. min(s1)
   12. ∀x:Var. x∈dom(s1) <=> x∈t
   13. ∃s:Sub. min(s) & s1⊂s & s2⊂s
               & ∀x:Var. x∈dom(s) => x∈dom(s1) ∨ x∈dom(s2)
   >> ∃s:Sub. s(t)=t2 & s(1)=12 & min(s) & (∀x:Var. x∈dom(s))
```

Figure 21: Can the substitutions be combined?.

References

[1] P. Aczel. The type theoretic interpretation of constructive set theory. In *Logic Collo-quium '77*. Amsterdam:North-Holland, 1978.

[2] W. Bledsoe and D. Loveland. *Automated Theorem Proving: After 25 Years*. American Math Soc., 1984.

[3] N. Bourbaki. *Theory of Sets*, volume I of *Elements of Mathematics*. Addison–Wesley, Reading, MA, 1968.

[4] R. Boyer and J. Moore. *A Computational Logic*. NY:Academic Press, 1979.

[5] R. Boyer and J. Moore. Metafunctions: proving them correct and using them effi-ciently as new proof procedures. In *The Correctness Problem in Computer Science.*, pages 103–84. NY:Academic Press, 1981.

[6] A. Bundy. *The Computer Modelling of Mathematical Reasoning*. NY:Academic Press, 1983.

[7] A. Bundy. A broader interpretation of logic in logic programming. In *Proc. 5th Sympo. on Logic Programming*, 1988.

[8] R. L. Constable *et al. Implementing Mathematics with the Nuprl Development System*. NJ:Prentice-Hall, 1986.

[9] M. Davis. The prehistory and early history of automated deduction. In *Automation of Reasoning 1*, pages 1–28. Springer-Verlag, NY, 1983.

[10] M. Davis and J. T. Schwartz. Metamathematical extensibility for theorem verifiers and proof checkers. *Comp. Math. with Applications*, 5:217–230, 1979.

[11] J. Gallier. Logic for computer science. In *Foundations of Automatic Theorem Proving*. Harper and Row, 1986.

[12] J.-Y. Girard. *Proof Theory and Logical Complexity, vol. 1*. Bibliopolis, Napoli, 1987.

[13] D. Good. Mechanical proofs about computer programs. In C. Hoare and J. Shepard-son, editors, *Mathematical Logic and Programming Languages*, pages 55–75. Springer-Verlag, NY, 1985.

[14] M. Gordon, R. Milner, and C. Wadsworth. Edinburgh LCF: a mechanized logic of computation. *Lecture Notes in Computer Science*, 78, 1979.

[15] D. M. Harper, R. and R. Milner. Standard ml. Technical report, Lab. for Foundations of Computer Science, University of Edinburgh, 1986. TR ECS-LFCS-86-2.

[16] S. Hiyashi and H. Nakano. *PX: A Computational Logic*. Foundations of Computing. MIT Press, Cambridge, MA, 1988.

[17] D. J. Howe. *Automating Reasoning in an Implementation of Constructive Type Theory*. PhD thesis, Cornell University, 1988.

[18] D. J. Howe. Computational metatheory in Nuprl. In E. Lusk and R. Overbeek, editors, *9th International Conference on Automated Deduction*, pages 238–257, New York, 1988. Springer-Verlag.

[19] T. Knoblock. *Mathematical Extensibility in Type Theory.* PhD thesis, Cornell University, 1987.

[20] T. B. Knoblock and R. L. Constable. Formalized metareasoning in type theory. In *Proc. of the First Annual Symp. on Logic in Computer Science.* IEEE., 1986.

[21] P. A. Lindsay. A survey of mechanical support for formal reasoning. *Software Engineering Journal*, page 27, January 1988.

[22] P. Martin-Lof. Constructive mathematics and computer programming. In *Sixth International Congress for Logic, Methodology, and Philosophy of Science*, pages 153–75. Amsterdam:North Holland, 1982.

[23] P. Mendler. *Inductive Definition in Type Theory.* PhD thesis, Cornell University, Ithaca, NY, 1988.

[24] Y. Moschovaski. *Elementary Induction on Abstract Structures.* North-Holland, Amsterdam, 1974.

[25] K. Mulmuley. The mechanization of existence proofs of recursive predicates. In *Seventh Conf. on Automated Deduction, LNCS 170*, pages 460–475. Springer-Verlag, NY, 1984.

[26] J. S. Newell, A. and H. Simon. Empirical explorations with the logic theory machine: A case study in heuristics. In *Proc. West Joint Computer Conf.*, pages 218–239, 1957.

[27] L. Paulson. Lessons learned from LCF: a survey of natural deduction proofs. *Comp. J.*, 28(5), 1985.

[28] L. Paulson. *Logic and Computation.* Cambridge University Press, NY, 1987.

[29] P. Rosenblum, J. Laird, and A. Newell. Metalevels in soar. In D. N. P. Maes, editor, *Meta-Level Architetures and Reflection.* North-Holland, 1988.

[30] N. Shanker. Towards mechanical metamathematics. *J. Automated Reasoning*, 1(4):407–434, 1985.

[31] R. M. Smullyan. *First–Order Logic.* Springer–Verlag, New York, 1968.

[32] H. Wang. Toward mechanical mathematics. *IBM J. Research and Development*, (4):2–22., 1960.

[33] L. Wos, R. Overbeek, L. Ewing, and J. Boyle. *Automated Reasoning.* Prentice–Hall, Englewood Cliffs, NJ, 1984.

Formal Techniques in Artificial Intelligence
A Sourcebook. R.B. Banerji (editor)
© Elsevier Science Publishers B.V. (North-Holland), 1990

Qualitative Physics

Stephen D. Grantham and Lyle H. Ungar

Department of Chemical Engineering
University of Pennsylvania
Philadelphia, PA 19104

1. Introduction

Much of how our world behaves is described by the laws of physics. Scientists and engineers express these laws through the language of continuous mathematics. State variables, which take on values in the space of real numbers, describe the world while differential and algebraic equations determine how it changes. It is common, however, to make inferences about the world without ever referring to differential equations or numerical values. For example, humans can deduce that a pan of water placed on a gas burner will heat up and eventually boil or that a glass bottle knocked off a table will fall to the floor and may shatter. Much of the analyses performed by scientists and engineers involves similar reasoning: mathematical calculations are a small part of designing a new chemical plant or diagnosing a fault in an electric circuit. Even when mathematical representations are used, there is a large amount of qualitative knowledge needed to set up equations and interpret the results of simulations. Qualitative reasoning systems are formal representations which support the description of such reasoning about the physical world.

1.1 Limitations of Continuous Mathematics

In order to describe the behavior of a system in formal mathematics, the exact numerical initial value of each variable and the exact form of the set of differential equations describing the physics of the system must be known. If not, it is impossible to infer anything about the system. In contrast, humans are able to make useful deductions when only partial, often very limited and non-numeric, information is known.

Even when a complete mathematical description is available, the resulting simulation of behavior (a complete set of numerical values for each state variable at every time instant) is not particularly informative and requires interpretation. This interpretation usually results in a qualitative description of the essential features of behavior - the temperature of a heated liquid rises to its boiling point or a piston in an engine cylinder oscillates between two end points etc. Thus, much of the numerical description is superfluous to useful descriptions of behavior; one wishes to abstract away from the numerical detail.

Furthermore, numerical descriptions fail to produce insight into why a system behaves as it does. One cannot ask a numerical simulation, "Why does the temperature of the reactor rise in this simulation?"; the answer would at best be a list of all the equations and data used in the simulation. The relations between parameters which represent the physical laws to which a system conforms are not explicitly represented in mathematics. They are irretrievably buried within the equations and mathematical analysis used to solve them. However, engineers and scientists are quite capable of explaining the results of a complex mathematical analysis. They do this by referring to qualitative descriptions of the physical laws governing the system.

Continuous mathematics is concerned with detail but much of this information is superfluous. It is clear that the important concepts and distinctions required to reason about the physical world are not quantitative but qualitative in nature. These features are inherent in the representation of continuous mathematics but are lost in its complexity. Commonsense reasoning about the physical world does not require the use of this mathematics but a much simpler representation explicitly referring to these important qualitative concepts.

1.2 Qualitative Representation

The aim of qualitative reasoning is to create and use representations of the world which are simplified so that irrelevant detail is ignored while maintaining enough resolution to distinguish and explain important features of behavior. For example, the temperature of water in a pan may be specified as either high, normal, or low rather than giving an exact numerical value and the effect of heating the water on a stove can be described as causing its temperature to increase rather than specifying the governing equations of heat transfer. In this sense, qualitative reasoning systems can be viewed as defining a *qualitative mathematics*: a rigorous methodology in which to make inferences from imprecise, qualitative knowledge of parameter values and relations in much the same way that continuous mathematics does with exact numerical values and differential equations.

When an engineer develops a mathematical model of some situation, he or she has already determined which physical laws are relevant, which parameters will be affected and which will remain unchanged. Qualitative reasoning systems which seek to operate in physical domains must carry the burden of producing qualitative models by a similar analysis and be able to produce convincing explanations of the results obtained by analyzing them. Such systems present a framework, or ontology, within which to represent the non-mathematical knowledge or *qualitative physics* which underlies reasoning about the behavior of physical systems - both the intuitive "Naive Physics" of the man in the street [34, 48, 49] and the more expert knowledge of scientists and engineers [18, 34]. We will discuss two major approaches: a *device-centered* ontology [18], which looks at the world as being composed of a number of pieces of equipment connected together and a *process-centered* ontology [34], which looks at the world as a number of interacting processes such as chemical reaction and heat transfer. These representations each offer a domain independent framework which supports reasoning about physical systems. The actual problem formulation - restating a domain description in a form compatible with a framework - is left to the modeler. The usefulness of a particular methodology depends on how naturally the domain of interest falls into its framework.

1.3 Uses of qualitative physics

For the most part, current expert systems for problems such as fault diagnosis and process control are based on "shallow" models which correlate observations of world and desired actions without considering the underlying mechanisms which cause the observed or desired behavior. These expert systems are typically hand-coded for a specific situation and a specific set of diagnoses. Such reasoning systems tend to be very inflexible and narrow in their scope [9]. Because they are made by interviewing human experts, their performance is limited to that of the expert upon whose reasoning the system is based. They are also notoriously difficult to test. By building systems based on first principles models, one can gain the same advantages that quantitative models offer: generality and rigor. It is widely expected that qualitative physics will form the basis of the next generation of expert systems which reason about physical domains [9, 18]. For many tasks, such as producing novels designs, experienced-based ("shallow") expert systems are not possible, and quantitative equations are not available or are hopelessly expensive to solve. Qualitative physics offers the only hope for automating such tasks.

Even when solutions can in theory be obtained numerically, qualitative reasoning offers advantages in speed. The simplified representations used in qualitative physics do not carry the computational overhead that continuous mathematics does. Thus, although they are substantially slower than expert systems based on the reasoning of human experts, they are still relatively attractive for use in real time expert systems where qualitative deductions are needed and numerical computation is too slow. The speed of qualitative reasoning can also be increased by compiling reasoning off-line.

There is a final reason for studying qualitative physics: all computer programs that reason about physical systems implicitly make some simplification of the world and some assumptions about the best way to represent objects and events. Often, explicit consideration of what is being modeled allows a more systematic approach. Even producing a standard production rule expert system composed of rules of the form:

    IF temperature of reactor is low
    AND feedstream flowrate is normal
    THEN suspect catalyst degradation

makes assumptions and raises questions: "What do low and normal mean?" "What if I want to reason about changing systems?" "How can physics be systematically added to the program?"

Qualitative reasoning systems have been created to perform reasoning in areas as diverse as mechanics [4, 7, 8, 11, 27, 28, 46, 66, 67], electronic circuit analysis [13, 14, 20, 85] and chemical engineering [68, 70]. Spatial reasoning, or *qualitative kinematics* [27, 28, 29, 30, 31, 43], in which one must describe the motion of objects in two or three dimensions, is a substantially different field and will not be treated here; there is good reason to believe that spatial reasoning is inherently at least partially quantitative, and will not fit well into the frameworks described below. For a review of the current status of qualitative kinematics see [38]. There is also a large body of work on *temporal logics*; formal systems of reasoning about changing systems [1, 2, 87]. Although all of these are useful for reasoning about physical systems, this chapter will concentrate on representing and reasoning about systems where the major problem is capturing the interrelationships of complex interacting systems, rather than reasoning about the timing of multiple events.

2. Representing Structure and Behavior

2.1 Essential Requirements of a Representation
In formal mathematics the world is described in terms of variables and equations. The values of the variables at a given instant describe the *state* of the world. The equations represent the physical laws which govern the way in which the state of the world changes. The variables and equations together describe the *structure* of the world. The solution of the equations produces a description of how the state changes with time - its *behavior*. Similarly, a qualitative representation must provide a framework to express the state and structure of the world and provide a means of inferring behavior from structure. In addition, it must be able to explain how the behavior arose from the structure.

2.2 Representing State
One of the major aims of qualitative reasoning is to produce a much simpler representation than that of continuous mathematics. Whereas in mathematics variables take on values in the continuous space of real numbers, qualitative representations split up this space into finite sets of intervals called *quantity spaces*. The value of a variable is represented by its position in this quantity space - either on an interval or on a boundary between intervals. The simplest quantity space contains only one boundary, 0, and allows a variable to take on three values: it can lie on the boundary (0), on the interval above it (+), or on the interval below it (-).

Because representations must be simple yet detailed enough to make important distinctions, the selection of intervals is crucial. The boundaries between intervals should correspond to points in the number space at which important events occur. These are called *landmark values*. A judicious choice of landmark values captures relevant distinctions while maintaining simplicity. For example, the temperature space of a substance should contain landmarks corresponding to its melting, boiling and critical points. Although it is not possible to express the exact numerical temperature of the substance in the quantity space, it is possible to infer whether it is a solid, liquid, gas (if the value is in an interval) or some equilibrium combination of phases (if the value is a landmark) - regions which exhibit distinct behaviors.

In addition to its value in a quantity space, the state of a variable is also defined by its direction of change (typically increasing, decreasing or stationary). The direction of change determines which landmark the variable is moving toward and hence the value (and consequently state) it will move to next. When a variable changes state it is said to undergo a *state transition*. The direction of change provides the link between structure and behavior, allowing sequences of state transitions to be predicted.

2.3 Representing the Physics - Qualitative Constraints

Physical laws define the relations that determine what combinations of variable values and directions of change constitute valid world states and what state transitions are possible. One formalism for representing these relations is the notion of *qualitative constraint equations*. These are a qualitative version of the differential and algebraic equations used in formal mathematics to constrain the space of possible behaviors. Just as traditional equations conform to the laws of algebra, qualitative constraints have their own, weaker qualitative algebras. An example is the notion of *confluences* [18]. In this notation [X] represents the sign of variable X and [dX] represents the sign of the derivative of X with respect to time, dX/dt. The quantity spaces of both variables and their rates of change thus consist of positive numbers, negative numbers, and zero (+,-,0).

An algebra can be specified which describes how qualitative values are combined:

addition

[x] + [y]		[y]		
		-	0	+
	-	-	-	?
[x]	0	-	0	+
	+	?	+	+

Entries denoted "?" indicate that all three values (+, -, 0) satisfy the condition.

multiplication

[x] [y]		[y]		
		-	0	+
	-	+	0	-
[x]	0	0	0	0
	+	-	0	+

A constraint

$$[a] + [b] + [c] + ... = [e] + [f] + ...$$

is satisfied if the expressions on both sides of the constraint evaluate to the same qualitative value. If either side is ambiguous (qualitative evaluation produces the value "?") then the constraint is automatically satisfied.

Notice that when adding quantities of differing sign the sum is not uniquely defined as relative magnitudes are required. No information is lost when signs are multiplied. Notice also, that this algebra does not form a ring (in particular, there is no inverse in addition), and so most of the nice properties one expects from algebras do not hold. For example, if

$$[x] + [y] = [a]$$

and

$$[x] + [z] = [a]$$

it does not follow that

$$[y] = [z]$$

the sign of [y] and [z] are completely unrelated. (To see this, pick values for x, y, z, and a; e.g. let x=4, y=-2, z= 1 and a=10)

Although addition has no inverse, subtraction can be defined by the equivalence

$$[x] - [y] <=> [x] + [-y]$$

which results in the following table:

subtraction

[x] - [y]

		[y]	
	-	0	+
-	?	-	-
[x] 0	+	0	-
+	+	+	?

It should be noted that this is just one possible algebra for one particular type of constraint system and one particular form of reasoning. For other possible algebras see, for example, [85, 88, 75, 77, 79, 21, 22, 57].

To see how confluences work in a simple system, consider the valve shown in figure 1 [18].

The laws of fluid flow constrain the flowrate, pressure drop and orifice area to change only in ways consistent with the following confluence:

[dP] + [dA] - [dQ] = 0

In addition, the flow must be in the same direction as the pressure drop i.e.

[P] - [Q] = 0

<u>Figure 1: A Simple Valve</u>

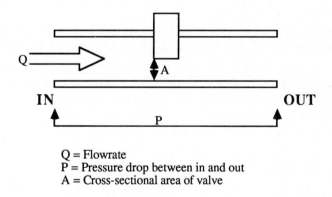

Q = Flowrate
P = Pressure drop between in and out
A = Cross-sectional area of valve

Any assignment of variables to values which satisfies the constraints represents a valid state. A constraint is satisfied when both sides of the equality have the same sign. The first of the above confluences illustrates the ambiguity that can arise: when both [dA] and [dQ] are positive ([+]), their difference could be +, - or 0, dependent on the relative magnitudes of the rates of change in the area and flow rate. In these cases the confluence is considered to be automatically satisfied for all values of other variables in the confluence.

All of the following sets of values satisfy the confluence:

[dP]	[dA]	[dQ]
0	0	0
+	+	+

+	-	+
+	0	+
+	-	0
-	+	+
-	+	-
-	0	-
-	+	0

Several techniques have been used by researchers to solve systems of qualitative constraint equations, including propagation through constraints [18], Gaussian elimination [21] and Waltz consistency filtering [56, 57].

Another type of qualitative constraint is the *monotonic function relationship* which constrains the values of the derivatives of two variables: The functional relationship between two variables, x and y, is said to be increasing monotonic if when one of them changes the other changes in the same direction and decreasing monotonic if they change in opposite directions. There are slight variations in the type of functional monotonicity different representations can handle. Kuipers, in his QSIM system [56], represents monotonic increasing relations in functions relating strictly two variables (such as $y = 4x$) as $M^+(x,y)$. An equivalent confluence representation would be $[dy] = [dx]$. Forbus' qualitative proportionality (or Q-prop) representation [34] is a little more flexible in that it can accommodate monotonic relations within functions containing an arbitrary number of variables. For example, the function $y = a + 1/b + x^2$ is represented by the following three relations:

$$y \propto_{Q+} a$$
$$y \propto_{Q-} b$$
$$y \propto_{Q+} x$$

$y \propto_{Q+} x$ represents an increasing monotonic relation between x and y assuming all other variables on which y is dependent are held constant. Similarly, $y \propto_{Q-} b$ represents a decreasing monotonic relation.

Yet another form of relation is that of inequalities or *order of magnitude reasoning*, which is discussed in section 5.1.

2.4 Deriving Constraints

Constraints can be obtain from an intuitive feel of how a system behaves based on experience or can be derived directly from the mathematical model of the system using the rules of qualitative algebra. Consider the confluences in the above valve example. The equation defining flow through an orifice is given by

$$Q = CA \sqrt{2P/\rho} \qquad P >= 0, A > 0$$

where ρ is the density and C is a constant. Using de Kleer and Brown's representation, the corresponding confluences can be derived as follows:

Take the sign of both sides of the equation and use the rule that the sign of the product of two numbers is the product of their signs.

$$[Q] = [C][A][\sqrt{2P/\rho}]$$

Note that C and A are always positive and that $\sqrt{2P/\rho}$ is zero if and only if P is zero and is positive if P is positive.

$$[C] = +$$
$$[A] = +$$
$$[\sqrt{2P/\rho}] = [P]$$

Thus, our equation reduces to

$$[Q] = [+][+][P]$$

or $\qquad [Q] - [P] = 0$.

To derive the relationships between the changes in quantities, take the derivative of the original equation with respect to time,

$$dQ/dt = C \sqrt{2P/\rho} \quad dA/dt + CA \sqrt{1/2P\rho} \; dP/dt$$

and take the signs of the resulting equations,

$$[dQ] = [C] [\sqrt{2P/\rho}] [dA] + [C][A] [\sqrt{1/2P\rho}] [dP]$$

As P>0, C>0 and A>0 this simplifies to

$$[dQ] = [dA] + [dP]$$

or

$$[dP] + [dA] - [dQ] = 0$$

A physical situation may behave differently at different states and so it may take several sets of confluences to model it's structure,each applicable under different circumstances. The confluences for the valve equation assume that the flow and pressure drop are always positive and that the valve is neither closed or fully open. A more complete model, which assumes no pressure drop in a fully opened valve, is:

CLOSED	:	$[A=0]$	, $[Q]=0$,	$[dQ]=0$
OPEN	:	$[A=A_{max}]$	, $[P]=0$,	$[dP]=0$
WORKING P<0	:	$[0<A<A_{max}]$	, $[Q]-[P]=0$,	$[dP]-[dA]-[dQ]=0$
WORKING P>0	:	$[0<A<A_{max}]$	, $[Q]-[P]=0$,	$[dP]+[dA]-[dQ]=0$

2.5 Expressing causality: Directed constraints

With the exception of qualitative proportionalities, the constraint relations discussed above are non-directed: they make no attempt to express a causal ordering of "what causes what". A confluence with n terms can be used to determine a qualitative value for any of its variables if the other n-1 variable values are known. $[A] = [B] + [C]$ could just as well be written as $[B] = [A] - [C]$ or $[C] = [A] - [B]$ and so we could say "changes in B and C cause changes in A", "changes in A and C cause changes in B" and "changes in A and B cause changes in C" with equal validity. However, qualitative proportionalities can be used to represent a causal ordering:

$$X \propto_{Q+} Y$$

means that a change in Y causes a change in X and not vice versa. Such constraints which force a direction of dependency are called *directed constraints*. They are more expressive than non-directed constraints because not only do they confer the relation between variables but in addition they give information as to which change must occur first. For example, consider a gas in a sealed container. The pressure of the gas (P) is a measure of the time averaged force exerted by gas molecules as they bombard a surface. Thus the pressure is dependent on the momentum of the gas molecules (M) and the number of molecules in the container (N) or

$$P=f(M, N)$$

In the Q-prop representation this can be represented as

$$P \propto_{Q+} M$$
$$P \propto_{Q+} N$$

which state that if the number of molecules changes the pressure will change in the same direction and similarly for momentum. Notice that while algebraic equations such as P=f(M,N) can be rearranged to M=f(P,N), Q-props cannot. Q-props represent causality and hence specify a direction of dependency; Pressure changes in response to a change in momentum never vice versa. The equivalent confluence representation, $[P] = [M] + [N]$, fails to capture this dependency.

A causal relation can be represented as an IF-THEN rule. The antecedent is either some ordinal relation between values in a quantity space or a direction of change of a variable. The consequent is always a direction of change for some variable. If the antecedent is true it "causes" the consequent to be true. In the gas example above, an equivalent representation of $P \propto_{Q+} M$ is:

If	$[dM] = +$	**Then**	$[dP] = +$
If	$[dM] = -$	**Then**	$[dP] = -$
If	$[dM] = 0$	**Then**	$[dP] = 0$

Notice how this causal representation forces a direction of dependency on variable changes: P will change if X changes but not vice versa. Note also that if a variable does not appear in the consequent section of any causal specification then it will never be changed due to changes in another variable (e.g. M in the gas example).

Unlike non-directed constraint equations it is not possible, in general, to derive these directed relations solely from mathematical expressions. This is because equations do not represent the notion of causality. Generating these relations requires a deeper understanding of the mechanism of the particular physical phenomena being modelled.

2.6 Inferring behavior from structure: Envisionment
Inferring behavior from structure is the qualitative equivalent of integrating time-dependent equations to determine the values of variables over time. In quantitative representations, initial variable values and differential equations are used to generate the numerical values of the parameters at the next time step. The qualitative equivalent takes a set of quantity spaces and some representation of the laws governing a system and produces the next qualitatively different state.

Two types of inference about the behavior of the system are needed. First, the current state of the world must be determined from a partial description (i.e. intrastate behavior must be determined). Secondly, the next state or states that the system can move to must be found (i.e. the interstate behavior). Specific mechanisms for calculating intra and inter-state behavior depend on the representation used and two such mechanisms are described in sections 3.3 and 4.5. Here we discuss common features of the rules governing interstate behavior:

Any variables which are moving toward a landmark can cause a *state transition*. It is frequently the case that within a world state many variables are candidates for change. In order to determine the next state it is necessary to find out which of the candidate transitions are valid and which of the valid ones are reached first. This is achieved by applying rules derived from the constraints imposed by a given qualitative representation. Many such rules have been used [18, 34, 56, 57, 85, 86, 74] but they all include variations on the following three principles.

Change rules: A parameter will only change state if it has a non-zero derivative.
Continuity conditions: All variables must change continuously through the quantity space - transitions can only occur to neighboring states in the quantity space. If the current value lies in an interval then its next value must be one of the landmarks bordering that interval. Similarly, values on landmarks must change to neighboring intervals. For example, a number or derivative cannot change from positive to negative without passing through zero.
Landmark rule: A change from a landmark always occurs before a change to a landmark. This is because movement off a point requires only an infinitesimal amount of time while movement to it requires finite time.

Even after applying these rules, there often remain several variables capable of transition. To determine which transition occurs first, the quantitative rate of change of each variable and the distance it is from its landmark must be known. Thus, the inference mechanism produces not a simulation of a single behavior but a branching tree of all behaviors that could happen for any combination of numerical parameter values. This tree of behaviors is called an *envisionment*, and any particular path through it is called a *history*.

The mechanism for inferring behavior is a simple cycle: Determine the current world state, perform a transition ordering to determine valid variable transitions and repeat for each one. This cycle repeats until the world becomes static or until a cycle is detected.
Consider the situation shown in figure 2.

A boy is crossing from the left to right bank of a stream by jumping from rock to rock. He progresses from the left to right by jumping from the rock he is on to the nearest rock to his right. Each rock represents a particular state and a valid state transition is one which moves him to the nearest state to his right. Notice that at two points in the river the next rocks are so close together that it is not possible to determine which is the nearest so he has a choice. This means there are 4 possible paths he can take to reach the right bank. The total envisionment for the crossing is shown in figure 3, with each of the four paths through the envisionment representing a possible history for the crossing.

Figure 2: Crossing a Stream

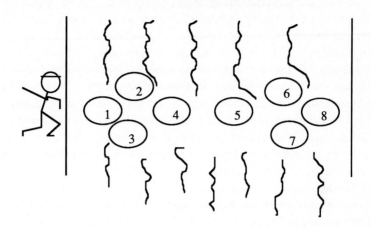

Figure 3: Envisionment for River Crossing

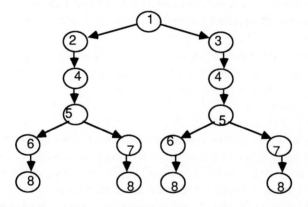

2.7 Ontology

So far we have considered the development of qualitative mathematics: methods of
representing and reasoning with qualitative information in an analogous way to traditional
mathematics and quantitative data. Examples of the types of qualitative mathematics
developed include order of magnitude reasoning [69, 63, 8], qualitative arithmetic [75, 88,
89] and qualitative integration (for example, the QSIM system of Kuipers [57]).
Just like their traditional counterpart, qualitative mathematical systems provide a
representation which can be used to model and analyze the behavior of physical systems.
Historically, the burden of creating mathematical models and producing a convincing

explanation of their solution has fallen on the scientist or engineer concerned. The aim of qualitative physics is to represent and utilize the knowledge required to achieve these additional tasks so they can be automated. But how are these models created in the first place? And how can we produce compelling explanations of the output from our (qualitative) mathematical analysis? Building and explaining models requires a commitment to some form of underlying, fundamental mechanism through which changes in the domain are brought about i.e. a commitment to some form of *ontology*. These ontologies provide a framework in which the physics of a domain can be expressed and used to model and explain phenomena. Ontologies used in qualitative physics systems are of two types [44]: a) *Explicit-mechanism* ontologies, in which all changes in the system are assumed to be caused either directly or indirectly by a specific class of objects, called agents of change (for example the process-centered ontologies of [34, 74, 82]).

b) *Implicit-mechanism* ontologies which do not have explicit agents of change. Rather the domain is represented by a set of devices connected together, the changes arising from the interaction between these devices [18,85].

Developing an explicit-mechanism representation is a much more difficult task than non-causal modelling as it requires a deep knowledge of the physical mechanisms underlying a domain. However, once obtained, they can more readily produce a compelling explanation of behavior (see below) and simplify reasoning [44]. Unfortunately, the underlying principles of many domains do not lend themselves to such explicit causal descriptions. For example, it would be difficult to causally represent thermodynamic principles such as "A system will seek its lowest free energy configuration". Obviously, in these cases implicit-mechanism modelling is appropriate. Thus, the choice of which type of representation to use will be heavily influenced by the domain of application.

2.8 Explaining Behavior

One way of explaining behavior is to generate a causal explanation for a particular history. The way in which a causal explanation is generated depends on the type of model used to represent a domain. For explicit-mechanism systems, explanation is reduced to identifying which agents of change are active for a given situation and tracing the propagation of their effects through a network of directed constraint relations. For implicit mechanisms, explanation is not so simple. Implicit -mechanism systems tend to represent domains as interacting groups of non-directed qualitative constraints. In order to generate explanations it is necessary to assume that the flow of information through the constraint satisfaction procedure is the same as the flow of causality in the modelled domain. This is considered in more detail in section 3.4.

The following sections consider in detail two examples which illustrate how different choices of ontology, qualitative relations and quantity space lead to very different reasoning systems.

3. Device-centered Ontology

3.1 Underlying philosophy

The fundamental premise behind the device centered ontology of de Kleer and Brown [18] is that all physical situations can be viewed as some kind of machine whose output represents the observed behavior of the world. The machine consists of a number of components (e.g. electronic devices or pieces of chemical plant equipment), which are connected together in some predetermined manner (e.g. as described by a process and instrumentation diagram or circuit diagram). The goal of this approach is to predict and explain the behavior of the "machine" as a whole using only a knowledge of the behavior of the individual components and how they are connected together. The device-centered approach to qualitative physics is perfectly suited to object-oriented programming. Libraries of objects such as heat exchangers, pumps and sensors can be built containing descriptions of the behavior of the objects. These can then be assembled to model specific plants. All of the advantages of, for example, a frame-based system in which specific parts inherit their characteristic from prototype parts arise naturally; complex models can easily be built from well understood building blocks.

In order that the models of the components be usable in different scenarios and under unanticipated operating conditions of neighboring components (e.g. the failure of a component attached to the component in question), the models for each component should be as universal as possible; in particular, the behavior of the component should not depend upon their intended function.

3.2 Representing Structure

A physical structure can be modelled as consisting of three constituents: *materials*, *components* and *conduits*. The materials are altered as they pass through a series of components. Conduits (pipes, conveyor belts, or wires) serve to pass the material between the components (pieces of equipment or electronic devices); hence they specify how the devices are connected together. Most materials can be described by two variables: one describing a flow rate (e.g. current, fluid flow, or heat flow) and the other describing a driving force (e.g. voltage, pressure, or temperature). It is these material variables which represent the observable features of a world. Variable values in device-centered representations are often represented in the simplest quantity space: that with the single landmark value of zero.

There are two types of laws governing behavior; both are represented as confluences. Firstly, there are the laws governing the behavior of each component which specify the relationships between the component variables and the changes in material variables as they pass through the device. Secondly, there are two laws based on device topology or network laws: The law of *continuity*, which demands that the material variables of the component ports on either side of a confluence have the same values, and the law of *compatibility*, which states that the change in the material potential variable between two points in the device must be the same irrespective of the route taken. These laws correspond to Kirchoff's laws for electric circuits and to conservation of mass and energy for chemical plants. Notice that it is not necessary to specify all of the continuity and compatibility conditions that arise from a particular topology: only a small subset are required to completely specify the system. Any others added are redundant and cause problems when constructing an explanation of how the device functions. Unlike formal mathematics there is no theory which specifies how many continuity and compatibility equations are required to completely specify the system. de Kleer and Brown use the heuristic of a continuity confluence for every component and a compatibility confluence for every three. Consider the simple frictionless spring and mass system shown in figure 4.

The device topology is very simple, consisting of only two components, a spring and a block, connected through a single conduit. The confluences describing the system are:

SPRING	1	$[F_s] = -[X_s]$
	2	$[dF_s] = -[dX_s]$
BLOCK	3	$[V_b] = [dX_b]$
	4	$[F_b] = [dV_b]$
CONTINUITY	5	$[X_s] = [X_b]$
	6	$[dX_s] = [dX_b]$
	7	$[F_s] = [F_b]$

The above confluences fully specify the structure of this very simple device.

Figure 4: Frictionless Spring

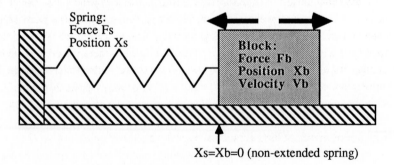

Spring:
Force Fs
Position Xs

Block:
Force Fb
Position Xb
Velocity Vb

Xs=Xb=0 (non-extended spring)

The equivalent device-centered representation is:

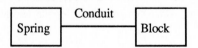

3.3 Inferring device behavior

As mentioned above, there are two aspects to determining the behavior of a device: determining valid states from a partial description (intrastate behavior) and determining valid state transitions (interstate behavior).

Any state which satisfies the set of confluences is a valid state. Thus the intrastate problem is that of finding assignments of variable values which satisfy the confluences. Several *constraint satisfaction* techniques have been developed to determine valid consistent solutions to a set of qualitative constraints. Most of these involve the use of *truth maintenance* techniques [80, 24, 37, 16, 15] to keep track of the assumptions upon which a deduced parameter value depends and revoke assumptions as needed to get a consistent solution.

A simple algorithm for finding a self-consistent intrastate behavior is:
   0) Start with a known variable value
   1) Find an unsatisfied confluence which contains this value
   2) See if it can be used to determine an as yet unknown value
   3) Repeat from 1).

Unfortunately, it is possible for this method to become stuck at confluences with three or more terms. Consider the following three confluences:

$$[A] = [B] + [C]$$
$$[D] = [B] - [C]$$
$$[E] = [B] + [C]$$

with $[A] = +$ and $[D] = -$ and $[E] = -$

Here we know the left hand side of all the confluences but propagation can go nowhere because all of the constraints have two unknowns. Consequently the propagation gets stuck even though the only consistent assignment is $[B] = - [C] = +$. de Kleer and Sussman call such systems *inherently simultaneous* [19]. If the confluences were governed by the laws of algebraic equations then one could use symbolic manipulation to get round this but, unfortunately, it is not the case. Instead one must randomly generate a plausible solution and then test the resulting deductions for consistency. Once a guess has been generated the constraint propagation resumes. Such guessing is not possible in quantitative systems, where there are an infinite number of possible guesses.

If our spring is is pulled to the left and held such that $[X_s] = +$ and $[V_b] = 0$ and then released, the initial intrastate is determine by constraint propagation to be:

Z	[Z]	[dZ]
X_s	+	0
X_b	+	0
F_s	-	0
F_b	-	0
V_b	0	-

A device changes state when either any of it's parameters change their qualitative value (i.e. cross a landmark in its quantity space) or when one of its components changes state (i.e. the component parameters move out of the operating range of the current component model confluences). In the spring each component has a single model so only parameter transitions need be considered.

In the spring's initial state only one derivative is non-zero, that of velocity and that is on its landmark of 0 so the parameter value immediately transitions to $[V_b] = -$. As the derivatives of the other parameters are zero they do not change state. Determining the new derivative values by constraint propagation gives the new state as:

Z	[Z]	[dZ]
X_s	+	-
X_b	+	-
F	-	+
F_b	-	+
V_b	-	-

In this state both the positions (X) and the forces (F) are moving towards their landmark and so there are four candidates for parameter transition (V_b is moving away from its landmark so is not a candidate). Any combination of these candidates can transition simultaneously, giving rise to 14 possible state transitions. Fortunately only the case in which all four transition simultaneously leads to a state consistent with the confluences. The new state is:

Z	[Z]	[dZ]
X_s	0	-
X_b	0	-
F_s	0	+
F_b	0	+
V_b	-	0

The process of determining possible parameter transitions and then filtering out ones inconsistent with confluences and transition rules is repeated until a state of quiescence (all derivatives zero) is reached or a cycle is detected. In the latter case the behavior consists of an infinite cycle of repeated states. The interstate behavior is represented on a state transition graph shown in figure 5.

3.4 Explaining Behavior

Explanation of interstate behavior is straight forward. Identification of which variable traverses which landmark suffices. Intrastate behavior is a little more problematic.What "caused" the variables to take on the values they did? An answer such as "because these are the values which satisfy the constraints" is hardly compelling. Our desire to produce a causal explanation requires producing an ordering of values, each value being justified by the existence of a previous one. This can be achieved, in part, by producing a trace of how information is propagated through constraints during the constraint satisfaction

Figure 5: State Transition Graph for the Frictionless Spring

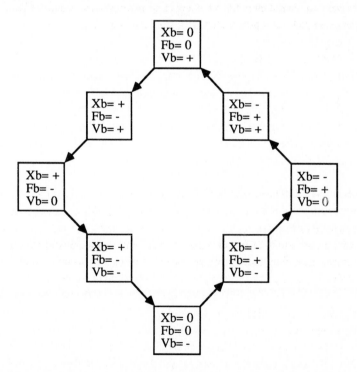

procedure. This, of course, assumes that the flow of information through the constraints is the same as the flow of causality in the modelled device. For instance, consider the first state in the spring example. Initially all we know is that $[V_b] = 0$ and $[X_s] = +$. The explanation proceeds as follows:

$[X_S] = +$ Given
$[X_S] = +$ and confluence 5 $\Rightarrow [X_b] = +$
$[X_S] = +$ and confluence 1 $\Rightarrow [F_S] = -$
$[F_S] = -$ and confluence 7 $\Rightarrow [F_b] = -$
$[F_b] = -$ and confluence 4 $\Rightarrow [dV_b] = -$
$[V_b] = 0$ Given
$[V_b] = 0$ and confluence 3 $\Rightarrow [dX_b] = 0$
$[dX_b] = 0$ and confluence 6 $\Rightarrow [dX_S] = 0$
$[dX_S] = 0$ and confluence 2 $\Rightarrow [dF_S] = 0$
$[dF_S] = 0$ and confluence 7 $\Rightarrow [dF_b] = 0$

In the above explanation the existence of a parameter value is justified as either being given or as being derived from a known value via a confluence and thus we have imposed a causal ordering. Unfortunately this causal linkage breaks down when a set of simultaneously inherent confluences is encountered. When this situation is encountered, it is necessary to guess a value to enable the constraint propagation scheme to continue. Such a guess would have no justification and so would defy any causal explanation. Thus, it is not possible, in general, to generate a causal explanation of intrastate behavior when such non-directed constraints are used.

A similar method, which derives causality from a set of equations using the methods of *causal ordering* and *comparative statics*, has been proposed [54]. The method works by successively identifying subgroups of the equation set which can be solved independently of the rest, the variables in these subgroups are said to causally influence the others. This approach suffers from the same problem as that discussed above i.e. the inability to impose a causal ordering for an inherently simultaneous equation set.

4. Process Centered Ontology

4.1 Underlying Philosophy
The process-centered ontology of Forbus [34] focuses on the agents which cause a world to change. Changes tend to occur when inequalities exist between variable values. For example when two objects of different temperatures are brought into contact the heat energy of the hotter one decreases and that of the colder one increases. If the two temperatures where equal then no change would occur. Similarly, if a rigid object is subject to the influence of opposing, unequal forces its velocity will increase in the direction of the stronger force while if the forces are of equal strength the object maintains its initial state of motion. Such phenomena are termed *processes* and are assumed to be the sole mechanism for change. Given a complete set of processes for a domain (a knowledge of when they occur, what they affect and when they stop) then it is presumed to be possible to predict

and explain the behavior of a world by identifying which processes are active, the changes they cause and how these changes are propagated through the system.

4.2 Representing States

The world consists of objects which are described by variables. These variables take on values in a partially ordered space of landmark values. Each variable is of a particular type (temperature, pressure, etc.). All variables of the same type may be taken to have values in the same quantity space to allow comparison. In addition, each variable is described by the value of its derivative, generally taken to be either +, - or 0.

Consider the situation shown in figure 6.

Figure 6: Oil and Ice Example

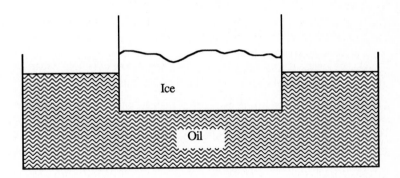

A lump of ice is contained in a beaker which is floating in a bath of hot oil. The landmarks defining the quantity space for temperature are

$(T_{melt-oil}, T_{melt-H_2O}, T_{boil-H_2O}, T_{boil-oil})$

Assuming that the temperature of the oil is somewhere between the melting point and boiling point of water and that the temperature of the ice is below its melting temperature, the quantity space looks as follows

$((T_{melt-oil}, T_{ice}), T_{melt-H_2O}, T_{oil}, T_{boil-H_2O}, T_{boil-oil})$

Notice that the space is only partially ordered. Both the melting point of the oil and the temperature of the ice are colder than the melting point of ice but not enough information has been given to determine their temperatures relative to each other. They are included within parenthesis to indicate an unknown ordering.

4.3 Representing the Physics
4.3.1 Individual Views

When a variable changes it tends to cause other variables to change with it. Such relations are represented by qualitative proportionalities (described in section 2.5). In a dynamic environment ordering relations change and objects appear and disappear. Thus Q-prop relationships do not necessarily hold under all circumstances and are conditional upon certain requirements being met. To account for this, Q-props are specified within an *individual view* which also contains three types of conditions which must exist for the relations to be valid:

Individuals	- The objects which must exist
Quantity Conditions	- Ordering relations which must hold between variable values of the individuals.
Preconditions	- Non-quantitative conditions which are expressed as predicates

For an example of these conditions, see Figure 7.

The Q-prop relations specified within an individual view only hold if that individual view is active i.e. if all of the three types of conditions are satisfied.

4.3.2 Processes

The representation so far can only describe relations where a variable changes in response to a change in some other variable. That is, it can represent the response of a system to perturbations but not the origin of these perturbations. Representing the primary causes of change is the job of processes.

Processes are just like individual views except they contain additional relationships - *influences* which specify changes that the process directly induces on variables. For example, consider the process Heat-Flow [34] shown in figure 7. There must exist two objects (src and dst) both of which contain heat. These objects must be connected by a path (path) which is capable of carrying heat between the two. In addition, one of the objects must have a higher temperature than the other. Only when all these conditions are satisfied is there heat flow between the two objects. The result of the process is to produce a flowrate which is proportional to the temperature difference between the objects. The heat of the hotter body decreases with a rate equal to the amount of the flowrate and the heat of the colder body increases at a rate equal to the amount of the flowrate.

Figure 7: Example of a Process

Process: Heat Flow
    Individuals:
               src an object, Has-Quantity(src,heat)
               dst an object, Has-Quantity(dst,heat)
               path a Heat-Path, Heat-Connection(path,src,dst)
    Preconditions:
               Heat-Aligned(path)
    Quantity Conditions:
               A[temperature(src)] > A[temperature(dst)]
    Relations:
               Let flowrate be a quantity
               A[flowrate] > zero
               flowrate $\propto_{Q+}$ (temperature(src) - temperature(dst))
    Influences:
               I- (heat(src), A[flowrate])
               I+ (heat(dst), A[flowrate])

In this representation the A[x] denotes the position of x in its quantity space.

Influences, represented as "I+(<quantity changing>, <flow causing change>)" as in "I+(mass, flowrate)", are much stronger representations than Q-props. A process positively influences a variable V by an amount n such that its derivative is equal to n. Thus if the variable is negatively influenced by another process by an amount m the resultant derivative is obtained by subtracting m from n (i.e. one can subtract outflows from inflows to determine whether the contents of a tank is increasing or decreasing.) It is not possible to make these resolutions in a Q-prop conflict as the Q-prop contains no information on the magnitude of the effect of changes in the independent variable on the derivative of the dependent variable. Influence relations are linearly proportional; Q-props are only monotonic.

The notions of Q-props and indirect influences divide the domain variables into two types: *independent variables* which can only change by the direct influence of a process and *dependent variables* which can only change through their Q-prop relations with another changing variable. Processes specify the root causes of change in a domain; individual views specify how these primary changes propagate through the domain. Note that this explicit-mechanism model has much stronger constraints than the implicit device-centered models. In addition to being directed constraints, many of the constraints approach quantitative relationships in strength.

4.4 Intrastate Behavior

Given a static qualitative description of a world state in terms of a set of quantity spaces and a library of all possible processes and individual views it is possible to

a) Identify all active processes and individual views.

b) Determine which dependent variables are changing and what direction they are changing in by referring to the influences of the active individual views.

c) Determine how these direct changes are propagated to independent variables by referring to the Q-prop relations in the active individual views and hence identify all variables which are changing and the directions they are changing in.

4.5 Inferring Behavior: An Example

Consider the beaker of ice floating in hot oil. The relevant processes and Individual Views for the domain are shown in figure 8 together with a description of the initial state. By referring to the quantity space for temperature it can be seen that the individual views solid(H_2O) and liquid(oil) are active and that the process Heat-Flow is active between the oil and the ice. Heat-Flow is the only active process and so is the sole driving force for change. The result is to cause the heat of the oil to decrease and that of the ice to increase. These changes propagate through the Q-prop relations in the active individual views and cause the temperature of the ice to increase and that of the oil to decrease.

At this stage the temperature of the ice is moving toward the landmark T_{melt,H_2O} from below and the temperature of the oil is moving toward it from above:

$$(T_{melt-oil}, T_{ice} \rightarrow, T_{melt-H_2O}, \leftarrow T_{oil}, T_{boil-H_2O}, T_{boil-oil})$$

What happens next depends upon whether the ice or the oil hits the landmark T_{melt,H_2O} first. If the ice reaches it first it will result in the activation of an additional process, melting. The result of this is that a new object, a liquid, is created in the beaker. The heat of the ice no longer changes but its amount decreases and that of the water increases. The temperature of the ice continues to decrease. Now we have to consider changes in the amount-of quantity space as well as the temperature space:

$$\text{Temperature}(T_{melt-oil}, \{T_{ice} = T_{melt-H_2O}\}, \leftarrow T_{oil}, T_{boil-H_2O}, T_{boil-oil})$$

$$\text{Amount-of}(zero, \leftarrow \text{amount-of(ice)})$$

Again we have a choice as to what variable will hit a landmark first, with different behaviors resulting in the different cases.

The inference mechanism is a repeated cycle of identifying active processes and individual views, determining the derivatives of the state variables and postulating which variables can change values by moving to or from landmarks. The mechanism stops when it reaches a state at which no processes are active.

The complete envisionment for this example is given in figure 9. For each path through the envisionment the mechanism produces a history of behavior. Histories are described from the perspective of an object and consist of:
a) *Parameter histories* - A description of the qualitative states that each parameter of the object pass through over some time span.
b) *Process histories* - A description of the processes which have influenced the object, and
c) *View histories* - A description of the individual views which the object has participated in.

Histories serve both to describe and explain behavior. Parameter histories express the behavior whilst process histories identify the active agents which are the root cause of change and View histories identify the active Q-prop relationships through which the root changes are propagated. One of the histories from our example is given in figure 10.

Figure 8: Processes and Individual Views of Domain

Process: Melting
> Individuals:
>> s a contained-solid
>> hf a process instance, process(hf)=heat flow and dst(hf)= s
> Quantity Conditions:
>> Status(hf, active)
>> Not A[temperature(s)] < A[t-melt(s)]
> Relations:
>> There exists l a piece of stuff
>> Liquid(l)
>> Substance(l) = Substance(s)
>> Temperature(l) = Temperature(s)
>> Let generation-rate be a quantity
>> A[generation-rate] > zero
>> generation-rate $\propto_{Q+}$ flowrate(hf)
> Influences:
>> I - (heat(s), A[flowrate])
>> I - (amount-of(s), A[generation-rate])
>> I+ (amount-of(l), A[generation-rate])

Individual View: Solid

Individuals:

        p a piece of stuff

Quantity Conditions:

        Not A[temperature(p)] > A[t-melt(p)]

        Not Liquid(p)

Relations:

        temperature(p) $\propto_{Q+}$ heat(p)

        Volume(p) $\propto_{Q+}$ Amount-of(p)

Individual View: Liquid

Individuals:

        p a piece of stuff

Quantity Conditions:

        Not A[temperature(p)] < A[t-melt(p)]

        Not A[temperature(p)] > A[t-boil(p)]

        Not Solid(p)

        Not Gas(p)

Relations:

        volume(p) $\propto_{Q+}$ amount-of(p)

        temperature(p) $\propto_{Q+}$ heat(p)

Individual View: Contained-Liquid (p)

Individuals:

        con a container

        sub a liquid

Preconditions:

        Can-Contain-Substance(con,sub)

Quantity Conditions:

        A[amount-of-in(sub,con)] > zero

Relations:

        There exists p, a piece of stuff

        amount-of(p) = amount-of-in(sub,con)

        made-of(p) =sub

        container(p) = con

The contained solid is represented similarly.

Figure 9: Envisionment for Oil and Ice

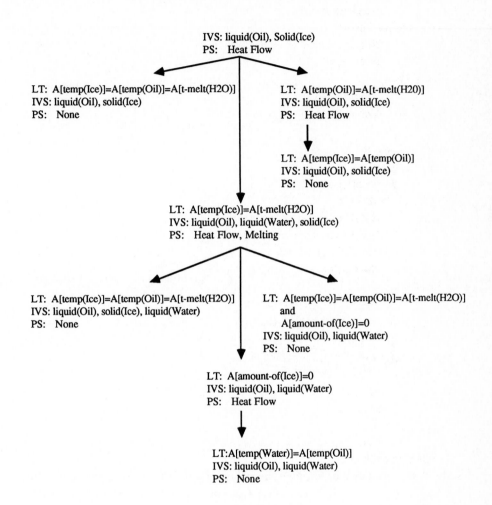

LT   = Landmark Transition
IVS = Individual View Structure
PS   = Process Structure

Figure 10: One History for Ice and Oil example

History for Ice:

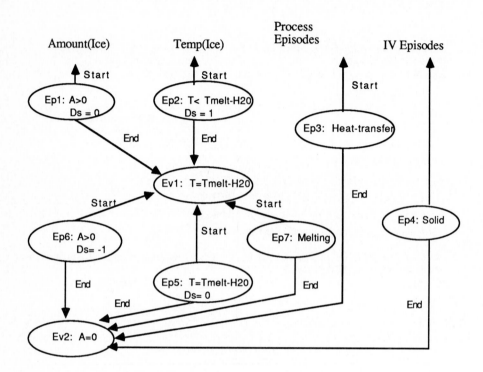

4.6 QPT and Logic

The physical knowledge represented in qualitative process theory could also be represented in logic. Figure 11 shows the equivalent logic notation for the individual view "contained-liquid" [34]. The advantage of using QPT is that it provides a domain independent *organizational structure* which facilitates more efficient representation and reasoning. In particular, the explicit representation of agents of change (through processes) and the notion that objects can only interact when their histories intersect, helps solve the frame problem [34].

Figure 11: Description in Logic of a Contained Liquid

$\forall$ c $\in$ container $\forall$ s $\in$ liquid

  Container(c) $\wedge$ Liquid(s) $\Rightarrow$

    ($\exists$ IV $\in$ view-instance

    ; names of individuals are used as selector functions

    con(IV) = c $\wedge$ sub(IV) = s

    ; logical existence of individual is timeless

    $\wedge$ ($\exists$ p $\in$ piece of stuff

      container(p) = c $\wedge$ made-of(p) = s)

    $\wedge$ ($\forall$ t $\in$ time

    ; it is active whenever Preconditions and Quantity Conditions hold

    (T Status(IV, Active) t)

    $\leftrightarrow$ [(T Can-Contain-Substance(con(IV), sub(IV)) t)

      $\wedge$ (T A[amount-of-in(sub(IV), con(IV))] > ZERO t)]

    ; when active, p exists physically and its amount is the

    ; amount of that kind of substance in the container

    $\wedge$ (T Status(IV, Active) t) $\Rightarrow$

      ((T Contained-Liquid(p) t)

      $\wedge$ Exists-In(p, t)

      $\wedge$ (M amount-of(p) t) = (M amount-of-in(s,c) t))))

; In general,

$\forall$ IV $\in$ view of instance $\forall$ t $\in$ time

  (T Taxonomy(Status(IV, Active), Status(IV, Inactive)) t)

----

5. Limits of Qualitative Reasoning

Analyzing the limits of qualitative representations has been, and continues to be, an active
area of research [56, 77, 79, 47]. Research has concentrated on two issues:

a) The ambiguity arising from weak representations and algebras.

b) The production of solutions not realizable in the modelled domain (spurious
solutions).

5.1 Ambiguity

As seen above, qualitative reasoning systems do not produce a single description of
behavior, but an envisionment of many possible behaviors. This is because the qualitative
representation does not carry enough information to resolve competing tendencies and so
remains ambiguous as to the outcome. This ambiguity manifests itself in two ways:

  1) Inability to determine which variable changes state first in transition
      analysis.

2)   Inability to determine the direction of change of a variable which is
     influenced by multiple competing tendencies.

Ambiguities, in general, can only be resolved through a knowledge of the exact numerical
values of the relevant parameters. This is, by definition, impossible in any qualitative
representation so ambiguity is an inherent part of qualitative reasoning. Although this is a
disadvantage in circumstances when it is desired to know what will happen for a given set
of parameter values (for example, simulation), it can also provide benefits. In design, for
example, a knowledge of how a system behaves for all parameter values and how that
behavior is produced for each would enable the designer to determine the most desirable
behavior possible and pick the parameter values required to achieve it.

In situations where ambiguity is undesirable it can be reduced by providing qualitative
information on relative magnitudes of influence. In many domains it is often the case that
certain types of influence are much weaker or stronger than others. This information can be
used to resolve the effect of competing influences. D'Ambrosio [6] proposes to incorporate
this information by the annotation of influences with linguistic sensitivities (small, large
etc). A similar method is to incorporate information about relative magnitudes of
influences. The use of several formalisms of reasoning about relative orders of magnitude
have been proposed [63,69]. In these formalisms influence magnitudes are related using
relations such as A is negligible compared to B, A is close to B and A is the same order of
magnitude as B. A set of inference rules then generates a partial ordering of values into
groups significantly different in magnitude.

5.2 Spurious Solutions

The equations in a formal mathematical description of the structure of a world can be
integrated to produce a single prediction of behavior. In contrast a qualitative description of
the structure (often derived directly from these equations) will produce multiple predictions
of behavior. The reason is that a single qualitative description is compatible with not one
but many different sets of differential equations. One would hope that all solutions
produced by an envisionment would correspond to that produced by at least one of its
compatible sets of differential equations i.e. that all solutions are physically realizable. This
is, unfortunately, not the case; physically impossible or *spurious solutions* arise from two
sources:

a) The weakness of qualitative representations.
b) Local generation schemes for inferring behavior in which the next state is determined by
consideration of the current state only (irrespective of previous trends).

Consider, for example, a solid object connected to a spring as shown in figure 4 [56]. The
object is initially pulled to the right so that the spring is extended beyond it's equilibrium
position and held. The extended spring exerts a force on the object so that when it is
released the object is pulled to the left and the spring contracts. Once the spring contracts to

a length equal to its rest length the spring no longer exerts any tensile force but the momentum of the block causes it to continue to contract. At this point the spring starts to exert a force on the object in the opposite direction causing it to decelerate and eventually move to the right. The system oscillates back and forth.

The system can be described mathematically by the following equation:

$$\frac{d^2x}{dt^2} = -\frac{K}{M}x$$

Where: x = spring extension from equilibrium position
t = time
K = spring constant
M = mass of the block

This produces a single behavior of stable oscillation for all parameter values. However, the corresponding qualitative constraints allow three behaviors: increasing, decreasing and stable oscillation. Only the latter is physically realizable. The problem arises because of an inability to order transitions. Consider the situation shown in figure 12.

As the object moves to the left, both the velocity and position are moving toward landmarks. Velocity is decreasing to zero and position is increasing towards its initial extension. It is not possible to determine whether the position reaches its landmark before, after or at the same time as the velocity reaches zero giving rise to the three distinct possibilities. In addition, because of the local nature of envisionment, the same choice is encountered at every cycle of oscillation. For example, if the oscillation decreased at the previous cycle it can increase, or stay the same at the next one. This leads to an explosion of possible behaviors.

The crucial physics here is the law of energy conservation, which states that the sum of kinetic and potential energies of the system remains constant at all times. The kinetic energy of the system is proportional to the velocity of the object and the potential energy is proportional to the extension or compression of the spring relative to its rest position. Thus whenever the object has zero velocity its energy consists only of potential energy, since this total energy is

S.D. Grantham and L.H. Ungar

Figure 12: Possible transitions for turning point

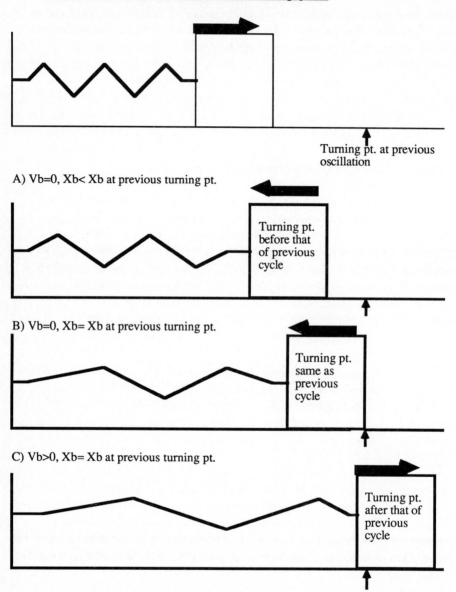

Turning pt. at previous oscillation

A) Vb=0, Xb< Xb at previous turning pt.

Turning pt. before that of previous cycle

B) Vb=0, Xb= Xb at previous turning pt.

Turning pt. same as previous cycle

C) Vb>0, Xb= Xb at previous turning pt.

Turning pt. after that of previous cycle

constant at all times the potential energy at zero velocity must always be constant and so the positions at which velocity is zero must remain constant as well. Hence the landmarks must be reached coincidentally. This knowledge is implicitly encoded in our formal mathematics (indeed it is on consideration of energy conservation that the equation was derived in the first place) but is lost when moving to a qualitative representation.

Researchers are actively seeking methods of reducing the number of spurious solutions. Kuipers suggests that remodelling the system from a different perspective can sometimes eliminate spurious solutions [56]. For example, remodelling the spring example above to explicitly represent the conservation of energy would eliminate the two spurious solutions. This puts the emphasis on creating relevant domain models. It is sometimes possible to further exploit the mathematical description in order to eliminate certain types of spurious solutions. For example, a qualitative phase plane analysis [78, 62] can be used to reduce the spring behavior to only three distinct possibilities: either increasing, decreasing or stable oscillation. A qualitative phase plane analysis makes use of the facts that trajectories cannot split or cross in order to rule out spurious solutions. Such an analysis eliminates all spurious solutions which result from local generation.

In addition, it has been shown that a knowledge of higher derivatives can, in some circumstances, be used to eliminate other types of spurious solutions [59, 61, 17, 85, 86]. Branching often occurs when the derivative of a variable equals zero. A knowledge of the sign of the second derivative can can often determine which is the correct option. For example, if a variable has decreased to a stationary point (i.e its derivative is zero) and its second derivative is negative then the variable value must increase (see figure 13).

Figure 13: Second Derivatives and their corresponding Trajectories

Trajectory	Sign of Second Derivative
	+
	-
	0

Another method is the addition of further constraints obtained from redundant equations derived from manipulation of the original equation set. Consider the following equations

$$C = A + B$$
$$E = 2C + A$$
$$D = C - E$$

In the confluence representation of de Kleer these give rise to the following qualitative constraints

[C] = [A] + [B]
[E] = [C] + [A]
[D] = [C] - [E]

Assume that we know that [A] = + and [B] = + then the qualitative constraints give three solutions

Solution	[C]	[D]	[E]
1	+	+	+
2	+	0	+
3	+	-	+

From our original equation set we see that for positive A and B, E > C always and so D is always negative. Thus the first two solutions predicted by our qualitative system are spurious. This arises because our representation is too weak to capture relative magnitudes. However, if we manipulate the original equation set by substituting for E in equation 3 with equation 2 we get

D = -C - A

Giving the confluence

[D] = - [C] - [A]

By adding this to our other three confluences the spurious solutions are eliminated.

Unfortunately there is no technique for determining which or how many "redundant" confluences are required to reduce the number of spurious solutions and it becomes infeasible to produce all redundant permutations for large equation sets. However, Kramer and Oyeleye have produced a set of heuristics for picking such equations and have proved them useful in reducing spurious solutions when modelling complex behavior of chemical plants [68].

Eliminating spurious solutions is still an area of active research, but it appears that qualitative descriptions derived from equations alone cannot, in general, provide adequate information to eliminate all spurious solutions; more situation-specific knowledge is required. This information must (so far) be deduced in an *ad hoc* manner.

6. Other Forms of Reasoning

Up to now the only form of reasoning we have considered is that of envisionment i.e. using a qualitative model of the structure of a system to infer how it can behave. Envisionment has been the most studied method of qualitative reasoning but there are several other forms. In particular, interest has recently grown in data interpretation, fault diagnosis and comparative analysis. These reasoning techniques are discussed below.

6.1 Data Interpretation
The essence of data interpretation is, given a time series of numerical data, describe the underlying qualitative model of behavior which produced it. Forbus has developed his ATMI technique to perform such an analysis [36, 40]. The procedure is as follows:
a) Map the quantitative time series into a sequence of intervals each consisting of a set of constant qualitative values.
b) For each interval determine the set of qualitative states which could produce such qualitative values.
c) Use the total envisionment for the system to provide constraints on valid state transitions and hence to produce compatibility constraints between the states in adjacent intervals.
d) Use these constraints to filter out incompatible sequences of qualitative states. All remaining state sequences are valid models for the behavior.

Data interpretation has important applications in design, monitoring and fault diagnosis. For example, in operating a chemical plant, interpretation of instrument measurements will identify if the plant is functioning as intended and enable the testing of fault hypothesis if there is a malfunction. In addition, when designing a new chemical plant, the numerical output of quantitative simulations have to be interpreted to produce a qualitative model of what the simulation is predicting.

6.2 Fault Diagnosis
A fault arises whenever the observed behavior of an artifact contradicts that predicted by its qualitative model. A fault is indicative that some aspect of the model is wrong and fault diagnosis is the reasoning process by which the defective part of the model is identified. Fault diagnosis can be broken down into three parts:
1) Discrepancy detection - determining which parts of the predicted behavior are inconsistent with observations.
2) Hypothesis generation - determining which aspects of the model, if defective, could produce the observed discrepancies.
3) Hypothesis testing - determining whether the hypothesized faults are consistent with all of the observed behavior.
This form of reasoning has received much attention in diagnosing faults in digital and analog circuits (see, for example, [3]) and a thorough review of model-based diagnosis is given in [10].

6.3 Comparative Analysis
After envisionment has produced a history of behavior it is often desirable to describe and explain how the behavior would change if one of the parameter values were altered. For example, how would the behavior of an oscillating spring and mass system change if its

mass were increased? Weld calls such reasoning *comparative analysis* and has developed
two techniques which perform such reasoning. The first, *differential qualitative analysis*
[83], works by changing the perspective from which parameters are viewed. Normally
parameters are viewed from the perspective of time but when comparing behaviors it is
useful to shift the perspective to that of some other parameter. In the spring and block
example by viewing force as a function of position the following explanation can be
generated [83 p 959].

> "Since force is inversely proportional to position, the force on the block
> will remain the same when the mass is increased. But if the block is heavier it won't
> accelerate as fast, then it will always be going slower and so will take longer to
> complete a full period."

The second technique is *exaggeration* [84] which works by exaggerating changes to their
extremes. It yields the following type of explanation for our spring system.

> "If the mass were infinite, then the block wouldn't move, so the period would be
> infinite. Thus, if you increase the mass by only a little bit, then the duration of the
> period would increase a little bit as well."

7. Extensions

One of the goals of qualitative reasoning systems is to emulate the performance of
engineers and scientists. In order to achieve this they must be able to perform the
mathematical analysis that the former do and be able to reason in complex domains.

7.1 Increasing the Power of the Qualitative Mathematics

The mathematical representation so far described is very simple. We can describe
parameters as increasing, decreasing and stable, but that is about it. Scientists and
engineers often describe the behavior of dynamic systems as "decreasing exponentially, "
asymptotes to some value ", "increases linearly ", and make use of sophisticated
knowledge of phase plane and bifurcation techniques to analyze these systems. If our
reasoning systems are to be able to make complex inferences about dynamical systems they
must use a more expressive representation and have a knowledge of sophisticated
mathematical techniques.

Sacks has developed a *Qualitative Mathematical Reasoner* [71] which provides more
expressive qualitative descriptions of the behavior of sets of linear differential equations. It
describes the systems by decomposing them into the sum or product of a set of interval
descriptors which contain information on the derivative and convexity of the function and
notes interesting behaviors such as singularities and inflexion points. Sacks has also
developed a technique called *Piecewise Linear Reasoning* [72] which produces a phase
plane analysis of the behavior of non-linear equation sets by constructing and examining a
piecewise linear approximation. Yip has sought to increase the sophistication of qualitative
reasoners by developing systems which perform reasoning in the phase plane [90, 91]. He

has produced a system KAM, which autonomously explores the phase space of non-linear equation sets - automatically setting up numerical simulations and producing high level qualitative interpretations of the results. His approach exploits a deep understanding of dynamical systems theory, using qualitative knowledge of bifurcation rules and valid types of dynamic trajectories.

7.2 Modelling Complex Domains

As qualitative reasoning systems have been applied to more realistic domains, two problems have become apparent. Firstly, as domains become more complex it is apparent that the domain must be modelled from more than one perspective in order to solve non-trivial problems. One approach is to compliment qualitative physics with other methodologies. For example, de Kleer [14] combines a qualitative physics approach with a *teleological analysis* (i.e. an assumption that a device has a purpose) in order to describe the behavior of electronic devices. A device is modelled in two ways: by a qualitative model and by a list of the ways in which it is commonly used. The use of this teleological information allows circuit behaviors to be ruled out which are predicted as valid by a qualitative physics analysis but which no sane designer would intend the circuit to perform. Similarly, Stanfil combines a qualitative analysis with knowledge of geometry and symbolic algebraic manipulation of standard equations to model the behavior of machines. He groups knowledge into a hierarchy of seven individual experts which interact to produce an overall qualitative description of machine behavior from a drawing [76].

Another approach is the use of *ontological shift* , that is, switching between different qualitative representations of the same system. For example, consider the switch between the contained-liquid ontology of Hayes [49] and the molecular collection (MC) ontology of Collins when analyzing the behavior of a refrigeration cycle [5]. The contained liquid ontology is used to determine which processes are active between which objects. Once the basic process structure has been identified, a switch to the MC ontology allows the performance of more complex inferences such as recognizing the refrigerator as a closed loop heat pump. The MC ontology takes the Lagrangian perspective of considering a group of molecules as they move with the fluid through the system while the contained liquid ontology takes a Eulerian approach. Switching between these two perspectives allows deductions to be made which would be impossible if only one perspective was considered.

As the qualitative models become more and more complex, both in their representation at multiple levels of detail and their ability to perform multiple reasoning tasks, it becomes necessary to provide focus to allow such systems to perform efficiently. It is not necessary to consider all transient behaviors of a system if only an explanation of its steady state behavior is desired. Neither is it necessary to perform a statistical mechanics analysis on the motion of gas particles being pumped into a container if we only want to know what pressure they are at. Thus, systems need to recognize which part of their knowledge is relevant to a particular task and ignore the rest. Falkenhainer and Forbus have proposed a set of conventions by which to set up such "large scale qualitative models" [26]. They suggest the key is to explicitly represent modelling assumptions. Specifically, simplifying assumptions which decompose the domain into a set of different levels of detail and perspective and operating assumptions which are used to filter out irrelevant predictions of qualitative simulation by focusing only on specific types of behavior. By making explicit the conditions under which these assumptions are applicable it is possible to increase the focus and efficiency of a system.

Murthy has attempted to solve the same problem by developing a system which reasons with a hierarchy of quantity spaces [65]. By dynamically shifting between quantity spaces of different resolution a system can focus in on details or abstract away to a higher level whenever necessary. Such efficiency considerations have thus far been less important for explicit-model systems, which already reason at a more abstract level.

8. Conclusions

Qualitative reasoning provides formal approaches to two aspects of reasoning about physical phenomena: Firstly, it provides a formal approach to representing and reasoning with qualitative information in much the same way that traditional mathematics provides a formal system for making inferences about numerical data. It provides qualitative inference techniques equivalent to integration (envisionment), arithmetic reasoning (qualitative arithmetics) and reasoning with inequalities (order of magnitude reasoning). Secondly, it provides formal approaches to producing models of physical systems and for producing causal explanations of behavior. Causality can either be represented implicitly (through the use of implicit mechanism ontologies and non-directed constraints), in which case it is derived as part of the inference procedure for determining behavior, or it can be represented explicitly (through the use of explicit mechanism ontologies and directed functional dependencies), in which case it is the imposition of causality which determines behavior. The major drawback of qualitative reasoning is that it produces ambiguous and, even worse, spurious solutions. Although special techniques can be applied to reduce ambiguity in certain cases, ambiguity is an unavoidable consequence of any qualitative representation. Whether or not all spurious solutions can be eliminated is a matter for future research to determine.

A variety of representations and reasoning strategies have been proposed and one might criticize the field of qualitative physics for not converging to a common standard in the way traditional mathematics has. However, it must be remembered that qualitative physics systems carry an additional burden in seeking to produce models and explain results. Experts in different fields utilize very different reasoning techniques when constructing and explaining models: doctors, engineers and lawyers all tend to approach problems in different ways as do specialist within each of these disciplines. Certain forms of representation and reasoning lend themselves to efficient computing in particular domains so it is hardly surprising that researchers working in different application areas have taken different approaches. As qualitative reasoning is applied to more and more domains an even greater variety of representations and ontologies may be expected. Different levels of abstraction are needed in different problems and different amounts of structure and organization at the level of devices or processes are required for different applications.

As the field of qualitative reasoning develops, it finds application in more and more domains. In the recent past, qualitative reasoning has been applied to areas as diverse as design [89], tutoring systems [33, 45, 53], producing systems which plan and learn in physical domains [14, 23, 25, 42, 50, 51, 52] and instilling robots with a qualitative physics of their environment [73]. Only by applying qualitative physics to more complex domains and trying to make more intricate deductions can its capabilities be increased and its potential explored.

9. References

1.   Allen, J. "Towards a general model of action and time" *Artificial Intelligence,* 23 (2), 1984.

2.   Allen, J. and Koomen, J. "Planning using a temporal world model," Proceedings of IJCAI-83, 1983.

3.   Bobrow, D. (Ed.) *Qualitative reasoning about physical systems*, MIT Press, Cambridge, 1984.

4.   Chiu, C. "Qualitative physics based on exact physical principles," presented at the 1st Qualitative Physics Workshop, Urbana, Illinois, 1987.

5.   Collins, J. and Forbus, K. "Reasoning about fluids via molecular collections," Proceedings of AAAI-87, Seattle, 1987.

6.   D'Ambrosio, B. "Extending the mathematics in Qualitative Process theory," Proceedings of AAAI-87, 1987.

7.   Davis, E. "A logical framework for solid objective physics" New York University Computer Science Department Technical Report no. 245, October, 1986. To appear in *International Journal of AI in Engineering*, 1988.

8.   Davis, E. "Order of magnitude reasoning in qualitative differential equation," New York University Computer Science Department Technical Report no. 312, 1987.

9.   Davis, R."Expert Systems: Where Are We? and Where Do We Go From Here?" *AI Magazine* 3(2), 1-22 (1982).

10.   Davis, R. and Hamscher, W. "Model-based reasoning: troubleshooting" In *Exploring Artificial Intelligence,* H. Shrobe editor, Morgan Kaufmann, 1988.

11.   de Kleer, J. "Qualitative and quantitative knowledge in classical mechanics," TR-352, MIT AI Lab, Cambridge, Mass, 1975.

12.   de Kleer, J. "The origin and resolution of ambiguities in causal arguments," Proceedings of IJCAI-79, 1979.

13.   de Kleer, J. "Causal and teleological reasoning in circuit recognition" MIT AI Lab Technical Report No. 529, 1979.

14.   de Kleer, J. "How Circuits Work," *Artificial Intelligence*, **24**, 1984.

15.   de Kleer, J. "Choices without Backtracking," AAAI-84, Austin, Texas, 1984.

16.   de Kleer, J. "An assumption-based truth maintenance system,"*Artificial Intelligence*, **28**, 1986.

17.   de Kleer, J. and Bobrow, D."Qualitative reasoning with higher order derivatives" AAAI-84, 1984

18.   de Kleer, J. and Brown, J. "A qualitative physics based on confluences," *Artificial Intelligence*, **24**, 1984.

19.   de Kleer, J. and Sussman G. J. "Propagation of constraints applied to circuit synthesis" *Circuit Theory and Application ,* **8,** (1980) 127 -144

20.   de Kleer, J., Williams, B. "Reasoning about Multiple Faults," Proceedings of AAAI-86, 1986.

21.   Dormoy, J. and Raiman, O. "Assembling a device" presented at the 1st Qualitative Physics Workshop, Urbana, Illinois,1987.

22.   Dormoy, J. and Raimam, O. "Assembling a device" *AI in Engineering*, To appear, 1989.

23.   Doyle, R. "Constructing and refining causal explanations from an inconsistent domain theory," Proceedings of AAAI-86, 1986.

24.   Doyle, R."Truth maintenance systems for problem solving" MIT AI Lab AI-TR-419, 1978.

25.   Falkenhainer, B. "Proportionality graphs, units analysis, and domain constraints: Improving the power and efficiency of the scientific discovery process" Proceedings of IJCAI-85, 1985.

26.   Falkenhainer, B., and Forbus, K. "Setting up large scale qualitative models" Proceedings of AAAI-88, 1988.

27.   Faltings, B. "A theory of qualitative kinematics in mechanisms," University of Illinois at Urbana-Champaign, Department of Computer Science Technical Report No. UIUCDCS-R-86-1274, 1986.

28.   Faltings, B. "Qualitative Place Vocabularies for Mechanisms in Configuration Space," University of Illinois at Urbana-Champaign, Department of Computer Science Technical Report No. UIUCDCS-R-87-1360, 1987.

29.   Faltings, B. "Qualitative kinematics in mechanisms," Proceedings of IJCAI-87, 1987.

30.   Forbus, K. "Spatial and qualitative aspects of reasoning about motion," AAAI-80, Palo Alto, California, 1980.

31.   Forbus, K. "A study of qualitative and geometric knowledge in reasoning about motion," MIT AI Lab Technical Report No. 615, 1981.

32.   Forbus, K. "Qualitative reasoning about physical processes" IJCAI-7, Vancouver, B.C., 1981.

33.   Forbus, K. "An interactive laboratory for teaching control system concepts," BBN Technical Report No. 5511, 1984.

34.   Forbus, K. "Qualitative process theory" *Artificial Intelligence*, **24**, 1984.

35.   Forbus, K. "Qualitative Process theory" MIT AI Lab Technical report No. 789, 1984.

36.   Forbus, K. "Interpreting measurements of physical systems," Proceedings of AAAI-86, 1986.

37.   Forbus, K. "The Qualitative Process Engine," Technical Report No. UIUCDCS-R-86-1288, 1986. To appear, *International Journal of AI in Engineering*, 1989.

38.   Forbus, K. " Qualitative Physics: Past, Present and Future" In *Exploring Artificial Intelligence,* H. Shrobe editor, Morgan Kaufmann, 1988.

39.   Forbus, K. "Intelligence Computer-Aided Engineering," Proceedings of the AAAI Workshop on AI in Process Engineering, Columbia University, New York,1987. *Submitted for publication.*

40.   Forbus, K. "Interpreting observations of physical systems," *IEEE transactions on systems, man, and cybernetics*, Vol. SMC-17, No. 3, 1987.

42.   Forbus, K. and Gentner, D. "Learning physical domains: Towards a theoretical framework" in Michalski, R., Carbonell, J. and Mitchell, T. *Machine Learning: An Artificial Intelligence Approach, Volume 2*, Tioga press, 1986.

43.   Forbus, K., Nielsen, P., and Faltings, B. "Qualitative Kinematics: A Framework," Proceedings of IJCAI-87, 1987.

44.   Forbus, K. and Gentner, D. "Causal reasoning about quantities," Proceedings of the Eighth annual conference of the Cognitive Science Society, Amherst, Mass., 1986.

45.   Forbus, K. and Stevens, A. "Using qualitative simulation to generate explanations," BBN Technical Report No. 4490, 1981. Also, Proceedings of the third annual meeting of the Cognitive Science Society, 1981.

46.   Gelsey, A. "Automated reasoning about machine geometry and kinematics" Third IEEE conference on AI applications, Orlando, Florida, 1987.

47.   Hall , R. J. "Spurious behaviors in qualitative prediction" MIT AI Lab. Working Paper 308 , 1988

48.   Hayes, P. "The naive physics manifesto" in *Expert systems in the micro-electronic age*, D. Michie (Ed.), Edinburgh University Press, 1979.

49.   Hayes P. "Naive Physics 1: Ontology for liquids" in Hobbs, R., Moore, R. (Eds.), *Formal Theories of the Commonsense World*, Ablex Publishing Corporation, Norwood, New Jersey, 1985.

50. Hogge, J. "Compiling plan operators from domains expressed in Qualitative Process theory," Proceedings of AAAI-87, 1987.

51. Hogge, J. "The compilation of planning operators from Qualitative Process theory models," Technical Report No. UIUCDCS-R-87-1368, 1987.

52. Hogge, J. "TPLAN: A temporal interval-based planner with novel extensions," Technical Report No. UIUCDCS-R-87-1367, 1987.

53. Hollan, J., Hutchins, E., and Weitzman, L., "STEAMER: An interactive inspectable simulation-based training system," *AI Magazine*, 1984.

54. Iwasaki, I. and Simon, H. "Causality in device behavior," Artificial Intelligence, **29**, 1986.

55. Kuipers, B. "Common sense Causality: Deriving behavior from Structure" *Artificial Intelligence*, **24**, 1984.

56. Kuipers, B. "The limits of qualitative simulation" Proceedings of Ninth Joint International Conference on Artificial Intelligence, 1985.

57. Kuipers, B. "Qualitative Simulation," *Artificial Intelligence*, **29**, 1986.

58. Kuipers, B. "Abstraction by time-scale in qualitative simulation," Proceedings of AAAI-87, 1987.

59. Kuipers, B. and Chiu, C. "Taming intractable branching in qualitative simulation," Proceedings of IJCA-87, 1987.

60. Kuipers, B. and Berleant, D. "Using incomplete quantitative knowledge in qualitative reasoning" Proceedings AAAI-88, 1988.

61. Lee, W.W., Chiu, C., and Kuipers, B.J. "Developments towards constraining qualitative simulation," University of Texas at Austin Artificial Intelligence Laboratory Technical Report No. AI TR87-44, 1987.

62. Lee, W. W., and Kuipers, B. J. "Non-intersection of trajectories in qualitative phase space: A global constraint for qualitative simulation" Proceedings AAAI-88, 1988.

63. Mavrovouniotis, M. and Stephanopolous, G., "Reasoning with orders of magnitude and approximate relations," Proceedings of AAAI-87, 1987.

64.   Mozetic, I. "The role of abstractions in learning qualitative models" Proceedings of the 4th International Workshop on Machine learning, *Morgan Kaufmann*, 1987.

65.   Murthy, S. S. "Qualitative reasoning at multiple resolutions" Proceedings AAAI-88, 1988.

66.   Nielsen, P. "The qualitative statics of rigid bodies," University of Illinois at Urbana-Champaign, Department of Computer Science Technical Report No. UIUCDCS-R-87-1354, 1987.

67.   Nielson, P. "A qualitative approach to mechanical constraint," Proceedings of AAAI-88, 1988

68.   Oyeleye, O. and Kramer, M. "Qualitative simulation of continuous chemical processes" Paper presented at AIChE National Meeting, New York, 1987.

69.   Raiman, O. "Order of magnitude reasoning," Proceedings of AAAI-86, 1986.

70.   Rich, S.H. and V. Venkatasubramanian, "Model-based reasoning in diagnostic expert systems for chemical process plants," Computers and Chem. Eng. 11(2), 111-122 (1987).

71.   Sacks, E. "Qualitative Mathematical Reasoning," Proceedings of IJCAI-85, 1985.

72.   Sacks, E. "Piecewise linear reasoning," Proceedings of AAAI-87, 1987.

73.   Schmolze, J. "Physics for robots," Proceedings of AAAI-86, 1986.

74.   Simmons, R. "Representing and reasoning about change in geologic interpretation," MIT Artificial Intelligence Lab TR-749, 1983.

75.   Simmons, R. "Commonsense arithmetic reasoning," Proceedings of AAAI-86, 1986.

76.   Stanfill, C. "The decomposition of a large domain: Reasoning about machines" AAAI-83, Washington, D.C., 1983.

77.   Struss, P. "The limitations of qualitative mathematics," presented at the first Qualitative Physics Workshop, Urbana, Illinois,1987.

78.   Struss, P. "Global filters for qualitative behaviors" Proceedings of AAAI-88, 1988.

79. Struss, P."Mathematical Aspects of Qualitative Reasoning" *AI* in Engineering, To appear, 1989.

80. Steele, G. L. and Sussman, G. J. "CONSTRAINTS- A language for expressing almost hierarchical descriptions," *Artificial intelligence*, **14** (1980) 1 - 39.

81. Weld, D. "Switching between discrete and continuous process models to predict genetic activity." MIT AI lab TR-749, 1984.

82. Weld, D. "The use of aggregation in qualitative simulation," *Artificial Intelligence*, 30(1), 1986.

83. Weld, D. "Comparative Analysis," Proceedings of IJCAI-87, 1987.

84. Weld, D. " Exaggeration" Proceedings of AAAI-88, 1988.

85. Williams, B. "Qualitative analysis of MOS circuits" *Artificial Intelligence*, **24**, 1984.

86. Williams, B."The use of continuity in a qualitative physics" AAAI-84, 1984.

87. Williams, B. "Doing time: Putting qualitative reasoning on firmer ground," Proceedings of AAAI-86, 1986.

88. Williams, B. "MINIMA : A symbolic Approach to qualitative algebriac reasoning" AAAI-88, 1988.

89. Williams, B. "Principled design based on topologies of interaction," PhD Thesis, MIT AI Lab, To appear, 1989.

90. Yip, K. "Extracting qualitative dynamics from numerical experiments," Proceedings of AAAI-87, 1987.

91. Yip, K. "Generating global behaviors using deep knowledge of local dynamics," Proceedings of AAAI-88, 1988.

Formal Techniques in Artificial Intelligence
A Sourcebook. R.B. Banerji (editor)
© Elsevier Science Publishers B.V. (North-Holland), 1990

Automatic Generation of Heuristics

J.P.E. Hodgson
Center for Machine Learning
Department of Mathematics and Computer Science
St. Joseph's University
Philadelphia. PA 19131. USA.

1 Introduction

1.1 Problem Solving in AI

Problem solving is one of the laboratories of artificial intelligence. Over the years a number of puzzles have become the "white mice"to which ideas for general methods have been applied. Many of the problems are of a combinatorial nature, ranging from the familiar Towers of Hanoi puzzle to the (far more difficult) Rubik's cube puzzle which occasioned much interest recently. In the course of this chapter we will discuss many of them in detail in connection with specific problem solving methods.

What these puzzles have in common is that they can be described in a fairly simple way and yet can be amazingly difficult to solve. The Towers of Hanoi may be by now so familiar to people that it hardly seems like a puzzle, but the fifteen puzzle with its sliding tiles is not trivial even for someone who "knows" how to solve it, while Rubik's cube is hard even for those who know it well.

These puzzles represent in microcosm some of of things that human intelligence is capable of. Usually solved by "taking thought"they are simple and yet complex enough to pose real difficulties. They thus provide us with a collection of problems on which we can try out our methods in a context that permits a more detailed analysis than is possible for larger problems. The methods which we shall discuss are referred to as weak methods, to distinguish then from those that use domain knowledge. They rely extensively upon ideas that reduce search to manageable proportions.

Many workers in Artificial Intelligence have objected that these kinds of problems are too simple-minded to be of any real assistance in building so- called "real world AI systems". They claim that the weak methods built for these problems cannot scale up to the size of any viable system. While the practical side of all of us will sympathize with this viewpoint, we should not lose sight of the value of sound theoretical underpinnings for what we do. The study of weak methods applied to "toy" problems is valuable because it provides the kind of closed domain needed for theoretical studies. In part this chapter tries to provide a theory based overview of heuristic generation methods as a basis for comparison of the various methods. With this in mind we begin with a discussion of a what we can call the "classical approach" to to problem solving.

1.2   Decomposition and GPS

To set the scene for our discussion of the automatic generation of heuristics we will describe first two very powerful ideas that in some way underlie most problem solving methodologies. The discussion will be somewhat informal. Formal definitions will be postponed until Section 2.

One of the most powerful ideas in computer science is that of decomposition. Modern software engineering principles teach us that large programs should be broken up into small units. Problem solving uses the same strategy. The solution to a complex problem can often be broken up into a sequence of solutions to simpler problems. Many of the heuristics of problem solving work because they generate such a decomposition. By the same token much of what makes problem solving an interesting area of research is the unfortunate fact that large numbers of interesting problems cannot be decomposed easily, if at all.

To describe decomposition a little more formally, and to enable us to discuss General Problem Solver (GPS, [26]). We will adopt the following semi-formal definition of a problem.

Definition 1.1 *A problem is a triple (I, M, G). Where I is a set of predicates which define the initial state of the problem. M is a set of operators that modify the state of the problem. G is a set of predicates which define the goal of the problem.*

A solution to a problem then consists in applying a sequence of operators from M which have the effect of making the predicates of G true. Suppose that the goal predicates have the form $G = A \wedge B$ then we can decompose the problem into the pair of problems (I,M,A) and (A,M,$A \wedge B$). If we can solve each of these problems then we can solve the original problem. In order for this decomposition to present an advantage we would want in some way to know that the two component problems are really simpler.

As examples of what we might mean by simpler we could for example ask that the set M of operators can be reduced for each component problem or that in one or both components some of the state variables can be ignored. Let us illustrate each of these possibilities with a simple example.

3	2	1	4
5	6		15
9	10	12	11
13	14	8	7

A Fifteen Puzzle Position

The above diagram shows a position in the well known fifteen puzzle. The object of the puzzle is to rearrange the tiles so that they appear in ascending order from the top left to the bottom right with the blank in the bottom right hand corner. The operators available for changing the state consist of sliding a tile into the blank slot.

One way in which the problem can be decomposed into two problems is illustrated by the diagram below which represents the final state for the first problem and the initial state for the second problem. In the terms of our definition of decomposition the diagram represents a state satisfying the predicate A. The asterisks indicate that the precise value of the tile in that location is irrelevant.

1	2	3	4
5	6	7	8
	*	*	*
*	*	*	*

Fifteen Puzzle Decomposition

In this case for the second problem we do not need to take into account any of the part of the puzzle appearing above the middle line. So that the second component is indeed simpler than the original puzzle. The first component is also simpler since the precise location of the tiles in the lower half is not specified. Here we have a case in which the states that need to be examined are reduced in each component. The operators for each component are the same as in the original[1].

For an example in which the number of operators is reduced we can take the example of the Towers of Hanoi.

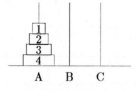

Towers of Hanoi

The problem is to move all the discs to pin C by moving individual discs between pins, but without ever placing a disc upon a smaller disc. We can decompose this problem into a pair of problems by choosing as intermediate position one in which

---

[1]At least in terms of the description that we have given, for a different problem description the operators might well be fewer for each component.

disc 4 is on pin C. In the second component of the problem we can then ignore the
moves that affect disc 4 as it does not need to be moved any more.

Given the desirability of decomposing problems one can then consider problem
solving from the view point that what one wants to do is find a suitable decomposition
of any given problem. Indeed this is so basic a principle that it is worth displaying it.

Heuristic 1.2 *Given any problem, try to decompose it into a collection of "simpler"
problems.*

As we saw in the two examples above the decomposition involves setting intermediate goals. We turn next to what is perhaps the most influential problem solving
paradigm. Our description follows that of [7] with some modifications.

General Problem Solver (GPS) [26] uses a technique called *means-end analysis.*
Given a problem state to work on it compares this state with the goal state. The
result of this comparison is to produce a set of "differences" between the current state
and the goal state. GPS then tries to reduce these differences. To see how this works
let us represent the states in the Towers of Hanoi puzzle pictured above by a list
of lists. Each component list represents the discs stacked on the corresponding pin.
Thus the initial configuration is represented by the list ((1 2 3 4) () ()) the goal state
is (() () (1 2 3 4)). The comparison step produces four differences.

- Disc 1 is on A, not C.

- Disc 2 is on A, not C.

- Disc 3 is on A, not C.

- Disc 4 is on A, not C.

The system then chooses a difference to reduce. Note that as we specify a difference
to reduce we specify an intermediate stage in the solution and thus a decomposition
of the problem. In order to make this choice we need to be more specific about the
operators. For GPS an operator has three parts

- Preconditions

- Transformation function

- Differences reduced

The preconditions are a list of conditions under which the operator is applicable.
The transformation function describes the effect of the operator and the differences
reduced is a list of those differences that the operator is good for reducing. It is
convenient to represent the information carried by this third part by means of a table
called the "connection table". If D is the set of possible differences and M is the set
of operators for the problem then the connection table is the subset $\Gamma \subset D \times M$ of
pairs (d, m) such that the operator m affects the difference d.

Returning to the preconditions we can now describe how GPS selects the difference
to be reduced. For each difference between the current state and the goal state we
can list the operators that reduce the difference:

- Move disc 1 to pin C.

- Move disc 2 to pin C.

- Move disc 3 to pin C.

- Move disc 4 to pin C.

Note that to solve the problem we will need to achieve the effect of every one of these operators. We list the preconditions for each of these operators.

Move	Preconditions
Move disc 1 to pin C.	None
Move disc 2 to pin C.	Disc 1 is on pin B
Move disc 3 to pin C.	Disc 1 and disc 2 are on pin B
Move disc 4 to pin C.	Disc 1, disc 2 and disc 3 are on pin B

The move with the largest number of preconditions, which we can reasonably call the most difficult difference, is then selected for reduction. It is at this point that GPS goes beyond simple problem decomposition. GPS now selects as a subgoal the goal of making the preconditions of "Move disc 4 to pin C" true. Moreover the moves that will be used to do this are to be only those applicable to the differences between the current state and this subgoal. GPS therefor decomposes the 4 disc Towers of Hanoi into the following sequence of subproblems.

1. Move discs 1,2 and 3 to pin B using only operators applied to these discs.

2. Move disc 4 to pin C.

3. Move discs 1,2 and 3 to pin C using only operators applied to these discs.

In general the aim of GPS is to order the differences so that as the differences are successively reduced the operators that are used become fewer. In particular once a difference has been reduced in its place in the ordering no operator that affects it should be applied again.[2] This is something that can be quite nicely captured in the connection table. It requires that when exhibited as matrix the table have a triangular form.

We can reformulate GPS in a more formal way as follows:

1. List the differences $D_1, \ldots, D_n$ between the initial state and the goal state.

2. Order the differences according to the number of preconditions for applying the operators that reduce them. Placing the most difficult first. (Assume that we renumber the differences at the same time.)

---

[2]The difference could be reduced earlier during the reduction of a difference placed earlier in the order but it may be necessary to unreduce the difference again.

3. The kth intermediate problem is then the reduction of the k most difficult differences, $D_1, \ldots, D_k$. The operators to be used are those that apply to the differences $D_k, \ldots, D_n$. (Since in the initial state for this problem the differences $D_1, \ldots, D_{k-1}$ will have been reduced we must not use the operators that affect those differences.)

A connection table for such a problem would thus appear as below.

Operator\Difference	D_1	D_2	D_3	D_4
m_1	1			
m_2	1	1		
m_3	1	1	1	
m_4	1	1	1	1

A triangular connection table.

For a particular problem some of the 1's below the diagonal could be zeros or the value could be state dependent, in this case the 1 should be replaced by a '?'.

It is important to note that the order of the columns in the connection table is determined by the ordering of the differences chosen at step 1. The ordering of the rows is chosen when trying to make the table triangular.

GPS serves as a paradigm for automatic problem solvers. We shall see a heavy reliance on differences and difference ordering as we describe the various problem solving heuristics. We take the view that most problem solving heuristics work by trying to find a suitable decomposition of the problem. Decomposition is at the heart of most problem solving methodologies. Our approach is to describe a general framework in which existing problem solvers can be seen from a common perspective.

1.3   Structure of the Chapter

In the next section we give a number of formal definitions that will be used in the rest of the chapter. We also describe a basic taxonomy of heuristics for problem solving. These are discussed in more detail in section 3. This section includes an exposition of Jean-Louis Lauriere's problem solving system [22] which is of interest because it is quite distinct in flavour from more traditional methods based upon GPS.

In section 4 we discuss how the heuristics can be used in combination. As examples we describe Korf's macro learning problem solver [18] and recent work by H.A. Guvenir on problem decomposition [11].

Section 5 discusses problem solving systems which use information gathered during their operation to improve their performance. In section 6 we discuss problem solvers based upon production systems. In particular we descibe **Soar** [21].

Section 7 considers questions of efficiency. We prove a result on the overhead required for learning by problem solving programs such as Korf's and Guvenir's which generate solutions that apply to generic examples of a problem.

The final section contains some concluding remarks.

2   Formal Definitions

In this section we describe the three structural heuristics of problem solving. Choice of one of these structural heuristics leads to an associated solution process for the problem. In each case the approach to solving the problem is quite different, so these three heuristics serve in part to classify problem solving techniques.

The three heuristics are relaxation, restriction, and abstraction[3] These three provide basic tools for problem solving strategies. We give informal descriptions first followed by a more formal framework.. We conclude the section with some general remarks on implementations of the methods. Detailed discussions of implementations and the implementation heuristics will be the subject of the later sections of the chapter. Informally we can describe the heuristics as follows.

A relaxation heuristic attempts to solve the problem by embedding it in a larger problem. Examples of this are the balloon heuristic in Gries [10] and the A^* [28] algorithm which will be discussed later in subsection 3.1.2. There is a sense in which GPS [26] can be regarded as being a relaxation heuristic, in that initially the interplay between the process of reduction of different goals is ignored. The simpler problem of describing the difference between the current state and the goal state is solved first.

A restriction heuristic is in some sense the opposite of a relaxation heuristic in that one tries to solve the problem by restricting the search space in some way. Examples of this are depth first iterative deepening [16] in which the restriction involves restricting the length of move sequences. Each of Lauriere's separation principles [[22] section 3.1 p59] falls into this category since they are used to select additional restrictions on the search domain. Alpha-Beta pruning [13] is another example of a restriction strategy, a detailed discussion of the whole family of search algorithms based on it is to be found in Pearl's book [28].

The third heuristic is abstraction [9], [17], [27]. Abstraction involves identifying states that are different in ways currently to be considered unimportant. Abstraction methods are often heavily influenced by GPS because like GPS abstraction seeks to decompose a problem into simpler parts which can be strung together to obtain a solution.

We can illustrate the method of abstraction with an application to the route finding problem. Suppose that one is given a map of the United States and asked to find a route from Oakland, California to Montauk, New York. One initially abstracts the problem to the consideration of only the interstate highway system. To do this each point in the US must be associated with its closest point of entry to the interstate highway system. Since this is still a complex problem it can be further abstracted by ignoring those intersates that are local service roads leaving only the major inter-city roads. So for example the ring of interstates around Washington DC are shrunk to a single point representing Washington. This simpler graph is then traversed between the point corresponding to Oakland and the point representing Montauk. This last part of the problem can be solved by an application of A^*. This is an example of mixing heuristics to which we shall return later.

---

[3] Decomposition is discussed in subsection 2.3.

2.1   Definitions

In order to formalize this material we need to give some definitions.

Definition 2.1 *A free problem P is a triple (S, Ω, a) where a is a partial map*

$$a : S \times \Omega \to S.$$

The set S is called the state space of the problem and the set Ω is the move set of the problem. The map a represents the effect of the moves on the state space. The effect of a move u on the state s is to give the state $a(s, u)$. The element $a(s, u)$ fails to exist precisely when (s, u) is not in the domain of a; that is when u cannot be applied to the state s.

   We illustrate this definition with a pair of examples. Since we discussed them in section 1 we use the Fifteen Puzzle and the Towers of Hanoi.

Example 2.2 *In the Towers of Hanoi puzzle with four discs the state space consists (to follow our earlier description) of all lists of three ordered lists (L_1, L_2, L_3), such that the elements 1,2,3,and 4 appear on exactly one of the lists.*

   To illustrate the moves consider the move ω = "move disc 3 from pin A to pin C" this is represented by the partial map.

state	ω(state)
((3 4) (1 2) ())	*((4) (1 2) (3))*
((3) (1 2 4) ())	*(() (1 2 4) (3))*
((3) (1 2) (4))	*(() (1 2) (3 4))*

   It is worth noting that this representation stores the information that a large disc cannot be placed on a smaller one in the descriptions of the moves. The ordering of the elements of the list is a way of avoiding duplications.

Example 2.3 *In the case of the fifteen puzzle the state space is much larger. It can be defined as the set of all permutations of the sixteen symbols.*

$$1, 2, 3, 4, 5, 6, 7, 8, 9, 10, 11, 12, 13, 14, 15, blank$$

(Note that this includes pairs of configurations that cannot be transformed into one another.)

   The moves can be represented by four maps D(own), L(eft), R(ight), U(p) corresponding to the direction in which the blank moves.

Moves can be combined by using the associativity of map composition[4]. Thus the totality of ways of moving about the state space is given by strings formed from the alphabet Ω. A string Σ is *admissible* whenever it represents a composable sequence of moves. By abuse of notation we write $a(s, \Sigma)$ for the effect of applying Σ to s.

   This notion of free problem does not as yet address the fact that problems represent things that must be solved. To incorporate this we need another definition.

---

[4] Associativity works just as well for partial maps as for maps defined on the whole of the state space. The composition of two partial maps may of course have a smaller domain than the first map in the composition.

Definition 2.4 *A problem instance PI is a quintuple*

$$(S, \Omega, a, s_0, G)$$

where (S, Ω, a) is a free problem, s_0 is a state in S called the initial state and G is a subset of S called the goal set.

A solution (sequence) for a problem instance is an admissible string Σ on the alphabet Ω such that $a(s_0, \Sigma) \epsilon G$.

This definition corresponds to the one used by Niizuma and Kitahashi [27].

Having defined the notion of problem we must turn to the question of when two such things are to be regarded as equivalent. We present here a definition of a notion which we call *strong homomorphism*. We use the modifier strong because there is a weaker notion that is also useful which is not required at this stage in the development but will be needed later when we discuss the work of Niizuma and Kitahashi in section 4. We will usually omit the modifier strong when the context makes it clear what is meant.

Definition 2.5 *Given two problems $P_1 = (S_1, \Omega_1, a_1)$ and $P_2 = (S_2, \Omega_2, a_2)$, with a pair of maps $f : S_1 \to S_2$ and $g : \Omega_1 \to \Omega_2$ then the domain of a_1 is partitioned into two sets*

$$K(a_1) = \{(s, \omega) | f(a_1(s, \omega)) = f(s)\}$$

and

$$M(a_1) = Domain(a_1) \setminus K(a_1)$$

The pair (f,g) defines a strong homomorhism $F : P_1 \Rightarrow P_2$ provided the equation

$$f(a_1(s, u)) = a_2(f(s), g(u))$$

is satisfied on $M(a_1)$. $K(a_1)$ is called the kernel of F.

Note that the sets K and M are really defined relative to the map f. We will therefor refer also to K as the kernel of f. The notion extends to problem instances by requiring that the map of state spaces maps the initial state of the domain problem to that of the range problem and the goal state of the domain problem into the goal of the range problem.

The division of the domain of a into two subsets is motivated by a desire to avoid reformulation. It would seem more natural to require that the commutativity holds on the whole of the doamin of a. We can illustrate the point with an example. Let P_1 be the fifteen puzzle and let f be the map on the state space that is given by the values of the tiles in the lower half of the puzzle. Then the move D which moves a tile downwards will sometimes change the state space in the image and sometimes not but when it does change the state it will do so in a way that is consistent. The notion of weak homomorphism that will be introduced later avoids this problem but at the price of effectively renaming all the moves so that they are labelled by the state to which they are applied.(See subsection 4.2.2).

Note that we do not require that the existence of a move in the range problem implies that it comes from the domain problem.

Problem homomorphisms can be used to map complicated problems into simpler ones allowing us the possibility of representing problems in terms of a collection of simple problems. There is another notion used in the representation of a problem that it will be convenient for use to define at this point.

Definition 2.6 *Given a (free) problem $P = (S, \Omega, a)$ a feature for P is a map*

$$f : S \longrightarrow T(f)$$

where $T(f)$ is a finite set. A collection $\{f_1, \ldots, f_n\}$ of features is called discriminating *if the map*

$$\prod f_i : S \longrightarrow \prod T(f_i)$$

given by

$$\prod f_i(s) = (f_1(s), \ldots, f_n(s))$$

is injective. A set $\{f_1, \ldots, f_n\}$ of features is called adequate *for a goal G, if given any goal state g and any non goal state s there is a feature f_i from the set such that $f_i(g) \neq f_i(s)$.*

A discriminating set of features thus provides a complete description of the state space.

We now turn to the notion of (strong) isomorphism.

Definition 2.7 *Two problems P_1 and P_2 are* strongly isomorphic *if there exists a pair of mutually inverse strong homomorphisms $F : P_1 \Rightarrow P_2$ and $H : P_2 \Rightarrow P_1$ between them.*

In other words if F is the pair of maps (f, g) and H is the pair (h, k) then we require that the compositions $f.h$, $h.f$, $g.k$ and $k.g$ are all identity maps. In particular this means that for every move in P_1 there is a corresponding move in P_2 and vice-versa.

We can use 1-1 homomorphisms in a natural way to define subproblems.

Definition 2.8 *Let $P = (S, \Omega, a)$ be a problem. A problem $P_0 = (S_0, \Omega_0, a_0)$ is a* (strong) subproblem *of P if there exists a problem homomorphism $(f, g) = F : P_0 \Rightarrow P$ such that $f : S_0 \to S$ and $g : \Omega_0 \to \Omega$ are monomorphisms.*

If Ω_0 is empty or just the identity the subproblem is called trivial.

A definition closely related to that of subproblem is that of problem extension. This will form the basis of the relaxation heuristic.

Definition 2.9 *A Problem Extension P^e of a problem P is given by a monomorphism $E : P \Rightarrow P^e$.*

An extension is just the opposite of a subproblem (which we could call a restriction). However there is a special kind of extension that we want to have which we will call an instance relaxation.

Definition 2.10 *An instance relaxation PI^r of a problem instance PI is a (strong) monomorphism $R : PI \Rightarrow PI^r$.*

An interesting (and important) example of an instance relaxation is one where the underlying map is the identity and the goal space is enlarged. This is the case in the balloon heuristic [10].

We next give the definition which is the underlying notion for the abstraction heuristic. Usually a quotient problem is defined by giving a description of how one goes about finding one, as for example in [27] or [14]. It is sufficient for us to give a definition in terms of the existence of an onto homomorphism from the given problem onto the quotient problem.

Definition 2.11 *A* Quotient Problem $P/R = (S/R, \Omega/R, a/R)$ *of a problem P is given by an epimorphism $\pi : P \to P/R$, thus the maps $S \to S/R$ and $\Omega \to \Omega/R$ which are induced by π are both onto.*

We use the notation P/R for the quotient problem to retain the idea that a quotient problem is associated with some kind of equivalence relation on the state space. This equivalence relation corresponds to the more usual notion of abstraction, in which inessential or less important aspects of the problem are ignored.

2.2   The Heuristics

We now describe the basic classification of the heuristics. We begin by giving what we call the pure heuristics. Each will be illustrated with a simple example based upon the problem of finding a path between two points in a graph. The rest of the chapter is devoted to a more detailed survey of the heuristics as they appear in the literature. This will involve a dicussion of how the basic heuristics can be combined to make more sophisticated heuristics. In addition we will develop a theory of how one can, in general, develop heuristcs for solving a particular problem.

The basic heuristics are the *relaxation* heuristic, the *restriction* heuristic and the *abstraction* heuristic. We give somewhat formal definitions. The definitions will be given in terms of problems rather than problem instances. Since it is instances that one solves this requires a brief justification. In part we justify this by the assertion that dealing with problems is cleaner than dealing with instances. The main reason is that we want to be able to talk about subproblems, where the start and goal may not map to the original start and goal. If we stick to instances this is impossible.

Heuristic 2.12 *A* Relaxation Heuristic *for solving a problem P consists of the following steps*

1. *Choose a problem extension $P \Rightarrow P^e$.*

2. *Solve the extension P^e.*

3. *Use the solution of P^e as a guide for solving P.*

This heuristic is sometimes called the "balloon heuristic" [10] because one allows the search space to balloon out and then lets the air out of the balloon to shrink the search space to the original. Each step of the heuristic requires some work, although it is usual to choose the extension in such a way that at least step 2 is easily solved. As an example we return to the problem of route finding in the traversal of a road map of the United States.

Example 2.13 *The problem space S can be taken to be a set of locations in the USA. The move set consists of the roads joining pairs of locations. (We do not want at the moment to consider the concatenation of two roads, say Washington-Baltimore and Baltimore-Wilmington as being a move Washington-Wilmington). The extended problem has the same problem space, but the move set consists of all (great circle!) lines joining each pair of locations in S as well as the original roads.*

This extended problem can be solved trivially, since for each instance of the original problem we have provided a solution, namely the great circle route. The main work is required to squeeze down the solution. This can be done by iteratively extending the current partial solution the road that is closest in direction to the solution to the remainder of the problem provided by the extended problem.

This is a case where we do want to make explicit that we can apply the idea to a problem instance as well. Specifically we have:

Heuristic 2.14 *A* Relaxation Heuristic *for solving a problem instance PI consists of the following steps.*

1. *Choose a problem instance relaxation $PI \Rightarrow PI^r$.*

2. *Solve the relaxed instance.*

3. *Use the solution of PI^r as a guide to find a solution of PI.*

This heuristic allows one the methodology of expanding the goal. This can be done by discarding some of the conditions that specify the goal. We shall see later that Lauriere's problem solver provides an example of this [22].

We turn next to the heuristic associated to reducing the search space.

Heuristic 2.15 *A* Restriction Heuristic *for solving a problem P is given by*

1. *Choose a subproblem P_0 of P.*

2. *Solve P_0.*

The subproblem should, of course have the same start and goal as the problem instance which is required to be solved.

Example 2.16 *This heuristic is sometimes called pruned search. As an example consider once again the route finding problem. If we replace the graph by a minimal spanning tree we have a subproblem whose solution is trivial, which provides a solution to the original problem.*

Note that in this case the generation of the subproblem requires the major effort, whereas in the case of the relaxation heuristic it was the squeezing down of the solution that takes the work.

It may seem in some cases that the relaxation heuristic and the restriction heuristic are not distinct techniques. Indeed since they are in some sense dual to one another it may sometimes be unclear which heuristic type one is dealing with. However there is an easy criterion that can be used to determine whether one is using a restriction heuristic or a relaxation one, which is the following. Each heuristic replaces the current problem by another problem whose solution is in some sense trivial. If the problem whose solution is trivial is a subproblem of the original problem then one has a restriction heuristic. If it is an extension then one has a relaxation heuristic.

The final heuristic type which we define is abstraction. This heuristic provides a basis for many of the methods that work by problem decomposition.

Heuristic 2.17 *An* Abstraction Heuristic *for the solution of a problem P is given by*

1. *Choose a quotient problem P/R.*

2. *Solve the quotient problem.*

3. *Lift the solution of P/R to P.*

Example 2.18 *Returning once more to the route problem, we can identify each location to its nearest point on the interstate highway system, with a similar identification for the routes between location. (There may be some ambiguities in this process but they can easily be resolved).*

One then finds a route between the terminal points in this simpler map. The solution to the original problem requires one to adjoin routes from the start to the interstate system and from the interstate system to the end. This corresponds to lifting the solution to the original problem.

Each of these heuristics is actually used in practice. Although they are most often combined in some way. The power of weak problem solving techniques derives precisely from the ability to combine and refine these heuristics.

2.3 Decomposition

Problem decomposition is often cited as a heuristic for problem solving. In our discussion we take a view that somewhat distinguishes decomposition from the other methods (which is why we have not listed it as one of the three structural heuristics). To draw an analogy with programming languages we see decomposition (or rather the putting together of the solutions to the components) as being comparable to the sequencing of statements. The three structural heuristics are comparable to the major control structures of a language.

Thus it will be the case that most problem solving techniques will involve decomposition at some stage. The nature of the decomposition (and indeed in many cases the decomposition itself) will be determined by the choice of structural heuristic. Abstraction heuristics often lead to decompositions of the problem. In [27] Niizuma and Kitahashi use abstraction to provide a decomposition. In [9] Ernst and Goldstein also use abstraction method to decompose Fool's Disc. GPS [26] , originally designed to model human problem solving, uses relaxation-restriction methods to decompose a problem into solvable pieces.

In a sense, as we indicated in section 1, we see decomposition as a more fundamental technique than the three structural heuristics to which we have referred. Just as sequencing is a fundamental construct in programming languages, which allows one to put together the other structures to obtain large programs, so decomposition is fundamental . Because of this viewpoint decomposition will appear throughout the chapter as a primary technique for combining the heuristics and as the basic method for combining solutions.

3   Search Reduction Techniques Without Decomposition

This section will discuss the use of the heuristics in unmixed form. We will describe a number of search algorithms that are used in AI applications. The most important of these are the A^* algorithm and depth-first iterative deepening.

The section will begin with more detailed descriptions of the use of relaxation and restriction heuristics in pure form. By contrast the abstraction heuristic does not seem to occur in pure form except as a strategy generating heuristic (it is in fact, as we remarked earlier, the driving heuristic behind many methods of finding decompositions.) The general discussion will be followed by a number of concrete examples.

In general relaxation heuristics provide either a function h for the A^* algorithm or they provide a strategy for ordering the goals. In this second case they are not of themselves powerful enough to solve the problem.

Restriction heuristics procede by trying to solve the problem by either restricting the state space directly or by restricting the move set. Typically a feature of the state is constrained to have a particular value in order to see whether a solution can be obtained without altering the value of this feature. In human problem solving this kind of heuristic is often used to try and avoid using "moves" that are difficult to execute, expensive or in some way distasteful. Here again the heuristic does not often work in pure form but must be combined with others.

The main part of this section will be devoted to an exposition of one of the most sophisticated problem solvers which uses a heuristic in more or less pure form. This is the work of Jean-Louis Lauriere [22]. We shall see this as a powerful example of a relaxation heuristic. An interesting aspect of Lauriere's methodology is that for many of the problems that it solves it provides solutions that differ quite radically in approach from those given by other problem solvers.

3.1   Search strategies

The most naive approach to problem solving is to use a straightforward search. In general this runs afoul of the combinatorial explosion and therefor one has heuristics to try and reduce the search. Let us review how the three heuristics modify search strategies.

3.1.1   Restriction Searches

A restriction search is one in which the search only takes place within a subproblem. We have already seen the example of the spanning tree as a subproblem of a graph used for the traversal problem. We can give some other examples here.

One of the more powerful problem solvers to appear recently is Korf's method of macro-generation [18]. While this is not a pure example of the restriction heuristic it makes very strong use of a restriction heuristic in its search for macros. Korf's search algorithm makes use of the fact that he is looking for macros that fix the values of a set of features and that set the value of one more feature. Therefor rather than look at arbitrary compositions of move sequences he restricts himself to composing elements from a list of moves sequences that fixes those features that he wants left invariant.

Korf's problem solver can be seen as a restriction method because the goal is to provide a small set of macros which can then be used to solve any instance of the problem. As he looks for macros that leave more and more features invariant Korf restricts the collection of moves used to construct these macros. He is thus able to reduce the search sufficiently.

The result of Korf's procedure is a to provide a much restricted search space (which he calls a macro table) in which the search problem is easy. The work is required to find the macros. We will give a detailed description of the method in the next section.

Another example of a restriction search strategy is given in [15]. In this case a cube like puzzle is solved by only searching for macros with desirable properties amongst move sequences generated by a subset of the moves. This method works when the problem exhibits symmetry.

We can give a general description of a "restriction search" as follows.

Heuristic 3.1 *To perform a restriction search*

1. *Restrict in some way either the number of generators of admissible move sequences or the length of acceptable macros.*

2. *If step 1 fails increase the number of moves or depth of the search.*

As an example of this we describe depth first iterative deepening [17]. This a restriction heuristic for coping with the memory requirements of breadth first search. Korf [18] relies heavily on iterative deepening in his search for macros.

Algorithm 3.2 *To perform a depth-first iterative deepening search*

1. *Set depth D equal to 1.*

2. *Traverse the search tree depth first to depth D.*

3. *Set D to D + 1.*

4. *Goto 2.*

This provides a method of performing what is almost a breadth first search but without the concomitant overhead.

Greedy algorithms and hill-climbing provide other examples of restriction searches. They fall into this category because they reduce the search space by pruning the search tree. We can describe these searches, which we may call evaluation searches, in this context in the following way.

Heuristic 3.3 *An evaluation search*

1. *Put the state state on OPEN.*

2. *If OPEN is empty, exit with failure.*

3. *Remove from OPEN and place upon CLOSED a state s for which the evaluation function is "best" according to some evaluation function.*

4. *If s is a goal state exit with success.*

5. *Otherwise evaluate all states accessible from s placing the one with the "best" evaluation function upon OPEN.*

6. *Go to step 2*

By placing only the best state on the list of open nodes we prune the search. If we were to place all the successor states on the OPEN list we would permit back-tracking.

The formal deductive Problem-solving system of Quinlan and Hunt [30] uses an evaluation search. The system formalizes problem solving in the manner of a term rewriting system. That is a problem is presented as the search for a sequence of operators which will rewrite one structure into another. Before a choice of operator to apply is made a limited form of look-ahead is used to evaluate the desirability of applying the operator. Thus the search space is pruned by only following those branches which seem to be leading somewhere.

It is amusing to note that both Prim's algorithm and Kruskal's algorithm for finding minimum cost spanning trees are greedy algorithms. The results of which can be used (as has been noted earlier) for quickly finding paths between two points in a graph. So here we have a double application of a restriction heuristic.

3.1.2 Relaxation Searches and the A^* Algorithm

The principle behind a relaxation search is that embedding the problem in a larger one provides guidance for the search in the original problem. This heuristic has been analysed at some length by Judea Pearl [28] so our coverage is necessarily a duplication of his work.

The critical issue in the use of relaxation for search guidance is that the enlarged problem should admit a simple solution for all of its instances. We can summarize the approach in the following.

Heuristic 3.4 *To perform a relaxation search in a problem P.*

1. *Choose an extension of the problem P^e.*

2. *At each choice point in the search tree for P choose the branch that is in some sense "nearest" to the branch of the search tree for P^e which is on the solution path in P^e joining the current node to the goal node.*

The use of the vague word nearest in the description of the heuristic requires some comment. It is motivated by the example of the graph search given in the previous section but it also covers the A^*-algorithm. Since in this case the estimating function (which will be the cost of the solution of the extended problem) is used to choose the best next node. This is the one which minimizes the excess over the solution to the extended problem. In more detail [28] we suppose that we are seeking the minimum cost path between two nodes, s for start and G for goal, of a graph. The function g(n) represents the minimum cost (so far) for going from s to n. The function h(n) is the cost of going from n to G in the extended graph. Thus $f(n) = g(n) + h(n)$ is an estimate of the cost of the path from s to g via n. In detail we have:

Algorithm 3.5 The A^*-Algorithm

1. *Put the start node s on OPEN.*

2. *If OPEN is empty, exit with failure.*

3. *Remove from OPEN and place upon CLOSED a node n for which f is minimum.*

4. *If n is a goal node, exit successfully.*

5. *Otherwise expand n, generating all its successors. For every successor n' of n:*

   a. *If n' is not already on OPEN or CLOSED evaluate h(n') (the cost from n' to the goal node in the extended problem) and calculate $f(n') = g(n') + h(n')$ where g(n') is the cost of this route to n' from s.*

   b. *If n' is already on OPEN or CLOSED place it upon OPEN if the route to n' via n lowers g(n').*

6. *Go to Step 2*

There is a considerable resemblance between this algorithm and the earlier heuristic 3.3. Since we have distinguished between restriction and relaxation searches we should comment on this. The essential difference is that in the case of the algorithm described above the function h(n) comes from the solution to the extended problem and is thus global in nature. In the case of the earlier heuristic the evaluation function is more local. Thus in hill-climbing one moves in the direction of steepest ascent not along the line towards the summit: these two directions need not be the same!

One advantage that relaxation heuristics have is that it is often easy to generate the extended problem mechanically. This is because one can enlarge the problem by adding moves and/or states by removing some of the specifications for a legal move or state. We give an example.

Suppose that we represent the positions in the fifteen puzzle by a set of predicates position(tile, location). For convenience let us introduce a predicate differentPlace(tile1,tile2) which is specified by

$$differentPlace(tile1, tile2) \Leftrightarrow position(tile1, location1)$$

$$\wedge position(tile2, location2) \wedge location1 \neq location2.$$

We can then specify a legal state in the fifteen puzzle by the conjunction

$$differentPlace(1,2) \wedge differentPlace(1,3) \wedge \ldots \wedge differentPlace(15, blank).$$

The state space for the fifteen puzzle is then given by all (tile,location) pairs that represent legal states, where tile is one of 1, 2, 3, 4, 5, 6, 7, 8, 9, 10, 11, 12, 13, 14, 15, blank and position is one of 1, 2, 3, 4, 5, 6, 7, 8, 9, 10, 11, 12, 13, 14, 15, 16 (see diagram below).

1	2	3	4
5	6	7	8
9	10	11	12
13	14	15	16

Fifteen Puzzle: Location Names

If we now discard all the conditions for a legal state having to do with the predicate *differentPlace*, (leaving only those related to tile names and location names) we have an expanded problem. In this problem a tile can be moved horizontally or vertically without regard to whether the adjacent location is empty. This is then the relaxed problem for which solutions are trivial to find. It gives us an h function as the number of moves in the enlarged problem between the current state and the goal.

A final important example of a relaxation methodology is given by chunking [21]. In this case the search space is enlarged by the addition of chunks of knowledge about how to resolve certain sub-problems. Therefor a methodology that deliberately sets out to look for useful chunks, as for example in [14], provides another instance of relaxation.

3.1.3   Abstraction Searches

We have already given the example of the interstate highway system as an instance of an abstraction search. Since this is fairly typical we shall keep the further discussion of abstraction searches brief.

The clumping of sub-networks of a network into nodes is a standard technique for keeping the routing problem manageable in large networks. This is supported by the use of network addresses that facilitate the clumping. (This method is used by the phone service, perhaps the most familiar application of this technique).

A major distinction between abstraction searches and the earlier examples is the fact that the "simplified" problem is not usually one in which the problem becomes trivial. Rather it is one in which the problem is an order of magnitude smaller.

3.2   Lauriere's Problem Solver

In a paper [22] which deserves to be much more widely known Jean-Louis Lauriere describes a language and a program for stating and solving combinatorial problems. We will give a fairly detailed description of his method here. The over-arching heuristic which guides his approach is that of relaxation. His perspective is drawn from operations research so that a reader of his paper who is more familiar with conventional AI work may have some difficulty in relating it to the more usual approaches.

Lauriere's work deals with combinatorial problems which he defines as follows find in a discrete space, a particular point which satisfies a given family of conditions.

In describing the method he borrows the language of operations research, so that a problem is solved in three steps. This flow is diagrammed follows:

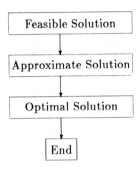

The feasible solution can be viewed as the solution to a relaxed problem, with the approximate solution as an intermediate step in the compression of the solution into the original problem.

The language in which Lauriere states his problems is called ALICE. The flavour of ALICE is perhaps best conveyed by giving a specific example of a problem statement in the language. We have chosen to present the fool's disk problem [2]. In this problem four concentric rings are divided into eight sectors each of which contains an integer. The rings are free to rotate about their common center. The problem is to rotate the discs so that the sum along each radius of the disc is 12. One reason for choosing this example is that Lauriere's problem solver provides a solution quite different in flavour from the one that appears in eg:disc. The ALICE description of Fool's disk is:

```
GIVEN   SET   D = INT      1    4           discs
              Q = INT      1    8           octants
        MAT   V ↪ PDT      D    Q Q         octants' values
FIND    FUN   ROT >--> D   Q                rotation
WITH    ∀     J ∈ Q        (    Σ I ∈       D ( V (
        I     1 + (        J    - ROT I     - 1 ) MOD
        8     ) ) = 12)
        ROT   1 = 8
END
```

```
2,1,3,4,2,5,1,3
3,2,3,4,1,3,4,5
3,4,5,3,3,2,2,1
5,1,5,3,4,3,2,4
```

As can be seen the problem statement is in four parts. The first three parts are introduced by the key words, GIVEN, FIND, and WITH. The last part occurs after the key word END. The GIVEN part declares the variable and constants. The FIND part specifies what is to be found in terms of the variables and constants from the GIVEN part and a number of language primitives of which FUN (function) is one. The WITH part specifies the constraints that must be satisfied. The section following the END specifies the initial condition. ALICE possesses a rich dictionary that allows it to handle a very diverse set of problems.

Besides this algebraic representation of the problem ALICE also uses a bipartite graphical scheme to represent information about the problem and the current state of the search. This is used because Lauriere interprets a problem in terms of finding a mapping of some kind (more generally a relation). The two types of nodes in the graph correspond to the domain and range respectively. So that the desired mapping then becomes a graph.

ALICE works by trying to satisfy the WITH conditions in some order. (There are several heuristics for ordering these constraints which we will discuss shortly). Thus ALICE uses a relaxation approach, specifically one of instance relaxation in which the goal is enlarged. For example if a (1-1) function between two sets A and B is wanted , the initial bi-partite graph will consist of the sets A and B in which every node in A is joined to every node in B, representing the fact that a priori any element of B could be an image of a given point in A. As the search progresses arcs will be removed from the graph until a graph representing a (1-1) function is obtained.

If we return to the diagram we gave at the beginning of the discussion the feasible solution corresponds to the solution to the extended problem. In many cases the approximate solution is good enough because we are not required to optimize.

Let us now turn to the heuristics that ALICE uses to choose the order in which it attempts to satisfy the constraints. Constraints are ordered by complexity, beginning with the simplest one. (There is a specific algorithm for determining the complexity of a constraint, which works by assigning weights to the symbols and variables that appear in the constraint.) The constraints are then subjected to a reasoning process in this order.

This process has as its goal the simplification and reduction in number of the constraints.For example given the pair of constraints

$$x_2 \geq 0, 0 \leq -4 - x_2 + x_1$$

the system will derive that x_1 must be equal to at least 4.

Having manipulated the constraints ALICE then attempts to satisfy them. This is the process of squeezing the solution to the extended problem down into a solution to the original problem. Constraints are satisfied, using a specific set of rules, in order of increasing complexity. This is based upon a heuristic that seems to be sufficiently prevalent that it is worth stating explicitly.

Heuristic 3.6 Principle of Deniability *When faced with a choice, make the choice that least restricts your future actions.*

As an example let us return to the case of Fool's disc and follow the ALICE solution. We quote from p 84 of [22].

At the time of the first choice, the program considers the constraint which has the largest second member. Taking the seventh one, as $v(1,7) = 1$, it searches the largest possible value for $(v(2,1) + (ROT(2))_{mod8})$ which gives $ROT(2) = 7$; then the choice $ROT(3) = 6$ implies $ROT(4) = 8$ but does not fit. $ROT(3) = 7$ implies $ROT(4) = 4$ and a solution is given.

One of the more interesting things about this method of finding the solution to fool's disc is that is quite different form the solution given elsewhere, for example in [2], which we will describe in section 4. The more conventional solution works by first moving the disks so that the sum on each pair of orthogonal diagonals is 48. This can be done using rotations through only 45 degrees. Then the sums on each diagonal are reduced to 24, using rotations through 90 degrees. The solution is then obtained by rotations through 180 degrees.

Lauriere applies his problem solver to a large number of other problems. A few of which we list here: The Eight Queens problem, Missionaries and Cannibals, Instant Insanity, the Travelling Salesman, graph colouring, resource allocation, scheduling and truck dispatching.

In closing our dissussion of Lauriere's work we reproduce two examples of what he calls meta-heuristics. They are closely related to the principle of deniability given above and serve as useful guides in the construction of heuristic problem solvers.

Heuristic 3.7 *When making choices*

1. *Make the most informative choice.*

2. *Make the least expensive choice.*

4   Programmed Generation of Strategies

In this section we will cover the methods that use combinations of the heuristics. The simplest examples of such mixed techniques are obtained by mixing the relaxation and restriction techniques. For example iterative deepening can be regarded as a combination of restriction followed by progressive relaxation. We will look at some other combinations in more detail here. It should be observed that the relaxation-restriction combinations are really fairly simple combination techniques. The interesting cases arise in the case where one of the heuristics is abstraction, which we regard as the primary problem decomposition technique.

4.1   Relaxation-Restriction Methods

These are methods that use relaxation to determine the overall strategy and follow it with restriction to solve the intermediate goals. In these cases the restrictions are to those moves that do not disturb already established goals. We can consider GPS [4] as an example of this.

Since we are now entering the realm of problem decomposition we will require some additional definitions to fix our terms. We begin by repeating a definition from section 2.

Definition 4.1 *Given a problem* $P = (S, \Omega, a)$ *a feature for P is a function* $f : S \rightarrow T(f)$, *where* $T(f)$ *is a finite set.*

The more familiar *difference* is simply the complement of an equivalence relation. Thus given a feature f, there is an associated difference D_f given by the equation

$$x D_f y \Leftrightarrow f(x) \neq f(y)$$

It is important to know when one has enough features to describe a problem.

Definition 4.2 *Given a problem* $P = (S, \Omega, a)$ *and a set* $\{f_i\}$ *of features for P. The set of features is called* discriminating *if given any two points* $x, y \in S$, *there is some feature* $j \in I$ *such that* $f_j(x) \neq f_j(y)$. *A set of differences is* discriminating *if the associated features are.*

For certain very simple kind of problems the differences do not interfere with one another. We can state this formally as follows.

Definition 4.3 *A problem P with discriminating difference set* $\{D_i\}$ *is said to be* totally decomposed *if there exist moves* $\{\omega_i\}$ *such that each* ω_i *reduces* D_i *without affecting any difference* D_j *for* $j \neq i$ *which is logically independent of* D_i.

We can always formally relax a problem with a discriminating set of differences to a totally decomposed one by adjoining moves designed to reduce the differences. For our purposes we do not need even to be able to specify the moves precisely, (as we shall see in the case of fool's disc this would amount to solving the problem) it is enough to hypothesize their existence.

As we saw in section 1 in GPS a problem is posed in terms of requiring that a set of differences be reduced. A relaxed problem is obtained by assuming that the differences can be reduced independantly. For example in the Towers of Hanoi problem one could relax the preconditions on the moves and assume that a disk can be moved directly to its destination pin.

The reason why this is not a pure relaxation heuristic is that once the goals have been ordered, which is of course crucial in making GPS work, one restricts oneself to moves that do not disturb the differences that have already been reduced.

We can give a high level description of the technique as follows.

Algorithm 4.4 *Given a problem. P*

1. *Relax P to* P^e *a totally decomposed problem which can be solved.*

2. *Order the states along the solution path for* P^e *as successive goals for restricted problems in P.*

3. *Solve each of the restricted problems.*

To illustrate the method we can refer to the four disk Tower of Hanoi Puzzle once more. We obtain a problem extension P^e by assuming that a disk can always be moved from its current pin to any other pin. This relaxed puzzle is then solved in four moves.

1. Move disc four to pin C.

2. Move disc three to pin C.

3. Move disc two to pin C.

4. Move disc one to pin C.

The intermediate problems are then the problems of making the preconditions for each step in the above list possible.

The essential new idea that makes GPS not just a relaxation heuristic is the restriction of the moves in each intermediate problem to those that do not disturb what has already been fixed up. The work involved in applying GPS comes in steps 2 and 3 of the above outline[5]. Step 2 is critical and is achieved (where GPS is successful) by the construction of the connection table, which should be triangular if GPS is to succeed. The connection table then provides the move sets for the restricted problems.

One can, of course, intercalate relaxation and restriction as often as is necessary. For example if Fool's disk is presented in the form in which only moves through 45 degrees are defined as the basic moves, and the differences to be reduced are defined as

D_1 = the sum along a pair of orthogonal diameters,

D_2 = the set of sums along the diameters,

D_3 = the set of sums along the radii.

then the second and third problems have no moves, so one must relax them by taking move sequences instead of moves.

4.1.1   Problem Decomposition Using Invariants

One notable example of problem decompsition is that found in [9]. Here it is shown how one can automatically generate subproblems by searching for invariants. This technique was used to automatically generate the differences given above for Fool's disk. The method has been considerably extended by Guvenir [11] and will be discussed in detail later. First we discuss a method based on the assumption that the differences are already in place.

4.1.2   Macro Generation and Serial Decomposability

In [18] Korf describes a problem solving technique that works by generating macro-operators. We can regard this as being a version of a relaxation-restriction heuristic if we take the view that the differences that have to be reduced as first regarded as independant. This relaxed version of the problem allows us to specify the set of macros that need to be learned in order to solve the problem. The learning of the macros is the restriction part. We will now describe Korf's work in more detail.

---

[5]There may also be some work in finding the differences. For the moment we ignore this problem, treating the differences as a given of the problem.

Korf uses a "state vector" representation of a problem. A point in the state space is accordingly represented by the values of a set of vectors. So to represent the states in Rubik's cube the variables are the cubies and their values encode both their position and orientation. In the language of features there is a feature for each cubie, and the values of each feature correspond to the location and orientation of the cubie. Features and state vectors are dual concepts (much as coordinate values and coordinate functions are), there is no difference in their informational content. A state vector is given by evaluating a set of features, the features are recoverable by taking specific coordinates of the state vector.

For a macro problem solver a solution to a problem comes in the form of a macro table. We reproduce here the macro table for the eight- puzzle. Note that in spite of a superficial similarity this is not the same as the connection table of GPS. In GPS the connection table specifies the moves relevant to removing a difference, there is no guarantee that they are applicable. In the macro table provided earlier differences have been reduced, the macro table provides a move sequence which will reduce the difference. The macro table thus encapsulates a solution to the problem whereas the connection table merely provides the moves to be used in seeking a solution.

TILES

	0	1	2	3	4	5	6
0							
1	UL						
2	U	RDLU					
3	UR	DLURRDLU	DLUR				
4	R	LDRURDLU	LDRU	RDLLURDRUL			
5	DR	ULDRURDLDRUL	LURDLDRU	LDRULURDDLUR	LURD		
6	D	URDLDRUL	ULDDRU	URDDLULDRRUL	ULDR	RDLLUURDLDRRUL	
7	DL	RULDDRUL	DRUULDRDLU	RULDRDLULDRRUL	URDLULDR	ULDRURDLLURD	URDL
8	L	DRUL	RULLDDRU	RDLULDRRUL	RULLDR	ULDRRULLDLURD	RULD

The primitive moves are represented by their first letter – Right, Left, Up, Down – giving the direction in which a tile is moved. The columns of the table correspond to the state variables of the problem. Each column contains the macro necessary to map its corresponding state variable to its goal value from a given position without disturbing the values of the state values that precede it in the solution order. The rows of the macro table correspond to the different possible values of the state variables. Thus by applying the appropriate sequence of macros any instance of the problem can be solved.

The two main issues that need to be discussed in the context of the macro- problem solver are thus the learning of macros and the question of when the method works. We review the learning of macros first. For this we assume that the order in which the differences are to be reduced has already been determined.

The basic strategy for discovering macros is depth-first iterative deepening [18]. This search strategy (recall 3.2)is a compromise between depth-first search and breadth first search, in which a tree is searched depth first, initially to depth one, then to depth two, etc.. Search begins by applying the move sequences to the final position. As each stage of the search is carried out the macros that are discovered are entered into the macro table. There is a difficulty with this brute force approach to macro generation in that one cannot simply run the program until all the locations in the macro table are filled, since it can happen that certain locations will never be filled (these correspond to impossible instances of the problem).

The brute force method is sufficient for The Towers of Hanoi, the Eight puzzle and Think-A-Dot. However for larger problems more sophisticated search methods are required. We have already mentioned that one can exploit the composition of macros with the same invariance to produce another macro of like invariance. This technique is fully exploited by Korf in [18]. The interested reader can find the details in sections 5.3 and 5.4 of his paper. We shall also see macro composition used in [11].

The other question addressed by Korf is that of the applicability of the technique to problems. Specifically which problems can be expected to yield to Korf's methods. There is a criterion for this, *serial decomposability*, which we now define.

Definition 4.5 *A solution order is a ordering of the state variables* $(s_1, \ldots, s_n)$ *of a state vector.*

Since each state variable corresponds to a feature we can also consider a solution order as an ordering of the features of the problem, or equivalently as a selection of the order in which the differences are to be reduced.

Definition 4.6 *A function f is* serially decomposable *with respect to a particular solution order iff there exists a set of vector functions f_i for $1 \leq i \leq n$, where each f_j is a function from V^j to V, and V^j is the set of i-ary vectors with components chosen from V, which satisfy the following condition:*

$$\forall s \epsilon S, f(s) = f(s_1, \ldots, s_n) = (f_1(s_1), f_2(s_1, s_2), \ldots, f_n(s_1, \ldots, s_n))$$

A macro is serially decomposable with respect to a solution order if each of the operators in it are.

Definition 4.7 *A problem is* serially decomposable *if there exists a solution order such that every move is serially decomposable with respect to it.*

In a serially decomposable problem there is some way of ordering the features of the problem so that the effect of a move on a feature depends only on the values of those features that precede it in the solution order. The significance of serial decomposability is in the following theorem.

Theorem 4.8 *If a problem is serially decomposable, then there is a macro table for it.*

This theorem provides a satisfying conclusion to Korf's work because it seems clear that it delimits effectively the domain of problems to which Korf's method applies.

4.2   Abstraction-Restriction-Relaxation Methods

In this section we give a framework that incorporates all three of the basic heuristics.
We will treat methods that mix abstraction and restriction as special cases of this
framework[6].

We have seen that abstraction methods seek to decompose the problem by ignoring
differences that are temporarily to be regarded as unimportant and dealing with them
later, restriction methods limit the moves that are to be used and relaxation methods
permit an increase in the number of moves that are used. The heuristic combination
that we will now describe is the most sophisticated combined methodology that we will
discuss. A high level description of an abstraction-restriction- relaxation algorithm
takes the following form.

Algorithm 4.9 *Given a problem P.*

1. *Choose an equivalence relation on P, giving a problem P/R.*

2. *Solve P/R, (Abstraction).*

3. *List the intermediate sub-problems P_i of P that need to be solved. (Restriction)*

4. *Solve each of the subproblems P_i using a relaxation method. (Relaxation)*

5. *Intercalate the solution of P/R with the solutions of the P_i to obtain a solution
   to P.*

We shall see that Refinement With Macros (RWM) [11] provides a good example
of this. RWM is a program that generates a strategy for solving a problem. The
strategy takes the form of a sequence of intermediate problems. The generation of
the strategy corresponds to steps 1 and 2 in algorithm 4.9. This is the refinement
portion of RWM. The macro portion corresponds to step 3.

Unlike GPS, RWM generates the intermediate problems in an adaptive manner,
rather than using a given set of differences. As the program progresses the strategy
is refined by introducing additional intermediate problems into the current strategy.
The refinement process is iterated using the current strategy as input. We do not
however regard RWM as a true adaptive problem solver since it does not learn new
moves, therefor we will discuss it here rather than in the next section.

4.2.1   Refinement with Macros

We will illustrate Guvenir's method of Refinement With Macros using the example
of the 2 x 2 x 2 Rubik's cube.

---

[6]The other methods could also have been treated this way, but they seem to have more independant
interest.

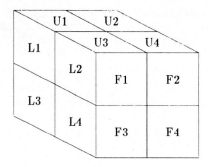

$2 \times 2 \times 2$ Rubik's Cube

In RWM the state space of a problem is defined using "atomic statements" which are binary predicates. The arguments to an atomic statement are constants or state components.

```
State Components are
        (F1 F2 F3 F4       ; Front Face
        L1 L2 L3 L4        ; Left Face
        R1 R2 R3 R4        ; Right Face
        U1 U2 U3 U4        ; Upper Face
        D1 D2 D3 D4        ; Down Face
        B1 B2 B3 B4 )      ; Back Face
```

In general an atomic statement asserts either the equality of two variables or the fact that a variable has a particular value. Thus a typical atomic statement for the cube problem is F1 = F2 where the equality is taken to mean that the colors of F1 and F2 are the same. The goal state can be expressed as a conjunction of such atomic statements, in the obvious way.

Each move is given as a triple (Move, Precondition, Effect). The effect of each move is specified in terms of the state variables. Continuing with our example we describe rotation of the front face through 90 degrees as follows

```
(oF  nil
    (F1 F2) (F2 F4) (F4 F3) (F3 F1)
    (L2 U4) (U4 R3) (R3 D1) (D1 L2)
    (L4 U3) (U3 R1) (R1 D2) (D2 L4))
```

The presence of a pair such as (F1 F2) in the description of the move's effect means that the face located at F1 moves to location F2.

RWM uses the following formalization of a problem.

Definition 4.10 *A problem is defined by a triple* $(I(s), M, G(s))$, *where I(s) is a statement that determines the initial position, M the set of moves and G(s) is the goal statement.*

The RWM method consists of two separate processes, which Guvenir calls *refinement* and *macro generation*. The refinement process corresponds to the abstraction-restriction part of the algorithm 4.9 and the macro generation is a use of relaxation to solve the restricted problems. We begin by describing how refinement works. We continue with the running example of the (2 x 2 x 2) Rubik's cube.

Refinement in RWM

Refinement is a procedure based upon four steps which will be described below. The object is to provide a sequence of intermediate problems forming a solution strategy. It is an iterative process. One pass through refinement (if sucessful) decomposes a problem $(I(s), M, G(s))$ into a pair of problems $(I(s), M_1, G_1(s))$ and $(G_1(s), M_2, G(s))$. In order to describe the method properly we need some definitions.

Definition 4.11 *A move m is* safe *over a statement Q(s) if when m is applied to a state s for which the statement Q(s) is true the resulting state m(s) also satisfies Q. Formally*

$$\forall s(Q(s) \Rightarrow Q(m(s)))$$

For example the move oFoF is safe over F1=F3.

Definition 4.12 *A move m is* irrelevant *to going from Q(s) to R(s) if m is safe over Q(s) and when applied to a state that satisfies Q(s) but not R(s) the resulting state m(s) will never satisfy R. Formally m is safe over* $Q(s) \wedge \neg R(s)$. *A move m is* relevant *to going from Q(s) to R(s) if it is safe over Q(s) and not irrelevant to going from Q(s) to R(s).*

For example oF is relevant to going from $R2 = R4$ to $R2 = R4 \wedge R1 = R2$.

With these definitions we can describe the process of refinement.

Step-1. The first step of the refinement process is to determine the relevant moves for going from the empty statement to each atomic statement of the goal. For example the moves relevant to the statement F1 = F2 are oF, oL, oU, and oR.

Step-2. At this step the atomic statements that have exactly the same set of relevant moves are grouped into one statement. This gives a pairing between sets of statements and sets of relevant moves.

Step-3. The goal $G_1(s)$ of the first subproblem will be the statement from the list of statements generated in step 2 with the largest number of safe moves over it. Therefore for each of the statements, the moves that are safe over that statement are determined. The moves that are safe over G_1 are the ones that will be used to solve the rest of the problem.

At this stage we have used two of the ideas that we mentioned earlier. Abstraction is used to lump together moves that are relevant to the same set of statements. (Two moves are "equivalent" if they are relevant to the same set of statements, or two sets of statements are equivalent if they have the same set of relevant moves.) Then we use the deniability principle to select one of these sets to define the goal by which we refine (or decompose) the problem. There is however one more detail to take care of: we need to know that we have a chance of solving the rest of the problem.

Step-4. To determine the adequacy of the moves that are safe over the goal G_1 chosen at step-3 we must check whether each of the atomic statements in the goal that are not part of the specification of this subproblem (that is in $G(s) \setminus G_1$) has at least one move relevant to it which is safe over the subproblem.

In the case of our 2 x 2 x 2 cube this first pass produces the subproblem. In which the moves listed are all the macro sequences relevant to solving the subproblem.

```
Goal:   (EQ L3 L4) (EQ D1 D3)
Moves:  (oF) (oFoF) (oUoF) (oFoFoF) (oRoFoF) (oRoFoFoF)
        (oUoFoF) (oUoUoF) (oFoRoFoFoF) (oFoFoRoFoFoF)
        (oRoRoFoF) (oUoUoUoF) (oRoUoUoF) (oUoFoUoFoF)
        (oFoUoFoUoUoF) (oFoFoUoFoUoUoF) (oRoUoFoUoUoF)
        (oUoUoFoF) (oUoUoFoFoUoFoF)
```

This refinement process continues on the rest of the problem until no more refinement is possible. That is to say one repeats the above four steps, except that the only moves that are used are those that are safe over the first subproblem.

It may well happen that this process of refinement alone fails to produce intermediate problems that are simple enough to solve. That is to say that the restriction portion of the heuristic leaves us with a problem that is too small to work with because it does not have enough moves. In this case we need to expand (relaxation) the subproblems in some way. This is where the process of macro generation comes in. We can describe this process as follows.

Macro Generation in RWM

Let I(s) be the statement that specifies the initial state of one of the intermediate problems. Let MS denote the set of all moves that are safe over I(s). Let M be the set of moves that are relevant to the goal G(s) of the problem, and let $MI = MS \setminus M$. Then we can form macros consisting of the compositions $MS \circ MS$ and $MI \circ MS$. These macros are added to the set of moves for the intermediate problem and fed into the refinement mechanism.

Guvernir gives details of the application of his method to several problems other than the 2 x 2 x 2 Rubik's cube puzzle. They are pyraminx, 3 x 3 x 2 domino, Trillion, the mod 3 puzzle, 3-disk Tower of Hanoi, Eight puzzle, Monkey and Bananas, Rubik's magic, and sorting.

The idea behind grouping together statements that have the same set of relevant moves is that such moves are likely to have a high degree of interaction. So that in trying to decompose the problem one does not want to split apart moves that interact strongly. Indeed the major challenge for abstraction problem solving techniques (as indeed for all these ideas) is coming up with the right equivalence relation. In this context Korf [18] cites a heuristic for decomposing a problem which is a version of our earlier deniability principle, namely: pick a set of state variables such that the freedom of the remaining variables is maximized. Clearly what is intended is that the decomposition should be into pieces that are as independant as possible. In any given case what is needed is a way of capturing this so that it can be exploited by the system.

Other problem solvers use only the first two steps of algorithm 4.9, we can call these abstraction-restriction problem solvers[7]. For example there is the work of Niizuma and Kitahashi [27]. Here the decomposition is based upon constructing the connection table for the problem, and then choosing a suitable set of differences to use for the abstraction. More accurately of course one is really selecting the features associated to the differences and using these to generate equivalence relations.

4.2.2   Problem Decomposition according to Niizuma and Kitahashi

To describe the approach of Niizuma and Kitahashi in more detail requires some definitions in addition to those we have already given. The most important of these is the notion of weak homomorphism.

Definition 4.13 *A weak homomorphism $F : P_1 \rightarrow P_2$ between two problems $P_1 = (S_1, \Omega_1, a_1)$ and $P_2 = (S_2, \Omega_2, a_2)$ is given by a pair of maps $f : S_1 \rightarrow S_2$ and $g : S_1 \times \Omega_1 \rightarrow \Omega_2$ such that if h is defined by the equation*

$$h(s, u) = (f(s), g(s, u))$$

the following diagram commutes:-

$$
\begin{array}{ccc}
a_1 : S_1 \times \Omega_1 & \longrightarrow & S_1 \\
\downarrow{h} & & \downarrow{f} \\
a_2 : S_2 \times \Omega_2 & \longrightarrow & S_2
\end{array}
$$

The commutativity of the diagram is to be taken in the sense that whenever the clockwise composition exists so does the counterclockwise one, and they are equal. We can write the commutativity condition as an equation thus:-

$$f(a_1(s, u)) = a_2(f(s), g(s, u))$$

Once again the right-hand side is to exist whenever the left hand side does. The essence of this definition is that we have allowed the image of a move to depend on the state to which the move is being applied.

Two problems P_1 and P_2 are *weakly isomorphic* if there exist inverse weak homomorphisms $F : P_1 \rightarrow P_2$ and $K : P_2 \rightarrow P_1$. The interested reader can translate this definition into equational form in a straightforward way.

In order to understand the significance of the difference between strong isomorhism as defined earlier in definitions 2.5 and 2.7 and this definition of weak isomorphism we can consider two descriptions of the Towers of Hanoi. We suppose that we have just

---

[7] If RWM does not need macros for a particular problem then it becomes only an abstraction-restriction heuristic

three discs 1,2, and 3 in order of increasing size and that the three pins are labelled A, B and C. The state space is described by giving the location of each pin. We have two possible ways of describing the moves. The first uses just pins:-Move a disk from Pin A to Pin B, etc.. The second uses a disc number and a pin name:-Move disc 1 to pin B, etc..

In the first case the problem is described with just six moves whereas the second uses nine moves. Thus the free problem descriptions cannot be strongly isomorphic, they are however weakly isomorphic.

Niizuma and Kitahashi use weak isomorphism as a mechanism for passing between problem representations. Indeed the significance of weak isomorphism is that it accurately captures the idea of problem reformulation. In order to see how they use the notion we need another definition.

Definition 4.14 *Suppose we are given a problem* $P = (S, \Omega, a)$ *and an equivalence relation R on the state space S. R is called Ω- admissible if $a \mid M(a)$ (recall from definition 2.5 that $M(a)$ is the subset of the domain of a on which a does not preserve the equivalence relation) induces an action on the set of equivalence classes S/R. If the equivalence relation R is derived from a feature $f : S \rightarrow T(f)$) in the usual way so that $xRy \Leftrightarrow f(x) = f(y)$ we say that f is Ω-admissible and similarly for the difference associated to R.*

We can give an alternative formulation of this definition which is more suitable for computation as follows.

Definition 4.15 *Suppose we are given a problem* $P = (S, \Omega, a)$ *and an equivalence relation R on the state space S. Let us write xRy to mean that x and y in S are R-equivalent. An equivalence relation R on S is then Ω -admissible if $xRy \Rightarrow$ whenever $a(x, \omega)$ and $a(y, \omega)$ both exist for a given ω and not $a(x, \omega)Rx$ then either $a(y, \omega)Ra(x, \omega)$ or $a(y, omega)Ry$.*

If we write $R[x]$ for the equivalence class of x, the action a/R is defined by the equation

$$a/R(R[x], \omega) = R[(a \mid M(a))(x, \omega)]$$

This definition is a reworking of condition 2.11 of page 126 of [27]. In the context of problem decomposition its relevance is clear. It can be informally related to the previous notions of relevance and safety in that an admissible move[8] is both safe with respect to an equivalence relation in that it preserves the equivalence of states and it is relevant in that it affects the states in an equivalence preserving way.

However Niizuma and Kitahashi use it together with weak isomorphism to state an interesting heuristic for choosing between problem representations.

Heuristic 4.16 *A primitive difference is one associated to a two valued feature. Given two weakly isomorphic problems choose the one with the larger number of admissible primitive differences.*

---

[8]Technically moves are not admissible, but if the equivalence relation is admissible with respect to the move the we can call the move admissible

It is not clear that one needs to restrict the applicability of this heuristic to primitive differences. Probably choosing the representation with the largest number of admissible features would do as well, provided largest takes into account the set of possible values of each feature.

The Niizuma-Kitahashi problem solving method can then be summed up as follows.

Algorithm 4.17   *1. Select an admissible difference d from the connection table for the problem.*

2. Solve P/R(d). Let $\omega_k \circ \omega_{k-1} \circ \ldots \circ \omega_1$ be a solution.

3. Decompose P into $P_1, \ldots, P_{k+1}$, where P_i is the problem of going from the image of ω_{i-1} to the domain of ω_i. (With appropriate modifications at the beginning and end of the chain).

Each of the P_i is a subproblem of the original problem. Indeed Niizuma and Kitahashi were the first to attempt a formal definition of subproblem. Much of the formalization that appears in this chapter is based upon the author's attempts to understand the work of Niizuma and Kitahashi.

Another look at this kind of problem decomposition method, where the subproblems are used to generate the decomposition rather than the differences is given in [14].

5   Adaptive Reduction Strategies

One weakness of most of the problem solving methods that we have described is that they do not learn from their experience. Or that if they do, the learning is not very sophisticated.

Korf's macro generation program could be said to learn in that it does not start again from the beginning when looking for macros that preserve more differences that any known one. Guvenir's RWM learns in as much as it uses the output of one pass through refinement as the input for the next. Ernst and Goldstein's program [9] that solved Fool's disc "learned" the correct differences to use. These are however fairly limited examples of learning. What we want to discuss here is some of the things that might be done to improve this.

One difficulty is that often a problem solving program will attempt to solve a subproblem which is equivalent to one that it has solved before except for a renameing of the variables involved. An intelligent problem solver should be able to make use of this.

In the language of the earlier part of the paper this is a special kind of relaxation heuristic. A program that stores "chunks" of knowledge based on previous experience is essentially enlarging its move set by incorporating additional moves that solve special instances of the problem or some subproblem.

The challenge for such a problem solver is deciding what to remember. We will review some results in this direction.

5.1 Chunking

The concepts behind the use of chunking are (like so many AI methods) based upon human learning techniques. In particular upon the following, drawn from work of Laird, Newell and Rosenbloom [21].

Hypothesis 5.1 *A human acquires and organizes knowledge of the environment by forming and storing expressions called chunks, which are structured collections of the chunks exisitng at the time of learning.*

The methodology of chunking is to use a hierarchical structuring of the goal as a basis for a divide and conquer technique which is used to reduce the goal to a set of elementary chunks. In the paper cited above Rosenboom illustrates the technique with a problem of responding to a stimulus consisting of a set of lights which the subject must reproduce by pressing an array of buttons. It is of some interest in our context however to see how the methods might be applied in more traditional problem solving areas.

There are several problems that lend themselves to the chunking approach but before we discuss specific examples it is appropriate to see how chunking fits into our general framework. Let us give a formal defintion of "chunk".

Definition 5.2 *Given a problem P a* chunk *for P is a solution to an instance of a subproblem P_0 of P. A* full chunk *is a complete set of solutions to every instance of some subproblem P_0.*

A problem solver that makes use of chunking must have an architecture that allows it to manage the chunks. We can suppose that incorporated into the system there is a Chunk Manager (CM). This would be responsible for storing and retrieving those chunks that are useful. In order to do this some heuristics are needed to determine which chunks are useful. One such heuristic is given in [21]. It is a natural reflection of the fact that small chunks are more likely to be useful than large ones.

Heuristic 5.3 Task Structure Assumption *The probability of recurrence of an environmental pattern decreases as the size of the pattern increases.*

On the other hand small chunks although more likely to occurr may not be rich enough to be useful in that there may simply be too many of them that one needs to remember. This problem is addressed in [14] where the following heuristic definition of a useful chunk is given.

Heuristic 5.4 *A chunk is useful if the associated subproblem*

1. *has a small set of discriminating features.*

2. *has a state space that is relatively large compared to the set of features.*

We need a more precise definition of relatively large. First however we need a technical definition.

Definition 5.5 *A subproblem P_0 of a problem P is called* split *if there is a problem homomorphism $r : P \Rightarrow P_1$ such that in the composition*

$$r \circ i : P_0 \Rightarrow P \Rightarrow P_1$$

P_0 is the inverse image of a point in P_1.

Split problems thus represent pieces of a problem that appear both as sub- problems and as inverse images in quotient problems.

Definition 5.6 *The state space of a problem P is relatively large compared to a discriminating set of features if any split subproblem of P associated has a state space whose size is comparable to the size of its set of discriminating features whereas P has a state space an order of magnitude larger than the set of features.*

This series of definitions somewhat distinguishes chunks from macros. Specifically it restricts chunks to small subproblems, whereas macros may deal with a large number of features. For example the macros used by Korf [18] eventually involve most of the features of the problem. The goal of chunking is to capture aspects of a problem that occur repeatedly during the solution of the problem. This approach is more likely to be effective in problems that exhibit a high degree of symmetry. That this is indeed the case can be seen in [15] and [14].

Chunking thus appears as an effective mechanism for learning pieces of solutions. The work of Rosenbloom ([21]) shows that programs that use chunking reproduce many characteristics of human learning. In [3] Banerji discusses the way in which a sophisticated Rubik's cubist will use solutions to one part of the problem to resolve other parts. All this indicates that problem solvers based upon the principle of chunking and macro generation can be expected to be effective. In each case what is required to make them work is some way of detecting the applicability of a given chunk or macro. This will often require more sophisticated applications of problem decomposition techniques than previous methods.

Methods that rely on chunking or macro generation have to limit in some way the amount of learning they attempt to do. This is in order to avoid getting tied up in learning to the exclusion of problem solving. Thus we saw that in [21] the chunks are restricted to those obtained by a hierachical decomposition of the goal state. The notion of useful chunk is another method of restricting the amount of learning that is done. Korf's macro problem solver only looks for macros of a specific type, which is specified by the problem decomposition. We may thus describe these kinds of learning problem solver structures in the following way.

Heuristic 5.7   *1. Select some set of subproblems which cover the given problem.*

2. Solve each of the subproblems.

3. Assemble the subproblem solutions into a solution for the original problem.

Having reviewed the overall ideas of chunking we will look in more detail at two problem solvers that actually use chunking.

5.1.1 Chunking of Goal Hierarchies

The problem used as an illustration in [21] is that of pressing a set of buttons in response to a stimulus. The system has to learn the correct response. The original human task was an experiment, reported in [8], in which the stimulus environment consisted of an oscilloscope on which a vertical line could appear in one of four horizontal positions. The response environment consisted of of a set of four buttons, lying under the fore and middle fingers of the subjects hands. On each trial of the task, one of the lines would appear on the oscilloscope, and the subject was to press an appropriate button. There were three conditions in the experiment, each of which specified a different mapping of line position to button.

Light Stimulus, Button Response

The program works by decomposing the goal of making the correct response into a goal hierarchy. To illustrate the idea suppose that the button that is to pressed is the one that is immediately under the stimulus line. Then we have the following hierarchical decomposition of the goal.

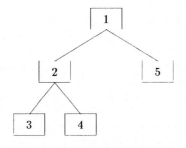

Goal Hierarchy

Where the subgoals are (the total goal is to press a the correct button in response to the stimulus.)

```
1. Press-Button-Under-Stimulus-Line
  2. Get-Horizontal-Location-Of-Stimulus-Line
    3. Get-Stimulus-Line
    4. Get-Horizontal-Location-Of-Stimulus
  5. Press-Button-At-Horizontal-Location.
```

Once the goal hierarchy is created the chunking mechanism is quite simple. In the above decomposition the method would chunk together goals 3 and 4 into a single goal, creating a chunk corresponding to the goal 2. Further learning will chunk goals 2 and 5 together. Thus the hierarchy provides a mechanism for glueing the chunks together. If we refer back to our general chunking heuristic we see that the hierarchical decomposition of the goal corresponds to the first step of decomposing the problem into elementary pieces. These pieces are then solved (or learned depending upon context) and final chunked together.

We can summarize the key aspects of chunking as it applies to goal hierarchies.

- Each chunk represents a specific goal with a specific set of parameter values. It relates the parameter values to the results of the goal.

- Chunks are created through experience with the goals processed.

- Chunks are created bottom-up in the goal hierarchy.

- A chunk consists of connection, encoding, and decoding components.

- Chunk encoding and decoding are hierarchical, parallel, goal-asynchronous processes that operate on goal parameters and results (respectively).

- Chunk connection is a serial, goal-synchronous process that generates (encoded) results from (encoded) parameters.

- Chunks improve performance by replacing normal processing of a goal (and its subgoals) with the faster process of encoding, connection, and decoding.

The architecture of Rosenbloom's system **XAPS3** is that of a production system. Chunks are therefore themselves productions. The chunk acquisition process consists of three parts. A chunk is only created after the system has decided to successfully terminate a goal, but before anything is done about it. At that point the goal is still active, and all of its information is still available.

Chunking is also used in **Soar** [21] which will be discussed in the section on expert problem solvers. For the moment we note that in adapting chunking to **Soar** some of the features above were done away with. In particular the bottom-up nature was dispensed with. **Soar** builds single production chunks for every subgoal that terminates.

The goal hierarchies introduced above are also used in a problem solving system being developed by Paul Benjamin [5]. The system works by carefully analyzing a solution to a problem with a view to generating a hierachical decomposition of the problem.

5.1.2   Chunking and Subproblem Equivalence

The other application of the chunking idea which we want to discuss is based upon [14]. Unlike the above methodology which begins with a hierachical decomposition of the goal, the approach is to find a collection of chunks which can be patched together to form a solution. This patching together uses a concept of hierachical decomposition of a problem which we explain. We will require some definitions.

Definition 5.8 *Given a pair $P = (S, \Omega, a)$ and $P' = (S', \Omega', a')$ of problems and a weak homomorphism $F : P \to P'$ with state map $f : S \to S'$, to each point $y \in S'$ associate the subset $Y = f^{-1}(y)$ of S and the subset $\Psi = (\omega \in \Omega | a'(g(\omega), y)) = y)$. The triple$(Y, \Psi, a)$ is a subproblem of P called the* inverse image problem *of y.*

With this preliminary we can give the definition of a two stage hierarchy.

Definition 5.9 *A (two-stage) hierarchy for a problem $P = (S, \Omega, a)$ consists of a weak problem homomorphism $F : P \to P'$ onto a problem $P' = (S', \Omega', a')$ and the collection $\{(Q(y), \Psi(y), a)\}$ of inverse image subproblems indexed by the points of S'.*

It is convenient to write this as $(P, \{Q(y)\}; P')$. We have the following theorem about the construction of two stage hierarchies.

Theorem 5.10 *Given a two-stage hierarchy $(P, \{Q(y)\}; P')$ on a problem P there exists an equivalence relation R on P such that P' is weakly isomorphic to P/R.*

Proof. Treat the map $f : S \to S'$ as a feature; R_f is the associated equivalence relation. •

It is important to note that the subproblems $Q(y)$ may well vary with y. In any case this two stage hierarchy allows the possibility of assembling a solution to the original problem from a solution to P' and solutions to each of the $Q(y)$'s. However the fact that the move sets of the $Q(y)$'s may have an effect outside of $Q(y)$ causes difficulties. It is this obstruction that we want to address now, through the notion of a split hierarchy. Split hierarchies turn out to be the kind of hierarchy that allow us the decomposition that we are looking for.

Definition 5.11 *A two stage hierarchy $(P, \{Q(y)\}; P')$ on a problem P is called* split *if for each subproblem $(Q(y), \Psi, a)$ and any move $\psi \in \Psi$, ψ is the identity outside $Q(y)$. (Recall that ψ is the restriction of a move on the whole of S.)*

There is a related notion of (split) multi-level hierarchy defined as a tree of sub-problems rooted at P.

It may seem that this is a very restrictive condition that will rarely be satisfied in practice. In fact this is not the case, and in [14] it is shown how one can extend the methodology outside the domain of this condition. Given a problem $P = (S, \Omega, a)$ there is an ideal situation in which by suitable choice of an equivalence relation R on S one gets a split two-stage hierarchy $(P, \{Q(y)\}; P/R)$ for which the Q(y)'s are up to strong isomorphism drawn from a small set of problems $(Q_1, \ldots, Q_k)$ – suppose k is one or two for concreteness. Under these circumstances having a complete set of solutions to the Q_i will allow one to solve the original problem. These Q_i are just the chunks we are looking for. Problems that can be covered by such a small set $(Q_1, \ldots, Q_k)$ of subproblems are called *uniform* for the set of subproblems.

Theorem 5.12 *Let P be a problem uniform for the finite set $(Q_1, \ldots, Q_k)$. If the state space for P can be covered by a disjoint collection of the problems from the model set then we have multi-level hierarchy enabling us to solve the problem.*

We can illustrate these ideas with the example of the fifteen puzzle.

Example 5.13 *The fifteen puzzle is uniform for the five puzzle. This means that every point in the configuration space of the fifteen puzzle can be contained in an image of the five puzzle.*

All this really says is that the blank can always be enclosed in some 2×3 *rectangle within the* 4×4 *square. Note that all the tiles outside the* 2×3 *rectangle are assumed to be fixed, so that in this case we can obtain the five puzzle by restriction.*

Thus if we consider the fifteen puzzle and the equivalence relation obtained by identifying two states if they can be connected by a sequence of 5-puzzle moves drawn from the horizontal five puzzle located in the top left hand corner. The states of the (weak) quotient puzzle are specified by giving the exact locations of the tile outside the top left hand region. The placement of the remaining tiles are all equivalent.

*	*	*	4
*	*	*	15
9	10	12	11
13	14	8	7

A Position in a Fifteen Puzzle Quotient

The diagram illustrates one such position. The asterisks indicate that the precise values appearing in the corresponding location are irrelevant in the quotient space. The corresponding function f into the quotient space is given by the values of the numbered tiles. f is thus the function corresponding to the features associated to the squares numbered 4,8,9,10,11,12,13,14,15,16 in the usual ordering. The moves in Ψ are those that permute the tiles whose values are indicated by asterisks.

Truly adaptive problem solvers would use the progress in solving the problem to add to the list of chunks or modify the strategy. Cases where this is done are the subject of the next section.

6   Production System Problem Solvers

The problem solvers we have discussed so far have tended to rely on single weak methods. Primarily these have been the heuristics derived from the basic three, restriction, relaxation, and abstraction. In this section we consider a problem solver that is based upon the paradigm of a production system.

6.1   Soar

We will illustrate the use of production systems in problem solving by a discussion of
Soar [21]. Soar is a problem solving architecture based upon the notion of *Universal
Subgoaling* this is the ability of a problem solver to treat any difficulty that arises
during problem solving as a problem in itself.

Soar is a large program consisting of many productions. In our overview we can
only illustrate some of the main ideas. We can perhaps best begin the description of
the architecture with the search control strategy.

1. Decide on Success (The state is a desired state).

2. Decide on Failure or Suspension (the goal will not be achieved on this attempt).

3. Select a goal.

4. Select a problem space.

5. Select a state from those currently available (if the current state is to be aban-
   doned).

6. Select an operator to apply to the state.

7. Apply the operator to obtain the new state.

The memory (or stock) of Soar consists of objects, their augmentations and a
current context which contains one slot for each of the Current Goal, the Current
Problem Space, the Current State, and the Current Operator. The augmentations
are many valued relations between objects in the stock. Typically if X27 and X56 are
states there might be an augmentation to X27 indicating that the application of the
operator A34 will transform X27 to X56.

The single generic control act available in Soar is the replacement of an object in
one of the Current slots by another object. This is implemented by an *elaboration-
decision* phase. Both the elaboration and decision parts are encoded using productions. The decision is based upon a voting procedure. This voting procedure does
not always produce a resolution. Depending on the stage in the list above at which
the *difficulty* arises one has a taxonomy of difficulties. For example corresponding to
"Select Operator" one finds the difficulty that there are no available operators. It is
at this point that Subgoaling is introduced.

Universal subgoaling is the ability to set up subgoals for all the difficulties that
the system can face. The Soar architecture permits the incorporation of many well-
known weak methods of problem solving as methods of difficulty resolution. On pages
67-8 of [21] an extensive list of the methods is given. We will reproduce part of this
here.

Operator Subgoaling. If an operator cannot be applied to a position, then set
up a sub-goal of making the operator applicable. This restriction heuristic is familiar
from such problem solvers as GPS. [4].

Constraint Satisfaction There are a set of constraints on a set of variables.
An assignemt of variables must be found that satisfies the constraints. A suitable
relaxation heuristic is used to search for the assignment.

Unification Given two patterns containing variables and functions with variables, find the most general unifying expression.

The weak methods are organized into a heirarchy which can be used to order them as productions for the system. The heirarchy is based upon the observation that each weak method arises from the addition of a small amount of new task dependant knowledge. Certain knowledge should be applicable to many methods, and as the knowledge becomes more specialized, fewer methods will share it.

This organization of the weak methods is therefor based upon a different perspective from the one that we have been using. The trunk of the tree represents the common knowledge with the branches occuring when there is a different task structure or knowledge available. Rather than explain the structure of the tree in detail, (which is done in pages 69-74 of la:chunk, we will show how the top level of the tree can be fitted into our perspective.

The root of the tree is **Soar** itself and there are three branches, leading to *operator subgoaling* , *Selection of problem space with evaluation operator* and *hypothesis and match, constraint satisfaction.* The first is an abstraction heuristic in that one has determined that the quotient problem in which a given operator has to be applied is relevant to the solution. The second corresponds to restriction since it is from this branch that the evaluation searches descend. The last branch is relaxation as has been observed before in the context of other solution methods that rely on constraint satisfaction such as Lauriere's.

Because **Soar** is a production based system it lends itself to adaptation and learning through chunking (as we have already indicated). Since the elaboration-decision phase of the system generates all the relevant knowledge for the decision it is possible to create chunks for each goal that is successfully concluded.

For each goal that is generated, the architecture maintains a *condition-list* of all data that existed before the goal was created and which was accessed in the goal. When a goal terminates the condition-list is used to build the conditions of a chunk. The actions of the chunk should be the results of the goal. This form of chunking is more than just caching of previous information because a task can share subgoals with another task.

The chunking mechanism was successfully applied to the eight puzzle and to tic-tac-toe. In the case of tic-tac-toe chunking was able to detect and make use of board symmetries. This happens because the condition list managed to ignore orientation information that was not used during problem solving. In the context of the remarks on chunking in the previous section [14] this is not entirely unexpected.

7   Efficiency Considerations

Efficiency is the area of greatest weakness in problem solving. Most workers have been content to report the observed time that a problem solver takes. This is essentially the approach taken by Lauriere [22]. He gives a table relating the size of the ALICE description of the problem, the number of seconds of CPU time (on an IBM370/168) and the number of backtracks. There does not seem to be any obvious correspondance between these numbers. For example Instant Insanity takes the same time as Missionaries and Cannibals even though its ALICE desrciption is much smaller and it uses fewer backtracks.

Korf gives a fairly detailed discussion of the question in both in his problem solving by macro generation paper [18] and in his paper on planning as search [17]. Guvenir [11] also discusses the question but is not able to come to many conclusions. Perhaps the most detailed discussion of efficiency of heuristics is given by Judea Pearl in his book [28]. Unfortunately much of his approach is not of great relevance to our point of view. In [21] there is some discussion of the overhead due to chunking in **Soar** and the attendant reduction in the number of decisions that have to be made.

The scattered nature of the results on efficiency will be reflected in the structure of this section. We will try to pull things together in the terms that we have set up for the dicussion of heuristics.

7.1   Framework for Estimating the Efficiency of a Heuristic

We can give a general description of the various heuristics that we have looked at as follows:

Heuristic 7.1   *1. Given a problem P, replace it by a (sequence of) problem(s) which can be solved.*

   2. Use the solution(s) to the problem(s) to solve the original problewm.

In order to estimate the efficiency of a heuristic we need therefore to estimate the time for each step. We can use the time for a brute force search to estimate the complexity of the problem itself. In making the comparison we need to bear in mind that the object of most problem solving systems is not just to solve one instance of the problem, rather it is to find a system that will be capable of solving many different instances. This means that one has to amortize some of the cost of the problem solving system over the number of cases to be solved. Thus a problem solver may use a depth-first iteratgive deepening search to look for macros as Korf does. Once the macros have been found however the solution to the problem is quickly found. Korf also uses lengths of the macros as a measure of the optimality of the solution found by his method.

In the terms of the outline heuristic given above this approach says that the cost of the first part, the solving of the replacement problem(s) is to be amortized over the solution of future instances of the problem. In part this is an accceptance of the inevitable, since it is much easier to estimate the costs of the second part than of the first. We can illustrate what we mean by considering the case of fool's disk.

In this problem, which we discussed earlier in section 3, four concentric rings are divided into eight sectors each of which contains an integer. The rings are free to rotate about their common center. The problem is to rotate the disks so that the sum along each radius is 12.

The usual solution to this problem uses a GPS type method following the outline given in section 1. The differences used are the following.

D_1 = the sum along a pair of orthogonal diameters,

D_2 = the set of sums along the diameters,

D_3 = the set of sums along the radii.

In [9] Ernst and Goldstein showed how the differences can be mechanically generated. Using this we can easily estimate the search reduction. Let us assume first that no backtracking is needed. Then to reduce the first difference requires us to examine at most eight moves. The second requires eight more and the last a final maximum of eight. Thus we can find a solution (if no backtracking is required) by examining no more than 24 moves. As opposed to examining all possible moves which is 8^3. This is a reduction of the search space to 3/64 of its original size.

It is of some interest to consider the effect of backtracking on the search. This is best analysed in the context of trying to find every solution to the problem. In which case the search strategy has to be a little different. One has to obtain all the solutions to the intermediate problems. We can describe it in detail as follows.

1. When reducing D_1 using only moves of rings through 45 degrees, store enough moves to switch between any pair of solutions to this first problem. (If there are n solutions this requires n moves including the identity move, the number of such solutions is necessarily a power of 2).

2. When reducing D_2, in addition to all rotations through 90 degrees use any of the moves that make the transition between solutions at step 1. Once again store enough moves to switch between any two solutions at this stage.

3. When reducing D_3, in addition to all rotations through 180 degrees use any of the moves that make the transition between the solutions at step 2.

Suppose that there are in fact two solutions at step 1 but only one solution to the problem. Then depending upon whether there are two solutions or one to step 2 the search requires on to examine either 40 or 32 moves. Still a substantial reduction. In any case the heuristic is effective at search reduction. In general for each partial solution found at one level there are 8 moves to be examined at the next level.

If we try to compare this method to the one given by Lauriere it is not clear that Lauriere's method necessarily achieves any search reduction except by aborting searches that are hopeless as soon as possible. This makes the efficiency of his method hard to estimate. On the other hand Lauriere's program does not have the overhead involved in discovering the differences. So for a true comparison we should have some way of estimating this overhead. Later in the chapter we will refine and prove the following conjecture which can be used as a heuristic for estimating the overhead required by the learning phase of a problem solver.

Conjecture 7.2 *The cost of finding a set of macros or learning a set of non-obvious differences can be estimated as the cost of solving an average instance of the problem by brute force search.*

The intuitive justification for this is that the methods for finding macros or non-obvious differences rely upon using symbolic representations for problem parameters. Put another way, a generic instance of the problem is solved with careful watch for certain kinds of patterns. It is exactly the kind of pattern sought that classifies the heuristic. Even problem solvers that work from the solution of a single instance [5] follow this pattern.

7.2   Estimates of search reduction

Since Korf gives the most detailed analysis of the efficacy of his problem solving technique we will begin with a review of his results [18].

Korf uses three criteria to gauge the performance of his method: the number of macros required to fill the macro table, the amount of time necessary to learn the macros and the number of primitive moves required to solve an instance of the problem. In this direction he presents three main results.

- The number of macros is equal to the sum of the number of values for each of the state variables (features), as compared to the product of the number of values which is the size of the state space.

- The total learning time is of the same order as the time required to find a single solution using conventional search techniques.

- The length of the solution is no greater than the optimal solution length times the number of state variables.

These results correspond well with the observations made above about fool's disc. This is interesting since fool's disk is one of the problems for which Korf's method is not suited. (This is because for Korf's method to work one would have to be able to specify the solution in terms of the values of the state variables, which is of course precisely the problem.)

Once stated the first and third of these results are fairly clear. The first follows because the macro table contains one column for each state vector and one row for each possible value of the vectors. The last result is simply a worst case analysis, at any stage the macro required could be as long as the optimal solution length (remember that the search method is depth-first iterative deepening).

We will say a little more about the middle result because it bears upon our earlier heuristic estimate. Korf gives the following more precise estimate of the time required for learning the macro table (his theorem 24 p 81 of [18]).

Theorem 7.3 *Given a serially decomposable problem P for which each primitive operator has an inverse primitive operator, an optimal macro table M for P can be generated in time $O(nD_sB_m^{D_s/2})$, where n is the number of state variables, B_m is the maximum branching factor of the space, and D_s is the maximum subgoal distance for the solution order embodied in the macrotable M.*

Korf shows that this is of the same order as the time to solve an instance of the problem by explicitly estimating the time to solve the problem using ordinary search with subgoals, with bi-directional search between the subgoals. This provides a proof of the conjecture for serially decomposable problems, but only by observing that two calculations give the same value.

We now turn to Guvenir's Refinement with Macros method [11]. The analysis of RWM is carried out only in terms of time complexity of the two parts of the method, the refinement process and the macro generation process. Estimates are given in terms of the size of the problem. Size being measure in terms of the number M of moves, the number $\mid G(s) \mid$ of atomic statements in the goal statement, and n_p the average number of preconditions of a move. In these terms the complexity of the refinement process is $O(\mid G(s) \mid^3 (2 + n_p).M)$, and the complexity of macro generation process (which may take place more than once) is $O(M^2)$.

In this form it is hard to compare Guvenir's results with Korf's. Before trying to do so we note the following major difference between the approaches. In Guvenir's method the intermediate subproblems are generated by the problem solving system itself, whereas in Korf's method the solution order predetermines a set of intermediate problems. On the other hand Guvenir's method produces a strategy not a solution.

One way in which we can compare the results is to look at a problem that both methods solve: The $2 \times 2 \times 2$ Rubik's cube. Korf's solution has 75 non-identity macros, the longest of which is 11 moves, and an average case solution length of 27 moves. Guvenir's solution has 6 subgoals with 19,17,14,11,8,and 5 moves respectively of which the longest is 91 primitive moves in length (bear in mind that a rotation through 270 degrees is not a primitive move for Guvenir). Guvenir's solution thus uses a total of 74 macros.

The corresponding running time estimates are

Korf	Guvenir Refinement	Guvenir Macro Generation
$24 \cdot 6^{23/2}$	$24^3 \cdot 3 \cdot 6$	6^3

In this case the cost of refinement is approximately the same as the cost of Korf's macro generation. This suggests that refinement does indeed take about as long as a solution to an average instance of the problem. This is rendered more plausible by observing that $\mid G(s) \mid$ is a reasonable estimate of the number of features in the problem. (Each atomic statement in the goal could be regarded as a two valued feature as in [27].) If the number of primitive moves is about the square root of the number of features then we would get this result.

7.3   Proof of the Conjecture

We now return to the earlier conjecture on the learning time that a problem solver requires. We are able to give a more precise formulation of the conjecture and show that in this form the conjecture is true.

We are going to be considering problem solvers in which a solution to a particular problem instance $PI = (P, s_0, G)$ of a problem P is obtained by first analysing the problem P and deriving a generic solution method. Korf's macro generator comes in this class through its generation of macros. Guvenir's refinement with macros and Ernst and Goldstein's [9] solution to fool's disk enter because they begin by seeking appropriate differences with which to decompose the problem. On the other hand Lauriere's problem solver does not belong to this class since it does not solve generic versions of the problem.

What all these two phase problem solvers have in common is that they work through the notion of difference. We can describe the methods generically in the following heuristic.

Heuristic 7.4 *Given a problem instance $PI = (P, s_0, G)$ of a problem P*

   1. Choose an ordered set $\{D_1, \ldots, D_k\}$ of adequate differences for the problem P.

(Recall that a set of differences is adequate if it distinguishes any non-goal state from any goal state.)

2. *Sequentially reduce the differences.*

In the problem solvers we have looked at that rely on differences the emphasis has been on either the first part of the heuristic ([11], [9]) with little consideration of the second or on the second one with little consideration of the first [18]. In each case however the part of the heuristic that is emphasized involves a discussion of the generic problem. The results of the analysis are then applied to specific instances.

We will refer to this analysis of the generic problem as the *learning phase* of the problem solver. This terminology is justified since its costs are to be amortized over the subsequent applications of the problem solver.

Definition 7.5 *A problem solver that uses the methodology of the heuristic given above will be called* difference oriented.

Note that there are difference oriented problem solvers across the various classes of heuristics that we discussed earlier so that this concept is in some sense independant of the earlier classification. We have the following theorem.

Theorem 7.6 *The time cost of the learning phase of a difference oriented problem solver is of the same order as the time taken to solve a single instance of the problem using a conventional search technique.*

We have seen that a case of this theorem was known to Korf in [18]. However Korf's proof was based upon giving independant calculations of the two quantities and showing that the results were the same. Our proof will be more conceptual.

Proof. The key to the proof is really interpreting what is meant by "conventional search technique". In fact we observe that whether the problem solver works by searching for the differences or by searching for macros (or other packaged difference reduction mechanism) this involves a search which will use "conventional search techniques" which could be applied directly to solve a generic instance of the problem. A generic instance being one in which the feature values are to be treated as symbols.

Thus by using the search technique used for the learning phase on a generic problem instance we solve the problem instance. Conversely if we use the problem instance as a template for applying the search method to the learning phase we solve the problem. This proves the theorem.

7.4 Storage penalties

Several of the problem solving systems that we have looked at use additional storage to record move sequences that are useful in solving problems. It is of some interest to assess the costs of this strategy. Whereas the learning time cost is a one time penalty that is amortised over the lifetime of the problem solver, storage used for special solutions is a permanent overhead in a problem solver. In the case of a problem solver that is continually adding to its knowledge base it can become the dominant part of the system.

Unfortunately little is known about this problem. The general problem of dynamic knowledge organization is an active area of AI research and a review would be out of place here.

There is however one case where some experimental data is available. In [21] there is a discussion of an application of chunking in a version of **R1** the configuration program. The program, which is referred to as **R1- Soar** was applied to small configuration tasks. The base system had 232 productions (95 come with **Soar**, 135 define **R1-Soar**). The program had two versions, one "Min S-C" had minimal search control and the other "Added S-C" had an additional 10 productions that remove much of the search. In the following table (which is reproduced from p295 of [21]), the number of search control decisions is used as the timing metric. This is a reasonable metric for a production system since the system is driven by these decisions. The run-time overhead of chunking (mostly to compile the new productions is approximately 15%.

Run Type	Initial Productions	Final Productions	Decisions
Min S-C	232	232	1731
Min S-C with Chunking	232	291	491
Min S-C after Chunking	291	291	7
Added S-C	242	242	150
Added S-C with Chunking	242	254	90
Added S-C after Chunking	254	254	7

One should not draw general conclusions from a single piece of experimental evidence. However the effectiveness of chunking in reducing the number of decisions is striking. The overhead in terms of added productions is in each case a small fraction of the original production base. Clearly this is an area where much work needs to be done.

8   Summary and Conclusions

We have examined a number of methods for problem solving. These methods have been classified using three basic heuristics, restriction, relaxation and abstraction. The methods can be combined to obtain more comprehensive problem solving techniques.

The most developed form that the combination of heuristics takes is that described in algorithm 4.9. Here all three basic techniques are put together to form a problem solving paradigm which encompasses many of the special methods that have been described in this chapter.

As a conclusion to this chapter we would like to discuss the role that the problem representation plays in the implementation of the heuristics. Our original definition of a problem in section 2 did not make explicit the way in which the state of a problem is represented. This was done so as to be able to move between different methods of problem representation as we described different problems. However different representations of the state space will lend themselves to different ways of applying the heuristics.

A method of describing the state space that uses logical predicates to define the problem state lends itself to relaxation heuristics because, as we saw in the case of the fifteen-puzzle, predicates can be dropped thus enlarging the search space. Such descriptions are also appropriate for restriction methods since additional predicates can be added to the state description. Descriptions that define the current state in terms of feature values lend themselves to abstraction techniques because they tend to facilitate the discovery of equivalence relations.

The problem of finding the appropriate description for a problem is one that has not been much discussed. Some work has been done by Amarel [1],Korf [19] and Niizuma and Kitahashi [27]. The notion of weak isomorphism defined in section 4 seems to capture the underlying notion adequately. However applications in which different representations are automatically examined do not seem to be ready yet.

Problem Solving will continue to provide a valuable laboratory for AI research. As we have indicated earlier there are many interesting questions in the areas of efficiency, overhead for learning and storing knowledge as well as questions about representation that remain to be resolved.

Acknowledgements

I am grateful to Ranan Banerji for his willingness to both listen to my ideas on these topics and to read the results. All errors are of course my responsibility not his. Some of the work described here was done with the generous support of the Benjamin Franklin Partnership of the Commonwealth of Pennsylvania.

References

[1] S. Amarel. On the Representations of Problems of Reasoning About Actions. In D.Michie (editor) Machine Intelligence. American Elsevir. New York 1968.

[2] R.B. Banerji. Artificial Intelligence: A Theoretical Approach. North-Holland. 1983.

[3] R.B. Banerji. GPS and the Psychology of the Rubik Cubist: A Study in Reasoning about actions. In Artificial and Human Intelligence A. Elithorn and R. Banerji Editors. North-Holland, Amsterdam, 1983.

[4] R.B. Banerji and G.W. Ernst. A Theory for the Complete Mechanization of a GPS Type Problem solver. Proc. 5th International Conference on Artificial Intelligence Cambridge MA. 1977.

[5] P. Benjamin. Private Communication.

[6] D. Chapman. Planning for Conjunctive Goals. AI 32 1987 333-377

[7] E. Charniak and D. McDermott. Introduction to Artificial Intelligence. Addison-Wesley Reading Massachusetts 1984.

[8] J. Duncan. Response Selection Rules in Spatial Choice Reaction tasks. In S. Dornic (Ed.) Attention and Performance VI. Hillsdale NJ. Lawrence Erlbaum Associates 1977.

[9] G.W. Ernst and M.M Goldstein. Mechanical Discovery of Classes of Problem Solving Strategies. J ACM 29 1 1-23 1982

[10] D. Gries. The Science of Programming. Springer Verlag

[11] H.A. Guvenir Learning Problem Solving Strategies Using Refinement and Macro Generation. Ph.D. Thesis. Case University. 1987.

[12] P.E. Hart, N.J. Nilsson and B. Raphael. A Formal Basis for the Heuristic Determination of Minimum Cost Paths. IEEE Trans. Systems Science and Cyberetics SSC-4(2):100-7. 1968.

[13] T.P. Hart and D.J. Edwards. The Tree Prune (TP) Algorithm. MIT Artificial Intelligence Project Memo #30, R.L.E. and Computation Center, MIT, Cambridge Mass. Reprinted in revised form as The Alpha-Beta Heuristic.

[14] J.P.E. Hodgson. Solving Problems by Subproblem Classification. Proceedings ISMIS Torino. 1988.

[15] J.P.E. Hodgson. Interactive Problem Solving. SIGART Newsletter. 1987.

[16] R. Korf. Depth First Iterative-Deepening: An Optimal admissible tree search. Artificial Intelligence 27 (1985) 97-109.

[17] R. Korf Planning as Search: A Quantitative Approach. AI 33 1987 65-88

[18] R. Korf. Learning to Solve Problems by Macro-generation. Pitman 1985.

[19] R. Korf. Toward a model of Representation Changes. AI. 14 41-78 1980.

[20] J.E.Laird, A. Newell, P.S. Rosenbloom . SOAR: An Architecture for General intelligence. AI 33 1987 1-64.

[21] J.E. Laird, A. Newell, P.S. Rosenbloom. Univesral Goaling and Chunking. Kluwer Academic publishers. 1986

[22] J-L. Lauriere. A Language and a Program for Stating and Solving Combinatorial Problems. AI 10 1978 29-127

[23] D. Lenat The nature of Heuristics II AI 21 (1-2) 1983 31-59

[24] D. Lenat The nature of heuristics III AI 21 1-2 61-98. 1983

[25] V. Lesser, Jasmin Pavlin and Edmund Durfee. Approximate Processing in Real Time problem Solving. AI Magazine. 9 1988 49-61.

[26] A. Newell and H.A. Simon. Human Problem Solving. Prentice- Hall. Englewood Cliffs. NJ. 1972.

[27] S. Niizuma and T. Kitahashi. A Problem Solving Method Using Differences or Equivalence Relations Between States. AI 25 1985 117-151

[28] J. Pearl Heuristics Addison-Wesley 1984.

[29] I. Pohl, First Results on the Effect of Error in Heuristic Search, In B. Meltzer and D. Michie (Eds.), Machine Intelligence 5 (American Elsevir) New York 1970. 219-236.

[30] J.R. Quinlan and E.B. Hunt. A Formal Deductive Problem- Solving System. Journal of the ACM. 15 (1968) 625-646.

[31] Sacerdoti. Earl D. The Non-linear Nature of Plans. Advance papers 4th International Joint Conference on Artificial Intelligence. Tbilisi 1975 Vol 1 206-214.

[32] Sussman Gerald J. A Computer Model of Skill Acquisition. American Elsevier. New York 1975.

Formal Techniques in Artificial Intelligence
A Sourcebook. R.B. Banerji (editor)
 Elsevier Science Publishers B.V. (North-Holland), 1990

A Survey of Computational Learning Theory

Philip D. Laird
Artificial Intelligence Research Branch
NASA Ames Research Center
Moffett Field, California 94035

1   Overview

I write this survey mainly for readers interested in machine learning, whose research methodology includes some amount of mathematical modeling. The scope of the article is limited to research that has a formal foundation and pertains to the problem of making computers "learn", whatever that means. I hope that readers new to the field find a roadmap to the recent literature, and that researchers already immersed in the field may gain some perspective about the relationship of their work to that of their colleagues.

Like most surveys, this article contains no new results, except perhaps for relating research that previously had not been compared. Most of the work is generally available in the published literature, or at least in technical research reports still available from the sponsoring institutions. The remarks in this introduction are my own thoughts and are not intended to express any consensus on the part of learning researchers.

The Nature of Learning. In thinking about the content and structure of this survey, I have once again been forced to confront the annoying question: what is learning? Many programs and models purport to learn in some fashion, but like intelligence, learning is easier to recognize than to define. The "Potter Stewart" mode of concept definition ("I know it when I see it") is of no help when an author is forced to declare his prejudices, as I am now.

What is the nature of a program that learns? Most programs P compute a relation: given x, output a value or set of values $y = P(x)$ with a specified property. We assume that the initial state of the program is always the same at the beginning of each computation, so that regardless of any previous computations, the output values $P(x)$ depend only on x. A *learning* program, however, also modifies its initial state: starting in state q, the result of the computation $P(x \mid q)$ is a sequence of values y and a new state q' from which subsequent computations will begin. It is this progression of states of the program that interests us, that is the result of learning. For cumulative changes of state to be considered learning, there must also be improvement in the computation.

For example, the time to compute y given x may decrease, or the likelihood that $P(x)$ has some desirable property (small size, greater accuracy) may increase.

Everyone reading this understands that a learning program is itself just a program, and that by redefining what we mean by input, program state, and output, we can just as easily view the entire computation over the "learning" phase as a single execution, with all the training data treated as one large input. The program is then just a search for an output with the desired properties. This image also has a converse: any search program, even a simple linear search, can be viewed as a learning program by changing what we think of as input or output and what we consider to be the program state.

The fundamental duality between learning and search permeates the research literature — theoretical, experimental, connectionist, and statistical. Those whose main interest is in algorithms think of learning as a combinatorial optimization problem. To problem-solvers, learning is a game between teacher and learner. To the statistician, it is a hypothesis-testing problem, and to the systems analyst, a nonlinear optimization problem. All of these are, fundamentally, search problems.

So is there really anything to say about learning that is not just a property of search? To judge from nearly thirty years of research in computational learning theory, one might have difficulty concluding that there is. There are algorithms, however, accepting contraints as input and returning a rule satisfying those constraints, that nonetheless make us uncomfortable when they are described as learning algorithms. We prefer to think of learning as occurring *incrementally* over time: as more constraints or evidence are obtained, our knowledge about the target grows more precise. By contrast a *ballistic* (or *batch*) algorithm processes all constraints together until it finally bursts forth with the result. A ballistic algorithm can, of course, be made to appear incremental by adding each new instance to a list and running the procedure on the full list. The distinction, therefore, between a truly incremental algorithm and a disguised ballistic one is the rate at which storage grows in comparison to the growth in size of the total set of input data. The storage in a ballistic program grows in proportion to the total input, while that of a truly incremental learning program grows much more slowly (e.g., space that grows logarithmically with the size of the input).

In summary, every learning program is also a search program, and most search programs can be seen as learning in some sense. For practical purposes, we seek learning algorithms whose performance criteria improve regularly as successive input data arrive, and yet whose space requirements increase slowly compared to the size of the input data. We shall find that few of the learning algorithms in the published literature achieve both these goals; true learning algorithms are not easy to find.

Formalism and Learning Research. We have no difficulty finding potential learning applications: learning human languages; learning to recognize classes of objects in scenes; learning to distinguish between important and unimportant events; learning an opponent's strategy by observing his moves; learning one's way about a new environment, and so on. What is, or should be, the role of formalism in attacking these types of problems?

In a field where the final concern is with what tasks can be accomplished by computer, one often hears complaints that formalism offers little or no insight. Such comments may reflect a misunderstanding of the term "formal"; in particular "formalism" and "mathematics" are commonly taken to be synonymous. But a well-designed machine or program requires the same insight, clarity of reasoning, and careful structure as the best mathematical work. "Formal" here refers to the careful expression of ideas in a manner suitable for succinct communication. The ideas we are most interested in are those with the broadest implications, whether for designing programs or reasoning about concepts.

Mathematical formalism can serve machine learning in several ways. By identifying fundamental concepts common to many learning problems, the theory reduces the number of ideas we must retain in order to solve problems. By modeling and simplifying problems so that we can reason formally about them and their solutions, we increase our understanding of the relevant elements of the problem domain and how they affect the solution. In the analysis of learning algorithms we discover their capabilities and limitations. Occasionally a negative result will show that acceptable solutions to the problem do not exist as specified, and thereby force us to revise our approach to the problem.

Not all formal work, however, serves us equally well in the task of enabling machines to learn. As new models proliferate, and algorithms for learning with respect to those models are published, people question the relevance of the research. When a theorist is asked, "Have you implemented any of your results?" one sometimes hears in response: "My results have been proved formally and rigorously; therefore, programming them is just an exercise that will not contribute any new ideas." Such comments demonstrate a misunderstanding of the role of theory. Mathematics, especially as a model of learning, is *just* a model. Models incorporate a host of assumptions and simplifications in order allow mathematical treatment. As a consequence, the theorems are merely suggestive of the true phenomenon being studied; only experience with implementation can determine whether the resulting concepts are useful. When the theory arises in response to experience – perceptron theory, for example – the mapping from theory to practice is usually fairly close. But since much of the learning theory to date has been concerned less with solving concrete problems than in formulating abstract models of learning, its relevance to machine learning remains to be demonstrated. The reason for this situation is not hard to find: under pressure to get results, theorists in all areas occasionally pursue a mathematically fertile theory beyond the limits of its usefulness.

Both mathematical and machine studies of learning are vulnerable to the "sirens of detail". Some theorists, for example, develop their ideas in increasingly abstract terms, with few of their colleagues able to understand, let alone utilize, the products of their research. Likewise there are those who derive pleasure from writing an enormously complex machine program, perhaps to emulate certain aspects of human intelligence or to display characteristics that even Potter Stewart would recognize as learning. In each case these "sirens" may be luring the researcher away from the true objective of the formal science of learning, which is to discover its conceptual kernel and to make these concepts part of the common knowledge of the community of computer scientists.

For such a theory to become common knowledge in the way that the periodic table and Newtonian mechanics are common knowledge, *there must exist simple, unified bases for the variety of behaviors collectively called learning.* No one knows whether such a theory exists. But we hope that it does, and we continue to direct our research efforts in its pursuit. One of the goals of this survey is to highlight the elements common to different learning models.

General Outline.   This article is in four parts. The first two sections view learning as an inductive, rather than a deductive, inference process. The first section treats induction in first-order logic, and the second does so in probabilistic logic. After that, we review research that treats learning as a combinatorial search problem in which the choice of representation is crucial to the time complexity of the problem. Finally we examine learning in networks of simple processing units that communicate only with other units nearby.

In each section, I describe the principal ideas, and some of the fundamental results when these can be stated without excessive exposition. I follow with a description of the representative literature so that the reader can begin to locate source materials in the area. I have not compiled a complete bibliography; nor is it possible in these few pages to do justice even to the results that are described.

The wealth of research results in learning has made the decision about what to include extremely difficult. No reader should presume that all the interesting and important work in formal learning theory has been listed here; equally, no researcher should attribute my omission of his or her results as a judgment of worth. I have included research results that, in my view, assist the reader to acquire a coherent picture of the field, understand the motivation for current research, and appraise its significance.

2   Induction

From the earliest days of AI, researchers have pursued two main approaches to the automation of intelligence:

- explicit knowledge representation, coupled with general inference algorithms for utilizing the consequences of that knowledge;

- "self-organizing systems" composed of massive assemblies of small-scale units, wherein knowledge is distributed throughout the system, and intelligence emerges as a macroscopic property of the system as a whole.

Mathematical logic forms the theoretical basis for the first approach. By contrast, no single branch of mathematics dominates the formal theory in the second, although thermodynamics and statistical mechanics have provided some of the inspiration.

In this section and the next we consider learning within the first paradigm, that of inference-based systems. The term "inference" refers generally to effective symbolic procedures for deriving new facts from known ones. That process is called *deductive* if it fits the schema of a process of logical deduction (axioms, rules of inference, etc.). Much of the philosophical research in learning has been devoted to developing a corresponding theory of *inductive* inference, a calculus for inferring generalizations from particular observations. Whereas theorems in a deductive calculus are subsumed by the axioms, in an inductive system the "facts" or examples are subsumed by the inferences.

Within the framework of the Church-Turing model of computation, a vigorous study of the absolute limits of inductive inference has been conducted for the past twenty years. The result is a rich and beautiful theory of the abstract complexity of learning. But this line of mathematics says little about the design of learning programs for real machines, and in accordance with the stated objectives of this survey, I shall not describe it further. See [62] for an introduction to this research.

Inductive Synthesis of Concepts. *Concept learning* has been one of the core problems of machine-learning research, for both theory and practice.[1] In its simplest form, a *concept* is a subset of some universe U of objects. Associated with the concept is a representation expressed in some chosen language $\mathcal{L}$. For example, "dog" denotes a particular subset of the set of all animals, and we can represent this subset by a logical relation over certain features (number of legs, has a tail, sensitivity of the olfactory sense, etc.). In a concept-learning task, the learner receives *examples* labeled "dog" or "not a dog" by a process we call the *teacher* already in possession of the target concept. Based on the examples, the learner offers a sequence of hypotheses, expressed as sentences in $\mathcal{L}$. This sequence should eventually converge to the target concept or to a close approximation. This informal characterization of concept learning can be formalized in many ways, depending on how the examples are represented, how the teacher selects the examples, what computational limitations apply to the learner, and so on.

Assuming the representation language $\mathcal{L}$ is recursively enumerable, there is a very simple procedure (called *identification by enumeration*) for finding the target concept from the examples. Let $L_1, L_2, \ldots$ be a list of the concepts. Suppose $x_1, x_2, \ldots$ is the list of examples presented by the teacher. After receiving the i'th example, the inference process chooses as its next hypothesis the first concept in the list that agrees with the i'th example. In response, the teacher chooses a counterexample (provided one exists). It is easy to see that, under very general conditions, this simple procedure *converges* — i.e., after some finite number of examples, the process outputs the correct concept. Moreover it enjoys two of the characteristics of a learning algorithm as set forth in the introduction: search and slow storage growth. The third requirement – gradual improvement in the hypotheses – is not fulfilled in this case, and for this reason identification by enumeration does not inspire much excitement as a learning algorithm.

It is equally apparent that, without considerable amplification, identification by

---

[1]Throughout this survey I use the problem of supervised concept learning to illustrate the main ideas and to facilitate comparison of the different approaches. Other learning tasks are treated in the references.

enumeration is not a practical inference procedure. Nevertheless it forms the basis for many learning algorithms, including the Inductive Synthesis method, to be described below. In any real problem a correct hypothesis is liable to be a large and complex expression; consequently any practical algorithm must have a technique for inferring the individual parts of the concept instead of searching sequentially through the entire concept space. Many clever techniques for accomplishing this had been devised for particular languages (automata, grammars, Turing machines, lisp functions, ...). Then Ehud Shapiro devised an elegant way to do inductive synthesis using first-order logic as a representation language. As a result we can now solve most of these other concept-learning problems in a unified way by representing the hypotheses in a first-order language.

I shall give an overview of Shapiro's theory, based on [76]. For this discussion, we represent concepts as first-order Horn sentences — that is, conjunctions of zero or more clauses of the form $(P_1 \wedge \ldots \wedge P_k) \rightarrow Q$, where P_i and Q are atoms (neither negated nor quantified). Each clause is universally quantified over its variables; existential quantification is not used. The P_i's are called the *premises* and Q the *conclusion* of the clause. For this discussion, the term "clause" means "Horn clause". **T** and **F** denote "true" and "false", respectively. As logical inference rules we allow resolution and substitution for equals.

For example, the following sentence, consisting of two clauses, defines the concept of plus as the set of triples (x, y, z) such that $x + y = z$. Zero (0) is a constant symbol in the language, and the intended interpretation of the function symbol succ is that $\mathrm{succ}(x)$ means $x + 1$ (successor function).

$$\mathbf{T} \rightarrow \mathrm{plus}(X_1, 0, X_1).$$
$$\mathrm{plus}(X_2, Y_2, Z_2) \rightarrow \mathrm{plus}(X_2, \mathrm{succ}(Y_2), \mathrm{succ}(Z_2)).$$

The first clause expresses the fact that $x + 0 = x$ for all (natural integers) x; the second says that $x + (y + 1) = (x + y) + 1$. Together these define inductively the concept plus over all terms of the form 0, $\mathrm{succ}(0)$, $\mathrm{succ}(\mathrm{succ}(0))$, etc. Note that the two clauses are implicitly quantified by $\forall X_1$, $\forall X_2$, $\forall Y_2$, and $\forall Z_2$ and conjoined together.

Let $\mathcal{L}$ be a fixed first-order language with equality and at least one constant symbol. $U_{\mathcal{L}}$ denotes the Herbrand universe of variable-free terms over $\mathcal{L}$. In the example above, $U_{\mathcal{L}}$ is the set $\{0, \mathrm{succ}(0), \mathrm{succ}(\mathrm{succ}(0)), \ldots\}$. Let p be an n-place predicate in $\mathcal{L}$; a *model* $M(p)$ of p is a set of atoms $p(t_1, \ldots, t_n)$, where each t_i is a term in $U_{\mathcal{L}}$. Thus the model associated with the predicate symbol p is a concept — namely, a subset of $U_{\mathcal{L}}$. A *model* M over $\mathcal{L}$ is the union of models $M(p)$ over all predicate symbols p in $\mathcal{L}$.

The objective of the Inductive Synthesis system is to find a sentence φ in $\mathcal{L}$ representing the model M in the following way: the set of variable-free atoms, or *facts*, that are logical consequences of φ is precisely the set M.

For example, the predicate plus defined above is one representation for the model consisting of the set of facts:

$$\mathrm{plus}(0, 0, 0)$$

$$\text{plus}(0, \text{succ}(0), \text{succ}(0))$$
$$\text{plus}(\text{succ}(0), 0, \text{succ}(0))$$
$$\text{plus}(\text{succ}(0), \text{succ}(0), \text{succ}(\text{succ}(0)))$$

$$\cdots$$

This same model can also be represented in many other ways.

We assume that there is a teacher who knows what M is and who can provide information about M in various ways. Among these is to give a counterexample to a hypothesis φ, if φ does not exactly represent M. For example, suppose our hypothesis for the plus concept above is

$$\mathbf{T} \to \text{plus}(X, Y, 0)$$

(i.e., for all x and y, $x + y = 0$). Then a counterexample to this hypothesis would be

$$-\text{plus}(0, \text{succ}(0), 0).$$

The flag "$-$" in the example signals that this atom is not in the target model $M(\text{plus})$. Again, in response to the hypothesis

$$\mathbf{T} \to \text{plus}(X, \text{succ}(Y), Y).$$

the teacher might return, as counterexamples, either of the following:

$$+\text{plus}(0, 0, 0)$$

$$-\text{plus}(0, \text{succ}(0), 0)$$

Note that we are expecting the teacher to have "superpowers", since in general no recursive computation exists that can answer correctly all such queries. However for many expressive domains of practical concern, these are either decidable questions or approximately decidable in the sense that an algorithm can provide the answers with high probability, or, at worst, answer, "I don't know".

The Inductive Synthesis algorithm is a variant of the idea of identification by enumeration, with an important change: when the hypothesis is found to be incorrect, the unit of modification is the clause, not the entire hypothesis. That is, when given a counterexample for its current hypothesis, the algorithm either discovers an incorrect clause and modifies it, or supplies an additional clause needed to account for additional positive examples.

A simplified version of the algorithm is as follows:

Inductive Synthesis Algorithm (Outline)

1. Initialize the current hypothesis φ to the empty sentence. (The empty sentence has no clauses and thus represents the null-set model.)

2. While φ is incorrect, repeat the following.

    2.1 Obtain from the teacher a counterexample $\pm e$ and store it.

2.2 Repeat the following until φ is correct for all stored facts.

   2.21 If φ fails to imply some stored *positive* example, find a predicate $p \in \mathcal{L}$ such that, for some fact $e \in M(p)$, e is not a consequence of φ. Then add to φ a clause that covers (implies) the fact e.

   2.22 If φ implies some stored *negative* example, find an incorrect clause in φ and remove it.

3. Write down φ as the solution.

As a slightly more elaborate example, consider the target sentence consisting of the two previous clauses defining plus, together with the following two clauses defining times:

$$\mathbf{T} \rightarrow \texttt{times}(X_3, 0, 0).$$
$$\texttt{times}(X_4, Y_4, W_4) \wedge \texttt{plus}(X_4, W_4, Z_4) \rightarrow \texttt{times}(X_4, \texttt{succ}(Y_4), Z_4).$$

We start the algorithm with the empty sentence as the current hypothesis, expressing the conjecture that no term is the sum of any other terms nor the product of any other terms. In response, assume the teacher returns the counterexample,

$$+\texttt{plus}(\texttt{succ}(0), \texttt{succ}(0), \texttt{succ}(\texttt{succ}(0))).$$

The algorithm, noting that this fact is not covered by the empty sentence, determines that the theory of the predicate plus is incomplete and adds a clause, say

$$\mathbf{T} \rightarrow \texttt{plus}(X, Y, Z),$$

to φ. Next, the teacher tells us this hypothesis is too general by providing the counterexample $-\texttt{plus}(0, 0, \texttt{succ}(\texttt{succ}(0)))$. In response the algorithm removes the clause, but is now back where it started since φ no longer covers the first example. So it searches again, this time for a less general clause that both implies the first example and fails to imply the second. For example, the clause

$$\texttt{plus}(X, Y, \texttt{succ}(X))$$

will cover these two examples.

Either this pattern of hypothesis-and-counterexample repeats forever, or the algorithm converges to a sentence equivalent to the target definitions of plus and times, at which point the teacher cannot return any counterexample and the algorithm halts with a correct sentence.

To complete the description of the algorithm, we also need

- a diagnosis procedure for finding an incomplete predicate or erroneous clause causing the failure;

- a search procedure to find an appropriate clause to cover a missing fact.

These I shall describe presently. Another requirement is that the algorithm be able to decide whether its hypothesis φ implies a given atom e. In general this problem is partially undecidable, but as a practical matter, useful concept representations often come with a bound on the time required to decide membership in that concept. If the algorithm cannot prove or disprove membership of an example within the bounded number of steps, it may conclude that the hypothesis fails on that example.[2]

Diagnosis procedure. The diagnosis problem is typical of the "credit assignment" dilemmas that often arise in search problems. Continuing the above example, suppose the algorithm has reached the point where the hypothesis φ has the correct definition of times, but has not yet acquired the full definition of plus. The example

$$+\texttt{times}(0, \texttt{succ}(\texttt{succ}(0)), 0)$$

will be a counterexample to φ if, for example, only the clause

$$\mathbf{T} \to \texttt{plus}(X, 0, X)$$

is missing from φ. The algorithm must somehow determine that it is the plus predicate that is in error, not times.

That the diagnosis problem is solvable depends on the following two lemmas:

- If φ implies a fact not in M, then φ contains an incorrect clause — more specifically, φ contains a clause C not valid in M.

- If φ fails to imply a fact in M, then φ is incomplete — more specifically, there exists a clause C valid in M but not implied by φ.

These are fairly obvious when the target concept has only one predicate (as in the plus example above), but with more than one, the interactions among the various clauses make it difficult to assign blame within φ. These simple lemmas are crucial in telling us that the problem can be traced to at least one predicate p and its target $M(p)$.

To diagnose a negative counterexample, proceed as follows. We assume the teacher can answer *membership queries* of the form: "Is the ground atom $p(\dots)$ in $M(p)$?". First, construct the resolution proof $\varphi \vdash e$ (where e is a negative example). Let $(P_1 \wedge \dots \wedge P_n) \to Q$ be the clause in which Q unifies with e via the substitution θ. For each of the premises P_i we ask the teacher if the fact $\theta(P_i)$ is in M. If the response is yes for all i, then this clause is erroneous, since true premises are implying a false result; diagnosis then returns this clause. Otherwise, let $\theta(P_i)$ be false in M. Since $\varphi \vdash \theta(P_i)$, we recursively diagnose this false example.

To diagnose a positive counterexample, proceed as follows. We assume the teacher can answer *existential queries*: given an atom $p(t_1, \dots, t_n)$ in which some of the terms t_i contain variables, enumerate the instantiations of the variables that yield atoms in $M(p)$. Let e be a positive example not covered by φ. Since $\varphi \not\vdash e$, one of two situations

---

[2] This formalizes a heuristic we use to decide whether our programs are looping endlessly or not.

must hold: (1) no clause in φ unifies with e — in which case the predicate p in the atom e is incompletely covered by φ, and the diagnosis returns p; or (2) every clause in φ whose conclusion unifies with e has at least one premise P_i not implied by φ. For each such premise, we ask the teacher to enumerate the instances of P_i that are true in M, and if φ fails to imply any of these, we recursively investigate these for incompleteness.

Refinement search. The search for a new clause to cover a missing fact $+e$ plays a vital role in the correctness and efficiency of the learning procedure. The search must be complete, in that no possible clause may be overlooked indefinitely as a candidate. The search must also be systematic: once a clause has been discarded it should never again be tried. Shapiro accomplishes this by defining a well-founded partial ordering $\preceq$ on clauses whose conclusion contains the predicate p. *Well-founded* means that the ordering should be semi-infinite, with no infinite descending chains. In addition, the relation $\preceq$ is chosen so that $C_1 \preceq C_2$ only if C_1 subsumes C_2. An ordering with these properties is called a *refinement* relation.

We use this ordering as follows:

- Whenever a clause is removed from a hypothesis, that clause is *marked*.

- When searching for a clause to cover a missing fact, we select from the unmarked clauses one that is minimal with respect to the ordering $\preceq$.

An example of a refinement on Horn clauses over the predicate plus is the following:

- The clause that is minimum with respect to $\preceq$ is $\mathbf{T} \to \text{plus}(X_1, Y_1, Z_1)$.

- Given the clause $C = (P_1 \wedge \ldots \wedge P_n) \to \text{plus}(t_1, t_2, t_3)$, we form the set of clauses directly beyond C in the ordering by applying one of the following modifications to C:

  - Unify two distinct variables in C. For example, from the clause

  $$\mathbf{T} \to \text{plus}(X_1, Y_1, Z_1)$$

  we obtain

  $$\mathbf{T} \to \text{plus}(X_1, X_1, Z_1)$$

  and

  $$\mathbf{T} \to \text{plus}(X_1, Y_1, Y_1).$$

  - Replace all occurrences of a variable $X \in C$ by a constant or a function in its most general instantiation. For example, from

  $$\mathbf{T} \to \text{plus}(X_1, Y_1, Y_1)$$

  we can obtain, among other clauses,

  $$\mathbf{T} \to \text{plus}(X_1, 0, 0)$$

  and

  $$\mathbf{T} \to \text{plus}(\text{succ}(X_1), Y_1, Y_1).$$

o Add as a new premise to the clause C an atom in its most general instantiation. For example, from

$$\mathbf{T} \rightarrow \text{plus}(\text{succ}(X_1), Y_1, Z_1)$$

we can obtain, among other clauses,

$$\text{plus}(X_2, Y_2, Z_2) \wedge \mathbf{T} \rightarrow \text{plus}(\text{succ}(X_1), Y_1, Z_1)$$

and

$$\text{times}(X_2, Y_2, Z_2) \wedge \mathbf{T} \rightarrow \text{plus}(\text{succ}(X_1), Y_1, Z_1).$$

With this refinement, we will eventually generate every possible clause (or an equivalent to every possible clause), and are thereby assured that search for a clause to satisfy a set of examples will terminate successfully.

Convergence properties.   We have now sketched the main features of the Inductive Synthesis algorithm: the basic algorithm itself, the requirements of the teacher, the diagnosis algorithm, and the search-for-clause mechanism using a refinement relation. The main theoretical result about this algorithm is that it works: *For any model M over $\mathcal{L}$ that can be expressed with a Horn sentence, the algorithm converges in a finite number of iterations to a Horn sentence φ such that, for any fact f, $\varphi \vdash f$ iff $f \in M$.*

The way the algorithm obtains just the information it needs from the teacher, locates errors within the current hypothesis, and searches systematically for the right combination of clauses are all highly original contributions to the theory and practice of inductive inference. Its limitations are that it stores all examples (violating the low-storage desideratum), relies on totally accurate information from the teacher, and requires explicit examples of all predicates $p \in \mathcal{L}$, not just examples of the target concept. For example, we might want the algorithm to see examples of the predicate **times** and infer that some intermediate predicate (**plus**) is required in the definition of **times**. The inference of auxiliary concepts is recognized as a difficult problem, for which no one has yet found a satisfactory solution.

Sources.   Identification in the limit was first defined and studied by Gold [33]. An excellent survey of inductive inference theory and techniques is to be found in the review article by Angluin and Smith [7]. The Inductive Synthesis algorithm began as the Model Inference System of Ehud Shapiro [78, 77], and was eventually recast as a system for synthesis of Prolog programs from examples of their input/output behavior [76]; the latter monograph also contains a detailed implementation.

The elegance of Shapiro's algorithm has inspired other authors to explore ways of generalizing and applying the ideas. The algebraic (as opposed to logical) basis of the algorithm was exposed by Laird [51]. Angluin [13] compares the power and complexity of several types of query capabilities in teachers, including the ones employed by Shapiro. Whereas Shapiro's refinement search replaces a clause by one that is more specific, others [39, 24] have employed generalization in their search, replacing a clause by one that covers more examples. Algorithms that are constructive (formulate hypotheses directly from the examples) rather than enumerative (like Shapiro's algorithm) are potentially more efficient; a few such algorithms have been found, including a subclass of logic programs [72] and linear grammars [82].

3   Bayesian Induction

As a representation language for AI, first-order logic leaves unresolved many difficulties, among them how to incorporate plausible deductions from uncertain premises in a formally consistent way. Indeed, the entire subject of uncertainty reasoning is an active research topic in AI. Curiously, the basis for much of the current research on plausible reasoning was discovered more than two centuries ago: Thomas Bayes's famous theorem on conditional probabilities has enabled scientists from Laplace and Gibbs to Keynes and Shannon to derive statistically sound inferences from noisy data.

In this section we continue with the general problem of how to make inferences by induction; but instead of first-order logic, we shall adopt *probabilistic logic*, with emphasis on the learning aspects. The general situation is familiar: we have some sample data, and we have a choice of hypotheses with which to explain the data. But now, because of noise and other random factors, the data can serve only as evidence for and against certain hypotheses, not as counterexamples to eliminate incorrect hypotheses. How, then, do we choose a hypothesis using the evidence? And as new data arrive, how can we revise our hypotheses so that eventually we converge? And finally, given that we converge, do we necessarily converge to a good hypothesis?

A Calculus of Beliefs.   A formal logic of plausible deduction extends Boolean logic by capturing formally the sorts of deductions that humans perform every day:

- if A frequently implies B and A occurs, then B is more plausible;

- if A implies B and B occurs, then A is more plausible;

- if A implies B and A is known to be false, then B becomes less plausible.

An essential requirement of such a logic is that it be *consistent*: from the same evidence, all paths of reasoning should produce the same conclusions. The logic should also subsume standard Boolean logic when all probabilities are 1 or 0.

In place of implications, we introduce *conditionals*. The conditional $(A \mid B)$ represents, roughly, the possibility that proposition A holds, given the certain knowledge that proposition B holds. Similarly the conditional $(A \wedge B \mid C \wedge D)$ represents the possibility that both A and B hold, given the certainty of both C and D. Probabilistic logic replaces the validity of propositions by a measure of belief, a function ("probability function") that assigns a value to every conditional.

The principal problem of probabilistic logic is to determine the requisite properties of every appropriate measure of belief. Formally this is the reverse of mathematical probability theory, where a probability measure is defined axiomatically, and theorems are obtained relating the measures of different sets. To serve as a useful model of a rational agent, a probability function should satisfy certain *desiderata*. For example, as the probability $p(A \mid B)$ increases, then $p(\neg A \mid B)$ should decrease. Again, if $(A' \mid C)$ is more probable than $(A \mid C)$, then for any event B, $(A' \wedge B \mid C)$ should be at least as probable as $(A \wedge B \mid C)$. Standard probability theory (assigning real numbers to measurable sets) satisfies these and other desiderata, and by general agreement fulfills the requirements of a calculus of beliefs. But is it the *only* such way to compute beliefs?

There have been many attacks on this question, starting with Keynes in 1921. Cox, in 1946, proposed a set of desiderata for a "rational" agent and asked whether all logics satisfying the same desiderata are isomorphic to probability theory. In effect his answer was "yes": if beliefs are real numbers, and if events are formulas in propositional logic, and we take as axioms the product rule[3]

$$p(A \wedge B \mid C) = p(A \mid B \wedge C)p(B \mid C)$$

and the sum rule

$$p(A \mid B) + p(\neg A \mid B) = 1$$

(where $1 \equiv p(B \mid B)$), then any consistent logic coincides with probability theory. But, as others have observed, humans carry out plausible inference quite well without real numbers — e.g., with just the values of "likely", "unlikely", "certain", and "impossible". Evidently the axioms proposed by Cox are too strong in their insistence that "probabilities" be real numbers.

Cox's work has since been generalized, most recently by Aleliunas [2]. An example of a set of axioms weak enough to construct a consistent belief logic based on non-numerical probabilities is shown in Figure 1. The set $\mathcal{L}$ of formulas is the collection of expressions over a finitely generated Boolean algebra, with propositions $\{A, B, \ldots, \mathbf{T}, \mathbf{F}\}$, maximum ($\mathbf{T}$) and operations $\wedge$, $\vee$, $\neg$. Conditionals are elements of $\mathcal{L} \times \mathcal{L}$. Probabilities are elements of a partially ordered set $(\mathbf{P}, \leq)$. For example, $\mathbf{P}$ could be the reals under the usual total ordering, or the set $\{impossible, possible, probable, certain\}^+$ with a partial ordering that extends the basic ordering $impossible \leq possible \leq probable \leq certain$ to this set. Probabilities are associated with formulas by a function $p : \mathcal{L} \times \mathcal{L} \to \mathbf{P}$, whose properties are governed by the axioms.

The axioms define the necessary properties of the family $\mathcal{P}$ of all such belief measures. Among the properties of $\mathcal{P}$ is that probabilities of complementary conditionals $p(\neg A \mid B)$ and $p(A \mid B)$ are related by a monotone non-increasing function c on $\mathbf{P}$. In the case of ordinary real probability, $c(x)$ is the function $1 - x$. Another property is the existence of an order-preserving dyadic function h, which in ordinary probability is multiplication. Many familiar properties of ordinary probability theory follow as theorems from the axioms, including the existence and uniqueness of probabilities $1 \equiv p(A \mid A)$ and $0 \equiv p(\neg A \mid A)$. But, in contrast to the Keynes/Cox formulation, these axioms admit models that are quite different from standard probability theory.

---

[3] Cox [27] argues semi-formally from desiderata that the product rule is the only axiom for computing $p(A \wedge B \mid C)$ from other conditionals, consistent with our common sense about causality and plausible reasoning. Similarly he argues that the sum rule is necessary, based primarily on the need to be consistent with the product rule.

A theorem of Aleliunas based on these axioms puts the Keynes/Cox results into perspective:

Suppose $\mathbf{P}$ *is totally ordered. For* $p \in \mathbf{P}$ *and any integer* $n > 0$, *let* p^n *denote the value* $h(p, p^{n-1})$, *with* $p^1 = p$. *Suppose also that the set* $\mathbf{P}$ *of probability values satisfies the following property: for any probabilities* $p \neq 1$ *and* $q \neq 0$, *there exists a positive integer* n *such that* $p^n < q$. *Then the structure of* $(\mathbf{P}, \leq)$ *is isomorphic to a subalgebra of real probabilities, with* $h(x,y)$ *corresponding to multiplication* $x \times y$ *and* $c(x)$ *to* $1 - x$.

Bayesian Learning Algorithms. Having chosen a belief function p (which, for clarity, we now assume is standard real probability), we can then take up the learning problem. In the Bayesian approach, the learning problem changes in three important ways.

- Whereas for Boolean logic every hypothesis is equivalent to a characteristic function on the set U with value 1 for points that are in the concept and 0 for points not in the concept, in the Bayesian framework a point is *in* the concept with a certain probability. Thus a concept hypothesis is equivalent to a generalized characteristic function that assigns $p(x) \in [0,1]$ to each point x in U.

- Whereas inductive synthesis has at each stage of the learning procedure a hypothesis that represents its current understanding of the target concept, the Bayesian approach does not single out any hypothesis as the current favorite. Instead, at each stage of a Bayesian learning procedure the algorithm assigns a probability to each hypothesis, representing its belief in that hypothesis as the target.[4]

- Whereas the Inductive Synthesis model assumes that a teacher provides counterexamples to any incorrect hypotheses, the notion of "counterexample" is meaningless in the probabilistic setting. Instead a teacher selects points from U according to some arbitrary process (unknown to the learner), and probabilistically classifies those examples as "in" or "out" according to some target hypothesis H_*.

Formally, we assume a set U of sample points and a set $\mathcal{H} = \{H_1, H_2, \ldots\}$ of hypotheses. The countability assumption for $\mathcal{H}$ is a matter of convenience, not necessity; but we do require that no two hypotheses in $\mathcal{H}$ be equivalent. Each hypothesis H_i assigns to each point x in U a probability, which we interpret as the probability that x is a member of the concept H_i. For concept learning this probability depends only on the hypothesis H_i and the point x; it is independent of any other events.[5] An example e is a point $x \in U$ together with a flag ($+$ or $-$). As usual, a "$+$" flag indicates that

---

[4]From a slight change of viewpoint, the "current hypothesis" in the Bayesian framework can be taken to be the function assigning a belief to each rule. However this view has not been used.

[5]Bayesian learning can also be applied to learning problems other than concept learning. In these situations temporal dependencies may become part of the hypotheses and the way that the sample is presented.

Aleliunas's axioms for a family P of belief functions over $(\mathbf{P}, \leq)$ and $\mathcal{L}$:

1. $\forall p \in P$, $A_1, B_1, A_2, B_2 \in \mathcal{L}$: if $A_1 \equiv B_1$ and $A_2 \equiv B_2$ then $p(A_1 \mid A_2) = p(B_1 \mid B_2)$.

2. $\forall p \in P$, $A \in \mathcal{L}$: $p(A \mid \mathbf{F}) = p(A \mid A)$.

3. $\forall p \in P, A, B \in \mathcal{L}$: $p(A \wedge B \mid B) = p(A \mid B) \leq p(B \mid B)$.

4. $\forall p_1, p_2 \in P$, $A \in \mathcal{L}$: $p_1(A \mid A) = p_2(A \mid A)$.

5. There exists a monotone non-increasing function $c : \mathbf{P} \to \mathbf{P}$ such that $\forall p \in P, A, B \in \mathcal{L}$: $c(p(A \mid B)) = p(\neg A \mid B)$, provided B is not logically equivalent to $\mathbf{F}$.

6. There exists a function $h : \mathbf{P} \times \mathbf{P} \to \mathbf{P}$ such that $\forall p \in P, A, B, C \in \mathcal{L}$:

   - h is order-preserving on each of its arguments;
   - $p(A \wedge B \mid C) = h(p(A \mid B \wedge C), p(B \mid C))$;
   - Let $0_{p,C} \equiv p(\neg A \mid A)$. If $p(A \wedge B \mid C) = 0_{p,C}$, then either $p(A \mid C) = 0_{p,C}$ or $p(B \mid A \wedge C) = 0_{p,C}$.

7. $\forall p \in P, A, B \in \mathcal{L}$: if $p(A \mid B) \leq p(A \mid \neg B)$, then $p(A \mid B) \leq p(A \mid \mathbf{T}) \leq p(A \mid \neg B)$.

8. $\forall x, y, z \in \mathbf{P}$, and distinct $A, B, C \in \mathcal{L}$: there exist functions $p_1, p_2, p_3 \in P$ (not necessarily distinct) such that

   - $p_1(A \mid \mathbf{T}) = x$, $p_1(B \mid A) = y$, and $p_1(C \mid A \wedge B) = z$.
   - $p_2(A \mid B) = p_2(A \mid \neg B) = x$ and $p_2(B \mid A) = p_2(B \mid \neg A) = y$.
   - $p_3(A \mid \mathbf{T}) = x$ and $p_3(A \wedge B \mid \mathbf{T}) = y$ whenever $y \leq x$.

Figure 1: Axioms of a probabilistic logic.

the point x is in the target concept, and vice versa for "$-$". *But in different examples, the same point x may be flagged with different signs by the teacher*, because (recall) x is in the concept only with some probability p and out with probability $1 - p$. If the target hypothesis assigns probability p to x, then on average the teacher will flag x "$+$" a fraction p, and "$-$" a fraction $1 - p$ of the times that x is presented.

The elementary propositions in $\mathcal{L}$ are of two types: (1) "H_i is the target hypothesis"; and (2) "the example e". The conditional $(+x \mid H_i)$ is the event that the teacher classifies the point x as "in" the concept, given that the target hypothesis is H_i. We ordinarily assume that $p(+x \mid H_i)$ can be computed from knowledge of both x and H_i. Clearly $p(-x \mid H_i) = 1 - p(+x \mid H_i)$. The conditional $(H_i \mid e)$ is the event that H_i is the target hypothesis used by the teacher, given the example e. $p(H_i \mid e)$ denotes our belief in H_i, given e. To compute this probability is the objective of the learning algorithm.

The basis of the learning algorithm is Bayes's Theorem. It may appear that we have lost Bayes's Theorem in the formalism above, but it can be found lurking in Axiom 6 of Figure 1:

$$p(A \wedge B \mid C) = h(p(A \mid B \wedge C), p(B \mid C)).$$

Since $A \wedge B \equiv B \wedge A$, we have (by the first axiom)

$$h(p(A \mid B \wedge C), p(B \mid C)) = h(p(B \mid A \wedge C), p(A \mid C)).$$

When h is ordinary multiplication, we immediately recognize Bayes's rule.

I shall first describe the general procedure without reference to Bayes's rule, and then consider what it all means. The learning algorithm proceeds in "stages" — receiving an example, updating beliefs in each hypothesis, receiving another example, and so forth. By the term "stage k" we refer to the interval after examining the k'th example e_k but before examining the $k + 1$'st. The symbol $\mathbf{e}_k$ indicates the sequence $e_1 e_2 \ldots e_k$ of examples examined in the first k stages. At each stage k in the learning process, including the initial stage ($k = 0$) before any data have been seen, there is a bias function $\beta_k \colon \mathcal{H} \to [0, 1]$ expressing the learner's preference for each of the hypotheses. This bias is normalized:[6]

$$\sum_i \beta_k(H_i) = 1. \tag{1}$$

At stage k, our bias β_k toward any hypothesis H_i will depend on the observations $\mathbf{e}_k$ as well as our initial bias β_0. A larger value for $\beta_k(H)$ indicates a stronger belief in the hypothesis H.

To compute the bias for any hypothesis H_i given the input sequence $\mathbf{e}_k$, the algorithm uses the following formula:

$$\beta_k(H_i) = c \, \beta_0(H_i) \, p(\mathbf{e}_k \mid H_i). \tag{2}$$

Here, c is a normalizing constant chosen to satisfy (1). The factor $p(\mathbf{e}_k \mid H_i)$ is called the *likelihood* of the evidence $\mathbf{e}_k$ given the hypothesis H_i. Thus we can interpret (2) as

---

[6] One sometimes allows β_0 to be unnormalized, a so-called *improper prior*.

changing the new bias for H_i in proportion to the prior bias $\beta_0(H_i)$ and the likelihood that the hypothesis H_i would have produced the observations. If both factors are large, our belief in the hypothesis is also large. But a large likelihood can be counteracted by a small prior bias, or vice versa. For example, in most locations our prior belief that an earthquake will occur is so small that, when the building shakes, we are much more likely to conclude that a truck has passed nearby, despite knowing that an earthquake would likely produce just such vibrations.

In (2) we have an algorithm for computing the bias function β_k from the example data, but what does this quantity mean? It is natural to interpret $\beta_k(H_i)$ as "the probability that the correct hypothesis is H_i", although this sentence makes no sense in the context of classical probability theory. By letting $\beta_k(H_i) \equiv p(H_i \mid e_k)$ in (2), and setting $1/c = \sum_j p(e_k \mid H_j)\beta_0(H_j)$, we again have a formal statement of Bayes's rule for the probability of (belief in) the hypothesis H_i given the evidence e_k. The initial bias β_0 should reflect our prior beliefs in the hypotheses. (See the discussion of priors, below.)

What is the result of this algorithm after processing a large sample of data? If one of our hypotheses H_i is correct, and if the teacher selects points in a reasonable way (e.g., selects them at random), then if the learning algorithm is sound we should expect $\beta_k(H_j)$ to converge uniformly to

$$\delta_{ij} = \begin{cases} 1 & \text{if } i = j \\ 0 & \text{otherwise} \end{cases}$$

in the limit as $k \to \infty$. To prove such a property we would need to know more about the domain, the choice of β_0, and the process for selecting examples; but given these, the requisite proof techniques are well known. Moreover, the convergence property usually holds regardless of the choice of prior bias β_0, provided that $\beta_0(H_*) > 0$ for the target hypothesis H_*.

For the Bayesian learning algorithm (2) to be a practical learning algorithm, we need to be able to compute $p(e_k \mid H_i)$ rather easily. In concept learning we already have a simplifying assumption that makes this possible, namely that the teacher classifies each example independently of the other examples. Thus

$$p(e_k \mid H_i) = p(e_1 \mid H_i) \ldots p(e_k \mid H_i).$$

Another useful feature of the Bayesian learning algorithm is the potential for incremental revision of beliefs. As more data are obtained, it may not be necessary to calculate the probability $\beta_{k+1}(H)$ from scratch using all $k + 1$ data values. Often we can use our previous result β_k and the new data value e_{k+1} to obtain β_{k+1}, and thereby free ourselves from having to store a complete history of the data. The idea is based on the following simple calculation:

$$
\begin{aligned}
\beta_{k+1}(H) &= p(H \mid e_{k+1}) \\
&= p(H \mid e_{k+1}, e_k) \\
&= c\, p(e_{k+1} \mid e_k, H)\, p(H \mid e_k) \\
&= c\, p(e_{k+1} \mid e_k, H)\, \beta_k(H) \\
&= c\, p(e_{k+1} \mid H)\, \beta_k(H).
\end{aligned}
$$

The last equality is a consequence of the independent-classification assumption. Again, c is some normalizing constant. Thus $\beta_{k+1}(H)$ can be computed knowing only β_k and the last example e_{k+1}. The independence assumption is critical to this argument and should therefore be examined carefully before adopting it in practice.

Bayesian Inferences   Now let us suppose that we employ a Bayesian learning algorithm in some domain, and that we are confident the algorithm converges in the limit to the correct hypothesis. At stage k what have we learned by computing β_k? Convergence in the limit is not particularly interesting unless we can draw useful inferences and make good decisions based on those inferences at finite times as well.

Following is an algorithm for inferring what we expect to observe at time $k+1$ in the way of concept membership. Let x be any point in U; write $p(+x_{k+1})$ to indicate the probability that x will be classified as "+" if selected by the teacher for presentation at stage $k + 1$. The probability of the example $+x_{k+1}$ given our current bias β_k is calculated from the formula:

$$p(+x_{k+1}) = \sum_i p(+x_{k+1} \mid H_i)\beta_k(H_i). \tag{3}$$

Computing $p(+x_{k+1})$ for one point x_{k+1} entails computing an average (over all hypotheses) of the likelihoods weighted by the biases. When $\mathcal{H}$ consists of a large number of hypotheses, this may not be a practical calculation to do exactly, but at least in theory we have the basis for making principled decisions from our predictions (by using a minimax strategy, for instance). Note that instead of choosing one of the hypotheses as our current favorite and making guesses based on that, we are basing predictions on all hypotheses, weighted by our beliefs in them. Thus the predictions may not coincide with those of any individual hypothesis in $\mathcal{H}$.

This is *one* algorithm for predicting concept membership, but is it a *correct* algorithm? After all, many algorithms are possible for choosing hypotheses and making inferences. If someone presented one of these other learning/inference algorithms, how might we argue that the Bayesian algorithm is as good or better?

Mathematically, of course, this question is nonsensical. We can point to our probability model and assert that our inference method is consistent with a rational agent based on certain axioms, and that these axioms satisfy certain desiderata specifying how a rational agent should act. But lacking formal criteria for the quality of an algorithm, we cannot prove one to be better than another.

For certain problems, however, useful criteria are available and formal results have been obtained. In many pattern recognition problems, examples are selected randomly by the teacher, and the stated objective is to minimize the mean squared difference between the true probabilities and those predicted by the target model H_*. Using this criterion, we can characterize an optimal algorithm as follows. For the point $x \in U$ let $F(+x)$ be the actual probability that x is classified as belonging to the concept. (F might not correspond to any hypothesis in $\mathcal{H}$.) Let $p(+x \mid e_k)$ be the probability predicted by an algorithm A based upon the data e_k. (When A happens to be the Bayesian algorithm, this is given by (3) above.) Then the *mean squared* error, $Err(A \mid F, \mathbf{e}_k)$, of the algorithm A based on $\mathbf{e}_k$ is given by

$$Err(A \mid F, \mathbf{e}_k) = \sum_{x \in U} [p(+x \mid \mathbf{e}_k) - F(+x)]^2,$$

and the *net mean squared error* $Err(A \mid F)$ is the expectation E_k of *Err* over all sequences $\mathbf{e}_k$ of k examples:

$$Err(A \mid F) = \mathsf{E}_k \sum_{x \in U} [p(+x \mid \mathbf{e}_k) - F(+x)]^2.$$

To quantify the overall error of A, we have to specify the distribution of the problems — i.e., the distribution $p'(F)$ of all possible F's. Then the error of the algorithm is:

$$Err(A) = \sum_F p'(F) Err(A \mid F). \tag{4}$$

We define an algorithm to be *optimal for the distribution $p'(F)$* if it minimizes $Err(A)$.[7]

For some classes of pattern recognition problems, the following has been proved: *Suppose a teacher selects a concept from the set $\mathcal{H}$, choosing H_i with probability $p'(H_i)$ $(1 \leq i \leq |\mathcal{H}|)$. Then the Bayesian algorithm based on (3), with prior $\beta_0(H_i) = p'(H_i)$, is an optimal algorithm for the distribution p' of problems. Moreover, this fact is independent of the number k of examples provided to the algorithm.* See [88] for more on this kind of analysis.

Priors. A significant point about the preceding theorem is that, to be optimal, the Bayesian algorithm needs to choose the prior β_0 to match the actual distribution of problem instances. But suppose there is *only one* problem instance? What, for example, is the probability of the destruction of the universe in the next century?

The Bayesian learning algorithm requires the learner, before seeing any data, to declare his bias for each of the hypotheses in the form of the function β_0. Besides making all such preferences explicit, this may help the learner to incorporate previous learning experiences and to express requirements external to the learning problem, such as a preference for simpler hypotheses over more complex ones. But this is also a source of controversy, for one must decide how to encode all prior information and preferences in the form of a real-valued function. And to be mathematically convincing, we must do so in a principled way.

Since Laplace, scholars have argued about the nature of *priors* (the function β_0), to the extent that for much of this century the field of statistical inference has been split into two camps: Bayesians, and those who reject Bayesian inference entirely because of the inherent subjectivity of choosing priors. To illustrate the problem, suppose we are trying to estimate the distance of a particular galaxy from Earth. We have, as data, the results of a small number k of independent astronomical experiments $\mathbf{e}_k = \{e_1, \ldots, e_k\}$, each of which produces a (noisy) estimate for the distance d. Being practiced Bayesians, we calculate for each experiment e_i the distribution $p(e_i \mid d)$ of

---

[7]Note that the number k of example points given as input to the algorithm is fixed. In effect we are comparing how well different algorithms do when given the same data.

observations given the distance d, and combine these into a distribution $p(d \mid \mathbf{e}_k)$ of distances using Bayes's rule:

$$p(d \mid \mathbf{e}_k) = c\,\beta_0(d)\,p(\mathbf{e}_k \mid d).$$

But what do we choose for $\beta_0(d)$, the prior distribution for d? If we assume total ignorance, we might choose a uniform "distribution" $\beta_0(d) = 1$ for $d > 0$.[8] But our ignorance is *not* total: we know that $d < \infty$; with even minimal knowledge of astronomy we can easily write down an upper bound $d_{\max}$ on this distance. Even if we could agree on a fixed value for $d_{\max}$, and choose $\beta_0(d)$ to be uniform over $[0, d_{\max}]$, we would have to admit that, if we are ignorant of d, we are equally ignorant of any function $f(d)$, so why shouldn't we choose $f(d)$ to be uniform over the interval $[0, f(d_{\max})]$? The problem here is one of quantifying ignorance in a consistent way: in different inference problems, each with the same prior information, we should choose the same prior β_0, even if we are inferring probabilities for different quantities.

No single satisfactory solution to this problem has been proposed, but a number of good ones have been suggested and applied successfully, particularly in domains of scientific inference. One is to select the prior distribution β_0 with maximum entropy $S(\beta_0) = -\sum_i \beta_0(H_i) \log \beta_0(H_i)$ satisfying all "testable" prior information. (A *testable* property of a distribution is one for which an effective decision procedure exists) Another is to construct priors so that the information is invariant under changes in scale (units of measurement) and translation of the coordinate system.

But just as evaluating an inference procedure depends on the definition of an optimal algorithm, any technique for choosing priors can be judged only by how successfully we derive inferences from them, and on no other basis. In all learning problems, we attack the problem by making prior assumptions about the nature of what we are learning; as a minimum this takes the form of choosing a representation for our hypotheses. The success of the learning algorithm depends strongly on the validity of these assumptions; and poor choices show up in the form of answers that predict and explain poorly. Bayesian priors are just another of these initial assumptions. A poor choice of priors is usually less critical than a poor choice of hypotheses, since the inferences become less dependent upon the priors as more data are obtained.

Sources. The probabilistic logic shown in Figure 1 and discussed in the surrounding text is due to Aleliunas [2, 3]; actually his axioms are slightly more general than the ones we have listed. Keynes [48], Cox [27], Aczél [1], and Tribus [83] contributed results leading up to this work. A different type of probabilistic logic, in which beliefs are probability ranges rather than point values, was explored by de Finetti [28] and independently by Nilsson [61]. Many techniques for drawing inferences from uncertain information have been devised, for which the book by Pearl [63] is an excellent, recent source.

Bayesian inference is a rich topic with many textbooks and references for both theory and application. As good examples we may cite the statistical texts by Berger [16] and Box and Tiao [22], and the pattern recognition texts by Duda and Hart [30]

---

[8] An improper prior; see footnote 6 above.

and Young and Calvert [90]. That Bayesian inference is no less than a general learning procedure has been noted [26] but not well documented, particularly in the theoretical literature. The book by Pearl [63] is perhaps the most complete central source to date for Bayesian inference techniques in AI. Applications of Bayesian inference abound; a good source for much of this work is the series of annual proceedings of the Maximum Entropy and Bayesian Inference Conference.

Polemics about the comparative merits of Bayesian learning *vis à vis* other methods are a constant source of entertainment, and no one entertains with more insight than Jaynes [40]. Closely related to Bayesian inference are the maximum-entropy method (due to Jaynes) and minimum-cross-entropy method (due to I. J. Good). This relationship is treated formally in [79]. Vapnik [88] discusses Bayesian and other methods for pattern recognition and proves the optimality result cited above.

[41] and [42] were breakthrough papers in the theory of choosing priors. Berger and Berry [17] argue cogently that classical statistical inference (of the Fisher-Neyman-Pearson school) is no less subjective than Bayesian statistics; they suggest that the Bayesian approach of including all subjective information explicitly in the form of priors is preferable to embedding it in the experimental procedure, where it is harder to identify.

4   Learnability

Although Bayesian learning is a powerful method for making inferences from sample data, little is known about how computationally difficult such an inference can be. In the past few years a series of formal learning models, often called learnability theory, has been used to study questions such as these:

- How complex is the learning problem in a particular domain? Particularly, what can be learned in (say) polynomial time or logarithmic space?

- If we change to a different representation, does the learning problem become quantifiably easier?

- How can a learning algorithm be designed with provable performance guarantees?

PAC-**Learnability.**   The *PAC*-learning[9] model differs from those we have considered until now by explicitly quantifying the running time of the learning algorithm and the accuracy of its result. We continue within the framework of concept learning, although the theory can be applied to other types of learning problems as well. The teacher in the *PAC*-learnability model selects points from the universe U independently and at random, with probabilities determined by some fixed probability distribution $\mathbf{P}$; the teacher then labels each one positive (if in the target concept) or negative (if not). The learner does not know what $\mathbf{P}$ is, and can make no assumptions about the distribution of the training data; hence the results are distribution independent.

---

[9] *PAC* is mnemonic for *probably approximately correct.*

Let $\mathcal{H} = \{H_1, H_2 \ldots\}$ be a family of concepts over U. The teacher selects a concept H_* from $\mathcal{H}$ and an arbitrary probability distribution $\mathbf{P}$ over the set U. The learner asks the teacher for some number m of examples. In response the teacher chooses m points from U, independently and randomly according to the distribution $\mathbf{P}$. The teacher then indicates for each point x whether x belongs to H_* and presents the set of labeled points to the learner.

The learner's task is to *approximate* the target concept H_* in finite time, to a specified accuracy. For any concept $H_i \in \mathcal{H}$, let $H_i \triangle H_*$ be the set $(H_i - H_*) \cup (H_* - H_i)$, the symmetric difference of the two concepts H_i and H_*. The concept H_i is said to be an *ϵ-approximation* of H_* if the probability $\mathbf{P}(H_i \triangle H_*)$ is at most ϵ. Such will be the case if the likelihood is small ($\leq \epsilon$) that another example from the teacher will be a counterexample to H_i. The learner may request any number m of examples, but he must output a hypothesis in $\mathcal{H}$ that ϵ-approximates H_*.

Note that the learner's success in approximating H_* is being measured by the same probability distribution used by the teacher to select examples. He is not penalized if his result incorrectly classifies points that occur only rarely. Thus *PAC*-learning mirrors the situation where we all have somewhat different versions of a concept (e.g., a "cup"), but agree on everyday instances of the concept (e.g., a coffeemug is a cup, but a tablespoon is not).

There is, in general, no way to guarantee that the learner will always produce an ϵ-approximation to the target concept as long as there is any possibility of drawing a wildly unrepresentative sample. The best we can require is that the learner do so on any run of the algorithm *with high probability*: if the algorithm is executed a large number of times, only a small fraction δ of them on average fail to output an ϵ-approximation.

Summarizing:

- A *PAC*-learning problem consists of four things: a concept family $\mathcal{H}$ over U, two parameters ϵ and δ, each in the range $(0, 1)$, and a teacher. The parameter ϵ is the required *accuracy* of, and δ the *confidence* in, the learner's output.

- The teacher selects a target concept $H_* \in \mathcal{H}$ and a probability distribution $\mathbf{P}$. Both of these are hidden from the learner.

- For every problem instance $(\epsilon, \delta, H_*, \mathbf{P})$, an algorithm for the *PAC*-learning problem requests a number of classified examples from the teacher, chooses a hypothesis $H_i \in \mathcal{H}$, and halts. The number of examples is called the *sample size*.

- The algorithm solves the problem if

$$\text{Prob}[(H_i \triangle H_*) > \epsilon] < \delta.$$

We say that the family $\mathcal{H}$ of concept representations is *(PAC-)learnable*[10] if there exists an algorithm to solve the *PAC*-learning problem.

---

[10]The appropriateness of the term *learnable* has been criticized, with justification. Along with other technical terms like *information*, it should be treated only as formal terminology.

Consider a simple example. Suppose U is the set $\{0,1\}^n$ of all Boolean n-tuples, and that we choose to represent concepts as Boolean formulas consisting of a single monomial. For example, the monomial $x_2(\neg x_3)$, which we shall write $x_2 x_3'$, represents the set of all n-tuples $(b_1, \ldots, b_n)$ with $b_2 = 1$ and $b_3 = 0$. Boolean variables x_i are commonly used to encode attributes of the target concept (e.g., "flies", "eats fish"). Suppose that the teacher selects the concept represented by the monomial $H_* = x_2 x_3'$ as the target, and chooses some probability distribution $\mathbf{P}$ over the n-tuples. Suppose also that the learning algorithm concludes by choosing $H = x_1 x_2$ for its hypothesis. This hypothesis agrees with the target on all points except those of the form $(1,1,1,*,\ldots,*)$ or $(0,1,0,*,\ldots,*)$; (where $*$ indicates either 0 or 1). This set of points is $H \triangle H_*$. If we sum the probabilities of each of these points and the result $\mathbf{P}(H \triangle H_*)$ is at most ϵ, then the learner's answer is an ϵ-approximation to the target. Suppose the algorithm requests lots of examples of the target concept, but by a quirk of probabilistic fate receives many copies of the same example $-(1,1,1,\ldots,1)$. Even though the probability of this happening may be extremely small, unless the probability of the point $(1,1,1,\ldots,1)$ is zero, it is still a possible sampling event. On the basis of this unrepresentative (and uninformative) sample, the learner may output a hypothesis that is not an ϵ-approximation to $x_2 x_3'$. But this is tolerable, provided this sample and others for which the algorithm does not produce an ϵ-approximation occur on any individual run of the algorithm with probability less than δ.

Polynomial-time PAC-learning. We have defined what it means for a domain to be learnable in the PAC framework, but we may also ask what domains are learnable using only "feasible" computational resources, especially time. According to current jargon, "feasible" means "bounded in running time by a polynomial in the parameters of the problem". Parameters here include the accuracy ϵ, the confidence δ, and some measure n of the problem size (such as the number of Boolean variables in the preceding problem). A family $\mathcal{H}$ of concept representations is *polynomial-time learnable* if it is learnable by an algorithm whose sample size is bounded by a polynomial in n, $1/\epsilon$, and $1/\delta$, and whose running time is bounded by a polynomial in the size of the sample.[11]

To explore these ideas, consider a concept class $\mathcal{H}$ of cardinality N. (N and n are usually different.) The following simple procedure, which we call the "filtering algorithm", is the basis for many PAC-learning algorithms. Request m examples from the teacher (where the value of m is still to be determined), and output any concept in $\mathcal{H}$ that is consistent with all m examples. The sample size m depends on ϵ, δ, and N. To compute a value for m, we reason as follows. If a hypothesis H is *not* an ϵ-approximation of the target, then the probability that a randomly chosen example will be consistent with H is no more than $1 - \epsilon$, and the probability that all m examples are consistent with H is at most $(1 - \epsilon)^m$. When $m = \epsilon^{-1} \ln(N/\delta)$, we have:

---

[11] We also assume that the learning algorithms are uniform for n, even though for some of the results cited this assumption is not necessary.

$$(1 - \epsilon)^m \leq e^{-\epsilon m}$$
$$= e^{-\ln(N/\delta)}$$
$$= \delta/N.$$

And since there are at most $N - 1$ concepts that are not ϵ-approximations, the probability is less than δ that any unacceptable hypothesis will survive the test of consistency with all m examples. Thus

$$m(N, \epsilon, \delta) = \frac{1}{\epsilon} \ln \frac{N}{\delta} \tag{5}$$

examples suffice to achieve *PAC*-learnability. The filtering algorithm is a poly-time *PAC*-learning procedure, *provided* that the teacher returns examples of polynomial length (in bits) and that the task of finding a consistent hypothesis in $\mathcal{H}$ can be solved in time polynomial in m. Whether or not these hold depends on the particular domain.

For the family of Boolean monomials used in the previous example, they do. With n attributes, there are 3^n monomial hypotheses, so it is infeasible to write them all down and scratch out the ones that disagree with some example. However, we can accomplish much the same thing by tracking each individual attribute. Initially we hypothesize the monomial $x_1 x_1' \ldots x_n x_n'$, the null concept. In response to a positive example $+(b_1, \ldots, b_n)$, for each i, if $b_i = 1$ then remove the variable x_i' from the hypothesis (if it has not already been removed); otherwise, if $b_i = 0$ then remove x_i. Negative examples will always be consistent with the current hypothesis, and may thus be ignored. After $m = \mathcal{O}[(n/\epsilon) \ln(1/\delta)]$ examples the resulting monomial satisfies the *PAC*-criteria.

But what about more complex domains where these do not hold? Note that the formula (5) is polynomial in $\log N$; thus as long as N, the number of hypotheses in $\mathcal{H}$, is $\mathcal{O}(2^{\text{poly}(n)})$, the sample size will be feasible. On the other hand, since there are 2^{2^n} Boolean concepts over $\{0,1\}^n$, this algorithm cannot be used to learn the family of arbitrary Boolean concepts. One is tempted to conclude that when $\log N$ is superpolynomial in n, the family $\mathcal{H}$ is not polynomial time learnable. But this is not so, since only a subset of $\mathcal{H}$ may be sufficient to provide an ϵ-approximation to any concept in $\mathcal{H}$.

Suppose the problem of finding a consistent formula is not feasible. We cannot conclude that the *PAC*-learning problem on $\mathcal{H}$ is infeasible, because there may be some other algorithm besides the filtering algorithm that solves the problem in polynomial time.

If neither the cardinality of $\mathcal{H}$ nor the difficulty of finding a consistent hypothesis determines whether a domain is polynomially *PAC*-learnable, we may ask what does. In [20], Blumer, Ehrenfeucht, Haussler, and Warmuth show that it is not the cardinality N, but the combinatorial property known as the Vapnik-Chervonenkis (VC) dimension of the family $\mathcal{H}$ that determines whether a polynomial size sample is likely to filter out all unacceptable hypotheses. Unfortunately space does not permit adequate definition or discussion of this quantity, other than to remark that the VC dimension is at most $\log_2 N$, but can be much smaller.[12] In the same paper, the authors also show

---

[12]For the important, but special, case of Boolean concepts families over n binary attributes, the same

that something very close to the consistency problem *is* the problem that, along with the VC dimension, determines whether the domain is polynomially *PAC*-learnable. Polynomial learnability of $\mathcal{H}$ is equivalent to the requirement that the VC dimension of $\mathcal{H}$ be bounded by a polynomial in n and that there exist a randomized poly-time algorithm taking a set of examples as input and producing, with probability at least $1/2$, a hypothesis in $\mathcal{H}$ consistent with the examples.

Change of representation. The learnability formalism also helps to quantify the impact of choosing a particular representation for concepts. A concept class is simply a family of subsets of U, but often there are many languages that can be used to represent the same family. For example, Boolean concepts — subsets of $\{0,1\}^n$— can be represented by arbitrary propositional formulas over n Boolean variables, or by disjunctive-normal-form formulas (DNF), or by conjunctive-normal-form formulas (CNF), etc. Similarly, concepts over binary strings can be represented by formal grammars, automata, and algebraic expressions.

Practitioners have long known that a mere change of representation can turn a difficult learning problem into an easy one and vice versa. The subset of the natural numbers, $\{1, 11, 1001, 110011, 1010001, \ldots\}$ in binary, is much easier to define in ternary: $\{1, 10, 100, 1000, 10000, \ldots\}$. Consider also the concept class $\mathcal{H}$ of concepts that can be represented by disjunctive normal form formulas with at most k terms. For example, $x_1 x_3' x_4 \vee x_2' x_4 x_8$ is a 2-term DNF formula but not a 1-term DNF. With growth measured by the number n of variables, this family is not *PAC*-learnable for any fixed $k > 1$ unless — contrary to conjecture — complexity classes NP and R are identical [64]. But by changing the problem to allow the learner to represent the same family of concepts in a different (and more expressive) language, called k-CNF (CNF formulas with at most k literals per conjunct), the class $\mathcal{H}$ becomes *PAC*-learnable. The reason for this turnabout is as follows. Concepts expressed in k-term DNF are hard to learn because the consistency problem is NP-hard, even though the requisite sample size is feasibly small. By contrast, the consistency problem for k-CNF requires only polynomial time [87]; moreover, every k-term DNF formula has an equivalent k-CNF formula of about the same size. Thus without any large increase in sample size over that needed for k-term DNF, we can quickly find a consistent k-CNF formula H' that ϵ-approximates the target concept. Of course since the k-term DNF family is properly contained in k-CNF, the algorithm may produce a k-CNF hypothesis that does not correspond to any k-term DNF concept. Neverthess, by this change of representation we satisfy the requirements of the *PAC*-learning problem: to find an ϵ-approximation of the target concept in polynomial time.

To summarize: For a given family C of possible target concepts (subsets of U), there are often many different languages (classes of formulas) for representing the concepts in C. The minimum requirement for such a language $\mathcal{H}$ is that every concept in C be represented by some formula in $\mathcal{H}$. It is possible that, for a class $\mathcal{H}$, the consistency problem is not tractable. In such cases it may help to change to a representation $\mathcal{H}'$ whose consistency problem is easier to solve. Let $\mathcal{H}$ and $\mathcal{H}'$ be representation

authors note that $\log N$ is bounded above by a polynomial in n iff the VC dimension is bounded above by a polynomial in n. This result also occurs in [57].

languages for a family of concepts over the same set U, We say that $\mathcal{H}$ *is* PAC-*learnable by* $\mathcal{H}'$ if there is an algorithm that solves the *PAC*-learning problem over $\mathcal{H}$ by choosing hypotheses from $\mathcal{H}'$. For every problem instance $(\epsilon, \delta, H_* \in \mathcal{H}, \mathbf{P})$, the algorithm must halt after obtaining some classified examples from the teacher and choosing a hypothesis $H_i' \in \mathcal{H}'$; and with probability at least $1 - \delta$, $\mathbf{P}(H_i' \triangle H_*) \leq \epsilon$. When $\mathcal{H}$ is *PAC*-learnable by $\mathcal{H}$, then $\mathcal{H}$ is *PAC*-learnable in accordance with our previous definition. One can easily show that if $\mathcal{H} \subseteq \mathcal{H}'$ and $\mathcal{H}'$ is polynomial-time *PAC*-learnable, then $\mathcal{H}$ is polynomial-time *PAC*-learnable by $\mathcal{H}'$.

Learnability of large concept classes. Learning $\mathcal{H}$ by a more expressive representation $\mathcal{H}'$ may not help if $\mathcal{H}'$ is *too expressive*. Consider concept classes that are regular sets of binary strings $\{0,1\}^*$. For any set of m examples, we can easily find a consistent hypothesis in the class of all deterministic finite automata (DFAs) by choosing an automaton that accepts precisely those strings occurring as positive examples. Yet rarely does a simple list of the positive examples qualify as learning, and the likelihood that this list ϵ-approximates the target DFA is probably rather small. In AI, this observation goes by the name of the *disjunction problem* [14]: representations that are expressive enough to include disjunctions (unions) of singleton concepts are too expressive because their consistency problem has a trivial solution.

In the terminology of learnability theory, domains with a disjunction problem (including DNF formulas and finite automata), are not *PAC*-learnable because the VC dimension increases too rapidly with the size parameter n. But here we encounter a serious weakness in our definition of *PAC*-learning: some domains that are not *PAC*-learnable according to the definitions and results cited above are, in actuality, quite learnable!

For example, consider again the class of DFAs accepting a subset of the binary strings $\{0,1\}^*$. The teacher picks a DFA of any size and a distribution over $\{0,1\}^*$, and presents a continual stream of classified examples. Can an algorithm *PAC*-learn this DFA? The VC dimension of the family of DFAs is infinite, so according to the main theorem of [20] it is not learnable from any finite sample size. But consider this algorithm:

1. Let H_1, H_2, ... be any enumeration of the DFAs. Set $i := 1$.

2. Obtain $m = \epsilon^{-1} \ln(2/\delta)$ examples, and test H_i for consistency with this sample.

3. If H_i disagrees with any example, increase i by 1, replace δ by $\delta/2$, and go to step 2.

4. Else write down the DFA H_i and halt.

It is not hard to show that this algorithm produces a *PAC*-approximation to the target. Thus DFAs *are* learnable. What is more, we have used no special properties of DFAs other than their enumerability and the ability to decide whether a DFA accepts an example string. Hence this argument applies equally to any recursively enumerable class with a decidable membership property, regardless of the VC dimension.

So where have we gone wrong? The problem is that our model of *PAC*-learning requires the learner to decide how many examples to obtain *before* testing any hypotheses.[13] This *a priori* sample size is the quantity that is determined by the VC dimension. Without that artificial requirement, some "unlearnable" classes become learnable and even polynomially learnable [53].

To correct this deficiency in our definitions we revise the learnability model as follows. Let C be a family of concepts — subsets of the (countable) set U. Let $\mathcal{H}$ be a family of representations for concepts in C such that every concept in C is represented by at least one hypothesis in $\mathcal{H}$. To each $H \in \mathcal{H}$ we assign an integer-valued measure $s(H)$ of simplicity, which we call *size*. We assume that $s(H) > 1$ and that $s(H)$ is easy to compute for all H. Let $\mathcal{H}_s$ be the subset of $\mathcal{H}$ consisting of all concept representations of size s; thus $\mathcal{H} = \bigcup_{s>0} \mathcal{H}_s$. A concept $C \in C$ *belongs to* $\mathcal{H}_s$ if s is the minimum size of any of its representations in $\mathcal{H}$; in this case we write $s(C) = s$. An instance of a PAC$_s$-*learning problem* is a concept $C_* \in C$, parameters ϵ and δ, and a teacher.

- The teacher chooses an arbitrary probability distribution $\mathbf{P}$ over U, and upon request, obtains a sample point x according to $\mathbf{P}$, classifies it as positive or negative according to C_*, and presents it to the learner.

- A learner takes the two parameters ϵ and δ, and outputs a hypothesis $H \in \mathcal{H}$, after obtaining a number of examples from the teacher. This number may depend on ϵ, δ, and the target C_*.

- We say that C *is* PAC$_s$-*learnable by* $\mathcal{H}$ if there exists a function $f(s, 1/\epsilon, 1/\delta)$ and a learner such that, for any problem instance, with probability at least $1 - \delta$, the learner requests at most $f(s(C_*), 1/\epsilon, 1/\delta)$ examples and writes down a hypothesis $H \in \mathcal{H}$ that ϵ-approximates C_*.

- We say that C *is polynomially* PAC$_s$-*learnable by* $\mathcal{H}$ if it is *PAC$_s$*-learnable by an algorithm for which the sample-size function $f(s, 1/\epsilon, 1/\delta)$ is polynomial in all three arguments, and which runs in time bounded by a polynomial in the size of the sample.

Note that the running time of the learner may increase with the size of the target concept. But since the learner does not know the size $s(C_*)$ in advance, he may need to keep increasing the sample size "on the fly" as he tests larger hypotheses.

Instead of the filtering algorithm, our prototype for designing efficient learning algorithm is as follows. Let $m(s)$ be a monotone increasing function with the property that $m(s)$ is an upper bound on the sample size needed to choose an ϵ-approximation to any concept of size at most s, with confidence $1 - \delta/2^s$. ($m(s)$ depends on the VC dimension of the domain.) Then

1. Initialize $s = 1$.

---

[13]This assumption in the definition of *PAC*-learnability and its implications went unnoticed by researchers for nearly two years.

2. Obtain enough additional examples so that a total of $m(s)$ examples are available.

3. If there exists a consistent hypothesis of size $\leq s$, write it down and halt.

4. Otherwise increase s by one and return to step 2.

Note the modified consistency problem in step 3. We can solve this problem if there is a polynomial-time algorithm to choose a hypothesis of minimum size consistent with the sample. And for many domains, the minimum-size consistency problem is polynomially related to the decision problem in step 3. Alas, for a number of interesting domains — including DNF and DFA — this problem is NP-hard. It may suffice, however, to find a consistent hypothesis *polynomially larger* than minimum, and this easier problem can sometimes be solved in polynomial time even when the minimum-size consistency problem cannot.

For example, an *Occam algorithm* is a procedure that finds a consistent hypothesis of size at most $s^c m^\alpha$ for some constant $c \geq 1$ and $\alpha < 1$, where s is the size of the minimum consistent hypothesis. Note the factor m^α: since $\alpha < 1$ the size of the resulting hypothesis is strictly smaller than the size of the sample (for all sufficiently large target concepts), so that the disjunction problem is eliminated. Upper bounds on the sample size $m(s)$ for Occam algorithms have been calculated as a function of the VC dimension [20].

Even with PAC_s-learnability some concept classes of particular interest remain hard to learn. For example, consider the class of Boolean concepts over $\{0,1\}^n$ represented in DNF. A convenient measure for the size s of a formula is the number of symbols. Boolean concepts are clearly PAC_s-learnable by DNF with an exponential sample size, but what about polynomial PAC_s-learnability? For any Boolean concept, there is a minimum-size DNF formula to represent it. Finding a minimum-size DNF formula consistent with a set of examples is NP-complete, so a minimum-size filtering algorithm is unlikely to lead to a poly-time algorithm. There may be an Occam or some other learning algorithm that requires polynomial time and a polynomial size sample, but none is known, and many researchers suspect that DNF is not polynomial PAC_s-learnable.

Arbitrary Boolean formulas (not just DNF) are a more compact representation than DNF. Hence the learning problem is more difficult, since the minimum-size formula is smaller and the allowable running time.correspondingly shorter. Recently Kearns and Valiant [47] showed that learning Boolean formulas is as hard as solving some number-theoretic problems (factoring Blum integers, deciding quadratic residuosity, etc.), all of them problems conjectured to be computationally infeasible.

The class of "regular" concepts (sets of binary strings accepted by DFAs) is of great practical significance. If we measure the size of a DFA by counting states, then each regular concept has a unique smallest representation as a DFA. We have seen that regular concepts are PAC_s-learnable by DFAs, but how complex is the learning problem? Finding the smallest DFA consistent with a set of examples is known to be NP-complete. Moreover, Pitt and Warmuth [66] have shown that learning regular concepts — whether by DFAs, NFAs, regular expressions, or regular grammars — is as hard as learning Boolean formulas, and recently they extended this to show that even finding a consistent DFA polynomially larger than the minimum is hard. An Occam algorithm is, therefore, unlikely to be found. Moreover, the results of [47] imply that the problems of learning acyclic DFAs and of learning a polynomial-size ϵ-approximation to a DFA are both as hard as the number-theoretic problems mentioned above. In short, the evidence is compelling that arbitrary Boolean formulas and finite automata are too general to be PAC_s-learnable.

Sources. The spark for the current interest in learnability theory was the pair of papers by Valiant [87, 86]. Statisticians have studied related models [29, 89]; recognition of the relevance of this work and applying it to concept learning was one contribution of the important paper by Blumer *et al.* [19]; the same paper also contains a proof that classes with infinite VC dimensions are not PAC-learnable. Others pointed out that this non-learnability property depends on the assumption that the sample size is independent of the target [53]. They showed that without this assumption any recursively enumerable hypothesis class with a decidable membership property is learnable.

To date the theory has accumulated more negative (non-learnability) results than positive. Hardness results for the consistency and other problems are given in [11, 12, 64, 46, 66, 65, 47]. Positive (learnability) results are available for k-CNF [87], k-decision lists [67], conjunctive and internal-disjunctive formulas [34], functions [58, 57], and others. Occam algorithms are introduced in [21]. When the learner can query actively, learning possibilities change substantially [13]. Even considering the known results for finite automata [5, 12, 69, 68], context-free grammars [73, 10], propositional Horn sentences [11], and problem-space operator heuristics [59], we have only begun to explore this learning problem. The recent volume [35] is a good source for recent research in learnability and other theoretical topics in learning.

An interesting model needs to be robust in the sense that minor variations in its definitions should leave the principal results intact. The PAC-model has many minor variations and several major ones; these are compared (and shown to be substantially equivalent) in [36]; see also [4]. An important variation, treated there and in [37], is the *prediction* model. The learner must predict membership of the randomly chosen point in the concept before the teacher informs him of the correct answer. Error is measured by the probability of making an incorrect prediction, as a function of the number of examples. Intuitively, a predictor that improves its prediction accuracy after polynomially many examples must be learning some way to approximate the target. Bounds on how well a predictor can do are closely related to bounds on how well a concept learner can do, independent of the choice of representation. This is especially useful in proving lower bounds for hard-to-learn concept classes.

In another important variation, the impact of errors in the teacher's training data has been examined. Errors can be deliberate (malicious errors) or random (noise), or in between. Errors can affect the choice of a point $x \in U$ or how the teacher classifies it ($+$ or $-$). Good bounds on several kinds of errors are known [45, 6, 75, 80, 52]. Closely related is the case where the target concept cannot be represented exactly by any hypothesis in the hypothesis class. Then the *closest approximating concept* becomes the objective of the learning process. Results on this problem are given in

[89], [53], and [4].

Most of the learnability research has been applied to concept learning, but some *PAC*-learning results are starting to appear in other areas too. Rivest and Schapire [69, 74] study the ability of a robot to model its environment using finite automata. Convergence of stochastic models is discussed in [9, 49, 50]. Sutton analyzes a class of incremental prediction models in [81]. Angluin [13] relates the *PAC*-learning model to that used by Shapiro and others, in which the learner must identify the target exactly while receiving from the teacher counterexamples to his hypotheses. Recently she has shown that DFA's and DNF formulas are not learnable in this model either [12, 8].

5   Network Models

Recall that AI has long had two competing representational paradigms:

- Explicit symbolic encoding of knowledge structures, coupled to inference algorithms for using that information; and

- A distributed network of rather simple processor nodes, wherein knowledge is an emergent property of the whole network and not necessarily apparent from its microstructure.

In the fifties, and again in the sixties, the latter, *connectionist* view, was aggressively explored, but the symbolic approach eventually assumed the more prominent part in research. The mid-eighties saw renewed interest in connectionist applications, fueled mainly by the (re-)discovery[14] of a learning algorithm known as *error back-propagation* and its application in several impressive experiments.

Actually this was not the first time that connectionist AI had been reinvigorated by the discovery of a learning algorithm: Rosenblatt's perceptron learning algorithm and the Adaline adaptation algorithm of Widrow and Hoff inspired a burst of research in the early sixties. Learning algorithms are critical to the vision of huge intelligent networks constructed of "dumb" elements, since explicitly programming a massive network of heterogeneous processors is clearly impractical.

A "neural" network is usually represented by a directed graph in which the nodes are associated with simple computational units (threshold logic units, finite-state automata, or the like) and the edges carry numerical messages between nodes, modified by fixed weights assigned to each edge. How can we explain the recurring interest in this model?

- The model is potentially massively parallel. In contrast, symbolic algorithms are often hard to adapt to parallel machines because they are conceived as serial procedures.

---

[14]The error back-propagation technique has apparently been found independently by several researchers, including P. Werbos (1974), D. Parker (1982), Y. LeCun (1985), and D. Rumelhart, G. Hinton, and R. Williams (1986).

- The model is distributed. Knowledge is a global property of the network, not concentrated in the high-information content of a few symbols. Consequently network performance may be less sensitive to local hardware failures and more tolerant of noise in the input.

- In some models the processor elements operate asynchronously and use continuous signals. With real-valued outputs and weights, it is possible to describe the network behavior using differential equations rather than combinatorial mathematics (something particularly appealing to scientists with a background in the physical sciences).

- In some models the network is sparsely connected: individual units communicate with only a relatively small subset of the nodes in the network. This suggests that large networks might be configured automatically by a simple learning algorithm that feeds error information back through the net, inducing local changes in connections or weights.

- The model is related to the Hebbian model of the brain. For some people this compatibility with neural models raises the hope that a simple theory might account for experimental observations about perception and cognition.

In both symbolic and connectionist AI research, the excitement over the potential of the ideas, fueled by festive funding levels, has led to a large body of desultory experimentation. At the same time, the progress of rigorous fundamental reseach based on formal foundations has been modest. As with learnability theory, many (but not all) of the mathematical results are negative ones. These negative results are valuable for guiding research away from less promising directions; unfortunately they are occasionally misinterpreted as discrediting the entire paradigm.

Perceptrons.   Perceptrons are a class of linear threshold devices. The name derives from their original use in studying the pattern-recognition problems associated with visual perception. Threshold logic is so closely related to Boolean logic that it would be surprising if many of the learnability results didn't have counterparts in threshold logic. Nevertheless the flavor of perceptron results is different from those of the previous sections. One reason is that the predicates of interest tend to be ones with topological characteristics (convexity, connectivity), and those that remain invariant under certain transformation groups. For example, the predicate $\mathbf{A}(x_1, \ldots, x_n)$ might be true on any input pattern containing the letter "A", no matter where it occurs within the input field $\mathbf{x}$; thus $\mathbf{A}$ is invariant under translations, rotations, etc.

Formally, the perceptron is defined as follows. Let R be a set of n binary inputs (a formalized "retina"). A predicate ϕ over R is a mapping from assignments X of the n input values into $\{0,1\}$, where 1 indicates concept membership (true) and 0 non-membership (false). Let Φ be a family of such predicates; a predicate F is said to be *linear with respect to* Φ if there exist integers α_ϕ (one for each $\phi \in \Phi$) and θ such that

$$\sum_{\phi \in \Phi} \alpha_\phi \phi(X) > \theta$$

iff $F(X) = 1$. The complement of such a function is also considered linear in Φ.

The family $L(\Phi)$ of functions linear with respect to Φ is easy to realize in hardware, provided Φ is not "too large" and the individual predicates $\phi \in \Phi$ are not "too complex" (terms to be made precise shortly). If the constant predicate $I(X) = 1$ is among those in Φ, then we can always take $\theta = 0$.

Let $\Phi = \{\phi_1, \phi_2\}$. The predicate $\phi_1 \vee \phi_2$ is easy to realize by letting $\alpha_1 = \alpha_2 = 1$ and $\theta = 0$. To represent the predicate $\phi_1 \wedge \phi_2$, let $\alpha_1 = \alpha_2 = 1$ and $\theta = 1$. For $\neg\phi_1$, set $\alpha_1 = -1$ and $\theta = -1$. In this manner one sees that any logical combination of the predicates Φ can be obtained by a threshold network of sufficient depth; perceptrons, however, are limited to a depth of one threshold unit.

The *support* of a predicate $\phi(X)$ is the smallest set of input units in R upon which ϕ depends. For example, the predicate $x_1 \vee (x_1 \wedge x_2)$ has support $\{x_1\}$. The class known as the set of *linear threshold functions* is $L(\Phi)$, where Φ is the set of predicates $\{x \mid x \in R\}$. A predicate of the form $x_{i_1} \wedge \ldots \wedge x_{i_k}$ $(k \leq n)$ is called a *mask* of order k. Since any predicate F can be written in disjunctive normal form, and $\neg x_i$ can be realized by $1 - x_i$, every predicate $F(X)$ over R is in $L(M)$, where M is the set of masks. This so-called *positive normal form for F* is unique. The *order of a predicate F* is the maximum order of any mask in its positive normal form.

There are 2^n possible masks. Any function whose positive normal form requires a substantial proportion of them surely cannot be considered realizable by perceptrons except for very small n. For this reason, functions of bounded order are of primary interest. Feasibility also requires that the coefficients α and θ be expressible with a reasonable number of bits. Together, these conditions impose limits on what can be feasibly represented with perceptrons. A well-known result of Minsky and Papert [56] states that the parity ("an odd-number of bits in X are 1") and connectedness predicates are not computable by finite-order perceptrons. Less familiar, but equally interesting, perceptron results are:

- The parity predicate requires $\Omega(2^n)$ bits to represent the coefficients α.

- The counting predicates $F_m(X) = $ "exactly m bits of R are one" are predicates of order 2.

- The "convex-figure" and "rectangular" predicates have order 3.

- Many low-order predicates cease to have bounded order when generalized to detect the property for some connected component of X. For example, "R consists of a hollow square" is of finite order, but "R contains a hollow square" is not.

Such results, and more significantly, the techniques developed to obtain such results, help to understand the types of pattern concepts that can be represented by perceptrons.

Given that a predicate is in $L(\Phi)$, how do we find a set of coefficients α_ϕ for it? (We assume henceforth that $\theta = 0$.) The remarkable *perceptron convergence theorem* of Rosenblatt states that a simple, intuitive, linear-feedback algorithm will eventually converge to a correct set of coefficients. This theorem is noteworthy, not because it is a learning algorithm — after all, direct enumeration of the coefficients will eventually converge, too — but because it is so simple, and because its running time is approximately proportional to the sum of the values of the coefficients it finds. In practice this is much faster on average than identification by enumeration.

A sketch of the algorithm is as follows. Examples are, again, points $\mathbf{x} = (x_1, \ldots, x_n)$ (with $x_i \in \{0, 1\}$), flagged + or - according to whether the target predicate is 1 or 0 on that point. The hypothesis maintained by the algorithm is represented by the set of coefficients α_i, for all $1 \leq i \leq n$. (Recall that $\theta = 0$.) The value predicted by the algorithm for the point $\mathbf{x}$ is the truth value (1 or 0) of the predicate: $\sum_i \alpha_i \phi_i(\mathbf{x}) > 0$. The teacher provides a counterexample to the current hypothesis as long as this remains possible. The learning procedure is as follows:

1. Initialize $\alpha_i = 0$ for $1 \leq i \leq n$. (Actually the initial values can be arbitrary.)

2. For each counterexample:

    2.1 If the example is positive $+\mathbf{x}$, then for each i such that $\phi_i(\mathbf{x}) = 1$, increase α_i by 1. (Promotion step.)

    2.2 If the example is negative $-\mathbf{x}$, then for each i such that $\phi_i(\mathbf{x}) = 1$, decrease α_i by 1. (Demotion step.)

The intuition behind the algorithm is immediate: for each counterexample, those predicates ϕ_i contributing to the error have their coefficient increased (if the false value is 0) or decreased (if 1). The convergence theorem says that after a finite number of counterexamples, the hypothesis will classify all points in R correctly, assuming that the target hypothesis is in $L(\Phi)$. Note that exponentially many counterexamples may be required — e.g., if every perceptron representing the target has an exponentially large coefficient (as does the parity predicate).

As discussed in the section on learnability, contemporary models of pattern discrimination treat predicates over variables x that represent binary-coded attributes ("is red", "breathes fire") rather than pixel activation as in a retina. In such problems, the geometry of the attributes is not a concern, and the predicates of interest are not expected to be invariant under group action. The set Φ of basic predicates is viewed as a set of abstract attributes, or *features*, rather than masks. Once the set of features Φ has been chosen, the problem of learning $L(\Phi)$ is formally identical to the perceptron learning problem, and Rosenblatt's algorithm can be used.

Recently Littlestone [55] has shown how the above learning algorithm can be improved. Whereas the coefficients α_i in Rosenblatt's algorithm are incremented by a constant amount (one) for each counterexample, in his algorithm they are *multiplied* by a constant when too small and divided by the constant when too large. As a result the convergence is potentially much faster. The price to be paid is that the program must be given some information about the subclass of linearly separable functions from which the target has been chosen. Call the function $F \in L(\Phi)$ Δ-*separable* if there exist coefficients $\alpha_i \geq 0$ such that

$$\sum_i \alpha_i \phi_i(\mathbf{x}) \; > \; 1 \text{ if } F(\mathbf{x}) = 1,$$

$$\leq \; 1 - \Delta \text{ if } F(\mathbf{x}) = 0.$$

Then his algorithm converges to a solution whenever the target is Δ-separable, after $\mathcal{O}((\log n/\Delta^2)\sum_i \alpha_i)$ counterexamples, where $n = |\Phi|$. Note that the resulting coefficients are all positive. Other classes of functions — including those for which negative coefficients may be necessary, and even functions that are not in $L(\Phi)$ — can be learned by first carrying out a change of representation $T : \Phi \to \Phi'$ to a new family of attributes defined in terms of the old, and running the learning algorithm for the new family. The resulting network is a perceptron (over Φ') preceded by a circuit for carrying out the transformation T.

Another intriguing property of the Littlestone algorithm is this: when the cardinality of the support (the minimum number of relevant attributes) of the target predicate F is small compared to n, the number of counterexamples required before the algorithm converges may also be quite small ($\mathcal{O}(\log n)$). Many learning algorithms run in time proportional to the total number of attributes (n), even when only a few of those attributes are needed to define the concept. But the number of counterexamples required by Littlestone's algorithm is $\mathcal{O}(\log n \sum_i \alpha_i)$. When most of the coefficients α_i are zero and the others are bounded, $\mathcal{O}(\log n)$ passes will be required. Thus for an important class of concepts that depend on only a small subset of a much larger collection of observed features, Littlestone's algorithm finds the target concept quickly by identifying those few relevant features and suppressing the many irrelevant ones.

Linear programming techniques can also be used to solve perceptron learning problems. We can store all the examples the teacher has shown us and treat each example as a constraint: $\sum_i \alpha_i \phi_i(\mathbf{x}) > 0$ for a positive example, ≤ 0 for a negative one. We then minimize $\sum_i \alpha_i$ using our favorite algorithm (e.g., simplex). But this algorithm stores all examples and constructs each new hypothesis from scratch rather than from the existing one. Thus we are unlikely to regard this "ballistic" algorithm as a learning algorithm, in the sense discussed in the introduction.

Multi-layer networks. By now perceptrons are fairly well understood, but the class of concepts that can be represented efficiently with a perceptron is limited. When we generalize in the natural way — by adding one or two additional layers of units between the inputs R and the output — we find that much less is known about the resulting networks. Comparison is complicated by the fact that most of the problems studied on these networks are *training* problems rather than concept-learning problems.

First some terminology: An acyclic threshold-logic network has *depth* k when the longest path from an input signal to the output passes through at most k threshold units (we also say that the circuit has k *layers*). Thus a perceptron has unit depth. When $\Phi = \{x_i \in R\}$, a depth of three suffices to realize every concept on R; we shall assume henceforth that Φ is this basic set. We also assume that there is a single output unit. Threshold nodes other than the output unit(s) are often called *hidden units*. Both the inputs x_i and outputs from hidden units are connected to threshold nodes via weighted edges, just as for perceptrons. Weights and thresholds can be

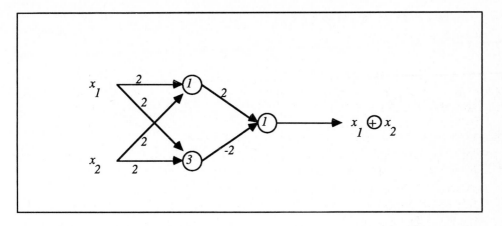

Figure 2: Two-input parity network. Thresholds are written in the nodes, weights beside the edges.

arbitrary real numbers (although integers generally suffice). A threshold unit with inputs s_i, weights α_i, and a threshold of θ outputs 1 if $\sum_i \alpha_i s_i > \theta$ and 0 otherwise. To illustrate, in Figure 5 we show a network with depth 2 that computes the parity function for $n = 2$: $F(x_1, x_2) = 1$ iff $x_1 \neq x_2$.

A *training problem* consists of a set S of examples of some function $F(x_1, \ldots, x_n)$, with the examples labeled as $+$ or $-$ in the usual way. In general the set S is a proper subset of all 2^n possible examples of the target F. The task is to construct a network that agrees with the examples by emitting 1 for each positive example and 0 for each negative example; for inputs not in S the output may be arbitrary. From the preceding section on learnability theory, we recognize this as a consistency problem, and know that if the examples have been selected randomly, and enough of them are provided, then we have a *PAC*-learning problem. But here we are required only to learn the set S.

The training problem has been shown to be NP-complete when the network configuration is given and the task is to choose the weights and thresholds. Thus, unlike the simple perceptron training problem (which is essentially a linear programming problem), the multi-layer training problem is unlikely to have any feasible algorithm — incremental or ballistic. [15]

In pursuit of an efficient algorithm we can try relaxing some of the requirements of the training problem. One is to require that it work for only some fraction of the examples; but if that fraction is more than 2/3, the problem remains NP-complete [44]. Another is to replace the linear-threshold function computed at each node by some other function. But if this is still a Boolean-valued function, the problem remains intractable [43].

---

[15]One reviewer pointed out that, from a *PAC*-learning perspective, the hardness results suggest that multi-layer threshold networks probably cannot learn (feasibly) the entire class of functions that they can represent when examples come from an arbitrary distribution. They may, however, be able to learn a useful subclass, or perhaps the entire class under a restricted set of distributions.

Suppose the nodes are allowed to compute a non-Boolean valued function. An example of such a function frequently used in practice is the so-called *logistic function*

$$f(x_1, \ldots, x_n \mid \alpha_1, \ldots, \alpha_n, \theta, \beta) = \frac{1}{1 + exp[-\beta(\sum \alpha_i x_i - \theta)]}.$$

The function f approaches the standard threshold transfer function as $\beta \to \infty$, but its output is always between zero and one. Complexity results for training with these functions are not available, but there is little reason to suspect that using the logistic transfer function in place of the θ-threshold function will reduce the computational complexity of the problem.

Another change that has been widely adopted is to replace the consistency criterion by a *least-mean-square error* (LMSE) procedure. This criterion is attractive in part because it is meaningful for continuous transfer functions, while "consistency" is not. Let $F(\mathbf{x})$ (where $\mathbf{x} \equiv (x_1, \ldots, x_n)$) be the target function and $H(\mathbf{x})$ the function computed by the current hypothesis machine. The error *Err* of H over the sample S is given by

$$Err(S) = \sum_{\mathbf{x} \in S} [F(\mathbf{x}) - H(\mathbf{x})]^2.$$

We seek a hypothesis H for which $Err(S)$ is minimum.

Apart from any question about the complexity of this optimization problem, we should ask whether this is a good criterion. Of course, without any applications in mind, all such judgments are subjective. But a recent paper [23] provides examples of networks using logistic transfer functions, for which a consistent solution exists, and yet the LMSE solution is inconsistent. Moreover the examples are for networks of unit depth. In response to this and other evidence that the LMSE criterion and associated hill-climbing algorithms may be unsuitable, still more modifications to the models are being studied. But after nearly thirty years of research, an ideal learning algorithm for threshold networks has yet to be found.

Sources. Historians will appreciate the view of connectionist AI in the early sixties available from the collection [91]; the paper by Widrow [89] describing the Adaline neural system is of particular interest. Early perceptron work is described in [70] and [60].

The classic work on perceptron theory by Minsky and Papert dates from 1969, but has been reissued with additional commentary [56]. A model of clarity and cogency, this book is as significant today as it was when it first appeared.

Littlestone's perceptron algorithm is clearly presented in [55] and [54].

A popular source for multi-layer network studies, including the back-propagation algorithm and the Boltzmann machine, is [71]. The intractability of training multi-layer threshold networks was proved by Judd [43, 44]. An extremely simple 2-layer 3-node network that nevertheless is NP-complete to train is described in [18]. See [23] for examples showing that least-mean-squared error algorithms can fail to find solutions when those solutions exist. As I write this, new results are being reported about the complexity of network learning (as distinct from training) in the *PAC*-learnability model, along with other topics. One can anticipate rapid progress in this field in the coming months and years.

Besides perceptrons, many other network models with learning procedures have been proposed and studied, both experimentally and theoretically. Among these are genetic algorithms [38], "structural" connectionism [32], adaptive resonance [25], and associative search networks [15].

6   Afterword

Control theory has produced a rich body of learning research that has not been included in this survey, partly for lack of space and partly because the motivation for this work comes from engineering rather than computer science. Nevertheless this research, often described as "adaptive control systems analysis", probably deserves the attention of learning theorists. Good starting places are the volumes by Tsypkin [84, 85] and the collection [31].

7   Acknowledgments

I owe a large debt to the people who took time away from their busy schedules to read drafts of this article, point out errors and offer suggestions: Peter Cheeseman, Silvano Colombano, Peter Dunning, Lol Grant, David Haussler, Nick Littlestone, and John Stutz. Any remaining errors are my responsibility. NASA's Ames Research Center and the AI Research Group under Peter Friedland provided me with the opportunity, incentive, and wherewithal to write this article.

References

[1] J. Aczél. *Lectures on Functional Equations and their Applications*. Academic Press, New York, 1966.

[2] Romas Aleliunas. A new normative theory of probabilistic logic. In *Proceedings, Canadian Society for Computational Studies of Intelligence*, pages 67–74, 1988.

[3] Romas Aleliunas. A summary of a new normative theory of probabilistic logic. In *Proceedings Uncertainty in AI Workshop*, pages 8–15, 1988.

[4] J. Amsterdam. Extending the valiant learning model. In *Proceedings, Fifth International Conference on Machine Learning*, pages 381–394, 1988.

[5] D. Angluin. Learning regular sets from queries and counterexamples. *Information and Computation*, 75:87–106, 1987.

[6] D. Angluin and P. Laird. Learning from noisy examples. *Machine Learning*, 2:343–370, 1987.

[7] D. Angluin and C. Smith. Inductive inference: theory and methods. *Comput. Surveys*, 15:237–269, 1983.

[8] Dana Angluin. *Equivalence queries and DNF formulas.* Technical Report YALEU/DCS/RR-659, Yale Univ. Dept. of Comp. Sci., 1988.

[9] Dana Angluin. *Identifying languages from stochastic examples.* Technical Report YALEU/DCS/RR-614, Yale University Dept. of Computer Science, 1988.

[10] Dana Angluin. *Learning k-bounded context-free grammars.* Technical Report YALEU/DCS/RR-557, Yale Univ. Dept. of Comp. Sci., 1987.

[11] Dana Angluin. *Learning propositional Horn sentences with hints.* Technical Report YALEU/DCS/RR-590, Yale Univ. Dept. of Comp. Sci., 1987.

[12] Dana Angluin. *Negative results for equivalence queries.* Technical Report YALEU/DCS/RR-648, Yale Univ. Dept. of Comp. Sci., 1988.

[13] Dana Angluin. Queries and concept learning. *Machine Learning*, 2:319–342, 1987.

[14] R. Banerji. The logic of learning. In *Advances in Computers*, pages 177 – 216, Elsevier, 1985.

[15] A. Barto, R. Sutton, and P. Brouwer. Associative search networks: a reinforcement learning associative memory. *Biological cybernetics*, 40(2), 1981.

[16] James O. Berger. *Statistical Decision Theory and Bayesian Analysis.* Springer-Verlag, New York, 1980.

[17] James O. Berger and Donald A. Berry. Statistical analysis and the illusion of objectivity. *American Scientist*, 76:159–165, 1988.

[18] A. Blum and R. Rivest. Training a 3-node neural network is NP-Complete. In *Proceedings, First Workshop on Computational Learning Theory*, Kluwer Academic Press, 1988.

[19] A. Blumer, A. Ehrenfeucht, D. Haussler, and M. Warmuth. Classifying learnable geometric concepts with the Vapnik-Chervonenkis dimension. In *Proc. 18th Symposium on Theory of Computing*, pages 273–282, ACM, 1986.

[20] A. Blumer, A. Ehrenfeucht, D. Haussler, and M. Warmuth. *Learnability and the Vapnik-Chervonenkis dimension.* Technical Report UCSC-CRL-87-20, University of California, Santa Cruz, 1987. To appear in *J. ACM*.

[21] A. Blumer, A. Ehrenfeucht, D. Haussler, and M. Warmuth. Occam's razor. *Inf. Proc. Letters*, 24:377–380, 1987.

[22] G. Box and G. Tiao. *Bayesian Inference in Statistical Analysis.* Addison-Wesley Publishing Company, Reading, Massachusetts, 1973.

[23] M. Brady, R. Raghavan, and J. Slawny. Gradient descent fails to separate. In *Proc. 2nd Int. Conf. Neural Networks*, pages 649 – 656, 1988.

[24] W. Buntine. Generalized subsumption and its applications to induction and redundancy. *Artificial Intelligence*, 36(2), 1988.

[25] G. Carpenter and S. Grossberg. Art 2: self-organization of stable category recognition codes for analog input patterns. *Applied Optics*, 26(3), 1987.

[26] P. C. Cheeseman. In defense of probability. In *Proc. Ninth IJCAI*, pages 1002–1009, 1985.

[27] R. T. Cox. Probability, frequency, and reasonable expectation. *American Journal of Physics*, 17:1–13, 1946.

[28] B. de Finetti. *Theory of Probability*. Wiley, New York, 1974.

[29] L. Devroye and T. J. Wagner. A distribution-free performance bound in error estimation. *IEEE Trans. Info. Theory*, IT-22:586–587, 1976.

[30] Richard O. Duda and Peter E. Hart. *Pattern Recognition and Scene Analysis*. Wiley-Interscience, 1973.

[31] K. S. Narendra (ed.). *Adaptive and Learning Systems: Theory and Applications*. Plenum Press, 1986.

[32] J. Feldman and D. Ballard. Connectionist models and their properties. *Cognitive Science*, 9:205–254, 1982.

[33] E. M. Gold. Language identification in the limit. *Information and Control*, 10:447–474, 1967.

[34] D. Haussler. Quantifying inductive bias: AI learning algorithms and Valiant's learning framework. *Artificial Intelligence*, 36(2):177–222, 1988.

[35] D. Haussler and L. Pitt (eds.). *Proceedings, 1st Computational Learning Theory Workshop*. Morgan Kaufmann, 1988.

[36] D. Haussler, M. Kearns, N. Littlestone, and M. K. Warmuth. Equivalence of models for polynomial learnability. In *Proceedings, 1st Computational Learning Theory Workshop*, 1988.

[37] D. Haussler, N. Littlestone, and M. K. Warmuth. Predicting {0,1}-functions on randomly drawn points (extended abstract). In *Proceedings, 1st Computational Learning Theory Workshop*, 1988.

[38] J. H. Holland. Escaping brittleness: the possibilities of general-purpose algorithms applied to parallel rule-based systems. In R. S. Michalski et al., editor, *Machine Learning II*, Morgan Kaufmann, 1986.

[39] H. Ishizaka. Model inference incorporating generalization. In *Proc. Symp. on Software Science and Engineering*, Kyoto, Sept., 1986.

[40] E. T. Jaynes. *Papers on Probability, Statistics and Statistical Physics.* Volume 158 of *Synthese Library*, D. Reidel, Boston, 1983.

[41] E. T. Jaynes. Prior probabilities. *IEEE Transactions on Systems and Cybernetics*, SSC-4(3):227–241, September 1968. (Reprinted in [40]).

[42] E. T. Jaynes. The well-posed problem. *Foundations of Physics*, 3:447–493, 1973. (Reprinted in [40]).

[43] J. S. Judd. Learning in networks is hard. In *Proceedings, First International Conference on Neural Networks*, I.E.E.E., 1987.

[44] J. S. Judd. Learning in neural networks (extended abstract). In *Proceedings, First Workshop on Computational Learning Theory*, Kluwer Academic Press, 1988.

[45] M. Kearns and M. Li. *Learning in the presence of malicious errors.* Technical Report TR-03-87, Harvard University Aiken Computation Lab, 1987.

[46] M. Kearns, M. Li, L. Pitt, and L. Valiant. On the learnability of boolean formulae. In *Proc. 19th ACM STOC*, 1987.

[47] M. Kearns and L. Valiant. *Learning Boolean Formulae or finite automata is as hard as factoring.* Technical Report TR 14-88, Harvard University, 1988.

[48] J. M. Keynes. *A Treatise on Probability.* MacMillan, London, 1921.

[49] P. Laird. Efficient unsupervised learning. In *Proc. 1st Comput. Learning Theory Workshop*, 1988.

[50] P. Laird. *Learning a probability distribution efficiently and reliably.* Technical Report RIA-88-10-10-0, NASA-Ames Research Center, AI Research Branch, 1988.

[51] P. Laird. *Learning by Making Models.* Technical Report RIA-88-4-12-0, NASA-Ames Research Center, AI Research Branch, 1988.

[52] P. Laird. *Learning from Good and Bad Data.* Kluwer Academic, 1988.

[53] N. Linial, Y. Mansour, and R. Rivest. Results on learnability and the Vapnik-Chervonenkis dimension (extended abstract). In *Proceedings, 1st Computational Learning Theory Workshop*, 1988.

[54] N. Littlestone. Learning in a layered network with many fixed-function hidden nodes. In *Proc. 1st International Conference on Neural Nets*, 1987.

[55] N. Littlestone. Learning quickly when irrelevant attributes abound: a new-linear threshold algorithm. *Machine Learning*, 2:285–318, 1987.

[56] M. Minsky and S. Papert. *Perceptrons: an introduction to computational geometry.* M.I.T. Press, 1988. (expanded edition).

[57] B. Natarajan. *Learning functions from examples.* Technical Report CMU-RI-TR-87-19, Carnegie-Mellon University Robotics Institute, 1987.

[91] M. C. Yovits, G. Jacobi, and G. Goldstein (eds.). *Self-Organizing Systems.* Spartan Books, Washington, DC, 1962.

Formal Techniques in Artificial Intelligence
A Sourcebook. R.B. Banerji (editor)
© Elsevier Science Publishers B.V. (North-Holland), 1990

A Primer on the
Complexity Theory of Neural Networks

*Ian Parberry**

Department of Computer Science,
333 Whitmore Laboratory,
The Pennsylvania State University,
University Park, Pa. 16802.

ABSTRACT

There is a growing dissatisfaction with the current generation of computers since they possess inherent inefficiencies which prevent the development of faster machines. It is argued by some scientists that a return to the brain analogy, which initiated early research into computing devices, may lead to more efficient architectures. Brain-like architectures, termed *neural networks,* have in recent years been the focus of a great resurgence of interest from researchers in many fields. This paper is an attempt to contribute to the communication between these fields by gathering together some "well-known" results on the computational complexity of neural networks. One hope for neural networks is that they will provide faster, more reliable computation at a reasonable cost. Applying the tools and techniques of computational complexity theory (the study of efficient computation) to neural networks, we obtain some indication of how conventional computers may be improved by emulating a few simple features of the brain which were previously ignored.

1. Introduction

Since we already possess a consummate computational device in the human brain, it is only sensible for us to turn to it for a role model when designing computing machines. The designers of computing machines work according to two types of specification. *Functional specifications* describe what the machine is supposed to achieve, and *technological specifications* describe the parts from which the machine can be constructed. The job of the designer is to come up with a design that satisfies both types of specifications. Unfortunately, Nature† does not provide us with either type of

---

* Research sponsored by the Air Force Office of Scientific Research, Air Force Systems Command, USAF, under grant number AFOSR 87-0400.

† Some readers may object to this anthropomorphic term. We use it as a convenient shorthand for the process, as yet little understood by scientists and theologians, by which the human brain was designed.

specification in a form that we can easily assimilate, although a compact, easily implementable description no doubt resides in our DNA. Even if functional specifications are devised for simple tasks, the problem of constructing an operational and denotational semantics for how the brain performs those tasks seems insurmountable given the vague technological specification "it's done with what we find in the brain".

Given the lack of precise specifications, the only way that we can hope to understand the brain is by direct observation and analysis. There are two principal types of phenomena which can be observed in the brain. *Denotational* phenomena relate to the brain as a static entity, and describe its physical construction. *Operational* phenomena relate to the brain as a dynamic entity, and describe how it operates. A simple denotational observation is that the brain is constructed from biological components, termed "wetware" by some. A simple operational observation is that electrical activity takes place in the brain. In short, denotational observations tell us how the brain is constructed and operational observations tell us how it works.

Some of the phenomena observed in the brain are crucial, and some may be side-effects of Nature's possibly crude attempt to meet functional and technological specifications simultaneously. Obvious questions in need of answers include:

> What are the functional specifications?
> What are the technological specifications?
> Which operational phenomena are crucial?
> Which denotational phenomena are crucial?

The first question very quickly spawns others such as "what is cognition?". This is a deep question which has occupied philosophers for millenia. The second is more of a bio-engineering question. The third and fourth questions involve clearing away the legacy of evolution and determining the "nuts and bolts" of how the brain works as a computational device. This is the realm of Computer Science. Other fields which have a stake in these questions include Artificial Intelligence, Biochemistry, Cognitive Science, Computer Engineering, Electrical Engineering, Mathematics, Neurobiology, Physics, and Psychology. True understanding of the brain can only come from a synergy of these fields.

Computer engineers currently work within technological specifications involving the feasibility and economy of doped silicon semiconductors. There is no guarantee that there is a design which satisfies Nature's functional specifications within these technological specifications. Given that computer designers operate under different technological specifications than Nature, it is imperative that we separate the crucial observations from side-effects, since a side-effect that is caused by Nature's technological specifications may not appear when the engineer attempts to find the best solution within his or her technological specifications. A mistaken identification of an operational phenomenon as being crucial may cause the abandonment of a computationally adequate model which does not exhibit it. We should not expect our brain-like computers to behave exactly like brains, but we must ensure that they behave like them in the computationally important ways.

Early computer engineers based their designs on the following denotational observations about the human brain:

> the brain is made up of small units (neurons),
> these units are interconnected;

and the following operational observations:

> the behaviour of the units is electrical, and discrete,
> the units perform simple Boolean operations.

All of these phenomena can be realized within the technological specifications of conventional electronics in the mid part of this century. Engineers were thus able to come up with a design for a type of self-directed electronic calculator which has served well for many decades, conventionally called the *von Neumann computer* after one of the principal scientists involved in the endeavour.

Although technological specifications have changed much since that time, the differences are in degree, not type. Apart from the above observations, the architecture of modern computers bears little resemblance to the brain. We have more recently begun to reach the point where we are confronting barriers to the production of faster, more powerful computers which are inherent in the von Neumann design. The most widely discussed barrier is the "von Neumann bottleneck", which refers to the fact that a large amount of data must typically be moved around inside the machine, a task which von Neumann computers do not perform well. Since the human brain does not share these shortcomings, it is apparent that Nature has found some better way of doing things. It is felt by some scientists that in order to produce better computers we must return to the brain analogy.

Since Nature operates under different technological specifications than human engineers, it is a misguided hope that we can construct a better computer by making random observations about the brain and attempting to construct computers which exhibit the same gross behaviours. It is imperative that we first understand in some degree *how* and *why* the brain is better than conventional computers. One approach is to abstract out the promising denotational and operational features of the brain and to demonstrate that they are capable of satisfying certain simple but attractive functional specifications. It is conceivable that the brain does so well because of the freedom allowed by the technological specifications of wetware as opposed to silicon. If this is found to be the case, a whole new technology must be developed for our new generation of brain-like machines.

The study of brain-like computers has developed into a new field, called *neural networks*. Although there has lately been an explosion of experimental work in the discipline, its theoretical foundations have not kept pace. Experimental evidence has repeatedly pointed to deep underlying truths which have yet to explained satisfactorily in theoretical terms. Nonetheless, theory is an important component of any scientific endeavour. Neural network researchers typically base their designs on the following denotational observations about the human brain:

> neuron interconnections are complex on a microscopic scale,
>
> regional interconnections are simple on a macroscopic scale,
>
> each neuron has large fan-in and fan-out;

(fan-in and fan-out refer to the number of inputs to a neuron and the number of places that an output gets routed to, respectively), and the following operational observations:

> neurons perform complicated operations,
>
> some behaviour of neurons is discrete,
>
> some behaviour of neurons is analogue,
>
> neurons operate in parallel,
>
> neurons have complicated behaviour over time.

Different groups of researchers naturally conflict in the degree of importance they attach to various operational and denotational phenomena.

Exactly what can we gain from making computers more brain-like? One reasonable expectation is efficiency. The human brain computes much faster than we have any right to expect. The reaction time of a typical neuron is in the millisecond range. The reaction time of a typical transistor is in the nanosecond range. Many complicated computational tasks (such as visual analysis, motion planning, motor control) are carried out in the brain within time intervals measured in seconds, that is, within an order of magnitude of a thousand times the reaction time of a neuron. We might expect then to perform the same computational tasks a million times faster on a conventional computer, given the relative speed of its components. Unfortunately we cannot even rival the speed of the brain on simple tasks. Obviously, then, the brain has a superior architecture for these tasks. The brain also realizes cheap fault-tolerance. Experimental evidence points to the fact that the brain can often continue to function satisfactorily even when a significant fraction of neurons are destroyed. There are methods known for giving conventional computers a similar fault-tolerant ability, but these remain impossibly expensive to implement. Apparently Nature has found a cheaper way to do it.

Perhaps not surprisingly, the expected synergy between the fields that make up neural network research has not become apparent in the short time that has passed since the latest resurgence of interest in brain-like computation. What is initially needed for the synergy is that elementary results from each field be broadcast to all neural networks researchers. This paper is an attempt to contribute to this sharing of information in a constructive fashion.

Theoretical Computer Science has made great progress since the early days of Church and Turing before electronic computers were seriously thought possible. For example, in the past two decades some interest has focussed on efficient computation, in particular on the fact that certain things are intrinsically more difficult to compute than others. The study of this phenomenon is called *computational complexity theory*. Since one of the potential advantages of neural networks is more efficient computation, it is natural to apply the techniques of complexity theory to them. Whilst it has been argued that conventional Computer Science, and in particular Theoretical Computer Science is fettered by the limitations of the von Neumann architecture, the opposite is actually the case. Computer Science provides a set of tools for reasoning about computation in any form.

The aim of this paper is to provide an overview of some of the application of complexity theory to neural networks. In it we abstract two operational observations and one denotational observation about the brain. The first is that neurons can behave in a discrete, or Boolean fashion. The second is that they compute a weighted binary threshold function of their inputs. The third is that the fan-in and fan-out of each neuron is large compared to the number of neurons used. We find that such a model is more powerful than classical computers in the sense that they can compute faster with only a reasonable increase in hardware, but perhaps not as powerful as some proponents of neural networks have conjectured. We will find that many of the questions raised by neural networks researchers have been partially answered by researchers in complexity theory, or at least the fundamental questions have been isolated and some facts about them enumerated.

One of the criticisms of this type of Theoretical Computer Science raised by neural networks researchers is that it uses the wrong computational paradigm. Church and Turing view a computer as a static device which receives a single input, produces a single output, and then resets itself. It does not modify its behaviour in response to a sequence of inputs and the order in which they are given, for instance, it gives the same answer whenever an input is repeated. In contrast, one of the major paradigms of neural networks research is that neural networks *learn from experience*. In defense against this criticism, it should be noted that current experiments on neural network learning consist of two phases. In the learning phase, educational data is presented to the machine. Then in a separate computation phase test data determines how well the machine has learned. The neural network uses the classical Church-Turing computational paradigm during the computation phase. Thus it is instructive to discover what neural networks can compute efficiently, before asking which of those things it can learn efficiently to compute efficiently*. We avoid question of the computational complexity of learning due to space limitations and the current volatility of the field, but the reader should keep in mind that a large body of theory on this subject has recently been developed from the seminal work of Valiant [72], much of which is relevant to neural networks. A second defense is that there may well be Church-Turing type computations going on in the brain as well as learning.

We are not claiming that the neural network models considered in this paper are a good model of the brain, nor that they are the only plausible type of brain-like computer. We are merely interested in abstracting certain observations about the brain and rigourously investigating their computational properties. It would be naive to claim that "this is how the brain works", or "this is how we should build the next generation of computers". Instead, we claim that computers based upon a particular abstraction of the brain are more powerful than von Neumann computers in certain formal senses. Some of the results can easily be applied to other models, and for some it remains an open problem.

In the interests of rigour, we will provide proofs for many of the results stated, particularly where the previously published proofs are more obscure, complicated or difficult to obtain than necessary. Many trivial proofs (defined to be those that the author could see instantaneously) have appeared with monotonous regularity in the literature and are not deemed worthy of reference. Some references are provided for easy proofs (defined to be those that the author could devise within an afternoon), and a small effort has been made to find the reference for the earliest publication or a particularly elegant version. Difficult or cumbersome proofs are sketched or omitted entirely to save space.

The remainder of this paper is broken up into six major sections. Section 2 consists of elementary definitions and notation; precision and rigour are important since this will be a formal exposition. Section 3 describes classical computational complexity theory in a form that will make it easy for us to contrast neural networks with

---

* Clearly there are two separate measures of efficiency in machine learning: efficiency of the learning algorithm, and efficiency of performance of the learned task. Clearly there ought to be some kind of trade-off between the two. The latter can be compared to the efficiency of a classical Church-Turing computer which is explicitly programmed to perform the same task. It would be acceptable for the learning machine to be slightly less efficient than the special-purpose one, but the degradation in performance must be kept within reasonable limits.

conventional computers. Section 4 defines our neural network model and investigates some equivalent variants of it. Section 5 is devoted to neural circuits, that is, neural networks without feedback. Section 6 contains some results about termination of neural network computations. Section 7 contains some conclusions and open problems.

2. Elementary Definitions and Notation

Throughout this manuscript R denotes the set of real numbers, R^+ denotes the set of positive real numbers, Z denotes the set of integers, and N denotes the set of non-negative integers. B denotes the Boolean set $\{0,1\}$; the integers "0" and "1" will be used to represent the Boolean values "false" and "true" respectively. If $x \in R$, then $|x|$ denotes the absolute value of x and

$$\text{sign}(x) = \begin{cases} 1 & \text{if } x \geq 0 \\ -1 & \text{otherwise.} \end{cases}$$

If $x \in R^+$, $\lfloor x \rfloor$ denotes the largest integer which does not exceed x, and $\lceil x \rceil$ denotes the smallest integer which is no less than x. If $x \in B$, $\bar{x}$ denotes the Boolean *complement*, or *negation,* of x, that is, $\bar{x} = 1-x$.

Two important Boolean operations are AND,OR:$B^n \rightarrow B$ and NOT:$B \rightarrow B$, called *conjunction, disjunction* and *negation* respectively. AND$(x_1,...,x_n) = 0$ iff $x_i = 0$ for some $1 \leq i \leq n$, OR$(x_1,...,x_n) = 1$ iff $x_i = 1$ for some $1 \leq i \leq n$, and NOT$(x) = \bar{x}$. Other important operations include NAND, MOD_p and MAJORITY where NAND$(x_1,...,x_n) = 1$ iff $x_i = 0$ for some $1 \leq i \leq n$, $\text{MOD}_p(x_1,...,x_n) = 0$ iff

$$\sum_{i=1}^{n} x_i = 0 \text{ mod } p,$$

and MAJORITY$(x_1,...,x_n) = 1$ iff

$$\sum_{i=1}^{n} x_i \geq n/2.$$

MOD_2 is often called *parity,* and MAJORITY is often called *consensus.* A *Boolean formula* is a formula made up from Boolean variables and binary (two-input) Boolean operations. It is *satisfiable* if there is an assignment of Boolean values to the variables such that the formula evaluates to 1. A *literal* is a variable or its complement. A *clause* is a disjunction of literals. A Boolean formula is said to be in *conjunctive normal form* if it is a conjunction of clauses. A Boolean formula is said to be in *disjunctive normal form* if it is the complement of a conjunctive normal form formula, that is, if it is a disjunction of conjunctions of literals.

In many different situations we will use $\|x\|$ to denote the intuitive concept of the "size" of x, to be defined formally for different classes of mathematical object x. For example, if S is a finite set, $\|S\|$ denotes the number of elements in S. All logarithms will be to base two unless explicitly stated otherwise. If $x \in \mathbf{N}$, $x > 0$, we write $\|x\|$ for the number of bits in the binary representation of x, that is, $\|x\| = \lfloor \log x \rfloor + 1$. For $x \in \mathbf{Z}$ we take $\|x\|$ to be the number of bits in the binary representation of $|x|$, and we set $\|0\| = 1$. If $f,g:\mathbf{N} \rightarrow \mathbf{N}$, then $f(n) = O(g(n))$ if there exists $c,d \in \mathbf{N}$ such that for all $n \geq c$, $f(n) \leq d.g(n)$, and $f(n) = \Omega(g(n))$ if there exists $d \in \mathbf{N}$ such that for all but finitely many $n \in \mathbf{N}$, $f(n) \geq d.g(n)$. Also, $f(n) = \Theta(g(n))$ if $f(n) = O(g(n))$ and $f(n) = \Omega(g(n))$. We will use $n^{O(1)}$ to denote a polynomial in n. An *exponential* in n means $2^{n^{O(1)}}$, and *polylog* means $(\log n)^{O(1)}$. The shorthand $\log^c n$ will be used for the polylog function $(\log n)^c$.

A *matrix* over a set S is a two-dimensional array of elements of S. Rows and columns are numbered consecutively, starting at one, from top-to-bottom and left-to-right respectively. We write m_{ij} or $m_{i,j}$ for the entry in the ith row and j^{th} column of a matrix $M = [m_{ij}]$. $M_{m,n}(S)$ denotes the set of m×n matrices over S. If $x^{(1)},...,x^{(m)} \in \mathbf{N}$ and $\|x^{(i)}\| \leq n$ for $1 \leq i \leq m$, then $matrix(x^{(1)},...,x^{(m)})$ is defined to be the matrix whose rows are the binary representations of the integers $x^{(1)},...,x^{(m)}$, that is, $matrix(x^{(1)},...,x^{(m)}) = [y_{ij}] \in M_{m,n}(\mathbf{B})$ where

$$x^{(i)} = \sum_{j=1}^{n} 2^{n-j} y_{ij}.$$

If $A \in M_{m,n}(\mathbf{R})$, $\det(A) \in \mathbf{R}$ denotes the determinant of A and $A^T \in M_{n,m}(\mathbf{R})$ denotes the transpose of A.

Let S be a set. A *string* over S is defined recursively as follows. The empty string (usually denoted ε or λ) is a string of length zero. If α is a string of length n and $s \in S$ then αs is a string of length n+1. We write $\|x\|$ for the length of x. S^n denotes the set of strings over S of length n. S^* denotes $\bigcup_{n=0}^{\infty} S^n$. If $x \in S^*$, we will write x_i for the ith symbol in x, counting consecutively from left to right starting at one. Thus $x = x_1 x_2 ... x_n$ where $x_i \in S$ for all $1 \leq i \leq n$. Where convenient we will write strings over S using tuple notation, that is, $x \in S^n$ will be written as $(x_1,...,x_n)$, and ignore the distinction between x and the row-vector corresponding to x, that is, we will take $x \in M_{1,m}(S)$. We will also ignore the distinction between $x \in \mathbf{N}$ and its binary representation $x_1 x_2 ... x_n \in \mathbf{B}^n$ where $n = \|x\|$ and

$$x = \sum_{i=1}^{n} 2^{n-i} x_i.$$

Let V be a finite set and $E \subseteq V \times V$. The ordered pair (V,E) forms what is commonly called a *directed graph*. If for all $u,v \in V$, $(u,v) \in E$ iff $(v,u) \in E$ then (V,E) is called an *undirected graph*. We will use the generic term *graph* whenever it is unnecessary to make the distinction between directed and undirected graphs. In graph-theoretic terminology, the elements of V are called *vertices* or *nodes*, and the elements of E are called *edges* or *arcs*. Let L:E→**Z**. The ordered triple (V,E,L) forms a *labelled directed graph*. If (V,E) is an undirected graph and for all (u,v)∈E, L(u,v)=L(v,u), then (V,E,L) is called a *labelled undirected graph*. If (V,E) is an undirected graph and v∈V, the *degree* of v is defined to be ∥{u∣(u,v)∈E}∥. If (V,E) is a directed graph and v∈V, the *in-degree* of v is defined to be ∥{u∣(u,v)∈E}∥, the *out-degree* of v is defined to be ∥{u∣(v,u)∈E}∥, and the *degree* of v is defined to be its in-degree plus its out-degree. The degree, in-degree and out-degree of a graph (directed or undirected in the first case, directed in the latter two cases) is defined to be the maximum degree, in-degree and out-degree respectively of its vertices. A graph is called *simple* if there are no self-loops, that is, for all v∈V, (v,v)∉E. A *bipartite graph* is an undirected graph (V,E) where $V = V_1 \cup V_2$, $V_1 \cap V_2 = \emptyset$ and $E \subseteq V_1 \times V_2$. A *cycle* in a graph (V,E) is a sequence of distinct vertices $(v_0, v_1, ..., v_{m-1})$ where $(v_i, v_{i+1}) \in E$ for $0 \le i < m$, and the addition in the subscripts is taken modulo m. If $\|V\| = m$ then it is called a *Hamiltonian cycle*. The *cost* of a cycle $(v_0, v_1, ..., v_{m-1})$ in a labelled graph (V,E,L) is defined to be

$$\sum_{i=0}^{m-1} L(v_i, v_{i+1}).$$

A directed graph which has no cycles is called *acyclic*.

3. Theory of Conventional Computation

This Section is divided into four subsections in which we provide a brief introduction to the theory of computation as it applies to conventional computation, specifically, computability theory, complexity theory, parallel complexity theory, and probabilistic complexity theory. In addition to the references cited there, we advise the reader who wishes more detailed information to consult Aho, Hopcroft and Ullman [2, 3], Garey and Johnson [23], Goldschlager and Lister [26], Harel [30], Hong [34], Hopcroft and Ullman [35], and Parberry [52].

3.1. Computability Theory

Intuitively, an algorithm is a method for evaluating a function f:**N**→**N**. The choice of **N** for the domain and range of the function is merely a matter of convenience. Any set which can be put into one-to-one correspondence with the natural numbers could equally well be used. Such a set is termed *countable*. We will use various mathematical objects such as integers, strings over a finite set, tuples of integers, and graphs, all of which are easily seen to be countable.

The above definition of an algorithm is not quite satisfactory since it is satisfied by an infinite list f(0),f(1),f(2),... together with the instructions "to find f(x), look at the xth

element of the list", yet such a formulation is impractical because we cannot reasonably be expected to carry around a list of outputs for every useful function (even for those inputs that we might reasonably be expected to encounter in everyday life). Furthermore, it offends an intuition that an algorithm should somehow be a deeper, more fundamental characterization of the function f than just a simple list of the values it takes on for all possible inputs. A more practical requirement is that an algorithm be a *finite* description of f that enables us to evaluate it on any input. We will say that any function which has a finite algorithm is *computable*.

It is clear that there are far more non-computable functions than computable ones since there is *a priori* only a countable number of finite algorithms, whereas there are uncountably many functions:

Theorem 3.1.1 There are uncountably many functions $f:N \to N$.

Proof. For a contradiction, suppose otherwise. Number the functions $f_1, f_2, \dots$. Define $f:N \to N$ by $f(x) = f_x(x) + 1$. Since f is a perfectly good function, it must appear somewhere in our list of functions. Suppose $f = f_k$. But then $f_k(k) = f(k) = f_k(k) + 1$, a contradiction. Therefore the functions cannot be enumerated, and so there are uncountably many functions. □

The above proof technique is called *diagonalization*.

The British mathematician Alan Turing was among the first to formalize the intuitive idea of a computable function. He suggested a model of computation called a *Turing machine* (see Turing [71]). The details of this model are not important here. What is important is that many other formalizations have been proposed (for example, Chomsky's type-0 grammars [15], Church's λ-calculus [16], Kleene's recursive functions [41], Post's production systems [59], and Sheperdson and Sturgis' Random Access Machines [66]) and yet all of them are equivalent in the sense that if a function is computable in one model, then it is computable in Turing's model (and vice-versa). Computer programs written in some modern high-level programming language such as Pascal [37] comprise one formal model of computation with which many readers will be familiar. This, too, can be proved equivalent to a Turing machine since a Turing machine can simulate a Pascal program and a Pascal program can be written to simulate any Turing machine.

Theorem 3.1.1 is not "constructible" in that it proves the existence of (an uncountably infinite number of) non-computable functions, but does not provide an explicit example. It is not difficult to construct a function which is not computable. Suppose we number all Pascal programs and all possible inputs to them. The following function is called the *halting function*: define $h:N \times N \to B$ by

$h(x,y) = 1$ iff the xth program halts on the yth input.

Theorem 3.1.2 (Turing [71]) The halting function is not computable.

Proof. (Sketch) For a contradiction, suppose that the halting function h defined above is computable. Then there exists a Pascal program which computes it. Modify this program to compute a second function $g:N \rightarrow N$ defined by $g(x) = h(x,x)$ for all $x \in N$. Further modify this program so that instead of outputting "1", it enters an infinite loop. This is a perfectly valid Pascal program, and so must appear in our enumerated list $p_1, p_2, \ldots$ of Pascal programs. Suppose that it is p_k for some $k \in N$. But what does p_k do on input k? It goes into an infinite loop if p_k halts on input k, and it halts and outputs "0" if p_k does not halt on input k, a contradiction. Therefore p_k cannot exist, which implies that there is no Pascal program to compute the halting function, so the halting function is not computable. □

While the above proof is by diagonalization, the use of diagonalization is not strictly necessary.

In summary, almost every model of computation invented to date is equivalent to the Turing machine in the sense that the same functions are "computable" under each model. There are, of course, models which are strictly more powerful. For example, consider adding an "oracle" for the halting function to one of the standard models of computation. An oracle is a "black-box" (in Pascal a *predefined function*) which can "magically" evaluate a specific function. This model is clearly more powerful than any we have met so far, but it is also clear where the power stems from: the added ability to compute a function which was previously not computable. This is regarded as cheating. Every *non-cheating* model of computation invented to date is equivalent to the Turing machine in the sense that the same set of functions are "computable" under each model. This observation is commonly called the *Church-Turing thesis* in honour of the contributions of Church and Turing.

3.2. Complexity Theory

The study of computability theory is of some considerable interest, but in practice we are not just interested in which functions are computable, but which functions are computable within a reasonable amount of resources. Complexity theory is the study of resource bounded computation. Resources of interest include *time* and *space*. These resources are defined differently for each different model of computation. For Pascal programs, the running-time of a particular program on a particular input can be taken to be the number of instructions executed, and space can be taken to be the number of bits of memory used. Typical models studied include the Turing machine [71], the Random-Access Machine [18], and the Storage Modification Machine [65]. It is reasonable to expect that the amount of resources required for a computation will increase with the size of the input. Therefore it is reasonable to measure resource requirements as a function of input size. For example, if $T:N \to N$, we say that a Pascal program runs in time $T(n)$ if for all inputs x with $\|x\| = n$, the program halts on x within time $T(n)$. This is called *worst-case* complexity.

It is clear that an algorithm which runs in exponential time is not very useful since it can only be used for very small input sizes. Even if the current rapid growth in technology were to result in a ten-fold increase in the speed of computers every year (and we were in a financial situation to take advantage of this increase), the input sizes for which our algorithm were to run in a reasonable amount of time would increase only marginally. Comparative figures can be found in any elementary textbook on complexity theory (for example, see Aho, Hopcroft and Ullman [2]). Polynomial-time algorithms are more useful. Although it may be argued that an algorithm which runs in time n^{100} is as useless as an exponential time algorithm, experience has shown that (with few exceptions) once a function has proved to be computable in polynomial time, the exponent has very quickly been reduced to a small constant. Functions which require exponential time to compute are termed *intractable*, whereas functions with polynomial time algorithms are termed *tractable*.

It is still possible to "cheat" using the above definitions. If an input is padded by adding sufficiently many zeros to the end of it, then any exponential time algorithm will be made to run in polynomial time. This does not, however, help us to compute more quickly in practice. We will henceforth assume the existence of a reasonable encoding scheme whereby various mathematical objects are mapped onto the natural numbers without padding. More on reasonable encoding schemes can be found in Garey and Johnson [23].

Our use of the terms "polynomial time" and "exponential time" above would be cavalier if they were dependent on a particular model of computation. Fortunately a stronger version of the Church-Turing thesis holds. Not only are all models of computation equivalent, all resources (such as running-time) are equivalent to within a polynomial (unless you cheat). This observation is called the *sequential computation thesis* by Goldschlager and Lister [26]. The term *sequential computation* is often used to describe the type of computation whose running-time is related by a polynomial to Turing-machine running-time.

Suppose we consider functions which, like the halting function, have range **B**, and consider the input to be a string over **B** in the natural fashion. The *language* of f is defined to be the set of strings x such that $f(x) = 1$. The process of computing such a function is called *language recognition*. If $f(x) = 1$, x is said to be *accepted*, and if $f(x) = 0$, x is said to be *rejected*. Many optimization problems, such as the Travelling

Salesman Problem, can be expressed as a language recognition problem.

THE TRAVELLING SALESMAN OPTIMIZATION PROBLEM (TSOP)
INPUT: A labelled directed graph $G = (V,E,L)$.
OUTPUT: The cost of the minimum-cost Hamiltonian cycle (if one exists).

THE TRAVELLING SALESMAN PROBLEM (TSP)
INSTANCE: A labelled directed graph $G = (V,E,L)$ and an integer A.
QUESTION: Does there exist a Hamiltonian cycle of cost at most A?

It is clear that if TSOP can be computed in polynomial time, then so can TSP. Furthermore, the converse is also true.

Theorem 3.2.1 TSOP can be solved in polynomial time iff TSP can be solved in polynomial time.

Proof. It is obvious that if TSOP can be solved in polynomial time then so can TSP. For the converse, suppose that TSP can be solved in polynomial time. Given a labelled, directed graph G, evaluate TSP with $A = 1,2,4,8,...$ in turn, until an upper-bound for the optimal cost Hamiltonian cycle is obtained. The exact cost can then be determined using TSP and binary search (for a description of the latter, see any standard text on algorithm design, such as Aho, Hopcroft and Ullman [2]). Since the cost is at most exponential, this algorithm must terminate in polynomial time. □

A similar relationship can also be demonstrated for a large number of interesting combinatorial optimization problems. Therefore we can concentrate on the sub-problem of language recognition without loss of generality. This realization is one of the seminal contributions of Cook [17].

Let P denote the class of languages which can be recognized in polynomial time. Let NP denote the set of languages of the form

$$\{x \mid \exists \ y \text{ such that } \|y\| = n^{O(1)} \text{ and } (x,y) \in L \text{ where } L \in P\}.$$

Clearly* TSP∈ NP. Furthermore, NP contains a large number of interesting problems. It is conjectured that P≠NP, but no proof has been produced in almost two decades of research (it is obvious that P⊆NP, but the converse is strongly suspected to be false). However, the hardest problems in NP have been identified. A problem is said to be *NP-complete* if it is among the hardest problems in NP in the sense that if it is a member of P then P=NP. A problem which has the latter property (and may not

---

* Here, x is an ordered pair consisting of the graph G and the integer A required as the input to TSP, and y is a Hamiltonian cycle in G of cost at most A.

necessarily be a member of NP) is called *NP-hard*. The seminal paper by Cook [17] contained a proof that the satisfiability problem is NP-complete:

THE SATISFIABILITY PROBLEM (SAT)
INSTANCE: A Boolean formula F in conjunctive normal form.
QUESTION: Is F satisfiable?

Karp [39] followed with proofs that many combinatorial problems are NP-complete. The book by Garey and Johnson [23] contains a list of three hundred NP-complete problems (including TSP). It is widely accepted that NP-completeness constitutes a certificate of intractability.

The NP-completeness of SAT was proved from first principles. The standard way of proving the NP-completeness of some new language $L \in NP$ is by "polynomial time reduction" from a known NP-complete language. A language X is polynomial time reducible to Y if Y is harder than X in the sense that an algorithm for Y can be used to help recognize X in polynomial time. More formally, X is *polynomial time reducible* to Y if there is a polynomial time algorithm for recognizing X which uses an oracle for Y.

Theorem 3.2.2 If an NP-complete language X is polynomial time reducible to $Y \in NP$, then Y is NP-complete.

Proof. If $Y \in P$, then we could replace all calls to the oracle which recognizes Y with a polynomial time procedure which recognizes Y. The resulting algorithm for X would then run in polynomial time, demonstrating that $X \in P$. But X is NP-complete, so if $X \in P$ then $P = NP$. We have shown that if $Y \in P$, then $P = NP$. That is, Y is NP-complete. $\square$

Intuitively, NP is the class of problems whose solution can be verified in polynomial time. Thus the $P \neq NP$ conjecture can be interpreted as saying that solution is harder than verification. Another interesting class is Co-NP, the class of complements of the languages in NP (the complement of a language L is the set of strings which are not members of L). Equivalently (noting that P is closed under complementation), Co-NP is the set of languages of the form

$$\{x | \bigvee y \text{ such that } \|y\| = n^{O(1)} \text{ and } (x,y) \in L \text{ where } L \in P\}.$$

It is widely conjectured that Co-NP $\neq$ NP. Note that $P = NP$ implies that Co-NP $=$ NP. It is also widely conjectured that NP $\cap$ Co-NP $\neq$ P. It is clear that P $\subseteq$ NP $\cap$ Co-NP and that $P = NP$ implies NP $\cap$ Co-NP $=$ P. The complements of NP-complete languages are complete for Co-NP. NP-complete languages are hard for Co-NP and their complements are hard for NP.

The definitions of NP and Co-NP can be extended by allowing a fixed number of alternating existential and universal quantifiers. The union of these classes is called the *polynomial-time hierarchy*. There are complete problems for every level of the hierarchy [44,70]. The polynomial-time hierarchy is properly contained in PSPACE, the class of languages recognizable using a polynomial amount of space.

3.3. Parallel Complexity Theory

A *classical circuit* is a 4-tuple $C = (V,I,O,E)$, where:

> V is a finite set of *gates*,
> (V,E) is a directed acyclic graph of in-degree 2,
> $I \subseteq V$ is an ordered set of *input gates*,
> $O \subseteq V$ is an ordered set of *output gates*, $O \cap I = \emptyset$.

We will usually take V to be $\{g_1,...,g_p\}$, but we will sometimes find it convenient to take V to be some other finite set which can easily be placed into one-to-one correspondence with the set $\{1,...,p\}$. For convenience, we will usually take $I = \{g_1,...,g_n\}$ and $O = \{g_{p-m+1},...,g_p\}$ where $\|V\| = p$. The graph (V,E) is often called the *interconnection graph* or *interconnection pattern* of C.

The *state* of $g \in V$, denoted $v(g) \in B$, is defined as follows. If $g \in I$, $g = g_i$, then $v(g) = x_i$. Otherwise

$$v(g) = 1 \text{ iff there exists } h \in V \text{ with } (h,g) \in E \text{ and } v(h) = 0^*.$$

The *output* of C on input x is then $(v(g_{p-m+1}),...,v(g_p))$. C can then be thought of as computing a function from B^n to B^m. The *size* of C is defined to be $|V|$, and the *depth* is defined to be the maximum depth of recursion needed to evaluate its output (equivalently, the minimum number of layers needed to lay out the circuit in such a manner that each gate receives inputs only from layers above it).

A classical circuit cannot be thought of as an algorithm since it fails one of our requirements: it does not produce a result for all inputs, only inputs of a fixed size. This can be partially remedied by thinking of a "circuit" as an infinite family of circuits $C = (C_1,C_2,...)$ where each C_n is a finite n-input circuit as defined above. The size and depth of the circuit family are defined to be the worst-case size and depth respectively of C_n expressed as a function of n. However, a circuit family again fails to be an algorithm since it does not have a finite description. Such a circuit family is often called a *nonuniform circuit*. A nonuniform circuit of exponential size can compute any

---

* Note that we define the classical circuit model using NAND gates. Any other complete basis would have sufficed. This substitution increases depth and size by only a small constant multiple.

function by encoding a list of outputs into its interconnection pattern. A polynomial size nonuniform circuit apparently loses this ability, although it may speed up certain computations to have a polynomial-size look-up table encoded nonuniformly into the circuit. C is made into a *bona fide* algorithm in the sense of Turing by insisting that the interconnection pattern of each C_n be computable from n. The algorithm for this computation then comprises the required finite description of C. In this case, C is called a *Turing-uniform* circuit. If queries about the interconnection pattern of C are computable in space logarithmic in its size*, C is called a *logspace-uniform* circuit.

Theorem 3.3.1 Polynomial size logspace-uniform classical circuits recognize exactly the languages in P.

Proof. (Sketch) Polynomial size logspace-uniform circuits must have polynomial depth. It is thus easy to construct an algorithm (for example, a Pascal program) which, given an input $x \in \mathbf{N}$, constructs C_n and then recursively evaluates $v(g_p)$. Since C_n has polynomial size and the depth of recursion is polynomial, this algorithm runs in polynomial time. The converse follows since it is an easy matter to construct a logspace-uniform circuit family which simulates a polynomial time algorithm such as a Turing machine. □

The depth of a circuit is a measure of parallel time. The concept of parallel time is well-defined to within a polynomial, regardless of the parallel machine model used. This observation is called the *parallel computation thesis* by Goldschlager [25]†. The size of a circuit is a measure of parallel hardware requirements. As expected, the concept of parallel hardware is also well-defined to within a polynomial. Furthermore, parallel hardware and time are well-defined to within a polynomial *simultaneously*. This observation is called the *extended parallel computation thesis* by Dymond [20]‡. Note that both parallel computation theses are conditional on the caveat "provided that you don't cheat". It is easy to produce counterexamples by "cheating" (see Blum [8] and Parberry [50, 51]). Other parallel machines studied include the alternating Turing machine [12], the shared memory machine [21, 25], and the vector machine [31, 60].

Parallel computers of polynomial size can sometimes give an exponential speedup over sequential algorithms. The class NC of languages which can be recognized in

---

* Suppose C has size Z(n). Number the gates of C consecutively using O(log Z(n)) bits. The *inter-connection language* of C is the set of ordered triples (i,j,n) such that gate i in the circuit with n inputs receives input from gate j. We require that this language be recognizable by a linear-space Turing machine, that is, in space logarithmic in Z(n).

† Goldschlager also noted that parallel time is polynomially equivalent to a conventional Turing machine resource, that of work-space.

‡ Pippenger [55] noted that parallel time and hardware are simultaneously polynomially equivalent to the conventional Turing machine resources of reversals and space.

polynomial size and polylog parallel time by logspace-uniform classical circuits (Pippenger [55]) is a surprisingly rich one. The parallel computation theses are generally interpreted as saying that NC is robust under various definitions of computation. It is also fairly robust under slightly stronger definitions of uniformity (Ruzzo [63]). Theorem 3.3.1 implies that NC$\subseteq$P. It is widely conjectured that NC$\neq$P. As with the question of whether NP$\neq$P, it is not known whether a proof (or disproof) of this conjecture can be obtained with the mathematical tools currently available. However, there is a growing catalogue of P-complete problems which play a role analogous to that of NP-complete problems. These are problems which are members of P, but if any one of them were shown to be member of NC, then P$=$NC. NC is often further broken down into the union of NC^k for k$\geq$1, where NC^k is the class of languages which can be recognized in polynomial size and depth O(log^{k}n). More information on NC and P-completeness can be found in Parberry [52].

Nonuniform analogues of uniform complexity classes are often studied. For example, nonuniform-P is the class of languages recognized by polynomial size nonuniform circuits and nonuniform-NC is the class of languages recognized by polynomial size, polylog depth nonuniform circuits. There is even a nonuniform analogue of the Turing machine (see Karp and Lipton [40]). Another natural but different variant of NC, called PUNC, is obtained by allowing the interconnection pattern to be *P-uniform,* that is, it must be computable by a deterministic Turing machine in time polynomial in its size (Allender [4]).

3.4. Probabilistic Complexity Theory

The standard deterministic models of sequential and parallel computation can be augmented with the ability to flip coins and make decisions based on their outcome. Such a probabilistic machine may perform different computations every time it is run (even with the same input), but we will be satisfied if it produces the correct answer most of the time. In particular, a probabilistic machine M is said to *recognize* a language L if there is some $\varepsilon \in \mathbf{R}$ such that M can determine whether or not an input x belongs to L with probability of error ε. More formally, we say that it *recognizes* L iff there is a real number $0 < \varepsilon < 0.5$ such that:

(i) for all x$\in$L, the probability that it rejects x is at most ε.

(ii) for all x$\notin$L, the probability that it accepts x is at most ε.

This is often called *two-sided bounded-error probabilism.*

The classical circuit model of the previous section can be made probabilistic by allowing the use of "random inputs", which are gates that randomly and independently take on values from **B** at the start of the computation. Two-sided bounded-error probabilism appears at first to be an unnatural choice of paradigm; for example, a language recognizer which answers correctly with probability 0.6 cannot be considered very reliable. However, by repeating a computation many times and taking the consensus, the error probability can be reduced to μ for arbitrarily small $\mu > 0$.

Lemma 3.4.1 (Chernoff [14]) In a sequence of N independent Bernoulli trials each with probability p of success, the probability that at least m trials succeed, denoted B(m,N,p), has the property

$$B(m,N,p) \leq \left[\frac{Np}{m}\right]^m \left[\frac{N-Np}{N-m}\right]^{N-m}$$

provided $m \geq Np$.

Theorem 3.4.2 For every probabilistic circuit of size z and depth d which recognizes L with error probability ε and every $\mu > 0$ there exists a probabilistic circuit of size

$$2z \frac{\log \mu}{\log (1-4\varepsilon^2)} + O(1)$$

and depth $d+O(1)$ which recognizes L with error probability μ.

Proof. Taking $p=0.5-\varepsilon$ and $m=N/2$ in Lemma 3.4.1 it follows that the probability of more than half of the N trials failing is given by

$$B(N/2,N,0.5-\varepsilon) \leq (1-4\varepsilon^2)^{N/2}.$$

Thus, for any $0 < \mu < \varepsilon$, if

$$N = 2 \frac{\log \mu}{\log (1-4\varepsilon^2)}$$

trials are made and the consensus taken, the probability of failure is reduced to μ. For example, a machine with only 60% chance of making the correct decision can be used to obtain 99.9% certainty with 339 trials, regardless of the size of the input.

The new circuit thus consists of N copies of the original circuit with the output from those copies input into a constant-size sub-circuit which outputs true iff a majority of its inputs are true. $\square$

Note that Theorem 3.4.2 conserves Turing-uniformity and logspace-uniformity. Perhaps surprisingly, probabilism does not add power to nonuniform circuits. Randomness in a circuit is removed by taking a sufficiently large nonuniform sample. The following result essentially says that the probability of substantially more than the expected number of failures happening is exponentially small in the size of the sample.

Lemma 3.4.3 (Angluin and Valiant [5], Valiant and Brebner [73])

If $k = Np(1+\beta)$ for some $0 \le \beta \le 1$ then $B(k,N,p) \le e^{-0.5\beta^2 Np}$.

Proof. The proof follows from Lemma 3.4.1. $\square$

Theorem 3.4.4 (Bennett and Gill [7]) For every probabilistic circuit of size $Z(n)$ and depth $D(n)$ there is a nonuniform classical circuit of size $O(n Z(n))$ and depth $D(n) + O(\log n)$ which recognizes the same language.

Proof. Let $C = (C_1, C_2, ...)$ be a classical circuit which recognizes some language L with error probability $0.5 - \varepsilon$, where $\varepsilon \in \mathbf{R}$, $0 < \varepsilon < 0.5$. A completely deterministic circuit family which recognizes L with no error will be constructed. If C_n is a finite circuit with n inputs, and r is a fixed string of zeros and ones of the appropriate size, let $C_n(r)$ be the circuit obtained by fixing the random-inputs according to r. That is, if the ith bit of r is 1, then the ith random input is replaced by a sub-circuit which outputs 1, otherwise by a sub-circuit which always outputs zero. Suppose cn such strings $r_1, ..., r_{cn}$ are picked at random, where $c > (1-2\varepsilon)(\log_e 2)/\varepsilon^2$, choosing each random bit independently with the appropriate probability. Let $\hat{C}_n$ consist of copies of $C_n(r_1), ..., C_n(r_{cn})$ with their outputs connected to the inputs of a consensus circuit which outputs 1 iff the majority of its inputs are 1 (the construction of such a circuit is left as an exercise for the reader). It will be demonstrated that there is a choice of $r_1, ..., r_{cn}$ such that $\hat{C}_n$ recognizes L.

If $x \in \mathbf{B}^n$, let Failures(x) = $\{(r_1, ..., r_{cn}) | \hat{C}_n$ gives the wrong output$\}$. By Lemma 3.4.1, if $r_1, ..., r_{cn}$ is picked at random, then the probability that it is in Failures(x) is less than 2^{-n}. Now, if any r_i is picked at random, the probability that it fails is $0.5 - \varepsilon$. Without loss of generality, assume that $\varepsilon \le 1/4$. If cn independent Bernoulli trials are performed to pick $r_1, ..., r_{cn}$, where $c > (1-2\varepsilon)(\log_e 2)/\varepsilon^2$, and we take $N = cn$, $p = 0.5 - \varepsilon$, $\beta = 2\varepsilon/(1-2\varepsilon)$, $k = cn/2$, then by Lemma 3.4.3 the probability that there are at least $cn/2$ failures out of cn trials is

$$B(cn/2, cn, 0.5-\varepsilon) \le e^{-0.5cn(0.5-\varepsilon)} < 2^{-n}.$$

Therefore if $r_1, ..., r_{cn}$ are picked at random, the probability that it is in $\bigcup_x$Failures(x) is less than one (since there are only 2^n possible strings x of length n). Hence there must be at least one choice of cn strings $r_1, ..., r_{cn}$ that make $\hat{C}_n$ work correctly for all inputs of size n. Therefore $\hat{C}$ recognizes the same language as C. $\square$

The exact relationship between nonuniform, Turing-uniform, logspace-uniform and probabilistic language classes for both sequential and parallel computation is not yet well understood.

4. A Neural Network Model

In the loosest terms, our neural network is an interconnected system of simple process-ing elements. The processors can be in one of two states, and change state indepen-dently according to simple rules. The processors compute weighted binary threshold functions.

4.1. The Basic Model

A *neural network* is a 6-tuple $M=(V,I,O,A,w,h)$, where:

> V is a finite set of *processors*,
> $I \subseteq V$ is a set of *input processors*,
> $O \subseteq V$ is a set of *output processors*,
> $A \subseteq V$ is a set of *initially-active processors*, $A \cap I = \emptyset$,
> $w: V \times V \rightarrow Z$ is a *weight assignment*,
> $h: V \rightarrow Z$ is a *threshold assignment*.

We will usually take V to be $\{v_1,...,v_p\}$ for some suitable $p \in N$. We will sometimes find it convenient to take V to be some other finite set which can easily be placed into one-to-one correspondence with the set $\{1,...,p\}$. Let $E \subseteq V \times V$ be defined by $E=\{(u,v)|w(u,v) \neq 0\}$. E represents the connections between processors. The ordered pair (V,E) forms a graph, which is often called the *interconnection graph* or *intercon-nection pattern* of M. The ordered triple (V,E,w) forms a labelled graph. We will often use graph-theoretic terminology to describe the relevant aspects of M. M will be called *symmetric* if its interconnection pattern is an undirected labelled graph, and M will be called *simple* if its interconnection pattern is simple. There are two measures of the amount of hardware needed to implement M which we will consider here. One is $\|V\|$, which we will call the *size* of M, and the other is

$$\sum_{u,v \in V} |w(u,v)|,$$

which we will call the *weight** of M. In a neural network with size z and weight w we will assume that $w \geq z+1$. This is a reasonable assumption since w is bounded below by the number of edges in the interconnection graph, which is greater than the size for all but degenerate graphs. We will use n to denote $\|I\|$, the number of inputs to M.

The processors of the neural network are relatively limited in computing power. Each processor can compute a weighted threshold function. A weighted threshold func-tion is a function $f(w_1,...,w_m,h):B^m \rightarrow B$, $m \in N$, $w_1,...,w_m,h \in Z$, defined as follows.

---

* In the neural networks literature it is customary to add the thresholds into the weight of M. It is clear that our definition differs from this one by at most a factor of two.

$$f(w_1,...,w_m,h)(x_1,...,x_m)=1 \text{ iff } \sum_{i=1}^{m} w_i x_i \geq h.$$

Each processor can be in one of two states, which we will call *active* and *inactive*. A neural network computes by having the processors change state according to certain rules. More formally, a *computation* of $M=(V,I,O,A,w,h)$ on an input $x\in B^n$ is defined as follows. Initially, the input processors of M are placed into states which encode x. That is, if $I=\{u_1,...,u_n\}$ then processor u_i is placed in the active state if $x_i=1$. The processors of A are also placed in the active state. All other processors are placed in the inactive state. The computation then begins.

Time is measured by dividing it into discrete intervals. These intervals are numbered consecutively, with time interval 0 denoting the period immediately before the computation begins. We will say "at time t" to denote the period immediately after interval t has ended and immediately before interval t+1 begins. During each interval, some or all of the processors are given the opportunity to update their states.

The state of an individual processor $v\in V$ is updated as follows. Let $S(v,t)\in B$ denote the state of processor v at time t. We will use the Boolean value "1" to denote the active state and "0" to denote the inactive state. Define the *input* to processor v at time t, $W(v,t)$, by

$$W(v,t)= \sum_{u\in V} w(u,v)S(u,t).$$

Define the state of processor v at time 0, $S(v,0)$, as follows. Suppose $I=\{u_1,...,u_n\}$. $S(u_i,0)=x_i$ for $1\leq i\leq n$. For $v\notin I$,

$$S(v,0)=\begin{cases} 1 & \text{if } v\in A \\ 0 & \text{otherwise.} \end{cases}$$

Suppose $v\in V$. Define the *potential state* of processor v at time $t\geq 0$, $S_{potential}(v,t)$ as follows.

$$S_{potential}(v,t)=1 \text{ iff } W(v,t)\geq h(v).$$

Processor $v\in V$ is said to be *stable* at time t if its state is consistent with its input, that is, $S(v,t)=S_{potential}(v,t)$, and *unstable* otherwise. The state of processor v at time $t>0$, $S(v,t)$, is then

$$S(v,t)=\begin{cases} \overline{S(v,t-1)} & \text{if } v \text{ is unstable at time } t-1 \text{ and updated during interval } t \\ S(v,t-1) & \text{otherwise.} \end{cases}$$

Suppose $U\subseteq V$, and $U=\{u_1,u_2,...,u_m\}$ for some $m\in N$. The *state* of U at time t is defined to be the string $S(U,t)=S(u_1,t)S(u_2,t)...S(u_m,t)$. A *configuration* of M at time t is defined to be $S_M(t)=S(V,t)$. The computation is said to be *terminated* by time t if it has reached a stable configuration, that is, $S_M(t)=S_M(t+1)$. Other terminology used to describe termination includes *halting, reaching a stable state,* and *converging.* The *running-time* (or *time requirement*) of M on input x, $\tau(M,x)$, is defined to be the smallest t such that the computation has terminated by time t. The *output* of M is defined to be $S(O,\tau(M,x))$. A neural network M_2 is said to be f(t)-*equivalent* to M_1 iff for all inputs x, for every computation of M_1 on input x which terminates in time t there is a computation of M_2 on input x which terminates in time f(t) with the same output. A neural network M_2 is said to be *equivalent* to M_1 iff it is t-equivalent to it.

4.2. Clamping

An alternative mode of computation commonly used in neural network literature involves *clamping* the input processors, that is, physically restraining them from participating in the computation by defining their states to be $S(u_i,t)=x_i$ for $1\le i\le n$, $t\ge 0$. The effect of clamping can easily be obtained in our model.

Theorem 4.2.1 For every clamped neural network M_1 of size z and weight w there exists an equivalent unclamped neural network M_2 of size z and weight w+n.

Proof. Let $M_1=(V,I,O,A,w_1,h_1)$ be a clamped neural network. Define $M_2=(V,I,O,A,w_2,h_2)$, where w_2 and h_2 are the same as w_1 and h_1 respectively except for the fact that $w_2(u,u)=1$ and $h_2(u)=1$ for all $u\in I$, and $w_1(v,u)=0$ for all $v\in V,u\in I$. Since the input processors of M_2 are always stable, any computation of M_1 can be duplicated in M_2. $\square$

4.3. Zero Thresholds

All non-zero thresholds in a neural network can be made zero with no increase in running-time and a small increase in both weight and size. First, add a new processor p to V. Put p in A. For each $v\in V$ with $h(v)=k\ne 0$, set h(v) to zero and add an edge of weight $-k$ from p to v. Since it has no inputs, processor p stays active during the entire computation. Thus p contributes weight $-k$ to W(v,t) at all times t, which means that the other processors connected to v must contribute weight at least k to cross the new threshold value of zero. Therefore the modified v has the same behaviour as the original. More formally, we have:

Theorem 4.3.1 For every neural network M_1 of size z and weight w there exists an equivalent neural network M_2 of size z+1 and weight 2w with zero thresholds.

Proof. Let $M_1=(V_1,I,O,A_1,w_1,h_1)$ be a neural network. Define $M_2=(V_2,I,O,A_2,w_2,h_2)$, where $V_2=V_1\cup\{p\}$, $A_2=A_1\cup\{p\}$, $h_2(v)=0$ for all $v\in V$ and w_2 is defined as follows. For all $u,v\in V_1$, $w_2(u,v)=w_1(u,v)$, and $w_2(p,v)=-h(v)$. For each computation of M_1, the corresponding computation of M_2 will update the same processors in each time interval.

Let $S_1(v,t)$ and $S_2(v,t)$ denote the state of processor v at time t in neural networks M_1 and M_2 respectively. Clearly for all $t \geq 0$, $S_2(p,t) = 1$. We claim that for $t \geq 0$, for all $v \in V_1$, $S_2(v,t) = S_1(v,t)$. The proof is by induction on t. The claim is certainly true for $t = 0$, since the same initial conditions hold. Now suppose that $t > 0$ and that the induction hypothesis is true at time $t-1$. By definition, $S_2(v,t) = 1$ iff

$$\sum_{u \in V_2} w_2(u,v)S_2(u,t-1) \geq 0$$

iff

$$\sum_{u \in V_1} w_1(u,v)S_1(u,t-1) + w_2(p,v)S_2(p,t) \geq 0$$

iff

$$\sum_{u \in V_1} w_1(u,v)S_1(u,t-1) \geq h(v)$$

iff $S_1(v,t) = 1$.

We can conclude that for each computation of M_1 on input $x \in B^n$ there is a corresponding computation of M_2 on x which terminates with the same output in the same running-time. Clearly M_2 has at most one more processor than M_1. Note that it can be assumed that for all $v \in V$,

$$|h(v)| \leq \sum_{u \in V_1} |w_1(u,v)|$$

since otherwise v would never change state (and thus could safely be removed from the neural network in the interests of efficiency). Hence

$$\sum_{v \in V_1} |h(v)| \leq \sum_{u,v \in V_1} |w_1(u,v)|, \tag{*}$$

that is, the sum of the thresholds of M_1 is bounded above by its weight. Therefore the weight of M_2 is given by the following.

$$\sum_{u,v \in V_2} |w_2(u,v)| = \sum_{u,v \in V_1} |w_2(u,v)| + \sum_{v \in V_1} |w_2(p,v)|$$

$$= \sum_{u,v \in V_1} |w_1(u,v)| + \sum_{v \in V_1} |h(v)|$$

$$\leq 2 \sum_{u,v \in V_1} |w_1(u,v)|. \tag{by (*)}$$

That is, the weight of M_2 is at most twice the weight of M_1. $\square$

4.4. Real Weights

Some versions of our model found in the literature allow real weights, whereas we have integer weights. However, all real weights can be replaced by integers since weighted binary threshold functions are robust under small perturbations to the weights. Each real weight can thus be replaced by a sufficiently close rational number. The resulting rational weights can be multiplied by the product of their denominators to give integer weights.

Theorem 4.4.1 (Minsky and Papert [45]) For every neural network M_1 with real weights there exists an equivalent neural network M_2 of the same size with integer weights.

Proof. Let $M = (V,I,O,A,w,h)$ be a neural network. Consider $v \in V$ with in-degree m, with weights $w_1,...,w_m$. Let $W(w_1,...,w_m):B^m \to Z$ be defined as follows.

$$W(w_1,...,w_m)(x_1,...,x_m) = \sum_{i=1}^{m} x_i w_i.$$

Processor v computes a weighted threshold function $f(w_1,...,w_m,h(v)):B^m \to B$ defined by

$$f(w_1,...,w_m,h(v))(x_1,...,x_n) = 1 \text{ iff } W(w_1,...,w_m)(x_1,...,x_m) \geq h(v).$$

Let δ be the largest value of $\{W(w_1,...,w_m)(x) | x \in B^m\}$ less than $h(v)$. If $0 < \varepsilon < \delta/m$, then for all $x \in B^m$,

$$W(w_1,...,w_m)(x) < h(v) \text{ iff } W(w_1+\varepsilon,...,w_m+\varepsilon)(x) < h(v).$$

But for each $w \in R$ there is a rational number $\hat{w}$ between w and $w+\varepsilon$. Therefore each real weight w_i can be replaced by a rational $\hat{w}_i$. Finally, integer weights can be obtained by multiplying each rational weight by the product of the denominators of all the weights. $\square$

4.5. The Role of Negative Weights

An edge with negative weight is an *inhibitory* one in the sense that if the source processor is active, then it contributes a negative value to the input of the destination processor, which may prevent the latter from becoming active. Thus it behaves much like a Boolean negation gate (which we will call a negation processor). A Boolean negation gate has in-degree one, with the incoming edge of weight one, and is active iff its input is zero. In fact, negative weights are in a sense equivalent to Boolean negation processors.

Lemma 4.5.1 For every neural network M_1 with negation processors there exists an equivalent neural network M_2 which has the same size and weight.

Proof. Let M_1 be a neural network with negation processors. Replace each negation processor with a standard processor, and set its threshold to zero and the weight of the edge into it to -1. $\square$

Lemma 4.5.2 (Muroga [46]) For every neural network M_1 of size z and weight w there exists a 2t-equivalent neural network M_2 of size 2z and weight w+z with negation processors and positive weights.

Proof. Let $M_1 = (V_1, I, O, A, w_1, h_1)$ be a neural network of size z and weight w. A neural network $M_2 = (V_2, I, O, A, w_2, h_2)$ is constructed from M_1 by modifying every edge of negative weight by making its weight positive, interposing a negation processor, and adding the absolute value of its weight to the threshold of the destination processor. More formally, $V_2 = V_1 \cup C$ where $C = \{\hat{u} | u, v \in V_1, w_1(u,v) < 0\}$ is the set of negation processors, and w_2, h_2 are defined as follows. If $w_1(u,v) > 0$ then $w_2(u,v) = w_1(u,v)$. If $w_1(u,v) < 0$ then $w_2(u,\hat{u}) = 1$, $w_2(\hat{u},v) = |w_1(u,v)|$. All other unspecified weights are zero. For all $v \in V_1$, let $to(v) \subseteq V_1$ be the set of vertices which are connected to v by edges of negative weight, that is, $to(v) = \{u \in V_1 | w_1(u,v) < 0\}$, and $from(v) \subseteq V_1$ be the set of vertices to which v is connected by edges of negative weight, that is, $to(v) = \{u \in V_1 | w_1(v,u) < 0\}$. Then

$$h_2(v) = h_1(v) + \sum_{u \in to(v)} |w_1(u,v)|.$$

For each computation of M_1, the corresponding computation of M_2 is as follows. For $V \subseteq V_1$ let

$$from(V) = \bigcup_{v \in V} from(v).$$

Let $U(t) \subseteq V_1$ be the set of processors which are updated during time interval t in M_1. Then for all $t > 0$, at time $2t-1$ update processors $U(t)$ in M_2, and at time $2t$ update processors (u,v) for all $v \in U(2t-1)$, $u \in from(U(2t-1))$.

M_2 has positive weights. It has one extra processor and an extra edge of weight one for each processor of M_1 that has negative weight edges from it. Therefore, M_2 has size at most 2z and weight at most w+z. $\square$

The following result is of some intrinsic interest, since it states that all connections can be made inhibitory.

Theorem 4.5.3 (Godbeer [24]) For every neural network M_1 of size z and weight w there exists a 2t-equivalent neural network M_2 of size 2z and weight 2w with negative weights.

Proof. Similar to Lemma 4.5.2. □

4.6. Networks of Bounded Weight

Although our model allows each weight to take on an infinite number of possible values, there are only a finite number of threshold functions (since there are only a finite number of Boolean functions) with a fixed number of inputs. Thus the weights of an n-input threshold function are bounded above by some function in n. In fact, $O(n \log n)$ bits are sufficient to describe each weight.

Theorem 4.6.1 For every neural network M_1 of size z there exists an equivalent neural network M_2 of size z and weight $z^{z+O(1)}$.

Proof. (Sketch) It is sufficient to prove that for every weighted threshold function $f(w_1,...,w_n,h):B^n \to B$ for some $n \in N$, there is an equivalent weighted threshold function $g(w_1^*,...,w_n^*,h^*)$ such that $|w_i^*| \le n^n$ for $1 \le i \le n$. To simplify the presentation, we will assume that $h = h^* = 0$. By Theorem 4.3.1 we can do this without loss of generality, and with a little thought the need for the extra processor required by that Theorem can be removed. We paraphrase the proof appearing in Muroga [46] (see Proposition 2.1.1, Theorem 3.1.2, and Theorem 9.3.2.1 of that reference) of a slightly stronger result from Muroga, Toda and Takasu [47]. Given a neural network M_1, convert it into a neural network with negation processors, arbitrary thresholds and positive weights by Lemma 4.5.2. The following procedure will demonstrate how to reduce the weights, assuming that they are positive, after which the negation processors can be removed by simply reversing the procedure of Lemma 4.5.2 (without recourse to the more expensive Lemma 4.5.1).

Consider a weighted threshold function $f(w):B^n \to B$ where $w \in N^n$, defined by

$$f(w)(x) = 1 \text{ iff } \sum_{i=1}^{n} w_i x_i \ge 0.$$

Consider the weight vector w to be a variable. The threshold function places constraints on w in the form of hyperplanes in hyperspace. In order to minimize the total weight of w, we need to find a minimal w subject to those constraints. More formally, define $S \in M_{2^n,2^n}(\{-1,0,1\})$ by $S_{ij} = 0$ if $i \ne j$ and

$$S_{ii} = \begin{cases} 1 & \text{if } f(w)(i) \ge k \\ -1 & \text{otherwise.} \end{cases}$$

Let $B \in M_{2^n,n}(\mathbf{Z})$ be defined to be the matrix product $B = SM$ where $M = matrix\,(0,1,...,2^n-1)$. Further define $h \in M_{n,1}(\mathbf{Z})$ to be the vector defined by

$$h_{i,1} = \begin{cases} k & \text{if } f(w)(i) \geq k \\ k-1 & \text{otherwise.} \end{cases}$$

Then the problem of finding minimal weights is reduced to the following: minimize

$$\sum_{i=1}^{n} w_i$$

subject to the constraints

$$Bw^T \geq h. \qquad (*)$$

Although the matrix B is exponentially large, most of it is irrelevant. There is a minimal solution to $(*)$ which satisfies exactly n of the vector inequalities in $(*)$ by equality. (Each inequality forms a hyperplane in hyperspace. The valid solutions w to $(*)$ are constrained by these hyperplanes into a polytope. The minimal w is in a sense the "lowest" point in the polytope. There must be at least one vertex of the polytope with no other part of the polytope "lower" than it, since a polytope is convex. A vertex of a polytope in n-dimensional space has exactly n hyperfaces meeting it, that is, it meets exactly n of the inequalities.) Cramer's rule can then be used to show that any solution w which satisfies these equalities has the property that w_i is bounded above by the maximum determinant of a matrix in $M_{n,n}(\{-1,0,1\})$. It is clear that this is bounded above by n!, which by Stirling's approximation gives the required result. The details are left to the interested reader. $\square$

Unfortunately, the best known lower-bound is the trivial $\Omega(n)$ bits.

Theorem 4.6.2 There are more than $2^{n(n-1)/2}$ n-input weighted threshold functions.

Proof. Let $H(n)$ be the number of weighted threshold function with n inputs. Consider an n-input weighted threshold function $f_n(w_1,...,w_n):B^n \rightarrow B$, $w_1,...,w_m \in \mathbf{Z}$; that is

$$f_n(w_1,...,w_n)(x_1,...,x_n) = 1 \text{ iff } \sum_{i=1}^{m} w_i x_i \geq 0.$$

Set $f_{n-1}(w_1,...,w_{n-1}) = f_n(w_1,...,w_{n-1},0)$ and further define

$$\hat{f}_n(w_1,...,w_n)(x_1,...,x_n) = \sum_{i=1}^{m} w_i x_i.$$

There are $H(n-1)$ ways of choosing f_{n-1}. For each of them there are $2^{n-1}+1$ ways of choosing w_n, respectively placing the j members of $\{x1 | x \in B^{n-1}\}$ which have largest $\hat{f}_n(x0)$ values (and therefore have largest $\hat{f}_n(x1)$ values) on or above the threshold for

$0 \leq j \leq 2^{n-1}$. It is clear that all weighted threshold functions constructed in this manner are distinct. We conclude that for $n > 0$,

$$H(n) \geq H(n-1)(2^{n-1}+1).$$

and $H(0) = 0$. Therefore $H(n) > 2^{n(n-1)/2}$. $\square$

The lower-bound can be improved to $H(n) > 2^{n(n-1)/2 + 32}$ (Muroga [46]) by observing that $H(8) > 2^{44}$ (Muroga, Tsuboi and Baugh [48]).

Corollary 4.6.3 There are weighted threshold functions which require weights of more than $(n-1)/2$ bits.

Proof. If all n-input weighted threshold functions could be expressed using weights of $(n-1)/2$ bits, then there would be at most $2^{n(n-1)/2}$ weighted threshold functions, contradicting Theorem 4.6.2. $\square$

4.7. Bipolar States

Our model has *binary* states, that is, states from the Boolean set **B**. Another alternative which is popular in the literature is to use *bipolar* states, that is, states from the set $\{-1,1\}$. The active state is denoted by "1" and the inactive state is denoted by "-1". The definition of the potential state of processor v at time t is then

$$S_{potential}(v,t) = sign(W(v,t)).$$

It is easy to see that this model is equivalent to ours:

Theorem 4.7.1 For every neural network M_1 of size z and weight w with bipolar states there exists an equivalent neural network M_2 of size z and weight 2w with binary states.

Proof. Let $M_1 = (V,I,O,A,w_1,h_1)$ be a neural network with bipolar states. Define $M_2 = (V,I,O,A,w_2,h_2)$ as follows. For each $u,v \in V$, $w_2(u,v) = 2w_1(u,v)$. For each $v \in V$,

$$h_2(v) = h_1(v) + \sum_{u \in V} w_1(u,v).$$

For each computation of M_1, the corresponding computation of M_2 will update the same processors in each time interval.

Let $S_1(v,t)$ denote the potential state of processor v at time t in M_1, that is,

$$S_1(v,t) = sign(\sum_{u \in V} w_1(u,v)S_1(u,t-1)).$$

Also let $S_2(v,t)$ denote the potential state of processor v at time t in M_2, that is,

$$S_2(v,t) = 1 \text{ iff } \sum_{u \in V} w_2(u,v)S_2(u,t-1) \geq h(v).$$

We claim that

$$S_2(v,t) = 1 \text{ iff } S_1(v,t) = 1,$$

or equivalently, that $S_2(v,t) = (S_1(v,t)+1)/2$. The proof is by induction on t. The induction hypothesis is certainly true for $t = 0$ by definition. Now suppose that the hypothesis is true at time $t-1$. Then $S_2(v,t) = 1$ iff

$$\sum_{u \in V} w_2(u,v) S_2(u,t-1) \geq h_2(v)$$

iff

$$2 \sum_{u \in V} w_1(u,v) S_2(u,t-1) \geq h_1(v) + \sum_{u \in V} w_1(u,v)$$

iff (by the induction hypothesis)

$$\sum_{u \in V} w_1(u,v) S_1(u,t-1) \geq h_1(v)$$

iff $S_1(v,t) \geq 0$. It is clear that M_2 has the same size as M_1, and weight double that of M_1. $\square$

Theorem 4.7.2 For every neural network M_1 of size z and weight w with binary states there exists an equivalent neural network M_2 with bipolar states which has size z and weight 2w.

Proof. The proof is similar to that of Theorem 4.7.1, and is left as an exercise for the reader. $\square$

4.8. Modes of Computation

When we gave a formal definition of a neural network, we divided time into discrete intervals and stated that "during each interval, some or all of the processors modify their respective states". However, we did not specify exactly which processors update their state within any particular interval. Two modes of computation are prevalent in the literature.

1. *Sequential operation,* in which a single processor updates its state within each interval. This processor may be chosen at random, or according to some deterministic rule.

2. *Parallel operation,* in which at least two processors update their state during each interval. For example, each processor could decide randomly and independently whether to update, or all processors could update during every interval. The former is called *random parallel,* and the latter *fully parallel* operation.

A computation is called *productive* if at least one unstable processor is updated in each interval. Note that many of the results of this section are robust under various modes of computation. We leave the exploration of the ramifications of this observation to the interested reader.

5. Neural Circuits

A directed acyclic neural network is called a *neural circuit*. A neural circuit can be divided into layers, with each layer receiving inputs only from the layers above it. As with classical circuits, the *depth* is defined to be the number of layers, and the *size* is the number of processors. In keeping with the circuit paradigm we will not count the input processors in either the depth or the size.

5.1. Neural Circuits and Neural Networks

Neural circuits have several nice properties that make them easier to deal with than neural networks, for example, all computations of a neural circuit terminate, and all computations on a given input terminate in the same configuration. Furthermore, all productive sequential computations of a neural circuit terminate within time bounded above by its size, and all fully parallel computations terminate within time bounded above by its depth. Neural circuits also have an elegant property that enables us to ensure that all weights are positive by insisting that both the inputs and their negations are available to the circuit.

Theorem 5.1.1 For every neural circuit of depth d, size z and weight w there is an equivalent neural circuit of depth d+1, size 2z+n and weight 2w+n in which the first layer consists of negation processors and all subsequent layers have positive weights.

Proof. The proof uses the standard "double-rail logic" (see, for example, Goldschlager and Parberry [27]) to push negations back to the inputs. $\square$

Using Theorem 5.1.1 we can restrict ourselves to a normal-form neural circuit with positive weights which is a function of literals. From this point onwards we will not charge for the first layer of negations*.

Neural circuits are surprisingly powerful despite the fact that they are a special case of neural networks.

---

* It is only necessary to add one to the depth bounds and n to the size and weight bounds of the subsequent results.

Theorem 5.1.2 (Parberry and Schnitger [53,54]) Every neural network of size z and weight w which halts in time t in fully parallel mode can be simulated by a neural circuit of size zt, weight wt and depth t.

Proof. A standard technique from Savage [64] (used more recently in Goldschlager and Parberry [27]) for removing cycles from a classical circuit can be used to make a neural network acyclic.

Suppose M_1 is a neural network of size z with running-time t when run in fully parallel mode. The acyclic machine M_2 consists of $T(n)+1$ "snapshots" of B, one at each point in time. As a consequence, M_2 will have size $z.(t+1)$ and run in time t. More formally, suppose $M_1 = (V_1, I_1, O_1, A_1, w_1, h_1)$. Then $M_2 = (V_2, I_2, O_2, A_2, w_2, h_2)$, where:

$$V_2 = \{(v,\tau) | 0 \leq \tau \leq t\},$$

$$I_2 = \{(u,0) | u \in I_1\},$$

$$O_2 = \{(u,t) | u \in O_n\},$$

$$A_2 = \{(u,0) | u \in A_2\},$$

$$w_2((u,\tau-1),(v,\tau)) = w_1(u,v) \text{ for } 1 \leq \tau \leq t,$$

$$h_2((v,\tau)) = h_1(v) \text{ for } 1 \leq \tau \leq t.$$

The correctness proof is left as an exercise for the reader. □

Theorem 5.1.3 For every neural circuit C of size z, weight w and depth d there is a symmetric neural network N with size z and weight $(2wz)^{d+O(1)}$ such that every computation of N terminates in the same configuration as C.

Proof. (Sketch) We make each edge of C bidirectional and increase the weights in such a manner that each processor is only affected by those edges which were formerly incoming. Suppose we draw C in a level-by-level fashion with each processor affected only by the level above it, and number the levels upwards from the final (output) level, starting at zero. The processors at level k have their thresholds multiplied by $(2w)^k$, and the edges between level $k-1$ and level k have their weights multiplied by the same amount. Thus the "outgoing" edges from a processor at level k can have combined weight at most $2^{k-1}w^k$, whereas in "incoming" edges each have weight at least $2^k w^k$. Therefore the "outgoing" edges cannot contribute enough weight to affect the processor. □

5.2. Threshold Circuits

A neural network with weights drawn from $\{\pm 1\}$ is called a *unit-weight* neural network. A unit-weight neural circuit is called a *threshold circuit*. The weight of the threshold circuit is equal to the number of edges, which is bounded above by the square of the size. Despite the apparent handicap of limited weights, threshold circuits are surprisingly powerful. A function $f:B^n \to B$ is called *symmetric* if its output remains the same no matter how the input bits are permuted.

Theorem 5.2.1 Any symmetric function can be computed by a threshold circuit with size $2n+1$ and depth 2.

Proof. (Sketch) A symmetric function can be uniquely defined by the set

$$S_f = \{m \in N \mid f(x) = 1 \text{ for all } x \in B^n \text{ with exactly m ones}\}.$$

The circuit uses $\|S_f\|$ pairs of gates. The ith pair has one processor active when the number of ones in the input is at least the ith member of S_f, and the other processor active when the number of ones in the input is at most the ith member of S_f. When given an input x such that $f(x) = 1$, exactly $\|S_f\| + 1$ of these gates are active, and when given an input x such that $f(x) = 0$, exactly $\|S_f\|$ of these gates are active. The output gate can therefore be a gate with threshold value $\|S_f\|+1$ whose inputs come from these gates. $\square$

We will also consider a limited version of a threshold circuit, called an *AND/OR circuit*. The layers of the circuit alternate between AND and OR gates*. This is clearly a special case of the neural circuit model since an n-input AND gate can be emulated by a single processor with unit weights on its inputs and a threshold of n, and an n-input OR gate can be emulated by a single processor with unit weights on its inputs and a threshold of 1.

Theorem 5.2.2 (Chandra, Stockmeyer and Vishkin [13])† Any Boolean function of n inputs can be computed by an AND/OR circuit with size $2^{n-1}+1$ and depth 2.

Proof. (Sketch) Express the Boolean function in disjunctive normal form essentially by listing (as conjunctions of literals) all of the inputs which make it true. Without loss of generality we can assume that the list has at most 2^{n-1} conjunctions in it. (There are at most 2^n conjunctions of literals. If more than half of these make the function true,

---

* The circuit may start with either kind of layer. Note that we are still assuming an "invisible" layer of negations.

† All of the results of this section that are attributed to Chandra, Stockmeyer and Vishkin [13] (Theorems 5.2.2, 5.2.3, 5.2.5, 5.2.6, and 5.2.8) have slightly worse bounds in that reference than are claimed here. We have made the obvious improvements.

compute the complement of f, negate it, and use Theorem 5.1.1.) Therefore the neural circuit consists of a layer of at most 2^{n-1} conjunctions followed by a single disjunction. □

We will now consider the problem of adding two n-bit integers represented in binary notation. For convenience we will limit ourselves to non-negative integers. The extension to negative integers is tedious but not difficult. Suppose we are to sum $x = x_1...x_n$ and $y = y_1...y_n$ to give $z = z_1...z_{n+1}$. Define c_i to be 1 if there is a carry into the ith position of the result, that is, into z_i. We define the *carry* of x and y to be $c_1...c_{n+1}$.

Theorem 5.2.3 (Chandra, Stockmeyer and Vishkin [13]) The carry of two n-bit natural numbers can be computed by an AND/OR circuit with size $O(n^2)$ and depth 3.

Proof. We use the standard elementary school algorithm. Define g_i to be 1 if there is a carry generated in the ith position of the operands, and define p_i to be 1 if there is a carry propagated in the ith position of the operands. Then

$$g_i = AND(x_i, y_i)$$

for $1 \le i \le n$,

$$p_i = OR(x_i, y_i)$$

for $1 \le i < n$, and

$$c_i = OR(g_i, AND(p_i, g_{i+1}), AND(p_i, p_{i+1}, g_{i+2}), \dots , AND(p_i, ..., p_{n-1}, g_n))$$

for $1 \le i \le n$, and $c_{n+1} = 0$. □

Theorem 5.2.4 The sum of two n-bit natural numbers can be computed by an AND/OR circuit with size $O(n^2)$ and depth 5.

Proof. First compute the carry of x and y in quadratic size and depth 3 using Theorem 5.2.3. Then, $z_1 = c_1$ and

$$z_i = MOD_2(x_i, y_i, c_i)$$

for $1 < i \le n+1$. A 3-input MOD_2 gate can easily be constructed from an AND/OR circuit of depth 2 using Theorems 5.1.1 and 5.2.2. □

Theorem 5.2.5 (Chandra, Stockmeyer and Vishkin [13]) The sum of n n-bit integers can be computed by a threshold circuit with size $O(n^3)$ and constant depth.

Proof. (Sketch) We will prove the result for non-negative integers. The extension to negative values is straightforward but tedious. Suppose we are to add $x^{(1)},...,x^{(n)} \in \mathbf{N}$ where $\|x^{(i)}\| \le n$ for $1 \le i \le n$.

1. Lay out the numbers as the rows of an n×n Boolean array, that is, construct *matrix* $(x^{(1)},...,x^{(n)})$.

2. Add the columns (using Theorem 5.2.1) and lay out the results as the rows of a Boolean array. The first row will be all zeros except for the last log n bits, which we will call the *dirty region*. Each subsequent row will have its dirty region shifted to the left by one bit.

3. Repeat step 2. The dirty regions will consist of log log n bits.

4. Divide the matrix into m×m submatrices, where $m = \sqrt{\log n}$. The only sub-matrices containing non-zero values will be the back diagonal and its superdiagonal.

5. Sum each submatrix independently (using Theorem 5.2.2). Observe that the overflow from each submatrix has less than m bits. We can even include with each diagonal submatrix the one directly above it. Thus we have effectively summed the array from step 3 in column strips of width m and obtained a result word and a collection of overflows which do not overlap and hence can be made into an overflow word.

6. Sum the result word and the overflow word (using Theorem 5.2.4). □

Theorem 5.2.6 (Chandra, Stockmeyer and Vishkin [13]) The product of two n-bit numbers can be computed by a threshold circuit with size $O(n^3)$ and constant depth.

Proof. Use the elementary-school shift-and-add multiplication algorithm, with Theorem 5.2.5 used to add the shifted values in cubic size and constant depth. □

Theorem 5.2.7 For every neural network M_1 of size z there exists an O(t)-equivalent unit-weight neural network M_2 of size $O(z^4\log^3 z)$.

Proof. By Lemma 4.5.2 we can make the weights of all non-unit edges positive, and then by Theorem 4.6.1 we can bound all weights to $O(z \log z)$ bits. By Corollary 5.2.5 we can replace every processor with non-unit weights by a threshold circuit of size $O(z^3\log^3 z)$ and constant depth. □

It is interesting to ask whether any improvement can be made in the size of Theorem 5.2.7, since it is a fairly large polynomial. It is clear that if the size of Theorem 5.2.3 can be improved to $Z(n)$, then the size of Theorem 5.2.7 will be improved to $p^2 Z(p \log p)$. Chandra, Fortune and Lipton [11] show by a sophisticated argument that $Z(n)$ can be reduced to almost a linear function*. Surprisingly, the authors also found a matching lower-bound [10].

---

* Define $f^{(1)}(x) = f(x)$, and for $i > 1$, $f^{(i)}(x) = f(f^{(i-1)}(x))$. Define $f_1(n) = 2^n$, and for $i > 1$, $f_i(n) = f_{i-1}^{(n)}(2)$. There is an AND/OR circuit for carry of depth O(d) and size $n.f_d^{-1}(n)$.

Theorem 5.2.7 states that we can assume unit weights by increasing the size by a polynomial and the running time by only a constant multiple. The result can also be combined with Theorem 5.1.2 if wished.

It is reasonable to ask whether neural circuits are faster than classical circuits. The answer is affirmative:

Theorem 5.2.8 (Chandra, Stockmeyer and Vishkin [13]) Any function which can be computed by a classical circuit of depth d and size z can be computed by an AND/OR circuit of depth $O(d/\varepsilon \log \log z)$ and size $z^{1+\varepsilon}$, for any $\varepsilon > 0$.

Proof. (Sketch) Divide the classical circuit horizontally into strips of depth $\varepsilon \log \log z$. Within each strip, each output gate can depend only on $\varepsilon \log z$ inputs, and thus its role can be played by an AND/OR circuit of size $O(z^{\varepsilon})$ and constant depth by Theorem 5.2.2. $\square$

Therefore neural networks speed up P and NC by a small amount:

Corollary 5.2.9 Any function which can be computed by a classical circuit of depth d and polynomial size can be computed by an AND/OR circuit of depth $O(d/\log \log n)$ and polynomial size.

5.3. Fault-Tolerance

One advantage that the brain has over conventional computers is its ability to perform reliable computations with unreliable hardware. Carver Mead (quoted in [33]) has observed that: "The brain has this wonderful property - you can go through and shoot out every tenth neuron and never miss them". A plausible interpretation of this observation is that correct computations can be carried out with high probability when neurons malfunction with probability one in ten. As we shall see, threshold circuits have such a fault-tolerant ability for language recognition. In particular, they can reliably simulate fault-free classical circuits with not much increase in size or depth.

Suppose $f: B^n \rightarrow B$ is a Boolean function and $g: B^n \rightarrow B$ is a stochastic Boolean function. We say that g is an ε-*approximation* to f if for all $x \in B^n$, the probability that $f(x) \neq g(x)$ is a fixed constant less than ε. Suppose $\mu, \varepsilon \in R^+$. A Boolean gate is an ε-*noisy* f-gate if it computes an ε-approximation to f. A finite circuit which computes f is said to be (μ, ε)-*resilient* if it computes an $(\varepsilon + \mu)$-approximation to f whenever its gates are replaced by their ε-noisy counterparts. Note that we can never hope to do better than an ε-approximation to f with ε-noisy gates, since the output gate is ε-noisy.

Theorem 5.3.1 Every Boolean function which can be computed by a finite classical circuit of size z and depth d can be computed by a (μ,ε)-resilient threshold circuit with size

$$\frac{2z}{\lambda}(\ln z + \ln \frac{2}{\mu}) + 1$$

and depth 2d+1, for all $1/12 \leq \varepsilon < 1/6$ and $\mu > 0$ where

$$\lambda = \frac{\varepsilon}{2}(\frac{1}{6\varepsilon}-1)^2.$$

Proof. Let C be a classical circuit of size z and depth d. Suppose $1/12 \leq \varepsilon < 1/6$. Each wire in C will be replaced by a *cable* of m wires (m will be given explicitly later). Each gate in C will be replaced by a sub-circuit with two input cables and one output cable. A wire in one of these cables will be called *correct* if it carries the same value as the wire in C corresponding to that cable, and a cable will be called *correct* if at most θm of its wires are incorrect (θ will be given explicitly later).

We will analyze the probability that the output cable of a sub-circuit corresponding to a gate is incorrect, given that its input cables are correct. Let g be a gate in C. The corresponding sub-circuit consists of two levels of gates. The first level consists of m ε-noisy copies of g, with the ith copy taking as input the ith wire from each of the two input cables. The probability that more than half of these gates are incorrect is $B((0.5-2\theta)m,m,\varepsilon)$ (see Section 3.4 for notation). The second level of the sub-circuit consists of m ε-noisy majority gates, each of which has m inputs, one from each of the ε-noisy copies of g. The outputs of these gates form the output cable for the sub-circuit. The probability that the output cable is incorrect given that less than half of the first-level gates are incorrect is $B(\theta m,m,\varepsilon)$. Therefore, taking $\theta = 1/6$, the probability of an output cable being incorrect given that its input cables are correct is

$$2\,B(m/6,m,\varepsilon) \leq 2e^{-\lambda m}$$

where

$$\lambda = \frac{\varepsilon}{2}(\frac{1}{6\varepsilon} - 1)^2$$

for $1/12 \leq \varepsilon < 1/6$ by Lemma 3.4.3.

Since there are z cables which may independently fail, the probability that the cable representing the output of C is incorrect is bounded above by

$$2ze^{-\lambda m}.$$

This is at most μ when

$$m = \frac{1}{\lambda}(\ln z + \ln \frac{2}{\mu}).$$

Thus the output cable of the new circuit is incorrect with probability at most μ. The circuit is completed by placing an m-input MAJORITY gate on the output cable. The probability that the output of this gate is incorrect is less than $\mu+\varepsilon$. $\square$

The result is only interesting when $\mu+\varepsilon < 0.5$ (see Section 3.4). Suppose we call a circuit ε-*resilient* if it is (μ,ε)-resilient for some $\mu \in \mathbf{R}^+$ such that $\mu+\varepsilon < 0.5$. Taking Carver Mead's example of $\varepsilon = 0.1$, we have:

Corollary 5.3.2 Every Boolean function which can be computed by a finite classical circuit of size z and depth d can be computed by a 0.1-resilient threshold circuit of size $63z \log z + 145z + 1$ and depth $2d+1$.

The most efficient circuits come from taking $\varepsilon \leq 1/12$.

Corollary 5.3.3 Every Boolean function which can be computed by a finite classical circuit of size z and depth d can be computed by an ε-resilient threshold circuit of size $48z \log z + 76z + 1$ and depth $2d+1$, where $\varepsilon \leq 1/12$.

We can draw three conclusions from Theorem 5.3.1. Suppose we call the value $1/\mu \in \mathbf{R}$ the *accuracy* of the circuit. Noisy gates can substitute for perfect ones by using a log-linear number of them. Accuracy can be increased arbitrarily by further adding a linear number of noisy gates. If gates with a higher noise level must be substituted in the resilient circuit, the same accuracy can be obtained (albeit with a higher error rate) by adding a further log-linear number of noisy gates.

The basic techniques of this section can be traced back to von Neumann [49]. Dobrushin and Ortyukov [19] have a non-constructive proof of Theorem 5.3.1 for resilient classical circuits (the depth increases to O(log n)). Pippenger [56] gives a constructive version of this proof.

5.4. Language Recognition

It is interesting to consider which classes of languages can be recognized by resource bounded neural networks. We might consider any or all combinations of the following.

1. Uniformity: Nonuniform, Turing-uniform, or logspace-uniform.

2. Size: Exponential, or polynomial.

3. Weight: Exponential, polynomial, logarithmic, or constant.

4. Running time: Polynomial, polylogarithmic, logarithmic, or constant.

All of the results described in Section 4 and thus far in Section 5 were for finite neural networks, but in Section 3 we learned that it makes more sense to talk about infinite families of finite machines, one for each input size. The results were expressed in a manner which makes it easy to generalize them to infinite families. Almost all of them are logspace-uniform, with the notable exception of Theorems 3.4.4, 4.6.1 and 5.2.2. The proof of Theorem 3.4.4 does not even appear to be Turing-uniform. The proof of Theorem 4.6.1 is certainly Turing-uniform, but appears to take time exponential in size. There is no corresponding result known for logspace-uniform neural networks. However, it is reasonable to restrict logspace-uniform neural networks to have weight bounded above by an exponential in size, so that the number of bits needed to describe each finite neural network in an infinite family is polynomial in the number of processors. Thus no weight larger than exponential is given in the list above. Theorem 5.2.2 is nonuniform when applied to arbitrary functions, but is clearly Turing-uniform when applied to computable functions and logspace-uniform when applied to polynomial-time computable functions.

In the remainder of this paper we will assume that the weight of a neural network is at most exponential (if the weight is at most polynomial we will say that it has *small weight*). With this assumption, Theorems 5.1.2 and 5.2.7 imply that it is sufficient to consider only threshold circuits, provided time is bounded above by a polynomial in size. It is easy to see that if a neural network terminates, then it must do so within time exponential in size. If a logspace-uniform polynomial size neural network is allowed to run for exponential time, then the class of languages that it recognizes is exactly PSPACE. This is immediately obvious for parallel operation, and requires slightly more work for sequential operation [42].

Logspace-uniform polynomial size threshold circuits are uninteresting since they recognize exactly the languages in P (the proof is similar to that of Theorem 3.3.1) and logspace-uniform polynomial size, polylogarithmic depth threshold circuits are uninteresting since they recognize exactly the languages in NC. Neither characterization seems to bring new knowledge about the standard complexity classes. Turing-uniform and nonuniform analogues of these results are also obvious. Threshold circuits of polynomial size and constant depth are interesting, however, since they differ radically from standard complexity classes. Any nondegenerate function requires depth $\Omega(\log n)$ to compute on the classical circuit model of Section 3.3. In contrast, we saw in Section 5.1 that any Boolean function can be computed in *constant* depth, and many useful functions can be computed in polynomial size and constant depth by threshold circuits (more exciting examples can be found in Reif [62]).

Other interesting classes include the functions computable by small weight, logspace-uniform, constant depth threshold circuits. Some results (including robustness) concerning exponential and polynomial size threshold circuits of this form were given by Parberry and Schnitger [53]. Exponential size circuits recognize exactly the languages in the polynomial-time threshold hierarchy of Wagner [74], which is the obvious generalization of the classical polynomial-time hierarchy using threshold quantifiers instead of the conventional existential and universal logic quantifiers. Polynomial size circuits recognize exactly the languages in the logarithmic-time threshold hierarchy, which is the corresponding generalization of Sipser's [67] logarithmic-time hierarchy.

The class of languages recognized by AND/OR circuits of polynomial size and $O(\log^k n)$ depth is called AC^k. AC^0 denotes the class of languages recognized by AND/OR circuits of polynomial size and constant depth. The corresponding class for threshold circuits is often called TC^k. It should be clear that for all $k \geq 0$,

$$AC^k \subseteq TC^k \subseteq NC^{k+1} \subseteq AC^{k+1}.$$

The proofs are trivial with perhaps the exception of the second containment, which requires the use of the technique of Theorem 5.2.4 to give a constant depth classical circuit which inputs three integers x_1, x_2, x_3 and outputs two integers y_1, y_2 with the property that $x_1 + x_2 + x_3 = y_1 + y_2$ (one of the outputs encodes the carry-generate and the other the carry-propagate).

5.5. Lower-Bounds

Very few lower-bounds for threshold circuits have been obtained. It appears that the more powerful the gates, the more difficult it is to prove lower-bounds. Even lower-bounds for limited versions of our neural network model have proved to be extremely deep. However, they hold even for nonuniform circuits.

Much effort has been spent in studying constant depth AND/OR circuits. It is clear that AND/OR circuits are more powerful than classical sequential and parallel machine models, since (by a cut-and-paste argument) classical circuits require depth $\Omega(\log n)$ to compute any function which depends upon all of its inputs, whereas by Theorem 5.2.2 AND/OR circuits can compute any Boolean function in constant depth. However, the construction of that Theorem uses exponential size for the computation of even simple functions such as the parity function (which has n Boolean inputs and is true when an odd number of its inputs are true). It is obvious that exponential size is required for some functions (any function which is not computable in polynomial time is an obvious example), but it is more interesting to ask exactly which functions require exponential size to compute in constant depth.

Furst, Saxe and Sipser [22] first demonstrated that the parity function cannot be computed in constant depth by a polynomial size AND/OR circuit. Yao [75] further showed that size $2^{n^{1-\lambda}}$ for some $\lambda \in \mathbf{R}$, $\lambda > 0$, is necessary to compute parity in constant depth. With a little thought, a simple divide-and-conquer argument together with Theorem 5.2.2 can be used to show that constant depth can be achieved with size $2^{n^{1-\lambda}}$ for any $\lambda > 0$. Yao's lower-bound implies that a polynomial size circuit for computing parity must have depth $\Omega(\log n / \log \log n)$. Theorem 5.2.8 can be used to provide a matching depth upper-bound for polynomial size. Hastad [32] further tightened and improved Yao's result. Sipser [67] has demonstrated a depth hierarchy for constant-depth, polynomial size AND/OR circuits. That is, he has found functions which can be computed by depth d, polynomial size circuits which require exponential size to compute in depth d−1.

A second group of problems which has elicited much research effort comes from the study of constant-depth, polynomial size circuits constructed from gates which compute symmetric functions with no bound on fan-in. Clearly every function which can be computed by such a circuit can be computed by a neural circuit of twice the depth and the same size to within a linear factor (Theorem 5.2.1). Razborov [61] has shown that polynomial size, constant depth circuits of AND and MOD_2 gates cannot compute the majority function. R. Smolensky [69] extended these results to show that polynomial size, constant depth circuits of AND, OR and MOD_p gates cannot compute MOD_q, where p and q are distinct primes. Barrington [6] has demonstrated that a two-level circuit with MOD_2 gates on the first level and MOD_3 gates on the second level cannot compute AND in polynomial size. The class of languages recognized by polynomial size circuits of AND, OR and MOD_p gates of $O(\log^k n)$ depth is called $AC^k(p)$. The union of $AC^0(p)$ for all $p \geq 2$ is denoted ACC. It should be clear from our discussions that for all $k \geq 0$, $p \geq 2$,

$$AC^k \subseteq AC^k(p) \subseteq TC^k,$$

and

$$AC^0 \subset AC^0(p) \subset ACC \subseteq TC^0 \subseteq NC^1.$$

The only non-trivial result for threshold circuits is for small weights. If $x, y \in B^n$, define the *inner product* of x and y to be

$$MOD_2(AND(x_1, y_1), ..., AND(x_n, y_n)).$$

Hajnal et al [29], prove that inner product, which can be computed in depth 3 and polynomial size, cannot be computed in depth 2 and polynomial size.

5.6. Probabilistic Neural Circuits

The results of Section 3.4 apply equally well to neural circuits. By Theorem 5.2.5 we can restrict ourselves to threshold circuits without paying more than a constant multiple in depth and a polynomial in size. Theorems 3.4.2 and 3.4.4 can easily be modified for neural circuits, the depth of the latter improving to D(n)+1. Similar results hold for small weight neural networks whose *processors* behave randomly (for example, Boltzmann machines [1], see Parberry and Schnitger [54]).

6. Termination

So far we have concentrated mainly on neural circuits, which have convenient termination properties. Whilst only neural networks which halt are useful for practical computation, there is no efficient general method for determining whether a given neural network halts on a given input. Symmetric neural networks are slightly easier to deal with, and are the subject of the first sub-section. The general case is the subject of the second sub-section.

6.1. Some Tractable Termination Problems

A neural network computation was deemed to have halted if it reaches a stable configuration. It is reasonable to ask whether all neural networks halt. Simple undirected networks operated in sequential mode always halt.

Theorem 6.1.1 (Hopfield [36]) Any productive sequential computation of a symmetric simple neural network will terminate in time proportional to its weight.

Proof. Let $M = (V, I, O, A, w, h)$ be a symmetric, simple neural network. Since Theorems 4.3.1 and 4.7.2 conserve productiveness, we can without loss of generality assume that M has bipolar states and zero thresholds. Define the *stability** of M at time t to be

$$\sigma(t) = \sum_{u \in V} S(u,t)W(u,t)/2.$$

We claim that for all $t > 0$, if some vertex $v \in V$ is unstable and is updated at time t, then $\sigma(t) \geq \sigma(t-1)+2$. There are two cases to consider. First, consider the case $S(v,t-1) < 0$ and $W(v,t-1) > 0$. Since M is symmetric, the contribution of vertex v to $\sigma(t-1)$ is $-W(v,t-1)$, and the contribution of v to $\sigma(t)$ is $W(v,t) = W(v,t-1)$. Therefore $\sigma(t) = \sigma(t-1) + 2W(v,t-1)$, and so $\sigma(t) \geq \sigma(t-1)+2$. The second case, $S(v,t-1) > 0$ and $W(v,t-1) < 0$, follows similarly.

Suppose M has weight w. Then for all $t \geq 0$, $-w \leq \sigma(t) \leq w$. Since, from the above, $\sigma(t) \geq \sigma(t-1)+2$, this implies that the computation must terminate in time w. $\square$

The above proof can easily be extended to cover symmetric neural networks which have positive weight self-loops.

It is an easy matter to design a non-simple symmetric neural network which does not halt when run in the sequential mode (for example, a negation processor with a self-loop) and a simple symmetric neural network which does not halt when run in the parallel mode (for example, two single-input OR gates connected together with a single wire). However, they will eventually flip-flop between two configurations.

---

* Stability is essentially the quantity that Hopfield calls *energy*, and P. Smolensky [68] calls *harmony*.

Theorem 6.1.2 Any productive computation of a symmetric neural network will eventually alternate between two configurations within time proportional to its weight.

Proof. The following elegant proof technique is borrowed from Bruck and Goodman [9]. Let $M = (V_1, I_1, O_1, A_1, w_1)$ be a symmetric neural network. Define a symmetric bipartite neural network $M_2 = (V_2, I_2, O_2, A_2, w_2)$ as follows. $V_2 = V_L \cup V_R$ where $V_L = \{(v,0) | v \in V_1\}$ and $V_R = \{(v,1) | v \in V_1\}$. $I_2 = \{(v,0) | v \in I_1\}$. $O_2 = \emptyset$, and $A_2 = \{(v,0) | v \in A_1\}$. For all $u, v \in V_1$, $w_2((u,0),(v,1)) = w_2((v,1),(u,0)) = w_1(u,v)$, with all other weights set to zero.

M_2 can be used to simulate M_1 as follows. For $t \geq 1$ let $\alpha(t) \subseteq V_1$ denote the processors of M_1 which were updated in time interval t. In time interval 1, update processors $(v,1)$ for all $v \in \alpha(1)$, sequentially in some order. If $x \in N$, let $\delta(x) \in B$ be zero if x is even and one otherwise. In each subsequent time interval t, update processors $(v, \delta(t))$ for all $v \in \alpha(t)$, sequentially in some order. Suppose $V = \{v_1, ..., v_p\}$. Let $S_1(t)$ denote the state of processor M_1 at time t. Let $S_2(v,t)$ denote the state of processor $v \in V_2$ of M_2 at time t, and for $i \in B$,

$$S_2^i(t) = S_2((v_1, i), t) ... S_2((v_p, i), t).$$

Then by induction on t, for all $t \geq 0$, $S_1(t) = S_2^{\delta(t)}(t)$ and for all $t \geq 1$, $S_1(t-1) = S_2^{\delta(t-1)}(t)$.

Since a bipartite graph is simple, all sequential computations of M_2 halt by Theorem 6.1.1. Thus the above simulation will eventually halt, and so there is some termination time τ proportional to the weight of M_2 (which is equal to the weight of M_1) for which $S_2^0(\tau) = S_2^0(\tau+2t)$ and $S_2^1(\tau+1) = S_2^1(\tau+2t+1)$ for all $t \geq 1$. Therefore, for all $t \geq 1$, $S_1(\tau) = S_1(\tau+2t)$ and $S_1(\tau+1) = S_1(\tau+2t+1)$. $\square$

The first occurrence of the above Theorem was for fully parallel operation [57].

6.2. Some Intractable Termination Problems

In the preceding section we learned that simple symmetric neural networks must terminate under sequential operation, but that they may instead enter a cycle of length two if they have negative weight self-loops or are not operated in sequential mode. It would be useful if we could tell exactly which neural networks can terminate under which conditions. Unfortunately, such a process is generally computationally intractable (Godbeer [24], Lipscomb [43] and Porat [58]). For example, consider the following problems.

> **THE STABLE CONFIGURATION PROBLEM (SNN)**
> INSTANCE: A neural network M.
> QUESTION: Is there a stable configuration of M?

There are two interesting cases of SNN. The first is for symmetric neural networks. SNN is NP-complete in this case even for neural networks of degree 3 with unit weights. Note that simple symmetric neural networks must have at least one stable configuration by Theorem 6.1.1, so this sub-case of SNN is a member of P. The second is for directed neural networks. SNN is NP-hard in this case even for neural networks of in-degree 2 with unit weights.

THE HALTING PROBLEM (HNN)

INSTANCE: A neural network M.

QUESTION: Is there a productive computation of M which halts?

There are many interesting cases of HNN. The first is under sequential operation, which has two interesting sub-cases. The first sub-case is that of symmetric neural networks, for which HNN is NP-hard even for networks of degree 3 with unit weights. Note that sequential computations of simple symmetric neural networks must halt on every input by Theorem 6.1.1, so this sub-case of HNN is a member of P. The second sub-case is that of directed neural networks, for which HNN is NP-hard even for neural networks of in-degree 2 with unit weights. The second case is under fully parallel operation, which also has two interesting sub-cases. The first sub-case is that of symmetric neural networks, for which HNN is NP-hard even for neural networks of degree 3 with unit weights. The second sub-case is that of directed neural networks, for which HNN is NP-hard even for neural networks of in-degree 2 with unit weights. We will see in both cases that the NP-hardness results hold even when the neural networks are restricted to run in polynomial time.

THE CYCLING PROBLEM (CNN)

INSTANCE: A neural network M.

QUESTION: Is there a productive computation of M which enters a cycle of length at most k?

By Theorem 6.1.2, any productive computation of a symmetric neural network must enter a cycle of length at most 2, but there is no guarantee that a directed neural network will enter a cycle of any given length since for every k there are neural networks which can enter a cycle of length at least k on some inputs (consider an odd-length cycle of processors with threshold 1 and all weights 1 when exactly one processor is active). CNN is NP-hard for all $k \geq 2$, even for neural networks of in-degree 2 with unit weights.

Theorem 6.2.1 SNN is NP-complete. HNN and CNN are NP-hard.

Proof. SNN$\in$NP since a stable configuration can be verified in polynomial time. Note that HNN may not be a member of NP because there is no guarantee that terminating computations do so in polynomial time. By Theorem 6.1.2, if there is a terminating computation of a symmetric neural network then there must be one which terminates in time bounded above by its weight. Thus symmetric neural networks with polynomial weight will have computations which terminate in polynomial time. The NP-hardness of these problems can be proved by reduction from SAT.

Given a Boolean formula F in conjunctive normal form, the corresponding neural network has three parts, or units, called the the "input unit", the "computation unit" and the "output unit". The *input unit* has the task of receiving the input to F and maintaining it throughout the computation, the *computation unit* evaluates F on the given input, and the *output unit* is unstable unless the computation unit reports that F is satisfied by the given input.

We will consider the case where M is directed first. Suppose F has variables $v_1,...,v_n$. The input unit consists of n input processors, one for each variable. The inputs are maintained by assigning each processor a unit threshold value and a self-loop of unit weight. The computation unit is a three-layer AND/OR circuit which evaluates F on the input stored in the input unit. The first layer computes the literals in F using at most n Boolean negation processors. The second layer computes the clauses of F using Boolean OR gates. The third layer computes the conjunction of the clauses of F using a single Boolean AND gate. The output unit consists of a single processor with threshold zero, a self-loop of weight −1 and an edge of unit weight from the output processor of the computation unit.

The input unit is stable. The computation unit is stable on a given input iff it evaluates F on that input. The output unit is stable iff the computation unit outputs one. Therefore M has an input for which there is a halting computation iff F is satisfiable. This holds true for all types of computation, including sequential and fully parallel. M has unit weights and can be constructed with in-degree 2 (all gates in the computation unit with fan-in greater than 2 can be replaced by a tree of two-input Boolean gates). If M is to be symmetric, all edges can be made bidirectional by using the technique of Theorem 5.1.3, but the resulting symmetric network does not have unit weights. The directed edges can be made bidirectional by the simple expedient of adding the fan-out of each processor in the computation unit to its threshold value.

We can conclude from the above that SNN and HNN are NP-hard. The NP-hardness of CNN can be demonstrated by substituting a cycle of the appropriate length (k+1 if k is odd and k+2 otherwise) for the output unit. Each processor has threshold 1, all edges have weight one and exactly one processor in the cycle is initially active. If the computation unit outputs zero, M will be locked into a cycle of length greater than k. Otherwise, all processors in the cycle become active and stable, and the computation terminates. Thus M enters a cycle of length at most k iff F is satisfiable.

Since the above constructions are based essentially on a shallow circuit, it is obvious that the reductions hold even if the neural networks are required to terminate in polynomial time. Any fully parallel computation of the bounded fan-in version which terminates must do so in logarithmic time, and any fully parallel computation of the unbounded fan-in version which terminates must do so in constant time. □

As we have already noted above, Theorem 6.1.1 tells us that simple symmetric neural networks have stable configurations, so SNN for simple symmetric neural networks is a member of P. Theorem 6.1.1 also gives an algorithm for finding a stable configuration; we just simulate a sequential computation of the neural network. However, this computation may take time up to the weight of the neural network, which may be exponential (though no larger, by Theorem 4.6.1). Unfortunately, this is likely to be the most efficient algorithm, since finding a useful stable configuration is difficult. Consider the following problems.

THE EVALUATION PROBLEM (ENN)

INSTANCE: A neural network M with a single output.

QUESTION: Is there a configuration of M with output 1?

THE OPTIMIZATION PROBLEM (ONN)

INSTANCE: A neural network M and an integer B.

QUESTION: Is there a configuration of M with stability greater than B?

Theorem 6.2.2 ENN and ONN are NP-complete.

Proof. Clearly ENN and ONN are members of NP. We will show by reduction from HNN that ENN is NP-hard even for symmetric neural networks with no negative weight self-loops. By Theorem 6.2.1, the halting problem for polynomial-time directed neural networks with unit weights is NP-hard. Suppose we are given an instance M of this problem. If there is an input such that there is a fully parallel computation of M which terminates, then that computation terminates in polynomial time. By Theorem 5.1.2 we can produce a polynomial size circuit which outputs the correct result on a given input if M terminates on that input, and may give an incorrect result otherwise. The insertion of an extra AND gate whose inputs come from the output unit of the final two layers of the circuit enables the circuit to determine whether or not M terminates on a particular input. This circuit can be transformed to a polynomial size symmetric network by the use of Theorem 5.1.3. It is easy to demonstrate by reduction from ENN that ONN is NP-hard even for symmetric neural networks with no negative weight self-loops. □

Another interesting problem is that of actually finding a stable configuration in a neural network which is guaranteed to have one.

THE IDENTIFICATION PROBLEM (INN)

INPUT: A simple symmetric neural network M.

OUTPUT: A stable configuration of M.

Godbeer [24] has observed that INN is unlikely to be NP-hard for simple symmetric
neural networks. Despite this, no polynomial time algorithm is known (Theorem 6.1.1
does not suffice since some sequential computations of simple symmetric neural networks may take time as large as their weight, which can be exponential; an example
attributed to Haken is given in [24]). Godbeer's reasoning is as follows. An optimization problem is said to be a *polynomial time local search* (PLS) problem if there is a
polynomial time algorithm which given one solution will find a better one, if one exists.
INN is a PLS problem since given a configuration of such a neural network, a "better"
configuration (that is, one with greater stability) can be found in polynomial time by
Theorem 6.1.1. Johnson, Papadimitriou and Yannakakis [38] note that no PLS problem
can be NP-hard unless NP = Co-NP.

7. Conclusion and Open Problems

We have studied a neural network model based on discrete neurons which compute
weighted binary threshold functions. We have found that these compare very favour-
ably with conventional models of computation, in that fast, reliable computations can be
carried out with a reasonable amount of hardware. Small speedups of the classes P and
NC can be obtained with polynomial hardware, and a surprisingly large number of functions can be computed with polynomial hardware in only a constant amount of time.
Although any function can be computed in constant time with exponential hardware, it
is clear that not all functions can be computed as fast with polynomial hardware (for
example, if an NP-complete language is computable in polynomial hardware then
P = NP). Many open problems remain. We list a few of the more interesting ones.

1. *The magnitude of the weights for weighted binary threshold functions (Section 4.6).*

Theorem 4.6.1 states that $O(n \log n)$ bits are sufficient to describe each weight. Corollary 4.6.3 states that $\Omega(n)$ bits are necessary. Can the gap between these bounds be narrowed? This result is important if some direct way of implementing weighted binary
threshold functions can be found, since it is reasonable to expect large weights to be
difficult to implement. Also, it is not enough to know that a small-weight threshold
function exists; we need to be able to find it efficiently. Theorem 4.6.1 is not logspace-
uniform. Are $n^{O(1)}$ bits sufficient for logspace-uniform circuits?

2. *Language classes for threshold circuits (Section 5.4).*

Investigate the structure of the logarithmic-time hierarchy, the polynomial-time threshold
hierarchy and the logarithmic-time threshold hierarchy. Since these hierarchies

respectively correspond to the languages computable in constant time by exponential hardware and polynomial hardware neural networks, more knowledge about them would provide some insight into whether our neural network model is appropriate for modelling various brain functions.

3.   *Lower-bounds for neural circuits (Section 5.5)*

Whilst neural circuits appear very powerful, the upper limits to their performance are only poorly delineated. Some of the interesting tasks which remain include the following. Find a *simple* function (of as low complexity as possible) which requires exponential size to compute in constant depth on a threshold circuit. Demonstrate a depth hierarchy for polynomial size threshold circuits, that is, show that for all $d > 3$ there are functions which can be computed in depth d and polynomial size but require exponential size to compute in depth $d-1$. There are also similar open problems for circuits of symmetric functions.

4.   *Convergence of directed neural networks (Section 6).*

Gotsman, Shamir and Lehmann [28] have shown that random directed networks with sufficiently high degree whose node functions are chosen randomly converge with probability one in sequential mode. Does a similar result hold for such networks when node functions are chosen at random from weighted binary threshold functions? One motivation for looking at this problem is that the brain appears to make use of random local connections. Perhaps an artificial neural network should have a similar structure.

5.   *Convergence of simple, symmetric neural networks (Section 6).*

Can INN be computed in polynomial time? It is unlikely to be PLS-complete (see Godbeer [24], Johnson, Papadimitriou and Yannakakis [38]), but perhaps some other theory of completeness can be developed for PLS problems whose neighbourhood structure can be computed in NC.

8. Acknowledgements

The author is grateful to Zoran Obradovic for proofing a rough draft, and most especially grateful to Mike Paterson and Paul Smolensky for their critical reading of the manuscript in its final stages. Thanks are also due to Ranan Banerji for his conscientious and professional management of the editorial process.

9. References

1.   D. H. Ackley, G. E. Hinton, and T. J. Sejnowski, "A learning algorithm for Boltzmann machines," *Cognitive Science,* vol. 9, pp. 147-169, 1985.

2.   A. V. Aho, J. E. Hopcroft, and J. D. Ullman, *The Design and Analysis of Computer Algorithms,* Addison-Wesley, 1974.

3. A. V. Aho, J. E. Hopcroft, and J. D. Ullman, *Data Structures and Algorithms,* Addison-Wesley, 1983.

4. E. W. Allender, "Characterizations of PUNC and precomputation," in *Proc. 13th Int. Colloquium on Automata, Languages and Programming,* Lecture Notes in Computer Science, vol. 226, pp. 1-10, Springer-Verlag, 1986.

5. D. Angluin and L. Valiant, "Fast probabilistic algorithms for Hamiltonian circuits and matchings," *Proc. 9th Ann. ACM Symp. on Theory of Computing,* 1977.

6. D. A. Barrington, "Bounded width branching programs," Ph. D. Thesis, Dept. of Mathematics, MIT, 1986.

7. C. H. Bennett and J. Gill, "Relative to a random oracle A, $P^A \neq NP^A \neq co\text{-}NP^A$ with probability 1," *SIAM J. Comput.,* vol. 10, no. 1, pp. 96-113, 1981.

8. N. Blum, "A note on the 'parallel computation thesis'," *Inform. Process. Lett.,* vol. 17, pp. 203-205, 1983.

9. J. Bruck and J. W. Goodman, "A generalized convergence theorem for neural networks and its applications in combinatorial optimization," *Proc. IEEE First International Conference on Neural Networks,* vol. III, pp. 649-656, San Diego, CA, June 1987.

10. A. K. Chandra, S. Fortune, and R. Lipton, "Lower bounds for constant depth circuits for prefix problems," in *Proc. 10th ICALP,* Springer-Verlag Lecture Notes in Computer Science, vol. 154, Barcelona, Spain, July 1983.

11. A. K. Chandra, S. J. Fortune, and R. Lipton, "Unbounded fan-in circuits and associative functions," *Proc. 15th Ann. ACM Symp. on Theory of Computing,* Boston, Mass., Apr. 1983.

12. A. K. Chandra, D. C. Kozen, and L. J. Stockmeyer, "Alternation," *J. Assoc. Comput. Mach.,* vol. 28, no. 1, pp. 114-133, Jan. 1981.

13. A. K. Chandra, L. J. Stockmeyer, and U. Vishkin, "Constant depth reducibility," *SIAM J. Comput.,* vol. 13, no. 2, pp. 423-439, May 1984.

14. H. Chernoff, "A measure of asymptotic efficiency for tests of a hypothesis based on the sum of observations," *Ann. of Math. Stat.,* vol. 23, pp. 493-507, 1952.

15. N. Chomsky, "On certain formal properties of grammars," *Information and Control,* vol. 2, no. 2, pp. 137-167, 1959.

16. A. Church, "The calculi of lambda-conversion," *Annals of Mathematical Studies,* vol. 6, Princeton University Press, Princeton, NJ, 1941.

17. S. A. Cook, "The complexity of theorem proving procedures," *Proc. 3rd ACM Symp. on Theory of Computing,* pp. 151-158, 1971.

18. S. A. Cook and R. A. Reckhow, "Time-bounded random access machines," *J. Comput. System Sci.*, vol. 7, no. 4, pp. 354-375, 1973.

19. R. L. Dobrushin and S. I. Ortyukov, "Upper bounds for the redundancy of self-correcting arrangements of unreliable functional elements," *Prob. of Info. Transm.*, vol. 13, pp. 203-218, 1977.

20. P. W. Dymond, "Simultaneous resource bounds and parallel computations," Ph. D. Thesis, Technical Report TR145/80, Dept. of Computer Science, Univ. of Toronto, Aug. 1980.

21. S. Fortune and J. Wyllie, "Parallelism in random access machines," *Proc. 10th Ann. ACM Symp. on Theory of Computing*, pp. 114-118, 1978.

22. M. Furst, J. B. Saxe, and M. Sipser, "Parity, circuits and the polynomial time hierarchy," *Math. Systems Theory*, vol. 17, no. 1, pp. 13-27, 1984.

23. M. R. Garey and D. S. Johnson, *Computers and Intractability: a Guide to the Theory of NP-completeness,* W. H. Freeman, 1979.

24. G. Godbeer, "The computational complexity of the stable state problem for connectionist models," M. S. Thesis, Dept. of Computer Science, Univ. of Toronto, Sept. 1987.

25. L. M. Goldschlager, "Synchronous parallel computation," Ph. D. Thesis, Technical Report TR-114, Dept. of Computer Science, Univ. of Toronto, Dec. 1977.

26. L. M. Goldschlager and A. M. Lister, *Computer Science: A Modern Introduction,* Prentice-Hall, 1983.

27. L. M. Goldschlager and I. Parberry, "On the construction of parallel computers from various bases of Boolean functions," *Theoret. Comput. Sci.*, vol. 43, no. 1, pp. 43-58, May 1986.

28. C. Gotsman, E. Shamir, and D. Lehmann, "Asynchronous dynamics of random Boolean networks," *Proc. IEEE Second International Conference on Neural Networks*, vol. I, pp. 1-7, San Diego, CA, June 1988.

29. A. Hajnal, W. Maass, P. Pudlak, M. Szegedy, and G. Turan, "Threshold circuits of bounded depth," *Proc. 28th Ann. IEEE Symp. on Foundations of Computer Science*, pp. 99-110, Los Angeles, CA, Oct. 1987.

30. D. Harel, *Algorithmics: The Spirit of Computing,* Addison-Wesley, 1987.

31. J. Hartmanis and J. Simon, "On the power of multiplication in random access machines," *Proc. 15th Ann. IEEE Symp. on Switching and Automata Theory*, pp. 13-23, 1974.

32. J. Hastad, "Improved lower bounds for small depth circuits," *Proc. 18th Ann. ACM Symp. on Theory of Computing*, pp. 6-20, Berkeley, CA, May 1986.

33. T. A. Heppenheimer, "Nerves of silicon," *Discover*, vol. 9, no. 2, pp. 70-79, Feb. 1988.

34. J. Hong, *Computation: Computability, Similarity and Duality,* Research Notes in Theoretical Computer Science, Pitman Publishing, London, 1986.

35. J. E. Hopcroft and J. D. Ullman, *Introduction to Automata Theory, Languages and Computation,* Addison-Wesley, 1979.

36. J. J. Hopfield, "Neural networks and physical systems with emergent collective computational abilities," *Proc. National Academy of Sciences*, vol. 79, pp. 2554-2558, Apr. 1982.

37. K. Jensen and N. Wirth, *Pascal User Manual and Report,* Springer-Verlag, New York, 1975.

38. D. S. Johnson, C. H. Papadimitriou, and M. Yannakakis, "How easy is local search?," *Proc. 26th Ann. IEEE Symp. on Foundations of Computer Science*, pp. 39-42, Portland, Oregon, Oct. 1985.

39. R. M. Karp, "Reducibility among combinatorial problems," in *Complexity of Computer Computations*, ed. J. W. Thatcher, Plenum Press, New York, 1972.

40. R. M. Karp and R. J. Lipton, "Turing machines that take advice," *L'Enseignment Mathematique*, vol. 30, Feb. 1980.

41. S. C. Kleene, *Introduction to Metamathematics,* D. Van Nostrand, Princeton, NJ, 1952.

42. M. Lepley and G. Miller, "Computational power for networks of threshold devices in an asynchronous environment," Unpublished Manuscript, Dept. of Mathematics, MIT, 1983.

43. J. Lipscomb, "On the computational complexity of finding a connectionist model's stable state vectors," M. S. Thesis, Dept. of Computer Science, Univ. of Toronto, Oct. 1987.

44. A. R. Meyer and L. J. Stockmeyer, "The equivalence problem for regular expressions with squaring requires exponential time," *Proc. 13th Ann. Symp. on Switching and Automata Theory*, pp. 125-129, IEEE Computer Society, Long Beach, CA, 1972.

45. M. Minsky and S. Papert, *Perceptrons,* MIT Press, 1969.

46. S. Muroga, *Threshold Logic and its Applications,* Wiley-Interscience, New York, 1971.

47. S. Muroga, I. Toda, and S. Takasu, "Theory of majority decision elements," *J. Franklin Inst.*, vol. 271, pp. 376-418, May 1961.

48. S. Muroga, T. Tsuboi, and C. R. Baugh, "Enumeration of threshold functions of eight variables," *IEEE Trans. Comput.*, vol. C-19, no. 9, pp. 818-825, Sept. 1970.

49. J. von Neumann, "Probabilistic logics and the synthesis of reliable organisms from unreliable components," in *Automata Studies*, ed. C. E. Shannon and J. McCarthy, pp. 43-98, Princeton University Press, 1956.

50. I. Parberry, "A complexity theory of parallel computation," *Ph. D. Thesis*, Dept. of Computer Science, Univ. of Warwick, May 1984.

51. I. Parberry, "Parallel speedup of sequential machines: a defense of the parallel computation thesis," *SIGACT News*, vol. 18, no. 1, pp. 54-67, 1986.

52. I. Parberry, *Parallel Complexity Theory,* Research Notes in Theoretical Computer Science, Pitman Publishing, London, 1987.

53. I. Parberry and G. Schnitger, "Parallel computation with threshold functions," *J. Comput. System Sci.*, vol. 36, no. 3, pp. 278-302, June 1988.

54. I. Parberry and G. Schnitger, "Relating Boltzmann machines to conventional models of computation," *Neural Networks*, vol. 2, no. 1, pp. 59-67, 1989.

55. N. Pippenger, "On simultaneous resource bounds," *Proc. 20th Ann. IEEE Symp. on Foundations of Computer Science*, pp. 307-311, Oct. 1979.

56. N. Pippenger, "On networks of noisy gates," *Proc. 26th Ann. IEEE Symp. on Foundations of Computer Science*, pp. 30-38, Portland, Oregon, Oct. 1985.

57. S. Poljak and M. Sura, "On periodical behaviour in societies with symmetric influences," *Combinatorica*, vol. 3, no. 1, pp. 119-121, 1983.

58. S. Porat, "Stability and looping in connectionist models with asymmetric weights," Technical Report TR 210, Dept. of Computer Science, Univ. of Rochester, March 1987.

59. E. Post, "Formal reductions of the general combinatorial decision problem," *Amer. J. Math.*, vol. 65, pp. 197-215, 1943.

60. V. Pratt and L. J. Stockmeyer, "A characterization of the power of vector machines," *J. Comput. System Sci.*, vol. 12, pp. 198-221, 1976.

61. A. A. Razborov, "Lower bounds for the size of circuits of bounded depth with basis AND, XOR," *Matematischi Zametki*, 1986.

62. J. Reif, "On threshold circuits and polynomial computation," *Proc. 2nd Structure in Complexity Theory Conference*, Ithaca, NY, June 1987.

63. W. L. Ruzzo, "On uniform circuit complexity," *J. Comput. System Sci.*, vol. 22, no. 3, pp. 365-383, June 1981.

64. J. E. Savage, "Computational work and time on finite machines," *J. Assoc. Comput. Mach.*, vol. 19, no. 4, pp. 660-674, 1972.

65. A. Schönhage, "Storage modification machines," *SIAM J. Comput.*, vol. 9, pp. 490-508, Aug. 1980.

66. J. C. Sheperdson and H. E. Sturgis, "Computability of recursive functions," *J. Assoc. Comput. Mach.*, vol. 10, no. 2, pp. 217-255, 1963.

67. M. Sipser, "Borel sets and circuit complexity," *Proc. 15th Ann. ACM Symp. on Theory of Computing*, pp. 61-69, Boston, Mass., Apr. 1983.

68. P. Smolensky, "Information processing in dynamical systems: foundations of harmony theory," in *Parallel Distributed Processing: Explorations in the Microstructure of Cognition*, vol. 1, pp. 194-281, MIT Press, 1986.

69. R. Smolensky, "Algebraic methods in the theory of lower bounds for Boolean circuit complexity," *Proc. 19th Ann. ACM Symp. on Theory of Computing*, pp. 77-82, New York, NY, May 1987.

70. L. J. Stockmeyer, "The polynomial time hierarchy," *Theoret. Comput. Sci.*, vol. 3, pp. 1-22, 1977.

71. A. M. Turing, "On computable numbers with an application to the Entscheidungsproblem," *Proc. London Math. Soc.*, vol. 2, no. 42, pp. 230-265, 1936.

72. L. G. Valiant, "A theory of the learnable," *Comm. ACM*, vol. 27, no. 11, pp. 1134-1142, 1984.

73. L. G. Valiant and G. J. Brebner, "A scheme for fast parallel communication," *SIAM J. Comput.*, vol. 11, no. 2, pp. 350-361, 1982.

74. K. W. Wagner, "The complexity of combinatorial problems with succinct input representation," *Acta Informatica*, vol. 23, no. 3, pp. 325-356, June 1986.

75. A. C. Yao, "Separating the polynomial-time hierarchy by oracles," *Proc. 26th Ann. IEEE Symp. on Foundations of Computer Science*, pp. 1-10, Portland, Oregon, Oct. 1985.

Formal Techniques in Artificial Intelligence
A Sourcebook. R.B. Banerji (editor)
© Elsevier Science Publishers B.V. (North-Holland), 1990

MECHANICAL THEOREM PROVING

David A. Plaisted
Department of Computer Science
CB# 3175, 352 Sitterson Hall
University of North Carolina
Chapel Hill, North Carolina 27599-3175[*]

1. Introduction

Formal logic is a means of expressing declarative, as opposed to procedural, knowledge. Declarative knowledge states what is true, without specifying how this knowledge is to be used. This permits knowledge to be used in new and creative ways but makes it harder to know which knowledge to use in a particular situation. Procedural knowledge specifies what is to be done in a particular situation. This leads to increased efficiency in well understood domains at the expense of a lack of deep understanding of the domain. Undoubtedly both kinds of knowledge are useful in different contexts. We will consider formal logic as a means of expressing declarative knowledge, and systems for reasoning using formal logic in a computer.

Virtually all of mathematics can be expressed in certain formal systems that have been developed, such as Zermelo-Fraenkel set theory. Not only formal mathematics but many other technical areas can be so expressed. First order logic is a particularly simple and well understood language which is adequate for many problems. It is even possible to express a version of set theory, von Neumann-Bernays-Gödel set theory [14], in first order logic, curiously enough, and this version of set theory is at least as powerful as Zermelo-Fraenkel set theory. However, this method of expressing set theory in first order logic is somewhat unnatural. We will concentrate on first order logic in this presentation, while mentioning other logics in addition.

There has been a good deal of controversy in the artificial intelligence community about the role of logic in artificial intelligence. It is certainly true that extensions of classical logic are needed to deal with common sense reasoning; such extensions include non-monotonic logic, logics of knowledge and belief, and probably certainties and temporal logic as well. But some have gone further and questioned whether logic is a suitable basis for

[*]This work was partially supported by the National Science Foundation under grant DCR-8516243.

artificial intelligence in general.

Our position is that axiomatic reasoning is of independent interest, regardless of whether it is the right foundation for artificial intelligence. Much of modern technical knowledge is or can be formalized in mathematical or logical terms, and much of the modern research endeavor involves axiomatic reasoning. Even much of artificial intelligence can be formalized in classical logic, possibly with extensions as mentioned above.

The automation of reasoning is particularly attractive because of the rapid and accurate inference which is possible on modern computers. Often one can obtain speeds of thousands of inferences per second. These are true first-order logic inferences, not the logical inferences per second (LIPS) measured for Prolog systems. The problem is not speed but control; the computer will generate relevant and irrelevant results with equal facility. The automation of reasoning is also desirable because constructing detailed proofs by humans is tedious and error prone. Indeed, one of the motivations of mathematical logic is to make reasoning as mechanical as possible, so logical systems are generally tailor made for computers.

One possible method of guiding the search in computer reasoning systems is human-computer interaction, with the human giving overall direction and the computer filling in the details and checking accuracy. This combination is attractive and has been and undoubtedly will continue to be useful. However, in this survey we will concentrate on methods that are fairly automatic. Such methods are useful in themselves, and can also be used to reduce the burden on the human in a human-computer reasoning system.

The possible applications of a theorem prover include expert systems, planning, common sense reasoning, proof checking, instruction, and aids to human mathematicians. Indeed, theorem provers can conceivably be used anywhere inference is used. One can view expert systems as specialized theorem provers; the well-known "brittleness" of expert systems might be alleviated by including more general axioms and reasoning capabilities, if efficient search strategies can be developed. Some of these applications may require non-monotonic logic or other extensions of classical logic. These areas are still the subjects of active research. However, much of the known methodology from first order logic should still apply to these extended logics. One can view a theorem prover as the ultimate declarative programming language, and so automated reasoning might be used to implement a programming language or to implement high-level supervision for a programming language. For such applications to materialize, it will be necessary to substantially advance the state of the art of mechanical theorem proving.

A number of applications of automated reasoning systems are already in existence. For example, program verifiers have been used to verify fairly complex programs. Examples of such verifiers include SRI's STP verifier [96], Stanford's verifier[108], and the Gypsy verifier [36] at the University of Texas at Austin. Also, the NuPrl system at Cornell[23] is really a logical system with a declarative and procedural interpretation in which guaranteed correct programs can be constructed; this system has certain automated reasoning features, but the search is primarily guided by human interaction. Certain expert systems can function as theorem provers; the ART expert system has been used to prove a non-trivial theorem in first-order logic.

Still, it must be admitted that the applications of mechanical reasoning systems have so far been sparse. The main reason may be that the state of the art in theorem proving is not sufficiently advanced. There appear to be other reasons as well: Many theorem provers do not incorporate heuristic search techniques that have been developed in artificial intelligence. Also, in any particular area, it is often possible to get better performance by writing a program just for that area. However, if general search is used, this leads to repeated work in building in search techniques for each area, and it also leads to brittleness as seen for example in expert systems. Part of the problem may be a lack of confidence that theorem provers can be useful, or a lack of familiarity with logic. Theorem provers may be seen as the next step beyond Horn clause logic programming, and as extensions to Prolog are explored, the user community may gradually become more accustomed to theorem proving and axiomatic reasoning. Another problem besides an unfamiliarity with logic is that the user interface is primitive in many theorem provers, and that programming language features such as inheritance have not been included in the logic. Often the logic is too limited in other ways, not including set theory or higher order logic. It seems likely that this situation will change with time, as theorem provers with better features and interfaces become available, as the state of the art advances, and as parameterized modules of axioms for various theories become widely available.

One problem with using theorem provers is that of insuring the correctness of the axioms given to the system. However, since the same axioms are used repeatedly, it pays to construct libraries which are widely available. Such well-tested libraries of axioms would help to reduce errors. There is also the problem of insuring the correctness of the proofs found by a theorem prover. Since theorem proving programs tend to be large and complex, it is difficult to ensure their correctness. However, since a theorem prover is a general program, it can be used repeatedly for many different problems, and so it pays to debug it well. Also, it is not necessary for the theorem prover to be bug-free; it is only necessary for the proofs, however obtained, to be correct. This may be shown by running the proofs through a proof checker. Most logical systems are constructed so that proof checking is simple. Thus it seems possible to write concise proof checkers that can be proven correct. Then a proof can be checked by running it through a number of different proof checkers written in different languages and run on different machines in widely separated locations. In this way, it should be possible to gain confidence in the correctness of even long proofs. The problem of the correctness of the initial specification given to the prover is still very real, however. A theorem to be proven often consists of standard axioms plus a specification of the problem. It may be that the specification does not accurately capture the intended intuition of the user. Furthermore, certain areas like preparing a business report, seem difficult to axiomatize. The best one can do is to develop methods of helping the user to see whether the problem specification accurately reflects his or her intentions. Finally, there are some philosophical and practical questions about whether logic is even in principle adequate for certain areas; many researchers in artificial intelligence feel that it is not. Not much can be concluded about this without more time and study and the development of mechanized inference systems powerful enough to make the formal approach seem at least potentially practical.

In this presentation I will concentrate on domain independent techniques, although specialized methods will be mentioned. I will also try to emphasize areas where my perspective can make the greatest contribution, and areas that are less well covered by others.

2. Propositional Calculus

There are a surprising number of issues that arise even in the propositional calculus, which is decidable. We assume some basic familiarity with logic and do not cover in detail some material that is easily omitted and readily available elsewhere. We first discuss syntax. We have "true" and "false", respectively, as propositional constants which are called *truth values*. We use **P, Q, R** et cetera for other propositional constants. These are also called atomic propositions. Propositional constants (other than true and false) are actually much like variables, except that they cannot be quantified. Note that Prolog typically uses upper case letters for variables and lower case letters for constants. We will not adhere to this convention. We consider the usual boolean connectives with the indicated meanings:

$\wedge$	conjunction (and)
$\vee$	disjunction (or)
$\neg$	negation (not)
$\supset$	implication (if then)
$\equiv$	equivalence (if and only if)
$+$	exclusive or (either but not both)

A *boolean expression* is a well formed expression composed of boolean constants and boolean connectives. The usual rules for precedence and omitting extra parentheses will be followed. Also, since $\wedge$ and $\vee$ are associative, we write **P** $\wedge$ **Q** $\wedge$ **R**, omitting parentheses, without ambiguity, and similarly for $\vee$. A *literal* is a propositional constant or the negation of a propositional constant. A boolean expression (also called a compound proposition) is in *conjunctive normal form* if it is of the form $A_1 \wedge \cdots \wedge A_n$ where each A_i is a disjunction of literals.

First, we informally discuss semantics. Suppose **P** is "It is raining" and **Q** is "I get wet." Then the expression **P** $\supset$ **Q** means "If it is raining then I get wet." Logic deals with rules for reasoning about such propositions **P** and **Q** that do not depend on the propositions themselves but only on the ways in which they are combined. The formal semantics of boolean expressions is defined as follows: The *domain* (set of possible values of an expression) is {true, false}. The meanings of the connectives are defined in the usual way. An *interpretation* (valuation) **I** is an assignment of truth values to propositions. Given an interpretation **I** and a boolean expression **A**, it is possible to assign **A** a truth value in **I** in the obvious way. We say **I** *satisfies* **A** if **A** is true in **I**, and we write **I** $\models$ **A** to indicate this. In such a case, we call **I** a *model* of **A**. So, **I** satisfies (**A** $\vee$ **B**) if **I** satisfies **A** or **I** satisfies **B**, **I** satisfies (**A** $\wedge$ **B**) if **I** satisfies **A** and **I** satisfies **B**, **I** satisfies $\neg$(**A**) if **I** does not satisfy **A**, and so on. If **A** is a proposition, then **I** satisfies **A** if **I** assigns "true" to **A**, that is, **I**(**A**) is "true". Note that there are 2^n interpretations for **n** atomic propositions. A formula **A** is *satisfiable* if there is some interpretation **I** such that **I** $\models$ **A**. The formula (**P** $\wedge$ **Q**) is satisfiable, but (**P** $\wedge$ $\neg$**P**) is not. A formula **A** is *valid* if it is true in all interpretations. In this case we write $\models$ **A**. For example, the formula (**P** $\wedge$ **Q**) $\supset$ **P** is valid. A formula is a *contradiction,* or *unsatisfiable,* if it is false in all interpretations. We say that formula **B** is a *logical consequence* of formula **A** if **B** is true in all interpretations making **A** true. We write this as **A** $\models$ **B**. For example, **P** $\models$ (**P** $\vee$ **Q**). Two formulas **A** and **B** are *equivalent* if they are true in the same interpretations, that is, they are logical consequences of each other. For example, (**P** $\vee$ **Q**) and (**Q** $\vee$ **P**) are equivalent. It is easy to see that for any formula **A** there is an equivalent formula **B** in conjunctive normal form. To obtain **B** from **A** it is only necessary to apply the following equivalence preserving rewrite rules as many times as possible:

$$\neg\neg A \rightarrow A$$
$$\neg(A \wedge B) \rightarrow \neg A \vee \neg B$$
$$\neg(A \vee B) \rightarrow \neg A \wedge \neg B$$
$$A \vee (B \wedge C) \rightarrow (A \vee B) \wedge (A \vee C)$$
$$(A \wedge B) \vee C \rightarrow (A \vee C) \wedge (B \vee C)$$

Also, we remove tautologies, that is, disjunctions like **P** $\vee$ **Q** $\vee$ $\neg$**P** that contain some propositional constant and its negation. For example, the conjunctive normal form of **P** $\vee$ (**Q** $\wedge$ **R**) is (**P** $\vee$ **Q**) $\wedge$ (**P** $\vee$ **R**), and the conjunctive normal form of $\neg$(**P** $\vee$ $\neg$**Q**) is ((¬**P**) $\wedge$ **Q**). It turns out that the conjunctive normal form of a formula is not unique. However, if "not", "and", and "exclusive or" are used instead to express an arbitrary boolean formula, it is possible to define a conjunctive normal form that is unique, interestingly enough. This idea goes back a long way, and a recent use of it may be found in [44] and [45].

2.1 Proof Procedures

We now consider methods of deciding whether a formula is valid. Since **A** is valid iff not(**A**) is unsatisfiable, it is of equivalent difficulty to decide unsatisfiability. The satisfiability problem is the most basic of the famous NP-complete problems [33], which no one can prove are hard but most people believe are. Many other problems of practical importance are also NP-complete. The best known methods to solve such problems take exponential time in the worst case. One decision procedure for validity is to calculate the truth value of **A** in all interpretations. This procedure is, naturally, of exponential complexity. A number of other decision procedures and proof systems exist for this problem. We first discuss some proof systems and then some decision procedures. Note that all are exponential in the worst case, but for certain kinds of formulas, some can be much faster than others. In fact, some procedures can be exponentially faster than others on certain kinds of formulas.

Many decision procedures can be classified as *affirmation* procedures or *refutation* procedures. An affirmation procedure shows that **A** is valid by constructing a proof of **A**, reasoning forward from axioms and successively generating new formulas using rules of inference. A refutation procedure shows that not(**A**) is unsatisfiable by deriving false from not(**A**) together with known axioms. In general, affirmation procedures seem to be more natural for humans. A proof procedure is in general a method of constructing a proof. For such procedures, an *axiom* is a formula that may be assumed without proof. We indicate the rules of inference for proof procedures in the format

$$A_1 \ A_2 \ ... \ A_n$$

$$A$$

indicating that if $A_1 \ A_2 \ ... \ A_n$ have already been derived or are axioms, then **A** may be concluded. Such a rule is called *sound* if A_1, A_2, ... , A_n together imply **A**. We are only interested in sound inference rules. A *goal* is a formula that we are trying to prove, and a *subgoal* is a goal that is attempted in the process of solving some other goal. An inference rule as above may be used in a forward chaining manner by concluding A if $A_1 \ A_2 \ ... \ A_n$ have already been derived. This rule may also be used in a backward chaining manner by making $A_1 \ ... \ A_n$ subgoals in turn if A is a goal. Now, affirmation procedures may use the rules of inference in either a forward or a backward chaining manner. Affirmation procedures that use inference rules in a back chaining manner are more goal-directed than refutation procedures, that is, they are more sensitive to the structure of the goal, and they also permit a more natural use of semantics to detect unachievable subgoals.

Many decision procedures require a formula to be in clause form, so we first define clause form, which is similar to conjunctive normal form. A *clause* is a disjunction of literals, expressed as a set. Thus {**P**, **Q**, not(**R**)} is a clause denoting the disjunction **P** $\vee$ **Q** $\vee$ $\neg$**R**. Since disjunction is associative and commutative and $(x \vee x) \equiv x$, this use of sets for disjunctions is an appropriate representation. A set of clauses {C_1, $\cdots$, C_n} represents the conjunction of the clauses in the set. This use of sets for conjunctions is also appropriate because conjunction is associative and commutative and $x \wedge x \equiv x$. It is easy to convert a formula in conjunctive normal form to clause form, and vice versa. For example, the clause form of **P** $\vee$ (**Q** $\wedge$ $\neg$**S**) is {{P,Q},{P, not(S)}}. A literal is called *positive* if it is a propositional constant, *negative* if it is the negation of a propositional constant. A *Horn clause* is a clause having at most one positive literal. Note that a Horn clause such as {not(**P**), not(**Q**), **R**} may be expressed as the implication **P** $\wedge$ **Q** $\supset$ **R**. A *Horn set* is a set of Horn clauses. A *positive clause* is a clause containing only positive literals; a *negative clause* is a clause containing only negative literals. A clause is a *tautology* if it contains both **P** and not(**P**) for some proposition **P**.

In the following discussion we emphasize decision procedures for formulas in clause form. One reason for this is that many theorems become trivial when converted to clause form. Also, many computer proof procedures require formulas to be in clause form. There are, however, disadvantages with clause form. The conversion to clause form can increase the size of a formula by an exponential amount. This can be avoided by introducing new propositional constants; for a discussion of this see for example [85]. Another disadvantage is that the structure of a formula is sometimes helpful in guiding the search for a proof; this structure is largely lost by the conversion to clause form. So, it is not evident that clause form is always the right representation of a formula. But, since clause form is a restriction on the form of the input, any proof procedure should be able to handle it well.

We consider a number of well known and less well known proof procedures for first order logic and their restrictions to propositional formulae in clause form. We evaluate these procedures based on the following criteria: 1) Do they support back chaining with caching? 2) Are they genuine support strategies? 3) Do they permit semantic deletion as in Gelernter's theorem prover [34]? 4) Is the cut rule or its equivalent well controlled during back chaining? 5) Does the procedure apply to an arbitrary first order formula in clause form? We now explain these features, which we feel are basic in a decision procedure for first order logic, though some good procedures may not use all of them. The basic ideas can be illustrated even for propositional logic, which we are now discussing.

We first illustrate back chaining with caching. Suppose we are considering the following set of Horn clauses, expressed as implications:

1.   **not R**
2. $Q_1 \wedge Q_2 \supset R$
3. $P_1 \wedge P_2 \supset Q_1$
4. $P_1 \wedge P_3 \supset Q_2$
5. $P_4 \supset P_1$
6. P_2
7. P_3
8. P_4

We may regard **R** as a goal. Using clause 2, we reduce **R** to the subgoals Q_1 and Q_2. Using clause 3, we reduce Q_1 to P_1 and P_2. We solve P_1 using clauses 5 and 8 and we solve subgoal P_2 using clause 6. We then use clause 4 to reduce Q_2 to subgoals P_1 and P_3. Now, P_1 has already been solved. We solve subgoal P_3 using clause 7. So, we work on the subgoals in the following sequence: **R**, Q_1, P_1, P_4, Q_2, P_1, P_3. At each step, one subgoal is being solved, and this subgoal is a single propositional constant. Caching means that a subgoal need not be solved more than once; if it is solved once, that solution is remembered. Also, if a subgoal fails, then it is not attempted again. Now, back chaining is not complete without a proper search strategy because it is possible to get into infinite loops and miss the proof. Therefore something like breadth-first search, best-first search, or depth-first iterative deepening[53,107] is needed. See [74] for a discussion of search methods.

A genuine support strategy is one that permits us to concentrate on the theorem, in the following way: Typically a theorem is of the form, Show **H** implies **R**, where **H** is a set of general axioms of number theory or some other domain, and **R** is the statement of the particular theorem. When we convert $H \supset R$ to clause form, we first negate to obtain $H \wedge \neg R$, and then obtain clauses for **H** and clauses for $\neg R$. A support strategy permits us to restrict inferences to those that depend on clauses from $\neg R$. Formally, we consider an interpretation **I** which is a model of **H**, and restrict inferences to those depending on clauses that are false in **I**. Now, some support strategies restrict **I**; for example, we could require that all inferences depend on a negative clause (which is equivalent to restricting **I** to a particular interpretation). We do not consider this to be a genuine support strategy. Support strategies are especially important when there are many assertions, because they focus attention on relevant assertions.

Semantic deletion is used with back chaining systems, and permits subgoals to fail if they are false in one of a collection of interpretations. With **H** and **R** as above, semantic deletion permits a subgoal **G** to fail (that is, no more attempts to solve the subgoal are made) if **G** is false in some model of **H**. The idea is that only clauses from **H** can be used to prove the subgoal; clauses from **R** cannot be used. Thus if **G** is false in some model **I** of **H**, then **G** cannot be a logical consequence of **H** and so **G** cannot be proven. This kind of semantic deletion is more suited to affirmation procedures than refutation procedures, but it can be adapted also to some refutation procedures. This method of subgoal deletion is important for the following reason: Each model **I** of **H** will tend to invalidate some subgoals. If many models are used, the chance that a subgoal will be invalidated becomes greater. The subgoals that pass all these semantic tests are likely to be logical consequences of **H**, and thus worth some effort to prove. This kind of semantic deletion was used by Gelernter's system for proving geometry theorems. His prover used diagrams of geometrical constructions and a subgoal would fail if it was false in the diagram. Thus one would not try to prove that two lines were parallel if in some diagram of the hypotheses, the lines were not parallel. Often in addition there is another kind of semantic deletion that can be applied, based on a single distinguished interpretation of **H**. This will be discussed later.

We now discuss the cut rule. Recall that we indicate rules of inference for proof procedures in the format

$$\mathbf{A_1} \ \mathbf{A_2} \ ... \ \mathbf{A_n}$$
$$------------$$
$$\mathbf{A}$$

In a sequent style system, the $\mathbf{A_i}$ and **A** are *sequents,* that is, of the form $\Gamma \rightarrow \Delta$ where Γ and Δ are lists of formulas. Also, $\Gamma \rightarrow \Delta$ means for our purposes that the conjunction of the formulas in Γ implies the disjunction of the formulas in Δ. Γ is called the *antecedent* and Δ is called the *succedent* of this sequent. The cut rule is the following inference rule in a sequent-style system:

$$\Gamma \rightarrow \Delta, \mathbf{A} \qquad \mathbf{A}, \Lambda \rightarrow \Theta$$
$$------------------------------------$$
$$\Gamma, \Lambda \rightarrow \Delta, \Theta$$

The cut rule is hard to control in a back chaining manner because **A** is not constrained; there is no guidance as to how **A** should be chosen, since **A** does not appear in the sequent $\Gamma, \Lambda \rightarrow \Delta, \Theta$. We feel that a mechanized proof system should control this rule in some way. The cut rule is very close to the resolution rule for clause form, actually.

Finally, some systems like Prolog style back chaining are good for Horn clauses but not in general. We are interested in systems that apply to an arbitrary set of clauses.

We now formalize the back chaining method given above in terms of a system of inference rules. The idea is to convert each Horn clause to an inference rule. Thus the clause

$$\mathbf{Q_1} \wedge \mathbf{Q_2} \supset \mathbf{R}$$

would be converted to the inference rule

$$\frac{Q_1 \qquad Q_2}{R}$$

The entire refutation may be expressed as follows:

$$\frac{\dfrac{P_4}{--}}{\dfrac{P_1 \quad P_2}{Q_1}} \qquad \frac{\dfrac{P_4}{--}}{\dfrac{P_1 \quad P_3}{Q_2}}$$
$$\frac{Q_1 \qquad\qquad Q_2}{R}$$

Note that the subgoal P_1 is represented twice in this proof. This expresses Prolog's back chaining style search if the inference rules are used in a back chaining manner. Note also that there is no search for this problem using this approach; there is only one way to solve each subgoal. However, this approach does not immediately extend to non-Horn clauses.

We next discuss Hilbert-style systems. In these systems, there is one inference rule, modus ponens, that permits us to conclude **B** given **A** and (**A** $\supset$ **B**). In the preceding format, this rule would be written

$$\frac{A \qquad A \supset B}{B}$$

Also, there are several axioms, which are not relevant here. If we represent a Horn clause $L_1 \wedge \cdots \wedge L_n \supset L$ as $(L_1 \supset (L_2 \supset \cdots (L_n \supset L) \cdots))$ then a Hilbert-style system, used in a back chaining manner, does not quite have the right properties. For the above problem, the goal is **R**, so the last inference rule used in the proof must have the form

$$\frac{A \qquad A \supset R}{R}$$

We can attempt to solve the subgoal **A** by using any one of the seven Horn clauses or the modus ponens rule again, giving a total of 8 choices. If we choose to solve **A** $\supset$ **R** first, we can use modus ponens again, or the implication $(Q_1 \supset (Q_2 \supset R))$, two choices in all. In either case, there will be still more choices later. This is more inefficient than Prolog, for which there is only one way to solve each subgoal. Also, it is not clear how to handle non-Horn clauses. If such a system is used in a forward chaining manner, there is little or no search. However, forward chaining in general is not sensitive to the goal being attempted.

Next we consider ground resolution. Given clauses **C** and **D** such that $P \in C$ and $\text{not}(P) \in D$, this inference rule permits us to conclude $(C - \{P\}) \cup (D - \{\text{not}(P)\}$. So we have the rule

$$\frac{C_1 \cup \{P\} \qquad C_2 \cup \{\text{not}(P)\}}{C_1 \cup C_2}$$

In this case, we say that the two clauses *resolve on* the predicate **P**. This rule is essentially the cut rule of Gentzen's system LK' if a clause is represented as a sequent $\Gamma \rightarrow \Delta$ where Γ

and Δ are lists of positive literals. For example, the clause {not P_1, not P_2, Q_1, Q_2} would be represented by the sequent P_1, $P_2 \rightarrow Q_1$, Q_2. Soundness of the above rule is easy to verify. Resolution is also complete, in the sense that a set S of clauses is unsatisfiable iff the empty clause { } is derivable by a sequence of resolutions.

In figure 1, we show a resolution proof of { } from the Horn clauses given above. We write each clause on a line without the set braces, so that for example {not **P**, not **Q**, **R**} would be written not **P**, not **Q**, **R**. This proof is a negative resolution proof. That is, in each resolution, one of the clauses used is a negative clause. This approximates back chaining. However, it does not implement caching, since the subgoal P_4 is solved twice. Also, this method explicitly combines more than one subgoal in a single clause. This can increase the search space significantly. For Horn sets, back chaining with caching takes polynomial time, but negative resolution can take exponential time. Of course, for some problems, especially in first order logic, negative resolution may be superior for other reasons. Also, caching does not make much difference on simple problems. Still, we feel that it is a significant issue. This lack of back chaining with caching is at least theoretically a fairly serious deficiency of resolution since back chaining with caching is such a basic problem solving strategy in AI. In our work, we have found that caching sometimes helps a lot on hard problems. The Argonne group has had significant success with UR (unit resulting) resolution [62] for Horn sets and even for many non-Horn sets. This method is polynomial for propositional Horn sets, but is not entirely a goal directed strategy. In a more general sense, for a set S of clauses over **n** propositional constants, there are 3^n non-tautologous clauses that may be generated by

---

1.	not R	given
2.	not Q_1, not Q_2, R	given
3.	not Q_1, not Q_2	1, 2 resolving on R
4.	not P_1, not P_2, Q_1	given
5.	not P_1, not P_2, not Q_2	3, 4 resolving on Q_1
6.	not P_4, P_1	given
7.	not P_4, not P_2, not Q_2	5, 6 resolving on P_1
8.	P_4	given
9.	not P_2, not Q_2	7, 8 resolving on P_4
10.	P_2	given
11.	not Q_2	9, 10 resolving on P_2
12.	not P_1, not P_3, Q_2	given
13.	not P_1, not P_3	11, 12, resolving on Q_2
14.	not P_4, not P_3	13, 6, resolving on P_1
16.	not P_3	14, 8, resolving on P_4
17.	P_3	given
18.	empty clause	16, 17 resolving on P_3

FIGURE 1

---

resolution. Thus the total work to do all possible resolutions may approach 9^n. If negative resolution is used, since there are 2^n negative clauses, the total work might approach 6^n. Since exhaustive testing (constructing a "truth table") only needs to consider 2^n interpretations, this seems like an excessive amount of work for propositional calculus. Possibly even more significant is the space saved by exhaustive testing; the space required is proportional to the number of propositions, whereas resolution might take exponential space. Of course, even when caching is used, known back chaining methods also take exponential time on non-Horn clauses. For first order logic, the disadvantages of resolution are not so clear, and resolution is more attractive than exhaustive testing. However, another drawback to resolution is that it does not permit semantic deletion with multiple interpretations as defined above.

We now consider Gentzen style systems. If the cut rule is not used, these systems generally are guided by the outermost connectdive of a formula. Such systems typically have rules of the form

$$\Delta \to \Gamma, A$$
$$\overline{}$$
$$\Delta \to \Gamma, A \vee B$$

For formulas in conjunctive normal form, such rules do not implement back chaining as desired, since back chaining requires simultaneous consideration of literals in different disjunctions. Even if Horn clauses are represented as implications, as mentioned above, Gentzen style systems do not implement back chaining as desired. The reason is that the only time that the antecedent and consequent are compared, or that symbols in different formulas are compared, is for axioms, using the rule that $\Delta \to \Gamma$ may be assumed if Δ and Γ have a common formula. However, this comparison of symbols in different formulas needs to occur all throughout the proof in order to properly model back chaining. If the cut rule is used, and clauses are represented as sequents of the form $\Gamma \to \Delta$ where both Γ and Δ are lists of positive literals, then a Gentzen style system is essentially equivalent to resolution. If such a system is used in a forward chaining manner, then it can simulate negative resolution as above, but this has the same problems as negative resolution, which we discussed above. If a Gentzen style system is used in a back chaining manner, then the cut rule is hard to control, as mentioned earlier.

The methods we now discuss can be viewed as adaptations of a sequent style system to implement back chaining. There may be other such adaptations as well. We can motivate these systems by representing a Horn clause $P_1 \wedge P_2 \wedge \cdots \wedge P_n \supset Q$ by the inference rule

$$P_1 \, P_2 \ldots P_n$$
$$\overline{}$$
$$Q$$

and using this rule in a back chaining manner, as was done earlier in this section. As mentioned above, this is essentially Prolog's proof method. This idea of representing each clause by an inference rule turns out to be fruitful, and can be extended to non-Horn clauses as well, but it is difficult to do it properly. The inference rules so obtained may be justified as sequences of applications of the cut rule, where clauses are represented as sequents as above, but the cut rule is more controlled than in Gentzen's system LK'. Thus the systems we present are really methods of controlling the cut rule in a backward chaining strategy. For Horn clauses, these methods are essentially the same as Prolog-style back chaining. We discuss a number of systems but only give the inference rules for one, for the sake of brevity.

The "simplified problem reduction format" of [81] has one inference rule per clause. This is essentially a sequent style system in which the sequents are of the form $\Gamma \to L$ where Γ is a list of positive literals and L is a positive literal. This system permits semantic deletion and back chaining with caching, but is not a genuine support strategy. Also, the cut rule is not well controlled. The "modified problem reduction format" of [83] is an attempt to improve on the simplified problem reduction format by controlling the cut rule better. This system implements back chaining with caching and semantic deletion, and the cut rule is controlled. However, the system is not a genuine support strategy. Also, the antecedents Γ of sequents $\Gamma \to L$ may contain both positive and negative literals. Both of these strategies have "semantic" variants, in which a particular distinguished interpretation I is chosen. The semantic variants are the same as the standard strategies except that instead of considering whether a literal is positive or negative, we consider whether it is true or false in I. Thus the standard strategies are special cases of the semantic versions, in which I is the interpretation making all positive literals true. In the simplified problem reduction format, the semantic variant only uses sequents of the form $\Gamma \to L$ where L and all literals in Γ are true in I. In the semantic variant of the modified problem reduction format, the semantic variant only uses sequents of the form $\Gamma \to L$ where L is true in I. Both variants are genuine support strategies and permit semantic deletion and back chaining with caching. The semantic variant of the simplified problem reduction format does not control the cut rule well, however. The semantic modified problem reduction format has all the desired properties, but the fact that the antecedent may contain literals false in I may be a disadvantage. The MESON procedure of [55], related to the model elimination strategy, is a support strategy and controls the cut rule well. However, caching cannot be done as directly with this method, and semantic deletion of subgoals is not possible. This strategy is the one which Stickel [106] has recently implemented so efficiently. Loveland's near-Horn Prolog [57] permits back chaining and controls the cut rule well. However, it does not seem to be a true support strategy and does not permit semantic deletion. This strategy is intended primarily as a programming language, not a theorem prover. We finally present a system, the constrained semantic simplified problem reduction format, which seems to meet all objections. The idea of this system is to add a means of controlling the cut rule in the semantic simplified problem reduction format. The rules are formulated to take advantage of caching, and a slightly different formulation may be better if caching is not used. In addition, the system is formulated to be applicable to first order logic; if the system is only intended for propositional logic, then some simplifications can be made. Many readers may want to skip the description of this system because of its complexity.

2.2 A Semantic Proof System

This system is a sequent style system in which the antecedents of sequents may contain propositional variables as well as propositional constants. The inference rules are used in a back chaining manner, so that if

$$A_1 \ A_2 \ ... \ A_n$$

$$A$$

is an inference rule, this means that if **A** is a subgoal, then **A** may be shown by proving A_1 ... A_n in turn recursively. We need to specify how variables are bound during this process, to give these rules a computational meaning as well as a declarative meaning. For this, we use the notation (**X**:**X**=**P**) to mean that **X** is bound to a value such that **X**=**P**, that is, **X** is bound to **P**. Also, (Λ Θ : Γ,**Y** = Λ,**L**,Θ) means that Λ and Θ are bound to values making the equation true. In a declarative reading, we can consider such variables to be replaced by their values, and read (**X**:**X**=**P**) as **X**=**P**.

We now discuss the semantics used in this system. Suppose we are trying to prove **H** implies **R**, where **H** is a set of general hypotheses and perhaps some particular hypotheses for this theorem, and **R** is the theorem we are trying to prove. We assume **H** is satisfiable, and moreover, that **H** has a number of known models. Let **P** be a new predicate symbol. We show that (**H** ∧ (**R** ⊃ **P**)) ⊃ **P**. We claim that this is equivalent to proving (**H** ⊃ **R**), as follows: If **H** implies **R**, then from **H** and (**R** ⊃ **P**) we may conclude **P** (since **H** implies **R** and **R** implies **P**). If (**H** ∧ (**R** ⊃ **P**)) ⊃ **P** is valid, then (**H** ∧ (**R** ⊃ **false**)) ⊃ **false**, since **P** is a new predicate symbol, hence **H** implies **R**. Thus it suffices to show (**H** ∧ (**R** ⊃ **P**)) ⊃ **P**. We assume **H** has a collection of known models. We negate the formula (**H** ∧ (**R** ⊃ **P**)) ⊃ **P** and convert to clause form. This gives a set S_1 of clauses for (**H** ∧ (**R** ⊃ **P**)) and the clause {not **P**}. Each model of **H** may be converted to a model of (**H** ∧ (**R** ⊃ **P**)) by interpreting **P** as **R** is intepreted. These will also be models of S_1. Let **I** be one such model, which we call the *distinguished* model. Let I_1 ... I_k be other models of S_1. In the following inference rules, we allow for the possibility that more than one clause may be false in **I**, and that these clauses may have more than one literal, even though in our case {not **P**} is the only clause that may be false in **I**. Let S be S_1 U {{not **P**}}. In the following rules, Ψ is a semantic test that is applied to subgoals before they are attempted. The subgoals in this system are sequents in which the antecedent is a list of literals and variables, and the succedent is a single literal.

Rules of inference

A1

$$\Psi(\Gamma \to L) \qquad L \ in \ \Gamma$$

$$\Gamma \to L$$

For clause {L_1 ... L_m} in S that is false in **I** the rule

G

$$\Psi(\Gamma \to \textbf{true}) \quad \Gamma \to \overline{L}_1 \quad ... \quad \Gamma \to \overline{L}_m$$

$$\Gamma \to \textbf{false}$$

For clause $\{L, L_1, L_2, ..., L_m\}$ in S the rules (m+1 in all)

H
$$\frac{\Psi(\Gamma \to L) \quad \Gamma \to \overline{L}_1 \quad ... \quad \Gamma \to \overline{L}_m}{\Gamma \to L}$$

Also for clause $\{L, L_1, L_2, ..., L_m\}$ in S the rules (m+1 in all)

A2
$$\frac{\Psi(\Gamma,\Delta \to L) \quad (\Gamma,\Delta \to \overline{L}_1) \text{ or } (I \models L_1) ...}{(\Gamma,\Delta \to \overline{L}_m) \text{ or } (I \models L_m) \quad (X:X=L)}{\Gamma \, X \, \Delta \to L}$$

Also for clause $\{L, L_1, L_2, ..., L_m\}$ in S the rules (m+1 in all)

NH
$$\frac{\Psi(\Gamma \to L') \quad \Gamma,Y \to L' \quad (\Lambda\,\Theta : \Gamma,Y = \Lambda,L,\Theta)}{(\Lambda,\Theta \to \overline{L}_1) \text{ or } (\Lambda,\Theta,L_1 \to L') ...}{(\Lambda,\Theta \to \overline{L}_m) \text{ or } (\Lambda,\Theta,L_m \to L')}{\Gamma \to L'}$$

D
$$\frac{P}{P \text{ or } Q} \qquad \frac{Q}{P \text{ or } Q}$$

Ψ
$$\frac{I \models (\Gamma \wedge L) \qquad (\forall j)\, I_j \models (\Gamma \supset L)}{\Psi(\Gamma \to L)}$$

We can show that S is unsatisfiable iff $\to$ false (with an empty antecedent) is derivable in this system. But first some explanation is necessary. This system is intended to be used in a back chaining manner. The interpretations I and $I_1 ... I_k$ are as above. In general, I is an arbitrary interpretation of S and each I_j must satisfy the condition that $I_j \models \{C \in S : I \models C\}$. The rule Ψ implements the semantic test that is applied to all sequents before they are attempted. For variables X in the antecedent, we assume that the semantic test succeeds, that is, we assume that $I \models X$ and $I_j \models X$, since X might be bound to a proposition P such that $I \models P$. The rule A1 is a standard assumption axiom. The rules G are goal rules, applied to clauses that are false in the distinguished interpretation I. These clauses are the support clauses. The rules H are applied to clauses that are Horn clauses, in a semantic sense of the term. We call a clause C a *semantic Horn clause* if at most one literal of C is true in I. The rules A2 are other assumption axioms that are used to add literals to the antecedent of a sequent. This is where the control of the cut rule takes place. These rules bind variables in the antecedent to specific literals. The rules NH are applied to clauses that are non-Horn clauses, in a semantic sense of the term. These rules add variables to antecedents of rules and check to see if these variables get bound to the proper literals. The rules D are for disjunction, at a meta-level, and the rule Ψ is for semantics, as mentioned above.

We now mention why it is important to require that in a sequent $\Gamma \to L$, both Γ and L be true in I. This prevents the generation of subgoals of the form $\Gamma \to L$ where not(L) is a logical consequence of S_1. If we could prove $\Gamma \to L$, then using not(L) we could prove $\Gamma \to$ false, so the subgoal $\Gamma \to L$ is not needed. Similarly, we do not want sequents of the form Γ, $\mathbf{L} \rightarrow \mathbf{M}$ where not($\mathbf{L}$) is provable from $\mathbf{S}_1$. Such sequents seem bothersome from an intuitive viewpoint, since they either assume or try to prove something that is "false."

So, it turns out that extending the problem reduction format to even full propositional logic is surprisingly subtle. However, it does seem that we have found a system having all the desirable theoretical properties we want. We still need practical evidence that semantics is helpful in guiding the search for a proof, and that problem reduction formats perform well.

2.3 Other Decision Procedures

We now discuss "model theoretic" as opposed to "proof theoretic" decision procedures for the propositional calculus, that is, methods based on deciding validity by searching through all interpretations, explicitly or implicitly. As mentioned above, it is of equivalent complexity to decide whether a formula is unsatisfiable. One of the earliest and best is the method of Davis and Putnam[24]. For this we assume S is in clause form. This method is like a recursive case analysis, where for a proposition $\mathbf{P}$, the cases are $\mathbf{P}$ being true or false. There are also some refinements: If $\{\mathbf{P}\}$ or $\{not(\mathbf{P})\}$ is a clause then only one case for $\mathbf{P}$ needs to be considered. Similarly, if $\mathbf{P}$ only occurs positively or negatively, only one case for $\mathbf{P}$ needs to be considered. Van Gelder [110] has developed a method that may be considered as a generalization of the Davis and Putnam method to non-clausal formulas. This method runs in approximately $O(2^{.25n})$ time for a formula with $\mathbf{n}$ occurrences of propositions. Another interesting and novel method is that of Bledsoe[7]. This is based on the idea of counting the number of interpretations in which S is false. It turns out that this can be done very efficiently if the number of predicates in S is not too large. However, for a formula with $\mathbf{n}$ propositional constants, the storage required is $2^{\mathbf{n}}$ bits, so the applicability of this method is limited for large $\mathbf{n}$.

We now present a possibly original method similar to the semantic tree method [55] but with lemma generation; this can dramatically speed it up in some cases. The idea is to check all interpretations and see if any satisfy S. This is improved by using a backtracking search to fail as soon as possible so that many interpretations need not even be examined; also, information about how failure occurs is saved to prevent repetitive parts of the search. Let |S| be the number of clauses in set S of clauses. Note that with a small amount of preprocessing of S, we can decide unsatisfiability in $O(2^{\mathbf{n}} |S|)$ time just by a search through all interpretations. This is actually a lot better than the worst case bound for resolution for propositional calculus. There are $3^{\mathbf{n}}$ non tautologous clauses over n propositional constants, and it is conceivable that there could be $\Omega(9^{\mathbf{n}})$ work to check pairs of clauses for new resolvents. So for propositional calculus, Davis and Putnam's method or something similar is usually a lot better than resolution. One might think that deleting subsumed clauses could help resolution; for our purposes a clause $\mathbf{C}$ subsumes $\mathbf{D}$ if $\mathbf{C}$ is a proper subset of D. However, it is easy to show that there are at least $3^{\mathbf{n}}/\mathbf{n}$ non-tautologous clauses, none of which subsumes any other. Thus the total work might still be large. Still, in practice, deletion of subsumed clauses in resolution theorem provers can help significantly.

2.3.1 The Semantic Tree Method with Lemma Generation

We first present the above-mentioned semantic tree method with backtracking. Let S be a set of clauses and let Atoms be the atoms (propositions) appearing in S. The procedure

---

```
tree_search(I,Remain,Tag)
    if ( ∃ D in S)(D ⊂ I)
    then   Tag := false
    else
    if Remain = { }
    then   [[satisfiable]]
           Tag := true
    else   pick L in Remain;
           tree_search(I U {L},Remain - {L},Tag1);
           if    Tag1
           then  Tag := true
           else  tree_search(I U {not(L)},Remain - {L},Tag2);
                 Tag := Tag2
           fi
    fi fi
```

FIGURE 2

"tree_search" given in figure 2 tests if S is satisfiable. When tree_search({ },Atoms,Tag) is called, if S is satisfiable this returns with Tag = true, else Tag = false. The symbol ∃ means "there exists," and is used in programs to indicate a search for a specified element of a finite set. The meaning of the arguments is as follows: **I** is the interpretation so far (the partial interpretation being considered) and Remain is the atoms not yet assigned truth values. For simplicity we reverse the signs of atoms in **I**; thus the partial interpretation being considered is the one that assigns all literals in **I** a truth value of false. The time required by this procedure is $O(2^n |S|)$, since there are $|S|$ clauses to check and at most $O(2^n)$ recursive calls to tree_search. A naive method of testing ($\exists$ D in S)(D ⊂ **I**) takes longer than $O(|S|)$ time since each clause may have many literals. However, if with each clause we store a count of how many literals have been so far falsified, this test can be done in $O(|S|)$ time.

The procedure "contradict" given in figure 3 tests if S is satisfiable, at the same time constructing a resolution proof and avoiding repetitive parts of the search by storing lemmas. The parameters S and Atoms are as above. When contradict({ },S,Atoms,Snew,C) is called, if S is satisfiable this returns with C = true, otherwise C is the empty clause and a resolution proof of the empty clause is constructed. **I**, **R**, and Remain are input parameters to this procedure, and Rnew and C are output parameters. The meaning of **I** and Remain is also as above. The meaning of the arguments to contradict is as follows: **R** is the set of clauses so far (the original clauses plus lemmas added); Rnew is **R** with more lemmas added during this call; and C is a clause that contradicts **I**. We reverse signs of literals in **I** as above.

The procedure ''contradict'' can be exponentially faster than the search without lemmas being saved. However, in the worst case it will still take exponential time. It is possible to modify this method to be similar to Davis and Putnam's method, by always choosing **L** in

---

```
contradict(I,R,Remain,Rnew,C)
        if ( ∃ D in R)(D ⊂ I)
        then   Rnew := R;
               C := D
        else
        if Remain = { }
        then   [[satisfiable]]
               C := true;
               Rnew := R
        else   pick L in Remain;
               contradict(I U {L},R,Remain - {L},R1,C1);
               if C1 = true or L not in C1
               then   C := C1 ;
                      Rnew := R1
               else   contradict(I U {not(L)}, R1, Remain - {L},R2,C2);
                      if C2 = true or L not in C2
                      then   C := C2 ;
                             Rnew := R2
                      else   C := (C1 - {L}) U (C2 - {not(L)});
                             Rnew := R2 U {C}
                      fi
               fi
        fi fi
```

FIGURE 3

Remain so that some clause in **R** contradicts **I** U {**L**} or **I** U {not(**L**)} when possible. It is also necessary to choose ''pure literals'' when possible. A literal **L** is *pure* if **L** appears in S but $\overline{L}$ does not. Instead of S, we consider the set of clauses that are not known to be satisfied by the partial interpretation at any point. Modified in this way, ''contradict'' is about as fast as Davis and Putnam's method and sometimes a lot faster, in terms of how many interpretations are seen. However, if many lemmas are generated, then the time to test (∃ **D** in **R**)(**D** ⊂ **I**) can increase, and this method can become slower than Davis and Putnam's method. We will analyze how much time this takes, below.

Note that the method constructs a resolution proof of { } from S; this proof can be output if sufficient information is recorded during the search.

We illustrate this method on the following example: Let S be {{**P,R**},{not **P**, **R**},{**P**,not **R**},{not **P**, not **R**},{not **Q,R**},{**Q**,not **R**}}. The method executes as follows:

```
I = {}
   I = {P}
      I = {P,Q}
         I = {P,Q,R}, contains clause {P,R}
         I = {P,Q, not(R)}, contains clause {P, not(R)}
      I = {P,Q}, contains resolvent {P}
   I = {P}, contains {P}

   I = {not(P)}
      I = {not(P),Q}
         I = {not(P),Q,R}, contains clause {not(P),R}
         I = {not(P),Q,not(R)}, contains clause {not(P),not(R)}
      I = {not(P),Q}, contains resolvent {not(P)}
   I = {not(P)}, contains {not(P)}
I = {}, contains resolvent {}
```

We now discuss the total work for this method. There are $O(2^n)$ partial interpretations and up to 2^n lemmas generated. The work to test if a partial interpretation is contradicted is therefore $O(2^n + |S|)$ since the number of lemmas and input clauses is bounded by $2^n + |S|$. The total work is therefore $O(4^n + 2^n |S|)$. This can be improved in a couple of ways. First, when a literal L is added to a partial interpretation I, all lemmas containing not(L) can be deleted from the set of lemmas used in partial interpretations extending I. Also, the only part of a lemma C that is relevant for a partial interpretation I is $C - I$; the literals in $C \cap I$ do not influence the method directly. Therefore it is not necessary to keep two lemmas C1 and C2 such that C1 - I = C2 - I. It turns out that the number of lemmas one needs to keep is $O(3^k)$ where k is the number of atoms that have not been assigned truth values yet. Thus the work for each call to "contradict," not counting work for recursive calls inside the call, is $O(3^k)$ where $k + |I| = n$, and the number of lemmas generated is never more than 2^n. Also, there are 2^n calls with k=0, 2^{n-1} calls with k=1, 2^{n-2} calls with k=2 et cetera. Using this, we can show that the method can be implemented so that the total work is $O(\alpha^n + 2^n |S|^{\log_3(1.5)})$, where α is $2^{2-\log_3(2)}$, which is about 2.583. Note that $2 < \alpha < 3$, and if S has no tautologies then $|S| \leq 3^n$ and this bound is then $O(3^n)$. If $|S| =< 2^n$ then this bound is $O(\alpha^n)$. Note that if S has no tautologies then each atom can either be positive, negative, or absent in a clause of S, so there are three possibilities per atom, and a total of 3^n possible non-tautologous clauses in S. It seems likely that not saving lemmas having small proofs will make the method run a lot faster, since lemmas with large proofs will tend to have many literals and will not be used often.

In figure 4 we give another method "contradict2" with worst case time $O(n^2 2^n + 2^n |S|^{\log_3(1.5)})$, which is not much worse than the bound for Davis and Putnam. Note that these methods sometimes do much better than Davis and Putnam by avoiding repeated work. The meaning of the parameters of the procedure is as above, except that Rnew is handled differently. The idea is to only consider lemmas that are recently generated, since they will include those lemmas for partial interpretations most like I. In this method, R is stored as a stack with the added operation of deletion of an arbitrary element from the middle of a stack. The most recently used or generated lemmas are nearest the top of the stack. When a lemma is used again, it is deleted from the stack and put on the top of the stack. Note that such a structure can be implemented as a linked list. Also, R is a global variable, so it is not listed among the parameters of "contradict2."

This procedure is called at the top level by contradict2({ },0,Atoms,C) where S is assigned the input clauses. and **R** is the empty stack. Note that the program is very similar to the previous one. The work for testing if a recently generated lemma is a subset of **I**, is smaller when |I| is larger. Since most of the calls have |I| near n, the total work for testing recently generated lemmas is small, and can be shown to be $O(n^2 2^n)$. The work for testing if some element of S is a subset of I can actually be more than this, since |S| may be $O(3^n)$. Using techniques as in the procedure "contradict", the work for S can be reduced to $O(2^n |S|^{\log_3(1.5)})$. Thus the total work is $O((n^2+|S|^{\log_3(1.5)})2^n)$. If S has no tautologies then as before this is $O(3^n)$. If $|S| \le 2^n$ then this bound is $O(\alpha^n)$ for α as above. For smaller |S|, the time can be less than α^n, and this bound is better than the bound for the previous method.

We present in figure 5 another, simpler procedure "contradict3" which has some interesting properties relating to its complexity. This procedure is like "contradict2", but it does not save any lemmas except the clause C. However, it sometimes performs much better

---

```
contradict2(I,M,Remain,C)
        if ( ∃ D in S)(D ⊂ I)
           or ( ∃ D in the first M elements of R)
              (D ⊂ I)
        then   delete D from R;
               push D on the stack R;
               C := D
        else
        if Remain = { }
        then   [[satisfiable]]
               C := true
        else   pick L in Remain;
               contradict2(I U {L},M,Remain - {L},C1);
               if C1 = true or L not in C1
               then   C := C1
               else   M1 := max(2^(|Remain|-1),|R|);
                      contradict2(I U {not(L)},M1,Remain - {L},C2);
                      if C2 = true or L not in C2
                      then   C := C2
                      else   C := (C1 - {L}) U (C2 - {not(L)});
                             push C on the stack R
                      fi
               fi
        fi fi
```

FIGURE 4

```
contradict3(I,Remain,C)
      if ( ∃ D in S)(D ⊂ I)
      then  C := D
      else
      if Remain = { }
      then  [[satisfiable]]
            C := true
      else  pick L in Remain;
            choose M1 in {L, not(L)} nondeterministically;
            let M2 be the other element of {L, not(L)};
            contradict3(I U {M1},Remain - {L},C1);
            if C1 = true or M1 not in C1
            then  C := C1
            else  contradict3(I U {M2},Remain - {L},C2);
                  if C2 = true or M1 not in C2
                  then  C := C2
                  else  C := (C1 - {M1}) U (C2 - {M2});
                  fi
            fi
fi fi
```

FIGURE 5

than the procedure "tree_search" given above. The saving of the single lemma **C** can mean that large sections of the search are avoided. The worst case running time is $O(2^n|S|)$ since there are at most 2^n interpretations to check and each takes at most $|S|$ time. Also, we can show that if the nondeterministic choices of M1 and M2 are properly done, and S is unsatisfiable, the procedure "contradict3" will halt in a time polynomial in the size of the proof it finds. Of course, a shortest proof may be of size exponential in n, and this procedure will not necessarily find a shortest proof. Also, for this we measure the size in a way that counts repeated lemmas repeatedly. Specifically, we define the *tree size* of a resolution proof as follows: Suppose $C_1 C_2 ... C_n$ is a resolution proof from set S of clauses. That is, each C_i is either in S or is a resolvent of C_j and C_k for j,k < i. Define t_i, $1 \le i \le n$, as follows: If C_i is in S then t_i is 1. If C_i is a resolvent of C_j and C_k for j,k < i then $t_i = t_j + t_k + 1$. Finally, the tree size of the proof is t_n. The procedure "contradict3" takes $O(|S|nt)$ time to construct a resolution proof of { } from S of tree size **t**, where **n** is the number of atoms (propositional constants) in S, if the nondeterministic choices are made properly.

A similar idea can be applied to the procedures "contradict" and "contradict2" given above, namely, we can choose nondeterministically whether to consider **P** or not(**P**) first, for each call of the procedure. It turns out that if the nondeterministic choices are properly made, then contradict and contradict2 both run in time polynomial in the size of the proof they find, where size is the number of axioms and lemmas in the proof, rather than the tree size defined above. Thus the size of a proof $C_1 \, C_2 \, ... \, C_n$ is n.

3. First Order Logic
3.1. Syntax

We now discuss first order logic, in which variables may be quantified. We first discuss syntax. We use **a, b, c** for individual constants, **x, y, z** for (individual) variables, **P, Q,
R** for predicate constants, **f, g, h** for function constants, and we have boolean connectives as
in propositional logic. Each predicate constant and function constant has an *arity,* which is a
non-negative integer telling how many arguments it takes. In sorted logic, the arity also
specifies the sorts of the arguments, but we will not discuss that formally here. We also have
quantifiers ∀ and ∃, read "for all" and "there exists," respectively. A *term* is a well formed
expression composed of individual constants, variables, and function constants. An *atom* is a
predicate constant followed by a list of terms. A *literal* is an atom or an atom preceded by a
negation sign. A *formula* is defined as follows: If A is a formula then (∀x)A and (∃x)A are
formulas, for any variable x, and formulas may also be constructed using boolean connectives
in the usual way. In a formula of the form (∀x)A, A is called the *scope* of the quantifier
(∀x); similarly, in a formula of the form (∃x)A, A is called the scope of the quantifier (∃x).
We sometimes write (**Q** x) to refer to either (∃x) or (∀x). A quantifier free formula is in
conjunctive normal form if it is a conjunction of disjunctions of literals (as in the propositional calculus); it is in *prenex conjunctive normal form* if it is of the form (Q x_1) (Q x_2) ...
(Q x_n) A where A is a quantifier free formula in conjunctive normal form. We sometimes
call A the *matrix* of this formula.

3.2. Semantics

An *interpretion* (structure) **I** consists of a *domain* **D**, which is a non-empty collection
(informally, a set) of objects, together with assignments I_v and I_c of meanings to variables and
constants. For a variable x, I_v assigns an element of **D** to x, for an individual constant **a**, I_c
assigns an element of **D** to **a**, for a function constant **f**, I_c assigns a function from D^n to **D**,
where **n** is the arity of **f**, and for a predicate constant **P**, I_c assigns a function from D^n to
{true, false}, where **n** is the arity of **P**. We indicate these objects by I_v (x), I_c (a), I_c (f), and
I_c (P), respectively. We assume that some first order language of (individual) constant, function, and predicate symbols is specified, that **I** assigns meanings to these symbols, and that no
other constant, function, and predicate symbols may appear in formulas. Given an interpretation **I** and a formula A, **I** assigns a truth value to A in the obvious way. Informally, boolean
connectives are interpreted as in propositional logic, and quantifiers are interpreted consistent
with their readings "for all" and "there exists." Formally, we define the meaning A^I of a
term A in interpretation **I** as follows:

> If A is a variable then A^I is I_v (A)
> If A is an individual constant then A^I is I_c (A)
> If A is a term of the form $f(t_1 \cdots t_n)$ where the t_i are terms, then A^I is
> $F(T_1 \cdots T_n)$ where T_i is t_i^I and F is I_c (f). Thus the meaning of f
> is a function that is applied to the T_i, which are the meanings of
> the t_i. So A^I is an element of D, the domain of I.

Also, we define the truth value of a formula A in an interpretation I. We write I $\models$ A, read
"I satisfies A", to indicate that A is true in interpretation I. We define $\models$ recursively as
follows:

> If A is an atom of the form $P(t_1 \cdots t_n)$ where the t_i are terms then
> I $\models$ A if $F(T_1 \cdots T_n)$ is true, where T_i is t_i^I and F is I_c (P).
> If A is a formula of the form $A_1 \lor A_2$ then I $\models$ A iff I $\models$ A_1 or
> I $\models$ A_2. The other boolean connectives are interpreted similarly.
> If A is a formula of the form $(\forall x)B$ then I $\models$ A iff J $\models$ B for all J like
> I except that $J_v(x)$ is an arbitrary element of the domain D.
> If A is a formula of the form $(\exists x)B$ then I $\models$ A iff J $\models$ B for some J
> that is like I except that $J_v(x)$ is an arbitrary element of the
> domain D.

For example, if the domain D of I is {0, 1, 2, ... } and I_c (f) is the successor function and I_c
(P) is the predicate testing if an integer is even, then I $\models$ $(\forall x)(P(x) \lor P(f(x)))$ but not
I $\models$ $(\forall x)(P(x) \supset P(f(x)))$. We write I $\not\models$ B to indicate that I $\models$ B does not hold, that is, I
does not satisfy B.

We say A is *satisfiable* if there is an interpretation I such that I $\models$ A; otherwise A is
unsatisfiable, or a contradiction. If I satisfies A, we call I a *model* of A. We say A is *valid*
if all interpretations I satisfy A. This is also written $\models$ A. We say that B is a *logical*
consequence (or a valid consequence) of A, written A $\models$ B, if all interpretations that satisfy
A also satisfy B. For example, P(a) $\models$ $(\exists x)P(x)$. We write $A_1 A_2 \cdots A_n \models$ B to indicate
that all models that satisfy all the A_i also satisfy B. It is known that validity in first order
logic is partially decidable but not decidable. This means that there is a procedure which,
given any valid formula, will eventually halt and state that the formula is valid, but given an
invalid formula, might not halt. However, it is known that there can be no recursive bound
on the running time of such a procedure on valid formulas; thus the procedure may run a
long time even on short formulas. We now discuss methods for partially deciding validity.

3.3. Proof Systems (Human Oriented)

One way to show that a formula is valid is to prove it using some suitable collection
of inference rules. Quite a few such sets of rules have been devised, and many are *complete,*
in the sense that every valid formula may be proven, and *sound,* in the sense that only valid
formulas may be proven. Hilbert style systems typically use modus ponens (given above) as
the inference rule and express axioms largely using the $\supset$ connective. Sequent style proof
systems, introduced by Gentzen, tend to have an inference rule to introduce each logical connective, so that the structure of a proof is largely determined by the structure of the formula
one is trying to prove. Such systems are attractive for backward chaining reasoning for this
reason. For a discussion of these systems, see Gallier [30]. A discussion of the 8 or 9

principle kinds of proof systems is given in [64]. "Natural deduction proofs" are something like sequent style proofs, except that there are "discharge" rules for removing assumptions. In the theorem proving community, the term "natural deduction" is sometimes used to refer to any backward chaining, subgoal oriented prover, that is, to any problem reduction format. Although we will not present many first order proof systems, we will give a method for converting some propositional proof procedures to first order proof procedures.

Complete mechanical proof systems exist for first order logic, but this is not true for number theory or higher order logic in general. Gödel showed that in any "mechanical" (computable) proof system that expresses properties of natural numbers, some valid formula is unprovable. Note that it is not possible to express all properties of the natural numbers in first order logic, essentially because it is not possible to do general mathematical induction in first order logic. The general induction scheme requires quantifying over a predicate, which requires a higher order logic. Gödel also showed that it is not possible to prove consistency of a sufficiently powerful logic within the logic itself. In order to show that a logical system is consistent, it is necessary to use some more powerful system. But then one still does not know that this more powerful system is consistent. This makes "Hilbert's program" unachievable in a strict sense; Hilbert's goal was to put all mathematical reasoning on a finite, mechanical basis, essentially. Still, such consistency proofs are common and give insight into the structure of formal systems. Also, formal logic is a useful tool for expressing exact reasoning, even though some properties of the logic may not be provable in it.

4. Computer Proof Systems

We now discuss theorem proving procedures that are adapted for a computer. These differ from human-oriented proof systems in that the inference steps may be more complex and less intuitive. Many computer oriented proof procedures are refutation procedures, and are therefore less natural for humans than affirmation procedures. These often require a formula to be in clause form, which is defined for first order formulas in a way similar to that given already for the propositional calculus. For a general discussion of mechanical theorem proving, see [3,17,21,30,116].

We introduce some terminology. An *atom* is a predicate constant followed by a list of terms. A *literal* is an atom or the negation of an atom. The literal is called *positive* if it is an atom, *negative* if it is the negation of an atom. A *clause* is a set of literals, representing the disjunction of the literals in the set. A first order formula is in *clause form* if it is a set of clauses, representing the conjunction of the clauses in the set. We say that this set of clauses is satisfiable if the corresponding conjunction of disjunctions of literals is satisfiable.

Free variables in a clause are regarded as universally quantified. To prove that a theorem **A** is valid in first order logic, we prove that not(**A**) is unsatisfiable. Many computer proof procedures require that not(**A**) be converted to clause form. There is a systematic procedure for converting any formula **B** to a set **S** of clauses such that **B** is satisfiable iff **S** is. This involves converting **B** to prenex conjunctive normal form and eliminating quantifiers by the use of Skolem functions. For example, suppose we are trying to prove that

$(\exists x)(\forall y)P(x,y) \supset (\forall y)(\exists x)P(x,y)$.   We   negate   this,   and   try   to   prove   that
$\text{not}((\exists x)(\forall y)P(x,y) \supset (\forall y)(\exists x)P(x,y))$ is unsatisfiable. This formula is equivalent to
$(\exists x)(\forall y)P(x,y) \wedge (\exists y)(\forall x) \neg P(x,y)$. The clause form of this is $\{\{P(a,y)\},\{\neg P(x,b)\}\}$,
which represents the conjunction of two clauses, each containing a single literal. The details
of this process are given in many standard texts, such as [21] and [55]. For a proof that
Skolemization preserves satisfiability, see [55]; validity is not necessarily preserved. Note
that this process removes the distinction between a set of axioms and the theorem to be proven; all are on a common footing. Thus, if a theorem is of the form $(H \supset R)$, its negation
is of the form $(H \wedge \neg(R))$. If R is regarded as the theorem and H as the axioms, then we
add the negation of the theorem to the axioms and convert everything to clause form. Thus
we obtain some clauses from H and some from $\text{not}(R)$. The latter ones are generally of more
interest than the former for the search. Some methods try to re-introduce the distinction
between the theorem and the axioms in various ways to focus attention on the theorem. One
of the virtues of Gentzen-style systems is that this distinction is inherent and need not be re-
introduced.

Proof procedures based on clause form depend on Herbrand's theorem, which is actually somewhat different than what Herbrand proved; his result was a purely syntactic result,
while the following result involves semantics. First we need some definitions.

Definition. A *substitution* is a mapping Θ from variables to terms, such that for only
finitely many variables x do we have $\Theta(x) \neq x$. We represent a substitution by a finite set $\{x_1
\leftarrow t_1, x_2 \leftarrow t_2, ..., x_n \leftarrow t_n\}$, indicating that $\Theta(x_i)$ is t_i and $\Theta(x) = x$ if x is a variable distinct
from the x_i. If t is a term, then by $t \Theta$ we indicate the result of simultaneously replacing all
variables x_i in t by t_i. Thus if x is a variable, $x \Theta$ is $\Theta(x)$, and if t is a term $f(t_1 ... t_n)$ then $t
\Theta$ is $f(t_1 \Theta ... t_n \Theta)$. Similarly, for a literal L and a clause C we indicate the result of apply-
ing Θ by $L \Theta$ and $C \Theta$. We say a term u is an *instance* of a term t if there is a substitution
Θ such that u is $t \Theta$, and similarly for literals and clauses.

The following result is popularly known as Herbrand's theorem.

Theorem 1. *A set S of clauses is unsatisfiable iff there is a set S' of ground clauses
such that a) S' is unsatisfiable and b) every clause C' in S' is an instance of some clause C
in S.*

For example, if S is the following set of clauses

$$\{\{P(a)\},\{\neg P(x),P(f(x))\},\{\neg P(f(f(x)))\}\}$$

then S' is the following:

$$\{\{P(a)\},\{\neg P(a),P(f(a))\},\{\neg P(f(a)),P(f(f(a)))\}, \{\neg P(f(f(a)))\}\}.$$

4.1 Unification

In order to generate the proper instances automatically, mechanical proof procedures
generally rely on a *unification* algorithm.

Definition. A substitution Θ is *as general as* a substution Γ if there is a substitution
Φ such that for all terms t, $t \Theta \Phi = t \Gamma$.

Definition. A *unifier* of two literals L and M is a substitution Θ such that $L \Theta$ and $M
\Theta$ are identical. A *most general unifier* of L and M, if it exists, is a unifier of L and M

which is as general as any other unifier of **L** and **M**.

It turns out that if **L** and **M** are unifiable, they have a most general unifier, and this unifier may be computed fairly efficiently. The most general unifier is unique up to renamings of variables. Most general unifiers are useful for theorem provers because they permit the instantiations to be as general as possible subject to the identification of two literals or other structures. This reduces the search space since less general structures need not be examined. One can also show that for a set **B** of literals, a most general unifier of **B** exists if any unifier of **B** exists, where a unifier of a set **B** of literals is a substitution Θ such that $\{$**L** Θ : **L** in **B**$\}$ contains one literal.

There are a fair number of algorithms known for finding most general unifiers. Probably the earliest unification algorithm known to computer science was due to Robinson[91], although unification was known earlier. The algorithm we present in figure 6 is one of the simplest such algorithms, while also permitting a reasonably efficient implementation.

Our algorithm is based on an equation solving paradigm. Suppose we are unifying two literals **L** and **M**. We may assume that **L** and **M** are both negative or both positive, for otherwise the unification fails. If they are both negative, we can remove the negation from both to obtain an equivalent problem. Let us assume **L** and **M** are atoms. If their predicates differ, the unification fails, so we assume their predicates are identical. Therefore **L** is $P(s_1 \dots s_n)$ and **M** is $P(t_1 \dots t_n)$ for some s_i and t_i. This unification problem is converted into the set of equations

$$\{s_1 = t_1, s_2 = t_2, \dots, s_n = t_n\},$$

which are solved using the procedure "solve". This procedure will eventually either fail or

---

procedure solve(equations)

An equation of the form x = x for a variable x may be deleted.

If some equation is of the form f(...) = g(...) and f and g are different (or have different numbers of arguments), then fail.

Otherwise, if some equation is of the form $f(s_1 \dots s_n) = f(t_1 \dots t_n)$, then delete it and replace it by the equations $s_1 = t_1, s_2 = t_2, \dots, s_n = t_n$.

Otherwise, if some equation is of the form x = t or t = x and t is not a variable and x occurs in t, then fail.

Otherwise, if some equation is of the form x = t or t = x and t is not x and x and t are not marked, then mark x and replace x by t everywhere except in this equation, and orient this equation x = t.
end solve.

FIGURE 6

generate a set of equations of the form $\{x_1 = t_1, x_2 = t_2, ..., x_n = t_n\}$ where all the x_i are marked and no x_i appears in any t_j. The final most general unifier is then the substitution $\{x_1 \leftarrow t_1, x_2 \leftarrow t_2, ..., x_n \leftarrow t_n\}$. For example, given the atoms $P(g(a),x)$ and $P(y,f(y))$, this procedure starts with the equations

$$g(a) = y, \; x = f(y)$$

and converts this to

$$y = g(a), \; x = f(g(a)) \text{ with } y \text{ marked}$$

and finally to

$$y = g(a), \; x = f(g(a)) \text{ with } x \text{ and } y \text{ marked.}$$

Thus the most general unifier is the substitution $\{y \leftarrow g(a), x \leftarrow f(g(a))\}$. This procedure can easily be extended to find the most general unifier of a set of literals. For example, to find the most general unifier of $\{P(r_1 \; ... \; r_n), P(s_1... \; s_n), P(t_1 \; ... \; t_n)\}$, we start with the equations $\{r_1 = s_1, s_1 = t_1, r_2 = s_2, s_2 = t_2, ..., r_n = s_n, s_n = t_n\}$.

We now give a general method for "lifting" propositional proof systems to first-order logic. For this, we assume that all first-order formulas are in quantifier-free form, that is, they contain no quantifiers, and free variables are assumed to be universally quantified (as in clause form). Suppose we have an inference rule

$$\frac{A_1 \; A_2 \; ... \; A_n}{B}$$

for propositional logic. Typically this rule will be a schema containing variables representing formulas. We convert this inference rule to the following first-order inference rule:

$$\frac{A_1' \; A_2' \; ... \; A_n'}{B \, \Theta}$$

where we assume that the A_i' have no common variables with each other or with the A_i, and that Θ is a most general substitution such that $A_i' \, \Theta = A_i \, \Theta$ for all i. If a propositional proof system contains more than one inference rule, each such rule is converted to a first-order inference rule in this way. We presented some proof systems in sections 2.1 and 2.2, which can be converted to first order logic proof systems in this way. For example, by applying this lifting method we obtain resolution for first order logic, as follows.

4.2 Resolution

Definition. If L is an atom then $\overline{L}$ is not(L). If L is not(M) then $\overline{L}$ is M.

Definition. Given two clauses C_1 and C_2 with subsets B_1 and B_2 such that $B_1 \cup \{\overline{L} : L \text{ in } B_2\}$ is unifiable, a *resolvent* D of C_1 and C_2 is $(C_1 - B_1) \, \Theta \cup (C_2 - B_2) \, \Theta$, where Θ is a most general unifier of $B_1 \cup \{\overline{L} : L \text{ in } B_2\}$. For this, we rename variables so that C_1 and C_2 have no common variables. Note that two clauses may not have any resolvents, or they may have one or more than one resolvent. We call B_1 and B_2 the *subsets of resolution* for this resolution operation. We say that C_1 and C_2 are *parents* of D. For example, resolving the clauses $\{P(a)\}$ and $\{\text{not } P(x), P(f(x))\}$, we obtain the resolvent $\{P(f(a))\}$. Also, resolving $\{P,Q\}$ and $\{\text{not } P, R\}$ in propositional logic, we obtain $\{Q, R\}$. Note that resolution is *sound*, that is, if **C** is a resolvent of C_1 and C_2, then **C** is a logical consequence of C_1 and C_2, interpreting free variables as universally quantified variables. A *resolution proof of C_n from* **S** is a sequence C_1 C_2 ... C_n of clauses such that for each i, either C_i is in **S**, or C_i is a resolvent of C_j and C_k for j, k < i. If C_n is the empty clause, this is called a *refutation from* **S**.

Sometimes a "factoring" operation is defined separately from resolution:

Definition. Suppose **C** is a clause and **B** is a subset of **C** having two or more literals. Let Θ be a most general unifier of **B**. Then **C** Θ is a *factor* of **C**.

The following "lifting theorem" is often used to prove completeness of resolution:

Theorem 2. *Suppose C_1 and C_2 are clauses and D_1 and D_2 are instances of C_1 and C_2, respectively. Suppose* **D** *is a resolvent of D_1 and D_2. Then there is a resolvent* **C** *of C_1 and C_2 such that* **D** *is an instance of* **C**.

It is possible to extend this to subsumption also:

Definition. A clause **C** *subsumes* clause **D** if there is a substitution Θ such that **C** Θ is a subset of **D**. Some authors require also that $|C| \leq |D|$ and call this Θ-subsumption.

Theorem 3. *Suppose C_1 and C_2 are clauses and C_1 and C_2 subsume D_1 and D_2, respectively. Suppose* **D** *is a resolvent of D_1 and D_2. Then there is a resolvent* **C** *of C_1 and C_2 such that* **C** *subsumes* **D**, *or else C_1 subsumes* **D**, *or C_2 subsumes* **D**.

This theorem can be used to show that it is not necessary to retain subsumed clauses when certain theorem proving methods are used.

Definition. We say a clausal inference system is *complete* if for every unsatisfiable set **S** of clauses, there is a proof of the empty clause from **S** using the system.

Theorem 4. *Resolution is complete.*

Proof. Suppose **S** is unsatisfiable. The idea is to show that ground resolution is complete for ground clauses, then to use Herbrand's theorem to show that there is a ground resolution refutation from suitable ground instances of clauses in **S**, and then use the lifting theorem to lift this to a resolution refutation from **S**.

Resolution can also be used for *answer extraction*. This idea was mentioned early by Green[37]. The idea is that if we prove a theorem of the form $(\exists x)P(x)$, then from the proof it is sometimes possible to construct a term **t** such that $P(t)$. If not, it is always possible from the proof to find a set t_1 ... t_n of terms such that $P(t_1)$ or $P(t_2)$ or ... or $P(t_n)$ by looking at the instances of the clauses used in the proof. This latter case is called an "indefinite answer." Sometimes it is possible also to find conditions under which each answer t_i will be correct. For a discussion of answer extraction, see [37].

There are a multitude of refinements to resolution which preserve completeness, and a number of other clausal theorem proving strategies. For example, one such is *tautology deletion*. Recall that a clause **C** is a tautology if for some atom **L**, **C** contains both **L** and not(**L**). For many (but not all) strategies, the strategy is still complete if clauses that are tautologies are not used in proofs. We mention some additional important refinements now.

Theorem 5. *Suppose* **S** U {**C**} *is a set of clauses and* **C** = C_1 U C_2 *where C_1 and C_2 have no common variables. Then* **S** U {**C**} *is unsatisfiable iff* **S** U {C_1} *is unsatisfiable and* **S**

U {C_2} *is unsatisfiable.*

Proof. S U {C} represents the first order formula (A $\wedge$ B) where A is a universally quantified conjunction of disjunctions representing S, and B is a universally quantified disjunction of literals in C. Now, B is equivalent to (B$_1$ $\vee$ B$_2$), where B$_1$ is the universally quantified disjunction of literals in C$_1$ and B$_2$ is the universally quantified disjunction of literals in C$_2$, since C$_1$ and C$_2$ have no common variables. Thus (A $\wedge$ B) is equivalent to (A $\wedge$ B$_1$) $\vee$ (A $\wedge$ B$_2$). Thus (A $\wedge$ B) is satisfiable iff (A $\wedge$ B$_1$) is satisfiable or (A $\wedge$ B$_2$) is satisfiable. But (A $\wedge$ B$_1$) is satisfiable iff S U {C$_1$} is satisfiable, and similarly for (A $\wedge$ B$_2$) and S U {C$_2$}.

This is the basis of "splitting," which is a powerful and too little used theorem proving method. The idea is that the problem S U {C} is decomposed into two independent subproblems. If C is {P(a), P(b)} then we can choose C$_1$ to be {P(a)} and C$_2$ to be {P(b)}, for example. Splitting can also be applied recursively to the subproblems. The clause C can either be an input clause or a clause derived from input clauses by resolution. Often splitting can be applied to derived clauses but not to clauses given in the original statement of the problem. Splitting can also be combined with ideas from section 2.3 about propositional calculus decision procedures to avoid unnecessary subcases when splitting is used recursively on subproblems. Especially the procedure "contradict3" is useful in this context.

Definition. A first-order clause is *positive* if it contains only positive literals.

Theorem 6. *If* S *is unsatisfiable then there is a resolution refutation from* S *in which each resolution is between clauses* C$_1$ *and* C$_2$ *such that* C$_1$ *is positive or* C$_2$ *is positive.*

This strategy is called *P1-deduction* [92] or *positive resolution*. Similarly, one can define negative resolution and prove its completeness; more general such restrictions can also be defined. For example, for an arbitrary interpretation I, one can require that when two clauses C$_1$ and C$_2$ are resolved, one of them must be false in I. This is the "semantic resolution" of [101]. If I is chosen as a standard model of the axioms of the theory being considered, this restriction prevents axioms from resolving together. This gives a kind of "set of support" stragegy which is very useful for focusing attention on the theorem to be proven rather than on the general axioms of whatever theory is being considered. For example, if we are trying to prove R from the axioms H, then we are trying to prove (H $\supset$ R), so a refutation method will attempt to prove that (H $\wedge$ not(R)) is unsatisfiable. Now, if I is a model of H, then only the clauses arising from not(R) will be false in I, and so this method focuses attention on the theorem R. However, testing if a clause is false in I can be expensive or impossible if I is non-trivial. The set of support strategy of [117] is a way of getting nearly the same effect without the need to use I explicitly. A sequence of positive resolutions can be combined into a hyper-resolution [92], which avoids explicitly generating intermediate results. This strategy is often used by the Argonne group.

Many refinements are based on some method of ordering the literals in a clause and restricting resolution so that the subset of resolution may only contain clauses that are maximal in the ordering. One such ordering is to order literals by their predicate symbols, some predicate symbols being considered as "smaller than" others. The A-orderings of [101] are another ordering method. For P1 deduction, it is possible to use such orderings in a different way. To be specific, if clauses C_1 and C_2 resolve, and C_1 is positive, then one can require that the subset of resolution for C_1 be maximal among all literals of C_1 in the ordering, and that the subset of resolution for C_2 be minimal in the ordering among the negative literals of C_2. Locking resolution [10] adds indices to the literals which may be used to order them.

Definition. A *unit clause* is a clause containing exactly one literal.

Unit resolution is the restriction in which resolutions are only performed between a unit clause and another clause. This strategy is not complete, but is often useful. A combination of unit resolution and something like hyper-resolution is called UR resolution, which is often used by the Argonne group.

Definition. An *input clause* is a clause in a set S of clauses, distinguished from a clause generated from S by resolution. *Input resolution* is the strategy in which one of the clauses resolved must always be an input clause. This is also not complete but is often useful. An equivalence between unit and input resolution is mentioned in [20].

There are also restrictions on *factoring*. These are restrictions on the size of the subsets of resolution or their contents. A particularly severe but still complete restriction is given in [90]. For P1 deduction, it is never necessary that a subset of resolution consisting of negative literals, contain more than one literal, for example.

4.3. Specialized Strategies

We now discuss theorem proving strategies suitable for certain subclasses of first order logic. Here we discuss syntactic subclasses; specialized decision procedures for particular theories (except equality) will be discussed in section 6.

Definition. A *Horn clause* in first order logic is a clause having at most one positive literal.

Such clauses are used in Prolog, and certain restricted strategies are complete for Horn clauses. For example, input resolution is complete for Horn clauses. Also, positive resolution without factoring is complete for Horn clauses [42]; this is a strategy in which clauses C_1 and C_2 are resolved only if C_1 or C_2 is a positive unit clause. Loveland [57] has developed methods good for near-Horn clauses, that is, clauses having not many positive literals, in the context of logic programming. Prolog has a negation by failure which gives an extension of Horn clause logic to non-Horn clauses, but this extension does not have the same semantics as first-order logic.

4.3.1. Equality

There are many specialized methods for equality. The equality axioms are the following:

$$x = x$$
$$x = y \supset y = x$$
$$x = y \land y = z \supset x = z$$
$$x_1 = y_1 \land \dots \land x_n = y_n \supset f(x_1 \dots x_n) = f(y_1 \dots y_n)$$
$$x_1 = y_1 \land \dots \land x_n = y_n \land P(x_1 \dots x_n) \supset P(y_1 \dots y_n)$$

Adding these axioms to a set of clauses usually results in cluttering up the search space with many equality clauses. Therefore it is often better to use specialized methods for equality. We have found, however, that for one prover, the equality axioms performed better than specialized methods on some problems from combinatory logic [102]. Some specialized methods require the use of the following "functionally reflexive" axioms for each function symbol **f**:

$$\mathbf{f}(\mathbf{x}_1 \ldots \mathbf{x}_n) = \mathbf{f}(\mathbf{x}_1 \ldots \mathbf{x}_n)$$

Such axioms, being instances of **x** = **x**, should be avoided when possible. Most specialized equality strategies do not require their use.

Definition. An *equational system* is a set of equations and negations of equations.

For equational systems, term rewriting methods can be much more efficient than general first-order methods; such methods are discussed in another chapter of this volume. The general idea of specialized strategies for equality is to allow the replacement of equals by equals; this is generalized into the so-called paramodulation rule for clauses. The idea of paramodulation is that if C[t] is a clause containing a term **t** and ((s = t) ∨ D) is another clause, then we can conclude (C[s] ∨ D), where C[s] is C with the occurrence of **t** replaced by **s**. If s = t, we can conclude C[s] by replacement of equals by equals. Otherwise, **D** is true. Thus in all cases we can conclude (C[s] ∨ D). Similarly, from C[t] and (t = s ∨ D) we can conclude (C[s] ∨ D). Paramodulation is a lifting of this rule to the general case: most general substitutions are applied to make such a replacement possible. Thus we have the following definition:

Definition. Suppose C[t] is a clause containing a non-variable term **t** and (**u** = **v** ∨ D) is another clause. Suppose these two clauses have no common variables (since variables can always be renamed). Suppose **t** and **u** are unifiable, and let ϴ be a most general unifier of **t** and **u**. Then (C ϴ [v ϴ] ∨ D ϴ) is a *paramodulant* of C[t] and ((u = v) ∨ D). Similarly, (C ϴ [v ϴ] ∨ D ϴ) is a paramodulant of C[t] and ((v = u) ∨ D).

For example, the clause (P(g(a)) ∨ Q(b)) is a paramodulant of P(f(x)) and ((f(a) = g(a)) ∨ Q(b)). Brand[15] showed that if **Eq** is the set of equality axioms given above and S is a set of clauses, then S U **Eq** is unsatisfiable iff there is a proof of the empty clause from S U {x = x} using resolution and paramodulation as inference rules. Thus, paramodulation allows us to dispense with all the equality axioms except **x** = **x**. A simpler proof was given by Peterson[78] and more recent and more general proofs are found in Hsiang and Rusinowitch [46] and elsewhere. These more recent proofs often show the refinement of restricted versions of paramodulation which considerably reduce the search space. Some early versions of paramodulation required the use of the functionally reflexive axioms, but this is now known not to be necessary. When **D** is empty, paramodulation is similar to "narrowing", which has been much studied in the context of logic programming and term rewriting.

Similar to paramodulation is the rewriting or "demodulation" rule[118], which is essentially a method of simplification:

Definition. Suppose C[t] is a clause containing a non-variable term **t** and **u** = **v** is another unit clause. Suppose **v** is "simpler" than **u**, in a sense too technical to precisely describe here. (See [25] for a discussion of "simplification orderings" and related topics.) Suppose these two clauses have no common variables (since variables can always be renamed). Suppose **t** is an instance of **u**, and let **Θ** be such that **t** is **u** **Θ**. Then **C** [**v** **Θ**] is a *demodulant* of **C**[**t**] and **u** = **v**. Similarly, **C** [**v** **Θ**] is a demodulant of **C**[**t**] and **v** = **u** if **v** is simpler than **u**. This idea can be generalized, to only require that **v** **Θ** be simpler than **u** **Θ**, rather than requiring that **v** be simpler than **u**.

The idea of saying that **v** is simpler than **u** is to ensure that demodulation terminates. For example, we would not say that **y** * **x** is simpler than **x** * **y**, since then the clause **a*b=c** could demodulate using the equation **x*y=y*x** to **b*a=c** and then to **a*b=c** and so on indefinitely. However, we can say that **x** is simpler than **x** * 1, so that the clauses **P(x*1)** and **x*1=x** have **P(x)** as a demodulant. Some of the proofs of completeness of paramodulation also permit demodulation. This is essential in practice, for without it one can generate expressions like **x*1*1*1** that clutter up the search space. There are also completeness proofs of paramodulation that permit demodulation and various restrictions on the order in which literals may resolve away, that is, they restrict which literals may be included in the subsets of resolution.

Another approach is to consider *conditional equations* such as **x/x=1** if **x≠0**. These are formally equivalent to first order clauses having at least one equality literal, but concepts similar to demodulation can be extended to them as well [122].

Still another approach to equality is to build an equational theory into the unification procedure. This idea was suggested by Plotkin[86], and leads to fairly efficient theorem provers. However, this approach also increases the complexity of the prover, and a large number of unification procedures for various equational theories are known[98,99]. Recent work has concerned systematic methods for combining unification algorithms for various theories; see for example [94]. Another paper in this volume deals with equational unification. There are also a number of other equality-based theorem proving methods, such as equality-based binary resolution [26].

4.4 Other Proof Procedures

There are some problems with resolution style proof precedures as we have described them. The conversion to clause form often destroys the structure of a formula, and this structure can be important. The conversion to clause form can increase the size of a formula by an exponential amount, but this can be avoided by adding new predicate symbols [85]. Difficulties with back chaining in the context of resolution have been mentioned in section 2.1. Mathematical induction does not naturally combine with resolution; for example, Manna and Waldinger use a non-clausal proof procedure to allow induction in their TABLOG system [59]. Explicit quantifiers are sometimes useful. If a predicate **P(x)** is defined using quantifiers, say as (∃**y**)**Q**(**x**, **y**), then it is useful to be able to replace occurences of **P** by their definition. This is not possible if quantifiers are not explicitly represented. A method that comes close, however, is given in Potter and Plaisted[87]. The set of support restriction is often essential, but it is not complete when used together with P1 deduction or hyper-resolution or locking resolution. Still, resolution has many advantages, and is often the strategy of choice.

We mention some clausal proof procedures that do implement back chaining. One of the earliest is the model elimination strategy of Loveland [54]. This is also a set of support strategy as defined in section 2.1, and permits a flexible ordering of the literals, giving this strategy many advantages. The MESON procedure of Loveland [55] is an adaptation of this strategy that is more like Prolog, and may be viewed as an extension of Prolog to full first order logic. In Plaisted[84], a sequent-style refinement of the MESON procedure is given that is even closer to Prolog in the structure of the proofs. In fact, this refinement of the MESON procedure may be viewed as a simple, satisfiability-preserving translation of an arbitrary set of first order clauses into a set of Horn clauses. Loveland's near-Horn Prolog[57] has already been mentioned. This permits back chaining but not set of support as defined in section 2.1, and avoids the need for contrapositives. For a definition and discussion of contrapositives, see Plaisted[83]. Similar methods are given in [83] and [81], where the emphasis is on complete theorem proving strategies rather than logic programming languages using depth-first search.

There are a number of connection-graph based methods that perform the search in a completely different way, keeping track of possible unifications or "connections" between literals. This avoids certain search redundancies due to the order in which unifications are performed. For a description of such procedures, see Bibel[5]; for some completeness and incompleteness results, see [27]; for a description of a connection graph based prover on which a large number of examples have been run and in which a large amount of effort has been invested, see [28]. Andrews' matings [2] are similar to connection graphs, but do not perform any unifications until a possible proof is found. Andrews[65] has implemented a higher order theorem prover using these ideas, and has obtained some impressive results.

Hsiang's method[44,45] reduces first-order logic to an equational theory using a term rewriting system that encodes boolean algebra using the connectives "and" and "exclusive OR." This method and its relation to resolution have been studied to some extent. It is not clear at this point how efficient this method is compared to resolution. Another novel equality-based method is that of Overbeek[77], which involves an efficient enumeration of the set of ground instances of a set of clauses using equations to simplify as much as possible. This method performs impressively well on some examples.

Finally, there are many methods that are not based on anything similar to clause form. We do not discuss these methods much. In general, the sequent style methods of Gentzen [30] have a lot to recommend them. Some work has been done recently on algorithms for unifying formulae with explicit quantifiers. Also, there are a number of provers which have languages in which the user can specify his own proof strategies. A recent example is [18]. This is an attractive idea because it provides one way of building knowledge into the theorem prover. However, it places an additional burden on the user who must be familiar enough with theorem proving strategies to state a method for attempting a proof. Many users do not have the required knowledge of theorem proving, and humans also seem to find proofs without having to know much about theorem proving strategies.

4.5 Complexity Bounds

We close this section by discussing the complexity of testing satisfiability of a set of clauses. We would like to say more about the performance of various provers than how efficiently they prove certain specific theorems. We would like to have a theoretical basis for comparing various theorem provers and strategies to help put the field on a firm theoretical basis. Although the validity problem for first order logic is partially decidable but not decidable, one can bound the complexity of a proof procedure in terms of the complexity of a smallest proof of unsatisfiability. Proof procedures with meaningful such bounds exist, since one proof procedure is just to enumerate possible proofs in order of their complexity. Using such a measure of complexity, one can say something about the asymptotic behavior of theorem provers. This should help to compare theorem provers in a machine independent way, and may also motivate the design of proof procedures with better asymptotic complexity. This may also give us some understanding about why various theorem provers perform as they do. In addition, such an analysis should lead to the study of various specialized classes of formulae on which better complexity bounds may be obtained. Of course, a theoretical analysis does not say how well a prover will do on a particular example, and so it is possible that a good prover may still have a large asymptotic time bound.

We bound the complexity of a clausal theorem proving procedure in terms of the complexity of the set of ground instances appearing in a proof. If S is an unsatisfiable set of clauses, then by Herbrand's theorem there is an unsatisfiable set G of ground instances of S. We can bound the complexity of various proof procedures in terms of properties of G, such as the sum of the sizes of the literals in G. If S is satisfiable then G does not exist. Also, there is no way that we can predict beforehand the size of G from S, since there can be no recursive bound on the size of G. This analysis therefore takes into account the fact that first-order logic is only partially decidable, and that any complete theorem prover will fail to halt on some inputs. We give separate bounds for Horn clauses and general clauses, since Horn clauses are easier to decide. Often we write $G(S)$ to indicate which set S is being referred to.

For the purposes of this analysis we define two complexity classes. These are in the spirit of polynomial time, exponential time, etc. and bound the time taken by a theorem proving procedure in terms of properties of G.

Definition. **EXPATOM** is the complexity class of problems involving sets S of first order clauses that can be solved in time $O(\|S\| + c^{dn})$ where $\|S\|$ is the length of S when written as a character string, c is a constant, n is the size of the largest literal in $G(S)$, and d is the maximum number of literals in any clause in $G(S)$. The size of a literal is the number of symbols in the literal when it is written as a character string. Note that although we are only interested in the satisfiability problem, the class **EXPATOM** is more general and refers to any problem whose input is a set of first order clauses.

Definition. **EXPSUM** is the complexity class of problems involving sets S of first order clauses that can be solved in time $O(\|S\| + c^{n})$, where $\|S\|$ is as above and c is a constant and n is the sum of the sizes of the different literals appearing in $G(S)$. Note that n is not the sum of the sizes of the clauses in $G(S)$, since only one of the different occurrences of the same literal is counted.

In both of the above definitions, c is a fixed constant which does not depend on S.

Theorem 7. *The unsatisfiability problem for Horn clauses is in* **EXPATOM**, *and the unsatisfiability problem for general first-order clauses is in* **EXPSUM**.

Proof. For both parts of the theorem we use a similar procedure, as follows:

$$R \leftarrow S \ ;$$
$$b \leftarrow 1;$$
while [the empty clause has not been derived] do
$$R \leftarrow I_b(R);$$
$$b \leftarrow b+1$$
od;

Here $I_b(R)$ is R together with all clauses derivable from R using inference system I, deleting formulas bigger than b. but saving their small factors. For Horn clauses, we take I to be positive unit resolution or hyper-resolution. We obtain the bound for Horn clauses by noting that when the bound b reaches the maximum literal size in $H(S)$, a proof will be found. When this happens, there can be c^b positive unit clauses derived for some c, since there are a finite number of non-variable symbols (more on this below). Positive unit resolution will never produce a clause having more than d literals. It is only necessary to keep clauses in which each literal has size at most b. There are at most c^{bd} such clauses, and each one can resolve against at most c^b positive unit clauses. Thus the number of possible inferences before the search is exhausted is $O(c^{b(d+1)})$. Each such inference takes polynomial time at most using typical unification algorithms [61]. The total time is $O(b^k c^{b(d+1)})$ for some k, which is $O(a^{bd})$ for some constant a. Since b is n as in the definition of **EXPATOM**, the first part of the theorem follows. We need also to look through S once to find which clauses are of various sizes; this takes time $O(\|S\|)$. For this we are assuming that all factors of clauses in S are also in S.

For non-Horn clauses the procedure is similar except that general resolution is used as the inference system instead of positive unit resolution. This part of the analysis makes use of the fact that it is never necessary to retain a lemma of size greater than n where n is the sum of the sizes of the literals in $G(S)$. Also, there are at most c^n such clauses for some constant c. For this part, it is also necessary that S contain its factors, and it is necessary also to retain all small factors of a clause that is larger than the size bound b.

For both procedures, there is a subtlety that must be dealt with. Suppose $P(a, \ a, \ a, \ \cdots, \ a)$ is in $H(S)$ for some large number of a's. The literal $P(x_1, x_2, ..., x_n)$ may appear in a proof. This literal takes $O(n \log(n))$ space to write down, since there are n variables and each one may take $\log(n)$ bits to write down. This would weaken the time bounds a little. To deal with this, we need to broaden the definition of factor so that $P(x, x, x, ..., x)$ would be considered as a factor of $P(x_1, x_2, ..., x_n)$. Such factors can be found by identifying pairs of variables, one pair at a time, to avoid an excessive running time.

If we know the optimum bound b in advance the above procedure can be improved, sometimes dramatically, just by starting with b set to the bound. This is because a proof may be found very quickly when the bound is big enough, but a lot of time may be spent when the bound is smaller. Of course, if the bound is set too big this can also cost a lot of time. Thus, knowing the optimum size bound is very important. Most provers allow the user to set various bounds, but this can be done automatically with a bounded degradation of performance compared to an optimal setting, as the following result shows.

Theorem 8. *Let* f(b,S) *be the time taken by an inference procedure for unsatisfiability if* b *is the size bound. Let* b(S) *be the optimal size bound for* S. *Then there is a partial algorithm which, for all* S, *test if* S *is unsatisfiable and if* S *is unsatisfiable runs in time* $O(\max(b(S),f(b(S),S))^2)$.

Proof. Let P_b be a process which tests unsatisfiability of S with maximum size bound b. Consider the following procedure which runs various P_b alternately:

> **for b ← 1 step 1 until [a refutation is found] do**
>   **start process P_b and run it for b steps;**
>   **for i ← 1 step 1 until b-1 or a refutation**
>   **is found do**
>   **run process P sub i for one step;**
>   **od**
> **od.**

This procedure runs in the indicated time bound, by the following argument. After each iteration of the inner loop, processes P_1 through P_b have each been run for b steps. The total work to do this is $O(b^2)$. When b reaches the optimum value b(S), then a proof will be found if the work f(b(S), S) required by P_b(S) is not larger than b(S). If f(b(S), S)) is larger than b(S), then it may be necessary to run the first f(b(S), S) procedures for f(b(S), S) steps. In either case, the specified time bound is obtained.

This can probably be improved, since the above method repeats work between various P_b. Also, there may be better ways of allocating effort than that used above. However, there are probably few (if any) provers in existence that perform even within the bound given above.

5. Hard Problems Solved by Theorem Provers

We now present some of the more well known and difficult problems solved by theorem provers, either automatically or with human assistance. This should help to give an idea of the current state of the art in mechanical theorem proving. We note that theorem provers have an advantage over humans in that the axioms needed for a proof are usually known by the user, while a human attempting to prove a theorem does not always know what axioms to use. Also, the form in which a theorem is stated to a prover is sometimes artificial. Still, some interesting proofs have been found. For an excellent survey of the history of theorem proving to 1984 and a collection of papers illustrating the state of the art at that time, see Bledsoe and Loveland[9] and the survey article by Loveland[56].

One of the earliest results is from Guard et al[41]. Their interactive semi-automated reasoning program derived a lemma in lattice theory, known as SAM's lemma, which had not been proven previously, and which was the key to an open problem. The Argonne prover [58] has also solved some open problem in mathematics, with human assistance. Some early examples are given in [115]. Although these problems are mostly fairly obscure, this is still an impressive achievement. Andrews' prover [65] has some higher order logic capability and has found a fully automatic proof of Cantor's theorem that the powerset of a set is larger than the set, even for infinite sets. It is remarkable that this proof is found in under a minute of computer time. Bledsoe's group at the University of Texas at Austin has found fully automatic proofs of a number of theorems in analysis, such as the intermediate value theorem, which states that a continuous function **f** such that **f(a)** < 0 and **f(b)** > 0 must have a zero between **a** and **b**. These proofs have made use of some specialized methods to handle reasoning about real numbers. Hunt[48] has used the Boyer-Moore theorem prover to give a correctness proof for a microcoded central processing unit called the FM8501. This prover has also been used (with human guidance) to prove mathematical theorems[12], such as the law of quadratic reciprocity in number theory, Gödel's incompleteness theorem, the Church-Rosser theorem for term rewriting systems[95], and the unsolvability of the halting problem for lisp programs. In addition, a property of the RSA encryption algorithm has been shown on this prover. Using techniques based on rewrite rules, Stickel[104] found an automatic and natural proof that in a ring, if $x^3 = x$ for all **x**, then the ring is commutative. Some incompleteness results in logic have been found fairly automatically on the Argonne prover[89]. An open problem in ring theory was recently solved automatically using a special theorem prover developed by Wang[113]. The Argonne group has used their theorem prover to suggest and verify some new results about solutions of equations in combinatory logic[63]. The fast theorem prover OTTER written by McCune found fully automatic proofs of a number of hard theorems in implicational logic. For a list of challenge problems for current theorem provers, see the last four papers in the 1988 International Conference on Automated Deduction [88]. It appears that theorem provers can be respectable aids to human mathematicians, although most of the significant results still require careful user guidance.

6. Specialized Decision Procedures

We now discuss a number of specialized decision procedures. These are theorem proving methods designed for subclasses of formulae from a particular domain. Formally, one considers formulas over a restricted language, in which the interpretations are restricted. For example, one might restrict the function symbols to + and - and the constant symbols to 0 and 1 and the predicate symbols to ≤. Also, one might restrict the interpretation to be the standard one for arithmetic, that is, the domain would be the real numbers and the function symbols would be given their standard meanings. This would lead to a special class of formulas, and we might be interested in methods for deciding validity of first-order formulas with the nonlogical symbols (predicate, function, and individual constant symbols) restricted as indicated. Although validity of general first-order formulas is undecidable, validity of special classes of formulas may be decidable. Specialized methods typically do not reason from the axioms, but use properties of the domain to decide if a formula is in the theory. Quite a number of such specialized classes of formulas have been considered, and many specialized decision procedures have been developed. Often quantifier-free formulas are studied; these are prenex normal form formulas in which all variables are universally quantified. For such formulas the validity problem is often much easier than for formulas with an arbitrary quantifier structure. Also, some general results are known[76, 71] about decision procedures for combinations of decidable theories. When specialized methods can be used, they are typically much more efficient than general first-order proof procedures. However, the cost for using them is the extra complexity of including a number of specialized decision procedures in a theorem prover. Also, an over-emphasis on specialized procedures may lead to a neglect of the hard and important problems that remain in general first-order logic.

One of the early decidability results concerns real arithmetic, in which the constants are 0 and 1, the functions are +, -, and *, the predicates are < and =, and the domain is the real numbers. The standard interpretation is assumed. This theory essentially involves statements of the form $p(\overline{x}) \geq 0$, where p is a polynomial, and was shown to be decidable by Tarski[109]. A recent, more efficient decision procedure for this problem is given in [40]. Another decidable theory is that of reals with addition, which is as above except that the multiplication operator may not appear. A proof that any decision procedure for this theory takes nondeterministic exponential time is given in [43]. The quantifier-free theory of reals with addition is essentially the same as linear programming. This is called ''Bledsoe real arithmetic'' by Bundy[17]. For this, the simplex method [67] is often used. Recently a polynomial time method was found by Khachian[51], but this method seems to be too slow for practical use. A faster method has been developed by Karmakar [50] and seems to be practically useful. A decision procedure for the quantifier-free theory of reals with addition that is based on intervals has been given by Bledsoe [6]; this method often works well on small formulas, though in general it may take exponential time. Another well known decidable theory is that of the integers with addition, or Presburger arithmetic. This is like the reals with addition except that the domain is the integers instead of the reals. This is decidable, but requires nondeterministic double exponential time to decide[29]. Other decidable theories include the theory of equality[73], in which the only predicate is =, the theory of lisp list structure, and the theory of arrays. All these theories permit uninterpreted function symbols. For a discussion of these theories see [43]. Under fairly general conditions, the combination of two theories is decidable if the two theories are decidable separately[72]. For an easy description of a method for deciding combinations of theories, see Nelson [71]. If the theories have the property of ''convexity,'' this method is especially efficient. For another method of combining decision procedures using rewrite rules, see Shostak [97].

A decision procedure for a subclass of elementary geometry was recently developed by Wu[121]. This is a very efficient method that transforms geometry theorems into systems of polynomial equations and applies algebraic methods. This method can also automatically find degenerate cases of theorems, that is, special cases in which the theorem is false. Quite a number of theorems have been proven using this procedure, and some possibly new theorems have been shown (although in a field as old as geometry it is hard to know for sure that something is new). For an easy introduction to this method, see Chou[22]. Wu's method has also been used to generate theorems in geometry. Wang[113] has recently developed a specialized theorem proving method for ring theory, and using it he has solved an open problem in this area. Though his method is not always applicable, it seems to be often applicable on typical problems, and has obtained a number of hard proofs fairly quickly.

We mention a number of other specialized methods: Moore[68] has found a way to encode logics of knowledge and belief in first order logic, making it possible to use first order systems to reason about knowledge and belief. Some decision procedures for fragments of set theory have been developed; see for example [19]. A decision procedure for some graph theory formulas is given in Moser[69]. A method of representing modal logic statements in first order logic with a special unification procedure is presented in Ohlbach[75]. Decision procedures for a number of temporal logics are known; see for example [100]. Special unification algorithms are often used to deal with particular sets of equations in theorem provers, the most notable being associative and commutative operators [103], but the technique is much more general than this; see another chapter in the present volume for a more detailed discussion of equational unification. A variation called "rigid E-unification" was introduced by Gallier et al [32] and shown to be NP complete [31]; this is interesting because the general E-unification problem is undecidable.

7. General Issues in Automatic Theorem Proving

We now discuss a number of general issues concerning theorem provers, such as search strategies, simplification, semantics, abstraction and analogy, finding relevant axioms, and some general software engineering issues. The first question has to do with completeness. Does it really matter if a theorem prover is complete? Human mathematicians may be incomplete but that does not seem to be a problem. In addition, certain specialized methods that are not complete are preferable to general methods in their domains of applicability. So it seems that there is a place for special methods and even for methods whose domain of applicability is not precisely known. But usually it does not require much modification to make a theorem prover complete, and incomplete provers often fail on embarrassingly simple problems.

Another issue is whether formal logic is in principle adequate for reasoning about the world. There are some problems in theoretical AI dealing with common sense reasoning, but people seem to get along just fine without knowing the theory at all. In addition, formalists often tend to emphasize simple, exhaustive methods and to ignore heuristic methods that are often necessary for success in real applications. Yet, much of the world can be expressed in logical terms, and logical deduction is of interest in its own right, so efforts to improve formal methods seems justified. To give up logic is really to give up a precise understanding of what one is talking about, and this seems to be a high price to pay.

7.1 Search Strategies

We now make some comments on search strategies. We have already commented on the importance of true back chaining with caching. Some problems are better for forward chaining than back chaining, so it makes sense to balance forward and backward chaining in some way. In order for back chaining to be complete, breadth-first search, best-first search, depth-first iterative deepening[53,107] (DFID), or some such strategy must be used. Depth-first iterative deepening has the advantage that it is much more storage efficient than the others. Also, under certain general conditions, it is about as time efficient as breadth-first search.

We have mentioned the importance of caching used together with DFID. However, it is not easy to do caching properly. The problem is that one wants to fail when a solution to a subgoal is generated twice. This makes some kind of bookkeeping necessary to know which solutions correspond to which subgoals. Another problem with DFID is to combine it with a priority system. In best-first search it is easy to choose the most promising subgoal at every step and work on it. This is not so easy with depth-first iterative deepening. Some kind of explanation based generalization[66] is also useful with back chaining, to ensure that solutions are as general as possible.

Another issue with back chaining is to do subgoal reordering intelligently. We found that this can be very important for some problems. One problem took 1000 seconds without subgoal reordering, 120 seconds with one method of subgoal reordering, and 20 seconds with another method. Similar behavior was observed on other problems. It is difficult to devise a good general method of ordering subgoals. We typically prefer large subgoals first, but we have found that subgoals that have more function symbols than the goal can cause trouble since back chaining can cause function symbols to proliferate.

7.2 Rewriting

Rewriting and simplification are essential for many problems. Rewriting (demodulation) permits expressions to be replaced by equivalent but simpler expressions. For example, x - x can be replaced by 0. The concept of simplification can also be extended to clauses. For example, a clause $L_1 \lor L_2 \lor \cdots \lor L_n$ can be simplified to $L_2 \lor L_3 \lor \cdots \lor L_n$ if not(L_1) has been derived; this can also be done if a literal more general than not(L_1) has been derived. Since unit clauses are used in such simplifications, it makes sense to adjust the search to favor the genaration of unit clauses. Such unit simplification is done automatically in rewrite based methods such as that of Hsiang[44]. Deleting clauses that are subsumed may be viewed as another kind of simplification. Still another kind of simplification is the replacement of predicates by their definitions. For example, the predicate subset(X,Y) can be replaced by the formula $(\forall Z)((Z \in X) \supset (Z \in Y))$. Using such replacements systematically, followed by simplification of the resulting formula using boolean equivalences, many simple set theory problems can be proven completely automatically without any search or with very little search. For example, showing that $P(X \cap Y) = P(X) \cap P(Y)$, where P(X) is the powerset of **X**, may easily be shown in this way. This cannot directly be done in a resolution theorem prover because the definitions involve explicit quantifiers, and resolution applies to clauses in quantifier free form. Unfortunately, explicit quantifiers make the unification algorithm more complicated, so it is not clear what is the best approach in general. If the axioms of set theory are directly given to a resolution theorem prover, such simple set theory identities often become intractable because the natural idea of replacing predicates by their definition is lost in a mass of skolem functions. One way to partially overcome this problem in a quantifier-free setting is given in Potter and Plaisted[87]. Also, it is not always best to replace predicates by their definitions, since this can unnecessarily complicate the search.

7.3 Priorities

The use of priorities to control the search is also important. Small clauses should generally be preferred to large clauses, where the size of a clause is the number of occurrences of symbols in it. Also, clauses that were generated with less effort should generally be preferred to those that required more effort. One nice implementation of the former idea is found in Argonne's provers, which at each step choose the smallest available clause and resolve it with everything else permitted by the strategy chosen by the user. This use of priorities helps to explain the generally good performance of these provers. Of course, it is often better to modify the priority so that some function symbols are weighted more than others, and some subterms are weighted more than others. The Argonne provers generally permit the user to assign these weights. Another good idea is to prefer clauses containing function symbols and predicates that occur in the theorem, since they are more likely to be relevant.

The hierarchical deduction prover of Wang[114] has an especially interesting priority structure. It measures the complexity of a proof by taking into account how the variables are bound in the unifications. This gives a fairly natural and intuitive measure of proof complexity which enables this prover to get some fairly hard problems automatically. This prover is essentially a combination of locking resolution [10] and set of support, and may be viewed as a refinement of ordinary resolution. In our modified problem reduction format prover, we have also gotten good results using a priority measure similar to that of Wang.

7.4 Semantics

Since humans use semantics (models) extensively in proving theorems, it seems natural that computer theorem provers should also. There have been some notably successful attempts in this direction, such as the geometry theorem prover of Gelernter[34], but so far it seems that not much has been gained in this way in other provers. The use of semantics corresponds to examples or pictures that people use to determine whether a lemma they are attempting, is true. Human mathematicians often do not attempt to prove a theorem until they are convinced on semantic grounds that it is true. The use of semantics and finite models has been beneficial in nonstandard logic theorem provers[64]; the provers mentioned in [64] use a problem reduction format and Gentzen-style proof systems. Wang's hierarchical deduction prover also can use semantics, but it seems to do pretty well without semantics. There are trivial uses of semantics, having to do with choosing signs for various predicates, but we are concerned instead with semantics that are natural and based on realistic interpretations. Closely related to the use of semantics is the use of examples; see [4] for a discussion of the use of examples.

7.5 Abstraction

It would seem to be useful for a theorem prover to learn from experience. One way of learning is learning by analogy: when a theorem is attempted, similar theorems that have been proven in the past may furnish information useful in guiding the search. Early work in this area was done by Kling[52]. The Austin group has done some more recent work in this area[16], although the analogies used so far are fairly restrictive and the improvement in search time is not dramatic. The idea of abstraction is closely related: to solve a problem **P**, we abstract **P** to obtain **Q**, solve **Q**, and invert the abstraction to map solutions to **Q** back to solutions to **P**. An abstraction will typically throw away some of the information in **P**; for example, the abstraction may ignore some of the preconditions of an action. Even if **Q** is solved, it is possible that the solutions to **Q** will fail to map back to a solution to **P**. Still, the idea seems attractive. Some early work in this area was done by Sacerdoti[93] and Plaisted[80]. Another method of abstraction was given in Plaisted[82]. More recently, D. Plummer has used abstractions to help decide which definitions will be useful in proving a theorem, with moderate success. It is also possible to use more than one abstraction at the same time, or to use more than one level of abstraction. For example, we can abstract P_1 to P_2, and abstract P_2 to P_3. We can then solve P_3, and map solutions back to solutions for P_2 and then P_1. This idea was actually implemented by Greenbaum and Plaisted at the University of Illinois. Although some reductions in search time were obtained, usually the performance was disappointing. The most notable successes were the rapid failures of the abstraction prover when a mistake had been made in the input. So, the abstractions we tried were most useful in quickly detecting when a proof could not be found. Direct use of resolution would not detect this, but would generate many clauses in attempting to find a proof. It is possible to combine the use of many levels of abstraction with the use of many abstractions at the same time, to get a "network" of abstractions to guide the search. Another idea is to relax the correspondence between the abstract space and the original space. Instead of requiring every inference in the original space to correspond to an inference in the abstract space, we can instead use the abstract space to modify the priorities, so that we prefer clauses in the original space that map onto useful clauses in the abstract space. Indeed, there is much to be tried and little that has been done in this area.

We now give an example of an abstraction mapping, to give a flavor of what can be done. This is an abstraction which has not been published until now, which we call the *joint subsumption abstraction*. This abstraction is defined as follows:

Definition. A set **T** of clauses *jointly subsumes* clause **C** if there is a set $\{D_1, \cdots, D_n\}$ of clauses such that each D_i is an instance of some clause in **T**, and such that $C = \cup_i D_i$.

Definition. If **S** is a set of clauses, let **Pr(S)** be the set of clauses appearing in refutations from **S**. That is, **Pr(S)** may include not only elements of **S** but also clauses generated from **S** by resolution. Let $\mathbf{Pr_d(S)}$ be the set of clauses appearing in depth **d** or less refutations from **S**.

Theorem 9. *If **S** is inconsistent, and **T** is a set of clauses which jointly subsume every clause in **S**, and **R** is a refutation from **S**, then every clause in **R** is jointly subsumed by* $\mathbf{Pr_d(T)}$*, where **d** is the depth of **R**.*

The idea is the following: Given a set **S** of clauses, we construct **T** as in the theorem. We then find refutations from **T**. These refutations are used to guide the search for a refutation from **S**, by use of the above theorem. This theorem permits us to restrict the search space by deleting resolvents **C** which are not jointly subsumed by $\mathbf{Pr_d(T)}$, where **d** is the maximum depth of search. We may consider **T** as an "abstraction" of **S** in which certain information is lost. Proofs from **T** are potential abstractions of proofs from **S**. These abstract proofs may be used to guide the search for a proof from **S**.

This abstraction does not require the use of "multiclauses", which are clauses in which the same literal can occur more than once; previous abstractions did require multi-clauses. Also, there is considerable flexibility in the choice of **T**. One way to choose **T** is to include for every clause **C** in **S** a clause **D** in **T** such that **C** is an instance of **D**. Another possibility is to choose for every clause **C** in **S**, clauses D_1 and D_2 in **T** such that **C** is the union of D_1 and D_2. Furthermore, this can be done independently for different clauses of **S**. We have never fully implemented this method, which seems to be one of the more promising abstractions we have studied.

7.6 Size of Inferences

Another issue for automated deduction is the size of the inference steps. There is some advantage in using larger inference steps, since then fewer intermediate lemmas will be saved and the search space will not grow so rapidly. Hyper-resolution[92] is one way of doing this to some extent. Another such approach is the linked inference of [119]. The theory resolution of Stickel[105] is also a realization of this concept.

7.7 Relevance Tests

Choosing relevant axioms is also essential for a mechanical theorem prover. There may be hundreds or thousands of facts which could conceivably be brought to bear in the search for a proof, and a reasoning system should be able to select those assertions that are likely to be relevant. Current provers have an advantage in that the human user does this selection in most cases. Set of support methods tend to choose relevant facts because they only perform inferences that depend on the theorem, directly or indirectly. By looking at theorems proven in the past, it might be possible to select facts likely to be relevant. The relevance criterion of Plaisted[79], implemented by Jefferson[49], is another possible approach. This method was strikingly successful in finding relevant clauses from a set of hundreds of input clauses in a couple of common sense reasoning problems, in which the proofs were fairly simple. The idea is that if two clauses **C** and **D** contain literals **L** and **M**, respectively, such that not(**L**) and **M** are unifiable, then **C** and **D** are closely related. If **C** and **D** are closely related, and **D** and **E** are closely related, then **C** and **E** are somewhat less closely related. In this way we can measure how closely related two clauses are. We also say that a set of clauses is *fully matched* if for every clause **C** in the set and every literal **L** in **C** there is a clause **D** in the set and a literal **M** in **D** such that **L** and not(**M**) unify. One can show that if there is a refutation from a set **S** of clauses, then the set of clauses used in the refutation must be closely related to the theorem and fully matched, where the measure of how closely related the clauses are, depends on the length of the refutation. This idea can be used to filter the set of clauses to find a set of clauses that can contribute to a short proof, in polynomial time. This idea also can be used to detect and generate relevant *instances* of a set of clauses. Attempts to extend this methodology to more mathematical problems with longer proofs have not yet been successful. A graph based relevance method such as that of Jefferson and Plaisted[49] seems most useful when the proofs are fairly short but there are many input clauses.

7.8. General Software Engineering Issues

Since theorem provers are computer programs, general software engineering issues arise in their design. It is important to have user friendly input and output, and to choose data structures carefully. The idea of "structure sharing" is important to prevent the prover from using too much memory on hard problems. Some kind of "discrimination net" is useful to rapidly locate potentially unifiable pairs of literals. This method was used successfully in the Franz lisp resolution prover of Greenbaum and Plaisted[39] as well as in the Otter theorem prover of McCune. The use of concurrency can speed up a prover; for some work in this area see [1]. It is important for the prover to have good default switch settings so that a naive user can still obtain good results. In developing a theorem prover, empirical testing is valuable. This helps to identify which mechanisms are sufficient to handle a problem area, and to reveal factors which have been overlooked. In testing a prover, one often finds that a simple problem succeeds, while a complicated problem, taking several hours on a successful run, fails. In this case, one wants to know whether the strategy is incomplete, whether the search strategy needs to be improved, or whether the program has a bug. In such a case, a fruitful approach is to make the simple problem more and more like the complicated problem until the failure occurs, to pinpoiint the problem. This is much more time efficient than modifying the complicated problem in the hope of finding a proof. For example, a simple problem might be obtained by choosing exactly the right instances of the right clauses to get a proof. The complicated problem might have additional clauses and might not have the instances chosen. One advantage of automated deduction research is that the same theorems can be run on many provers, making a comparison of different theorem provers easy. This is not so simple in other areas of artificial intelligence, where different programs may use diffferent formalisms.

7.9. Extensions

We now consider various extensions to first order logic which may be useful in a theorem prover. One extension is that of sorts and order sorted algebra. The use of sorts can significantly improve the efficiency of a theorem prover, as well as permitting simpler axiomatizations, although order sorted logic requires a more complicated unification algorithm. For a general discussion of sorts in theorem proving, see [112]; for an example of increased efficiency due to sorts, see [111]. A theoretical discussion is given in [3]. Another extension is mathematical induction. Certain theorems are not provable without mathematical induction. For example, in first order logic it is not possible to prove that addition is commutative from the axioms defining addition in terms of the successor relation. Even though all ground instances of the equation $x+y=y+x$ may be shown, the equation cannot be derived, since in first order logic it is not possible to specify that an element is finite. The most notable example of a prover using induction is the Boyer-Moore prover[11]. This prover requires guidance from the user in the statement of a series of lemmas leading up to the theorem. The lemmas need to be chosen carefully to make proper use of the heuristics used by the program. In this prover, theorems are rewrite rules, nicely constraining the search. Also, general existential quantifiers cannot be used in this prover. The non-clausal theorem prover used in the

TABLOG system[60] also permits mathematical induction. Another extension is higher order logic, which permits quantification over functions and predicates, and permits some theorems to be stated much more naturally than first order logic. One of the more well known provers with some higher order logic capability is the prover of Andrews[65] at Carnegie-Mellon University. This prover uses Huet's unification algorithm[47] to unify higher order expressions. Lambda calculus permits higher order functions to be expressed; the lambda-Prolog system of [70] permits lambda calculus expressions to be used. This is valuable because it provides a formalism for bound variables, which are useful for formalising logic and computer programs. Finally, set theory itself is useful in a prover; it is convenient to be able to directly refer to sets of elements and prove their properties. An interesting way of embedding set theory in first order logic is given in [14]; however, this encoding is unnatural. Possibly more natural such encodings exist.

There are so many possible extensions and features for theorem provers that it becomes a problem to know how to combine them in the best way. This may be more of an engineering problem than a problem in basic research. It is surprising that theorem proving is so complicated, because the mathematical formalism on which it is based, is so simple. Many theorem provers ignore some of the important features mentioned above, such as priorities or back chaining. It is not clear that any one method will perform well on all problems. It may be possible to get a lot of intelligence into a theorem proving program simply by having a large collection of methods and alternating between them. This seems to be the approach used by humans. Some kind of meta-knowledge about which methods to apply on which problems would be useful in this context.

8. Major Theorem Proving Programs

We now discuss some of the more well known theorem proving programs, while omitting many others. We have already mentioned the Boyer-Moore theorem prover several times. This prover has recently been extended[13] to handle bounded quantifiers and partial functions. In this prover, priorities are not as important as in other provers, since rewriting controls the search fairly well. Some care is necessary, however, in stating the theorem in such a way that the prover will obtain a proof. The Argonne provers have also been mentioned several times. These are among the most user friendly and widely distributed provers in existence, and are based on resolution with many options. Andrews' prover has also been mentioned; this prover uses natural deduction higher order logic, and sorts. It uses something called "matings"[2] instead of resolution. It uses "negation normal form" rather than clause form to express the assertions. Mark Stickel has recently implemented a "Prolog technology theorem prover" that implements a version of model elimination and can perform several thousand inferences per second. Ed Clarke's PARTHENON prover[1] implements essentially the same strategy on 15 processors and obtains tens of thousands of inferences per second. Both provers are very impressive. However, the fact that the same subgoal may be solved many times without remembering the previous solutions, may be a drawback. Also, these provers do not permit term rewriting or any specialized inference rules. Bledsoe's group at the University of Texas at Austin has proven a number of respectable theorems in set theory, calculus (limit theorems), intermediate analysis, and elementary topology[8]. Most of this work has been done on "natural deduction" provers; by this term, Bledsoe denotes what Loveland calls "problem reduction formats," that is, provers that decompose a goal into subgoals and work on the subgoals recursively. Bledsoe's use of the term "natural deduction" differs from the use of this term in logic as a technical term denoting a particular proof system. Many of the proofs found by Bledsoe's provers were obtained using rewrite rules, and some of them also required specialized inference rules or heuristics for inequalities or limits. T. C. Wang has implemented a hierarchical deduction prover[114], which is essentially a combination of locking resolution[10] and set of support. This prover has obtained some impressive proofs fully automatically, without any specialized inference rules. His prover has a fairly sophisticated measure of proof complexity, which is largely responsible for its success. However, on some easier problems it does not perform as well. The NuPrl system at Cornell[23] is used for program development in a constructive logic, and is more a proof checker than a proof finder. It permits the user to specify methods to be applied to subgoals of various forms. The Prolog theorem prover of Plaisted[83] uses true back chaining, depth-first iterative deepening, and caching of solutions to subgoals to avoid repeated work. This prover solves almost as many problems as does Stickel's prover from his test set[106], but usually takes longer. By incorporating a measure of proof complexity similar to that of Wang, we are able to find proofs for many of his theorems too, such as **gcd**, **lcm**, and **am**8. By using semantics, we can obtain an automatic proof of a first order version of the intermediate value theorem. By incorporating a priority system to favor small subgoals, we can obtain three moderately hard theorems that we cannot prove otherwise. This prover also has specialized inference rules for equality and rewriting. Richard Potter[87] has obtained a number of simple set theory theorems automatically on this prover using a special method of rewriting. We have also found an automatic subgoal reordering method which reduces the average proof time for the examples we have tested. This prover is remarkably compact, in addition, and is designed to be reliable with a minimum of user guidance. The Markgraph Karl prover[28] has been mentioned earlier. In addition, there are many other provers which various researchers (including the author) have developed and which we cannot cover here.

9. Implications for Artificial Intelligence

We comment on the implications of theorem proving research for the field of artificial intelligence. We feel that there is a need to understand theorem proving in general before concentrating on specific applications. The author has been working in this area for over ten years, and only now is he starting to understand the right approaches. There is simply not time for AI researchers in various areas to develop a good general search method for each application. The generality of logic, however, makes it possible and even desirable to develop a general search program for logic and then specialize it for various applications. For this to be successful, it will be necessary to combine insights from theorem proving and artificial intelligence. In the past, theorem proving has suffered at times by not incorporating AI techniques such as heuristic search, back chaining, and semantics. Similarly, AI has at times been handicapped because its programs could not handle quantifiers, true variables, case analysis, or subsumption checks to delete specific assertions when more general ones become known.

9.1 The Frame Problem and Contexts

We now present a representation that may help to deal with the frame problem in artificial intelligence, without recourse to non-monotonic logic. This representation may also help to mechanize reasoning relative to various contexts. The representation is based on the situation calculus[38]. The "frame problem"[35] is to find a good method of specifying what does not change when an action is performed. A straightforward representation is awkward, requiring many separate "frame axioms" stating what does not change when each action is performed. The idea of our approach is that a situation has locations, and that predicates and actions refer to particular locations or sets of locations in a situation. To handle the frame problem, we specify that actions at certain locations do not influence predicates at certain other locations. Thus, by a small number of axioms about the manner in which locations interact, it is possible to constrain a large number of interactions between actions and predicates.

This general approach may be formalized as follows: We write $P(x,y,Loc(l,s))$ to indicate that predicate $P(x,y)$ holds in location l of situation s. We write $Act(a(x,y),Loc(m,s))$ to indicate the situation resulting from performing action $A(x,y)$ at location m in situation s. These locations need not be physical locations, but rather "logical" locations, used as a means of grouping together similar actions and predicates. It is then possible to specify frame axioms by a conditional equation like

$$Loc(l,Act(a,Loc(m,s)))=Loc(l,s) \text{ if not } Interfere(l,m)$$

where "interfere" is a predicate indicating which locations may influence on each other. This equation specifies that after performing action a at location m, location l has not changed, so that predicates at location l have not changed, if l and m do not interfere. Thus, if l and m do not interfere, then an action at location l will not change the truth values of predicates at location m. Also, restrictions may be placed on which actions can take place at which locations. There are a number of ways that the "interfere" relation may be axiomatized. For example, it is possible that if l and m are distinct then they do not interfere. Or the locations can be organized into a hierarchy so that an action at a location l may influence all locations m below l in the hierarchy, but no others. Or, any desired constraints between the locations may be expressed by properly axiomatizing the interfere predicate. This can be done more economically than by considering all pairs of actions and predicates on situations which is required in the usual first order representation. This is more economical because many actions and predicates can have a given location and can all be handled at once by specifying how this location interferes with others. Other possibilities are to give a predicate more than one location, possibly a set of locations. In general, this approach permits considerable flexibility in concise representations of collections of frame axioms.

10. References

[1]   Allen, P.E., Bose, S., Clarke, E.M., and Michaylov, S., PARTHENON: A parallel theorem prover for non-Horn clauses, system abstract, Proceedings of the 9th International Conference on Automated Deduction, E. Lusk and R. Overbeek, eds., Lecture Notes in Computer Science vol. 310, G. Goos and J. Hartmanis, eds. (Springer-Verlag, New York, 1988), pp. 764 - 765.

[2]   Andrews, P.B., Theorem proving via general matings, J. ACM 28 (1981)193 - 214.

[3]   Andrews, P.B., An Introduction to Mathematical Logic and Type Theory: To Truth Through Proof (Academic Press, New York, 1986).

[4]   Ballantyne, A., and Bledsoe, W., On generating and using examples in proof discovery, Machine Intelligence 10 (Harwood, Chichester, 1982) 3-39.

[5]   Bibel, W., Automated Theorem Proving, Vieweg, 1982.

[6]   Bledsoe, W.W., The sup-inf method in Presburger arithmetic, Memo ATP-18, Mathematics Dept., University of Texas at Austin, 1974.

[7]   Bledsoe, W.W., Ground resolution using anti-clauses, Report No. ATP-72, Departments of Mathematics and Computer Sciences, The University of Texas at Austin, April, 1983.

[8]   Bledsoe, W., Some automatic proofs in analysis, in Automated Theorem Proving: After 25 Years, W. Bledsoe and Donald Loveland, eds., Contemporary Mathematics, Vol. 29, American Mathematical Society, 1984, pp. 89-118.

[9]   Bledsoe, W.W., and Loveland, D.W., eds., Automated Theorem Proving: After 25 Years (American Math. Society, Providence, R.I., 1984).

[10] Boyer, R., Locking, a restriction of resolution, Ph.D. thesis, University of Texas at Austin, TX (1971).

[11] Boyer, R. and Moore, J., A Computational Logic, Academic Press, New York, 1979.

[12] Boyer, R. and Moore, J.S., Proof checking, theorem proving, and program verification, in Automated Theorem Proving: After 25 Years, W. Bledsoe and Donald Loveland, eds., Contemporary Mathematics, Vol. 29, American Mathematical Society, 1984, pp. 119 - 167.

[13] Boyer, R. and Moore, J.S., The addition of bounded quantifiers and partial functions to a computational logic and its theorem prover, J. Automated Reasoning 4 (1988) 117 - 172.

[14] Boyer, R., Lusk, E., McCune, W., Overbeek, R., Stickel, M., and Wos, L., Set theory in first order logic: clauses for Godel's axioms, Journal of Automated Reasoning 2 (1986) 287 - 327.

[15] Brand, D., Proving theorems with the modification method, SIAM J. Comput. 4 (1975) 412-430.

[16] Brock, B., Cooper, S., and Pierce, W., Anological reasoning and proof discovery, Proceedings of the 9th International Conference on Automated Deduction, E. Lusk and R. Overbeek, eds., Lecture Notes in Computer Science vol. 310, G. Goos and J. Hartmanis, eds. (Springer-Verlag, New York, 1988), pp. 454 - 468.

[17] Bundy, A., The Computer Modelling of Mathematical Reasoning (Academic Press, New York, 1983).

[18] Bundy, A., The use of explicit proof plans to guide inductive proofs, Proceedings of the 9th International Conference on Automated Deduction, E. Lusk and R. Overbeek, eds., Lecture Notes in Computer Science vol. 310, G. Goos and J. Hartmanis, eds. (Springer-Verlag, New York, 1988), pp. 111 - 120.

[19] Cantone, D., Ghelfo, S., and Omodeo, E., The automation of syllogistic I. Syllogistic normal forms, J. Symbolic Computation 6 (1988) 83 - 98.

[20] Chang, C.L., The unit proof and the input proof in theorem proving, J. ACM 17 (1970) 698 - 707.

[21] Chang, C. and Lee, R., Symbolic Logic and Mechanical Theorem Proving (Academic Press, New York, 1973).

[22] Chou, S.-C., Proving elementary geometry theorems using Wu's algorithm, in Automated Theorem Proving: After 25 Years, W. Bledsoe and Donald Loveland, eds., Contemporary Mathematics, Vol. 29, American Mathematical Society, 1984, pp. 243 - 286.

[23] Constable, R.L., Allen, S.F., Bromley, H.M. et al, Implementing Mathematics with the Nuprl Proof Development System (Prentice-Hall, Englewood Cliffs, N.J., 1986).

[24] Davis, M. and Putnam, H., A computing procedure for quantification theory, J. ACM 7:3 (1960) 201 - 215.

[25] Dershowitz, N., Orderings for term-rewriting systems, Theoretical Computer Science 17(1982)279-301.

[26] Digricoli, V. and Harrison, M., Equality-based binary resolution, J. ACM 33 (1986) 253 - 289.

[27] Eisinger, N., What you always wanted to know about clause graph resolution, Proceedings of the 8th International Conference on Automated Deduction, J. Siekmann, ed., Lecture Notes in Computer Science vol. 230, G. Goos and J. Hartmanis, eds. (Springer-Verlag, New York, 1986), pp. 316 - 336.

[28] Eisinger, N. and Ohlbach, H.J., The Markgraf Karl refutation procedure, Proceedings of the 8th International Conference on Automated Deduction, J. Siekmann, ed., Lecture Notes in Computer Science vol. 230, G. Goos and J. Hartmanis, eds. (Springer-Verlag, New York, 1986), pp. 681 - 682.

[29] Fischer, M. and Rabin, M., Super-exponential complexity of Presburger arithmetic, Proc. Symposium on the Complexity of Real Computation Processes (1973).

[30] Gallier, J., Logic for Computer Science: Foundations of Automatic Theorem Proving (Harper and Row, Philadelphia, 1986).

[31] Gallier, J., Narendran, P., Plaisted, D., and Snyder, W., Rigid E-unification is NP-complete, Proceedings of the Third Annual Symposium on Logic in Computer Science (IEEE, Piscataway, N.J., 1988), pp. 218 - 227.

[32] Gallier, J., Raatz, S., and Snyder, W., Theorem proving using rigid E-unification: equational matings, invited paper, Colloquium on the Resolution of Equations in Algebraic Structures, May 4-6, 1987, Austin, Texas.

[33] Garey, M. and Johnson, D., Computers and Intractability: A Guide to the Theory of NP-Completeness (Freeman, San Francisco, 1979).

[34] Gelernter, H., Hansen, J.R., and Loveland, D.W., Empirical explorations of the geometry theorem proving machine, in: E. Feigenbaum and J. Feldman, eds., Computers and Thought (McGraw-Hill, New York, 1963) 153 - 167.

[35] Genesereth, M. and Nilsson, N., Logical Foundations of Artificial Intelligence (Kaufmann, Los Altos, Calif., 1987).

[36] Good, D.I., London, R.L., and Bledsoe, W.W., An interactive program verification system, Proceedings of International Conference on Reliable Software, Los Angeles, California, April, 1975.

[37] Green, C., Theorem proving by resolution as a basis for question-answering systems, Machine Intelligence 4 (American Elsevier, New York, 1969), pp. 183 - 205.

[38] Green, C., Application of theorem proving to problem solving, in Webber, B.L. and Nilsson, N.J., eds., Readings in Artificial Intelligence (Kaufmann, Los Altos, Calif., 1981).

[39] Greenbaum, S., and Plaisted, D., The Illinois prover: a general purpose resolution theorem prover, extended abstract, Eighth Conference on Automated Deduction, July, 1986.

[40] Grigor'ev, D. Y. and N. N. Vorobjov, Solving systems of polynomial inequalities in subexponential time, J. Symbolic Computation 5 (1988) 37 - 64.

[41] Guard, J.R., Oglesby, F.C., Bennett, J.H., and Settle, L.G., Semi-automated mathematics, J. ACM 18 (1969) 49 - 62.

[42] Henschen, L. and Wos, L., Unit refutations and Horn sets, J. ACM 21 (1974) 590-605.

[43] Hopcroft, J. and Ullman, J., Introduction to Automata Theory, Languages, and Computation (Addison-Wesley, Reading, Mass., 1979).

[44] Hsiang, J., Refutational theorem proving using term rewriting systems, Artificial Intelligence 25 (1985) 255 - 300.

[45] Hsiang, J. and Dershowitz, N., Rewrite methods for clausal and non-clausal theorem proving, Proc. 10th EATCS Intl. Colloq. on Automata, Languages, and Programming, Barcelona, Spain, 1983.

[46] Hsiang, J. and Rusinowitch, M., A new method for establishing refutational completeness in theorem proving, Proceedings of the 8th International Conference on Automated Deduction, J. Siekmann, ed., Lecture Notes in Computer Science vol. 230, G. Goos and J. Hartmanis, eds. (Springer-Verlag, New York, 1986), pp. 141 - 152.

[47] Huet, G., A unification algorithm for typed lambda calculus, Theoretical Computer Science 1 (1975) 27-57.

[48] Hunt, Warren A., FM8501: A Verified Microprocessor, Institute for Computing Science, The University of Texas at Austin, Austin, Texas 78712, Technical Report 47, February, 1986, 254 pp.

[49] Jefferson, S. and Plaisted, D., Implementation of an improved relevance criterion, First Conference on Artificial Intelligence Applications, Denver, Colorado, December, 1984, 7 pp.

[50] Karmakar, N., A new polynomial time algorithm for linear programming, Combinatorica 4 (1984) 373 - 395.

[51] Khachian, L.G., A polynomial algorithm in linear programming, Doklady Akademii Nauk, USSR, Nova Seria, 244 (1979) 1093 - 1096, translated in Soviet Mathematics Doklady 20 (1979) 191 - 194.

[52] Kling, R., A paradigm for reasoning by analogy, Artificial Intelligence 2 (1971) 147-178.

[53] Korf, R.E., Depth-first iterative deepening: an optimal admissible tree search, Artificial Intelligence 27 (1985) 97 - 109.

[54] Loveland, D., A simplified format for the model elimination procedure, J. ACM 16 (1969) 349 - 363.

[55] Loveland, D., Automated Theorem Proving: A Logical Basis (North-Holland, New York, 1978).

[56] Loveland, D., Automated theorem proving: a quarter century review, in Automated Theorem Proving: After 25 Years, W. Bledsoe and D. Loveland, eds., (American Mathematical Society, Providence, RI, 1984), pp. 1-45.

[57] Loveland, D., Near-Horn Prolog, Proceedings of the Fourth International Conference on Logic Programming, Melbourne, Australia, 1987, pp. 456 - 469.

[58] Lusk, E., McCune, W., and Overbeek, R., ITP at Argonne National Laboratory, 8th International Conference on Automated Deduction, Oxford, England, 1986, pp. 697 - 698.

[59] Malachi, Y., Manna, Z., and Waldinger, R., TABLOG: The deductive-tableau programming language, in ACM Symp. LISP and Functional Prog., Austin, Texas, 1984, pp. 323-330.

[60] Malachi, Y., Manna, Z., and Waldinger, R.J., TABLOG: The deductive tableau programming language, in Logic Programming, D. DeGroot and G. Lindstrom, eds. (Prentice-Hall, Englewood Cliffs, N.J., 1986), pp. 365 - 394.

[61] Martelli, A., and Montanari, U., An efficient unification algorithm, ACM Trans. Programming Languages and Systems 4 (1982) 258 - 282.

[62] McCharen, J., Overbeek, R., and Wos, L., Problems and experiments for and with automated theorem proving programs, IEEE Transactions on Computers C - 25 (1976) 773 - 782.

[63] McCune, W. and Wos, L., A case study in automated theorem proving: finding sages in combinatory logic, Journal of Automated Reasoning 3 (1987) 91 - 107.

[64] McRobbie, M., Meyer, R., and Thistlewaite, P., Towards efficient "knowledge based" automated theorem proving for non-standard logics, Proceedings of the 9th International Conference on Automated Deduction, E. Lusk and R. Overbeek, eds., Lecture Notes in Computer Science vol. 310, G. Goos and J. Hartmanis, eds. (Springer-Verlag, New York, 1988), pp. 197 - 217.

[65] Miller, D., Cohen, E., and Andrews, P.B., A look at TPS, Proceedings of the 6th Conference on Automated Deduction, D.W. Loveland, ed., Lecture Notes in Computer Science vol. 138, G. Goos and J. Hartmanis, eds. (Springer-Verlag, New York, 1982), pp. 50 - 69.

[66] Mitchell, T.M., Keller, R.M., and Kedar-Cabelli, S.T., Explanation-bsed generalization: a unifying view, Machine Learning 1 (1986) 47 - 80.

[67] Mitra, G., Tamiz, M., and Yadegar, J., Experimental investigation of an interior search method within a simplex framework, C. ACM 31 (1988) 1474 - 1482.

[68] Moore, R.C., A formal theory of knowledge and action, in Hobbs, J.R. and Moore, R.C., eds., Formal Theories of the Commonsense World (Ablex, Norwood, N.J., 1985).

[69] Moser, L., A decision procedure for unquantified formulas of graph theory, Proceedings of the 9th International Conference on Automated Deduction, E. Lusk and R. Overbeek, eds., Lecture Notes in Computer Science vol. 310, G. Goos and J. Hartmanis, eds. (Springer-Verlag, New York, 1988), pp. 344 - 357.

[70] Nadathur, G. and Miller, D., An overview of lambda Prolog, in 5th International Logic Programming Conference, Seattle, Wash., August, 1988, pp. 810 - 827.

[71] Nelson, G., Combining satisfiability procedures by equality sharing, in Automated Theorem Proving: After 25 Years, W. Bledsoe and D. Loveland, eds., Contemporary Mathematics, Vol. 29, American Mathematical Society, pp. 201 - 211.

[72] Nelson, G. and Oppen, D., Simplification by cooperating decision procedures, ACM Transactions on Programming Languages and Systems 1 (1979) 245-257.

[73] Nelson, G. and Oppen, D. Fast decision procedures based on congruence closure, J. ACM 27(1980)356 - 364.

[74] Nilsson, N.J., Principles of Artificial Intelligence (Tioga, Palo Alto, Calif., 1980).

[75] Ohlbach, H., A resolution calculus for modal logics, Proceedings of the 9th International Conference on Automated Deduction, E. Lusk and R. Overbeek, eds., Lecture Notes in Computer Science vol. 310, G. Goos and J. Hartmanis, eds. (Springer-Verlag, New York, 1988), pp. 500 - 516.

[76] Oppen, D., Complexity, convexity, and combinations of theories, Theoretical Computer Science 12 (1980) 291 - 302.

[77] Overbeek, R., A new class of automated theorem-proving algorithms, J. ACM 21 (1974) 191-200.

[78] Peterson, G.E., A technique for establishing completeness results in theorem proving with equality, SIAM J. Computing 12 (1983) 82-100.

[79] Plaisted, D., An efficient relevance criterion for mechanical theorem proving, Proceedings of the First Annual National Conference on Artificial Intelligence, Stanford University, August, 1980, pp. 79-83.

[80] Plaisted, D., Theorem proving with abstraction, Artificial Intelligence 16 (1981) 47 - 108.

[81] Plaisted, D., A simplified problem reduction format, Artificial Intelligence 18 (1982) 227-261.

[82] Plaisted, D., Abstraction using generalization functions, Eighth Conference on Automated Deduction, Oxford, England, July, 1986.

[83] Plaisted, D., Non-Horn clause logic programming without contrapositives, Journal of Automated Reasoning 4 (1988) 287 - 325.

[84] Plaisted, D., A sequent style model elimination strategy and a positive refinement, May, 1988, to appear in Journal of Automated Reasoning.

[85] Plaisted, D., and Greenbaum, S., A structure-preserving clause form translation, Journal of Symbolic Computation 2 (1986) 293 - 304.

[86] Plotkin, G.D., Building-in equational theories, Machine Intelligence 7 (Meltzer and Michie, eds.), Halsted Press, New York, 1972, 73 - 90.

[87] Potter, R. and Plaisted, D., Term rewriting: some experimental results, Proceedings of the 9th International Conference on Automated Deduction, E. Lusk and R. Overbeek, eds., Lecture Notes in Computer Science vol. 310, G. Goos and J. Hartmanis, eds. (Springer-Verlag, New York, 1988), pp. 435 - 453.

[88] Proceedings of the 9th International Conference on Automated Deduction, E. Lusk and R. Overbeek, eds., Lecture Notes in Computer Science vol. 310, G. Goos and J. Hartmanis, eds. (Springer-Verlag, New York, 1988), pp. 704 - 734.

[89] Quaife, A., Automated proofs of Löb's theorem and Gödel's two incompleteness theorems, J. Automated Reasoning 4 (1988) 219 - 231.

[90] Rabinov, A., A restriction of factoring in binary resolution, Proceedings of the 9th International Conference on Automated Deduction, E. Lusk and R. Overbeek, eds., Lecture Notes in Computer Science vol. 310, G. Goos and J. Hartmanis, eds. (Springer-Verlag, New York, 1988), pp. 582 - 591.

[91] Robinson, J., A machine oriented logic based on the resolution principle, J. ACM 12 (1965) 23-41.

[92] Robinson, J., Automatic deduction with hyper-resolution, Int. J. Comput. Math. 1 (1965) 227-234.

[93] Sacerdoti, E., Planning in a hierarchy of abstraction spaces, Artificial Intelligence 5 (1974) 115-135.

[94] Schmidt-Schauss, M., Unification in a combination of arbitrary disjoint equational theories, Proceedings of the 9th International Conference on Automated Deduction, E. Lusk and R. Overbeek, eds., Lecture Notes in Computer Science vol. 310, G. Goos and J. Hartmanis, eds. (Springer-Verlag, New York, 1988), pp. 378 - 396.

[95] Shankar, N., A mechanical proof of the Church-Rosser theorem, J. ACM 35 (1988) 475 - 522.

[96] Shostak, R., Schwartz, R., and Melliar-Smith, P.M., STP: a mechanizable logic for specification and verification, Proceedings of the 6th Conference on Automated Deduction, D.W. Loveland, ed., Lecture Notes in Computer Science vol. 138, G. Goos and J. Hartmanis, eds. (Springer-Verlag, New York, 1982), pp. 32 - 49

[97] Shostak, R.E., Deciding combinations of theories, J. ACM 31 (1984) 1 - 12.

[98] Siekmann, J, Unification theory, Proceedings of European Conference on Artificial Intelligence, 1986.

[99] Siekmann, J. and Szabo, P., Universal unification and a classification of equational theories, 6th Conference on Automated Deduction, New York, 1982, in Lecture Notes in Computer Science 138, G. Goos and J. Hartmanis, eds. (Springer-Verlag, New York, 1982), pp. 369-389.

[100] Sistla, A.P. and Clarke, E.M., The complexity of propositional linear temporal logics, J. ACM 32 (1985) 733 - 749.

[101] Slagle, J.R., Automatic theorem proving with renamable and semantic resolution, J. ACM 14 (1967) 687 - 697.

[102] Smith, M. and Plaisted, D., Term-rewriting techniques for logic programming I: completion, Report No. TR88 - 019, University of North Carolina at Chapel Hill, April, 1988.

[103] Stickel, M., A unification algorithm for associative-commutative functions, J. ACM 28 (1981)423 - 434.

[104] Stickel, M., A case study of theorem proving by the Knuth-Bendix Method: discovering that $x^3 = x$ implies ring commutativity, Proceedings of the 7th Conference in Automated

Deduction, R. Shostak, ed., Lecture Notes in Computer Science 170, G. Goos and J. Hartmanis, eds. (Springer-Verlag, New York, 1984), pp. 248-258.

[105] Stickel, M., Automated deduction by theory resolution, Journal of Automated Reasoning 1 (1985) 333 - 355.

[106] Stickel, M., A PROLOG technology theorem prover: implementation by an extended PROLOG compiler, Proceedings of the Eight International Conference in Automated Deduction, Oxford, England, July 1986, pp. 573-587.

[107] Stickel, M. and Tyson, W.M., An analysis of consecutively bounded depth-first search with applications in automated deduction. Proceedings of the Ninth International Joint Conference on Artificial Intelligence, Los Angeles, California, August, 1985, pp. 1073 - 1075.

[108] Suzuki, N., Verifying programs by algebraic and logical reduction, Proceedings of International Conference on Reliable Software, Los Angeles, California, April, 1975, pp. 473 - 481.

[109] Tarski, A., A Decision Method for Ordinary Algebra and Geometry, (University of California Press, 1951).

[110] Van Gelder, A., A satisfiability tester for non-clausal propositional calculus, Proceedings of the 7th International Conference on Automated Deduction, R. E. Shostak, ed., Lecture Notes in Computer Science vol. 170, G. Goos and J. Hartmanis, eds. (Springer-Verlag, New York, 1984).

[111] Walther, C., Schubert's Steamroller - a case study in many sorted resolution, technical report, Institut for Informatik, May, 1984.

[112] Walther, C., A Many-sorted Calculus Based on Resolution and Paramodulation, Research Notes in Artificial Intelligence (Kaufmann, Los Altos, Calif., 1987).

[113] Wang, T.C., Elements of Z module reasoning, Proceedings of the 9th International Conference on Automated Deduction, E. Lusk and R. Overbeek, eds., Lecture Notes in Computer Science vol. 310, G. Goos and J. Hartmanis, eds. (Springer-Verlag, New York, 1988), pp. 21 - 40.

[114] Wang, T.C. and Bledsoe, W.W., Hierarchical deduction, Journal of Automated Reasoning 3 (1987) 35 - 77.

[115] Winker, S., Generation and verification of finite models and counterexamples using an automated theorem prover answering two open questions, J. ACM 29 (1982) 273 - 284.

[116] Wos, L., Overbeek, R., Lusk, E., and Boyle, J., Automated Reasoning: Introduction and Applications (Prentice-Hall, New Jersey, 1984).

[117] Wos, L., Robinson, G., and Carson, D., Efficiency and completeness of the set of support strategy in theorem proving, J. ACM 12 (1965) 536 - 541.

[118] Wos, L., Robinson, G., Carson, D., and Shalla, L., The concept of demodulation in theorem proving, J. ACM 14 (1967) 698-709.

[119] Wos, L., Veroff, R., Smith, B., and McCune, W., The linked inference principle, II: the user's viewpoint, Proceedings of the 9th International Conference on Automated Deduction, E. Lusk and R. Overbeek, eds., Lecture Notes in Computer Science vol. 310, G. Goos and J. Hartmanis, eds. (Springer-Verlag, New York, 1988), pp. 316 - 332.

[120] Wos, L. and Winker, S., Open questions solved with the assistance of AURA, in Automated Theorem Proving: After 25 Years, W. Bledsoe and D. Loveland, eds., American Mathematical Society, Providence, RI, 1984, pp. 73-88.

[121] Wu, Went-tsün, On the decision problem and the mechanization of theorem proving in elementary geometry, Scientia Sinica 21 (1978) 159 - 172.

[122] Zhang, H. and Kapur, D., First order theorem proving using conditional rewrite rules, Proceedings of the 9th International Conference on Automated Deduction, E. Lusk and R. Overbeek, eds., Lecture Notes in Computer Science vol. 310, G. Goos and J. Hartmanis, eds. (Springer-Verlag, New York, 1988), pp. 1 - 20.

Formal Techniques in Artificial Intelligence
A Sourcebook. R.B. Banerji (editor)
© Elsevier Science Publishers B.V. (North-Holland), 1990

Semantic Issues in Deductive Databases and Logic Programs

Halina Przymusinska
Department of Computer Science
The University of Texas at El Paso
(fp00@utep.bitnet)

Teodor Przymusinski
Department of Mathematical Sciences
The University of Texas at El Paso
(teodor%utep.uucp@cs.utexas.edu)

To our sons Lukasz and Marcel with love

1   Introduction

The theory of *deductive databases* traces its beginnings to the fundamental paper written by Codd [Codd, 1970] in which formal foundations of the so called *relational databases* have been first outlined. A relational database is a collection of *individual facts (data)*, equipped with the capability to efficiently manipulate (update) its contents and to answer queries about it. Typically, *relational algebra* is used to implement those functions.

In the middle of 1970's it was realized, however, that, in spite of their great usefulness, the capabilities of relational databases are severely limited by their inability to handle *deductive* and *incomplete* information. The need for *deductive reasoning* stems from the fact that we often want to be able to deduce *new* information from the *facts* already present in the database and from *deductive rules*, which are known to us and which we could include in the database. Unfortunatelly, relational databases do not have the capability to store and handle sufficiently general deductive rules. The necessity to deal with *incomplete information* is due to the fact that our knowledge is often incomplete and therefore we are forced to derive conclusions in the absence of complete information. This phenomenon is particularly evident in the case of *disjuctive* and *negative* information. Again, relational databases do not provide the capability to deal with this problem.

The above realization led to the concept of *deductive databases*, which, in addition to storing individual facts (extensional data), can store and manipulate deductive rules of reasoning (intensional data) and are able to answer queries based on logical derivation coupled with some mechanism for handling incomplete information. The initial impetus to the new field has been given by the first Workshop on Logic and Databases held in Toulouse in 1977 [Gallaire and Minker, 1978]. Several years later, Reiter made a first attempt at providing a theoretical foundation for deductive databases [Reiter, 1984] and the first survey of the field appeared [Gallaire *et al.*, 1984]. The area has been developing rapidly during the following years. In particular, the first comprehensive book on the subject [Ullman, 1988] has been recently published and implementation of large experimental database systems [Morris *et al.*, 1986; Zaniolo, 1988] has begun.

More information on the historical perspective of the field can be found in [Minker, 1988b].

Logic programming was introduced in the early 1970's by Colmerauer [Colmerauer et al., 1973] and Kowalski [Kowalski, 1974] and the first Prolog interpreter was implemented by Roussel in 1972 [Roussel, 1975]. Logic programming introduced to computer science the important concept of *declarative* – as opposed to *procedural* – programming. It is based on Kowalski's principle of *separation of logic and control* [Kowalski, 1974; Kowalski, 1979]. Ideally, a programmer should be only concerned with the *declarative meaning* of his program, while the procedural aspects of program's execution are handled automatically.

Late 1970's witnessed the beginning of the development of formal foundations of logic programming, starting with the classical papers by Van Emden and Kowalski on the least model semantics [Van Emden and Kowalski, 1976], Clark's work on program completion [Clark, 1978] and Reiter's paper on the closed world assumption [Reiter, 1978]. Further progress in this direction was achieved in the early 1980's (e.g., [Apt and Van Emden, 1982; Jaffar et al., 1983]) leading to the appearance of the first book devoted to foundations of logic programming [Lloyd, 1984; Lloyd, 1987]. The selection of Prolog as the underlying language of the Japanese Fifth Generation Computers Project in 1982 led to a much greater visibility of logic programming and rapid proliferation of various logic programming languages – especially Prolog.

It has quickly become clear that logic programming and deductive databases are closely related [Reiter, 1984; Gallaire et al., 1984; Lloyd and Topor, 1985; Lloyd and Topor, 1986; Minker, 1988a] and that they are based on very similar theoretical foundations. Their introduction and subsequent development of their formal foundations has been an outgrowth and an unquestionable success of the *logical approach* to *knowledge representation*. This approach is based on the idea of providing intelligent machines with a *logical specification* of the knowledge that they possess, thus making it independent of any particular implementation, context-free, and easy to manipulate, exchange and reason about.

Consequently, a precise *meaning* or *semantics* must be associated with any logic or database program in order to provide its declarative specification. The performance of any *computational mechanism* is then evaluated by comparing its behavior to the *specification* provided by the declarative semantics. This does not mean that such a computational mechanism must necessarily be based on some logical proof procedure, such as, for example, resolution. It implies however, that *logic is the final arbiter of its correctness* [Reiter, 1984].

Finding a suitable declarative or intended semantics of deductive databases and logic programs is one of the most important and difficult research problems and is the main topic of this paper. In particular, the paper reports on a very significant progress made recently in this area. It also presents some results which have not yet appeared in print.

The paper is organized as follows. In the next two sections we define deductive databases and logic programs. Subsequently, in Sections 4 and 5, we discuss model theory and fixed points, which play a crucial role in the definition of semantics. Section 6 is the main section of the paper and is entirely devoted to a systematic exposition and comparison of various proposed semantics. In Section 7 we discuss the relationship between declarative semantics of deductive databases and logic programs and non-monotonic reasoning. Section 8 contains concluding remarks.

2 Deductive Databases

By a *deductive database* $\overline{P}$ we mean a triple:

$$\overline{P} =< P, SEM(P), IC >$$

where P is a *logic program* (also called a *database program*), SEM(P) is the *declarative semantics* of P and IC represents the *integrity constraints*.

Logic (or database) programs P consist of finitely many clauses and are defined in the next section. Semantics SEM(P) of a program P is the intended meaning of P and usually is defined either as a completion COMP(P) of the program P or as an intended model M_P or a set of intended models $MOD(P)$ of P. The problem of finding a suitable semantics $SEM(P)$ for a program P and a discussion of some of the proposed solutions is the main topic of this paper and is investigated in great detail in the sequel. However, any semantics is assumed to logically imply all formulae from P:

$$SEM(P) \models P.$$

Integrity constraints usually consist of a finite set of (closed) first order formulae and are supposed to be at all times satisfied by the semantics SEM(P) of the program P:

$$SEM(P) \models IC.$$

Although there is no way to precisely differentiate between formulae which should be considered as integrity constraints and those which should be made part of the program, nevertheless the overall distinction between the respective roles of the program P and the integrity constraints IC is quite essential:

- Integrity constraints do not directly affect the semantics SEM(P) of the database $\overline{P}$, which is entirely determined by the program P. Instead, they are used only to verify the integrity of the program P. Namely, any program P whose semantics SEM(P) does not satisfy the integrity constraints IC is considered to violate the imposed constraints and is therefore rejected. This is in contrast to the fact that updates (changes) to the program P itself generally lead to immediate changes of the semantics SEM(P).

- Once the integrity of the program P has been established, integrity constraints are no longer needed for query answering, which depends entirely on SEM(P).

- Integrity constraints describe properties and relations which are supposed to be satisfied at all times by the program and therefore they remain largely static. On the other hand, the database program P usually changes frequently due to various updates (deletions, insertions etc.).

- Integrity constraints may, in general, include arbitrary first order formulae, whereas programs usually consist of sets of clauses.

For example, if P is any logic program, then we could define the semantics SEM(P) of P as the Clark completion *comp(P)* of the program [Clark, 1978] and the integrity constraints IC to consist of the so called Clark Equality Axioms (see [Lloyd, 1984; Kunen, 1987; Przymusinski, 1989c]).

3   Logic Programs

By an *alphabet* $\mathcal{A}$ of a first order language $\mathcal{L}$ we mean a (finite or countably infinite) set of *constant, predicate* and *function* symbols[1]. In addition, any alphabet is assumed to contain a countably infinite set of *variable* symbols, connectives $(\wedge, \vee, \neg, \leftarrow)$, quantifiers $(\exists, \forall)$ and the usual punctuation symbols. A *term* over $\mathcal{A}$ is defined recursively as either a variable or a constant or an expression of the form $f(t_1, \ldots, t_k)$, where f is a function symbol and t_i's are terms. An *atom* over $\mathcal{A}$ is an expression of the form $p(t_1, \ldots, t_k)$, where p is a predicate symbol and t_i's are terms. The *first order language* $\mathcal{L}$ over the alphabet $\mathcal{A}$ is defined as the set of all well-formed first order formulae that can be built starting from the atoms and using connectives, quantifiers and punctuation symbols in a standard way. A *literal* is an atom or its negation. An atom A is called a *positive literal* and its negation $\neg A$ is called a *negative literal*. An expression is called *ground* if it does not contain any variables. The set of all ground atoms of $\mathcal{A}$ is called the *Herbrand base* $\mathcal{H}$ of $\mathcal{A}$. If G is a quantifier-free formula, then by its *ground instance* we mean any ground formula obtained from G by substituting ground terms for all variables. For a given formula G of $\mathcal{L}$ its *universal closure* or just *closure* $(\forall)G$ is obtained by universally quantifying all variables in G which are not bound by any quantifier. Unless otherwise stated, all formulae are assumed to be *closed*.

By a *logic program* we mean a finite set of universally closed *clauses* of the form

$$A \leftarrow L_1 \wedge \ldots \wedge L_m$$

where $m \geq 0$, A is an atom and L_i's are literals. Literals L_i are called *premises* and the atom A is called the *head* of the clause. Conforming to a standard convention, conjunctions are replaced by commas and therefore clauses are written in the form

$$A \leftarrow L_1, \ldots, L_m.$$

Logic programs constituting parts of deductive databases will be also called *database programs*. A program P is *positive* (or definite or Horn) if all of its clauses contain only positive premises. A positive program P without function symbols is called a *datalog* program and a function-less program which is not positive is called a *datalog program with negation (datalog$\neg$)*.

If P is a program then, unless stated otherwise, we will assume that the alphabet $\mathcal{A}$ used to write P consists precisely of all the constant, predicate and function symbols that explicitly *appear* in P and thus $\mathcal{A} = \mathcal{A}_P$ is completely determined[2] by the program P. We can then talk about the first order *language* $\mathcal{L} = \mathcal{L}_P$ *of the program* P and the *Herbrand base* $\mathcal{H} = \mathcal{H}_P$ *of the program*.

It is always possible, by means of a simple transformation of a given database program P, to assume that the set S of all predicate symbols in the alphabet $\mathcal{A}$ is decomposed into two disjoint subsets S_E and S_I of the so called *extensional* and *intensional* predicates so that if P_E is the set of all clauses from P, whose heads belong to S_E and if P_I is the remaining set of clauses, namely those clauses whose heads belong to S_E, then P_E consists entirely of ground atomic formulae and P_I does not contain any

---

[1] The set of function symbols may be empty while the sets of constant and predicate symbols are assumed to be non-empty.

[2] If there are no constants in P then one is added to the alphabet.

ground atomic formulae. The subprogram P_E is called the *extensional part* of P and P_I is the *intensional part* of P. This division is quite important for data menagement and query processing. The intensional part P_I is usually assumed to be relatively small and fairly static and it represents the *deductive* component of the program. The extensional part P_E is normally relatively large, subject to extensive changes (insertions, deletions etc.) and represents the *relational* component of the database. From the semantic point of view, however, the distinction between extensional and intensional parts is irrelevant.

4 Model Theory

Throughout most of the paper, we consider only *Herbrand* interpretations and models; the *equality predicate* = (if present) is interpreted as identity. In Section 6.8 we discuss the role and importance of non-Herbrand interpretations.

Definition 4.1 *By a* (2-valued) Herbrand interpretation I *of* $\mathcal{L}$ *we mean any set of ground atoms, i.e., any subset of the Herbrand base* $\mathcal{H}$.

Clearly, any (2-valued) interpretation I can be equivalently viewed as a tuple $< T, F >$, where T and F are disjoint subsets of the Herbrand base $\mathcal{H}$, T is the set of atoms which are true in I (i.e., those that belong to I) and F is the set of atoms which are false in I (i.e., those that do not belong to I). Interpretations I defined above are called *2-valued* because they satisfy the condition $\mathcal{H} = T \cup F$ and thus assign to every ground atom either the value *true* or *false*.

Interpretations or, more precisely, models of a given theory T can be thought of as "possible worlds" representing possible states of our knowledge about T. Since, at any given moment, our knowledge about the world is likely to be incomplete, we need the ability to describe possible worlds in which some facts are neither true nor false but rather *unknown or undefined*. That is why we need *3-valued* interpretations and models to describe possible states of our knowledge.

The notion of a 3-valued interpretation is a straightforward extension of the 2-valued definition obtained by removing the requirement that $\mathcal{H} = T \cup F$.

Definition 4.2 *By a* 3-valued Herbrand interpretation I *of the language* $\mathcal{L}$ *we mean any pair* $< T; F >$, *where* T *and* F *are disjoint subsets of the Herbrand base* $\mathcal{H}$. *The set* T *contains all ground atoms true in I, the set* F *contains all ground atoms false in I and the truth value of the remaining atoms in* $U = \mathcal{H} - (T \cup F)$ *is unknown (or undefined).*

Thus a 3-valued interpretation is 2-valued iff $\mathcal{H} = T \cup F$ or, equivalently, iff $U = \emptyset$. The following proposition is obvious.

Proposition 4.1 *Any interpretation* $I = < T, F >$ *can be equivalently viewed as a function* $I : \mathcal{H} \to \{0, \frac{1}{2}, 1\}$, *from the Herbrand base* $\mathcal{H}$ *to the 3-element set* $\mathcal{V} = \{0, \frac{1}{2}, 1\}$, *defined by:*

$$I(A) = \begin{cases} 0, & \text{if } A \in F \\ \frac{1}{2}, & \text{if } A \in U \\ 1, & \text{if } A \in T. \end{cases}$$

An interpretation I *is 2-valued iff* I *maps* $\mathcal{H}$ *into the 2-element set* $\{0,1\}$.

Unless stated otherwise, 3-valued interpretations will be viewed as 3-valued functions into $\mathcal{V}$. The function (interpretation) $I : \mathcal{H} \to \mathcal{V}$ can be be recursively extended to the truth valuation $\hat{I} : C \to \mathcal{V}$ defined on the set C of all closed formulae of the language.

Definition 4.3 *If I is an interpretation, then the truth valuation $\hat{I}$ corresponding to I is a function $\hat{I} : C \to \mathcal{V}$ from the set C of all (closed) formulae of the language to $\mathcal{V}$ recursively defined as follows:*

- *If A is a ground atom, then $\hat{I}(A) = I(A)$.*

- *If S is a formula then $\hat{I}(\neg S) = 1 - \hat{I}(S)$.*

- *If S and V are formulae, then*

$$\hat{I}(S \wedge V) = min(\hat{I}(S), \hat{I}(V));$$
$$\hat{I}(S \vee V) = max\{\hat{I}(S), \hat{I}(V)\};$$
$$\hat{I}(V \leftarrow S) = \begin{cases} 1, & if \ \hat{I}(V) \geq \hat{I}(S) \\ 0, & otherwise. \end{cases}$$

- *For any formula $S(x)$ with one unbounded variable x:*

$$\hat{I}(\forall x \ S(x)) = min\{\hat{I}(S(A)) : A \in \mathcal{H}\};$$
$$\hat{I}(\exists x \ S(x)) = max\{\hat{I}(S(A)) : A \in \mathcal{H}\};$$

where the maximum (resp. minimum) of an empty set is defined as 0 (resp. 1).

Truth valuations assign to every formula F a number $0, \frac{1}{2}$ or 1, which reflects the *degree of truth* of F, ranging from the lowest, namely *false* (0), through *unknown* ($\frac{1}{2}$), to the highest, namely *true* (1).

Remark 4.1 *Our definition of the truth valuation $\hat{I}$ for the connectives $\vee, \wedge, \neg$ and for the quantifiers $\forall, \exists$ uses the so called Kleene tables [Kleene, 1952] and the truth valuation for the connective $\leftarrow$ uses the so called weak Kleene table (suggested earlier by Lukasiewicz) [Kleene, 1952]. In this respect, our approach essentially coincides with the approach proposed in [Fitting, 1985] and later applied in [Kunen, 1987]. However, since the primary goal of [Fitting, 1985; Kunen, 1987] was to define 3-valued extensions of the Clark predicate completion semantics, Fitting and Kunen considered 3-valued models of the Clark completion comp(P) of a logic program P rather than 3-valued models of the program P itself. They also considered a different ordering of truth values based on the degree of information rather than on the degree of truth. Under this ordering, the 'unknown' value is less than both values 'true' and 'false', with 'true' and 'false' being incompatible. As we will see below, this discrepancy immediately leads to different notions of minimality of a model.*

Definition 4.4 *A theory over $\mathcal{L}$ is a (finite or infinite) set of closed formulae of $\mathcal{L}$. An interpretation I is a (2-valued or 3-valued) model of a theory R if $\hat{I}(S) = 1$, for all formulae S in R.*

Clearly, every program P is a theory. The following proposition is immediate.

Proposition 4.2 *An (Herbrand) interpretation M is a model of a program P if and only if for every ground instance*

$$A \leftarrow L_1, \ldots, L_m$$

of a program clause we have

$$\hat{M}(A) \geq min\{\hat{M}(L_i) : i \leq m\}.$$

Thus, M is a model of a program if and only if the degree of truth of the head of every clause is at least as high as the degree of truth of the conjunction of its premises. By a *ground instantiation* of a logic program P we mean the (possibly infinite) theory consisting of all ground instances of clauses from P.

Corollary 4.1 *An (Herbrand) interpretation M is a model of a program P if and only if it is a model of its ground instantiation.*

The above corollary shows that for model-theoretic purposes (as long as only Herbrand interpretations are considered) one can identify any program P with its ground instantiation. Whenever convenient, we will assume, without further mention, that the program P has already been instantiated.

We now define additional connectives $(\leftrightarrow, \Leftarrow, \Leftrightarrow)$ in the usual way

$$\begin{aligned} S \leftrightarrow V &\equiv (S \leftarrow V) \wedge (V \leftarrow S); \\ V \Leftarrow S &\equiv V \vee \neg S; \\ S \Leftrightarrow V &\equiv (S \Leftarrow V) \wedge (V \Leftarrow S); \end{aligned}$$

where V and S are any two formulae.

Notice, that, although the two implications "$V \leftarrow S$" and "$V \Leftarrow S$" have the same 2-valued models, in general, they have different 3-valued models. Indeed, $\hat{M}(V \leftarrow V) = 1$ no matter what the truth value of V under $\hat{M}$ is, but $\hat{M}(V \Leftarrow V) = \frac{1}{2}$ if $\hat{M}(V) = \frac{1}{2}$. This reflects the fact that in 3-valued logic we have at least two natural notions of implication, which are applicable in different contexts. Similar remarks apply to the two associated equivalence connectives $\leftrightarrow$ and $\Leftrightarrow$.

Observe, however, that in the definition of a program clause we use the implication symbol $\leftarrow$ rather than $\Leftarrow$, because we want the trivial clause $S \leftarrow S$ to be satisfied in every interpretation, regardless of the truth value of S.

Definition 4.5 *[Przymusinski, 1989a] If I and J are two interpretations then we say that $I \preceq J$ if*

$$I(A) \leq J(A) \quad (or, \ equivalently, \quad \hat{I}(A) \leq \hat{J}(A))$$

for any ground atom A. If $\mathcal{I}$ is a collection of interpretations, then an interpretation $I \in \mathcal{I}$ is called minimal *in $\mathcal{I}$ if there is no interpretation $J \in \mathcal{I}$ such that $J \preceq I$ and $J \neq I$. An interpretation I is called* least *in $\mathcal{I}$ if $I \preceq J$, for any other interpretation $J \in \mathcal{I}$. A model M of a theory R is called* minimal *(resp.* least*) if it is minimal (resp. least) among all models of R.*

Proposition 4.3 *If* $I =< T; F >$ *and* $I' =< T'; F' >$ *are two interpretations, then* $I \preceq I'$ *iff* $T \subseteq T'$ *and* $F \supseteq F'$. *In particular, for 2-valued interpretations,* $I \preceq I'$ *iff* $I \subseteq I'$.

Thus $I \preceq I'$ if and only if I has no more true facts and no less false facts than I'. This means that minimal and least models of a theory R minimize the *degree of truth* of their atoms, by minimizing the set T of true atoms and maximizing the set F of false atoms F. In particular, the least interpretation in the set of all interpretations is given by $I =< \emptyset, \mathcal{H} >$.

As we mentioned above, [Fitting, 1985] considers a different ordering of truth values based on the *degree of information* rather than on the *degree of truth*. Under this ordering, the 'unknown' value is less than both values 'true' and 'false', with 'true' and 'false' being incompatible. This immediately leads to a different ordering between interpretations and to different notions of minimal and least models.

Definition 4.6 *[Fitting, 1985] If* $I =< T; F >$ *and* $I' =< T'; F' >$ *are two interpretations, then we say that* $I \preceq_F I'$ *iff* $T \subseteq T'$ *and* $F \subseteq F'$. *We call this ordering the F-ordering. If* $\mathcal{I}$ *is a collection of interpretations, then an interpretation* $I \in \mathcal{I}$ *is called F-minimal in* $\mathcal{I}$ *if there is no interpretation* $J \in \mathcal{I}$ *such that* $J \preceq_F I$ *and* $J \neq I$. *An interpretation* I *is called F-least in* $\mathcal{I}$ *if* $I \preceq_F J$, *for any other interpretation* $J \in \mathcal{I}$. *A model M of a theory R is called F-minimal (resp. F-least) if it is F-minimal (resp. F-least) among all models of R.*

In particular, the F-least interpretation in the set of all interpretations is given by $I =< \emptyset, \emptyset >$. The notions of *F-minimal* and *F-least* models are different from the notions of *minimal* and *least* models (see Definition 4.5). While minimal and least models of a theory R minimize the *degree of truth* of their atoms, by minimizing the set T of true atoms and maximizing the set F of false atoms F, F-minimal and F-least models minimize the *degree of information* of their atoms, by jointly minimizing the sets T and F of atoms which are either true or false and thus maximizing the set U of unknown atoms. For example, the F-least model of the program $p \leftarrow p$ is obtained when p is undefined, while the least model of P is obtained when p is false. As it will be seen in the sequel, this distinction reflects fundamental differences between the semantics based on Clark's completion and model-theoretic semantics, such as the least model semantics, perfect model semantics or well-founded semantics, which are the main topic of this paper.

5 Fixed Points

Declarative semantics of logic programs is often defined using fixed points of some natural operators Ψ acting on *ordered* sets of interpretations. Suppose $\leq$ is an ordering on the set $\mathcal{I}$ of interpretations of a given language, $\mathcal{J}$ is a subset of $\mathcal{I}$ and Ψ is an operator $\Psi : \mathcal{I} \to \mathcal{I}$ on $\mathcal{I}$.

Definition 5.1 *The operator* Ψ *is called* monotone *if* $I \leq J$ *implies* $\Psi(I) \leq \Psi(J)$, *for any* $I, J \in \mathcal{I}$. *An interpretation* $I \in \mathcal{I}$ *is a* fixed point *of* Ψ *if* $\Psi(I) = I$. *By the least upper bound* $\Sigma \mathcal{J}$ *of* $\mathcal{J}$ *(resp. the greatest lower bound* $\Pi \mathcal{J}$ *of* $\mathcal{J}$) *we mean an interpretation* $I \in \mathcal{I}$ *such that* $J \leq I$, *for any* $J \in \mathcal{J}$ *and* $J \leq J'$ *for any other*

J' with this property (resp. $I \leq J$, for any $J \in \mathcal{J}$ and $J' \leq J$ for any other J' with this property). By the smallest *interpretation (under the given ordering)* we mean an interpretation I_0 such that $I_0 \leq I$, for any other interpretation I.

Least fixed points of monotone operators Ψ are often generated by *iterating* the operator Ψ starting from the *smallest interpretation* I_0 and obtaining the (possibly transfinite) sequence:

$$\Psi^{\uparrow 0} = I_0;$$
$$\Psi^{\uparrow \alpha+1} = \Psi(\Psi^{\uparrow \alpha});$$
$$\Psi^{\uparrow \lambda} = \Sigma_{\alpha < \lambda} \Psi^{\uparrow \alpha};$$

for limit ordinals λ. Clearly, an iteration $\Psi^{\uparrow \alpha}$ is a fixed point of Ψ if and only if

$$\Psi^{\uparrow \alpha} = \Psi^{\uparrow \alpha+1}.$$

In the sequel we will consider two principal orderings among interpretations, namely the *standard* ordering $\preceq$ (see Definition 4.5) and the *F-ordering* $\preceq_F$ (see Definition 4.6). Operators acting on sets of interpretations ordered by the standard ordering, will be denoted by Ψ or Θ, while those acting on sets of interpretations ordered by the F-ordering, will be denoted by Φ or Ω. Recall that $I_0 = < \emptyset, \mathcal{H} >$ (resp. $I_0 = < \emptyset, \emptyset >$) is the smallest (resp. F-smallest) interpretation in the set of all interpretations ordered by $\preceq$ (resp. $\preceq_F$).

For a subset $\mathcal{J}$ of I, we will denote by $\Sigma \mathcal{J}$ (resp. $\Pi \mathcal{J}$) the least upper bound (resp. the greatest lower bound) of $\mathcal{J}$ with respect to $\preceq$. Similarly, we will denote by $\Sigma_F \mathcal{J}$ (resp. $\Pi_F \mathcal{J}$) the least upper bound (resp. the greatest lower bound) of $\mathcal{J}$ with respect to $\preceq_F$.

Observe, that if $\mathcal{J} = \{J_s : s \in S\}$, with $J_s = < T_s, F_s >$, then:

$$\Sigma \mathcal{J} = < \bigcup_{s \in S} T_s, \bigcap_{s \in S} F_s >;$$
$$\Pi \mathcal{J} = < \bigcap_{s \in S} T_s, \bigcup_{s \in S} F_s >;$$
$$\Sigma_F \mathcal{J} = < \bigcup_{s \in S} T_s, \bigcup_{s \in S} F_s >;$$
$$\Pi_F \mathcal{J} = < \bigcap_{s \in S} T_s, \bigcap_{s \in S} F_s > .$$

Although $\Sigma \mathcal{J}$, $\Pi \mathcal{J}$ and $\Pi_F \mathcal{J}$ are always well-defined interpretations, $\Sigma_F \mathcal{J} = < T, F >$ may not be an interpretation, because the sets T and F may not be disjoint. However, $\Sigma_F \mathcal{J}$ is always an interpretation, provided that $\mathcal{J}$ is an *F-directed* set of interpretations, i.e., such that for any $J, J' \in \mathcal{J}$ there is a $J'' \in \mathcal{J}$ satisfying $J \preceq_F J''$ and $J' \preceq_F J''$.

6   Declarative Semantics of Deductive Databases and Logic Programs

A precise meaning or *semantics* must be associated with any logic or database program P in order to provide a declarative specification of the program. *Declarative semantics* provides a mathematically precise definition of the meaning of the program in a manner, which is independent of procedural considerations, context-free, and easy to manipulate, exchange and reason about.

Procedural semantics of a logic program, on the other hand, usually is given by providing a procedural mechanism that, at least in theory and perhaps under some additional assumptions, is capable of providing answers to a wide class of queries. The performance of such a mechanism (in particular, its correctness) is evaluated by comparing its behavior to the *specification* provided by the declarative semantics. Without a proper declarative semantics the user needs an intimate knowledge of procedural aspects in order to write correct programs.

Finding a suitable declarative or intended semantics is one of the most important and difficult problems in logic programming and deductive databases. The importance of this problem stems from the declarative character of logic programs and deductive databases, whereas its difficulty can be largely attributed to the fact that there does not exist a precisely defined set of conditions that a 'suitable' semantics should satisfy. While all researchers seem to agree that any semantics SEM(P) must reflect the intended meaning of a program or a database and also be suitable for mechanical computation, there is no agreement as to which semantics best satisfy these criteria.

One thing, however, appears to be clear. Logic programs and deductive databases must be as easy to write and comprehend as possible, free from excessive amounts of explicit negative information and as close to natural discourse as possible. In other words, the declarative semantics of a program or a database must be determined more by its *commonsense meaning* than by its purely logical contents. For example, given the information that 1 is a natural number and that $n+1$ is a natural number if so is n, we should be able to derive a non-monotonic or commonsense conclusion that neither 0 nor *Mickey Mouse* is a natural number. Similarly, from a database of information about teaching assignments, which only shows that John teaches Pascal and Prolog this semester, it should be possible to reach a common sense conclusion that John does not teach Calculus. Clearly, none of these facts follow logically from our assumptions.

The intended semantics must therefore be *non-monotonic*, i.e., SEM(P) cannot monotonically increase with the theory P. For example, after learning (adding to P) the fact that 0 is also a natural number, we have to withdraw the previously reached conclusion to the contrary. Consequently, the problem of finding a suitable semantics for logic programs and deductive databases can be viewed as the problem of finding a suitable non-monotonic formalization of the type of reasoning used in logic programs and deductive databases. We briefly discuss the relationship between the proposed semantics and non-monotonic formalisms in Section 7. The problem of a suitable semantics for *negation* is just a special case of the more general problem of the intended semantics of a program or a database.

Declarative semantics SEM(P) of a program can be specified in various ways, among which the following two are most common. One that can be called *proof-theoretic*, associates with P its first order completion $COMP(P)$ (e.g., $COMP(P)$ can be P itself or the Clark predicate completion comp(P) of P). A formula V is said to be *implied* by the semantics SEM(P) if and only if it is logically implied by the completion

$$COMP(P) \models V,$$

i.e., if V is satisfied in all 2-valued (Herbrand or not) models of $COMP(P)$.

Another method of defining the declarative semantics SEM(P) of a program is *model-theoretic.* The semantics is determined by choosing a set $MOD(P)$ of *intended* models of P (in particular, one intended model M_P). For example, MOD(P) can be the set of all minimal models of P or the unique least model of P. A formula V is said to be *implied* by the semantics SEM(P) if and only if it is satisfied in all intended models:

$$MOD(P) \models V \quad \text{(in particular,} \quad M_P \models V).$$

Observe, that the proof-theoretic approach can be viewed as a *special case* of the model-theoretic approach. Other approaches to defining the declarative semantics are possible, e.g., a combination of proof-theoretic and model-theoretic methods has been used in [Kunen, 1987; Fitting, 1985].

It is important to point out that the terms *model-theoretic* and *proof-theoretic* are used here in a different sense than. e.g., in [Reiter, 1984; Gallaire *et al.*, 1984]. In those papers a model-theoretic approach to deductive databases was described to mean *viewing a deductive database as an interpretation* and it was contrasted with a proof-theoretic approach, which means *viewing a deductive database as a first order theory*. We always view a deductive detabase or a logic program P as a first order theory, but using a proof-theoretic approach we define its *semantics* by means of a first order completion of P, whereas using a model-theoretic approach we define the semantics be selecting one or more intended models of P.

In the remainder of this section we will review and discuss some of the proposed declarative semantics for logic programs and deductive databases. Our discussion is not meant to be exhaustive and the selection of semantics clearly reflects the authors' preferences. We will begin with a discussion of the Clark predicate completion semantics and its 3-valued extensions. Subsequently, we will concentrate on model-theoretic semantics, including the least model semantics, the perfect model semantics, the stable model semantics, the weakly perfect model semantics and the well-founded semantics. We finish with a brief discussion of the role and importance of semantics based on *non-Herbrand models*. Throughout our presentation, we will strive to explore relationships existing between various approaches.

6.1 Clark's Predicate Completion Semantics

The most commonly used declarative semantics of logic programs, although less popular in the context of deductive databases, is based on the so called *Clark predicate completion comp(P)* of a logic program P [Clark, 1978; Lloyd, 1984].

Clark's completion of P is obtained by first rewriting every clause in P of the form:

$$q(K_1, \ldots, K_n) \leftarrow L_1, \ldots, L_m,$$

where q is a predicate symbol and $K_1, \ldots, K_n$ are terms containing variables $X_1, \ldots, X_k$, as a clause

$$q(T_1, \ldots, T_n) \leftarrow V,$$

where T_i's are variables,

$$V = \exists X_1, \ldots, X_k \ (T_1 = K_1 \wedge \ldots \wedge T_n = K_n \wedge L_1 \wedge \ldots \wedge L_m)$$

and then replacing, for every predicate symbol q in the alphabet, the (possibly empty[3]) set of all clauses

$$q(T_1, \ldots, T_n) \leftarrow V_1$$
$$\cdots$$
$$\cdots$$
$$q(T_1, \ldots, T_n) \leftarrow V_s$$

with q appearing in the head, by a single universally quantified logical equivalence

$$q(T_1, \ldots, T_n) \leftrightarrow V_1 \vee \ldots \vee V_s.$$

Finally, the obtained theory is augmented by the so called *Clark's Equality Axioms* (see Section 6.8), which include unique names axioms and axioms for equality. These axioms are essential when considering non-Herbrand models of Clark's completion.

Clark's approach is mathematically elegant and founded on a natural idea that in common discourse we often tend to use 'if' statements, when we really mean 'iff' statements. For example, we may use the following program P_1 to describe natural numbers:

$$natural\_number(0)$$
$$natural\_number(succ(X)) \leftarrow natural\_number(X).$$

The above theory P_1 is rather weak. It does not even imply that, say, *Mickey Mouse* is *not* a natural number. This is because, what we really have in mind is

$$natural\_number(T) \longleftrightarrow \exists X\,(T = 0 \vee (T = succ(X) \wedge natural\_number(X)))$$

which is in fact Clark's completion of P_1 and it indeed implies

$$\neg natural\_number(MickeyMouse).$$

Unfortunately, Clark's predicate completion semantics has some serious drawbacks. One of them is the fact that *Clark's completion is often inconsistent*, i.e., it may not have any *2-valued* (Herbrand or not) models, in which case Clark's semantics is undefined. For example, Clark's completion of the program $p \leftarrow \neg p$ is $p \leftrightarrow \neg p$, which is inconsistent. The situation can be even worse, e.g., Clark's completion of the program P_2:

$$p \leftarrow \neg q, \neg p$$

is:

$$p \leftrightarrow \neg q, \neg p$$
$$\neg q$$

---

[3]If there are no clauses involving the head $q(T_1, \ldots, T_n)$, then the corresponding disjunction is empty and thus always false. The resulting completion contains therefore a universal negation of $q(T_1, \ldots, T_n)$.

which is inconsistent. However, after adding to P_2 a 'meaningless' clause $q \leftarrow q$ its completion becomes:

$$p \leftrightarrow \neg q, \neg p$$
$$q \leftrightarrow q$$

which has a model in which q is true and p is false. On the other hand, after adding to P another 'meaningless' clause $p \leftarrow p$ its completion becomes:

$$p \leftrightarrow p \vee (\neg q \wedge \neg p)$$
$$\neg q$$

which has a different model in which q is false and p is true.

6.1.1 Three-Valued Extensions

[Fitting, 1985] showed that the inconsistency problem for Clark's semantics, as well as some other related problems, can be elegantly eliminated by considering *3-valued* Herbrand models of the Clark predicate completion $comp(P)$, rather than 2-valued models only.

Theorem 6.1 *[Fitting, 1985] Clark's completion $comp(P)$ of any logic program P always has at least one 3-valued Herbrand model. Moreover, among all 3-valued models of $comp(P)$ there is exactly one* F-least *model M_P.*

This result gave rise to Fitting's 3-valued extension of Clark's semantics.

Definition 6.1 (Fitting's Semantics) *[Fitting, 1985] Fitting's 3-valued extension of the Clark predicate completion semantics is the semantics determined by the unique intended model M_P or, equivalently, by the set $MOD(P)$ of intended models, consisting of all 3-valued Herbrand models of $comp(P)$.*

For example, the program P_2 defined before has a unique 3-valued model in which q is false and p is undefined. Fitting also provided an elegant fixed-point characterization of 3-valued models of $comp(P)$.

Definition 6.2 (The Fitting Operator) *[Fitting, 1985] Suppose that P is a logic program. The Fitting operator $\Phi : \mathcal{I} \to \mathcal{I}$ on the set $\mathcal{I}$ of all 3-valued interpretations of $comp(P)$ is defined as follows. If $I \in \mathcal{I}$ is an interpretation of $comp(P)$ and A is a ground atom then $\Phi(I)$ is an interpretation given by[4]:*

(i) $\Phi(I)(A) = 1$ if there is a clause $A \leftarrow L_1, \ldots, L_n$ in P such that $\hat{I}(L_i) = 1$, for all $i \leq n$;

(ii) $\Phi(I)(A) = 0$ if for every clause $A \leftarrow L_1, \ldots, L_n$ in P there is an $i \leq n$ such that $\hat{I}(L_i) = 0$;

(iii) $\Phi(I)(A) = \frac{1}{2}$, otherwise.

---

[4]According to the conventions adopted in Section 4, P is assumed to be instantiated and interpretations are viewed as 3-valued functions.

Theorem 6.2 *[Fitting, 1985] An interpretation I of comp(P) is a model of comp(P) if and only if it is a fixed point of the operator Φ. In particular, M_P is the F-least fixed point of Φ.*

Moreover, the model M_P can be obtained by iterating the operator Φ, namely, the sequence $\Phi^{\uparrow\alpha}$ of iterations[5] of Φ is monotonically increasing and it has a fixed point

$$\Phi^{\uparrow\lambda} = M_P.$$

Kunen [Kunen, 1987] showed that the set of formulae implied by Fitting's semantics is not recursively enumerable and he proposed the following modification of Fitting's approach.

Definition 6.3 (Kunen's Semantics) *[Kunen, 1987] Kunen's 3-valued extension of the Clark predicate completion semantics is the semantics determined by the set $MOD(P)$ of intended models, consisting of all 3-valued (Herbrand or not) models of comp(P).*

Kunen showed that his semantics is recursively enumerable and closely related to the Fitting operator Φ.

Theorem 6.3 *[Kunen, 1987] A closed formula V is implied by Kunen's 3-valued extension of the Clark predicate completion semantics if and only if it is satisfied in at least one finite iteration $\Phi^{\uparrow n}$ of the Fitting operator Φ, $n = 0, 1, 2, \ldots$. Moreover, the set of formulae implied by this semantics is recursively enumerable.*

It is easy to see that Fitting's semantics is stronger than Kunen's semantics, i.e., any closed formula implied by Kunen's semantics is also implied by Fitting's semantics.

6.1.2   Drawbacks of Clark's Completion Semantics

Unfortunately, Clark's predicate completion does not always result in a satisfactory semantics. For many programs, it leads to a semantics which appears *too weak*. This problem applies both to standard Clark's semantics as well as to its 3-valued extensions and it has been extensively discussed in the literature (see e.g. [Shepherdson, 1988; Shepherdson, 1984; Przymusinski, 1989c; Van Gelder *et al.*, 1990]). We illustrate it on the following three examples.

Example 6.1 *Suppose that to the program P_1 defined before we add a seemingly meaningless clause:*

$$natural\_number(X) \leftarrow natural\_number(X).$$

It appears that the newly obtained program P_1' should have the same semantics. However, Clark's completion of the new program P_1' is:

$$natural\_number(T) \longleftrightarrow$$

$$(natural\_number(T) \vee T = 0 \vee \exists X\ (T = succ(X) \wedge natural\_number(X)))$$

from which it no longer follows that MickeyMouse (or anything else, for that matter) is not a natural number.

---

[5]According to the convention from Section 5, Φ is defined on the F-ordered set of interpretations and the iteration begins from the F-smallest interpretation $I = <\emptyset, \emptyset>$.

Example 6.2 (Van Gelder) *Suppose, that we want to describe which vertices in a graph are reachable from a given vertex a. We could write the following program P_3:*

$$edge(a, b)$$
$$edge(c, d)$$
$$edge(d, c)$$
$$reachable(a)$$
$$reachable(X) \leftarrow reachable(Y), edge(Y, X).$$

We clearly expect vertices c and d not to be reachable. However, Clark's completion of the predicate 'reachable' gives only

$$reachable(X) \longleftrightarrow (X = a \lor \exists Y \ (reachable(Y) \land edge(Y, X)))$$

from which such a conclusion again cannot be derived. Here, the difficulty is caused by the existence of symmetric clauses edge(c, d) and edge(d, c).

Example 6.3 *Suppose that program P_4 is given by the following clauses:*

$$bird(tweety)$$
$$fly(X) \leftarrow bird(X), \neg abnormal(X)$$
$$abnormal(X) \leftarrow irregular(X)$$
$$irregular(X) \leftarrow abnormal(X).$$

The last two clauses merely state that irregularity is synonymous with abnormality. Based on the fact that nothing leads us to believe that tweety is abnormal, we are justified to expect that tweety flies, but Clark's completion of P_4 yields

$$fly(T) \longleftrightarrow (bird(T) \land \neg abnormal(T))$$
$$abnormal(T) \longleftrightarrow irregular(T),$$

from which it does not follow that anything flies. On the other hand, without the last two clauses (or without just one of them) Clark's semantics produces correct results.

The above described behavior of Clark's completion is bound to be confusing for a thoughtful logic programmer, who may very well wonder why, for example, the addition of a seemingly harmless statement *"natural_number(X) ← natural_number(X)"* should change the meaning of the first program. The explanation that will most likely occur to him will be *procedural* in nature, namely, the fact that the above added clause may lead to a loop. But it was the idea of replacing *procedural* programming by *declarative* programming, that brought about the concept of logic programming and deductive databases in the first place, and therefore it seems that such a procedural explanation should be flatly rejected.

Some of the problems mentioned above are caused by the difficulties with the representation of transitive closures when using Clark's semantics (e.g., in the program P_3). Recently, [Kunen, 1988] formally showed that Clark's semantics is not sufficiently expressive to naturally represent transitive closures.

In the following sections we discuss model-theoretic approaches to declarative semantics of logic programs which attempt to avoid the drawbacks of Clark's semantics discussed above.

6.2   Least Model Semantics

The model-theoretic approach is particularly well-understood in the case of *positive logic programs*. In this section we assume that all interpretations are 2-valued.

Example 6.4 *Suppose that our program P consists of clauses:*

$$able\_mathematician(X) \leftarrow physicist(X)$$
$$physicist(einstein)$$
$$businessman(iacocca).$$

This program has several different models, the largest of which is the model in which both Einstein and Iacocca are at the same time businessmen, physicists and good mathematicians. This model hardly seems to correctly describe the intended meaning of P. Indeed, there is nothing in this program to imply that Iacocca is a physicist or that Einstein is a businessman. In fact, we are inclined to believe that the lack of such information indicates that we can assume the contrary.

The program also has the unique least *model M_P:*

$$\{physicist(einstein), businessman(iacocca), able\_mathematician(einstein)\},$$

in which only Einstein is a physicist and good mathematician and only Iacocca is a businessman. This model seems to correctly reflect the semantics of P, at the same time incorporating the classical case of the closed-world assumption [Reiter, 1978]: if no reason exists for some positive statement to be true, then we are allowed to infer that it is false.

It turns out that the existence of the unique least model M_P is the property shared by *all* positive programs.

Theorem 6.4 *[Van Emden and Kowalski, 1976] Every positive logic program P has a unique least (Herbrand) model M_P.*

This important result led to the definition of the so called least model semantics for positive programs.

Definition 6.4 (Least Model Semantics) *[Van Emden and Kowalski, 1976] By the least model semantics of a positive program P we mean the semantics determined by the least Herbrand model M_P of P.*

The least Herbrand model semantics is very intuitive and it seems to properly reflect the intended meaning of positive logic programs. The motivation behind this approach is based on the idea that we should minimize positive information as much as possible, limiting it to facts explicitly implied by P, and making everything else false. In other words, the least model semantics is based on a natural form of the *closed world assumption*.

The least model semantics avoids the drawbacks of the Clark predicate completion discussed in the previous section. For example, the least Herbrand model M_P of the programs P_1 and P_1' given above is:

$$\{natural\_number(0), natural\_number(succ(0)), natural\_number(succ(succ(0))), \ldots\}$$

which is exactly what we intended. Similarly, the least Herbrand model M_P of the program P_3 above is:

$$\{edge(a,b), edge(c,d), edge(d,c), reachable(a), reachable(b)\},$$

which is again exactly what we would expect.

Least model semantics also has a natural fixed point characterization. First we define the Van Emden-Kowalski immediate consequence operator $\Psi : I \to I$ on the set I of all interpretations of P (ordered by $\preceq$).

Definition 6.5 (The Van Emden-Kowalski Operator) *[Van Emden and Kowalski, 1976] Suppose that P is a positive logic program, $I \in I$ is an interpretation of P and A is a ground atom. Then $\Psi(I)$ is an interpretation given by:*

(i) $\Psi(I)(A) = 1$ if there is a clause $A \leftarrow A_1, \ldots, A_n$ in P such that $I(A_i) = 1$, for all $i \leq n$;

(ii) $\Psi(I)(A) = 0$, otherwise.

Theorem 6.5 *[Van Emden and Kowalski, 1976] The Van Emden-Kowalski operator Ψ has the least fixed point, which coincides with the least model M_P.*

Moreover, the model M_P can be obtained by iterating ω times the operator Ψ, namely, the sequence $\Psi^{\uparrow n}$, $n = 0, 1, 2, \ldots, \omega$, of iterations[6] of Ψ is monotonically increasing and it has a fixed point

$$\Psi^{\uparrow \omega} = M_P.$$

The least model semantics is strictly stronger than Clark's semantics:

Theorem 6.6 *Suppose that P is a positive logic program. If a closed formula is implied by the Clark predicate completion semantics (or by one of its 3-valued extensions) then it is also implied by the least model semantics.*

The only serious, drawback of the least model semantics seems to be the fact that it is well defined for a very restrictive class of programs. Programs which are not positive, in general, do not have least models. For example, the program $p \leftarrow \neg q$ has two minimal models $\{p\}$ and $\{q\}$, but it does not have the least model. Similarly, the program P_4 from Example 6.3 does not have the least model.

6.3 Perfect Model Semantics

As we have seen above, although the least model semantics seems suitable for the class of positive programs, it is not adequate for more general programs, allowing *negative premises* in program clauses. The inclusion of negation in program clauses increases the expressive power of logic programs and thus is of great practical importance. At the same time, the problem of finding a suitable semantics for programs with negation becomes much more complex. In this section we discuss the perfect model semantics, which extends the least model semantics to a wider class of logic programs. Throughout most of this section by an interpretation (model) we mean a *2-valued* interpretation (model).

---

[6] With respect to the standard ordering $\preceq$ of interpretations and beginning from the smallest interpretation $< \emptyset, \mathcal{H} >$. Here ω denotes the first infinite ordinal.

Example 6.5 *Suppose that we know that physicists are able mathematicians, whereas typical businessmen tend to avoid (advanced) mathematics in their work, unless they somehow happen to have a strong mathematical background. Suppose also that we know that Iacocca is a businessman and that Einstein is a physicist. We can express these facts using a logic program as follows:*

$$avoids\_math(X) \leftarrow businessman(X), \neg able\_mathematician(X) \quad (1)$$
$$able\_mathematician(X) \leftarrow physicist(X) \quad (2)$$
$$businessman(iacocca) \quad (3)$$
$$physicist(einstein). \quad (4)$$

This program does not have a unique least model, but instead it has two *minimal* models. In both of them Iacocca is the only businessman, Einstein is the only physicist and he is also an able mathematician, who uses advanced mathematics. However, in one of them, say in M_1, Iacocca avoids advanced mathematics, because he is not an able mathematician and in the other, M_2, the situation is opposite and Iacocca is an able mathematician, who uses advanced mathematics in his work.

Since any intended semantics for logic programs must include some form of the closed world assumption, and thus it must in some way *minimize positive information*, it is natural to consider *minimal models* of P [Minker, 1982; Bossu and Siegel, 1985; McCarthy, 1980] as providing the desired meaning of P. It seems clear, however, that *not both* minimal models capture the intended meaning of P. By placing negated predicate *able_mathematician(X)* among the premises of the rule, we intended to say that businessmen, in general, avoid advanced mathematics *unless* they are known to be good mathematicians. Since we have no information indicating that Iacocca is a good mathematician we are inclined to infer that he does not use advanced mathematics. Therefore, only the first minimal model M_1 seems to correspond to the intended meaning of P.

The reason for this asymmetry is easy to explain. The first clause (1) of P is logically (classically) equivalent to the clause

$$able\_mathematician(X) \lor avoids\_math(X) \leftarrow businessman(X) \quad (5)$$

and models M_1 and M_2 are therefore also minimal models of the theory P' obtained from P by replacing (1) by (5). However, the intended meaning of these two clauses seems to be different. The clause (5) does not assign distinct *priorities* to predicates (properties) *able_mathematician* and *avoids_math* and thus treats them as equally plausible. As a result the semantics determined by the two minimal models M_1 and M_2 seems to be perfectly adequate to represent the intended meaning of P'. On the other hand, the program clause (1) intuitively seems to assign distinct *priorities for minimization* to predicates *able_mathematician* and *avoids_math*, essentially saying that the predicate *ablemathematician* has to be first assumed *false* unless there is a compelling reason to do otherwise. We can say, therefore, that the clause (1) assigns a *higher priority* for minimization (or *falsification*) to the predicate *able_mathematician* than to the predicate *avoids_math*.

We can easily imagine the above priorities reversed. This is for instance the case in the following clause:

$$able\_mathematician(X) \leftarrow physicist(X), \neg avoids\_math(X)$$

which says that if X is a physicist and if we have no specific evidence showing that he avoids mathematics then we are allowed to assume that he is an able mathematician. Here, the predicate *avoids_math* has a higher priority for minimization than the predicate *able_mathematician*, i.e., it is supposed to be first assumed *false* unless there is a specific reason to do otherwise.

Also observe, that if $B \leftarrow A$ is a clause, then minimizing B (i.e., making B false) immediately results in A being minimized, too. Consequently, A is always minimized before or at the same time when B is minimized. The above discussion leads us to the conclusion that the *syntax* of program clauses determines relative *priorities* for minimization among ground atoms according to the following rules:

I. Negative premises have *higher* priority than the heads;

II. Positive premises have priority *no less* than that of the heads.

To formalize conditions I and II, we assume that the program is already instantiated and we introduce the *dependency graph G_P* of P (cf. [Apt *et al.*, 1988; Van Gelder, 1989b]), whose vertices are *ground atoms*, i.e., elements of the Herbrand base $\mathcal{H}$. If A and B are atoms, then there is a directed edge in G_P from B to A if and only if there is a clause in P, whose head is A and one of whose premises is either B or $\neg B$. In the latter case the edge is called *negative*.

Definition 6.6 (Priority Relation) *[Apt et al., 1988] For any two ground atoms A and B in $\mathcal{H}$ we define B to have a* higher priority[7] *than A $(A < B)$ if there is a directed path in G leading from B to A and passing through at least one negative edge. We call the above defined relation $<$ the priority relation between (ground) atoms. We will write $A \leq B$ if there is a directed path from B to A.*

Analogously, we can define the *predicate priority relation $<_P$* between predicate symbols, replacing in the above definition ground atoms by predicate symbols. Having defined the priority relation, we are prepared to define the notion of a *perfect model*. It is our goal to define a minimal model in which atoms of higher priority are *minimized* (or *falsified*) first, even at the cost of including in the model (i.e., making true in it) some atoms of lower priority. It follows, that if M is a model of P and if a new model N is obtained from M, by adding and subtracting from M some atoms, then we will consider the new model N *preferable* to M if and only if the addition of any atom A is always *justified* by the removal of a higher priority atom B (i.e. such that $A < B$). A model M of P will be considered *perfect*, if there are *no* models of P preferable to it. More formally:

Definition 6.7 (Perfect Models) *[Przymusinski, 1988b; Przymusinski, 1989c] Suppose that M and N are two distinct models of a logic program P. We say that N is preferable to M (briefly, N $<<$ M), if for every atom $A \in N - M$ there is a higher priority atom B, $B > A$, such that $B \in M - N$. We say that a model M of P is perfect if there are no models preferable to M. We call the relation $<<$ the preference relation between models.*

---

[7] There is no consensus in the literature as to whether to describe this property as having 'higher' or 'lower' priority and, accordingly, as to whether to denote it by $A < B$ or $A > B$.

It is easy to prove

Theorem 6.7 *[Przymusinski, 1988b] Every perfect model is minimal. For positive programs the concepts of a least model and a perfect model coincide.*

Example 6.6 *Only model M_1 in Example 6.5 is perfect. Indeed (using obvious abbreviations):*

$$M_1 = \{physicist(e), able\_mathematician(e), businessman(i), avoids\_math(i)\}$$

$$M_2 = \{physicist(e), able\_mathematician(e), businessman(i), able\_mathematician(i)\}$$

and we know that able_mathematician > avoids_math and therefore $M_1 << M_2$, while not $M_2 << M_1$. Consequently, M_1 is perfect, but M_2 is not.

Unfortunately, not every logic program has a perfect model:

Example 6.7 *The program:*
$$p \leftarrow \neg q \ , \ q \leftarrow \neg p$$
has only two minimal Herbrand models $M_1 = \{p\}$ and $M_2 = \{q\}$ and since $p<q$ and $q<p$ we have $M_1 << M_2$ and $M_2 << M_1$, thus none of the models is perfect.

The cause of this peculiarity is quite clear. The concept of a perfect model is based on relative priorities between ground atoms and therefore we have to be consistent when assigning those priorities to avoid priority conflicts (cycles), which could render our semantics meaningless. This observation underlies the approaches of Apt, Blair and Walker [Apt *et al.*, 1988] and Van Gelder [Van Gelder, 1989b], who argued that *when using negation we should be referring to an already defined relation*, so that the definition is not circular, or, as Van Gelder puts it, we should avoid *negative recursion*. This idea led them to the introduction of the class of *stratified* logic programs (see also [Chandra and Harel, 1985; Naqvi, 1986]). The class of stratified logic programs has been later extended [Przymusinski, 1988b] to the class of *locally stratified* programs.

Definition 6.8 *[Apt et al., 1988; Van Gelder, 1989b; Przymusinski, 1988b] A logic program P is* stratifed *(resp.* locally stratified*) if it is possible to decompose the set S of all predicate symbols (resp. the Herbrand base $\mathcal{H}$) into disjoint sets $S_1, S_2, \ldots, S_\alpha, \ldots,$ $\alpha < \lambda$, called* strata, *so that for every clause (resp. instantiated clause):*

$$C \leftarrow A_1, ..., A_m, \neg B_1, ..., \neg B_n$$

in P, where A's, B's and C are atoms, we have that:

(i) for every i, stratum(A_i) $\leq$ stratum(C),

(ii) for every j, stratum(B_j) $<$ stratum(C),

where stratum(A) $= \alpha$, if the predicate symbol of A belongs to S_α (resp. if the atom A belongs to S_α). Any particular decomposition $\{S_1 ,\ldots, S_\alpha,\ldots\}$ satisfying the above conditions is called a stratification of P *(resp.* local stratification of P*).*

In the above definition, stratification determines priority levels (strata), with lower level (stratum) denoting higher priority for minimization. For example, the program from Example 6.5 is stratified and one of its stratifications is $S_1=\{$able_mathematician$\}$, $S_2=\{$businessman, physicist, avoids_math$\}$.

The difference between the definitions of stratification and local stratification is that in the first case we decompose the set S of all predicate symbols, while in the second case we decompose the Herbrand base $\mathcal{H}$. Since every program can effectively refer only to a finite set of predicate symbols, stratifications can be always assumed to be finite. On the other hand, if the program uses function symbols then its Herbrand universe is infinite and its local stratifications can, in general, be infinite. The following fact is obvious:

Proposition 6.1 *Every stratified program is locally stratified.*

The next proposition characterizes (local) stratifiability.

Proposition 6.2 *[Apt et al., 1988; Przymusinski, 1988b] A logic program P is stratified if and only if its predicate priority relation $<_P$ is a partial order[8].*

A logic program P is locally stratified if and only if its priority relation $<$ is a partial order and if every increasing sequence of ground atoms under $<$ is finite[9].

All programs described so far in this paper, with the exception of Example 6.7, are stratified. The program in Example 6.7 is not even locally stratified. We now present an example of a locally stratified program which is not stratified.

Example 6.8 *The following program defines even numbers:*

$$even(0)$$

$$even(s(X)) \leftarrow \neg even(X).$$

Here $s(X)$ is meant to represent the successor function on the set of natural numbers. This program is not stratified because the predicate even is involved in negative recursion with itself, i.e., even $<_P$ even. However, P is locally stratified, because the priority ordering $<$ between ground atoms is easily seen to be a partial order and every increasing sequence of ground atoms is of the form:

$$even(s(s(s(...)))) < even(s(s(...))) < even(s(...)) < ... < even(s(0)) < even(0)$$

and therefore it must be finite.

The following basic result shows that every locally stratified program has the least model M_P with respect to the preference relation $<<$.

Theorem 6.8 *[Przymusinski, 1988b] Every locally stratified program P has a unique perfect model M_P. Moreover, M_P is preferred to any other model M of P, i.e., $M_P << M$, for any other model M.*

---

[8] By a *partial order* we mean an irreflexive and transitive relation.
[9] The last condition is only essential when the Herbrand base is infinite.

For stratified programs, models M_P have been first introduced under the name of 'natural' models in [Apt *et al.*, 1988; Van Gelder, 1989b] and defined in terms of iterated fixed points and iterated least models. In general, a (locally) stratified program may have many stratifications, however, the notion of a perfect model is defined entirely in terms of the priority relation $<$ and thus it does not depend on a particular stratification. Now we can define the perfect model semantics of locally stratified logic programs.

Definition 6.9 (Perfect Model Semantics) *[Apt et al., 1988; Van Gelder, 1989b; Przymusinski, 1988b] Let P be a locally stratified[10] logic program. By the perfect model semantics of P we mean the semantics determined by the unique perfect model M_P of P.*

It follows immediately from Theorem 6.7 that for positive logic programs the perfect model semantics is in fact equivalent to the *least model semantics* and thus the perfect model semantics *extends* the least model semantics.

The following result, slightly generalizing [Apt *et al.*, 1988], shows that the perfect model semantics is strictly *stronger* than the semantics defined by Clark's completion.

Theorem 6.9 *(cf. [Apt et al., 1988]) If P is a locally stratified logic program, then Clark's completion comp(P) is consistent and if a closed formula is implied by the Clark predicate completion semantics (or by one of its 3-valued extensions) then it is also implied by the perfect model semantics.*

The perfect model semantics eliminates various unituitive features of Clark's semantics discussed before. For example, the unique perfect model of the program P_4 discussed in Example 6.3 consists of:

$$\{bird(tweety), \; fly(tweety)\},$$

leading to the expected intended semantics. The perfect model semantics is actually used in two large experimental deductive database systems, namely in the LDL system, implemented at MCC [Zaniolo, 1988], and in the NAIL! system, which is currently under development at Stanford [Morris *et al.*, 1986].

6.3.1   Perfect Models As Iterated Fixed Points and Iterated Least Models

Least models of positive programs have been characterized as fixed points of the Van Emden-Kowalski operator. It turns out that perfect models of locally stratified programs can be also characterized as *iterated least fixed points* and as *iterated least models* of the program. In the remainder of this section we consider both 2-valued and 3-valued interpretations.

First we need a generalization of the Van Emden-Kowalski operator Ψ defined in Section 6.2. For any interpretation J we define a corresponding operator Ψ_J as follows:

Definition 6.10 (The Generalized Van Emden-Kowalski Operator) *Suppose that P is any logic program, $I, J \in \mathcal{I}$ are interpretations and A is a ground atom. Then $\Psi_J(I)$ is a (2-valued) interpretation given by:*

---

[10]Perfect model semantics can be defined for a significantly larger class of programs, but for the sake of compatibility with its extensions discussed in the following sections, we limit it to the class of locally stratified programs.

(i) $\Psi_J(I)(A) = 1$ *if there is a clause* $A \leftarrow L_1, \ldots, L_n$ *in* P *such that, for all* $i \leq n$, *either* $\hat{J}(L_i) = 1$ *or* L_i *is an atom and* $I(L_i) = 1$;

(ii) $\Psi_J(I)(A) = 0$, *otherwise.*

Intuitively, J represents facts currently known to be true or false and $\Psi_J(I)$ contains all atomic facts whose truth can be derived *in one step* from the program P assuming that all facts in J hold and assuming that all positive facts in I are true. The Van Emden-Kowalski operator Ψ coincides with Ψ_J, where $J = < \emptyset, \emptyset >$. Observe, that operators Ψ_J are asymmetric in the sense that they *do not* treat negative and positive information symmetrically. In Section 6.7 devoted to the well-founded semantics we will introduce analogous, but completely symmetric operators.

Proposition 6.3 *[Apt et al., 1988] For every interpretation J, the operator* Ψ_J *is monotone and it has the least fixed point given by* $\Psi_J^{\uparrow\omega}$ *(recall that* ω *stands for the first infinite ordinal).*

Intuitively, the least fixed point $\Psi_J^{\uparrow\omega}$ contains all positive (atomic) facts which can be derived from P knowing J. Now we give an iterated fixed point characterization of perfect models. Let $\{S_1, S_2, \ldots, S_\alpha, \ldots\}$, $\alpha < \lambda$, be a local stratification of a program P, i.e., a decomposition of the Herbrand base $\mathcal{H}$. For every $\beta \leq \lambda$ let

$$\mathcal{H}_\beta = \bigcup_{\alpha < \beta} S_\alpha.$$

Clearly,

$$\mathcal{H} = \mathcal{H}_\lambda.$$

Since the result of applying an operator Ψ_J to an arbitrary interpretation I is always a 2-valued interpretation $\Psi_J(I)$, we can identify interpretations $\Psi_J(I)$ with subsets of the Herbrand base. We construct the following (transfinite) sequence $\{I_\alpha : \alpha \leq \lambda\}$ of interpretations:

$$
\begin{aligned}
I_0 &= < \emptyset, \emptyset > \\
I_{\alpha+1} &= < \Psi_{I_\alpha}^\omega, \mathcal{H}_{\alpha+1} - \Psi_{I_\alpha}^\omega > \\
I_\delta &= \Sigma_F \{I_\alpha : \alpha < \delta\},
\end{aligned}
$$

for limit δ. At any given step α, the next iteration $I_{\alpha+1}$ is obtained by:

- Taking the least fixed point $\Psi_{I_\alpha}^\omega$ of the operator Ψ_{I_α} as the set of positive facts. This is justified by the fact that the least fixed point $\Psi_{I_\alpha}^\omega$ contains those positive facts whose truth can be deduced from P assuming I_α.

- Taking the complement of $\Psi_{I_\alpha}^\omega$ in $\mathcal{H}_{\alpha+1}$ as the set of false facts. This is justified by the fact that the program is locally stratified and thus atoms from $\mathcal{H}_{\alpha+1}$, whose truth cannot be deduced at the level $\alpha + 1$ can be assumed to be false.

One can show that the sequence $\{I_\alpha\}$ is F-increasing and, clearly, the last interpretation in this sequence is I_λ. Observe again, that the above definition of iterations I_α does not treat negative and positive information symmetrically. In Section 6.7 devoted to the well-founded semantics we will give an analogous, but symmetric definition.

The following two theorems generalize results obtained in [Apt *et al.*, 1988; Van Gelder, 1989b] from the class of stratified programs to the class of locally stratified programs. The approach presented here is slightly different from those given in [Apt *et al.*, 1988; Van Gelder, 1989b].

Theorem 6.10 *(cf. [Apt* et al.*, 1988; Van Gelder, 1989b]) The unique perfect model M_P of a locally stratified program coincides with I_λ. Moreover, M_P is itself the least fixed point of the operator Ψ_{M_P}.*

Thus perfect models of locally stratified programs can be viewed as iterated least fixed points of operators Ψ_J. Perfect models can be also described as *iterated least models* of the program.

Let us first denote by P_α the set of all (instantiated) clauses of P whose heads belong to $\mathcal{H}_\alpha$. Clearly, $P_\lambda = P$. It is easy to see that if in the above definition of the sequence I_α we replace the definition of $I_{\alpha+1}$ by:

$$I_{\alpha+1} = < \mathcal{H}_{\alpha+1} \cap \Psi^\omega_{I_\alpha}, \mathcal{H}_{\alpha+1} - \Psi^\omega_{I_\alpha} >$$

i.e., if we restrict true atoms to the elements of $\mathcal{H}_{\alpha+1}$ then we will still have $M_P = I_\lambda$. For the so modified sequence I_α the following result holds.

Theorem 6.11 *(cf. [Apt* et al.*, 1988; Van Gelder, 1989b]) For every $\alpha \leq \lambda$, I_α is the least model of the program P_α, which extends all models I_β of programs P_β, for $\beta < \alpha$ (i.e., such that $I_\beta \preceq_F I_\alpha$).*

Thus M_P can be viewed as an iterated least model of P.

6.4   Extensions of the Perfect Model Semantics

The class of perfect models of locally stratified logic programs has many natural and desirable properties. However, the fact that it is restricted to the class of locally stratified programs is a significant drawback. Several researchers pointed out that there exist interesting and useful logic programs with natural intended semantics, which are not locally stratified [Gelfond and Lifschitz, 1988; Van Gelder *et al.*, 1990].

Example 6.9 *[Gelfond and Lifschitz, 1988] Consider the program P given by:*

$$p(1,2) \leftarrow$$
$$q(X) \leftarrow p(X,Y), \neg q(Y).$$

After instantiating, P takes the form:

$$p(1,2) \leftarrow \tag{6}$$
$$q(1) \leftarrow p(1,2), \neg q(2) \tag{7}$$
$$q(1) \leftarrow p(1,1), \neg q(1) \tag{8}$$
$$q(2) \leftarrow p(2,2), \neg q(2) \tag{9}$$
$$q(2) \leftarrow p(2,1), \neg q(1). \tag{10}$$

This program is not locally stratified. Indeed, the priority relation $<$ between atoms is not a partial order, because $q(1) < q(2)$ and $q(2) < q(1)$. On the other hand, it seems clear that the intended semantics of P is well-defined and is characterized by the 2-valued model $M = \{p(1,2), q(1)\}$ of P. The same results would be produced by Prolog, which further confirms our intuition.

The cause of this peculiarity is fairly clear. Program P appears to be semantically equivalent to a locally stratified program P^* consisting only of clauses (6) and (7). The remaining clauses seem to be entirely irrelevant, because atoms $p(1,1)$, $p(2,1)$ and $p(2,2)$ can be assumed false in P. At the same time, they are the ones that destroy local stratifiability of P.

Three different extensions of the perfect model semantics have been proposed: the *stable model semantics* [Gelfond and Lifschitz, 1988] (equivalent to the *default model semantics* [Bidoit and Froidevaux, 1988]), the *weakly perfect model semantics* [Przymusinska and Przymusinski, 1988] and the *well-founded semantics* [Van Gelder *et al.*, 1990]. While the first two semantics are 2-valued and are defined only for restricted classes of programs, the well-founded semantics is 3-valued and is defined for *all* logic programs. Although the three semantics approach the problem from three different angles (see Section 7), it appears, that the well-founded semantics is the most adequate extension of the perfect model semantics. In the next section we discuss the weakly perfect model semantics. The remaining two semantics will be discussed in the following sections.

6.5 Weakly Perfect Model Semantics

As it was the case with locally stratified programs and perfect models, *the weakly perfect model semantics* is based on the decomposition of the program into *strata* and its semantics is based on the *iterated least model approach*, however, the decomposition is performed *dynamically* rather than *statically*. In the case of a single stratum the weakly perfect semantics is equivalent to the *least model semantics*. In this section all interpretations are assumed to be 2-valued.

The main idea behind the concept of the weakly perfect model semantics is to remove 'irrelevant' relations in the dependency graph G_P of a logic program and to substitute *components* of the dependency graph for its *vertices* in the definitions of stratification and perfect models. First, we define the notion of a component.

Definition 6.11 *[Przymusinska and Przymusinski, 1988] Let $\sim$ be the equivalence relation between ground atoms of P defined as follows:*

$$A \sim B \equiv (A = B) \vee (A < B \wedge B < A).$$

We will call its equivalence classes components *of G_P. A component is* trivial *if it consists of a single element A, such that $A \not< A$.*

According to the above definition, two distinct ground atoms A and B are equivalent if they are related by *mutual negative recursion*, i.e., recursion passing through negative literals. Mutual negative recursion is the primary cause of difficulties with a proper definition of declarative semantics of logic programs. We now introduce an order relation $\prec$ between the *components* of the dependency graph G_P.

Definition 6.12 *[Przymusinska and Przymusinski, 1988] Let C_1 and C_2 be two components of G_P. We define:*

$$C_1 \prec C_2 \equiv C_1 \neq C_2 \wedge \exists A_1 \in C_1, \exists A_2 \in C_2 \ (A_1 < A_2).$$

We call a component C_1 maximal, if there is no component C_2 such that $C_1 \prec C_2$.

Clearly, the relation $\prec$ and therefore the maximal components of P are completely determined by the syntactic form of the program P. The order relation $\prec$ between the components of the dependency graph G_P corresponds to the dependency relation $<$ between its vertices, but, as opposed to $<$, it has the added advantage of *always being a partial order*. It easily follows from Proposition 6.2, that a logic program P is locally stratified if and only if all components of G_P are trivial and there is no infinite increasing sequence of components. For any logic program P we introduce the following definitions.

Definition 6.13 *[Przymusinska and Przymusinski, 1988] By the* bottom stratum S(P) *of P we mean the union of all maximal components of P:*

$$S(P) = \bigcup \{C : \ C \text{ is a maximal component of } G_P\}.$$

By the bottom layer L(P) *of P we mean the corresponding subprogram of P:*

$$L(P) = \quad \text{the set of all clauses from } P, \text{ whose heads belong to } S(P).$$

Observe that, if the instantiated program is *infinite*, then it may not have any maximal components and thus its bottom stratum may be empty. For example, the bottom stratum of the program $p(X) \leftarrow \neg p(f(X))$ is empty.

Example 6.10 *Consider the program P from Example 6.9. The dependency ordering is given by the following relations:*

$$q(1) < q(2), \ q(2) < q(1),$$

$$q(1) \leq p(1,2), \ q(1) \leq p(1,1), \ q(2) \leq p(2,2), \ q(2) \leq p(2,1).$$

Program P has five components: $C_1 = \{q(1), q(2)\}, C_2 = \{p(1,2)\}, C_3 = \{p(1,1)\}, C_4 = \{p(2,2)\}$ and $C_5 = \{p(2,1)\}$. Clearly, $C_1 \prec C_k$, for any $2 \leq k \leq 5$. Consequently, the bottom stratum S(P) of P – defined as the union of maximal components of P – is given by:

$$S(P) = \{p(1,2), p(1,1), p(2,2), p(2,1)\},$$

and the bottom layer L(P) of P, i.e., the set of all clauses from P whose heads belong to S(P), is:

$$L(P) = \{p(1,2) \leftarrow\}.$$

Observe, that the bottom layer L(P) of the above program P has the least model

$$M = < \{p(1,2)\}, \ \{p(1,1), p(2,2), p(2,1)\} >$$

i.e., the model in which $p(1,2)$ is true and $p(1,1)$, $p(2,2)$, $p(2,1)$ are false.

If the bottom layer L(P) of P has the least model M then we can use it to remove from P all 'irrelevant' clauses and literals. More generally, we will now introduce an operation of reduction, which reduces a given program P modulo its 3-valued interpretation I, by essentially applying the Davis-Putnam rule to P [Chang and Lee, 1973].

Definition 6.14 *[Przymusinska and Przymusinski, 1988] Let P be a logic program and let I be its interpretation. By a* reduction *of P modulo* I *we mean a new program $\frac{P}{I}$ obtained from P by performing the following two reductions:*

- *removing from P all clauses which contain a premise L such that $\hat{I}(L) = 0$ or whose head A satisfies $I(A) = 1$;*

- *removing from all the remaining clauses those premises L which satisfy $\hat{I}(L) = 1$.*

Finally, we also remove from the resulting program all non-unit clauses, whose heads already appear as unit clauses (facts) in the program. This step ensures that the set of atoms appearing in unit clauses, also called extensional *atoms, is disjoint from the set of atoms appearing in heads of non-unit clauses, also called* intensional *atoms.*

The so reduced program $\frac{P}{I}$ does not contain any literals which are true or false in I. In the Example 6.10 the reduced program $P' = \frac{P}{I}$ consists only of the clause:

$$q(1) \leftarrow \neg q(2).$$

Clearly, P' does not contain any literals from $S(P)$. Observe that in the reduced program we got rid of all the 'irrelevant' clauses.

For 3-valued interpretations, $I_1 = < T_1, F_1 >$ and $I_2 = < T_2, F_2 >$, by their *F-union* $I_1 \cup_F I_2$ we denote the tuple $< T_1 \cup T_2, F_1 \cup F_2 >$. Clearly, $I_1 \cup_F I_2 = \Sigma_F\{I_1, I_2\}$. The idea behind the construction of weakly perfect models is as follows. Take any program $P = P_0$ and let $M_0 = < \emptyset, \emptyset >$. Let $P_1 = \frac{P}{M_0}$, find the least model M_1 of the bottom layer $L(P_1)$ of P_1 and reduce P modulo $M_0 \cup M_1$ obtaining a new program $P_2 = \frac{P}{M_0 \cup M_1}$. Find its bottom layer $L(P_2)$ and its least model M_2 and let $P_3 = \frac{P}{M_0 \cup M_1 \cup M_2}$. Continue the process until either the resulting k-th program P_k is empty, in which case $M_P = M_1 \cup \ldots \cup M_{k-1}$ is the weakly perfect model of P, or, otherwise, until either $S(P_k)$ is empty or $L(P_k)$ does not have a least model, in which case the weakly perfect model of P is undefined.

We now formalize the above approach, by giving a transfinite definition of a weakly perfect model M_P of a logic program P.

Definition 6.15 *[Przymusinska and Przymusinski, 1988] Suppose that P is a logic program and let $P_0 = P$, $M_0 = < \emptyset, \emptyset >$. Suppose that $\alpha > 0$ is a countable ordinal such that programs P_δ and interpretations M_δ have been already defined for all $\delta < \alpha$. Let*

$$N_\alpha = \Sigma_F\{M_\delta : 0 < \delta < \alpha\},$$

$$P_\alpha = \frac{P}{N_\alpha}, \quad S_\alpha = S(P_\alpha), \quad L_\alpha = L(P_\alpha).$$

- *If the program P_α is empty, then the construction stops and $M_P = N_\alpha$ is the* weakly perfect model *of P. The ordinal α is called the* depth *of P and is denoted by $\lambda(P)$. For $0 < \alpha < \lambda(P)$, the set S_α is called the α-th* weak stratum *of P and the program L_α is called the α-th* layer *of P.*

- *Else, if the bottom stratum $S_\alpha = S(P_\alpha)$ of P_α is empty or if the least model of the bottom layer $L_\alpha = L(P_\alpha)$ of P_α does not exist, then the construction also stops and the weakly perfect model of P is undefined.*

- *Otherwise, the interpretation M_α is defined as the least model of the bottom layer $L_\alpha = L(P_\alpha)$ of P_α and the construction continues.*

In the process of constructing the strata S_α, some ground atoms may be eliminated by the reduction and not fall into any stratum. Such atoms should be added to an arbitrary stratum, e.g. the first, and assumed false in M_P.

It is easy to see that the construction always stops after countably many steps. A particularly important case of the above definition occurs when all the strata S_α consist only of trivial components or – equivalently – when all the program layers L_α are *positive* logic programs.

Definition 6.16 *[Przymusinska end Przymusinski, 1988] We say that a logic program P is* **weakly stratified** *if it has a weakly perfect model and if all of its strata S_α consist only of trivial components or – equivalently – when all of its layers L_α are positive logic programs. In this case, we call the set of program's strata $\{S_\alpha : 0 < \alpha < \lambda(P)\}$ the* **weak stratification** *of P.*

Remark 6.1 *Observe, that since every positive logic program has the least model, a program P is weakly stratified if and only if whenever P_α is non-empty, $S_\alpha = S(P_\alpha)$ is also non-empty and consists only of trivial components.*

Example 6.11 *Consider the program P from Example 6.10. We obtain:*

$$P_1 = P, \quad S_1 = S(P) = \{p(1,2), p(1,1), p(2,2), p(2,1)\},$$

$$L_1 = L(P) = \{p(1,2) \leftarrow\},$$

and therefore

$$M_1 = <\{p(1,2)\}, \{p(1,1), p(2,2), p(2,1)\}>.$$

Consequently, $P_2 = \frac{P_1}{M_1} = \{q(1) \leftarrow \neg q(2)\}$, $S_2 = S(P_2) = \{q(2)\}$ is the union of maximal components of P_2 and $L_2 = L(P_2) = \emptyset$ is the set of clauses from P_2 whose heads belong to S_2. Therefore, $M_2 = <\emptyset, \{q(2)\}>$. As a result,

$$P_3 = \frac{P_2}{M_1 \cup M_2} = \{q(1) \leftarrow\}, \quad S_3 = \{q(1)\}, \quad L_3 = P_3 \quad and \quad M_3 = <\{q(1)\}, \emptyset>.$$

Since $P_4 = \frac{P_3}{M_1 \cup M_2 \cup M_3} = \emptyset$, the construction is completed, P is weakly stratified, $\{S_1, S_2, S_3\}$ is its weak stratification and

$$M_P = M_1 \cup M_2 \cup M_3 = <\{p(1,2), q(1)\}, \{p(1,1), p(2,2), p(2,1), q(2)\}>$$

is its weakly perfect model.

The class of programs having weakly perfect models is much broader than the class of weakly stratified programs.

Example 6.12 *Let P consist of clauses:*

$$p \leftarrow q, \quad q \leftarrow \neg p.$$

Then P has a single component and therefore its weakly perfect model is the least model of P, namely $M_P = < \{p\}, \{q\} >$ (see Corollary 6.14). Clearly, P is not weakly stratified. See [Przymusinska and Przymusinski, 1988, Example 3.4] for a discussion of this example.

Example 6.13 *Let P be as follows:*

$$
\begin{aligned}
p &\leftarrow q, \neg r \\
q &\leftarrow r, \neg p \\
r &\leftarrow p, \neg q
\end{aligned}
$$

The definition of propositions p, q and r is mutually circular, P has a single component and therefore its weakly perfect model is the least model of P, which is empty. Naturally, P is not weakly stratified.

The class of weakly stratified programs extends the class of (locally) stratified programs.

Theorem 6.12 *[Przymusinska and Przymusinski, 1988] Every locally stratified program is weakly stratified. Moreover, for locally stratified programs, the notions of a perfect model and a weakly perfect model coincide.*

Therefore, the weakly perfect model semantics *extends the perfect model* semantics from the class of locally stratified programs to a broader class of logic programs. Weakly perfect models also share the property of minimality with perfect models.

Theorem 6.13 *[Przymusinska and Przymusinski, 1988] Every weakly perfect model is minimal.*

It can be easily seen that the weakly perfect model semantics is based on the principle of *iterated (2-valued) least model semantics*. In particular, for programs with a single stratum the weakly perfect model semantics coincides with the least model semantics.

Corollary 6.14 *If a logic program P consists of a single stratum (in particular, if it consists of a single component), then for a model M of P:*

$$M \text{ is weakly perfect} \equiv M \text{ is perfect} \equiv M \text{ is the least model of } P.$$

The advantages of the weakly perfect model semantics include the facts that it extends the perfect model semantics, is patterned after the stratified approach and is based on the iterated least model approach. It is also closely related to the circumscriptive approach in non-monotonic reasoning (see Section 7). However, the weakly perfect model semantics also has some important drawbacks, namely, it is defined only for a restricted class of logic programs.

Example 6.14 *[Van Gelder et al., 1990] Let P be as follows:*

$$p \leftarrow q, \neg r, \neg s$$
$$q \leftarrow r, \neg p$$
$$r \leftarrow p, \neg q$$
$$s \leftarrow \neg p, \neg q, \neg r.$$

If we ignore the premise $\neg s$ in the first clause, then the first three clauses define p,q and r in a mutually circular fashion (see Example 6.13) and therefore we are compelled to assume the falsity of p, q and r and thus the intended semantics should imply s. The presence of the negative premise $\neg s$ does not seem to modify this conclusion. Unfortunatelly, it is easy to see that P consists of a single component and does not have the least model. Therefore, instead of producing the expected model $< \{s\}, \{p, q, r\} >$, the weakly perfect model semantics is undefined.

6.6 Stable Model Semantics

Stable models have been introduced in [Gelfond and Lifschitz, 1988] by means of a fixed point definition, which uses a natural transformation of logic programs. We first introduce the *Gelfond-Lifschitz* operator Γ acting on *2-valued* interpretations of a given program P. All interpretations and models in this section are 2-valued.

Definition 6.17 (The Gelfond-Lifschitz Operator) *[Gelfond and Lifschitz, 1988] Let P be a logic program and let I be its 2-valued interpretation. By a GL-transformation of P modulo I we mean a new program $\frac{P}{I}$ obtained from P by performing the following two reductions:*

- *removing from P all clauses which contain a negative premise $L = \neg A$ such that $\hat{I}(L) = 0$;*

- *removing from all the remaining clauses those negative premises $L = \neg A$ which satisfy $\hat{I}(L) = 1$.*

Since the resulting program $\frac{P}{I}$ does not contain any negative premises, it is positive and thus, by Theorem 6.4, it has a unique least model J. We define $\Gamma(I) = J$.

It turns out that fixed points of the Gelfond-Lifschitz operator Γ for a program P are always models of P.

Proposition 6.4 *[Gelfond and Lifschitz, 1988] Fixed points of the Gelfond-Lifschitz operator Γ for a program P are minimal models of P.*

This result leads to the definition of the *stable model semantics*.

Definition 6.18 (Stable Model Semantics) *[Gelfond and Lifschitz, 1988] A 2-valued interpretation I of a logic program P is called a stable model of P if $\Gamma(I) = I$. If a program P has a unique stable model M_P, then its stable model semantics is determined by this unique intended model M_P.*

Stable model semantics is closely related to the *autoepistemic* approach to non-monotonic reasoning (see [Gelfond, 1987] and Section 7). The same semantics has been independently discovered in [Bidoit and Froidevaux, 1988], where it is defined in terms of *default logic* and thus can be called the *default model semantics*.

Example 6.15 *Consider the program P in Example 6.9 and let*

$$M =< \{p(1,2), q(1)\}, \{p(1,1), p(2,2), p(2,1), q(2)\} >$$

be the unique weakly perfect model of P (see Example 6.11). The application of GL-transformation to P modulo M results in the following positive program $\frac{P}{M}$:

$$p(1,2) \leftarrow \tag{11}$$
$$q(1) \leftarrow p(1,2) \tag{12}$$
$$q(2) \leftarrow p(2,2) \tag{13}$$

whose least model is M itself. Therefore, $\Gamma(M) = M$, i.e., M is a fixed point of the operator Γ, and thus M is a stable model of P. It is easy to see that M is the only stable model of P. Consequently, the stable model semantics and the weakly perfect model semantics coincide in this case.

In general, a logic program may have one, none or many stable models. For example, the program $p \leftarrow \neg p$ does not have any stable models, while the program $p \leftarrow \neg q$, $q \leftarrow \neg p$ has two such models. However, in case of weakly stratified programs stable models are always unique.

Theorem 6.15 *[Przymusinska and Przymusinski, 1988] Every weakly stratified logic program P has a unique stable model M_P, which coincides with the unique weakly perfect model of P.*

In particular, the stable model semantics extends the perfect model semantics.

Corollary 6.16 *[Gelfond and Lifschitz, 1988] Every locally stratified program P has a unique stable model which coincides with the unique perfect model of P.*

In general, beyond the class of weakly stratified programs, the stable model semantics and the weakly perfect model semantics are different.

Example 6.16 *The program P in Example 6.12 has a weakly perfect model but it is easily seen not to have any stable models.*
On the other hand, the program in Example 6.14 has the expected (intended) unique stable model $M_P =< \{s\}, \{p, q, r\} >$, but its weakly perfect model is undefined.

The advantages of the stable model semantics include the fact that it extends the perfect model semantics, has an elegant and simple definition and is closely related to autoepistemic and default approaches to non-monotonic reasoning (see Section 7). However, the stable model semantics also has some important drawbacks. First of all, it is defined only for a restricted class of programs and, secondly, it does not always seem to lead to the expected (intended) semantics.

Example 6.17 ([Van Gelder *et al.*, **1990**]) *Let P be given by:*

$$b \leftarrow \neg a$$
$$a \leftarrow \neg b$$
$$p \leftarrow \neg p$$
$$p \leftarrow \neg a.$$

Although its weakly perfect model is undefined, this program has a unique stable model $M = \{p, b\}$. However, the unique stable model M seems unintuitive [Van Gelder et al., 1990] in view of the fact that, in 2-valued logic, p is a consequence of the third clause and therefore the last clause can be considered meaningless. The first two clauses, however, do not seem to have any reasonable (2-valued) intended semantics.

Moreover, it is easy to see that it is impossible to derive b from P using any Horn-resolution procedure. This is because any Horn-resolution procedure beginning with the goal $\leftarrow b$ will reach only the first two clauses of P, from which b cannot be derived.

As we will see in the next Section, the well-founded model semantics, which can be viewed as *3-valued stable model semantics* seems to avoid the difficulties encountered with the weakly perfect model semantics and the stable model semantics.

6.7   Well Founded Model Semantics

The well-founded semantics has been introduced in [Van Gelder *et al.*, 1990] and it seems to be the most adequate extension of the perfect model semantics to the class of *all* logic programs, avoiding various drawbacks of the other proposed approaches. Well-founded semantics also has been shown to be equivalent to suitable forms of 3-valued formalizations of all four major non-monotonic formalisms [Przymusinski, 1989d] (see Section 7).

One of the important features of well-founded models, and a strong indication of their naturality, is the fact that they can be described in many different, but equivalent, ways (see [Van Gelder *et al.*, 1990; Przymusinski, 1989a; Przymusinski, 1989d; Van Gelder, 1989a; Bry, 1989]). In this paper we use the (iterated) least fixed point approach proposed in [Przymusinski, 1989a], which seems to be a natural extension of least fixed point definitions of least models and perfect models and is also closely related to Fitting's extension of Clark's semantics. As opposed to the original definition proposed in [Van Gelder *et al.*, 1990], the iterated fixed point definition given here is constructive. In the second part of this section we will show that the well-founded semantics can be also viewed as *3-valued stable model semantics*.

First, for any interpretation J of a program P, we introduce the operator $\Theta_J : \mathcal{I} \to \mathcal{I}$ on the set $\mathcal{I}$ of all 3-valued interpretations of P, ordered by the standard ordering $\preceq$. The operator can be viewed as a cross between the Fitting operator Φ (Section 6.1) and Generalized Van Emden-Kowalski operators Ψ_J (see Section 6.3).

Definition 6.19 *[Przymusinski, 1989a] Suppose that P is a logic program and J is its interpretation. The operator $\Theta_J : \mathcal{I} \to \mathcal{I}$ on the set $\mathcal{I}$ of all 3-valued interpretations of P is defined as follows. If $I \in \mathcal{I}$ is an interpretation of P and A is a ground atom then $\Theta_J(I)$ is an interpretation given by:*

(i) $\Theta_J(I)(A) = 1$ if there is a clause $A \leftarrow L_1, \ldots, L_n$ in P such that, for all $i \leq n$, either $\hat{J}(L_i) = 1$ or L_i is positive and $I(L_i) = 1$;

(ii) $\Theta_J(I)(A) = 0$ if for every clause $A \leftarrow L_1, \ldots, L_n$ in P there is an $i \leq n$ such that either $\hat{J}(L_i) = 0$ or L_i is positive and $I(L_i) = 0$;

(iii) $\Theta_J(I)(A) = \frac{1}{2}$, otherwise.

Intuitively, the interpretation J represents facts *currently known* to be true or false. The *true* facts in $\Theta_J(I)$ consist of those atoms which can be derived *in one step* from the program P assuming that *all* facts in J hold and that all *positive* facts in I are true. The *false* facts in $\Theta_J(I)$ consist of those atoms whose falsity can be deduced *in one step* (using the closed world assumption) from the program P assuming that *all* facts in J hold and that all *negative* facts in I are true. Observe, that, as opposed to Van Emden-Kowalski operators Ψ_J, the operators Θ_J are completely *symmetric* in the sense that they treat negative and positive information symmetrically (dually).

Theorem 6.17 *[Przymusinski, 1989a] For every interpretation J, the operator Θ_J is monotone and it has a unique least fixed point*[11] *given by $\Theta_J^{\uparrow\omega}$.*

We will denote this least fixed point of Θ_J by $\Omega(J)$, i.e.

$$\Omega(J) = \Theta_J^{\uparrow\omega}.$$

Clearly, Ω constitutes an operator on the set of all interpretations of P.

Observe that, although the operators Θ_J resemble the Fitting operator Φ, they do not coincide with it. Moreover, the above Theorem is very different from Theorem 6.2. This is a consequence of the fact that the operators Θ_J are defined on the set of all interpretations ordered by the standard ordering $\preceq$ and not by the F-ordering $\preceq_F$ and thus the iterations begin from the smallest interpretation $I_0 = <\emptyset, \mathcal{H}>$ and not from the F-smallest interpretation $<\emptyset, \emptyset>$. As a result, as opposed to Φ, least points of operators Θ_J can be always obtained after only ω steps, where ω is the first infinite ordinal.

Intuitively, the least fixed point $\Omega(J) = \Theta_J^{\uparrow\omega}$ of Θ_J contains all facts, whose truth or falsity can be deduced (using the closed world assumption) from P knowing J. The operator Ω turns out to have a unique F-least fixed point.

Theorem 6.18 *[Przymusinski, 1989a] The operator Ω always has a unique F-least fixed point M_P, i.e. the F-least interpretation M_P such that*

$$\Omega(M_P) = M_P.$$

Moreover, all fixed points of Ω are minimal models of P.

As we will see below, the F-least fixed point of Ω can be simply obtained as a suitable iteration $\Omega^{\uparrow\lambda}$ of Ω. First, we give a definition of well-founded models.

---

[11]Recall that ω stands for the first infinite ordinal and that the iteration begins from the smallest interpretation $I_0 = <\emptyset, \mathcal{H}>$.

Definition 6.20 *[Przymusinski, 1989a] We call the unique F-least fixed point M_P of Ω the* well founded model *of P.*

Since the well-founded model of P is defined as the F-least fixed point of the operator Ω, which is itself defined by means of least fixed points of Θ, well founded models can be viewed as *iterated least fixed points* of the operator Θ. Although our definition of well-founded models is different from the original definition given in [Van Gelder *et al.*, 1990], the two notions are equivalent.

Theorem 6.19 *[Przymusinski, 1989a] Well founded models introduced above coincide with well-founded models originally defined in [Van Gelder et al., 1990].*

Now we can introduce the well-founded semantics of logic programs.

Definition 6.21 (Well-Founded Semantics) *[Van Gelder et al., 1990] The well founded semantics of a logic program is determined by the unique well-founded model M_P.*

In order to obtain a *constructive* definition of the well-founded model M_P of a given program P, we define the following (transfinite) sequence $\{I_\alpha\}$ of interpretations of P:

$$
\begin{aligned}
I_0 &= \ <\emptyset,\emptyset> \\
I_{\alpha+1} &= \ \Omega(I_\alpha) = \Theta_{I_\alpha}^{\uparrow\omega} \\
I_\delta &= \ \Sigma_F\{I_\alpha : \alpha < \delta\},
\end{aligned}
$$

for limit δ. Clearly, for any α, I_α coincides with $\Omega^{\uparrow\alpha}$, where the F-ordering of interpretations is used to generate consecutive iterations, i.e., we have:

$$I_\alpha = \Omega^{\uparrow\alpha}.$$

At any given step α, the next iteration $I_{\alpha+1}$ is obtained as the least fixed point $\Omega(I_\alpha) = \Theta_{I_\alpha}^\omega$ of the operator Θ_{I_α}. This is justified by the fact that, as we observed before, the least fixed point $\Omega(I_\alpha) = \Theta_{I_\alpha}^\omega$ contains all facts, whose truth or falsity can be deduced from P knowing I_α.

One can show that the sequence $\{I_\alpha\}$ is well-defined and F-increasing and therefore, since all interpretations are countable, there must exist the smallest λ, such that I_λ is a fixed point , i.e., such that:

$$I_{\lambda+1} = \Omega(I_\lambda) = I_\lambda$$

i.e., I_λ is a fixed point of the the operator Ω. We call $\lambda = \lambda(P)$ the depth of the program P. It turns out that I_λ is in fact the F-least fixed point of Ω and thus it coincides with the well-founded model M_P of P.

Theorem 6.20 *[Przymusinski, 1989a] The interpretation $I_\lambda = \Omega^{\uparrow\lambda}$ is the F-least fixed point of the operator Ω and thus it coincides with the well-founded model M_P of P:*

$$M_P = I_\lambda = \Omega^{\uparrow\lambda}.$$

Observe, that the above description of well-founded models is very similar to the iterated fixed point definition of perfect models given in Section 6.3, but it treats negative and positive information completely symmetrically (dually) and does not require the advance notion of (local) stratification.

Example 6.18 *Consider the program P from Example 6.9 given by:*

$$
\begin{aligned}
p(1,2) &\leftarrow \\
q(1) &\leftarrow p(1,2), \neg q(2) \\
q(1) &\leftarrow p(1,1), \neg q(1) \\
q(2) &\leftarrow p(2,2), \neg q(2) \\
q(2) &\leftarrow p(2,1), \neg q(1).
\end{aligned}
$$

We have $I_0 = < \emptyset, \emptyset >$ and $I_1 = \Omega(I_1) = \Theta_{I_0}^{\uparrow \omega}$. Since $\Theta_{I_0}^{\uparrow 0} = < \emptyset, \mathcal{H} >$ it follows from the definition of Θ that:

$$
\Theta_{I_0}^{\uparrow 1} = \Theta_{I_0}(< \emptyset, \mathcal{H} >) = < \{p(1,2)\}, \{p(2,1), p(1,1), p(2,2), q(1), q(2)\} > .
$$

Similarly,

$$
\Theta_{I_0}^{\uparrow 2} = \Theta_{I_0}(\Theta_{I_0}^{\uparrow 1}) = < \{p(1,2)\}, \{p(2,1), p(1,1), p(2,2), q(2)\} >
$$

and it is easy to see that $\Theta_{I_0}^{\uparrow 2}$ is a fixed point of Θ_{I_0}, i.e.,

$$
\Theta_{I_0}^{\uparrow 2} = \Theta_{I_0}^{\uparrow \omega} = I_1.
$$

Now, $I_2 = \Omega(I_1) = \Theta_{I_1}^{\uparrow \omega}$ and since $\Theta_{I_1}^{\uparrow 0} = < \emptyset, \mathcal{H} >$ it follows from the definition of Θ that:

$$
\Theta_{I_1}^{\uparrow 1} = \Theta_{I_1}(< \emptyset, \mathcal{H} >) = < \{p(1,2), q(1)\}, \{p(2,1), p(1,1), p(2,2), q(2)\} >
$$

and it is easy to see that $\Theta_{I_1}^{\uparrow 1}$ is a fixed point of Θ_{I_1}, i.e.,

$$
\Theta_{I_1}^{\uparrow 1} = \Theta_{I_1}^{\uparrow \omega} = I_2.
$$

Moreover, it is clear that the construction stops here because $I_3 = \Omega(I_2) = I_2$ and the well founded model of P is 2-valued and given by:

$$
M_P = I_2 = < \{p(1,2), q(1)\}, \{p(2,1), p(1,1), p(2,2), q(2)\} > .
$$

The well-founded model coincides therefore with the weakly perfect model and the unique stable model of P. Moreover, the depth of the program is $\lambda(P) = 2$.

A particularly important class of logic programs consists of those programs which have a *2-valued* well-founded model.

Definition 6.22 *[Przymusinski, 1989a] We call a logic program P saturated if its well-founded model M_P is 2-valued.*

For example the above discussed program is saturated. For saturated logic programs, the well-founded and the stable model semantics coincide.

Theorem 6.21 *[Van Gelder et al., 1990] If a program has a 2-valued well-founded model M_P then it also has a unique stable model and the two models coincide.*

For weakly stratified programs, all three extensions of the perfect model semantics coincide.

Theorem 6.22 *[Przymusinska and Przymusinski, 1988] For weakly stratified logic programs, well-founded models coincide with weakly perfect models and with unique stable models.*

In particular, the well-founded model semantics extends the perfect model semantics.

Corollary 6.23 *[Van Gelder et al., 1990] The well-founded model of a locally stratified program coincides with its perfect model.*

In general, the well-founded semantics, the stable model semantics and the weakly perfect model semantics are different. The fact that the well-founded semantics is different from the weakly perfect semantics follows immediately from Theorem 6.21 and from the examples illustrating the differences between the stable model semantics and the weakly perfect model semantics given in the previous section. Moreover, the program $p \leftarrow \neg p$ does not have any stable models, but its well-founded model is $< \emptyset, \emptyset >$. There exist also programs, which admit unique (2-valued) stable models that do not coincide with well-founded models. For example, the well-founded model of the program presented in Example 6.17 is $< \emptyset, \emptyset >$, which seems to be more intuitive than its stable model $M = < \{p, b\}, \{a\} >$.

In [Przymusinski, 1989a] the iterated fixed point definition of well founded models is used to introduce the so called *dynamic stratification* of an *arbitrary* logic program P, with properties analogous to local stratification. Using dynamic stratification, [Przymusinski, 1989a] showed that the well-founded model M_P can also be viewed as an *iterated least model* of a program and that well-founded models can be defined by means of a suitable *preference relation* between atoms, in a manner analogous to the definition of perfect models.

6.7.1 Well-Founded Semantics Coincides With 3-Valued Stable Semantics

In this section we give a definition of *3-valued stable models* which is exactly analogous to the definition of 2-valued stable models given in the previous section. Every 2-valued stable model is a 3-valued stable model, so our definition extends the notion of stable models.

We show that the well-founded model M_P of a program P is the *F-least stable model* of P. In particular, every logic program has at least one 3-valued stable model, namely M_P.

As we mentioned before, models of a program can be thought of as *possible worlds* representing possible states of our knowledge. Since, at any given moment, our knowledge about the world is likely to be incomplete, we need the ability to describe possible worlds in which some facts are neither true nor false and thus their status is unknown. This explains the need to use 3-valued logic or 3-valued possible worlds to describe our knowledge.

Before defining 3-valued stable models we need to expand our language by adding to it the proposition **u** denoting the property of being *unknown* or *undefined*. We assume that every interpretation I satisfies $I(\mathbf{u}) = \frac{1}{2}$ and thus $\hat{I}(\neg \mathbf{u}) = \frac{1}{2}$. We can therefore always replace $\neg \mathbf{u}$ by $\mathbf{u}$. By a *non-negative* program we mean a program, whose premises are either positive atoms or $\mathbf{u}$. First, we need the following generalization of the Kowalski-Van Emden Theorem 6.4:

Theorem 6.24 *Every non-negative logic program P has a unique least 3-valued model.*

We now extend the Gelfond-Lifschitz operator Γ to a 3-valued operator Γ^* as follows:

Definition 6.23 *Let P be a logic program and let I be its 3-valued interpretation. By the extended GL-transformation of P modulo I we mean a new program $\frac{P}{I}$ obtained from P by performing the following three operations:*

- *Removing from P all clauses which contain a negative premise $L = \neg A$ such that $\hat{I}(L) = 0$;*

- *Replacing in all the remaining clauses those negative premises $L = \neg A$ which satisfy $\hat{I}(L) = \frac{1}{2}$ by $\mathbf{u}$;*

- *Removing from all the remaining clauses those negative premises $L = \neg A$ which satisfy $\hat{I}(L) = 1$.*

Since the resulting program $\frac{P}{I}$ is non-negative thus, by Theorem 6.24, it has a unique least 3-valued model J. We define $\Gamma^*(I) = J$.

Fixed points of the operator Γ^* for a program P are defined as 3-valued stable models.

Definition 6.24 *A 3-valued interpretation I of a logic program P is called a 3-valued stable model of P if $\Gamma^*(I) = I$. The 3-valued stable model semantics of a program P is determined by the set $MOD(P)$ of all 3-valued stable models of P.*

It is easy to see that the above definition is a strict extension of the standard definition of stable models. In fact, standard stable models coincide with 2-valued stable models introduced above.

Example 6.19 *Suppose that P is:*

$$
\begin{aligned}
c &\leftarrow \neg d \\
a &\leftarrow \neg b \\
b &\leftarrow \neg a
\end{aligned}
$$

and let $M = <\{c\}, \{d\}>$. Then the transformed program is:

$$
\begin{aligned}
c &\leftarrow \\
a &\leftarrow \mathbf{u} \\
b &\leftarrow \mathbf{u}
\end{aligned}
$$

and its least model $\Gamma^*(M)$ coincides with M which shows that M is a 3-valued stable model of P.

Well-founded models are F-least stable models.

Theorem 6.25 *The well-founded model M_P of a program P is the F-least 3-valued stable model of P. Consequently, the well-founded semantics coincides with the 3-valued stable model semantics.*

We can say, borrowing from Horty and Thomasson's inheritance network terminology, that the well founded model is the most *skeptical* 3-valued stable model or possible world for P. For example, if P is given by $a \leftarrow \neg b$, $b \leftarrow \neg a$, then P has three stable models. One, in which a is true and b is false, the second, exactly opposite and the third in which both a and b are undefined. The last model, the most 'skeptical' one, is the well-founded model of P.

Corollary 6.26 *Every logic program has at least one 3-valued stable model, namely, the well-founded model M_P.*

Recall, that not every logic program has 2-valued stable models. Also, observe that although the characterization of well founded models as F-least 3-valued stable models is mathematically elegant it does not provide any constructive way of building such models.

6.8   Semantics Based on Non-Herbrand Models

Throughout the paper, with the exception of Clark's semantics and its 3-valued extension due to Kunen, we restricted ourselves to *Herbrand* interpretations and models. This approach is very convenient, in most cases leads to semantics based on *one* intended Herbrand model and is often quite suitable for *deductive database* applications. However, from the point of view of *logic programming*, the Herbrand approach has an important drawback, which was called the *universal query problem* in [Przymusinski, 1989c].

Suppose that our program P consists of a trivial clause $p(a)$. The program is positive and has only one (2-valued) Herbrand model $M_P = \{p(a)\}$. Therefore all model-theoretic semantics of P based on Herbrand models coincide and are determined by the model M_P. Consequently, all such semantics imply $\forall X\, p(X)$, because

$$M_P \models \forall X\, p(X).$$

In addition to not being very intuitive, this conclusion causes at least two negative consequences:

- Since $\forall X\, p(X)$ is a positive formula, not implied by P itself, all semantics based on Herbrand models of P violate the principle that *no new positive information should be introduced by the semantics of positive programs*, which – as it was explained in [Przymusinski, 1989c] – seems to be a natural and important requirement in logic programming.

- They also seem to *a priori* prevent standard unification-based computational mechanisms, typically used in logic programming, from being complete with respect to this semantics.

Indeed, when we ask the query $p(X)$ in logic programming, we not only want to have an answer to the question 'is there an X for which p(X) holds?', but, in fact, we are interested in obtaining *all* most general bindings (or substitutions) θ for which our semantics implies $\forall X\, p(X)\theta$. Therefore, in this case, if we ask $\leftarrow p(X)$, we should expect simply the answer 'yes' indicating that p(X) is satisfied for all X's or – in other words – signifying, that the empty substitution is a correct answer substitution. Unfortunately, standard unification-based computational mechanisms will be only capable of returning the special case substitution $\theta = \{X|a\}$.

It is sometimes argued that logic programming should only be concerned with Herbrand models rather than with general models of P. This conclusion is motivated by the belief that the role of logic programming is to answer existential queries and by the well-known fact that an existential formula F is derivable from a given (universal) theory T if and only if it is satisfied in all Herbrand models of T. This argument is only partially correct. In reality, *logic programming is not only concerned with answering existential queries, but it is primarily concerned with providing 'most general' bindings (substitutions) for the answers.* For example, if our program is

$$parent(X, father(X))$$
$$parent(X, mother(X))$$
$$grand\_parent(X, Y) \quad \leftarrow \quad parent(X, Z), parent(Z, Y)$$

and we ask $\leftarrow grand\_parent(X, Y)$, then we expect to obtain answers:

$$Y = mother(father(X)), \; Y = mother(mother(X))$$

etc., signifying that

$$\forall X \; grand\_parent(X, mother(father(X)))$$
$$\forall X \; grand\_parent(X, mother(mother(X))), \ldots$$

In other words, we expect to obtain 'most general' substitutions for which the given query holds and, as a result, we are in fact interested in answers to universal queries, like *'Is it true that for every X grandparent(X,mother(father(X)))?'*, to which general models and Herbrand models often provide different answers, as it was illustrated above.

There are two natural solutions to the universal query problem:

1. One can stick to Herbrand models of the program, but in addition:

   - Either *extend the language* of the program by asserting the existence of *infinitely* many function symbols (or constants) (see e.g. [Kunen, 1987]);

   - Or *extend the language* by asserting the existence of one or more 'dummy' functions (see e.g. [Van Gelder *et al.*, 1990]), which exist in the language, but are not used in the program.

From the semantic point of view these two approaches are essentially equivalent, but they also share a common problem, namely in some cases they may not be very natural. The reason is that one may not wish to automatically assume the *existence of objects* that are not mentioned *explicitly* in the program. Such an assumption can be called an *infinite domain assumption* and can be viewed as being in some sense *opposite* to the closed world assumption. In its presence, if we know only that $p(a)$ holds, then we are forced to conclude that there are many x's for which $p(x)$ is false, which may not always be desirable.

2. Another approach (see [Przymusinski, 1989c]) is to *extend the definitions of intended models* to include *non-Herbrand* models, thus leading to the definitions of non-Herbrand perfect models (resp. non-Herbrand stable models, non-Herbrand well founded models, etc.). One then defines the corresponding semantics to be determined by the set $MOD(P)$ of all, *Herbrand and non-Herbrand*, perfect models (resp. stable models, well founded models, etc.). Using this approach and knowing only that $p(a)$ holds, the answer to the query 'Does there exist an x for which p(x) is false?' is undefined, which in some contexts may seem more reasonable.

The extension of the definition of intended models, so that they include non-Herbrand models, is usually quite straightforward. For the perfect model semantics it has been done in [Przymusinski, 1989c] and for the other semantics it can be done in an analogous way.

However, when using non-Herbrand models in the context of logic programming, one has to additionally assume that they satisfy to so called *Clark's Equational Theory* (CET) [Kunen, 1987]:

CET1. $X = X$;

CET2. $X = Y \Rightarrow Y = X$;

CET3. $X = Y \wedge Y = Z \Rightarrow X = Z$;

CET4. $X_1 = Y_1 \wedge ... \wedge X_m = Y_m \Rightarrow f(X_1, ..., X_m) = f(Y_1, ..., Y_m)$, for any function f;

CET5. $X_1 = Y_1 \wedge ... \wedge X_m = Y_m \Rightarrow (p(X_1, ..., X_m) \Rightarrow p(Y_1, ..., Y_m))$, for predicate p;

CET6. $f(X_1, ..., X_m) \neq g(Y_1, ..., Y_n)$, for any two different function symbols f and g;

CET7. $f(X_1, ..., X_m) = f(Y_1, ..., Y_m) \Rightarrow X_1 = Y_1 \wedge ... \wedge X_m = Y_m$, for any function f;

CET8. $t[X] \neq X$, for any term $t[X]$ different from X, but containing X.

The first five axioms describe the usual *equality axioms* and the remaining three axioms are called *unique names axioms* or *freeness axioms*. The significance of these axioms to logic programming is widely recognized [Lloyd, 1984; Kunen, 1987].

The equality axioms (CET1) – (CET5) ensure that we can always assume that the *equality predicate* = *is interpreted as identity* in all models. Consequently, in order to satisfy the CET axioms, we just have to restrict ourselves to those models in which the equality predicate – when interpreted as identity – satisfies the unique names axioms (CET6) – (CET8).

For more information about the relationship between approaches based on Herbrand and on non-Herbrand models see [Gelfond *et al.*, 1988; Przymusinski, 1989c].

7 Relationship to Non-Monotonic Formalisms

Non-monotonic reasoning, logic programming and deductive databases are areas of crucial and growing significance to Artificial Intelligence and to the whole field of computer science. It is therefore important to achieve a better understanding of the relationship existing between these three fields.

There is no doubt that the three areas are related. Logic programming and database systems implement negation using various non-monotonic negation operators, such as the negation as failure mechanism of Prolog. The non-monotonic character of those operators closely relates logic programming and deductive databases to non-monotonic reasoning. Conversely, because of the non-monotonic character of such procedural operators, they can often be used to implement other non-monotonic formalisms [Reiter, 1986], thus opening the possibility for using logic programming and deductive databases as inference engines for non-monotonic reasoning.

In spite of the close relationship between non-monotonic reasoning, on the one hand, and logic programming and deductive databases, on the other, in the past these research areas have been developing largely independently of one another and the exact nature of their relationship has not been closely investigated or understood. One possible explanation of this phenomenon is the fact that, traditionally (see [Lloyd, 1984]), the declarative semantics of logic programs has been based on the Clark predicate completion (see Section 6.1). Clark's formalism, although very elegant and natural, is not sufficiently general to be applied beyond the realm of logic programming and therefore does not play a major role in formalizing general non-monotonic reasoning in AI.

The situation has changed significantly with the introduction of stratified logic programs and the perfect model semantics (see Section 6.3). For locally stratified logic programs, the perfect model semantics has been shown (see [Przymusinski, 1988a] for an overview) to be *equivalent* to natural forms of *all four* major formalizations of non-monotonic reasoning in AI:

- McCarthy's circumscription [Przymusinski, 1989c; Lifschitz, 1988];

- Reiter's default theory [Bidoit and Froidevaux, 1987];

- Moore's autoepistemic logic [Gelfond, 1987];

- Reiter's CWA [Gelfond *et al.*, 1989].

These results shed a new light on the semantics of logic programs and deductive databases and established a closer link between non-monotonic reasoning, logic programming and deductive databases.

As we know, three essentially different extensions of the perfect model semantics have been proposed:

- *Stable model semantics* (or, equivalently, *default model semantics*) (see Section 6.6) has been shown to be equivalent to natural forms of autoepistemic logic and default theory [Gelfond, 1987; Bidoit and Froidevaux, 1988].

- *Weakly perfect model semantics* (see Section 6.5) has been shown to be equivalent to natural forms of circumscription and CWA [Przymusinska and Przymusinski, 1988].

- *Well-founded model semantics* (see Section 6.7): originally, its relationship to non-monotonic formalisms was unclear.

In view of this situation, it initially appeared that it will not be possible to extend the result stating the equivalence of the perfect model semantics to suitable forms of all four major non-monotonic formalisms to much broader classes of programs. Nevertheless, Przymusinski has shown in [Przymusinski, 1989d] that the well-founded semantics is in fact also *equivalent* to natural forms of *all four* major formalizations of non-monotonic reasoning. However, in order to achieve this equivalence, *3-valued extensions of non-monotonic formalisms* had to be introduced, which is natural in view of the fact that the well-founded semantics is also 3-valued.

This above mentioned results will likely contribute to a better understanding of relations existing between various formalizations of non-monotonic reasoning and, hopefully, to the eventual discovery of deeper underlying principles of non-monotonic reasoning. They also pave the way for using *efficient computation methods*, developed for logic programs and deductive databases, as inference engines for non-monotonic reasoning.

For more information about the relationship between non-monotonic reasoning, logic programming and deductive databases, the reader is referred to [Przymusinski, 1988a; Przymusinski, 1989b].

8   Conclusion

In the paper we have described various proposed semantics for deductive databases and logic programs and discussed their mutual relations. We have particularly emphasized recent research work in this area which appears to be very significant and lead to a change of perspective. As a result a fairly clear picture seems to emerge:

- Fitting's and Kunen's semantics both appear to be suitable 3-valued *extensions of Clark's predicate completion semantics* to the class of all logic programs. The differences between the two approaches simply reflect the differences existing between semantics based exclusively on Herbrand models and those including non-Herbrand models (see Section 6.8). Consequently, Kunen's semantics may be preferred in the context of logic programming, while Fitting's semantics may be more suitable for deductive databases. Both semantics inherit the drawbacks of Clark's semantics and do not closely relate to non-monotonic reasoning.

- There are two essentially different *2-valued model-theoretic* semantics of logic programs, both of which are closely related to non-monotonic formalisms. One of them is the *stable model semantics* [Gelfond and Lifschitz, 1988], which coincides with the *default model semantics* [Bidoit and Froidevaux, 1988] and is based on autoepistemic logic or default theory. The other is the *weakly perfect model semantics* [Przymusinska and Przymusinski, 1988], based on circumscription or CWA.

- There is a unique *3-valued model-theoretic* semantics, namely the *well-founded semantics* [Van Gelder *et al.*, 1990], which is equivalent to suitable forms of all 3-valued non-monotonic formalisms and appears to be the most adequate semantics for logic programs and deductive databases.

- The well-founded semantics is defined for all logic programs, whereas the 2-valued semantics are restricted to more narrow domains. All the three model-theoretic semantics extend the *perfect model semantics* of stratified programs and coincide in the class of *weakly stratified programs* [Przymusinska and Przymusinski, 1988].

Acknowledgments

The authors are grateful to Michael Gelfond, Vladimir Lifschitz and Allen Van Gelder for helpful discussions on the subject of this article.

References

[Apt and Van Emden, 1982] K. Apt and M. Van Emden. Contributions to the theory of logic programming. *Journal of the ACM*, 29:841–862, 1982.

[Apt *et al.*, 1988] K. Apt, H. Blair, and A. Walker. Towards a theory of declarative knowledge. In J. Minker, editor, *Foundations of Deductive Databases and Logic Programming*, pages 89–142, Morgan Kaufmann, Los Altos, CA., 1988.

[Bidoit and Froidevaux, 1987] N. Bidoit and C. Froidevaux. Minimalism subsumes default logic and circumscription in stratified logic programming. In *Proceedings of the Symposium on Principles of Database Systems*, ACM SIGACT-SIGMOD, 1987.

[Bidoit and Froidevaux, 1988] N. Bidoit and C. Froidevaux. General logical databases and programs: default logic semantics and stratification. *Journal of Information and Computation*, 1988. (in print).

[Bossu and Siegel, 1985] G. Bossu and P. Siegel. Saturation, nonmonotonic reasoning and the closed world assumption. *Journal of Artificial Intelligence*, 25:13–63, 1985.

[Bry, 1989] F. Bry. Logic programming as constructivism: a formalization and its application to databases. In *Proceedings of the Symposium on Principles of Database Systems*, pages 34–50, ACM SIGACT-SIGMOD, 1989.

[Chandra and Harel, 1985] A. Chandra and D. Harel. Horn clause queries and generalizations. *Journal of Logic Programming*, 1:1–15, 1985.

[Chang and Lee, 1973] C. Chang and R.C. Lee. *Symbolic Logic and Mechanical Theorem Proving*. Academic Press, New York, 1973.

[Clark, 1978] K.L. Clark. Negation as failure. In H. Gallaire and J. Minker, editors, *Logic and Data Bases*, pages 293–322, Plenum Press, New York, 1978.

[Codd, 1970] E. F. Codd. A relational model of data for large shared data banks. *Communications of the ACM*, 13(6):377–387, 1970.

[Colmerauer *et al.*, 1973] A. Colmerauer, H. Kanoui, P. Roussel, and R. Passero. *Un Systeme de Communication Homme-Machine en Francais*. Research report, Groupe de Recherche en Intelligence Artificielle, Universite d'Aix-Marseille, 1973.

[Fitting, 1985] M. Fitting. A Kripke-Kleene semantics for logic programs. *Journal of Logic Programming*, 2(4):295–312, 1985.

[Gallaire and Minker, 1978] H. Gallaire and J. Minker. *Logic and Data Bases.* Plenum Press, New York, 1978.

[Gallaire *et al.*, 1984] H. Gallaire, J. Minker, and J. Nicolas. Logic and databases: a deductive approach. *ACM Computing Surveys*, 16:153–185, 1984.

[Gelfond, 1987] M. Gelfond. On stratified autoepistemic theories. In *Proceedings AAAI-87*, pages 207–211, American Association for Artificial Intelligence, Morgan Kaufmann, Los Altos, CA, 1987.

[Gelfond and Lifschitz, 1988] M. Gelfond and V. Lifschitz. The stable model semantics for logic programming. In R. Kowalski and K. Bowen, editors, *Proceedings of the Fifth Logic Programming Symposium*, pages 1070–1080, Association for Logic Programming, MIT Press, Cambridge, Mass., 1988.

[Gelfond *et al.*, 1988] M. Gelfond, H. Przymusinska, and T. Przymusinski. Minimal model semantics vs. negation as failure: a comparison of semantics. In *Proceedings of the International Symposium on Methodologies for Intelligent Systems*, pages 335–343, ACM SIGART, 1988.

[Gelfond *et al.*, 1989] M. Gelfond, H. Przymusinska, and T. Przymusinski. On the relationship between circumscription and negation as failure. *Journal of Artificial Intelligence*, 38:75–94, 1989.

[Jaffar *et al.*, 1983] J. Jaffar, J-L. Lassez, and J. Lloyd. Completeness of the negation as failure rule. In *Proceedings AAAI-83*, pages 500–506, American Association for Artificial Intelligence, Morgan Kaufmann, Los Altos, CA, 1983.

[Kleene, 1952] S.C. Kleene. *Introduction to Metamathematics.* Van Nostrand, Princeton, 1952.

[Kowalski, 1974] R. Kowalski. Predicate logic as a programming language. In *Proceedings of IFIP-74*, pages 569–574, 1974.

[Kowalski, 1979] R. Kowalski. Algorithm = logic + control. *Communications of the ACM*, 22:424–436, 1979.

[Kunen, 1987] K. Kunen. Negation in logic programming. *Journal of Logic Programming*, 4(4):289–308, 1987.

[Kunen, 1988] K. Kunen. Some remarks on the completed database. In R. Kowalski and K. Bowen, editors, *Proceedings of the Fifth Logic Programming Symposium*, pages 978–992, Association for Logic Programming, MIT Press, Cambridge, Mass., 1988.

[Lifschitz, 1988] V. Lifschitz. On the declarative semantics of logic programs with negation. In J. Minker, editor, *Foundations of Deductive Databases and Logic Programming*, pages 177–192, Morgan Kaufmann, Los Altos, CA., 1988.

[Lloyd, 1984] J.W. Lloyd. *Foundations of Logic Programming.* Springer Verlag, New York, N.Y., first edition, 1984.

[Lloyd, 1987] J.W. Lloyd. *Foundations of Logic Programming.* Springer Verlag, New York, N.Y., second edition, 1987.

[Lloyd and Topor, 1985] J.W. Lloyd and R.W. Topor. A basis for deductive database systems. *Journal of Logic Programming,* 2:93–109, 1985.

[Lloyd and Topor, 1986] J.W. Lloyd and R.W. Topor. A basis for deductive database systems II. *Journal of Logic Programming,* 3:55–67, 1986.

[McCarthy, 1980] J. McCarthy. Circumscription – a form of non-monotonic reasoning. *Journal of Artificial Intelligence,* 13:27–39, 1980.

[Minker, 1982] J. Minker. On indefinite data bases and the closed world assumption. In *Proc. 6-th Conference on Automated Deduction,* pages 292–308, Springer Verlag, New York, 1982.

[Minker, 1988a] J. Minker. *Foundations of Deductive Databases and Logic Programming.* Morgan Kaufmann, Los Altos, CA., 1988.

[Minker, 1988b] J. Minker. Perspectives in deductive databases. *Journal of Logic Programming,* 5(1):33–60, 1988.

[Morris *et al.*, 1986] K. Morris, J.D. Ullman, and A. Van Gelder. Design overview of the NAIL! system. In *Proceedings of the Third International Conference on Logic Programming, London, July 1986,* Association for Logic Programming, Springer Verlag, 1986.

[Naqvi, 1986] S.A. Naqvi. A logic for negation in database systems. In J. Minker, editor, *Proceedings of the Workshop on Foundations of Deductive Databases and Logic Programming, Washington, D.C.,* pages 378–387, August 1986.

[Przymusinska and Przymusinski, 1988] H. Przymusinska and T. Przymusinski. Weakly perfect model semantics for logic programs. In R. Kowalski and K. Bowen, editors, *Proceedings of the Fifth Logic Programming Symposium,* pages 1106–1122, Association for Logic Programming, MIT Press, Cambridge, Mass., 1988.

[Przymusinski, 1988a] T. Przymusinski. Non-monotonic reasoning vs. logic programming: a new perspective. In D. Partridge and Y. Wilks, editors, *Formal Foundations of Artificial Intelligence,* Cambridge University Press, London, 1988. In print. (Extended abstract appeared in: T. Przymusinski. On the relationship between non-monotonic reasoning and logic programming. In *Proceedings AAAI-88,* pages 444–448, American Association for Artificial Intelligence, Morgan Kaufmann, Los Altos, CA, 1988.).

[Przymusinski, 1988b] T. Przymusinski. On the declarative semantics of stratified deductive databases and logic programs. In J. Minker, editor, *Foundations of Deductive Databases and Logic Programming,* pages 193–216, Morgan Kaufmann, Los Altos, CA., 1988.

[Przymusinski, 1989a] T. Przymusinski. Every logic program has a natural stratification and an iterated fixed point model. In *Proceedings of the Eighth Symposium
on Principles of Database Systems*, pages 11–21, ACM SIGACT-SIGMOD, 1989.

[Przymusinski, 1989b] T. Przymusinski. Non-monotonic formalisms and logic programming. In , editor, *Proceedings of the Sixth Logic Programming Symposium*,
Association for Logic Programming, MIT Press, Cambridge, Mass., 1989. (in
print).

[Przymusinski, 1989c] T. Przymusinski. On the declarative and procedural semantics
of logic programs. *Journal of Automated Reasoning*, 5:167–205, 1989.

[Przymusinski, 1989d] T. Przymusinski. Three-valued non-monotonic formalisms and
logic programming. In R. Brachman, H. Leveque, and R. Reiter, editors, *Proceedings of the First International Conference on Principles of Knowledge Representation and Reasoning (KR'89), Toronto, Canada*, pages 341–348, Morgan
Kaufmann, 1989.

[Reiter, 1978] R. Reiter. On closed-world data bases. In H. Gallaire and J. Minker,
editors, *Logic and Data Bases*, pages 55–76, Plenum Press, New York, 1978.

[Reiter, 1984] R. Reiter. Towards a logical reconstruction of relational database theory.
In M. Brodie and J. Mylopoulos, editors, *On Conceptual Modelling*, pages 191–233,
Springer Verlag, New York, 1984.

[Reiter, 1986] R. Reiter. Nonmonotonic reasoning. *Annual Reviews of Computer Science*, 1986.

[Roussel, 1975] P. Roussel. *PROLOG, Manuel de Reference et d'Utilisation*. Research
report, Group d'Intelligence Artificielle, U.E.R. de Marseille, France, 1975.

[Shepherdson, 1984] J. Shepherdson. Negation as finite failure: a comparison of Clark's
completed data bases and Reiter's closed world assumption. *Journal of Logic
Programming*, 1:51–79, 1984.

[Shepherdson, 1988] J.C. Shepherdson. Negation in logic programming. In J. Minker,
editor, *Foundations of Deductive Databases and Logic Programming*, pages 19–88,
Morgan Kaufmann, Los Altos, CA., 1988.

[Ullman, 1988] J.D. Ullman. *Database and Knowledge-Based Systems*. Computer Science Press, Rockville, Md., 1988.

[Van Emden and Kowalski, 1976] M. Van Emden and R. Kowalski. The semantics of
predicate logic as a programming language. *Journal of the ACM*, 23(4):733–742,
1976.

[Van Gelder, 1989a] A. Van Gelder. The alternating fixpoint of logic programs with
negation. In *Proceedings of the Symposium on Principles of Database Systems*,
pages 1–10, ACM SIGACT-SIGMOD, 1989.

[Van Gelder, 1989b] A. Van Gelder. Negation as failure using tight derivations for general logic programs. *Journal of Logic Programming*, 6(1):109–133, 1989. Preliminary versions appeared in *Third IEEE Symp. on Logic Programming* (1986), and *Foundations of Deductive Databases and Logic Programming*, J. Minker, ed., Morgan Kaufmann, 1988.

[Van Gelder *et al.*, 1990] A. Van Gelder, K. A. Ross, and J. S. Schlipf. The well-founded semantics for general logic programs. *Journal of the ACM*, 1990. (to appear). Available from first author as UCSC-CRL-88-16. Preliminary abstract appeared in Seventh ACM Symposium on Principles of Database Systems, March 1988, pp. 221–230.

[Zaniolo, 1988] C. Zaniolo. Design and implementation of logic-based language for data intensive applications. In R. Kowalski and K. Bowen, editors, *Proceedings of the Fifth Logic Programming Symposium*, pages 1666–1688, Association for Logic Programming, MIT Press, Cambridge, Mass., 1988.

Formal Techniques in Artificial Intelligence
A Sourcebook. R.B. Banerji (editor)
© Elsevier Science Publishers B.V. (North-Holland), 1990

An Introduction to Unification Theory

JÖRG H. SIEKMANN
Universität Kaiserslautern, FB Informatik
Postfach 3049
D-6750 Kaiserslautern
WEST GERMANY

ABSTRACT: Most knowledge based systems in artificial intelligence (AI), with a commitment to a symbolic representation, support one basic operation: "matching of descriptions". This operation, called unification in work on deduction, is the "addition-and-multiplication" of AI-systems and is consequently often supported by special purpose hardware or by a fast instruction set on most AI-machines. Unification theory provides the formal framework for investigations into the properties of this operation. This article gives a tutorial introduction to the field and surveys some of its results.

1. INTRODUCTION

> *Überhaupt hat der Fortschritt das an sich, daß er viel*
> *größer ausschaut, als er wirklich ist.*
>
> *J.N.Nestroy, 1859*

Not least because of its numerous applications in artificial intelligence (AI) and computer science, the field of **unification theory** is currently witnessing intense activity. This field is concerned with problems of the following kind: Let f and g be binary functions, a and b constants, and x and y variables, and consider the two *first order terms* s and t built from these symbols as follows:

$$s = f(x\ g(a\ b)) \qquad t = f(g(y\ b)\ x)$$

The decision problem is whether or not there exist terms which can be substituted for the variables x and y in s and t so that the two terms thus obtained are identical. In this example g(a b) and a are two such terms and we write

$$\delta = \{x \leftarrow g(a\ b), y \leftarrow a\}$$

to represent this unifying substitution.

We say that δ is a *unifier* for s and t, since $\delta s = \delta t = f(g(a\ b)\ g(a\ b))$.

In addition to the above *decision problem* there is also the problem of finding a *unification algorithm,* which enumerates the unifiers for a given pair of terms. Such algorithms are at the very heart of present day computing, in fact they form part of the central processing unit of the "fifth generation computers" (ICOT, 1984). For efficiency reasons they are often implemented in silicon or at least supported by an abstract machine, such as the Warren Abstract Machine (Gabriel et al., 1984), into whose instruction set the terms to be unified are compiled.

Consider a variation of the above problem, which arises when we assume that f is commutative:

$$\text{(C)} \quad f(x\ y) = f(y\ x)$$

Now δ is still a unifier for s and t. However $\sigma = \{y \leftarrow a\}$ is also a unifier for s and t since

$$\sigma s = f(x\ g(a\ b)) =_C f(g(a\ b)\ x) = \sigma t.$$

But σ is *more general* than δ, or put another way δ is an *instance* of σ, since it is obtained as the composition of the substitutions $\lambda \circ \sigma$ where $\lambda = \{x \leftarrow g(a\ b)\}$. Hence a unification algorithm only needs to compute σ.

In some cases there is a single and unique least upper bound in the lattice of unifiers, called the *most general unifier* or alternatively the principal unifier. For example for every pair of uninterpreted terms as above there is at most *one* general unifying substitution. Under commutativity however, there are pairs of terms which have more than one most general unifier, but they always have at most *finitely* many.

The problem becomes entirely different, when we assume that the function f is associative:

$$\text{(A)} \quad f(x\ f(y\ z)) = f(f(x\ y)\ z)$$

In this case δ is still a unifying substitution, but $\tau = \{x \leftarrow f(g(a\ b)\ g(a\ b)), y \leftarrow a\}$ is also a unifier, since

$$\tau s = f(f(g(a\ b)\ g(a\ b))\ g(a\ b)) =_A f(g(a\ b)\ f(g(a\ b)\ g(a\ b))) = \tau t.$$

But $\tau' = \{x \leftarrow f(g(a\ b)\ f(g(a\ b)\ g(a\ b))), y \leftarrow a\}$ is again a unifying substitution and it is not difficult to see, that there are *infinitely* many unifiers, all of which are most general: just substitute g(a, b) twice, three times, four times .... etc.

Finally, if we assume that both axioms (A) and (C) hold for f, the situation changes yet again and for any pair of terms there are at most *finitely* many most general unifiers under (AC).

The above examples as well as the many practical applications of unification theory (see section 1.1.) share a common problem, which in its most abstract form is as follows: Let L be a formal language with variables and two words s and t in that language. Then for a given binary relation $\approx$ defined in L find a substitution σ such that $\sigma s \approx \sigma t$ (provided of course that σs and σt are welldefined).

If the relation $\approx$ can be specified by a set E of equational axioms and if L is the language of first order terms, unification of s and t in E amounts to solving the equation $s = t$ in the variety defined by E. For example if E consists of the associative axiom and the idempotence axiom $f(x,x) = x$, and s and t are terms, then unification of s and t amounts to solving equations in free idempotent semigroups. A better known example may be the following: if E is an axiomatization of the natural numbers and s and t are appropriate terms, unification of s and t amounts to solving Diophantine equations.

The mathematical investigation of equation solving is a subject as old as mathematics itself and right from the beginning was very much at the heart of it. It dates back to Babylonian mathematics (about 2000 B.C.) and has dominated much of mathematical research ever since. Unification theory carries this activity on in a more abstract setting. Just as universal algebra abstracts from certain properties that pertain to specific algebras and investigates issues that are common to all of them, unification theory addresses problems, which are typical for equation solving as such. And just as traditional equation solving drew much of its impetus from its numerous applications (for example the, for the times, complicated procedure for deviding legacies in Babylonian times or the applications in physics in more modern times), unification theory derives its impetus from its numerous applications in AI and computer science.

Central to unification theory are the notions of a ***set of most general unifiers*** μU and the ***unification hierarchy*** based on the cardinality of μU. Both notions will be formally introduced in section 2, where we define a ***unification problem*** for an equational theory E. However for many practical applications unification is too general a concept, instead it is of interest to know for two given terms s and t if there exists a ***matcher*** μ (a one-side-unifier) such that $\mu(s)$ and t are equal in E. In other words, in a ***matching problem*** we are allowed to substitute into one term only (into s using the above convention) and we say s matches t with matcher μ.

1.1. Applications

There is a wide variety of areas in AI and computer science where unification problems arise.

Databases

A deductive database (Gallaire & Minker, 1978) does not store every fact explicitly. Instead it contains only certain facts, from which other facts can be deduced by some inference rule. Such inference rules (deduction rules) heavily rely on unification algorithms.

The user of a relational database (Date, 1976) may logically *and* the properties he wants to retrieve or else he may be interested in the *natural join* of two stored relations. But *and* is an associative and commutative operation and the *natural join* obeys an associative axiom, which distributes over some other operation, hence both can be built into a unification algorithm (Snelting & Henhapl, 1985).

Information Retrieval

A patent office may store all known electric circuits (Bryan & Carnog, 1966) or all recorded chemical compounds (Sussenguth, 1965) as some graph structure, and the problem of checking whether a given circuit or compound already exists is an instance of a test for graph isomorphism (Ullman, 1976; Unger, 1964; Corneil, 1968). More generally, if the nodes of such graphs are labelled with universally quantified variables ranging over subgraphs, then these problems are instances of a *graph matching problem* (Rastall, 1969).

Computer Vision

It has become customary in this field to store the internal representation of external scenes as some net structure (Ballard & Brown, 1982; Winston, 1975). The problem to find a particular object represented in a given scene, is then also an instance of a graph matching problem (Ballard & Brown, 1972; Rastall, 1969). Here one of the main problems is to specify exactly what constitutes a successful match (since a test for endomorphism is too rigid for most applications): matching is carried out with respect to some distance function (or some metric), that is usually not formally defined, but depends on the application in mind. This kind of problem was called paraunification in (Szabo 1982).

Natural Language Processing

The processing of natural language by a computer (Winograd, 1972; Winograd, 1983; Tennant, 1981) is often based on transformation rules, which for example translate the surface structure of the input sentence into a more appropriate form for internal representation within the computer. Inference rules are used to derive the semantics of an input sentence and to disambiguate it. The knowledge about the external world that a natural language processing system must have, is represented by some machine oriented descriptions and it is of paramount importance to detect if two descriptions describe the same object or fact.

Transformation rules, inference rules and the matching of descriptions are but a few places where unification theory is applied within this field.

The meaning of a natural language utterance has to be represented in some internal representation language, which in turn should have a well defined semantics. Recently developed formalisms such as situation semantics (for which see (Barwise & Perry, 1983)) or discourse representation theory (Kamp, 1981) no longer use elementary set theoretical operations for the manipulation of natural language utterances, but rely on one basic operation, namely unification with respect to certain constraints.

Also special functional grammars have been designed for parsing natural languages, called unification grammars (Shieber, 1986), that depend on one fundamental operation: feature unification (Ait-Kaci, 1984; Smolka & Ait-Kaci, 1987).

Expert Systems

An expert system is a computer program (Brachmann & Schmolze, 1985), whose performance largely depends on its ability to represent and manipulate the knowledge within its field of expertise. Commonly this knowledge is represented in the form of production rules, such that if the preconditions of a production rule are fulfilled, its action part will be executed. Special languages such as OPS5 (Forgy, 1981) and others have been developed for the implementation of such systems. In OPS5 the conditional part of a production rule is matched against the entries in the knowledge base and if the match succeeds, the preconditions are considered true and the rule will fire.

The efficiency of this matching process is of crucial importance and special techniques, e.g. the Rete-algorithm (Forgy, 1982) and even hardware realisations (Ramnarayan & Zimmermann, 1985), have been proposed which are similar to efficient implementations of the unification algorithm in logic programming languages .

Text Manipulation Languages

The fundamental mode of operation in programming languages like SNOBOL (Farber et al., 1964) is to detect the occurrence of a substring within a larger string of characters (which may be a program or some other text), and there are methods known for doing this, which require less than linear time (Boyer & Moore, 1977). If these strings contain the SNOBOL "don't-care"- variable, the occurrence problem is an instance of the string unification problem (Siekmann, 1975).

Planning Systems

Computerbased generation of plans for actions, such as a plan for a robot action or plans for appropriate language generation, is an important subfield of AI. The methods for finding a plan can be viewed as a deduction process. In a recent paper Z.Manna and R.Waldinger show, how a tableau-based inference system with an extended unification algorithm (for additional equations and equivalences) can be used to generate such plans (Manna & Waldinger, 1986).

Pattern Directed Programming Languages

An important contribution to programming language design is the mechanism of pattern-directed invocation of procedures (Böhm et al. 1977; Hewitt, 1972; Rulifson et al., 1972; Beilken et al., 1982). Procedures are identified by patterns, instead of procedure identifiers as in traditional programming languages, and these patterns usually express goals to be achieved by executing the procedure. Incoming messages are tested for matching against the invocation patterns of procedures in a procedural data base, and a procedure is activated after a successful match between message and pattern is achieved. Here matching is carried out to find an appropriate procedure that helps to accomplish an intended goal and also for transmitting information to the invoked procedure. For these applications (often called demons, censors, agents, etc.) it is particularly desirable to have methods for the description and matching of objects in high level data structures such as strings, sets, multisets, lists and others.

A little reflection will show that for very expressive matching languages, as e.g. MATCHLESS in PLANNER (Hewitt, 1972), the matching problem is undecidable. This presents a problem for the designer of such languages: on the one hand, very rich and expressive languages are desirable, since they form the basis for the invocation and deduction mechanism. On the other hand, drastic restrictions will be necessary, if matching algorithms are to be found. The question is just how severe do these restrictions have to be.

Knowledge Representation Languages

Based on frame-like techniques to structure and represent knowledge (Minsky, 1975), special purpose programming languages such as KRL (Bobrow & Winograd 1977) or KL-ONE (Brachman & Schmolze, 1985) have been designed for this task. Apart from their respective commitment to the representation and structuring issue, they all support one central operation: "matching of descriptions" (Brachmann & Levesque, 1985). In a sense unification theory relates to these new kinds of programming languages - and hence to knowledge based systems - as formal language theory relates to traditional programming languages.

Logic Programming Languages

The discovery of the close relationship between logical deduction and computation, which means that logic enjoys a role in computer science analogous to that of analysis in physics, is certainly one of the outstanding scientific achievements of the later part of this century.

However there is a more specific point to this, namely that predicate logic itself can be viewed as a programming language (Kowalski, 1979) given a suitable machine to execute it. Predicate logic relates to a deduction system as for example LISP relates to EVAL. This insight opened up a new technological race for logic programming languages and appropriate machines on which to execute them. The Japanese coined the name "fifth generation computers" for such machines. The central computation performed in logic programming machinery is unification. In fact the unification algorithm - be it implemented in software or in silicon - is the central processing unit, the CPU, of these machines. Hence the speed of these machines is no longer expressed in MIPS (Millions of Instructions Per Second) as for conventional machines, but in KLIPS (thousands of Logical Inferences Per Second), which is in effect a measure of the number of unifications performed per second.

Term Rewriting Systems

The manipulation of terms in equationally defined theories, traditionally called demodulation (Wos et al., 1967), is based on matching and has always played an important role in deduction systems. If in addition the equations can be transformed into a confluent and finitely terminating rewriting system (Huet & Oppen, 1980, see also the article by Avenhaus and Madlener in this volume), they can be used to compute a unique normal form for any term. The test for confluence can be carried out by a procedure known as the Knuth-Bendix completion procedure (Knuth & Bendix, 1979), which uses a unification algorithm as its central component.

Certain equational axioms, such as associativity or commutativity, are notoriously difficult to handle using these systems. Therefore a given equational theory T can sometimes be separated into two constituent parts, $T = R \cup E$, such that only R needs to be transformed into a canonical rewriting system and E (the difficult equations) can be built into a special purpose unification algorithms (Peterson & Stickel, 1981).

Term rewriting systems are of considerable interest in computer science (Buchberger, 1987) and have now found a place in most computer science curricula, since they provide for a convenient computational treatment of equational logics. Not the least important among the many applications these systems have, is their foundational role in new programming languages which elegantly combine functional with logic programming. Term rewriting systems that operate on the word monoid are called Semi-Thue-Systems, for a survey see R.Book (Book, 1985).

Computer Algebra

In computer algebra, matching and unification algorithms also play an important role. For example the integrand in a symbolic integration problem (Moses, 1971) may be matched against certain patterns in order to detect the class of integration problems to which it belongs. A succesful match then triggers the appropriate action for its solution (which in turn may involve several quite complicated matching attempts (Blair et al., 1971; Fateman, 1971). Hence most computer algebra systems like REDUCE (Hearn, 1971), MACSYMA (Moses, 1974) or MATHLAB (Manove et al., 1968) make extensive use of unification or matching algorithms.

Algebra

A famous decidability problem, which inspite of many attacks remained open for over twenty years, has been solved. The Monoid Problem (also called Löb's Problem in western countries, Markov's Problem in eastern countries and the String Unification Problem in the field of automated deduction (Hmelevskij, 1964; Hmelevskij, 1966; Hmelevskij, 1967; Markov, 1954; Plotkin, 1972; Siekmann, 1975; Livesey & Siekmann, 1975), is the problem of deciding whether or not an equational system over a free semigroup possesses a solution. This problem has been shown to be decidable (Makanin, 1977). The Monoid Problem has important practical applications inter alia for deduction systems (string unification (Siekmann, 1975) and second order monadic unification (Huet, 1976; Winterstein, 1976)), for formal language theory (the crossreference problem for van Wijngaarden Grammars (van Wijngaarden, 1976) and for pattern directed invocation languages in AI as mentioned above.

Without surveying classical equation solving as such, one "unification problem" that should be mentioned is Hilbert's Tenth Problem (Davis, 1973), which is known to be undecidable (Matiyasevich, 1970). The problem is whether or not a given polynomial $P[x_1,x_2,...,x_n] = 0$ has an integer solution (a Diophantine solution). Although this problem was posed originally within the framework of traditional equation solving, unification theory has shed new light upon this problem (Siekmann & Szabo, 1986).

Semigroup theory (Clifford & Preston, 1961; Howie, 1976) is the field that traditionally poses the most important unification problems, i.e. those involving associativity. Although more established than unification theory is today, some interesting semigroup problems have been solved using techniques from unification theory and term rewriting systems (see e.g. (Siekmann & Szabo, 1982; Lankford, 1980; Lankford, 1979; Baader, 1987)).

Deduction Systems

All present day deduction systems - whether they are based on resolution (Robinson, 1965) or not - have a unification algorithm for first or higher order terms as their essential component: it is the "addition and multiplication of deduction work".

For almost as long as attempts at proving theorems by machines have been made, it has been well known that certain equational axioms, if left unconstrained in the data base of a deduction system, may force it to go astray. In 1967 J.A.Robinson proposed that substantial progress ("a new plateau") could be achieved, by removing these troublesome axioms from the data base and building them directly into the inference rules of the deductive machinery. One technique that has become important for deduction systems, is to build these axioms, which often define common data structures, into the unification algorithm itself. G.Plotkin has shown in a pioneering paper (Plotkin, 1972), that a deduction system is refutation complete, whenever its extended unification procedure generates a set of unifiers satisfying the three conditions of completeness, correctness and minimality. These properties are now used to axiomatically define the set of most general unifiers.

Nonclassical Logics

Knowledge representation systems in AI are often based on nonclassical logics that model temporal information, modality, probability or beliefs more adequately than ordinary first order logic (Brachmann & Levesque, 1985). As it turned out, the nonclassical aspect of a logic can often be accounted for using special terms and the mechanization of such logics amounts to finding appropriate unification algorithms. For example various forms of modal and temporal logics have been coded this way (Wallen, 1987; Nonnengart, 1987; Ohlbach, 1987) and particular unification algorithms for some standard modal logics (like S4,T etc) are reported in (Ohlbach, 1988).

It is the field of automated deduction systems (the series of Conferences of Automated Deduction, CADE, proceedings in Springer Lecture Notes in Computer Science), where unification problems first became of general importance and that has historically contributed most to unification theory.

1.2. Early History

Allowing for some exceptions we take 1976 as the (not entirely arbitrary) date before which work is considered early history, whereas later contributions are recorded under the heading 'Results' in sections 3.1. and 3.2.

The visionary thoughts about the nature of mathematics, symbols and human reasoning that Emil Post recorded in his diary and notes (partially published in (Davis, 1965)) contain the first hint as early as the 1920s of the concept of a unification algorithm that computes a most general representative as opposed to all possible instantiations (p.370 in (Davis, 1965)).

The first explicit account of a unification algorithm was given in J. Herbrand's thesis "Recherches sur la theorie de la demonstration" in 1930 (Herbrand, 1930), where he introduced three concepts with respect to the validity of formulas. He called them A, B and C. Concept B and C were the basis for the wellknown Herbrand Theorem, whereas concept A was by and large consigned to oblivion. In order to calculate that property A holds for a formula, he gave an algorithm which computes it. This was the first published unification algorithm and was based on a technique later rediscovered by A. Martelli and U. Montanari (Martelli & Montanari, 1976) and that is still much in use today.

Based on Herbrand's idea of a finite counterexample, i.e. that only a finite number of instantiations are necessary in order to show the unsatisfiability of a set of formulas, early theorem proving programs were developed, but it was not until 1960 when D.Prawitz (Prawitz, 1960) suggested a way out of these "British Museum Techniques" as they were called later on, which was to compute a most general representative for the abundant number of instantiations that are possible otherwise. However, as his logic did not contain any function symbols, there was little in fact to compute. In 1963 M.Davis published (Davis, 1963) a proof procedure that combined the virtues of Prawitz's procedure with those of the Davis-Putnam procedure. The implementation of this new proof procedure on an IBM 7090 at Bell Telephone Laboratories November 1962 used a unification algorithm to compute the "matings" and appears to be the first fully implemented unification algorithm in actual use.

It was not until 1965, however, when the seminal paper on the resolution principle by J.A.Robinson was published (Robinson, 1965), that a formal account of a unification algorithm for first order terms, which computes a unique, single representative (i.e. the most general unifier) first appeared in print. This has been the most influential paper in this field and firmly established the concept of unification in automated deduction systems (including systems not based on resolution).

The work for this paper was done essentially in 1963 at Argonne National Laboratory, a time when another group headed by J.R. Guard at the Air Force Cambridge Lab developed a deduction system based on a Gentzen-style sequent logic that also incorporated a unification algorithm. The work was published in some internal reports (Guard, 1964) and later in (Guard & Oglesby, 1969). However, although their algorithm was correct and complete, this was not proved. They also suggested extensions of the algorithm to higher order logic as well as first order extensions to incorporate axioms like commutativity and associativity. The algorithms used for these latter extensions were heuristically motivated (reordering of terms, rebracketing etc.) and were incorrect and incomplete in general.

The basic unification algorithm was discovered again by D.Knuth and published in a paper (Knuth & Bendix, 1970) that became a classic in the field of term rewriting systems. In order to turn a given set of equations into a canonical rewriting system, a completion process is described that depends heavily on a unification algorithm, whose theoretical properties (computation of the most general unifier) were recognised and demonstrated.

In 1967 J.A.Robinson proposed to build certain troublesome axioms directly into the deductive machinery of an automated theorem prover and in 1972 G.Plotkin (Plotkin, 1972) showed how this can be done without losing completeness. From the point of view of unification theory this paper contained two major contributions: first the definition of a set of most general unifiers, which became (in particular through the work of G.Huet) a central notion of the field, and second the discovery that there are equational theories (e.g. the associativity axiom) which induce an infinite set of most general unifiers.

M.Stickel presented special unification algorithms for associativity, commutativity and their combination in his thesis (Stickel, 1975; Stickel 1977), this work was essentially motivated by the matching problem in pattern invocated programming languages as already descibed above.

The work of G.Plotkin was taken up in my own thesis (Siekmann, 1978), which described several unification algorithms for the axioms of associativity, commutativity and idempotence and their combinations. This thesis also suggested that unification theory, at that stage a collection of special purpose algorithms, was worthy of study as a field in its own right and as an important branch of theoretical AI, centering around the unification hierarchy, a concept which was first introduced here along with some preliminary results concerning it.

While these developments were taking place in first order unification theory, there was also important work going on in higher order unification around the same time. Based on the theorem proving system of J.R.Guard and his associates mentioned above, W.F.Gould (Gould, 1966) investigated the most general common instance of two higher order terms and discovered that there are infinitely ascending chains of most general unifiers (i.e. a minimal set of most general unifiers does not exist for ω-order logics).

Influenced by P.Andrews, whose work was seminal for higher order deduction systems (Andrews, 1971), G.P.Huet developed a "constrained resolution method" (Huet, 1972) for higher order theorem proving, based on an ω-order unification algorithm. This work was then further developed in his "thèse d'état" in 1976 (Huet, 1976), which became of fundamental importance in shaping the field of first and higher order unification theory as it is known today.

2.   NOTIONS AND NOTATION

Unification Theory rests upon the notational conventions of Universal Algebra (see e.g. Grätzer, 1979; Burris, 1981) and of Computational Logic (see e.g. (Loveland, 1978; Huet & Oppen, 1980; Buchberger, 1987), which we shall briefly review in the following paragraphs. If the reader feels that this is too much formalism and too heavy for a first pass it may be advisable to continue with section 3 and come back to this formal treatment later on.

Given a set S with elements $\sigma, \delta, \tau, \dots$ and a *quasi ordering* $\leq$ on S, we say that two elements $\sigma, \tau \in$ S are *equivalent*, $\sigma \equiv \tau$, iff $\sigma \leq \tau$ and $\tau \leq \sigma$. A subset $U \subseteq$ S is called an (upper) *segment* or a *filter* of S, iff for $\sigma \in$ S and $\tau \in$ U and $\tau \leq \sigma$ we have $\sigma \in$ U. We say U is generated by a set cU iff U consists exactly of those elements of S that are greater than some elements of cU, i.e. $cU \subseteq U$ and $\forall \tau \in$ U there exists $\sigma \in$ cU with $\sigma \leq \tau$. A minimal generating set μU is called a *base* of U or the *μ-set* of U if it is a generating set for U with the following additional property: $\forall \ \sigma, \tau \in \mu U$: $\sigma \leq \tau$ implies $\sigma = \tau$. A segment does not necessarily have a base, but if the bases exist they are all equivalent.

We are interested in the existence, uniqueness and cardinality of such μ-sets in the more specific context of unification .

2.1. Computational Logic

Our starting point is the familiar concept of an *algebra* as a pair (A, $\mathbb{F}$), where A is the *carrier* and $\mathbb{F}$ is a family of *operators* (the *signatur*) given with their arities.

For $\mathbb{F}$ and a denumerable set of variables $\mathbb{V}$, we define $\mathbb{T}$, the set of first order terms, over $\mathbb{F}$ and $\mathbb{V}$, as the least set with   (i) $\mathbb{V} \subseteq \mathbb{T}$, and if arity(f) = 0 for f $\in \mathbb{F}$ then f$\in \mathbb{T}$ and

(ii) if $t_1, \dots, t_n \in \mathbb{T}$ and arity(f) = n then $f(t_1 \dots t_n) \in \mathbb{T}$.

Let $\mathbb{V}(t$) be the variables occurring in term t, a term t is *ground* if $\mathbb{V}(t) = \emptyset$. The algebra with carrier $\mathbb{T}$ and with operators corresponding to the term constructors of $\mathbb{F}$ is the absolutely free (term) algebra, i.e. it just gives an algebraic structure to $\mathbb{T}$. If the carrier is the set of ground terms it is called the initial algebra (Goguen & Thatcher, 1977) or Herbrand Universe (Loveland, 1978).

A *substitution* σ: $\mathbb{T} \to \mathbb{T}$ is an endomorphism on the term algebra $\mathbb{T}$, which is identical almost everywhere on $\mathbb{V}$ and hence can be represented as a finite set of variable-term pairs:

$$\sigma = \{x_1 \leftarrow t_1, \dots, x_n \leftarrow t_n\}.$$

Equational Logic

Although unification theory is not restricted to equationally defined theories, most results have been obtained within this frame.

An *equation* is a pair of terms, usually written as s = t. Given a set of equations E and a single equation s = t, we denote by E ⊨ s = t that s = t is true in every model of E (s = t is a modeltheoretical consequence of E). An *equational theory* T is a set of equations with T ⊨ s=t iff (s = t)∈ T, i.e. T consists of all its consequences. For a given set of equations E, the least equational theory T(E) is the finest congruence on the term algebra containing all pairs σs = σt, for all equations in E and all substitutions σ (the substitution invariant congruence generated by E). We say s and t are *E-equal,* abbreviated as s =$_E$ t, iff the terms s and t are in this congruence. E is a *presentation* of the congruence =$_E$ or an *axiomatization* of the equational theory T(E). Usually we say ´theory E´ and mean the equational theory T(E) axiomatized by E.

Obviously the axiomatization for an equational theory is not unique. A theory that has a finite axiomatization is called *finitely generated*, otherwise it is infinitely generated. E-equality is not decidable in general; however in unification theory we are usually only interested in equational theories with a decidable word problem. Another natural restriction is that we consider only consistent theories, i.e. theories, which do not collapse into a single equivalence class. A theory is *c o n s i s t e n t* if for all v,w∈ $\mathbb{V}$: v =$_E$w implies v = w.

A standard set of inference rules for equational logic is the following:

$$s = s$$
$$\text{if } s = t \text{ then } t = s$$
$$\text{if } r = s \text{ and } s = t \text{ then } r = t$$
$$\text{if } s_i= t_i , 1 \leq i \leq n, \text{ then } f(s_1,s_2, ...,s_n) = f(t_1,t_2, ... ,t_n)$$
$$\text{if } s = t \text{ then } \sigma s = \sigma t \text{ for all substitutions } \sigma.$$

An equation s = t can be *derived* or *proved* from an axiomatization E, E⊢ s = t , if it can be obtained in finitely many steps from E using the above rules. G.Birkhoff gave the first completeness proof for this derivation system (Birkhoff, 1935):

Theorem :   E⊢ s = t   iff   E ⊨ s = t

For a survey on classical equational logic see e.g.(Tarski, 1968; Taylor, 1979); sequences of replacement are used in (McNulty, 1976).

Term Rewriting Systems

Since neither ⊢ nor ⊨ are particularly convenient for a computational treatment of =$_E$, two computer oriented techniques for equational axioms called paramodulation (Wos & Robinson, 1973) and demodulation (Wos & Robinson, 1967) are extensively used in the

field of automated deduction. Suppose the equational theory is actually presented as
$E=\{l_1=r_1, l_2=r_2,..., l_n=r_n\}$, with the assumption that the r_i are in some sense smaller than
the l_i. A term s is said to be *demodulated* to t , if there is a subterm s´ in s and a pair $l_i = r_i$
in E such that s´$= \mu l_i$ for some substitution μ and term t is obtained from s by replacement
of s´ by μr_i.

A term s is said to be *paramodulated* to t, if there is a subterm s´ in s and a pair $l_i = r_i$ in
E such that $\sigma l_i = \sigma s´$ for a substitution σ; term t is obtained from σs by replacement of σs´
by σr_i. Note that this is only a special case of paramodulation, in the context of full
predicate logic a little extra machinery is required (Loveland, 1978). The problem is of
course how to find a presentation, such that the righthand side of the equations is smaller
than the lefthand side. This problem has been addressed in a paper by D.Knuth (Knuth &
Bendix, 1970), which is now a classic in this field. The essential observation is that it is
often possible for a given set of equations E to find an equivalent set in the sense of the
definition below, which is directed from left to right $R_E = \{l_1 \Rightarrow r_1, l_2 \Rightarrow r_2, ..., l_n \Rightarrow r_n\}$
with $Var(r_i) \subseteq Var(l_i)$ such that the r_i are smaller than the l_i. This is called a *term
rewriting system* (TRS). A TRS can be used to define a reduction relation on terms by:
$s \mapsto_R t$ if s can be demodulated to t using R. If there are no infinite sequences
$s_1 \mapsto s_2 \mapsto ...$ the relation $\mapsto_R$ is said to be terminating or *Noetherian*. The relation $\mapsto_R$
is called *confluent* if for every r, s, t with $r \mapsto_R s$ and $r \mapsto_R t$ there exists a term u such
that $s \overset{*}{\mapsto} u$ and $t \overset{*}{\mapsto} u$. A confluent, Noetherian relation is called *canonical* ; similarily a
TRS is called canonical, if the relation it is based upon is canonical. Canonical TRS´s are an
important basis for a computational treatment of equational logic, since they define a unique
normal form ‖t‖ for every term t given by: $t \overset{*}{\mapsto}$ ‖t‖ and there does not exist a term s with ‖t
‖ $\mapsto$ s. ‖t‖ exists because of the finite termination property and it is unique because of
confluence. The TRS R_E is *equivalent* to E if: $s =_E t$ iff ‖s‖ = ‖t‖. A terminating term
rewriting system can sometimes be completed to a canonical system with the Knuth-Bendix
completion procedure (Knuth & Bendix, 1970). Because of the great importance of TRS
for computer science, there is intensive research now on methods of how to obtain a
canonical TRS from a given set of equations (see Huet & Oppen, 1980; Buchberger, 1987
and Avenhaus & Madlener in this volume). Rewrite systems in the word monoid are known
as Semi-Thue Systems (Book, 1985).

Similar to the above rewrite relation $\mapsto_R$, we can define a relation $\rightsquigarrow_R$, often called
narrowing (Hullot, 1980) , such that $s \rightsquigarrow_R t$ holds, if s can be paramodulated to t. This
relation is of particular importance for universal unification algorithms.

2.2. Unification Theory

A *substitution* $\sigma: \mathbb{T} \to \mathbb{T}$ is an endomorphism on the term algebra $\mathbb{T}$, which is identical almost everywhere on $\mathbb{V}$ and hence can be represented as a finite set of pairs $\sigma = \{x_1 \leftarrow t_1, ..., x_n \leftarrow t_n\}$. The restriction $\sigma|_V$ of a substitution to a set of variables V is defined as $\sigma|_V x = \sigma x$ if $x \in V$ and $\sigma|_V x = x$ otherwise. SUB is the set of substitutions on $\mathbb{T}$ and ε the identity. The application of a substitution σ to a term t is written as σt. The composition of substitutions is defined as the usual composition of mappings: $(\sigma \circ \tau)t = \sigma(\tau t)$ for $t \in \mathbb{T}$. Hence SUB is a substitution monoid, it is the set of finitely representable endomorphisms on the term algebra $\mathbb{T}$: $\varepsilon \in SUB$ and if $\sigma, \tau \in SUB$ then $\sigma \circ \tau \in SUB$ (identity and composition); if $c \in \mathbb{F}_0$, $f(t_1,...,t_n) \in \mathbb{T}$ then $\sigma c = c$ and $\sigma f(t_1,...,t_n) = f(\sigma t_1,...,\sigma t_n)$ (homomorphism); $card(\{v \in V: \sigma v \neq v\}) < \infty$ for $\sigma \in SUB$.

The domain of a substitution is $\mathbb{T}$; by a slight abuse of language we define the special ´domain´ (the ´codomain´) of a substitution σ as the set of variables actually moved by σ (the terms introduced by σ):

$$DOM\sigma = \{x \in V: \sigma x \neq x \} \quad \text{(domain of } \sigma)$$
$$COD\sigma = \{\sigma x : x \in DOM\sigma\} \quad \text{(codomain of } \sigma)$$
$$VCOD\sigma = V(COD\sigma) \quad \text{(variables of codomain of } \sigma)$$

If $VCOD\sigma = \emptyset$ then σ is a *ground substitution.* A substitution ρ is called a *renaming substitution* iff $COD\rho \subseteq V$ and $\rho x = \rho y$ implies $x = y$ for $x,y \in DOM\rho$. A *permutation* is a bijective renaming substitution.

Given a set of variables $W \subseteq V$, E-equality in $\mathbb{T}$ is extended to the set of substitutions SUB by :

$$\sigma =_E \tau [W] \quad \text{iff} \quad \forall x \in W \quad \sigma x =_E \tau x$$

We say σ and τ are *E-equal on W* or the restrictions $\sigma|_W$ and $\tau|_W$ are E-equal.

A term s is an *E-instance* of t (or t is *more general* than s), $t \leq_E s$, iff there exist $\lambda \in$ SUB with $\lambda t =_E s$; s is *E-equivalent* to t, $s \equiv_E t$, iff $s \leq_E t$ and $s \geq_E t$. These notions are extended to substitutions by : A substitution τ is *more general* than σ on W (or σ is an *E-instance* of τ on W):

$$\tau \leq_E \sigma [W] \quad \text{iff} \quad \exists \lambda \in SUB \text{ with } \lambda \tau =_E \sigma [W].$$

Two substitutions σ, τ are *E-equivalent* on W :

$$\sigma \equiv_E \tau [W] \quad \text{iff} \quad \sigma \leq_E \tau [W] \text{ and } \tau \leq_E \sigma [W].$$

Given two terms s, t in $\mathbb{T}$ and an equational theory E, an *E-unification problem* is denoted as $<s=t>_E$. Note that a unification problem is not only characterized by the equational theory E, but also by the signature out of which s and t are built. In particular the type of a unification problem, as defined below, depends on both E and $\mathbb{T}$.

The problem $<s = t>_E$ is *E-unifiable* iff there exists a substitution $\sigma \in$ SUB such that $\sigma s =_E \sigma t$, σ is called an *E-unifier* of s and t. The set of all E-unifiers of s and t is written $U_E(s,t)$, which is a left ideal in the substitution monoid SUB, since $U_E =_E$ SUB$\circ$ U_E [W]. In particular U_E is a filter or an (upper) segment of SUB, since if $\sigma \in$ SUB and $\tau \in U_E$ and $\tau \leq_E \sigma$ then $\sigma \in U_E$.

Without loss of generality we assume the unifiers of s and t to be idempotent, i.e. $\sigma \cdot \sigma = \sigma$, since if not, we can always find equivalent ones which are. For a given unification problem $<s = t>_E$, it would be of little avail to compute the whole set of unifiers $U_E(s, t)$, which is always recursively enumerable for a decidable theory E, but instead smaller sets useful in representing U_E.

Therefore we define a generating set of U_E, called $cU_E(s,t)$ the *complete set of unifiers of s and t on W* = $\mathbb{V}(s,t)$, as:

  (i) $cU_E \subseteq U_E$ (correctness)
  (ii) $\forall \, \delta \in U_E \; \exists \, \sigma \in cU_E: \quad \sigma \leq_E \delta$ [W]   (completeness)

The base $\mu U_E(s,t)$, called the *set of most general unifiers*, is defined as the μ-set of $U_E(s,t)$ with respect to $\leq_E$ [W]:

  (iii) $\forall \, \sigma,\tau \in \mu U_E(s,t): \quad$ if $\sigma \leq_E \tau$ [W] then $\sigma = \tau$.   (minimality)

A set of substitutions $S \subseteq$ SUB is said to be *separated on W away from Z*, with $W \subseteq$ Z, iff the following two conditions are satisfied:

  • DOMσ = W   for all $\sigma \in$ S
  • VCOD$\sigma \cap Z = \emptyset$ for all $\sigma \in$ S.

For substitutions σ separated on W we have in paticular DOM$\sigma \cap$ VCOD$\sigma = \emptyset$, which is equivalent to the idempotence of σ. This property is often technically useful and we usually require μU_E to be separated on W = $\mathbb{V}(s,t)$ away from some $Z \supset W$. The set μU_E does not always exist (Fages & Huet, 1983; Schmidt-Schauß, 1986; Baader, 1986); if it does then it is not unique. However it is unique up to the equivalence $\equiv_E$ (see for example (Fages & Huet, 1983)) and hence it is sufficient to compute just one μU_E as a representative of the equivalence class $[\mu U_E]_{\equiv E}$.

A possible reason for the non-existence of minimal sets of unifiers is that the quasi order $\leq_E$ [W] on U_E is not well-founded. Obviously if it is well-founded (i.e. every strictly decreasing chain in U_E is finite), a minimal subset will always exist. More generally, if every decreasing chain of unifiers -including infinite ones - has a lower bound in U_E , then U_E has a μ-set. Although sufficient, this condition is not necessary for the existence of minimal sets of E-unifiers.

The above definitions are given for a unification problem that consists just of one equation, but unfortunately we have the following theorem : there is a theory E, where all single unification problems (as defined above) have minimal sets of unifiers, but for a finite set of problems this is not the case, the minimal set of E-unifiers does not even exist (Bürckert et al., 1986). For that reason we extend the definition of a unification problem to a finite system of equations $\Gamma = \{s_i=t_i: 1 \le i \le n\}$. Γ is called an *E-unification problem* or an equation system and is then denoted as:

$$<s_i = t_i : 1 \le i \le n >_E$$

A substitution σ is an *E-unifier of Γ*, or a solution of Γ, iff $\sigma s_i =_E \sigma t_i$, for $1 \le i \le n$. The set of E-unifiers is denoted accordingly as $U_E(\Gamma)$, similarly $cU_E(\Gamma)$ for a complete set of unifiers and $\mu U_E(\Gamma)$ for a minimal one.

Based on the cardinality of μU, we can classify unification problems and equational theories according to the following *unification hierarchy,* which turned out to be a backbone of unification theory just as the Chomsky-hierarchy for formal language theory. A *unification problem* Γ for an equational theory E is of type:

(i) **unitary**   if $\mu U_E(\Gamma)$ exists and has at most one element
(ii) **finitary**   if $\mu U_E(\Gamma)$ exists and is finite
(ii) **infinitary**   if $\mu U_E(\Gamma)$ exists and is infinite
(iv) **nullary** (or *zero*)   if $\mu U_E(\Gamma)$ does not exist.

Similarily we say an *equational theory* E is unitary (is finitary) if for all Γ, $\mu U_E(\Gamma)$ is unitary (is finitary), and E is infinitary (is nullary) if there exists some Γ such that $\mu U_E(\Gamma)$ is infinitary (is nullary).The unitary, finitary, infinitary and nullary classes of equational theories are $\mathcal{U}_1$, $\mathcal{U}_\omega$, $\mathcal{U}_\infty$ and $\mathcal{U}_0$ respectively.

We say that $\mathcal{U} = \mathcal{U}_1 \cup \mathcal{U}_\omega \cup \mathcal{U}_\infty$ the class of unitary, finitary and infinitary theories is *μ-based,* whereas $\mathcal{U}_0$ is not μ-based.

A *unification algorithm* for a given theory E is an algorithm that takes a set of equations Γ as input and generates some subset of $U_E(\Gamma)$. A *complete* unification algorithm generates a complete set $cU_E(\Gamma)$ and a *minimal* unification algorithm generates a base $\mu U_E(\Gamma)$. An important task of the field is to find minimal unification algorithms for a given theory, however for many applications the notion of a minimal algorithm is not strong enough, since it does not imply that the algorithm terminates even for a finite μU_E. On the other hand for a finitary theory the minimality requirement is often too strong, since an algorithm which generates a superset of μU may be far more efficient than a minimal one and hence sometimes preferable.

For that reason we say a unification algorithm is *type conformal* if it generates a set Ψ with:

      (i) $\mu U \subseteq \Psi \subseteq cU$, i.e. Ψ is a complete set of unifiers.

      (ii) If E is finitary then Ψ is finite and the algorithm terminates.

      (iii) If E is infinitary then $\Psi \equiv_E \mu U$, i.e. Ψ is a μ-base.

The aim of Unification Theory is to give an answer to the following three mayor problems:

PROBLEM ONE: For a given equational theory E, is it decidable whether two terms are unifiable in E ?

PROBLEM TWO: Given an equational theory E, what is its unification type ?

PROBLEM THREE: For a given μ-based equational theory E find an (efficient) unification algorithm that enumerates μU_E; respectively find an algorithm that is type conformal.

3.   RESULTS

The development of unification theory into a scientific field of its own was hallmarked by the slow emergence of a general theory, that addresses the above mentioned problems in a rather general setting. It was motivated inter alia by the comparatively late realization, that unification is equation solving in varieties, however the abstract nature of the theories under investigation as well as the computeroriented approach account for its destinct syntactic flavor.

Typical questions that are asked in this field are: How and under what conditions can unification algorithms be combined? Why is the combination of a finitary and an infinitary theory sometimes finitary and sometimes infinitary? How is a unification problem influenced by the choice of its signature, in particular when order sorted signatures are taken into account? Is it possible to find a Universal Unification Algorithm (similar to a Universal Turing Machine), which takes as input a pair of terms *and* an equational theory? What is the exact relationship between matching and unification? Is it possible to develop a general theory that classifies equational theories with respect to the unification hierarchy?

It is this general aspect of unification theory, where we currently witness the most dynamic developments. However given the tutorial nature of this article, we shall not present these results here. The interested reader may like to consult (Siekmann 1989) for a survey of these results.

3.1.   First Order Unification

Unification in the Absolutely Free Termalgebra.

The historical experience with the early deduction systems clearly revealed that "the unification computation occurs at the very heart of most deduction systems. It is the addition and multiplication of deduction work. There is accordingly a very strong incentive to design the last possible ounce of efficiency into a unification program. The incentive is very much the same as that for seeking maximally efficient realizations of the elementary arithmetic operations in numerical computing - and the problem is every bit as interesting" (Robinson, p.64, 1971).

Let us look at the actual algorithm in more detail, taking as a starting point the example from the beginning:

$$s = f(x \ g(a \ b))$$
$$t = f(g(y \ b) \ x)$$

The original algorithm of A. Robinson moves a pointer from left to right and compares the actual symbols. If they are already equal, then the pointer is moved on, till the first disagreement occurs: if none of the symbols is a variable, the algorithm reports failure otherwise the nonvariable term is substituted for the variable and recorded as a substitution component.

Looking at the example above, the pointer is initialized to the function symbol f. The corresponding symbols are equal, hence the pointer is moved on, till it finds the first disagreement pair. In this case: x and g(y b). Thus the substitution component

$\{(x \leftarrow g(y\ b))\}$ is generated and applied, leading to:

$s' = f(g(y\ b)\ g(a\ b))$

$t' = f(g(y\ b)\ g(y\ b))$

Now the pointer is moved on till it encounters a and y as the next disagreement pair and the final unifier is:

$\{(x \leftarrow g(y\ b)),\ (y \leftarrow a)\}$

One point deserves mentioning: before the disagreement term is substituted into the variable there is in fact a check – called the OCCUR-IN-CHECK – if that variable occurs within the term, in which case the algorithm reports failure. This is in agreement with the observation that under these circumstances the two terms are not (finitely) unifiable. However if we allow infinite terms the situation in fact changes, the two terms may become unifiable and it is this line that is taken now in some logic programming languages (Colmerauer 1982).

The following example is usually taken to demonstrate that the above algorithm is exponential (i.e. 2^n):

$$s = f(g(x_0, x_0),\ g(x_1, x_1),\ \dots,\ (x_{n-1}, x_{n-1}))$$
$$t = f(\quad x_1\quad,\quad x_2\quad,\ \dots,\quad x_n\quad)$$

Below is a version of a unification algorithm (its actual syntax is taken from (Knight 1989)) that is slightly different in spirit: it takes the structure of terms more into account and unifies the arguments one by one. This idea was taken even further in the decomposition algorithms of Martelli-Montanari (1979) and in fact the very first algorithm in Herbrand's thesis (1930) worked that way.

```
function UNIFY(t1, t2) ⇒ (unifiable: Boolean, σ: substitution)
begin
    if t1 or t2 is a variable then
        begin
            let x be the variable, and let t be the other term
            if x = t, then (unifiable, σ) ← (true, ∅)
            else if occur(x, t) then unifiable ← false
            else (unifiable, σ) ← (true, {x ← t})
        end
    else
        begin
            assume t1 = f(x₁, ... , xₙ) and t2 = g(y₁, ..., yₘ)
            if f ≠ g or m ≠ n then unifiable ← false
            else
                begin
                    k ← 0
                    unifiable ← true
                    σ ← nil
                    while  k < m and unifiable do
                        begin
                            k ← k + 1
                            (unifiable, r) ←  UNIFY(σ( xₖ), (σ( yₖ))
                            if unifiable then σ ← compose(r, σ)
                        end
                end
        end
    return (unifiable, σ)
end
```

A first and influential paper that investigated the efficiency problems of unification was published in 1971 by J.A.Robinson (Robinson, 1971), who proposed a table-driven implementation technique that derived its strength from an ingenious manipulation of pointer structures, which is - with some improvements - still at the heart of many current techniques. The manipulation of pointers, instead of the objects themselves, was also proposed by R.Boyer and J.S.Moore and became known as structure sharing (Moore, 1973).

Another problem with the above algorithm is, that its representation is far too close to an actual implementation and theoretical properties like correctness, termination and the important invariant that indeed it generates the *most general* unifier are cumbersome to show. For that and other reasons a less machine-oriented representation based on **transformations** that abstract from the control structure has become more common in the field. It stresses the point that unification is seen as solving equations (in analogy to solving say $x + 3 = y + 5$).

To compute a most general unifier of term lists $(p_1,..., p_k)$ and $(q_1,..., q_k)$ start from the set of equations $\{p_1 = q_1,..., p_k = q_k\}$ and transform as follows while possible (where x stands for a variable, t for a term, and E for a set of equations):

$\{t = t\} \cup E$	$\rightarrow E$	(tautology)
$\{x = t\} \cup E$	$\rightarrow \{x = t\} \cup E[x/t]$	(application)
if x occurs in E but not in t		
$\{t = x\} \cup E$	$\rightarrow \{x = t\} \cup E$	(orientation)
if t is a non-variable term		
$\{f(s_1,...s_n) = f(t_1,...,t_n)\} \cup E$	$\rightarrow \{s_1=t_1,..., s_n=t_n\} \cup E$	(decomposition)
$\{f(s_1,...s_n) = g(t_1,...,t_m)\} \cup E$	$\rightarrow$ failure	(clash)
$\{x = t\} \cup E$	$\rightarrow$ failure	(cycle)
if x occurs in t		

The race for the fastest algorithm started in 1973 with a proposal by L.D.Baxter (Baxter, 1973), that was further improved by M.Venturini-Zilli (Venturini-Zilli, 1975) in 1975, by G.P.Huet (Huet,1976) in 1976 and by A.Martelli and U.Montanari (Martelli & Montanari, 1979) in 1979, who presented an almost linear algorithm. These algorithms gain their efficiency by a graph like representation and some of them by an ingenious use of additional pointers. The following algorithm of G. Huet (the syntax is taken from (Knight 1989)) gives the flavour:

```
function UNIFY(t1, t2) ⇒ (unifiable: Boolean, σ: substitution)
begin
    pairs-to-unify ← {(t1, t2)}
    for each node z in t1 and t2,
        z.class ← z
    while pairs-to unify ≠ ∅ do
        begin
            (x, y) ← pop (pairs-to unify)
            u ← FIND(x)
            υ ← FIND(y)
            if u ≠ υ then
                if u and υ are not variables, and u.symbol ≠ υ.symbol or
                    numberof(u.subnodes) ≠ numberof(υ.subnodes) then
                        return (false, nil)
            else
                begin
                    w ← UNION(u, υ)
                    if w = υ and u is a variable then
                        u.class ← υ
                    if neither υ nor u is a variable then
                        begin
                            let (u1,...,un) be u.subnodes
                            let (υ1,...,υn) be υ.subnodes
                            for i ← 1 to n do
                                push ((u1, υ1), pairs-to-unify)
                        end
                end
        end
From a new graph composed of the root nodes of the equivalence classes.
This graph is the result of the unification.
If the graph has a cycle, return (false, nil), but the terms are infinitely unifiable.
If the graph is acyclic, return (true, σ), where σ is a substitution in which any variable x is
    mapped on to the root of its equivalence class, that is FIND(x).
end
```

Its actual complexity is $O(n*f(n))$ where n is the number of nodes and f(n) is a very slow growing (the inverse of Ackermann) function. This is why these algorithms are called "almost linear" and are in actual fact often preferable to linear algorithms.

The first linear unification algorithm was found in 1977 by M.Paterson and W.Wegman and finally published in (Paterson & Wegman, 1978). They used a particular data structure, directed acyclic graphs (dags), to represent the terms. Linearity is achieved by moving an additional pointer structure through these dags.

Although this result appeared to settle the problem once and for all, the issue was taken up again, when it became apparent that maintaining the dags and the pointer structure can be expensive and for most practical cases (i.e. short and usually not deeply nested terms) too inefficient.

A recent improvement was published by D.Kapur, M.S.Krishnamoorthy and P.Narendran (Kapur et al., 1982), other improvements or specific implementation techniques are published among others in (Bidoit & Corbin, 1983; Escalada & Ghallab, 1987). A comparison of several algorithms in terms of empirical findings was carried out by G.Winterstein (Winterstein, 1977).

Unification in Equational Theories.

The following table summarizes most of the results that have been obtained for unification problems in special equational theories E. The special theories consist of combinations of the following equations:

A:	$f(f(x,y), z) = f(x, f(y,z))$	U:	$1 * x = x * 1 = x$
FPAG:	Finitely Presented Abelian Group	QG:	Quasi-Groups
AG:	Abelian Groups	H10:	Hilbert´sTenthProblem
ABS:	Signed Binary Trees	BR:	Boolean Rings
D_R:	$f(x, g(y,z)) = g(f(x,y), f(x,z))$	C:	$f(x,y) = f(y,x)$
D_L:	$f(g(x,y), z) = g(f(x,z), f(y,z))$		
H:	$\varphi(x \circ y) = \varphi(x) \circ \varphi(y)$	I:	$f(x,x) = x$
T:	$f(g(x,y), g(y,z)) = f(g(x,y), g(x,z))$		
C_L:	$f(f(x,y), z) = f(f(x,z), y)$	MINUS:	$-(-x) = x; -(x * y) = (-y)*(-x)$
C_R	$f(x, f(y,z)) = f(y, f(x,z))$	FH:	$1*x = x, \ q(x*y) = q(y)$

The column under A_E indicates whether or not a type conformal algorithm is known.

Except for Hilbert's Tenth Problem, we have not included the classical work on equation solving in common structures such as rings and fields, which is well known. Let us comment on a few entries in the table below:

The **Robinson Unification Problem**, i.e. unification in the absolutely free algebra of terms or unification under the empty theory Ø, has attracted most attention so far and was already discussed in the previous paragraph

Theory	Type of E	Unification decidable	A_E	References
Ø	$\mathcal{U}_1$	Yes	Yes	(Herbrand, 1930; Robinson, 1965, 1971; Knuth &Bendix, 1970; Guard, 1964; Prawitz, 1960; Baxter, 1973; Huet, 1976; Martelli & Montanari, 1979; Paterson & Wegmann, 1978; Kapur et al., 1982)
A	$\mathcal{U}_\infty$	Yes	Yes	(Hmelevskij, 1967; Plotkin, 1972; Siekmann, 1975; Livesey & Siekmann, 1975; Makanin, 1977)
C	$\mathcal{U}_\omega$	Yes	Yes	(Herold, 1987; Kirchner, 1985; Siekmann, 1976)
I	$\mathcal{U}_\omega$	Yes	Yes	(Raulefs & Siekmann, 1978; Hullot, 1980; Herold, 1986)
A+C	$\mathcal{U}_\omega$	Yes	Yes	(Stickel, 1981; Livesey & Siekmann, 1976; Hullot, 1979; Fages, 1983; Huet, 1978; Herold & Siekmann, 1986; Büttner, 1985)
A+I	$\mathcal{U}_\omega$	Yes	?	(Siekmann & Szabo, 1982; Schmidt-Schauß, 1986; Baader, 1986)
C+I	$\mathcal{U}_\omega$	Yes	Yes	(Raulefs & Siekmann, 1978; Jouannaud et al., 1983)
A+C+I	$\mathcal{U}_\omega$	Yes	Yes	(Livesey & Siekmann, 1976; Büttner, 1986)
D	$\mathcal{U}_\infty$	?	Yes	(Szabo ,1982; Arnborg & Tidén, 1985; Mzali, 1986; Szabo & Unvericht, 1978)
D+A	$\mathcal{U}_\infty$	No	Yes	(Szabo, 1982; Siekmann & Szabo, 1986)
D+C	$\mathcal{U}_\infty$	?	Yes	(Szabo, 1982)
D+A+C	$\mathcal{U}_\infty$	No	Yes	(Szabo, 1982)
D+A+I	?	Yes	?	(Szabo, 1982)
H	$\mathcal{U}_1$	Yes	Yes	(Vogel, 1978)
T	$\mathcal{U}_\omega$	Yes	Yes	(Kirchner, 1985)
T+C	$\mathcal{U}_\omega$	Yes	Yes	(Kirchner, 1985)
T+C+C	$\mathcal{U}_\omega$	Yes	Yes	(Kirchner, 1985)
$C_{R,L}$	$\mathcal{U}_\omega$	Yes	Yes	(Jeanrond, 1980)
QG	$\mathcal{U}_\omega$	Yes	Yes	(Hullot, 1980)
AG	$\mathcal{U}_\omega$	Yes	Yes	(Lankford, 1979; Lankford et al., 1984)
H10	?	No	?	(Matiyasevitch, 1970; Davis, 1973)
FPAG	$\mathcal{U}_\omega$	Yes	Yes	(Lankford, 1980; Kandry-Rody et al., 1985)
FH	$\mathcal{U}_0$	Yes	?	(Fages & Huet, 1983)
MINUS	$\mathcal{U}_\infty/\mathcal{U}_\omega$	Yes	Yes	(Kirchner, 1985)
ABS	$\mathcal{U}_\infty/\mathcal{U}_\omega$	Yes	Yes	(Kirchner, 1982)
BR	$\mathcal{U}_1$	Yes	Yes	(Martin & Nipkow, 1986, 1987; Büttner & Simonis, 1986)
D_l+A+U_r		No		(Arnborg & Tidén, 1985)
D_l,D_r		Yes		(Arnborg & Tidén, 1985)
U		Yes		(Arnborg & Tidén, 1985)

Unification under Associativity is the famous monoid problem quoted in section 1.1. G.Plotkin gave the first unification algorithm for this theory (Plotkin, 1972) and used it to demonstrate the existence of infinitary equational theories. The example used in the introduction can serve as a point in case that there are infinitely many unifiers: the difficulty is of course to prove that the infinite chain of unifiers given there is in fact most general, i.e. that there is no upper bound. Completeness, correctness and minimality proofs were presented in (Siekmann, 1978), more recently in (Jaffar, 1985). J.Hmelevskij (Hmelevskij, 1967) and others worked on the decidability problem, which was finally positively settled by G.S.Makanin (Makanin, 1977) .

Unification under Commutativity has a trivial solution, which is however insufficient for practical applications. The trivial solution is as follows: compute all permutations of the subterms and apply Robinson's algorithm to the terms thus obtained.
For example: $\qquad$ s= f(x, y)

$$t = f(a, b)$$

has the permutations

$$s'= f(y, x)$$
$$t' = f(b, a)$$

and hence four unifiers can be computed, two of which are identical, leaving the two:

$$\sigma_1 = \{x \to a, \ y \to b\}$$
$$\sigma_2 = \{x \to b, \ y \to a\}$$

This algorithm can be improved considerably, but minimality presents a hard problem; type conformal algorithms are presented in (Siekmann, 1976; Herold, 1987; Kirchner, 1985). The main interest in this theory derives from its being finitary, which is in contrast for example to the infinitary theory of associativity. A nice characterization of this difference is possible in terms of universal unification algorithms. However, a deeper theoretical explanation, of why two apparently rather similar theories belong to entirely different unification classes, is still an open research problem.

Terms under **Associativity and Commutativity** closely resemble the datastructure multisets (sets which may contain multiple occurrences of the same element), which is used in the matching of patterns (pattern directed invocation) in many programming languages of Artificial Intelligence. This pattern matching problem for multisets (often called **bags** in the AI-literature) was investigated by M.Stickel in (Stickel, 1975; Stickel, 1977), who observed that it can be reduced to the problem of solving homogeneous linear diophantine equations over positive integers, with the additional proviso that only positive linear combinations of the solution set are admissible. His results were finally published in (Stickel, 1981).

Building upon the work of G.Plotkin (Plotkin, 1972), M.Livesey and J.Siekmann (Livesey

& Siekmann, 1976) investigated these axioms also, since they so frequently occur in applications of automated theorem proving. Independently of M.Stickel they observed the close relationship between the AC-unification problem and solving linear diophantine equations and proposed a reduction to inhomogeneous linear diophantine equations.

However an important problem remained open: the extension of the AC-unification algorithm to the whole class of first order terms turned out to be more difficult than anticipated. The suggestions for such an extension in (Stickel, 1976) as well as the sketch of an extension in (Livesey & Siekmann, 1976) were missing a crucial point, namely that the subformulas of a term to be AC-unified can have more symbols, than the original term. Hence the termination of the extended AC-unification procedure became a major problem, which remained open for many years. It was finally positively solved by F. Fages (Fages, 1984), who invented a particular complexity measure for this purpose.

G.P.Huet (Huet, 1978), A.Fortenbacher (Fortenbacher, 1983), D.Lankford (Lankford, 1985) and W.Büttner (Büttner, 1985) give efficient algorithms to solve homogeneous linear equations, where only positive linear combinations are admissible. Such an algorithm, originally investigated in (Gordan, 1873), is an important component of every AC-unification algorithm. A comparison of the algorithms of G.P.Huet and A.Fortenbacher and an extension of these algorithms to the case of inhomogeneous equations can be found in (Guckenbiehl & Herold, 1985).

J.M.Hullot (Hullot, 1980), F.Fages (Fages, 1984) and A.Fortenbacher (Fortenbacher, 1983; Fortenbacher, 1985) discuss computational improvements of the original Stickel-algorithm.

Recently another approach to AC-unification based on the decomposition technique of A.Martelli and U.Montanari was proposed by C.Kirchner (Kirchner, 1985; Kirchner, 1987)

G.E.Peterson and M.E.Stickel (Peterson & Stickel, 1981) present a generalisation of the Knuth- Bendix completion algorithm based inter alia on AC-unification. The practical advantage of a special purpose AC-unification algorithm is particularily well demonstrated for term rewriting systems in (Stickel, 1984).

Apart from interest in a practical and fast algorithm, which computes the set of unifiers, there is the main theoretical observation that the set of most general unifiers is always *finite* for AC-unification problems. This fact was independently discovered in (Stickel, 1985; Livesey & Siekmann, 1976). However, since the set of most general unifiers corresponds to the set of nonnegative solutions of certain linear diophantine equations, the finiteness of the μ-set of unifiers follows immediately from a theorem of Dickson (Dickson, 1913).

Two recent papers by A.Herold, J.Siekmann (Herold & Siekmann, 1986) and W.Büttner (Büttner, 1985) improved on the original work of (Livesey & Siekmann, 1976). In (Herold & Siekmann, 1986) an extension of the algorithm to the whole class of first order terms is presented using a modification of the Fages-complexity measure in the proof of termination.

Since the axioms of associativity and commutativity so frequently occur in practice, the AC-unification algorithm has become just as important for most applications as the original Robinson algorithm for free terms. However there are still annoying efficiency problems and substantial progress is still to be expected (see for example (Bürckert et al, 1988)).

Unification under **Distributivity and Associativity** provides a point in case that the combination of two infinitary theories is an infinitary theory. Is this always the case? The (D+A)- Unification Problem is of theoretical interest with respect to Hilbert´s Tenth Problem, which is the problem of Diophantine solvability of polynomial equations. An axiomatization of Hilbert´s Tenth Problem would involve the axioms (A) and (D) plus additional axioms for integers, multiplication, etc. Calling the union of these axioms H10, Y.Matiyasevich´s celebrated result (Matiyasevich, 1970) shows in fact the undecidability of the H10-unification problem. Now the undecidability of the (D+A)-Unification Problem demonstrates that all Hilbert axioms in H10 can be eliminated except for (D) and (A) and the problem still remains undecidable. Since A-unification is known to be decidable, the race is open as to whether or not (A) can be eliminated as well, such that (D) on its own presents an undecidable unification problem. More generally it is an interesting and natural question for an undecidable unification problem to ask for its "minimal undecidable substructure". Whatever the result may be, the (D+A)-problem already highlights the advantage of the abstract nature of unification theory in contrast to the traditional point of view, with its reliance on intuitively given entities (like integers) and structures (like polynomials).

An important recent discovery is that unification in **Boolean Rings** is unitary (Büttner & Simonis, 1986; Martin & Nipkow, 1986; Martin & Nipkow, 1987) which is likely to speed up a new technology race: Boolean rings are a common datastructure in computer science, e.g. they can be used advantageously to describe logical circuits or to build sets as data structure into logic programming languages. The fact that the unification of this data structure is *unitary* holds great practical potential in particular for programming languages, however the combination with free function symbols is unsettled.

It is important to realize that the results recorded in the above table do not always hold for the whole class of first order terms, but mostly only for some subset. The extension to the whole class of terms (assuming the empty theory for every function symbol that is not part of the known unification result) is nothing but a special case of the *Combination Problem* of theories. From the above table we already have:

A infinitary,	I finitary	and A+I	nullary,	i.e. $\infty + \omega = 0$
D infinitary,	A infinitary	and D+A	infinitary,	i.e. $\infty + \infty = \infty$
D infinitary,	C finitary	and D+C	infinitary,	i.e. $\infty + \omega = \infty$
A infinitary,	C finitary	and A+C	finitary,	i.e. $\infty + \omega = \omega$
C finitary,	I finitary	and C+I	finitary,	i.e. $\omega + \omega = \omega$
H unitary,	A infinitary	and H+A	infinitary,	i.e. $1 + \infty = \infty$
D_L unitary,	C finitary	and D_L+C	infinitary,	i.e. $1 + \omega = \infty$
D_L unitary,	D_R unitary	and D_L+D_R = D	infinitary,	i.e. $1 + 1 = \infty$

Here we assume that for example (C) and (A) hold for the same function symbol and the combination of these axioms is denoted as (C+A). But what happens if (C) and (A) hold for two different function symbols, say (C) for f and (A) for g? The known results for these combination problems are recorded in (Siekmann 1989).

Summarizing we notice that unification algorithms for different theories appear on first sight to be based on entirely different techniques. They provide the experimental laboratory for the general unification theory and it is paramount to obtain a much larger experimental test bed than is currently known .

Disunification

Given a unification problem <s = t>, we are interested in all unifiers,i.e. all substitutions σ such that $\sigma s = \sigma t$. Given a *disunification problem* <s ≠ t>, we are interested in inequality, i.e. we are interested in all substitutions σ such that $\sigma s \neq \sigma t$.

Such problems are relevant for logic programming, sufficient completeness of algebraic specifications and ´inductionless induction´ and have been investigated by A.Colmerauer (Colmerauer, 1984) and H.Comon (Comon, 1986) and C.Kirchner and P.Lescanne (Kirchner & Lescanne, 1987). We say a disequation is satisfied iff $\forall \sigma$. $\sigma s \neq \sigma t$, i.e. s=t is not unifiable. A substitution σ unifies the disequation s ≠ t iff $\forall \delta.\delta\sigma s \neq \delta\sigma t$. The problems with disequations are: (i) To find a disunification algorithm for a solution of the disunification problem of uninterpreted terms, (ii) How to represent the set of disunifiers. For example the problem <x ≠ b>, where x is a variable and b a constant, has infinitely many solutions that can not be represented by a single most general idempotent unifier (disunifier). But "x not b" *is* an intuitively satisfactory representation. For that reason it has become customary to represent the solutions in ´solved form´,that is as variable/term-pairs of the form x = t or x ≠ t . Using this more expressive representation <x ≠ b> is now unitary.

The open research problems in this area are the extension of disunification of uninterpreted terms to E-disunification problems.

3.2. Unification In Order Sorted Logics

Most programming languages are typed, i.e. usually a variable declaration ensures that the variable ranges over integers, reals, lists or such like. Similarly most practical applications of predicate logic utilize some sorted variant. For example we like to write formulas like

$$\forall \ x:\text{REAL}, \ \exists y:\text{COMPLEX}. \ \ y^2 = x$$

and treat them formally as an abbreviation for

$$\forall \ x.\text{real}(x) \Rightarrow \exists y.\text{complex}(y) \wedge y^2 = x,$$

since the explicit representation of sorts as unary predicates has many practical disadvantages. Hence the sort information should be "built-in". Sorting (or typing) terms also provides a way of building taxonomical knowledge into the logic.

The idea is to represent the sort (or taxonomical) hierarchy separately and also to provide an algorithm,which computes the sort of every term. For example a variable x of sort REAL stands for real numbers and can only be instantiated by a term t that also represents a real number or a number of a lower type in the sort hierarchy.This restricted instantiation has to be taken into account by an extended unification algorithm, which exploits the given information and computes a set of well-sorted unifiers for two terms. The remarkable increase in efficiency of a deduction system based on sorted unification is due to the fact that two syntactically unifiable terms may not be sort-unifiable and hence many redundant deduction steps can be avoided (Walther, 1983).

There are different kinds of sorted signatures with respect to their expressiveness. The simplest version requires that the sort structure is flat, i.e. the domain is just partitioned into subdomains that do not have any subsorts. Such sort structures are called many-sorted and are often used in algebraic specifications and also for term rewriting systems. Unification with proper sort-hierarchies, but restricted to one assignment f: $S_1 \times S_2 \times ....\times S_n \rightarrow S$ for every function symbol, is called order-sorted unification and was first investigated by Ch.Walther (Walther, 1983) and A.G.Cohn (Cohn, 1987), although the idea to build sorts into the logic is older (Herbrand, 1930; Oberschelp, 1962). Signatures as considered by Ch.Walther in (Walther, 1985) ensure that there is a single and unique most general unifier for two terms, if the sort structure is a semilattice. Otherwise see (Walther, 1986), where it is shown that there is a respective sort hierarchy such that the corresponding unification problem is unitary, finitary and even infinitary. When more than one sort assignment per function symbol (i.e. polymorphism) is allowed, there may be more than one but at most finitely many most general unifiers (Schmidt-Schauß, 1985; Schmidt-Schauß, 1987). Signatures with a sort-hierarchy and multiple sort assignments per function symbol are useful for automated reasoning systems, algebraic specifications and functional and logic programming languages. If in addition, not only function assignments, but also term declarations are used to specify the sort of a term as proposed in (Goguen, 1978; Wadge,

1982) then unification may become undecidable and the set of most general unifiers may be infinite (Schmidt-Schauß, 1985).

The combination of sorted signatures with equational theories was also first investigated by M.Schmidt-Schauss,who showed that, with some restrictions, the unification algorithms for an unsorted equational theory can be used to solve unification problems in the sorted equational theory. A most recent account of order sorted unification with term declarations is (Schmidt-Schauß, 1987), which also contains a complete bibliography of the work on sorted unification.

3.3 Unification In Logic Programming Languages

The close relationship between logic and computation (Hoare & Shepherdson, 1985) and the fact that predicate logic itself can be viewed as a programming language, was already discussed in section 1.1.

There are some specific problems for logic programming languages however: Terms like f(x,g(x)) and f(y,y) are not unifiable in the classical sense: although both terms are "standardized apart" (i.e. have different variables), once the first arguments of f are unified the second arguments share the same variable in y and g(y) and the socalled "occur-in-check" reports failure. In order to avoid this (expensive) checking two approaches are possible: either to admit infinite terms (Colmerauer, 1982; Mukai, 1983; Martelli & Rossi, 1984) or else to accept the occasional error as for example in most PROLOG implementations (Clocksin & Mellish, 1981).

Since unification is *the* central operation of logic programming languages, more elaborate schemes have been designed for speed up. Most prominent is currently the WARREN-Machine (Warren, 1983; Gabriel et al., 1984), which consists of an abstract set of machine instructions into which a logic programming language can be compiled. This set constitutes an abstract machine and each instruction can then either be supported by actual hardware or else by some sequence of microcode instructions of a more or less conventional machine. Using these techniques current LIPS-rates (number of unifications per second) are around 100 K LIPS and estimated to be in the order of 10^4 to 10^6 K LIPS in about ten years (Lusk & Overbeek, 1984; Gabriel et al., 1984).

Combining Logical and Functional Programming

Universal unification algorithms take an equational theory T *and t*wo terms as input and return the set of most general unifiers for the two terms under T. They are the basis of an interesting new approach to programming languages that combines the virtues of functional programming with logic programming. The idea is to have logic with equality (Goguen & Meseguer, 1986; Dershowitz & Plaisted, 1986; Fribourg, 1985) as a programming language and to use the predicates (i.e. the nonequality relations) for the standard logic programming aspects. The functional programming aspect is taken care of by an appropriate term rewriting system that computes the values of terms and handles the equality relation. In other words the equations are used in just the same way as they are used in the *narrowing* algorithms (see section 3.7.) and interest is in finding equational classes and narrowing strategies, such that it can be done efficiently.

For example B.Fribourg (Fribourg, 1985) discusses normalized innermost narrowing, whereas narrowing for nonterminating rewriting systems based on lazy unification (Bürckert, 1987) (lazy functional programming) was investigated by J.H.You and P.A.Subrahmanyam (You & Subrahmanyam, 1986) and S.Hölldobler (Hölldobler, 1987). A recent improvement was published by W.Nutt, R. Réty and G.Smolka (Nutt et al., 1987).

Alternatives to narrowing are presented among others by A.Martelli, C. Moiso and G.Rossi (Martelli et al., 1987) and also by J.Gallier and S.Raatz (Gallier & Raatz, 1986).

An interesting recent development called *feature unification* was motivated by unification grammars and knowledge representation schemes.The aim is to build socalled **feature terms**, an important datastructure that is used in AI to represent taxonomical knowledge as well as certain grammars,into a logic programming language (Smolka & Ait-Kaci, 1987) (see section 3.4. below).

The field of logic programming was in many ways influential in the development of unification theory, not the least important influence is the view that a logic program is in fact a special purpose unification algorithm that computes its answer values as appropriate bindings of the output variables, i.e. as 'most general unifiers'. This view that originated with the question answering systems (Rulifson et al., 1972) of the sixties can be captured by the slogan that "relational programming is unification".

Unification Chips

Anticipating the upcoming technological demand for ultrafast unification, there were early attempts to "compile the unification algorithm into silicon"; for example there was a special unification processor called the SUM (Robinson, 1985).

Similarly, if the Warren instruction set is directly supported by suitable hardware, this can be viewed as a unification machine.Current experiments use a pipeline of unification processors or else try to marry the Warren machine with a (set of) special unification processor(s) .

3.4. Unification-based Grammars

Recently developed grammar formalisms for natural languages such as Categorical Grammar, Head Grammars, Lexical Functional Grammars, Functional Unification

Grammars and Definite Clause Grammars rely on a feature/value system to represent the linguistic information about some sentence (Shieber, 1986). These approaches to grammar formalisms have been called *unification-based,* since they employ unification as a central operation to manipulate the feature/value structures.

The central idea is the following: Linguistic information such as "the number (of a pronoun) is singular and its person feature has the value third" can be expressed in a *feature structure* as:

$$
\begin{bmatrix}
\text{number}: & \text{singular} \\
\text{person}: & \text{third}
\end{bmatrix}
$$

or as

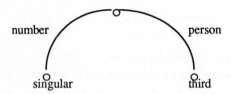

Here 'number' and 'person' are *features* and 'singular' and 'third' are their respective *values*. The feature values may themselves be structured as for example in:

$$
\begin{bmatrix}
\text{cat:} & \text{NP} \\
\text{agreement:} & \begin{bmatrix} \text{number}: & \text{singular} \\ \text{person}: & \text{third} \end{bmatrix}
\end{bmatrix}
$$

or in graph notation:

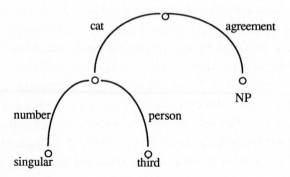

The essential difference between these feature structures and first order terms is the selection of arguments by attributes or features. Consider the following example taken from (K. Knight 1989): Suppose we want to represent the facts that John is a person, his name is John, his age is 23 and he is 180 cm tall. He is also married and his spouse's name is Mary and her age is 25. The feature structure to represent these facts would look like:

$$
\begin{bmatrix}
\text{type:} & \text{person} \\
\text{name:} & \text{john} \\
\text{age:} & 23 \\
\text{hight:} & 180 \\
\text{spouse:} & \begin{bmatrix} \text{name :} & \text{mary} \\ \text{age :} & 25 \end{bmatrix}
\end{bmatrix}
$$

Of course we could represent the same information by a first order term as:

person (john, 23,180, spouse (mary, 25))

where we would have to remember what each argument position actually stands for.

Apart from this practical inconvenience there are theoretical differences however:

(i)   There is no fixed arity in a feature structure and for many applications (mainly in natural language processing) this is important.

(ii) There is no distinguished head function symbol (like 'person' in the above example) and again for linguistic applications this is essential.

(iii) And finally the most important distinction: we may wish to express certain properties on features, i.e. we may have relations on these selectors. For example if John is to be exactly as old as his spouse, a *coreference maker* is inserted into the appropriate palce, indicating that the values of these two features ought to be equal.

This could be expressed in first order terms as

person (john, X, 180, spouse (mary, X))

i.e. by using the same variable name. But what happens, as K. Kevin (1989) argues in his very readable introduction to the subject, if there is a structured object involved? For example if we want to express the fact that John married his best friend? A possible representation is:

person (john, 23, 180, spouse (mary, 25)) <u>and</u> bestfriend (john, mary)

but this can become tedious for large structures.

There is a natural partial order on such feature structures called **subsumption** , which is based on their information content: a feature structure D_1 subsumes a feature structure D_2, $D_1 \le D_2$, if D_1 contains a subset of the information in D_2. Since there is now a partial order, which was the basic concept underlying the formal framework of unification theory as presented above, a unification based formalism can be developed for these grammars as well: two feature structures D_1 and D_2 can be unified, if there exists a feature structure D that contains the information of both D_1 and D_2, i.e. if $D \leq D_2$ and $D \leq D_1$.

Feature structures as introduced above are not only useful for the representation of grammatical and linguistic knowledge, but can in fact be used for the representation of any knowledge (as they are nothing but nested records with a particular interpretation). This is a particularily useful datastructure, when it is combined with an appropriate inheritance hierarchy (Touretzky, 1987) as used in semantic networks, frames and some programming languages like SMALLTALK. *Feature unification* is then an operation that, given two feature terms A and B, computes a feature term C denoting the intersection of the denotations of A and B (Smolka & Ait-Kaci, 1987).

Consider the following example (Ait-Kaci's ψ-terms as discussed in K. Kevin 1989), where we have a taxonomical hierarchy:

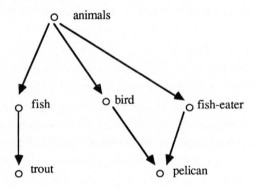

and properties are inherited from the more general to the more specific concept (i.e. in the direction of the arrows).

Given this information the following two ψ-terms are unifiable:

        fish-eater (likes : trout)

        bird (colour : brown; likes: fish)

and yield the new ψ-term:

        pelican (colour: brown; likes: trout)

The exciting prospect is that the parsing of a natural language sentence can be based on unification grammars as discussed above, the construction of its semantics can also be based on the unification of feature structures (Moore 1989) and finally, the representation of the meaning may be based on *frames* (a feature structure very common in AI, where the feature names and values are called slot names and values respectively). Frame-based representation formalisms like KL-ONE (Brachmann, Levesque 1985) are currently very popular. Finally if the generation of a natural language utterance is again based on unification grammars we have come full circle: syntactical analysis, semantical analysis, representation of meaning and finally generation of the response all rely essentially on one data structure, namely *feature structures,* and one operation, namely *unification of* feature structures. For this and other reasons, feature terms and inheritance have attracted widespread interest recently. LOGIN (Ait-Kaci & Nasr, 1986) is an extension of PROLOG, where ordinary terms are replaced by some special feature terms, called ψ-terms, and ordinary unification is replaced by ψ-unification. K.Mukai´s language CIL (Mukai, 1985) bears many similarities with LOGIN. L.Cardelli (Cardelli, 1984) gives a semantics of higher order feature types and inheritance in the framework of functional programming and denotational semantics.Recent work by W.C.Rounds and R.Kasper (Rounds & Kasper, 1986) gives an automata-theoretic formalization of feature terms. Actual feature unification algorithms have been reported by G.Smolka, H.Ait-Kaci and R.Nasr in (Ait-Kaci, 1984; Ait-Kaci & Nasr, 1986; Smolka & Ait-Kaci, 1987); if they are incorporated into a logic programming language, like for example in TEL (W. Nutt, G. Smolka 1988), these languages are likely to become essential tools not only in natural language processing, but in AI in general.

3.5. Higher Order Unification

Higher order logics, most prominently represented in the work of A.Church (Church, 1940), have provided a logical basis for many deduction systems: just as mathematics is more conveniently expressed in some higher order calculus, many automated reasoning systems exploit the expressiveness of higher order constructs.

An early higher order deduction system was built under the guidance of J.R.Guard, W.F.Gould developed its ω-order unification algorithm and presented it in his thesis (Gould, 1966). The potential advantage of a higher order deduction system and its mechanization was also discussed by J.A.Robinson in (Robinson, 1969). Since the number of unifiers of ω-order terms can be prolific, G.P.Huet developed an ω-order unification algorithm and a deduction system based on a "constraint resolution" method (Huet, 1972), whose characteristic is to postpone the computation of unifiers as long as possible (lazy unification). The unification algorithm was further elaborated in (Huet, 1975) and finally in (Huet, 1976).

Independently of C.L.Lucchesi (Lucchesi, 1972), G.P.Huet (Huet, 1973) discovered that ω-order unification is undecidable for $\omega \geq 3$; later D.Baxter (Baxter, 1978) showed the same result with a different proof technique, and D. Goldfarb (Goldfarb, 1981) showed, that in fact ω-order unification is undecidable for $\omega \geq 2$, thus providing yet another characterization of the gulf between first and higher order logics.

P.Andrews work (Andrews, 1971) on higher order deduction systems was most influential in this area, a most recent account of his work and that of his students D.A.Miller,E.L.Cohen and F.Pfenning is given in (Andrews, 1984)

Another unification algorithm for ω-order terms was developped by D.Jensen and T.Pietrzykowski and reported in (Jensen & Pietrzykowski, 1973, 1976; Pietrzykowski, 1971).

3.6. Complexity Results

In this section, which is taken from D.Kapur and P.Narendran´s survey paper (Kapur & Narendran, 1987) we give a brief overview of results obtained in studying the complexity of matching and unification problems. Both matching and unification problems for first-order terms built solely from uniterpreted function symbols have been known to be linear in the sum of the sizes of the input terms (Paterson & Wegman, 1978) as discussed in section 3.1.2. When function symbols have properties such as associativity, idempotency, etc., both problems turn out to be much harder, in fact intractable in most cases.

In the following table, symbols are used to stand for theories. The associated axiom(s) with each of the symbols is given below. For example, the symbol A implies that some of the function symbols in the terms under consideration are associative.

$$A: \ f(x,f(y,z)) = f(f(x,y),z)$$
$$C: \ f(x,y) = f(y,x)$$
$$I: \ f(x,x) = x$$
$$U: \ f(x,1) = x$$
$$D: \ f(x,g(y,z)) = g(f(x,y),f(x,z))$$

When more than one symbol is used to stand for a theory, it means that the axioms corresponding to each of the symbols are conjuncted as in section 3.1. For example, ACI, stands for the theory in which some function symbols appearing in the theory are assumed to be associative, commutative and idempotent. AC matching is an NP complete problem even if each variable in the pattern is restricted to have only at most two occurrences. AC1 stands for the theory in which function symbols may be associative-commutative and terms under consideration for unification and matching have unique occurences of each variable.

The set matching problem is defined as the problem of checking, given a set of patterns (sp) and a set of subjects (ss), whether there exists a substitution σ such that the set of terms obtained by applying σ on sp is the same as the set ss. Similarly, a set unification problem is defined as the problem of checking, given two sets of terms st and ss, whether there exists a substitution σ such that the set of terms obtained after applying σ on st is the same as the set of terms obtained after applying σ on ss. Bag matching and bag unification are defined analogously except that bags of terms (instead of sets of terms) are considered, i.e., number of occurrences of a term also becomes relevant.

As the table indicates, in most cases, both matching and unification problems turn out to be of the same order of complexity (except for associativity, where the two problems are really different).The complexity does not seem to grow even when additional properties of function symbols are assumed in some cases.

It also appears that for linear terms (terms in which every variable appears uniquely), both matching and unification problems are easier than for nonlinear terms (for matching, only the pattern has to be linear). This suggests that one of the main sources of complexity is the nonlinearity of terms.

There is one anomaly in this table, which is with respect to associative matching and unification. As the table states, associative matching is NP-complete, whereas associative unification (solvability of word equations over free semigroups) is only known to be decidable. The only complexity result known about associative unification is that it is primitive-recursive. A better upper bound is not known.

In the table, results are also given for unification problems over finitely presented algebras. In a finitely presented algebra, the presentation consists of a finite set of generators, a finite set of relations expressed using generators and the operator symbols of the algebra. Variables are not allowed in the relations. Terms under consideration for unification are „elementary terms", i.e., they can have variables but they do not have any uninterpreted function symbols. For example, FPAG is a finite presentation of abelian groups generated by a finite set of generators with a finite set of relations expressed in terms of generators and the operators of abelian groups. FPBR stands for finitely presented boolean rings. FPCSG stands for finitely presented commutative semigroups. FPA stands for arbitrary finitely presented algebras. If a finitely presented algebra does not have any relation, it is said to be freely generated. FCSG stands for finitely generated free commutative semigroups; FCSGI stands for finitely generated free commutative semigroups with idempotency; similarly, FCMI stands for finitely generated free commutative monoids with idempotency. FBR stands for finitely generated free boolean rings. SR is a theory presented by a finite complete (canonical) term rewriting system in which for each rule, the right-hand-side is either a ground term or a subterm of the left-hand-side.

Table: Complexity of Matching and Unification Problems

E	Matching		Unification	
Φ	linear		linear	(Paterson & Wegmann, 78)
U	NP-complete	(Arnborg & Tidén, 85	NP-complete	(Arnborg & Tidén, 85)
I	NP-complete	(Kapur & Narendran, 87)	NP-complete	(Kapur & Narendran, 87)
C	NP-complete	(Benanav et al., 85)	NP-complete	(Set 79)
A	NP-complete	(Benanav et al., 85)	decidable	(Makanin, 77)
CU	NP-complete	(Kapur & Narendran, 87)	NP-complete	(Kapur & Narendran, 87)
CI	NP-hard	(Kapur & Narendran, 86)	NP-hard	(Kapur & Narendran, 86)
AU	NP-complete	(Kapur & Narendran, 87)	decidable	(Makanin, 77)
AI	NP-hard	(Kapur & Narendran, 86)	NP-hard	(Kapur & Narendran, 86)
AC	NP-complete	(Kapur & Narendran, 86)	NP-complete	(Kapur & Narendran, 86)
ACU	NP-complete	(Kapur & Narendran, 86)	NP-complete	(Kapur & Narendran, 86)
ACI	NP-complete	(Kapur & Narendran 86)	NP-complete	(Kapur & Narendran, 86)
D	NP-hard	(Arnborg & Tidén, 85)	NP-hard	(Arnborg & Tidén, 85)
DU	NP-hard	(Arnborg & Tidén, 85)	NP-hard	(Arnborg & Tidén, 85)
Set	NP-complete	(Kapur & Narendran, 86)	NP-complete	(Kapur & Narendran, 86)
Bag	NP-complete	(Kapur & Narendran, 87)	NP-complete	(Kapur & Narendran, 87)
AC1	P	(Benanav et al., 85)	P	(Kapur & Narendran, 86)
FPCSG	decidable	(Kapur & Narendran, 87)	decidable	(Kapur & Narendran, 87)
FCSG	NP-complete	(Kapur & Narendran, 86)	NP-complete	(Kapur & Narendran, 86)
FCSGI	P	(Kapur & Narendran, 87)	P	(Kapur & Narendran, 87)
FCMI	P	(Kapur & Narendran, 87)	P	(Kapur & Narendran, 87)
FPAG	P	(Kapur et al., 85)	P	(Kapur et al., 85)
FBR	NP-complete	(Kapur et al., 85)	NP-complete	(Kapur et al., 85)
FPBR	NP-hard	(Kapur et al., 85)	NP-hard	(Kapur et al., 85)
FPA	NP-complete	(Kozen, 76)	NP-complete	(Kozen, 76)
SR	NP-complete	(Kapur & Narendran, 87)	NP-complete	(Kapur & Narendran, 87)

3.7. Universal Unification

As unification algorithms for different theories are usually based on entirely different techniques it would be interesting to have a universal unification algorithm for a whole class of theories: a ***universal unification algorithm*** for a class of theories $\mathbb{E}$, is an algorithm which takes as input a pair of terms (s, t) and a theory $E \in \mathbb{E}$ and generates a complete set of unifiers for $<s = t>_E$. In other words just as a Universal Turing Machine takes as its input the description of a special Turing Machine and its arguments, a universal unification algorithm accepts an (equational) theory E *and* two terms to be unified under E.

In a sense classical work on the mechanisation of deductive calculi constitutes a "universal unification algorithm": for example resolution is complete on pure equations (as long as the equality axioms are present) and hence is an undeterministic universal algorithm. Similarily paramodulation, E-resolution and the methods developed for equational reasoning (see (Bläsius & Siekmann, 1988) for recent references) can be seen as universal algorithms.

Although in some cases (like logic programming) this is an interesting view, it is of course too general to be of any practical use and in the sequel we shall just concentrate on the more specific techniques that have been proposed. There are currently two approaches:

Narrowing

To show the essential idea, this class of universal algorithms is based upon, suppose $<s = t>_E$ is the unification problem and R is a canonical rewrite system for E. Let h be a "new" binary function symbol then h(s,t) is a term and we have the following observation:

There exists $\sigma \in$ SUB with $\sigma s =_E \sigma t$ iff there exist terms p, q and $\delta \in$ SUB such that h(s,t) $\overset{*}{\Vdash}_R$ h(p,q) with $\delta p = \delta q$,where $\Vdash_R$ is the narrowing relation as defined above.

A first move towards an application of this result is a proper organization of the narrowing steps $\Vdash_R$ into a tree, with the additional proviso that variables are never narrowed:

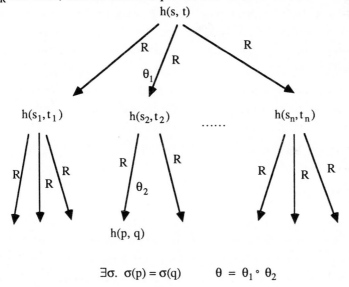

$$\exists \sigma. \ \sigma(p) = \sigma(q) \qquad \theta = \theta_1 \circ \theta_2$$

Then we have: if h(p, q) is a node in the narrowing tree, such that p, q are Robinson-unifiable with σ, i.e. $\sigma p = \sigma q$ then $\delta = \sigma \circ \theta$ is a correct E-unifier for s and t, where θ is the combination of all the narrowing substitutions obtained along the path from h(s,t) to h(p,q). And vice versa, for every E-unifier τ for s and t there exists a node h(p,q) in the narrowing tree, such that p and q are Robinson-unifiable with σ and $\sigma \circ \theta \leq_E \tau$ (Hullot, 1980).

Of course the set of unifiers obtained with this tree is far too large to be of any practical interest and the work of D.Lankford (Lankford, 1979) and J.-M.Hullot (Hullot, 1980) based on (Fay, 1979), is concerned with prunig this tree while maintaining completeness. J.-M.Hullot (Hullot, 1980) shows the close correspondence between rewriting steps and narrowing, some recent literature on narrowing.

Decomposition

An alternative approach towards a universal algorithm, developed by C. and H.Kirchner, is based on a generalisation of A.Martelli and U.Montanari´s decomposition technique that was already used for the combination problem.For a given unification problem and an equational theory E, the terms are fed into a cycle of three operations:

(i)   decomposition
(ii) merging
(iii) mutation relative to E.

Essentially, the first step decomposes the terms to be unified as far as possible into its subterms (similar to the fourth rule in the transformation based formulation of the unification algorithm in section 3.1.), the second step merges those variable/value pairs that eventually constitute the same mapping and only the third step is specific for a particular given theory. For a class of equational theories,called syntactic theories,there is a general method for this final mutation step (see (Kirchner, 1987) for an overview and (Kirchner, 1985) for details). This is an interesting result, as it demonstrates that most unification algorithms are not totally different after all, but have a common structure.

Right now it appears that narrowing is preferable for certain theories, whereas decomposition is good for others: for example the decomposition technique does not work for collapse axioms like idempotence, while narrowing does (Herold, 1986). On the other hand narrowing presupposes a canonical rewriting system for the equational theory, whereas decomposition does not.

Minimality

The set of unifiers U_E is recursively enumerable for any decidable theory E: just enumerate all substitutions and check if each one unifies the given terms, which is possible as E is decidable. Hence there is the important requirement that a universal unification algorithm should either generate a minimal set μU_E or at least should be type conformal. Since such a result is unattainable in general, there is the problem to find classes of theories, such that a universal unification algorithm is minimal (is type conformal) for every theory within this class. Ideally such a class should be large enough to contain most theories of practical interest, and still admit a correct, minimal and complete universal unification algorithm for this class. J.Siekmann and P.Szabo proposed a class of equational theories as a first step in this direction (called ACFM-theories) in (Siekmann & Szabo, 1981), A.Herold (Herold, 1982) gives an extension of this result.

The next 700 Unification Algorithms.

These general results can often be applied in practice for the design of an actual unification algorithm. So far the development of a special purpose algorithm was more of an art than a science, since for a given theory there was no indication whatsoever, of how the algorithm might actually work.

Using a universal unification algorithm as a starting point, this task is now much easier: first isolate the crucial parts and possible sources of inefficiency in the universal algorithm and then extract a practical and efficient special solution. A collection of canonical theories (Hullot, 1980) is a valuable source for this purpose and has already been used to find the first unification algorithms for Abelian group theory and quasi group theory (Lankford, 1979; Hullot, 1980) as well as an improvement of the algorithm for idempotence (Herold, 1986).

In closing the introduction to unification theory I should mention two current surveys of the field (K. Knight 1989) and (J. Siekmann 1989), which the reader may like to consult in addition.

Acknowledgements: I had many helpful suggestions and hints to the literature from P.Andrews, M.Davis, C.Kirchner, K. Knight, M.McRobbie, J.P.Jouannaud and J.A.Robinson. I am grateful to D.Kapur and P.Narendran for a preliminary version of their survey on complexity results, upon which section 3.1.6. is based. I also like to acknowledge the active involvement and the contributions of the members of my research group on unification H.J.Bürckert, A.Herold, W.Nutt, G.Smolka and M.Schmidt-Schauß without whose help this article would have been impossible.

4. REFERENCES

Andrews, P. (1971)
"Resolution in Type Theory".
J. of Symbolic Logic, vol 36.

Andrews, P., Miller, D., Cohen, E., Pfenning, E. (1984)
"Automating Higher Order Logic"
in: Contemparery Mathematics, American Math. Soc.

Aït-Kaci, H. (1984)
"A Lattice-Theoretic Approach to Computation Based on a Calculus of
Partially Ordered Type Structures".
Ph.D. Thesis, Department of Computer and Information Science, University
of Pennsylvania, Philadelphia.

Aït-Kaci, H., Nasr, R., LOGIN (1986)
"A Logic Programming Language with Built-In Inheritance".
Journal of Logic Programming, vol. 3.

Arnborg, A., Tiden, E. (1985)
"Unification Problems with One-Sided Distributivity".
Proc. of the 1st International Conference on Term Rewriting Techniques and
Applications, Dijon, France, May 1985, Springer LNCS 202, 398-406.

Baader, F. (1986)
"Unification in Idempotent Semigroups is of Type Zero".
J. of Automated Reasoning, vol. 2, 283-286.

Baader, F. (1987)
"Unification in Varieties of Idempotent Semigroups".
Internal Report, Institut für Mathematische Maschinen und
Datenverarbeitung, Universität Erlangen, 1987, also in: Semigroup Forum,
vol. 36.

Baader, F. (1988)
"Unification in Commutative Theories".
Institut für Informatik 1, Universität Erlangen, Interner Bericht.

Baader, F., Büttner, W. (1988)
"Unification in Commutative, Idempotent Monoids".
To appear in J. of Theor. Comp. Sci.

Ballard, D., Brown, Ch. (1982)
"Computer Vision".
Prentice Hall, New Jersey.

Barrow, Ambler, Burstall (1972)
"Some techniques for recognizing Structures in Pictures".
Frontiers of Pattern Recognition, Academic Press Inc.

Barwise, J., Perry, J. (1983)
"Situations and Attitudes".
Cambridge, MIT Press.

Baxter, L. D. (1973)
"An Efficient Unification Algorithm".
Report CS-73-23, University of Waterloo, Ontario, Canada, Department of
Analysis and Computer Science.

Baxter, L. D. (1977)
"The Complexity of Unification".
Internal Report CS-77-25, University of Waterloo, Ontario, Canada,Faculty
of Mathematics.

Baxter, L. D. (1978)
"The Undecidability of the Third Order Dyadic Unification Problem".
Information and Control, vol. 38, no. 2.

Beilken, Ch., Mattern, F., Spenke, M. (1982)
    "Entwurf und Implementierung von CSSA".
    Vol. A-E, SEKI-Memo-82-03, University of Kaiserslautern.
Benanav, D., Kapur, D., Narendran, P. (1985)
    "Complexity of Matching Problems".
    Proc. of the 1st International Conference on Term Rewriting Techniques and
    Applications, Dijon, France, May 1985, Springer LNCS 202, 417-429.
Bidoit, M., Corbin, J. (1983)
    "A Rehabilitation of Robinson's Unification Algorithm".
    In R.E.A. Pavon (ed.), Information Processing 83, North Holland 1983,
    909-914.
Birkhoff, G. (1935)
    "On the Structure of Abstract Algebras".
    Proc. Cambridge Phil. Soc., vol.31.
Blair, F. et al. (1971)
    "SCRATCHPAD/1: An interactive Facility for Symbolic
    Mathematics".
    Proc. of the 2nd Symposium on Symbolic Manipulation, Los Angeles.
Bläsius, K.H., Siekmann, J. (1988)
    "Partial Unification for Graph based Equational Reasoning".
    Proc. of 9th Intern. Conf. on Automated Deduction,Springer LNCS, vol .
    310.
Bobrow, D., Winograd, T. (1977)
    "An Overview of KRL"
    Cognitive Science, vol.1, no.1.
Böhm, H. P., Fischer, H. L., Raulefs, P. (1977)
    "CSSA: Language Concepts and Programming".
    M., 1977
Book, R. (1985):
    "Thue Systems as Rewriting Systems",
    in: Proc. of Rewriting Techniques, Springer Lecture Notes in Comp. Sci.,
    vol.202.
Book, R., Siekmann, J. (1986)
    "On Unification: Equational Theories are not bounded".
    J. of Symbolic Computation, vol. 2, 317-324.
Boyer, R., Moore, J. S. (1977)
    "A Fast String Searching Algorithm".
    CACM vol.20, no.10.
Brachman, R., Levesque, H. (1985)
    "Readings in Knowledge Representation".
    Will. Kaufmann Inc.
Brachman, R., Schmolze, J. (1985)
    "An Overview of KL-ONE".
    Cognitive Science, vol.9, no.2.
Bryan, H., Carnog, J. (1966):
    "Search Methods used with Transistor Patent Applications".
    IEEE Spectrum 3, 2.
Buchanan, B., Shortliffe, R. (1985)
    "Rule Based Expert Systems".
    Addison Wesley.
Buchberger, B. (1987)
    "History and Basic Features of the Critical-Pair Completion Procedure".
    Journal of Symbolic Computation, vol 3, no 1.

Bürckert, H.-J., Herold, A., Schmidt-Schauß, M. (1986/87)
        "On Equational Theories, Unification and Decidability".
        Proc. of the 2nd International Conference on Term Rewriting Techniques
        and Applications, Bordeaux, France, May 1987, Springer LNCS 256,
        204-215.
        Also SEKI Report, SR-86-19, Fachbereich Informatik, Universität
        Kaiserslautern, 1986.
Bürckert, H.-J. (1987)
        "Matching: A Special Case of Unification".
        Seki-Report SR-87-6, Fachbereich Informatik, Universität Kaiserslautern.
Bürckert, H.-J. et al. (1988)
        "Opening the AC-Unification Race".
        Journal of Automated Reasoning, vol 4, pp. 465-474.
Burris, S., Sankappanavar, H. P. (1981)
        "A Course in Universal Algebra", Springer Verlag.
        CADE see: Proceedings of the International Conference on Automated
        Deduction, Springer
Büttner, W. (1985)
        "Unification in the Datastructure Multisets".
        J. of Automated Reasoning, vol. 2, 1986, 75-88. Also SEKI-Report MEMO
        SEKI-85-V-KL, Fachbereich Informatik, Universität Kaiserslautern.
Büttner, W. (1986)
        "Unification in the Datastructure Sets".
        Proc. of the 8th Conference on Automated Deduction, Oxford, July 1986,
        Springer LNCS 230, 470-488.
Büttner, W., Simonis, H. (1986)
        "Embedding Boolean Expressions into Logic Programming".
        To appear in Journal of Automated Reasoning.
        Also Internal Report, Siemens, München.
Büttner, W. (1988)
        "Unification in Finite Algebras is Unitary (?)"
        Internal Report, SIEMENS AG, Corporate Labs, München.
CADE   see: Proceedings of the International Conference on Automated Deduction,
        Springer Lecture Notes in Computer Science, biannually,Springer Verlag.
Cardelli, L. (1984)
        "A Semantics of Multiple Inheritance".
        Proc. of Symposium on Semantics of Data Types, Springer LNCS, vol
        173.
Church, A. (1940)
        "A Formulation of the Simple Theory of Types".
        Journal of Symbolic Logic, vol 5.
Clifford, A., Preston, G. (1961)
        "The Algebraic Theory of Semigroups" ,
        vol.I and vol. II.
Clocksin, W., Mellish, C.(1981):
        "Programming in PROLOG", Springer.
Cohn, A.G. (1987)
        "A More Expressive Formulation of Many Sorted Logic".
        Journal of Autom. Reasoning, vol 3, no 2.
Colmerauer, A. (1984)
        "Equations and Inequations on Finite and Infinite Trees".
        Proc. of the International Conference on Fifth Generation Computer
        Systems, Tokyo 1984, North Holland, 85-99.
Colmerauer, A. (1982)
        "Prolog and infinite Trees",
        in: K. Clark, S.T. Tarnlund (eds), Logic Programming, Academic Press.

Comon, H. (1986)
"Sufficient Completeness, Term Rewriting Systems and 'Anti-Unification'".
Proc. of the 8th Conference on Automated Deduction, Oxford, July 1986,
Springer LNCS 230, 128-140.

Comon, H. (1987)
"About Disequations Simplification".
Internal Report RR 645-I-IMAG-55, Laboratoire d'Informatique
Fondamentale et d'Intelligence Artificielle, St. Martin d'Hères, France.

Corneil, D. G. (1968)
"Graph Isomorphism",
Ph.D., Dept. of Computer Science, University of Toronto.

Date, C. J. (1976)
"An Introduction to Database Systems".
Addison-Wesley Publ. Comp. Inc.

Davis, M. (1963)
"Eliminating the Irrelevant from Mechanical Proofs".
Symposia of Applied Math., vol.15, American Mathematical Society.

Davis, M. (1965): "The Undecidable".
Hewlett, New York, Raven Press.

Davis, M. (1973)
"Hilbert's Tenth Problem is Unsolvable".
American Mathematical Monthly, vol. 80.

Dershowitz, N., Plaisted, D. A. (1985)
"Logic Programming cum Applicative Programming".
Proc. of the 1985 Symposium on Logic Programming, Boston, July 1985,
54-67.

Dickson, L. (1913):
"Finiteness of the Odd Perfect and Primitive Abundant Numbers".
Amer. Journal of Maths, vol 35.

Dwork, C., Kannelakis, P. C., Mitchell, J. C. (1984)
"On the sequential Nature of Unification".
J. of Logic Programming I, 1984, 35-40. Also Technical Report CS-83-26,
Brown University.

Escalada, G. Ghallab, M. (1987)
"A Practically Efficient and Almost Linear Unification Algorithm".
(Draft) Laboratoire d'Automatique et d'Analyse des Systemes, Toulouse,
France.

Fages, F. (1984)
"Associative Commutative Unification".
Proc. of 7th International Conference on Automated Deduction, Napa,
California, May 1984,Springer LNCS 170, 194-208.

Fages, F., Huet, G. P. (1983)
"Complete Sets of Unifiers and Matchers in Equational Theories".
Theoretical Computer Science 43, 1986, 189-200. Also Proc. of the
Colloquium on Trees in Algebra and Programming 1983, Springer LNCS
159.

Farber, D. J., Griswald, R. E., Polonsky, I. P. (1964)
"SNOBOL as String Manipulation Language".
JACM, vol.11, no.2.

Fateman, R. (1971)
"The User-Level Semantic Matching Capability in MACSYMA".
Proc. of the 2nd Symposium on Symbolic Manipulation, Los Angeles.

Fay, M. (1979)
"First Order Unification in an Equational Theory".
Proc. of the 4th Workshop on Automated Deduction, Austin, Texas 1979,
161-167.

Forgy, C. (1981)
>   "OPS5 User Manual".
>   Carnegie Mellon University, Techn. Report, CMU-CS-81-135.
Forgy, C. (1982)
>   "Rete: A Fast Algorithm for the Many Pattern/Object Match Problem".
>   J. of Art. Intelligence, vol.19, no.1.
Fortenbacher, A. (1983)
>   "Algebraische Unifikation".
>   Diplomarbeit, Universität Karslruhe.
Fortenbacher, A. (1985)
>   "An Algebraic Approach to Unification under Associativity and
>   Commutativity".
>   Proc. of the 1st International Conference on Term Rewriting Techniques and
>   Applications, Dijon, France 1985, Springer LNCS 202, 381-397.
Franzen, M., Henschen, L. J. (1987)
>   "A New Approach to Universal Unification and its Application to
>   AC-Unification",
>   Northwestern University, Dep. of Comp. Sci., Illinois, Internal Report.
Fribourg, L. (1984)
>   "A Narrowing Procedure with Constructors".
>   Proc. of the 7th International Conference on Automated Deduction, May
>   1984, Napa, California, Springer LNCS 170, 259-281.
Fribourg, L. (1985)
>   "SLOG: A Logic Programming Language Interpreter Based on Clausal
>   Superposition and   Rewriting".
>   Proc. of the 1985 Symposium on Logic Programming, Boston, July 1985,
>   172-184.
Gabriel, J. (et al.) (1984)
>   "A Tutorial on the Warrren Abstract Machine".
>   Argonne National Lab., ANL-84-84.
Gallaire, H., Minker, J. (1978):
>   "Logic and Databases".
>   Plenum Press.
Gallier, J. H., Snyder, W. (1987)
>   "A General Complete E-unification Procedure".
>   Proc. of the 2nd International Conference on Rewriting Techniques and
>   Applications, Bordeaux, France, May 1987, Springer LNCS 256, 216-227.
Gallier, J. H., Raatz, S., Snyder, W. (1987)
>   "Theorem Proving Using Rigid E-Unification: Equational Matings".
>   Proc. of the Colloquium on the Resolution of Equations in Algebraic
>   Structures, Lakeway, Texas, May 1987. Also Internal Report, Department
>   of Computer and   Information Science, University of Pennsylvania,
>   Philadelphia.
Goguen, J. A., Thatcher, J., Wagner, E., Wright, J. (1977)
>   "Initial Algebra Semantics and Continuous Algebras".
>   JACM, vol.24, no.1.
Goguen, J. A. (1978)
>   "Order Sorted Algebra".
>   Techn. Report No 14, UCLA, Comp. Sci.Dept.
Goguen, J. A., Meseguer, J. (1986)
>   "Eqlog: Equality, Types and Generic Modules for Logic Programming",
>   in: DeGroot, Lindstrom (eds), Logic Programming, Functions and
>   Equations, Prentice Hall.
Goguen, J. A. (1988)
>   "What is Unification? A Categorical View".
>   Comp. Sci. Lab., SRI International, SRI-CSL-88-2.

Goldfarb, D. (1981)
"The Undecidability of the Second Order Unification Problem".
Theoretical Computer Science, vol. 13, 1981, 225-230.

Gordan, P. (1873)
"Über die Auflösung linearer Gleichungen mit reellen Coefficienten".
Mathematische Annalen, 23-28.

Gould, W. E. (1966)
"A Matching Procedure for ω-Order Logic".
Scientific Report no.4, Air Force Cambridge Research Laboratories,
Bedford, Massachusetts.

Grätzer, G. (1979)
"Universal Algebra".
Springer Verlag.

Guard, J. R. (1964)
"Automated Logic for Semi-Automated Mathematics".
Scientific report no.1, Air Force Cambridge Research Labs., AD 602 710.

Guard, J. R., Oglesby, F.C., Benneth, J.H., Settle, L.G. (1969)
"Semi-Automated Mathematics",
JACM, vol.18, no.1

Guard, J. R. (1964)
"Automated Logic for Semi-Automated Mathematics",
Scientific Report no 1, Air Force Cambridge Research Lab, AD 602 710.

Guckenbiehl, T., Herold, A. (1985)
"Solving Diophantine Equations".
Internal Report, MEMO SEKI-85-IV-KL, Universität Kaiserslautern.

Hearn, A. (1971)
"REDUCE2, A System and Language for Algebraic Manipulation".
Proc. of the 2nd Symposium on Symbolic Manipulation, Los Angeles.

Heilbrunner, S., Hölldobler, S. (1986)
"The Undecidability of the Unification and Matching Problem for Canonical
Theories".
Technical Report, University of the Federal Armed Forces, München.

Herbrand, J. (1930)
"Recherches sur la Théorie de la Démonstration", (thesis)
in: W. Goldfarb (ed), Logical Writings, Cambridge.

Herold, A. (1983)
"Some Basic Notions of First Order Unification Theory".
Internal Report MEMO-SEKI 15-83, Institut für Informartik I, Universität
Karlsruhe.

Herold, A. (1986)
"Narrowing Techniques Applied to Idempotent Unification".
Internal Report SEKI-Report SR-86-16, Fachbereich Informatik, Universität
Kaiserslautern.

Herold, A., Siekmann, J. (1985)
"Unification in Abelian Semigroups".
Internal Report MEMO-SEKI 85-III-KL, Fachbereich Informatik Universität
Kaiserslautern. Journal of Automated Reasoning,vol. 3,pp 247-283,1987

Herold, A. (1986)
"Combination of Unification Algorithms".
Proc. of the 8th Conference on Automated Deduction, Oxford, July 1986,
Springer LNCS 230, 450-469.
Also MEMO-SEKI 86-VIII-KL, Universität Kaiserslautern.

Herold, A. (1986)
"Narrowing Techniques Applied to Idempotent Unification".
Internal Report Seki-Report SR-86-16, Fachbereich Informatik, Univirsität
Kaiserslautern.

Herold, A. (1987)
    "Combination of Unification Algorithms".
    Dissertation, Universität Kaiserslautern.
Hewitt, C. (1972)
    "Description and Theoretical Analysis of PLANNER, a Language for
    Proving Theorems and Manipulation Models in a Robot".
    Dept. of Mathematics, Ph.C. Thesis, MIT.
Hmelevskij, J. I. (1964)
    "The Solution of certain Systems of Word Equations".
    Dokl. Akad. Nauk SSSR, vol. 156, 1964, 749ff = Soviet Math. Dokl., vol.
    5, 724-729.
Hmelevskij, J. I. (1966)
    "Word Equations without Coefficients".
    Dokl. Akad. Nauk SSSR, vol. 171, 1966, 1047ff = Soviet Math. Dokl.,
    vol.7, no. 6, 1966, 1611-1613.
Hmelevskij, J. I., (1967)
    "Solution of Word Equations in three Unknowns".
    Dokl. Akad. Nauk SSSR, vol. 177, 1967, no.5 = Soviet Math. Dokl., vol.
    8, 1967, no.6, 1554-1556.
Hoare, C. R. A., Shepherdson, J. C. (eds.) (1985)
    "Mathematical Logic and Programming Languages".
    Prentice Hall.
Howie, J. (1976)
    "Introduction to Semigroup Theory".
    Academic Press.
Huet, G. P. (1972)
    "Constrained Resolution: A Complete Method for Higher Order Logic".
    Ph.D. Thesis, Case Western Reserve University.
Huet, G. P. (1973)
    "The Undecidability of Unification in Third Order Logic".
    Information and Control, vol. 22, no. 3, 1973, 257-267.
Huet, G. P. (1975)
    "A Unification Algorithm for Typed λ-Calculus".
    Theoretical Computer Science, vol. 1, 1975, 27-57. Also Proc. of the
    Symposium on λ-Calculus and Computer Science Theory, 1975, Rome,
    LNCS 37. Also Rapport de Recherche No. 23, INRIA Le Chesnay.
Huet, G. P. (1976)
    "Résolution d'équations dans des langages d'ordre 1,2,...,ω".
    Thèse d'État, Université de Paris VII.
Huet, G. P. (1978)
    "An Algorithm to Generate the Basis of Solutions to Homogenous Linear
    Diophantine Equations".
    Information Processing Letters, vol. 7, no. 3, 144-147.
Huet, G., Oppen, D. (1980):
    "Equations and Rewirte Rules".
    R.Book (ed.), Formal Language Theory: Perspectives and Open Problems,
    New York, Academic Press.
Hullot, J.-M. (1979)
    "Associative Commutative Pattern Matching".
    Proc. of the 6th International Joint Conference on Artificial Intelligence,
    Tokyo, 406-412.
Hullot, J.-M. (1980)
    "Canonical Forms and Unification".
    Proc. of the 5th Conference on Automated Deduction, Les Arcs, France,
    1980, Springer LNCS 87, 318-334. Also Technical Report CSL-114,
    SRI-International.

ICOT, (1984)
"Fifth Generation Computer Systems".
North Holland Publ. Comp.

Jaffar, J. (1984)
"A Decision Procedure for Theorems about Multisets".
Internal Report, Monash University, Clayton, Victoria, Australia.

Jaffar, J. (1985)
"Minimal and Complete Word Unification".
Internal Report , Monash University, Clayton, Victoria, Australia.

Jensen, D. Pietrzykowski, T. (1973)
"Mechanizing ω-Order Type Theory through Unification".
Internal Report CS-73-13, Department. of Applied Analysis and Computer

Jouannaud, J. P., Kirchner, C., Kirchner, H. (1982)
"Incremental Unification in Equational Theories".
Proc.of the Allerton Conference on Communication, Control and Computation, University of Illinois, Urbana Champaign, 396-405.

Jouannaud, J. P., Kirchner, C., Kirchner, H. (1983)
"Incremental Construction of Unification Algorithms in Equational Theories".
Proc. of the 10th International Conference on Automata, Languages and Programming, Barcelona, Spain 1983, Springer LNCS 154, 361-373 .
Also Internal Report 82-R-047, Centre de Recherche en Informatique de Nancy, France.

Kamp, H. (1981)
"A Theory of Truth and Semantic Representation",
in: J.Groenendijk et. al.(eds), Formal Methods in the Study of Language.

Kandri-Rody, A., Kapur, D., Narendran, P. (1985)
"An Ideal-Theoretic Approach to Word Problems and Unification Problems over Finitely Presented Commutative Algebras".
Proc. of the 1st International Conference on Rewriting Techniques and Applications, Dijon, France, May 1985, Springer LNCS 202, 345-364.

Kapur, D., Krishnamoorthy, M.S., Narendran, P. (1982)
"A New Linear Algorithm for Unification".
Internal Report, no. 82CRD-100, General Electric, New York

Kapur, D., Narendran, P. (1987)
"Matching, Unification and Complexity" to appear in Journal of Autom. Reasoning.

Kirchner, C., Kirchner, H. (1981)
"Solving Equations in the Signed Trees Theory. Application to Program Derecursivation".
Internal Report 81-R-056, Centre de Recherche en Informatique de Nancy, France.

Kirchner, C., Kirchner, H. (1982)
"Contribution à la résolution d'équations dans les algèbres libres et les variétés équationelles d'algèbres".
Thèse de 3ème cycle, Université de Nancy I, France.

Kirchner, C. (1984)
"A New Equational Unification Method: A Generalisation of Martelli-Montanari's Algorithm".
Proc.of the 7th International Conference on Automated Decuction, Napa, California, May 1984, Springer LNCS 170, 224-247.
Also Proc. of the NSF Workshop on the Rewrite Rule Laboratory, 1983.

Kirchner, C. (1984)
"Standardizations of Equational Unification: Abstract and Examples".
Internal Report 84-R-074, Centre de Recherche en Informatique, Nancy, France.

Kirchner, C. (1985)
"Méthodes et outils de conception systématique d'algorithmes d'unification dans les théories equationelles".
Thèse d'État, Université de Nancy I, France.

Kirchner, C. (1986)
"Computing Unification Algorithms".
Conference on Logic in Computer Science, 206-216.

Kirchner, C., Lescanne, P. (1987)
"Solving Disequations".
Proc. of the 2nd IEEE Conference on Logic in Computer Science, Ithaca, New York.

Kirchner, C. (1987)
"Methods and Tools for Equational Unification".
Proc. of the Colloquium on the Resolution of Equations in Algebraic Structures, Lakeway, Texas, May .

Knight, K (1989)
"A Multidisciplinary Survey"
ACM Computing Surveys, vol. 21, no 1

Knuth, D. E., Bendix, P. B. (1970)
"Simple Word Problems in Universal Algebras".
In J.Leech (ed.), Computational Problems in Abstract Algebra, Pergamon Press, Oxford.
Amsterdam, Mathematical Centre.

Kowalski, R. (1979)
"Logic for Problem Solving".
North Holland.

Kozen, D. (1976)
"Complexity of Finitely Presented Algebras".
Int. Report 76-294, Dept. of Comp. Sci, Cornell University.

Kühner, S., Mathis, Ch., Raulefs, P., Siekmann, J. (1977)
"Unification of Idempotent Functions".
Proc. of the 5th International Joint Conference on Artificial Intelligence, MIT, Cambridge,Massachusetts.

Lankford, D. S. (1979)
"A Unification Algorithm for Abelian Group Theory".
Internal Report MTP-1, Louisiana Tech University, Ruston.

Lankford, D. S. (1980)
"A New Complete FPA-Unification Algorithm".
Internal Report MTP-8, Louisiana Tech University, Ruston.

Lankford, D. S. (1985)
"New Non-Negative Integer Basis Algorithms for Linear Equations with Integer Coefficients".
Internal Report, Louisiana Tech University, Ruston.

Lankford, D. S., Butler, G., Brady, B.(1984)
"Abelian Group Unification Algorithms for elementary Terms",
in: Contemporary Mathematics, vol. 29.

Lassez, J.-L., Maher, M. J., Marriott, K. (1986)
"Unification Revisited".
Internal Report RC 12394 (#55630) 12/16/86, IBM, Yorktown Heights.

Livesey, M., Siekmann, J. (1975)
"Termination and Decidability Results for Stringunification".
Internal Report Memo CSM-12, University of Essex.

Livesey, M., Siekmann, J. (1976)
"Unification of Sets and Multisets".
Internal Report MEMO SEKI-76-II, Institut für Informatik I, Universität Karlsruhe.

Loveland, D. (1978)
      "Automated Theorem Proving".
      North Holland.
Makanin, G. S. (1977)
      "The Problem of Solvability of Equations in a Free Semigroup".
      Math. USSR Sbornik, vol. 32, no.2, 129-198.
Makanin, G. S. (1983)
      "Equations in a Free Group ".
      Math. USSR Izvestiya, vol. 21, no. 3, 483-546.
Manna, Z., Waldinger, R. (1986)
      "How to clear a block: Plan formation in situational logic".
      Proc. CADE, Springer LNCS, vol 230.
Manove, Bloom, Engelmann (1968)
      "Rational Functions in MATHLAB".
      IFIP Conf. on Symb. Manipulation, Pisa.
Markov, A. A. (1954):
      "Trudy Mat. Inst. Steklov",
      no.42, Izdat. Akad. Nauk SSSR, 1954, NR17, 1038.
Martelli, A., Montanari, U. (1976)
      "Unification in Linear Time and Space: A structured Presentation".
      Technical Report B76-16, University of Pisa.
Martelli, A., Montanari, U. (1979)
      "An Efficient Unification Algorithm".
      ACM Transactions on Programming Languages and Systems, vol. 4, No. 2, 258-282.
Martelli, A., Rossi, G. F. (1984)
      "Efficient Unification with Infinite Terms in Logic Programming".
      Proc. of the International Conference on Fifth Generation Computer Systems, North Holland, 202-209.
Martin, U. (1986)
      "Unification in Boolean Rings and Unquantified Formulae of the First Order Predicate Calculus".
      Internal Report, University of Manchester.
Martin, U., Nipkow, T. (1986)
      "Unification in Boolean Rings".
      Proc. of the 8th International Conference on Automated Deduction, July 1986, Oxford, Springer LNCS 230, 506-513, to apperar in: Journal of Autom. Reasoning.
Martin, U., Nipkow, T. (1987)
      "Boolean Unification - A Survey", University of Manchester, Internal Report, 1987, to appear in: Journal of Symb. Computation.
Matiyasevich, Y. (1970)
      "Diophantine Representation of Recursively Enumerable Predicates".
      Ak. Nauk USSR, Ser. Math.vol. 35, 1971, 3-30.
McNulty, G. (1976)
      "The Decision Problem of Equational Bases of Algebras, Annals of Mathem. Logic, vol 10.
Meseguer, J., Goguen, J., Smolka, G. (1987)
      "Order-Sorted Unification".
      Proc. of the Colloquium on the Resolution of Equations in Algebraic Structures, Lakeway, Texas, also: Report CSLI-87-86, Centre for the Study of Language and Information, Stanford University, 1987.
Minsky, M. (1975)
      "A Framework for Representing Knowledge" ,
      in: P.Winston: "The Psychology of Computer Vision", McGraw Hill.

Moore, J. S. (1973)
  "Computational Logic: Structure Sharing".
  Ph.D. thesis, Univ. of Edinburgh.
Moses, J. (1971)
  "Symbolic Integration: The Stormy Decade".
  CACM 14, 8.
Moses, J. (1974)
  "MACSYMA - the fifth Year".
  Project MAC, MIT, Cambridge.
Mukai, K. (1983)
  "A Unification Algorithm for Infinite Trees".
  Proc. of the 8th International Joint Conference on Artificial Intelligence,
  Karlsruhe, 547-549.
Mukai, K. (1985)
  "Unification over Complex Indeterminates in Prolog".
  Technical Report TR-113, ICOT.
Murray, N. U. (1979)
  "Linear and almost-linear Methods for the Unification of First Order
  Expressions",
  (Ph.D. thesis) School of Comp. Sci., Syracuse University.
Mzali, J. (1983)
  "Algorithme de Filtrage Associatif Commutatif".
  Inernal Report 83-R-60, Centre de Recherche en Informatique de Nancy,
  1983.
Nelson, G., Oppen, D. (1980)
  "Fast Decision Procedures based on Congruence Closure".
  JACM, p.356-364.
Nevins, A. (1974)
  "A Human Oriented Logic for ATP", JACM 21.
Oberschelp, A. (1962)
  "Untersuchungen zur mehrsortigen Quantorenlogik".
  Mathematische Annalen, vol 145, pp 297-333.
Ohlbach, H. J. (1988)
  "A Resolution Calculus for Modal Logics".
  University of Kaiserslautern, SEKI-Report (Ph.D.thesis).
Ohlbach, H. J. (1988)
  "A Resolution Calculus for Modal Logics".
  (Ph.D. thesis), Universität Kaiserslautern.
Paterson, M., Wegman, M. (1978)
  "Linear Unification".
  J. of Computer and System Sciences, vol. 16, 158-167.
Peterson, G., Stickel, M. (1981)
  "Complete Sets of Reductions for Equational Theories with Complete
  Unification Algorithms".
  J. of the ACM, vol. 28, no. 2, 1981, 233-264.
  Also Technical Note 269, SRI International.
Plotkin, G. (1972)
  "Building in Equational Theories".
  Machine Intelligence, vol.7, Edinburgh University Press, 73-90.
Prawitz, D. (1960)
  "An Improved Proof Procedure".
  Theoria 26.
Prawitz, D. (1960):
  "An Improved Proof Procedure",
  Theoria 26.

Ramnarayan, R., Zimmermann, G. (1985)
"PESA, A Parallel Architecture for OPS5 Production
Systems".
19th Annual Hawaii International Conference on Systems Sciences.
Rastall, J. (1969)
"Graph Family Matching".
University of Edinburgh, MIP-R-62.
Raulefs, P., Siekmann, J. (1978)
"Unification of Idempotent Functions".
Internal Report MEMO SEKI-78-I, Universität Karlsruhe.
Robinson, J. A. (1965)
"A Machine Oriented Logic Based on the Resolution Principle".
J. of the ACM, vol. 12, no. 1, 23-41.
Robinson, J. A. (1969)
"Mechanizing Higher Order Logic",
Machine Intelligence, vol 4, Edinburgh University Press, pp. 151-170.
Robinson, J. A. (1971)
"Computational Logic: The Unification Computation".
Machine Intelligence, vol. 6, Edinburgh University Press 1971, 63-72.
Robinson, P. (1985)
"The Sum: An AI Coprocessor".
Byte, vol 10, no 6.
Robinson, J. A. (1969)
"Mechanizing Higher Order Logic",
in: Machine Intelligence, vol 4, Edinburgh Univ. Press.
Rounds, W.C., Kasper, R. (1986)
"A Complete Logical Calculus for Record Structures Representing Linguistic
Information",
Proc. of IEEE Symp. on Logic in Comp.Sci.
Rulifson, Derksen, Waldinger (1972)
"QA4: A Procedural Calculus for Intuitive
Reasoning".
Stanford Univ., Nov.
Schmidt-Schauß, M. (1985)
"Unification in a Many-Sorted Calculus with Declarations".
Proc. of the 9th German Workshop on Artificial Intelligence 1985, Springer
IFB 118, 118-132.
Schmidt-Schauß, M. (1985)
"A many Sorted Calculus with Polymorphic Functions Based on Resolution
and Paramodulation".
Proc. of the 9th International Joint Conference on Artificial Intelligence, Los
Angeles, 1985, 1162-1168.Also Internal Report MEMO SEKI-85-II-KL,
Fachbereich Informatik, Universität Kaiserslautern.
Schmidt-Schauß, M. (1986)
"Unification under Associativity and Idempotence is of Type Nullary".
J. of Automated Reasoning, vol. 2, no. 3, 277-282.
Schmidt-Schauß, M. (1987)
"Unification in Permutative Equational Theories is Undecidable".
Internal Report Seki-Report SR-87-03, Fachbereich Informatik, Universität
Kaiserslautern.
Schmidt-Schauß, M. (1987)
"Computational Aspects of an Order Sorted Logic with Term Declarations",
(thesis) University of Kaiserslautern.
Shieber, S. (1986)
"An Introduction to Unification-Based Approaches to Grammar".
CSLI Lecture Notes, no. 4, CSLI, Stanford University.

Shieber, S., Karttunen, L., Pereira, F. (1984)
        "Notes from the Unification Underground".
        Technical Report SRI-International, TN327.
Shostak, R. (1984)
        "Deciding Combinations of Theories",
        JACM, vol.31, no.1. Springer Lecture Notes Comp. Sci., vol.87
Siekmann, J. (1975)
        "String-Unification".
        Internal Report Memo CSM-7, Essex University.
Siekmann, J. (1976)
        "Unification of Commutative Terms".
        Proc. of the International Symposium on Symbolic an Algebraic
        Manipulation, EUROSAM'79, Marseille, France, June 1979, Springer
        LNCS 72, 531-545. Also Internal Report SEKI, Institut für Informatik I,
        Universität Karlsruhe, Germany.
Siekmann, J. (1978)
        "Unification and Matching Problems".
        Ph.D. Thesis, Essex University, Memo CSA-4-78.
Siekmann, J. (1984)
        "Universal Unification".
        Proc. of the 7th International Conference on Automated Deduction, Napa,
        California, Springer LNCS 170, 1-42.
Siekmann, J., Szabo, P. (1982)
        "A Noetherian and Complete Rewirte System for Idempotent Semigroups".
        Semigroup Forum, vol. 25.
Siekmann, J. (1986)
        "Unification Theory".
        Proc. of the 8th European Conference on Artificial Intelligence, Brighton,
        vol. 2, vi-xxv.
Siekmann, J., Szabo, P. (1981)
        "Universal Unification and Regular ACFM Theories".
        Proc. of the 7th International Joint Conference on Artificial Intelligence,
        Vancouver, 532-538.
        Also Internal Report MEMO SEKI-81-III, Universität Karlsruhe.
Siekmann, J., Szabo, P. (1982)
        "Universal Unification and a Classification of Equational Theories".
        Proc. of the 6th Conference on Automated Deduction, New York,
        Springer LNCS 87, 369-389.
        Also Internal Report MEMO SEKI-81-II, Universität Karlsruhe.
Siekmann, J., Szabo, P. (1982)
        "Universal Unification".
        Proc. of the 6th German Workshop on Artificial Intelligence, Bad Honnef,
        Germany 1982, Springer IFB 58, 177-190.
Siekmann, J., Szabo, P. (1986)
        "The Undecidability of the D_A-Unification Problem".
        Internal Report SEKI-Report, SR-86-19, Fachbereich Informatik,
        Universität Kaiserslautern, 1986, full paper appears in the Journal of
        Symbolic Logic (June 1989).
Siekmann, J., (1989)
        "Unification Theory"
        J. of Symbolic Computation, vol.7, pp 207-274.
Slagle, J. R. (1972)
        "ATP with built-in Theories including Equality, Partial Ordering and Sets".
        JACM 19, 120-135, 1972

Smolka, G., Aït-Kaci, H. (1987)
   "Inheritance Hierarchies: Semantics and Unification".
   MCC Technical Report no. AI-057-87, Microelectronics and Computer
   Technology Corporation, Austin, Texas.
Stickel, M. E. (1975)
   "A Complete Unification Algorithm for Associative-Commutative
   Functions".
   Proc. of the 4th International Joint Conference on Artificial Intelligence,
   Tblisi, 71-82.
Stickel, M. E. (1977)
   "Mechanical Theorem Proving and Artificial Intelligence Languages",
   Ph.D. Thesis, Carnegie-Mellon University, Pittsburgh.
Stickel, M. E. (1981)
   "A Unification Algorithm for Associative Commutative Functions".
   J. of the ACM, vol.28, no.3, 423-434.
Stickel, M. E. (1984)
   "A Case Study of Theorem Proving by the KB-Method".
   Proc. of CADE, Springer LNCS, vol 170, Springer Verlag.
Sussenguth, A. (1965)
   "A Graph-theoretical Algorithm for Matching Chemical Structures".
   J. Chem. Doc.5, 1.
Szabo, P. (1982)
   "Theory of First Order Unification".
   Ph.D. Thesis, Universität Karlsruhe, (in German).
Szabo, P. (1979)
   "Undecidability of the D_A-Unification Problems".
   Proc. of the 3rd German Workshop on Artificial Intelligence.
Szabo, P., Unvericht, E. (1978)
   "The Unification Problem for Distributive Terms".
   Internal Report SEKI-78-05, Institut für Informatik I, Universität Karlsruhe,
   Germany.
Tarski, A. (1968)
   "Equational Logic and Equational Theories of Algebra",
   Schmidt et al (eds), Contributions to Mathematical Logic, North Holland.
Taylor, W. (1979)
   "Equational Logic",
   Houston J. of Math. , 5.
Tennant, H. (1981)
   "Natural Language Processing",
   Petrocelli Books.
Tidén, E. (1986)
   "First-Order Unification in Combinations of Equational Theories".
   Ph D. Thesis, Stockholm.
Touretzky, D. S. (1987)
   "The mathematics of Inheritance Systems".
   M. Kaufman, Publishers, Los Altos, Research Notes in Art. Intelligence
Ullman, J. R. (1976)
   "An Algorithm for Subgraph Isomorphism".
   JACM, vol.23, no.1.
Unger, S. H. (1964)
   "GIT - Heuristic Program for Testing Pairs of Directed Line Graphs
   for Isomorphism".
   CACM, vol.7, no.1.
Venturini-Zilli, M. (1975)
   "Complexity of the Unification Algorithm for First Order Expressions".
   Calcolo vol. 12, no. 4, 361-371.

Wadge, W. (1982)
        "Classified Algebras".
        Internat. Report No 46, Univ. of Warwick, England.
Wallen, L. (1987)
        "Matrix Proof Methods for Modal Logics".
        Proc. of Intern. Joint Conf. on Art. Intelligence, Milan, Italy.
Walther, Ch. (1983)
        "A Many-Sorted Calculus Based on Resolution and Paramodulation".
        Proc. of the 8th International Joint Conference on Artificial Intelligence,
        Karlsruhe, Germany, 1983, 882-891, full version reprinted in: Research
        Notes in Artificial Intelligence, M. Kaufmann Publishers, Los Altos.
Walther, Ch. (1985)
        "Unification in many-sorted theories".
        Proc. of 6th ECAI, pp. 593-602.
Walther, Ch. (1986)
        "A Classification of Many Sorted Unification Problems".
        Proc. of the 8th International Conference on Automated Deduction, Oxford,
        Springer LNCS 230, 525-537.
        Also Internal Report 10/85, Institut für Informatik I, Universität Karlsruhe.
Walther, Ch. (1988)
        "Many Sorted Unification". J. of the ACM, vol 35, no 1, pp. 1-17.
Warren, D. H. (1983):
        "An Abstract Prolog Instruction Set",
        SRI Technical Note 309, SRI-International.
van Wijngaarden (et al.) (1976)
        "Revised Rep. on the Algorithmic Language ALGOL68".
        Springer Verlag, Berlin, Heidelberg, N.Y.
Winograd, T. (1972)
        "Understanding Natural Language". Edinburgh Univ. Press.
Winograd, T. (1983)
        "Language as a Cognitive Process", vol.1, Addison Wesley.
Winston, P. (1975)
        "The Psychology of Computer Vision".
        McGraw Hill.
Winterstein, G. (1976)
        "Unification in Second Order Logic".
        Bericht No 3, University of Kaiserslautern.
Winterstein, G. (et al) (1977)
        "A Comparison of Several Unification Algorithms".
        University of Kaiserslautern, Internal Report.
Wos, L., Robinson, G. A., Carson, D., Shalla, L. (1967)
        "The Concept of Demodulation in Theorem Proving". JACM, vol.14, no.4.
Wos, L., Robinson, G. A. (1973)
        "Maximal Models and Refutation Completeness: Semidecision Procedures in
        Automatic Theorem Proving",
        in: Word Problems (W.W.Boone, F.B. Cannonito, R.C.Lyndon, eds),
        North Holland.
Yelick, K. (1985)
        "A Generalized Approach to Equational Unification".
        Internal Report MIT/LCS/TR-344, Massachusetts Institute of Technology.

You, J.-H., Subrahmanyam, P. A. (1985)
        "E-Unification Algorithms for a Class of Confluent Term Rewriting
        Systems".
        Technical Report, Department of Computer Science, University of Alberta,
        Edmonton, Canada.

Index

A^* algorithm 129, 136, 138
A-orderings 297
a priori 191
absolute value 223, 241
abstract datatype specification 4
abstraction 129, 133, 135, 140, 308
abstraction–restriction–relaxation algorithm 148
AC^0 255, 256
ACC 256
accept 228, 233
accuracy 193, 253
AC^k 255, 256
$AC^k(p)$ 256
$AC^0(p)$ 256
active 237, 240, 244, 259, 260
acyclic graph 225, 231
acyclic neural network 246, 247
Aczel, J. 192
Adaline 202, 208
adaptive resonance 209
adequate 132
admissible move composition 130
admissible relation 153
affirmation procedure 273
Aleliunas, R. 185, 192
algorithm 225, 226, 228–232, 261, 262
ALICE 141, 142, 162
α-th layer 347
α-th weak stratum 347
Alpha–Beta pruning 129
alternating Turing machine 232
Amarel, Saul 169
analogue 220
analogy 308
analysis 313
AND 223, 255, 256, 260, 261
AND/OR 251
AND/OR circuit 248, 249, 251, 255, 256, 260
Andrews 300, 303, 312
Angluin, D. 202
answer extraction 295

antecedent 276
applications 270
approximating concept 201
approximation 251
arc 225
architectures 45, 217, 219, 220
array 224, 260
artificial intelligence 45, 218, 313
associative search network 209
atom 47, 289
atomic proposition 272
atomic symbols 47, 50
autotactic 58, 59
axiom 274
axiomatization 381

Back-chain 60
back-chaining 278, 299, 306
backtracking 283
backward chaining 274
ballistic 174
Banerji, Raman 156, 169
base 224
basis 231
batch 174
Bayesian learning 186
Bayes's Theorem 188
belief 184
Benjamin, Paul 158
Berger, J.O. 193
Bernoulli trial 234, 235
Berry, D. 193
best-first search 275
bias 188
Bibel 300
bidirectional edge 247, 260
binary
– representation 224
– search 229
– states 244, 245
binding occurrences 49
Biochemistry 218

bipartite
- graph 225, 258
- neural network 258
bipolar states 244, 245, 257
Birkhoff theorem 5
Bledsoe 283, 303–305, 313
Bledsoe real arithmetic 305
B(m, N, p) 234, 235, 252
Boltzmann machine 208, 256
Boolean
- array 250
- circuit 260
- concept 195–200
- expression 272
- formula 223, 230, 260
- function 242, 248, 251, 253, 255
- gate 240, 251, 260
- negation 240, 260
- operation 219, 223
- Rings 395
- set 223, 244
- value 223, 237, 255
- variable 223
bottleneck 219
bottom
- layer 347, 348
- stratum 347, 348
bounded quantifiers 312
Boyer–Moore theorem prover 304, 311, 312
brain 217, 222, 251
Brand 298
breadth first search 137, 275
Bundy 305

cable 252, 253
cartesian 47
- product 50
chunking 140, 155, 158, 162, 168
clause 223, 260, 325
- head 325
- premises 324
clause form 274, 291
closed world assumption 336, 338
CNF, *see* Conjunctive Normal Form
CNN 259, 260
Co-NP 230, 231
- complete 230
- hard 230
cognitive science 218
coin flip 233

column 250, 2224
combinatory logic 298, 304
combining unification algorithms 299
comparative analysis 111
comparative statics 96
complement 223, 230
complete 229, 231, 233, 259, 263, 290, 295
- basis 231
- set of R-unifiers 26
- set of unifiers 384
completeness 306
completion procedures 10, 11
completion sequence 12
complexity 165
- bounds 300
- theory 217, 221, 222, 225, 227
component 345, 349
- maximal 346
- trivial 346, 348
computability 225, 227
computable 226, 228, 232, 254, 255, 262
computable function 48
computation 24, 237, 239, 241, 244, 251, 257, 260
computation unit 260
computational complexity theory 217, 221, 222, 225, 227
computer design 217, 218
computer engineering 218
computer proof systems 291
computer science 218
concept 177
concurrency 311
conditional 184
- equations 299
- rewriting 19
confidence 194
configuration 237, 246, 247, 258, 259, 261, 262
confluences 81
confluent 6, 7, 382
congruence closure 47
conjunction 223, 249, 272
Conjunctive Normal Form (CNF) 223, 230, 260, 272, 289
connected 204
connection-graph 300
connection table 126, 128, 145, 146
connectionism 202, 209
consensus 223, 234, 235

consistency 291
consistency problem 197
– modified 200
consistent 381
constant depth 249, 251, 254, 256, 263
constant time 253, 262
constant weight 254
constrained semantic simplified reduction
  format 280
constraint 242, 243
constraint satisfaction 90, 161, 162
constructive 46–57
context-free grammar 201
contextual critical pair 19
contradiction 273, 290
contrapositive 300
contrapositive law 53
converge 263
convergent 6
convergent modulo 16
convex 204
convexity 305
correct cable 252
correctness proofs 271
cost 225, 229
countable 225, 226
counterexample 179
Cox, R.T. 185, 192
Cramer's rule 243
credit assignment 181
critical pair 8
– lemma 8
cut rule 275
cycle 225, 229, 247, 258, 260
cyclic 231

database program 323, 324
Davis and Putnam's method 283
Davis–Putnam rule 347
de Finetti, B. 192
decidable 272
decision 54
decision list 201
decision procedure 62, 273
declarative
– knowledge 269
– programming 270, 322, 335
– semantics 323
decomposition 124, 135, 143

deductive
– component 325
– database 322, 323
– reasoning 321
– rule 321
degenerate graph 236
degree 225, 231, 240, 259, 263
– of information 328
– of truth 326, 328
demodulant 299
demodulated 382
demodulation 298, 307
denotational
– phenomenon 218
– semantics 218
dependency graph 339
depth 231, 235, 246, 255, 263
depth first iterative deepening 129–137,
  146, 275, 306
depth of the program 347, 355
determinant 224
deterministic 233, 235, 245
diagnosis 181
diagnosis procedure 181
diagonal 250
diagonalization 226, 227
Diamond lemma 8
difference 126, 144, 146, 154, 169
– discriminating 144
– ordering 128
– primitive 153
differential qualitative analysis 112
dimension 243
dimensional 224
directed constraints 86
directed graph 224, 225, 229, 231
directed neural network 259, 261, 263
dirty 250
discrete behaviour 218, 219, 221
discrimination net 311
disjoint union 48
disjunction 223, 249, 272
disjunction problem 198
disjunctive information 321
disjunctive normal form 223, 249
distinguished model 281
disunification 396
divide-and-conquer 255
DNA 218
domain 272, 289

E-equal 35
E-equal on W 383
E-equivalent 383
E-instance 383
E-unification problem 383, 385
E-unifier 384
edge 225, 236, 238, 240, 241, 247, 248, 250,
  260
eight puzzle 146
electrical 218, 219
electrical engineering 218
electronic 219
elementary geometry 305
elimination 60
– tactic 60
empirical testing 311
energy 257
Engineering 218
ENN 261
envisionment 87, 88
ϵ-approximation 194
equality 297
– axioms 297, 360
equation 4, 381
equation solving 293
equational
– system 4, 298
– theory 381
– unification 306
equivalence 272
equivalence relation 144, 160
equivalent 238, 240, 242, 244, 273
Ernst, George 135, 154, 164, 166
error 191, 208, 233, 235, 253
– back-propagation 201
– malicious 201
– teacher 201
evaluation function 139
evaluation search 137
evolution 218
exaggeration 112
examples 308
exclusive or 272
existential quantifier 231, 255
expert systems 270
explanation based generalization 307
explicit-mechanism ontology 90
exponential 224, 243
– cost 229
– hardware 262

exponential (*cont'd*)
– size 231, 253, 256, 263
– speedup 232
– time 228, 254, 261, 262
– weight 254, 261, 262
extended parallel computation thesis 232
extension 133
extensional
– atom 348
– part of a program 325
– predicate 325

F-union 347
fact
– false 353
– negative 353
– positive 353
– true 353
factor 295
factoring 295, 297
fail 231, 235, 252
failure 234
fairness 12
false 223
fan-in 220, 221, 256, 260, 261
fan-out 220, 221
fault tolerance 220, 234, 251, 262
feasible 195
feature 132, 144, 146, 165, 166
– discriminating 132
– structure 400
– unification 399, 402
fifteen puzzle 125, 130, 131, 139, 160, 169
filtering algorithm 195
finitary 385
finite automaton 201
finite description 231, 232
finitely generated 381
first-order 52, 58
– logic 289
– terms 369
fixed point 329
– F-least 354
– iterated least 342, 343, 354
– least 329, 343, 354
flip-flop 257
FM8501 304
fool's disc 135, 141, 142, 144, 154, 163, 165
formula 223, 230, 289
forward chaining 274, 306

frame problem 314
freeness axioms 360
f(t)-equivalent 238, 250
fully matched 310
fully parallel operation 245, 247, 258, 261
functional specification 217, 218
functionally reflexive axioms 298

Gallier 290, 306
gate 231, 232, 240, 248, 251, 253, 255, 260
Gelernter 275, 308
General Problem Solver 126, 129, 145, 146, 148
genetic algorithm 209
Gentzen 277, 290, 300
Gentzen-style proof system 308
Gentzen-style system 279
genuine support strategy 275
globally finite 17
goal 124, 139, 155, 161
Godel 291, 304
Goldstein, M.M. 135, 154, 164, 166
Good, I.J. 193
graph 142, 224, 225, 229, 231, 236, 258
graph theory 306
greatest lower bound 329
Green 295
Greenbaum 309
Gries, David 129
Groebner basis 33
ground
– atom 324
– expression 324
– instance 324
– instantiation 327
– resolution 277
– substitution 24, 383
– term 4, 380
Guard 303
Guvenir, Halil 128, 145, 148, 150, 151, 154, 163, 165, 166

halt 227, 228, 238, 247, 257, 261
halting function 226, 227
halting problem 304
Hamiltonian cycle 225, 229
hard problem 229, 230
hardware 221, 236, 262
hardware verification 45
harmony 257

Herbrand base 324
Herbrand universe 178
Herbrand's theorem 292
hidden unit 206
hierarchical deduction prover 308, 313
hierarchy 155, 158, 159
– split 159
high-level programming language 226
higher order logic 312
Hilbert-style system 290
Hilbert's program 291
Hilbert's system 277
history 88
HNN 259, 261
Hoff, M.E. 202
homomorphism
– strong 131
– weak 131, 152
Horn 178
– clause 274, 297, 300
– resolution procedure 352
– set 274
Hsiang 298, 307
Hsiang's method 300
Huet 312
human–computer interaction 270
Hunt 304
hyper-resolution 296, 299, 310
hyperface 243
hyperplane 242, 243
hyperspace 242, 243
hypothesis 179

identification by enumeration 177
implication 272
implicit-mechanism ontology 90
in-degree 225
inactive 237, 244
incompleteness theorem 304
incremental 174, 189
individual view 98
induction 176
– inductionless 25
– list 49
– mathematical 51
– on recursive type 51, 61
– tactic 59, 60
inductionless induction 25
Inductive Synthesis Algorithm 179

Inductive Synthesis Method 178
inductive theorem 24
inductively defined 49
inductively reducible 25
inference
- Bayesian 190
- deductive 177
- inductive 176, 177
- rules 12
infinitary 385
infinite domain assumption 360
infinite loop 227
inhibitory 240
initial model 24
initially-active processor 236
injections (inject) 48, 61
INN 262, 263
inner product 256
input 220, 221, 226, 228, 231, 240, 242, 243, 246, 248, 251, 253, 255, 257, 259, 261
- clause 297
- processor 236, 237
- resolution 297
- size 228, 231, 234, 235, 253
- unit 260
instance 292, 370
instruction 227
integrity constraints 323
intensional
- atom 348
- part of a program 325
- predicate 325
interconnection graph 231, 236
interconnection pattern 231, 232, 236
intermediate value theorem 304, 313
internal-disjunctive formula 201
interpretation 272, 289
- 2-valued 325
- 3-valued 325
- F-least 328, 354
- F-minimal 328
- F-smallest 329
- Herbrand 325, 358
- least 328
- minimal 328
- smallest 328
interreduced 11
intractable 228, 258
invariant 147

isomorphism
- strong 132, 254
- weak 254

Jaynes, E.T. 193
Jefferson 310
joinable 6
joint subsumption abstraction 309
Judd, J.S. 208
justified proof 13

Karmakar 305
Kearns, M. 200
Keynes, J.M. 185, 192
Khachian 305
Kitahashi, T. 135, 152, 153, 169
Kleene tables 326
Kling 308
Knuth–Bendix completion 6
Korf, Richard 128, 137, 145, 154, 156, 163, 165, 166, 169

label 225, 229, 236
Laird, J.E. 155–183
lambda-calculus 226, 312
lambda-Prolog 312
landmark values 80
language 228, 235, 251, 253, 255, 262
language recognition 228, 235, 251, 253, 255
Lauriere, Jean-Louis 128, 129, 136, 140, 162, 164
layer 206–261, 401
learn 221, 222
learnable 194
- polynomial-time 195
learning 173, 256
- incremental 174
least upper bound 329
lemma generation 284
library 58, 59
lifting 294
lifting theorem 295
likelihood 188
linear programming 206, 305
linear threshold function 204
linked inference 310
list of outputs 226, 232
lists 48, 49

literal 223, 260, 272, 289, 291, 324
– negative 324
– positive 324
Littlestone, N. 205, 209
LK' 277
local coherence 16
local search 262
locally confluent 7
locking resolution 297, 299, 308
logarithm 224
logarithmic
– time 253
– weight 253
logarithmic-time hierarchy 255, 262
logarithmic-time threshold hierarchy 255, 262
logic
– engineer 45
– probabilistic 184, 192
– programming 271
– threshold 203
logic program 324
– locally stratified 340, 341
– positive 324, 336, 337
– stratified 340, 341
logical consequence 273, 290
logistic function 208
logspace-uniform
– circuit 232, 233, 262
– language 235
– neural network 254
– threshold circuit 254
logspace-uniformity 234, 254
Loveland 280, 297, 300, 303

macro 137, 145, 148, 154, 156, 163, 165
– table 137, 147
majority 223, 234, 235, 252, 253, 256
Markgraph Karl prover 313
mask 204
matcher 371
matching algorithm 65
matching problem 371
mathematical induction 299, 311
Mathematics 218
matings 300, 312
matrix 224, 243, 250, 289
maximum entropy 192
McCune 304, 311
means–end analysis 126

membership query 181
MESON procedure 280, 300
metamathematics 46
metatheorem 56, 75
millisecond 220
minimal spanning tree 134
minimum cost 139
– spanning tree 138
Minsky, M. 204, 208
MOD 223, 249, 256
modal logic 306
model 272, 290
– 2-valued 327
– 3-valued 327
– 3-valued stable 356, 358
– elimination 280, 300
– F-least 328
– F-least 3-valued stable 358
– F-least stable 356
– F-minimal 328
– Herbrand 327, 358
– Inference System 183
– intended 331, 360
– iterated least 342, 344, 356
– least 328
– minimal 328, 338
– non-Herbrand 331, 360
– perfect 339, 342
– preferable 339
– smallest 329
– stable 351, 352
– weakly perfect 348
– well-founded 352, 355
modified problem reduction format 280, 308
modus ponens 277
monadic 31
Moore 306
more general 383
Moser 306
most general unifier 292, 370
motion planning 220
motor control 220
move 130
– irrelevant 150
– relevant 150
– safe 150
multiclauses 310

NAND 223, 231

nanosecond 220
narrowing 27, 298, 382
- sequence 27
- substitution 27
natural deduction proof 291
Nature 217, 219
NC 233, 251, 254, 262, 263
NC^1 233
NC^k 233, 255
near-Horn clause 297
near-Horn prolog 280, 300
negate 249
negation 240, 241, 246, 257, 260, 272, 275
- by failure 297
- normal form 312
- processor 240, 241, 246, 257, 260
negative 291
- clause 274
- edge 339
- example 180
- information 321
- literal 274
- recursion 340, 345
- resolution 279, 296
- weight 240, 241, 257, 258, 261
neighbourhood 263
Nelson 305
network
- multi-layer 206
- neural 202
neural circuit 223, 251, 254, 257, 260, 263
neural network 236
- acyclic 246, 247
- bipartite 258
- clamped 238
- directed 259, 261, 263
- logspace-uniform 253, 254
- non-uniform 254
- simple 236, 237, 259, 263
- symmetric 236, 247, 257, 263
- Turing-uniform 254
- unit-weight 248, 250, 261
Neurobiology 218
neuron 219, 220, 251, 262
Newell, Alan 155
Niizuma, Seizabro 135, 152, 153, 169
Nilsson, N. 192
node 225, 263
Noetherian 6, 382
noise 253

noisy 251, 253
non-clausal
- proof procedure 299
- theorem proving 311
non-monotonic
- formalisms 330, 361
- logic 314
- reasoning 351, 361
- semantics 330
nondegenerate function 254
nonstandard logic 308
nonuniform
- circuit 231, 235, 255
- complexity class 233
- language 235
- neural network 253
- Turing machine 233
nonuniform-NC 233
nonuniform-P 233
nonuniformity 233, 254
normal form 6
NOT 223
NP 229–231, 262
NP-complete 229, 230, 259, 262
- problem 273
NP-hard 230, 259, 262
nullary (or zero) 385
Nuprl 57, 59, 60, 71, 313

Occam algorithm 200
Ohlbach 306
ONN 261
ontology 89
operational phenomenon 218, 221
operational semantics 218
operations research 141
operator
- fitting 333, 334
- Gelfond–Lifschitz 350, 357
- monotone 329, 353
- subgoaling 161
- Van Emden–Kowalski 337
- - generalized 324
optimization 229, 262
OR 223, 248, 249, 256, 257, 260
oracle 227, 230
order 204
order-of-magnitude reasoning 106
order sorted
- algebra 311

order sorted (*cont'd*)
- logics 397
- rewriting 20
- specification 21
ordering
- F-ordering 329
- literals 296
- standard 329
OTTER 304
out-degree 225
output 220, 221, 226, 227, 231, 234, 235, 238, 239, 247, 248, 251, 253, 261
- processor 236
- unit 237, 260
Overbeek 300

P 229, 230, 233, 251, 262
P-complete 233
P1 deduction 296, 297, 299
PAC-learnability 193
padding of input 228
Papert, S. 204, 208
parallel
- complexity theory 225
- computation 232, 235, 245, 246, 255, 261
- computation thesis 232
- hardware 232
- operation 220, 245, 254, 257
- time 232
paramodulant 298
paramodulated 382
paramodulation 298
parent 294
parity 204, 223, 255
PARTHENON 312
partial functions 312
partial reflection 72
Pascal 226, 228, 232
Pearl, Judea 163, 192
perceptron 203
- convergence theorem 204
permutation 383
permute 248
persistent
- equations 12
- rules 12
Peterson 298
Philosophy 218
Physics 218
Pitt, L. 200

Plaisted 299, 307, 309, 310, 313
Plotkin 299
PLS 262, 263
PLS-complete 263
Plummer 309
polylog 224, 233
- depth 233, 254
- time 253
polynomial 224
- depth 232
- hardware 262
- orderings 10
- rewriting 32
- size 232, 233, 251, 254, 256, 261, 263
- time 228, 230, 232, 253, 255, 260, 265
- time local search 262, 263
- time reduction 230, 260, 261
- weight 253, 254, 260
polynomial-time hierarchy 231, 254
polynomial-time threshold hierarchy 254, 262
polytope 243
positive 291, 296
- clause 274
- example 180
- inductive 50
- literal 274
- normal form 204
- resolution 296
Post production system 226
potential state 237, 244
Potter 299, 307, 313
precondition 126, 149
prediction 201
preference relation 339
prenex 46
prenex conjunctive normal form 289
Presburger arithmetic 305
prime 256
prior 191
priorities 308
priority for minimization
- higher 338
- predicate 338, 339
- relative 338, 339, 341
priority system 307
probabilism 234
probabilistic
- circuit 233, 235
- computation 233

probabilistic (*cont'd*)
- language recognition 233, 235, 251
problem 124
- extended 139
- extension 132, 144, 234
- free 130
- instance 131
- inverse image 159
- quotient 133
- reduction format 283, 313
- relatively large 156
- split 159
- totally decomposed 144
- uniform 159
procedural
- knowledge 269
- programming 322, 335
- semantics 330
processes 97
production system 160
productive computation 246, 257, 259
program 226, 228, 232
- database 323
- datalog 324
- datalog with negation 324
- extended positive 357
- locally stratified 341, 342
- logic 324
- positive logic 324, 336, 337
- saturated 355
- stratified logic 341, 342
- verification 45
- verifiers 45
- weakly stratified 349, 363
Prolog 279, 297, 300
- Prolog technology theorem prover 312
proof
- by consistency 25
- checking 271
- classical 47
- constructive 62
- equality 5
- refinement 58
- systems (human oriented) 290
- tableaux 56
propagate 249
propositional
- calculus 272
- constant 272
- formulas 53

propositional (*cont'd*)
- Horn sentence 201
pruning 138
PSPACE 231, 254
Psychology 218

QSIM 84
quadratic reciprocity 304
qualitative
- constraint 81
- mathematics 78
- physics 78
quantifier 231
quantity space 80
query 181, 201
quotient 160
quotient problem 133

R1-Soar 168
R-unifier 26
random 233, 235, 245, 256, 263
Random-Access Machine 226, 227
random parallel operation 245
real arithmetic 305
reals with addition 305
reasonable encoding scheme 228
reasoning 45, 52, 60
recognition 228, 235, 251, 253, 255
rectangular 204
recursive
- decomposition ordering 10
- function 226
- path ordering 10
reducible 6
reduction 230, 261
reduction of program modulo interpretation 347
reduction ordering 9
reductive system 20
refinement 58, 182
refinement with macros 148, 150, 154, 165
reflection 75
refutation 295
- procedure 273, 291
regular concept (DFA) 200
reject 228, 233
relational
- algebra 321
- component 325
- database 321

relaxation 129, 133, 134, 138, 139, 142, 143
- heuristic 134
relevance tests 310
reliable computation 217, 220, 234, 245, 251, 254, 257, 262
renaming substitution 383
representation 197
resilient 251, 253
resolution 277, 294
- proof 295
resolvent 294
resource 227, 228, 232, 253
restriction 129, 136, 139, 143
- heuristic 134
rewrite proof 11
rewrite rules 313
rewriting 312
rewriting modulo congruence 15
rigid E-unification 306
ring theory 304, 305
Rivest, R. 202
Robinson 293
Robinson unification 392
Rosenblatt, F. 202
Rosenbloom, Paul 155, 158
row 224
RSA encryption algorithm 304
Rubik's Cube 123, 146, 148, 156, 166
rules of inference 47, 58
Rusinowitch 298

Sacerdoti 309
SAM's lemma 303
SAT 230, 260
satisfiability 230
satisfiable 223, 230, 260, 290, 291
satisfies 272
satisfy 290
Schapire, R. 202
scope 289
search 174
search strategies 306
self-loop 225, 257, 258, 260, 261
self-organizing system 176
semantic
- deletion 275
- Horn clause 282
- resolution 296
- tree method 283

semantics 272, 289, 308, 323, 340
- declarative 329, 331
- default model 345, 351, 362
- least model 336, 337
- model-theoretic 331
- non-monotonic 331
- of 3-valued stable model 352, 358
- perfect model 337, 342, 363
- procedural 330
- proof-theoretic 331
- stable model 345, 351, 361, 362
- weakly perfect model 345, 361, 362
- well-founded 352, 355, 362
semiconductor 218
separated on W away from Z 384
sequent style
- methods 300
- proof system 290
- system 276
sequential
- computation 228, 232, 235, 245, 255, 257, 259, 261, 262
- - thesis 228
- operation 245, 257
sequents 57, 276
serial decomposability 147
serially decomposable 165
set of most general unifiers 371, 384
set of support 296, 299, 308
set theory 306, 312, 313
Shapiro, E.Y. 178
shared memory machine 232
Shostak 305
side-effect 218
signature 4
silicon 218, 220
simple
- graph 225, 258
- interconnection pattern 236
- neural network 236, 257, 259, 261, 263
simplex method 305
simplification 59
simplification ordering 298
simplified problem reduction format 280
simulate 226, 232, 247, 251, 258, 261
situation calculus 314
size 223, 224, 230–232, 235, 238, 244, 256, 261, 263, 288
Skolem function 291, 307
skolemization 292

small weight 254, 256
snapshot 247
SNN 258, 261
Soar 128, 158, 161, 162, 168
software engineering 311
solution 131
sort decreasing 22
sorts 311
sound 290, 295
space 227, 231
special 31
specialized decision procedures 304
speedup 232, 262
splitting 296
spurious solutions 106
stability 257
stable
– configuration 238, 257, 259, 261, 262
– processor 137, 237, 246, 257, 260
– state 237
– unit 260
state 80, 231, 236, 239, 244, 245, 257, 258, 262
– space 130
– transition 81, 87
– vector 146
Stickel 280, 304, 310, 312
stochastic function 251
Storage Modification Machine 227
strategy 136
stratification 341
– dynamic 356
– weak 349
string 224, 225, 228, 230, 235, 237
– rewriting 30
strip 250, 251
structural modulo 26
structure 290
– sharing 311
subgoal 127, 157, 274
– reordering 307, 313
subproblem 127, 132, 140, 145, 151, 154, 155
subset of resolution 294
substitution 5, 52, 292, 380, 383
subsumes 295
subsumption 295, 401
succedent 276
succeed 234
superdiagonal 250

support 204
Sutton, R. 202
symmetric
– function 248, 256
– graph 236
– neural network 236, 247, 257, 263
synergy 218, 221
syntax 289

tableau 56
– decision 54
TABLOG 312
tactic 58, 59
tactical 60
target 194
Tarski 305
tautology 46, 54, 274
– deletion 295
TC^0 256
TC^k 255, 256
teacher 179
technological specification 217, 220
technology 220
temporal logic 306
term 4, 289
– rewriting 16, 298, 307
– rewriting system 5, 304, 382
terminate 229, 237, 238, 246, 247, 254, 257, 258, 260, 261
terminating 6
theorem proving 28, 45, 46
theory resolution 310
three-valued extensions 363
threshold 247
– assignment 236
– circuit 248, 251, 253, 256, 262, 263
– function 221, 236, 240, 242, 244, 262, 263
– quantifier 254
– value 238, 241, 243, 248, 260
Thue congruence 30
time 227, 228, 238, 239, 246, 247, 253, 255, 257, 263
tolerant 251
topology 313
Towers of Hanoi 123, 125, 126, 130, 147, 152
tractable 228
training problem 206
transformations 389
– extended Gelfond–Lifschitz 357

transformations (*cont'd*)
– Gelfond–Lifschitz 350
transistor 220
Travelling Salesman Problem 229
tree size 288
Tribus, M. 192
true 223
truth
– maintenance 93
– valuation 325
– value 272
TSOP 229
TSP 229, 230
tuple 224, 225, 231, 236
Turing machine 226, 227, 232, 233
Turing-uniform
– circuit 232
– language 235
– neural network 254
Turing-uniformity 234, 254
two-sided bounded-error probabilism 233
type conformal 386

uncountable 226
undirected graph 224, 225, 236
unfailing completion 18
unification 162, 292
– algorithm 292, 370, 385
– hierarchy 371, 385
– problem 371
unifier 292, 369
uniform complexity class 233
uniformity 233
unique names axioms 360
unit
– clause 297
– resolution 297
– simplification 307
– weight 248, 250, 260, 261
unit-weight neural network 248, 250, 261
unitary 385
universal c
– closure 324
– quantifier 255

universal c (*cont'd*)
– query problem 358, 359
– subgoaling 161
– unification 406
unsatisfiable 273, 290
unstable
– processor 237, 246
– unit 260
UR resolution 278, 297

Valiant, L. 200, 201
valid 273, 290
valid consequence 290
validity problem 5
Van Gelder 283
Vapnik, V. 193
Vapnik–Chervonenkis dimension 196
vector 242, 243
vector machine 232
verification 230
vertex 225, 243, 257
vertices 241
von Neumann bottleneck 219
von Neumann computer 219, 221, 222
von Neumann–Bernays–Gödel set theory 269

Wang 304, 305, 308, 313
Warmuth, M. 200
weight 236, 238, 248, 250, 254, 256
– assignment 236
weighted binary threshold function 221, 236, 240, 242, 244, 262, 263
wetware 218, 220
Widrow, B. 208
width 250
worst-case analysis 165
worst-case complexity 228
Wu 305

XAPS3 158

Zermelo–Fraenkel set theory 269